Shannon Pratt
Alina V. Niculita

The Lawyer's Business Valuation Handbook

Understanding Financial Statements, Appraisal Reports, and Expert Testimony

Second Editio

AMERICAN BAR ASSOCIATION
Defending Liberty
Pursuing Justice

SECTION OF FAMILY LAW

Cover design by ABA.

18 17 7 6

Library of Congress Cataloging-in-Publication Data

Pratt, Shannon P.
The lawyer's business valuation handbook : understanding financial statements, appraisal reports, and expert testimony / by Shannon Pratt, Alina V. Niculita.
p. cm.
Includes bibliographical references and index.
ISBN 1-60442-803-1 (978-1-60442-803-2)
1. Corporations—Valuation—Law and legislation—United States. 2. Appraisers—Legal status, laws, etc.—United States. 3. Evidence, Expert—United States. I. Niculita, Alina V. II. Title.

KF1416.P73 2010
346.73'065—dc22 2010014019

Discounts are available for books ordered in bulk. Special consideration is given to state bars, CLE programs, and other bar-related organizations. Inquire at Book Publishing, ABA Publishing, American Bar Association, 321 N. Clark Street, Chicago, Illinois 60654.

www.ShopABA.org

Dedication

To all the lawyers
who work on business valuation matters:

We hope this book
will make your lives a little easier
and more productive
in dealing with business valuations.

Contents

Chapter 6

Chapter 7

Chapter 8

Chapter 15

Chapter 16

Reconciliation of Value Indications 239

Chapter 17

Valuations for Federal Tax Matters 249

Chapter 18

Chapter 28

Table of Exhibits

Foreword—Tax Law Perspective

Ronald D. Aucutt*

Taxes are everywhere in life, and value is everywhere in tax law. We think immediately of the estate and gift tax, of course. But the value of assets for which there is no established market can also matter greatly in measuring compensation income; in calculating and documenting charitable deductions; in determining the tax treatment or tax-free status of the formation, restructuring, combination, or dissolution of corporations and other entities; in qualifying for special tax treatment reserved for certain entities; in allocating income among taxpayers, especially in cross-border contexts; and in allocating income, basis, and other tax attributes among participants in business enterprises. And those are just a few prominent examples.

Nor are valuation issues limited to the actual determination of tax liability. In my own focus on estate planning, I often encounter clients who need to know the right amount to pay for a business, the right amount to accept in selling a business, or the best way to structure ownership, compensation, or buy-sell arrangements. Value is often critical. We lawyers are "counselors at law," and our clients often look to us for holistic counsel about these real-world decisions.

That is why *The Lawyer's Business Valuation Handbook* will be so useful. Most lawyers do not become appraisal experts and should be careful about appearing to express a professional "opinion" about value when they are not qualified to do so. Nevertheless, a working familiarity with this volume will reassure the lawyer in finding the best appraiser for the occasion, communicating with the appraiser, reviewing the appraisal, and explaining the implications of the appraisal to the client.

A lawyer has many responsibilities to the client relating to the determination of value. Typically, especially when attorney work-product status is important, the lawyer will initially interview and engage the appraiser and needs to know what to look

* Ronald D. Aucutt is a partner in the McLean, Virginia (Tysons Corner), office of McGuireWoods LLP and is the chair of the firm's Private Wealth Services Group. He concentrates on planning and controversy matters involving estate and gift tax and related disciplines, including the tax-efficient succession of family-owned businesses. He is a fellow and former president of the American College of Trust and Estate Counsel (ACTEC), an academician of the International Academy of Estate and Trust Law and former member of its Executive Council, a former vice chair (Committee Operations) of the American Bar Association's Section of Taxation, and a fellow of the American College of Tax Counsel. He is a co-author of *Structuring Estate Freezes*, published by Warren, Gorham & Lamont.

for and what questions to ask. Often the lawyer will receive the appraiser's preliminary findings, sometimes a written draft and sometimes an oral update, and needs to provide the reality check the client expects and most appraisers welcome. In the course of all this, the lawyer must be able to read with understanding the relevant source documents, such as financial statements and SEC reports, and must have at least a passing familiarity with the arcane world of "adjustments" to the data in those documents. Finally, even the best expert help cannot guarantee that there will be no controversy with the Internal Revenue Service. When there is, the lawyer will need to know how best to use expert valuation evidence and how to anticipate and work around possible IRS challenges and judicial misgivings.

This book will help the lawyer perform all those functions. In an orderly and accessible fashion, it explains how to spot valuation issues, how to engage an appraiser, how to read appraisals and attached documents, how to use an appraisal, and how to defend an appraisal if necessary. Make no mistake, there is no substitute for experience in dealing with valuation issues. But whether a seasoned practitioner seeking to sharpen client-service skills or a beginner wondering where to start, a lawyer will acquire an invaluable framework from this *Handbook*.

Speaking of experience, there is Shannon Pratt, the dean of the business appraisal profession. His experience is legendary and his teacher's instincts are unequalled. From basic definitions to real-world cases to checklists to litigation road maps, Shannon's experience and wisdom permeate these chapters. And there is a "premium": The lawyer, IRS examiner, or judge who consults these pages to learn how to read an appraisal or financial statement will find the *Handbook* itself very readable.

Foreword—Family Law Perspective

By Ronald L. Brown*

The second edition of *The Lawyer's Business Valuation Handbook* is indeed a handbook; but it is also an authoritative text, a reference guide, and a treatise. It is an overview and an in-depth analysis. It is both general and specialized. It is a valuable resource for both new matrimonial attorneys and those with considerable experience. It is not easy to be two seemingly different things at the same time. It takes special skills to accomplish this. Superman did it. Spiderman did it. And Shannon Pratt has done it. This book is all those things mentioned above, and more.

Shannon Pratt, the legendary business valuation guru and author of numerous books, has updated this important volume on a subject that has become one of the most important in the practice of family law during the past 25 years. Indeed, business valuation is often the critical component in a marital dissolution case. The valuation of a family business can determine the future course of the lives of both parties. In my 30 years of editing family law publications, business valuation has become a dominant theme and a key point of focus, and the name Shannon Pratt appears regularly in court opinions as a source of reliable information. Although Dr. Pratt has performed valuation engagements in a wide variety of legal areas (e.g., mergers and acquisitions, employee stock ownership plans (ESOPs), gift and estate taxes, corporate and partnership dissolutions, and dissenting stockholder actions), his insight has also played an important role in the marital dissolution arena. I have been fortunate to have had the opportunity to publish some articles authored by Dr. Pratt and am honored to write this Foreword.

Among the topics covered in this useful volume of particular interest to matrimonial attorneys are those that provide general background, such as Chapter 3, "Overview of Business Valuation Approaches, Methods, and Procedures"; Chapter 4, "Financial Statement Terminology Used in Business Appraisal"; Chapter 30, "Business Valuation Standards and Credentials"; and Appendix A, "Glossary of Business Valuation Terms."

A long section, Chapter 19, is devoted exclusively to marital dissolution valuations; it also offers a list of references for further consultation. This portion of the

* Ronald L. Brown is editor-in-chief of the *American Journal of Family Law.* He is the former editor of *Fairshare: The Matrimonial Law Monthly* (1980–2000). His family law publications include *Valuing Professional Practices & Licenses: A Guide for the Matrimonial Practitioner*, 3d ed., and *Drafting Prenuptial Agreements* (with Skoloff and Singer).

book begins with an explanation of the standard of value for marital dissolution business valuations with examples of the different approaches taken by different states. It covers a myriad of other critical issues, such as the valuation date—with extensive footnotes to case law; goodwill, including the distinction between personal and professional or enterprise goodwill—of great significance in the valuation of professional practices as well as businesses; the role of buy-sell agreements; covenants not to compete; minority and marketability discounts; and the problem of "double-dipping." Several separate chapters elaborate, addressing such important areas as personal versus entity goodwill and the valuation of professional practices and small service businesses.

Other sections of the work provide useful information for litigation, including Chapter 30, on business valuation standards and credentials; Chapter 31, covering the cross-examination of a business valuation expert; and Appendix B, which explains the alphabet soup of business valuation organization that figures in an expert's credentials.

Overall, the book presents a practical and highly readable discussion of a subject that divorce attorneys cannot afford not to be familiar with, since it will be cited by your opponent as well as courts. It is written in clear, nontechnical language despite the complexity of the subject. Although it can be consulted as needed, it would not be a bad idea to read through the text, or at least become familiar with its contents, so that it is more accessible when needed.

The second edition of *The Lawyer's Business Valuation Guide* is a valuable book that should be on the shelf of every family law attorney.

Foreword—Corporate Law Perspective

Francis G.X. Pileggi[1]

Business valuation is an essential component of most corporate law practices, but value is a relative estimate of worth that can be determined by a variety of methods.

As with many corporate law questions, attorneys across the country look for answers from the Delaware Court of Chancery, widely recognized as the nation's leading forum for corporate and business disputes. The court's members are regarded as experts on Delaware corporate law, which governs the internal affairs of over 60 percent of *Fortune* 500 companies and more than half of all publicly traded companies in the United States. So when the Delaware Chancery Court cites Dr. Shannon P. Pratt as a leading authority in business valuation, it carries great weight.

Praise for First Edition

A respected valuation authority and prolific author, Dr. Pratt is well known for writing an extensive collection of resources on business valuation issues, including *Valuing a Business,* one of the world's most widely cited valuation references. Adding to his noteworthy body of work, Pratt authored the first edition of *The Lawyer's Business Valuation Handbook* in 2000. Appraisers, attorneys, and judges predicted that the *Handbook* would be the "go-to" valuation reference guide for practitioners and jurists. The first edition was cited in multiple cases recently by Delaware's Court of Chancery, the nation's preeminent business court.[2] With its straightforward language, the book demystified the valuation process and facilitated communication between legal professionals and appraisers.

Improvements in Second Edition

In this new edition, Pratt and his co-author, Alina Niculita, maintain the pragmatic approach and understandable language, while delving deeper into relevant issues and expanding upon the *Handbook*'s original themes. The fundamentals of valuation remain at the book's center, with chapters discussing basic terminology, accepted valuation approaches and methodology, and business appraiser credentials and standards.

1. Francis G.X. Pileggi is the founding partner of the Wilmington, Delaware, office of Fox Rothschild LLP, an AmLaw 200 firm. He authors a blog at www.delawarelitigation.com that summarizes key corporate cases from Delaware's Chancery Court and Supreme Court.

2. *See, e.g., In re* PNB Holding Co. Shareholders Litig., 32 Del. J. Corp. L. 654 (Del. Ch. 2006); Delaware Open MRI Radiology Assoc., P.A. v. Kessler, 898 A.2d 290 (Del. Ch. 2006); Gesoff v. IIC Indus., Inc., 902 A.2d 1130 (Del. Ch. 2006).

However, the sections addressing valuation for different purposes, such as tax or corporate matters, have been expanded to create a comprehensive guide to the practical application of valuation. For instance, the corporate law practitioner will find relevant and invaluable information in the chapters addressing shareholder disputes and employee stock ownership plans. The new edition also includes chapters on buy-sell agreements, valuing S corporations, and valuation reports, thus creating a broader, more inclusive discussion of valuation and corporate law.

In addition to a more extensive examination of the role valuation plays in different practice areas, this treatise taps into the expertise of a number of recognized valuation professionals. Pratt and Niculita welcome the contributions of their peers, incorporating their skilled insights to create a balanced approach to the field and its applications.

Recommendation of the Second Edition

Referenced by the country's leading corporate law experts and hailed by attorneys and appraisers, *The Lawyer's Business Valuation Handbook* is a valuable tool for understanding the complexities of business valuation. Those practitioners who relied on the first edition will find new and expanded information in the latest edition, proving the book to be a worthy addition to their library. New readers, wondering how they managed so long without the *Handbook* in their arsenal, will find that it offers a comprehensive and practical guide to business valuation issues.

About the Authors

Shannon P. Pratt, CFA, ARM, ABAR, FASA, MCBA, CM&AA, is a well-known authority in the field of business valuation and has written numerous books that articulate many of the concepts used in modern business valuation around the world. He is chairman and CEO of Shannon Pratt Valuations, Inc., a business valuation firm headquartered in Portland, Oregon. He is also a member of the board of directors of Paulson Capital Corporation, an investment banking firm that specializes in small-cap IPOs.

Over the last 40 years, Dr. Pratt has performed valuation engagements for mergers and acquisitions, employee stock ownership plans (ESOPs), fairness opinions, gift and estate taxes, incentive stock options, buy-sell agreements, corporate and partnership dissolutions, dissenting stockholder actions, damages, marital dissolutions, and many other business valuation purposes. He has testified in a wide variety of federal and state courts across the country and frequently participates in arbitration and mediation proceedings.

He holds an undergraduate degree in business administration from the University of Washington and a doctorate in business administration, majoring in finance, from Indiana University. He is a Fellow of the American Society of Appraisers, a Master Certified Business Appraiser, a Chartered Financial Analyst, a Master Certified Business Counselor, and is certified in mergers and acquisitions.

Dr. Pratt's professional recognitions include being designated a life member of the Business Valuation Committee of the American Society of Appraisers, a life member of the American Society of Appraisers, past chairman and a life member of the ESOP Association Advisory Committee on Valuation, a life member of the Institute of Business Appraisers, the Magna Cum Laude in Business Appraisal award from the National Association of Certified Valuation Analysts, and the distinguished service award of the Portland Society of Financial Analysts. He recently completed two three-year terms as trustee-at-large of the Appraisal Foundation. Dr. Pratt also is certified by the American Society of Appraisers in Appraisal Review and Management (ARM), and by the Institute of Business Appraisers in Accredited in Business Appraisal Review (ABAR), enabling him to conduct multidisciplinary valuation reviews.

Dr. Pratt is the author, with Alina V. Niculita, of *Valuing a Business: The Analysis and Appraisal of Closely Held Companies,* 5th edition, published by McGraw-Hill; the co-author with Roger Grabowski of *Cost of Capital: Applications and Examples,*

3d edition; the co-author with Jay Fishman and William Morrison of *Standards of Value*; author of *The Market Approach to Valuing Businesses,* 2d edition; *Business Valuation Body of Knowledge,* 2d edition; *Business Valuation Discounts and Premiums,* 2d edition; and co-author with the Honorable David Laro of *Business Valuation and Taxes: Procedure, Law and Perspective*, all published by John Wiley & Sons. He is also co-author of *Guide to Business Valuations*, 19th edition, published by Practitioners Publishing Company, and is the co-author of *Valuing Small Businesses and Professional Practices*, 3d edition, published by McGraw-Hill.

He is publisher emeritus of a monthly newsletter, *Business Valuation Update* (primarily for the professional appraisal community).

Dr. Pratt develops and teaches business valuation courses for the American Society of Appraisers and the American Institute of Certified Public Accountants, and frequently speaks on business valuation at national legal, professional, and trade association meetings. He also developed and often teaches a full-day seminar (sometimes divided into two partial days) on business valuation for judges and lawyers.

Alina V. Niculita, CFA, ASA, MBA, is president and COO of Shannon Pratt Valuations, Inc., in Portland, Oregon. She is a Chartered Financial Analyst, a member of the CFA Institute, and an Accredited Senior Appraiser in business valuation of the American Society of Appraisers. At Shannon Pratt Valuations, Ms. Niculita works on all aspects of case management, including the fundamental aspects of business valuation and economic analysis and report writing. She has been involved in business valuation engagements for various purposes, such as transactions in company stock, estate and gift taxes, and litigation support. Ms. Niculita has also worked on business valuation reviews, valuations of intangible assets, and fairness and solvency opinions. She is the assistant author of *Valuing a Business: The Analysis and Appraisal of Closely Held Companies,* 5th edition, and co-author of *Business Valuation Body of Knowledge Workbook,* 2d Edition; *Cost of Capital Workbook*; *Closely Held Business Valuation*; and BNA Tax and Accounting Portfolio 5147, Mastracchio and Niculita, *Closely Held Business Valuation* (Accounting Policy and Practice Series). She is also a contributor to *BVR's Guide to Personal v. Enterprise Goodwill* (2009).

About the Contributing Authors

Frances (Xudong) Fan is a financial analyst at Shannon Pratt Valuations, Inc., in Portland, Oregon. She passed the Chartered Financial Analyst (CFA) Level I test and is a non-accredited member of the American Society of Appraisers. At Shannon Pratt Valuations, Ms. Fan works on the essential aspects of business valuation, such as economic analysis, financial statement analysis, discount rate development, and report writing. Ms. Fan holds an MBA with an emphasis in finance from Portland State University and a master's with a major in material science and engineering from Tsinghua University, China. She also received an undergraduate degree with a double major in material science and computer science from Zhejiang University, China.

Noah J. Gordon is legal counsel for Shannon Pratt Valuations, Inc., in Portland, Oregon, where he is regularly involved with business valuations. He has served as a contributing author and editor of several legal treatises and publications, and regularly contributes to various business valuation publications. Most recently, he has contributed to *Business Valuation Discounts and Premiums,* 2d edition (2009); *Guide to Business Valuations,* 19th edition (2009); *BVR's Guide to Personal v. Enterprise Goodwill* (2009); *BVR's Annual Guide to Fair Value in Dissent, Oppression and Marital Dissolution* (2009); *Valuing a Business: The Analysis and Appraisal of Closely Held Companies,* 5th edition (2008); *Employee Stock Option Plans: ESOP Planning, Implementation, Law and Taxation* (2007 update); *Standards of Value* (2006); and *The Market Approach to Valuing a Business*, 2d edition (2005). He also maintains a freelance editorial business. Mr. Gordon is admitted to the bars of Oregon, New York, New Jersey, the District of Columbia, and the United States Supreme Court.

Kimberly Linebarger is a financial analyst with Shannon Pratt Valuations, Inc. Ms. Linebarger has managed or assisted on valuation projects for a variety of purposes, including marital dissolution, merger and acquisition, report review, litigation, and damage actions. She has contributed to multiple publications on business valuation, including *Valuing a Business: The Analysis and Appraisal of Closely Held Companies*, 5th edition; *Business Valuation Discounts and Premiums*, 2d edition; and *BVR's Guide to Personal vs. Enterprise Goodwill* (2009). She was the project manager of *Cost of Capital: Applications and Examples*, Third Edition. She holds a bachelor of science in business administration, with an emphasis in finance, from Portland State University.

Angelina McKedy is a senior analyst for Shannon Pratt Valuations, Inc., in Portland, Oregon. She has assisted in performing valuation assignments for litigation support and dispute resolution (including dissenting stockholder suits and marital dissolution cases), solvency opinions, and fairness opinions. In addition to her business valuation work, she also provides stock portfolio management. She has contributed to many of Shannon Pratt's books and regularly contributes to *Guide to Business Valuations.* She is also a contributor to *BVR's Guide to Personal vs. Enterprise Goodwill* (2009). She holds a bachelor of science, business administration with an emphasis in finance, from Portland State University, and is a candidate member of the American Society of Appraisers.

Nicholas J. Mastracchio, Jr., CPA, holds a Ph.D. from Union College, where his studies and dissertation were in the area of valuation of closely held companies. He has been practicing accounting since 1964 and was managing director of Charles L. Marvin and Company, a CPA firm with offices in Albany and Schenectady, New York, from 1976 to 1991. He taught at the University at Albany for 30 years and was the Arthur Andersen Alumni Professor of Accounting. He now has emeritus status. In August 2006, he began teaching at the University of South Florida and has taught a graduate-level course in business valuations for two years. Dr. Mastracchio has been performing valuations for small professional firms as well as multimillion-dollar businesses since 1976. His valuation methodology has become case law in

New York state. His valuation work has included sales, mergers and acquisitions, gift and estate tax planning, buy-sell agreements, ESOP valuations, pension plan valuations, and litigation in the areas of matrimonial and minority shareholder actions, licenses, loss of income, and breach of contract. He has testified in numerous federal and state courts and arbitration hearings and limits his practice to these and related areas. He has written five books and 32 articles on valuations. Dr. Mastracchio is past chairman of the New York State Board of Public Accountancy, which oversees licensure and the conduct of the profession in New York state. He is on the education committee of the National Association of State Boards of Accountancy and is a past member of the American Institute of Certified Public Accountants' (AICPA) Board of Examiners, which is responsible for the CPA exam, including content and administration. He is a member of the AICPA Auditing Standards Board, which is responsible for setting auditing standards for all companies that do not file with the SEC. He is also a member of the AICPA, the New York State Society of Certified Public Accountants, and the American Academy of Economic Experts. He has been appointed to the American Arbitration Association Roster of Neutrals and is on its Commercial Panel.

Chad P. Phillips, CFA, is a financial consultant specializing in business and intangible asset valuation for business succession, estate planning, mergers and acquisitions, marital dissolution, shareholder disputes, financial reporting, and corporate planning since 1997. Phillips is a Chartered Financial Analyst (CFA) and has presented on a number of valuation-related topics to industry groups, professional organizations, and business executives alike.

Preface

This book is for lawyers who frequently, occasionally, or even for the first time encounter disputed (or potentially disputed) business valuation issues. It serves all of the above because it is written and organized both as a tutorial and as a reference manual.

The authors have over 40 years of combined experience in transactional matters (e.g., mergers and acquisitions, going public, going private) and also litigation or potential litigation (e.g., tax matters, shareholder disputes, marital dissolutions). All of these have elements in common, and many have specialized elements, thus requiring generalized chapters and also chapters addressing a particular valuation purpose.

Same Shares May Have Different Values

It is important to recognize that the same block of shares may have different values, even on the same day, depending on the statute and the case law governing the transaction. For example, an increasing number of states are not allowing discounts for lack of control and/or lack of marketability in dissenting stockholder suits, whereas federal, gift, estate, and income tax statutes universally use the standard of *fair market value*, which the courts have interpreted to allow such discounts.

Personal versus Enterprise Goodwill

One area in which we have done a great deal of work lately is the distinction between personal and enterprise goodwill. Entrepreneurs are invoking the *Martin Ice Cream*[1] case, where the income tax on the sale of the company was less to the extent that it encompassed personal goodwill. Also, there is a trend among state courts to take the position that the value of the enterprise attributable to personal goodwill is excluded from the marital estate in marital dissolutions. We have added a new chapter on personal versus enterprise goodwill.

One issue that arises in almost every business and professional practice valuation case is reasonable compensation, and we have added a chapter on that.

Premiums and Discounts

A major issue in many cases is premiums and discounts, especially discounts for lack of marketability (DLOM). There has been great progress in empirical DLOM data-

1. Martin Ice Cream, Co. v. Comm'r, 110 T.C. 189, 1998 U.S. Tax. Ct. LEXIS 17 (1998).

bases, and today most courts prefer that the analyst go into the databases and select the transactions most resembling the subject company rather than just use the average discounts. Other discount and premium issues that we see often are discounts for lack of control (minority interests) or premium for control.

The Tax Court in recent years has fully embraced discounts for trapped-in capital gains, and today it is not a question of whether but a question of how much. Other courts, however, have been slow to follow suit. Other discounts include voting versus nonvoting stock, key person discounts, discounts for nonhomogeneous assets (portfolio discount), and discounts for environmental litigation and other contingent liabilities.[2]

S Corporations and Other Pass-Through Entities

Almost half the valuations that our company has done lately involve S corporations or other pass-through entities, and we have added a chapter on those. We have also added a chapter on valuing professional practices and small service businesses.

"Fair Value" for Financial Reporting

One valuation purpose that has come to the fore lately is valuation for financial reporting. Financial Accounting Standard (FAS) 157 says that the standard of value for financial reporting is "fair value," but its definition of fair value comes closer to fair market value than to fair value as used in state statutes governing shareholder disputes (and interpreted through case law). We have added a chapter on fair value for financial reporting.

Buy-Sell Agreements

In the course of reviewing valuation reports pursuant to buy-sell agreements, we see many ambiguous valuation provisions in buy-sell agreements. Many even omit the applicable definition of value (the subject of Chapter 1). To assist lawyers in drafting unambiguous valuation provisions in such agreements, we've added a chapter on buy-sell agreements.[3]

Report Reviews

One of the most frequent (and hard to catch) categories of errors in business valuation reports is errors of omission. We've added two chapters on valuation reports—a gen-

---

2. *See also* SHANNON P. PRATT, BUSINESS VALUATION DISCOUNTS AND PREMIUMS, 2d ed. (John Wiley & Sons 2009).

3. *See also* Z. CHRISTOPHER MERCER, BUY-SELL AGREEMENTS: TICKING TIME BOMBS OR REASONABLE RESOLUTIONS? (Peabody Publishing, LP 2007).

eral chapter (what a good report should have) and a "working chapter" for reviewing reports. The report review chapter is free of copyright restrictions and is meant to be copied and the blanks filled in for each report. Two or more copies may be utilized for comparing your expert's report with that of the opposing expert and identifying the differences.

Cross-Examining Business Valuation Experts

And finally, in response to popular demand, we've added a chapter on cross-examining a business valuation expert.

Court Positions Cited, Sometimes Challenged

Illustrative court cases are cited throughout to illustrate courts' positions on many issues. On some issues various courts are unanimous in their positions, but on other issues courts' positions vary according to jurisdiction. For those that vary, we cite from decisions on either side of an issue. Occasionally, when we feel that one court's treatment of an issue is sounder than another, we say so, and tell you why. We believe that lawyers should know court precedents and usually should follow them, but sometimes it pays to challenge an unsound precedent and make new law.

The appendixes include a glossary, a list of business appraisal professional organizations with contact information, and a bibliography that includes business valuation databases.

We welcome questions and comments at Shannon Pratt Valuations, Inc., www.shannonpratt.com, (503) 459-4700, 6443 S.W. Beaverton Hillsdale Highway, Suite 432, Portland, Oregon 97221.

Shannon Pratt
Portland, Oregon
May 2010

Alina Niculita
Portland, Oregon
May 2010

Acknowledgments

This book has benefited immeasurably from an extraordinary amount of peer review from a blue-ribbon Editorial Advisory Board that provided valuable comments and suggestions. The book is far richer as a result of the contributions of these reviewers:

Ronald D. Aucutt
McGuire Woods LLP
McLean, Virginia
raucutt@mcguirewoods.com

Stephen J. Bravo, ASA, CBA, CPA/ABV/PFS, CFP, MST
Apogee Business Valuations, Inc.
Framingham, Massachusetts
sbravo@apogeebv.com

Roberto Castro, JD, MST, MBA
Faisal Alsayrafi, ASA, CM&AA, MBA, CVA
Financial Transaction House (a Saudi Arabia–based investment banking firm focusing on cross-border M&A, fairness opinions, and reorganizations)
Salt Lake City, Utah
Jeddah, Saudi Arabia
roberto.castro@fthgulf.com
faisal.alsayrafi@fthgulf.com

Gilbert E. Matthews, CFA
Sutter Securities Inc.
San Francisco, California
gil@suttersf.com

Linda B. Trugman, CPA/ABV, ASA, MCBA, MBA
Trugman Valuation Associates, Inc.
Plantation, Florida
linda@trugmanvaluation.com

Peter M. Walzer
Walzer & Melcher
Woodland Hills, California
pmw@walzermelcher.com

Richard M. Wise, FASA, MCBA, CVA, FCBV, FCA
Wise, Blackman LLP
Montreal, Canada
rmwise@wiseblackman.com

Several members of the staff of Shannon Pratt Valuations, Inc., Portland, Oregon, provided assistance with this edition, and we would like to express our gratitude for their professional and outstanding assistance.

Frances Fan, financial analyst, assisted with tracking the multiple iterations of the manuscript and conducting research. Along with Frances, Angelina McKedy, senior financial analyst, and Kim Linebarger, financial analyst, also assisted with research.

The glossary was updated by Kim Linebarger, and the bibliography was prepared by Frances Fan.

Paul Anthony, executive assistant to Dr. Pratt, assisted with logistic support and typing.

Last, but not least, the project manager on this book was Noah Gordon, legal counsel. He acted as a liaison and coordinator with the authors, the contributing authors, the reviewers, and the publisher. He also edited and proofread the manuscript. He was assisted in these endeavors by Frances Fan. This book could not have been completed without them.

We also would like to thank the editorial and production staffs at the American Bar Association for their assistance with this revision.

Finally, we wish to thank those who have written letters and had discussions with us about many conceptual and technical points since the last edition.

Shannon Pratt
Alina Niculita
Portland, Oregon

Chapter 1

Defining Value in the Relevant Context: Definitions of Value

It may come as a shock to some clients to learn that there may be two or more definitions of value for the same property at the same time. Furthermore, one definition may legitimately lead to an amount that is more than twice as much as the amount from another definition.

For example, the phrase "fair market value of these shares" is frequently found in buy-sell agreements. Usually, the minority parties to the agreements just assume that "fair market value" means a proportionate share of the value of the enterprise as a whole. When the triggering event occurs, they are shocked to find out that the term implies discounts for minority interest and lack of marketability, sometimes totaling 50 percent!

The oft-quoted expression "value lies in the eye of the beholder" is not very helpful when there is a legal need for a definition of value. Unquestionably, value is defined differently in different legal contexts. Unfortunately, the quest for the appropriate definition in any particular legal context is often a very difficult one. Therefore, identifying the correct definition of value in the legal context is a crucial beginning step in an appraisal.

The appraiser and the lawyer should agree on the definition of value at the outset, and the definition should be included in the written assignment. It is best to define and cite the source of definition and, if appropriate, to include such details in a buy-sell or arbitration agreement.

The valuation practitioner can bring experience to bear in helping the lawyer at this step. However, there is a strong concern that the definition of value is, ultimately, a legal question and therefore is the responsibility of the lawyer.

If an expert's procedures do not follow the pertinent legal definition of value, the judge may disallow the entire testimony.[1]

Commonly Used Definitions of Value[2]

The two most common expressions indicating definitions of value found in U.S. statutes are *fair market value* and *fair value*. There are other significant terms that appear in court case opinions, such as *market value, true value, true cash value, intrinsic value, investment value, marital value,* and more. These opinions rarely explain the meaning of the term or include authority or precedent for its use.

Other than fair market value and fair value, business appraisers and investment bankers will also frequently use *investment value* and *intrinsic* or *fundamental value.* These three terms are often found in court opinions, but again, usually without definition.

Fair Market Value

In the United States and Canada, the most widely recognized and accepted standard of value is *fair market value*. It is the standard that applies to most U.S. federal and state tax matters, such as estate taxes, gift taxes, inheritance taxes, income taxes, and ad valorem taxes. It is also the legal standard of value in some other valuation situations, primarily those involving taxes. The U.S. Treasury regulations define fair market value of a business interest as "the net amount which a willing purchaser, whether an individual or a corporation, would pay for the interest to a willing seller, neither being under any compulsion to buy or to sell and both having reasonable knowledge of relevant facts."[3]

There is general agreement that the definition implies that the parties have the ability—as well as the willingness—to effectuate this hypothetical cash transaction. The "market" in this definition can be thought of as all the potential buyers and sellers of like businesses or professional practices.

In the legal interpretations of fair market value, the willing buyer and willing seller are hypothetical persons, dealing at arm's length, rather than any particular buyer or seller. In other words, a price would not be considered representative of fair market value if it is influenced by special motivations not characteristic of a typical buyer or seller.

---

1. *See, e.g.,* Matter of Slant/Fin. Corp. v. The Chicago Corp. (N.Y. Sup. Ct. Oct. 5, 1995), *aff'd,* 236 A.D.2d 547, 654 N.Y.S.2d 627 (N.Y. App. Div. Feb. 18, 1997); Le Beau v. M.G. Bancorporation, Inc., 1998 Del. Ch. LEXIS 9, 1998 WL 44993 (Del. Ch. Jan. 29, 1998).

2. For a thorough discussion of definitions of value, *see* JAY FISHMAN ET AL., STANDARDS OF VALUE: THEORY AND APPLICATIONS (Wiley 2006).

3. 26 C.F.R. 20.2031–3. *See also* Rev. Rul. 59-60.

In Canada, however, fair market value may include the value of synergies with a particular buyer.[4]

The fair market value concept, however, which assumes an open and unrestricted market, does not preclude identifying groups of willing participants. Quite the contrary the valuer should be able to identify categories of willing purchasers. Furthermore, the analyst cannot ignore the position of the seller. However, the seller is assumed to be willing to sell under conditions that exist as of the valuation date.

The concept of fair market value also assumes prevalent economic and market conditions at the date of the particular valuation. You have probably heard it said many times: "I couldn't get anywhere near the value of my house if I put it on the market today," or "The value of XYZ Company stock is really much more (or less) than the price it's selling for on the New York Stock Exchange today." The standard of value that those people have in mind is some standard other than fair market value. This is because the concept of fair market value means the price at which a transaction could be expected to take place under conditions existing at the valuation date. In other words, one could say that the fair market value buyer is looking for the best risk/reward relationship available in the market at a given time.

The terms *market value* and *cash value* are sometimes used interchangeably with *fair market value*. Real estate appraisers generally use the term market value rather than fair market value. The Appraisal Foundation in its *Uniform Standards of Professional Appraisal Practice* (USPAP) defines market value as follows:

> A type of value, stated as an opinion, that presumes the transfer of a property (i.e., a right of ownership or a bundle of such rights), as of a certain date, under specific conditions set forth in the definition of the term identified by the appraiser as applicable in an appraisal.
>
> *Comment*: Forming an opinion of market value is the purpose of many real property appraisal assignments, particularly when the client's intended use includes more than one intended user. The conditions included in market value definitions establish market perspectives for development of the opinion. These conditions may vary from definition to definition but generally fall into three categories:
>
> 1. the relationship, knowledge, and motivation of the parties (i.e., seller and buyer);
> 2. the terms of sale (e.g., cash, cash equivalent, or other terms); and

4. For a thorough discussion of this issue, *see* Richard M. Wise, *The Effect of Special Interest Purchases on Fair Market Value in Canada*, 22:4 BUS. VALUATION REV., at 196–202 (American Society of Appraisers 2003).

3. the conditions of sale (e.g., exposure in a competitive market for a reasonable time prior to sale).

Appraisers are cautioned to identify the exact definition of market value, and its authority, applicable in each appraisal completed for the purpose of determining market value.[5]

As you can see from the above, market value as defined by USPAP is virtually synonymous with fair market value as defined in the U.S. Treasury regulations.

Judge David Laro, in a U.S. Tax Court decision, articulated the following as some guiding principles regarding the estimation of fair market value:

1. The willing buyer and the willing seller are hypothetical persons, rather than specific individuals or entities, and the characteristics of these hypothetical persons are not necessarily the same as the personal characteristics of the actual seller or a particular buyer.
2. Fair market value is determined as of the valuation date, and no knowledge of unforeseeable future events, which may have affected the value is given to the hypothetical persons.
3. Fair market value equals the highest and best use to which the property could be put on the valuation date, and fair market value takes into account special uses that are realistically available due to the property's adaptability to a particular business. Fair market value is not affected by whether the owner has actually put the property to its highest and best use. The reasonable, realistic, and objective possible uses for the property in the near future control the valuation thereof. Elements affecting value that depend upon events or a combination of occurrences which, while within the realm of possibility, are not reasonably probable, are excluded from this consideration.[6]

It is generally understood that fair market value means a value in cash or cash equivalents (as indicated in The Appraisal Foundation definition of market value) unless otherwise stated.

It is important to recognize that the fair market value of an equity interest in a business is *not* the pro rata share of the fair market value of the equity of the entire business. The value of equity interests can be impacted by such factors as liquidity discounts, minority discounts and blockage.

5. THE APPRAISAL FOUNDATION, UNIFORM STANDARDS OF PROFESSIONAL APPRAISAL PRACTICE 2010–2011 Edition.

6. Pabst Brewing Co. v. Comm'r, T.C. Memo. 1996-506 (1996).

Fair Value under State Statutes

The expression *fair value* is an excellent example of ambiguous terminology used in the field of commercial appraisal. To understand what the expression means, one has to know the context of its use. In the context of a standard of value in business valuation, the term fair value is a term found in state statutes governing dissenting stockholder and minority oppression actions. Its meaning is quite different from the term as used in Generally Accepted Accounting Principles, where until recently fair value and fair market value were used almost interchangeably.[7] Courts have given very different interpretations to the term fair value as a statutory business value standard.

Presently, fair value is the statutory standard of value provided for by state law. Courts will apply this statutory standard in cases involving dissenting stockholders' appraisal rights. These rights of action arise where the aggrieved party alleges that he or she is being forced to accept less than adequate consideration for his stock following a merger or sale of the business. Here, the aggrieved party seeks to enforce his or her right to have his/her shares appraised and to receive fair value in cash.[8]

Revisions made to the *Model Business Corporation Act of 1950* and adoption of the same, in part or in full, by 35 states has led to uniformity before the 1984 revision and being called the *Revised Model Business Corporation Act* (RMBCA). Prior to the 1999 the RMBCA defined fair value as:

> The value of the shares immediately before the effectuation of the corporate action to which the shareholder objects, excluding any appreciation or depreciation in anticipation of the corporate action unless exclusion would be inequitable.

In 1999, the definition changed to:

> "Fair value" means the value of the corporation's shares determined:
> (i) immediately before the effectuation of the corporate action to which the shareholder objects;
> (ii) using customary and current valuation concepts and techniques generally employed for similar businesses in the context of the transaction requiring appraisal; and
> (iii) without discounting for lack of marketability or minority status except, if appropriate, for amendments to the articles.

7. SFAS 157, Fair Value Measurements.
8. For a complete listing of states' dissenters' rights statutes, *see* www.BVLibrary.com.

Although many states adopted the RMBCA pre-1999 definition,[9] only a few of the states have adopted the 1999 version.[10] A minority of states that adopted the pre-1999 definition did so without the "unless exclusion would be inequitable" phrase;[11] other states omit this phrase but, in addition, add a clause that states that all relevant factors should be considered in determining value.[12] Florida and Illinois use a hybrid of the pre-1999 and 1999 definitions.

Despite the revisions, there is no clearly recognized consensus about the definition of fair value in the context of dissenting shareholder statutes.[13] However, the judicial precedents of most states certainly have not equated it to fair market value. When a situation arises of actual or potential stockholder dissent, it is important to carefully research the legal precedents applicable to each case and to take note of the date.

The term fair value is also found in the dissolution statutes of those states that have such statutes (for example, California Corporations Code Section 2000). An increasing number of states have enacted such statutes in recent years. Under these statutes, stockholders can trigger a corporate dissolution under certain circumstances. The company can avoid dissolution by paying the stockholders the fair value of their shares. Even within the same state, however, a study of case law precedents does not necessarily lead one to the same definition of fair value under a dissolution statute as under that state's dissenting stockholder statute.[14]

The term fair value in the context of state statutes is more extensively discussed in Chapter 18.

In summary, *fair market value* is a willing buyer/willing seller standard, whereas *fair value* does not necessarily assume a "willing" seller and/or a "willing" buyer.

Fair Value for Financial Reporting[15]

The Financial Accounting Standard Board (FASB) has another definition of fair value. Here, the term is used for financial reporting purposes; specifically, to report the fair values of certain assets and liabilities appearing on financial statements.

---

9. Alabama, Arizona, Arkansas, Colorado, Hawaii, Indiana, Kentucky, Massachusetts, Michigan, Missouri, Montana, Nebraska, Nevada, New Hampshire, North Carolina, Oregon, South Carolina, Vermont, Washington, and Wisconsin.

10. Connecticut, Idaho, Iowa, Maine, Mississippi, South Dakota, Virginia, West Virginia, and Wyoming.

11. Georgia, New Mexico, Rhode Island, Tennessee, and Utah.

12. Delaware, Oklahoma, and Pennsylvania.

13. *See* Model Business Corporation Act 2007 (4th ed. American Bar Association 2008).

14. *See, e.g.*, Lawson Mardon Wheaton, Inc. v. Smith, 160 N.J. 383, 734 A.2d 738 (1999); Balsamides v. Protameen Chemicals, Inc., 160 N.J. 352, 734 A.2d 721 (1999).

15. This section is excerpted from Shannon P. Pratt & Alina V. Niculita, Valuing a Business (5th ed. 2007).

The fair value definition was promulgated in Statement of Financial Accounting Standards (SFAS) 157.[16] It is effective for financial statements issued for fiscal years beginning after November 15, 2007, and for interim periods within those years.

The SFAS 157 definition is as follows:

> The price that would be received to sell an asset or paid to transfer a liability in an orderly transaction between market participants at the measurement date.

The important feature of this definition is that it is an *exit* price, *not* the price that would be paid to acquire the asset or to assume the liability (an *entry* price). SFAS 157 emphasizes that assets should not be valued at cost (an *entry* price) unless they can be disposed of at cost.

The "market" referred to in this definition is "the market in which the reporting entity would transact for the asset or liability, that is, the principal or most advantageous market for the asset or liability." Thus, the definition specifies an orderly transaction in the most advantageous market. Market participants are buyers and sellers in the principal (or the most advantageous) market for the asset or liability. These market participants are (1) unrelated, (2) knowledgeable about factors relevant to the asset or liability and the transaction, (3) able to transact (i.e., have the legal and financial ability to do so), and (4) willing to transact (i.e., motivated but not forced or otherwise compelled to transact). SFAS 157 clarifies that the term *fair value* is intended to mean a market-based measure, not an entity-specific measure.

The fair value premise for an asset is the asset's highest and best use from the perspective of market participants, which would maximize a company's future cash flows. A company's intended use of an asset is not necessarily indicative of the highest and best use of that asset as determined by a market participant; the fair value measure is *not* an entity-specific measure that reflects only the company's expectations for the asset. SFAS 157 requires that fair value measures consider the perspectives of market participants and the assumptions that those participants would use to price an asset or a liability.

The market price on the valuation date is fair value if there is an active market for the subject asset or liability, but not if the market is thin. The FASB identifies three levels in the hierarchy of measurements to quantify fair value, with the highest level available to be used:

16. Compare IFRS 3 (defining "fair value" as "the amount for which an asset could be exchanged or a liability settled between knowledgeable, willing parties in an arm's-length transaction").

Level 1	(highest-priority) inputs are quoted prices in active markets for identical assets or liabilities.
Level 2	inputs are those other than quoted prices included within Level 1 that are directly or indirectly observable.
Level 3	inputs are unobservable inputs that reflect assumptions about what market participants would use in their pricing analyses.

This would imply that, if there is an active market for the subject asset, the quoted price on the valuation date would apply. For those assets for which there is not an active market, but for which there is an active market for close comparables, the prices for the comparables, with appropriate adjustments for differences, could be used as inputs. The standard clearly favors observable market data. For other subject assets (Level 3 assets), other valuation methods, including the discounted cash flow (DCF), could be used as inputs. The company may use its own assumptions, but Level 3 inputs must be adjusted if information is available that indicates that market participants would use different assumptions.

Although the FASB emphasizes "market participant assumptions at the measurement date," there are differences between "fair value" for financial reporting purposes and "fair market value." For example, SFAS 157 apparently makes a (perhaps unintended) distinction between legally imposed restrictions on sale (e.g., restricted stock, which normally *should* be discounted) and market-imposed restrictions (e.g., blocks of stock that are too large to be sold without depressing the market, which *should not* be discounted for what the market refers to as "blockage"). Blocks of stock are to be valued at price times quantity, with no discount applied for the size of the block. However, there is the contrary opinion that no discounts are applied for SFAS 123R.[17] The FASB says that it did not adopt the definition of fair market value because it did not want the definition of fair value to be saddled with the nuances of court interpretations of fair market value.

Investment Value

The primary distinguishing characteristic of *investment value* is that it denotes *value to a particular owner or investor.* This is in contrast to fair market value, which is a concept of value in exchange, assuming hypothetical, typically motivated buyers and sellers. In other words, investment value is the value to a particular individual or entity, considering that individual's or entity's situation, perceptions, and motivation, not necessarily value in the marketplace. This is also essentially the same way that investment value is defined in the context of real estate appraisal.[18]

17. Scott Beauchene & Robert Duffy, *Getting Ready for 409A: Some Practical Considerations*, Business Valuation Update, May 2007.

18. *See* Appraisal Institute, The Appraisal of Real Estate 26 (12th ed. 2001).

Investment value is generally a "subjective" value, whereas *fair market value* is an "objective" value.

There are many valid reasons for the investment value to one particular owner or prospective owner to differ from the fair market value. Investment value considers the following unique factors:

1. Synergies with other operations owned or controlled—for example, buyer has a particular use for the particular property;
2. Relationships with other owners;
3. Differences in estimates of future earning power and/or perception of degree of risk;
4. Differences in aversion to or willingness to accept degrees of risk; and
5. Differences in income tax status.

Whether or not the term investment value is actually used, the concept is found frequently in business valuations for marital dissolution. That is, the courts often focus on value to the spouse who operates the business as opposed to value that could be realized in the market.

Finally, investment value has a slightly different meaning when used in the context of dissenting stockholder suits. In this context, it means a value based on earning power. However, the appropriate present value discount rate or the direct capitalization rate is usually considered to be a consensus rate rather than a rate peculiarly appropriate for any specific investor.

Intrinsic or Fundamental Value

Financial analysts that follow and report on publicly traded stock commonly use *Intrinsic value* (sometimes called *fundamental value*) to estimate value. Intrinsic value differs from investment value in that it represents an analytical judgment of value based on the investment characteristics perceived by a financial analyst rather than on how the characteristics comport to the circumstances of a particular investor.

Concurrence on the meanings of intrinsic value and fundamental value is found in the following definitions from an authoritative reference in the accounting field.

- *Intrinsic value:* The amount that an investor considers, on the basis of an evaluation of available facts, to be the "true" or "real" worth of an item, usually an *equity security*. The value that will become the market value when other investors reach the same conclusions. The various approaches to determining intrinsic value of the *finance* literature are based on expectations and discounted cash flows. See *expected value; fundamental analysis; discounted cash flow method.*[19]

- *Fundamental analysis:* An approach in security analysis which assumes that a security has an "intrinsic value" that can be determined through a rigorous evaluation of relevant variables. Expected earnings is usually the most important variable in this analysis, but many other variables, such as dividends, capital structure, management quality, and so on, may also be studied. An analyst estimates the "intrinsic value" of a security on the basis of those fundamental variables and compares this value with the current market price of this security to arrive at an investment decision.[20]

In the analysis of securities, intrinsic value is generally considered the appropriate price for a stock according to a financial analyst who has completed a fundamental analysis of the company's assets, earning power, and other factors. Two University of Chicago professors comment on the notion of intrinsic value as follows:

> The purpose of security analysis is to detect differences between the value of a security as determined by the market and a security's "intrinsic value"—that is, the value that the security *ought* to have and will have when other investors have the same insight and knowledge as the analyst.[21]

If the market value is below what the analyst concludes is the intrinsic value, then the analyst considers the stock a "buy." If the market value is above the assumed intrinsic value, the analyst suggests selling the stock.

It is important to note that the concept of intrinsic value cannot be entirely disassociated from the concept of fair market value. This is because the actions of buyers and sellers based on their *specific* perceptions of intrinsic value eventually lead to the *general* consensus market value and the constant and dynamic changes in market value over time.

Case law often refers to intrinsic value. However, almost universally, such references do not define the term other than by reference to the language in the context in which it appears. Such references to intrinsic value can be found both in case opinions where there is no statutory standard of value and also in case decisions where the statutory standard of value is specified as fair value or even fair market value. When references to intrinsic value appear in the relevant case law, the court usually is refer-

19. KOHLER'S DICTIONARY FOR ACCOUNTANTS 285 (6th ed. 1983) (W.W. Cooper & Yuri Ijiri eds.), *reprinted by permission.*

20. *Id.* at 228.

21. JAMES H. LORIE ET AL., THE STOCK MARKET; THEORIES AND EVIDENCE (2d ed. (1984).

ring to notions such as those discussed in this section. It is also common to find court cases that use the term intrinsic value to mean the inherent worth of the stock to the owner—in other words, to equate the term to investment value, as defined earlier.

Other Terms Referring to Value

Acquisition Value

The term *acquisition value* means the value to a particular acquirer. It is a term that is very similar to strategic value (see below). In this sense, the term falls within the concept of investment value, as described in the previous section.

The term may also be used to denote the actual price at which a transaction occurred. In this sense, it would be the same as transaction value, described more fully below.

Book Value

The term *book value* is an accounting term, not a financial term, and is not necessarily, or even usually, indicative of any of the definitions of value discussed in the previous section. It is not related to any concept of economic value.

The term represents historical costs of assets owned by the entity, less any depreciation or amortization deducted in the accounting system used by that entity. The American Society of Appraisers defines book value as follows:

> With respect to a business enterprise, the difference between total assets (net of accumulated depreciation, depletion, and amortization) and total liabilities as they appear on the balance sheet (synonymous with shareholders' equity). With respect to a specific asset, the capitalized cost less accumulated amortization or depreciation as it appears on the books of account of the business enterprise.[22]

It is noteworthy that many of a company's most valuable assets, especially if goodwill and other intangible assets are developed internally rather than purchased,[23] may not appear on the balance sheet at all. Similarly, there may be liabilities, especially those of a contingent nature, that do not appear on the balance sheet.

22. American Society of Appraisers Business Valuation Standards, Glossary (July 2008).
23. IPR&D generally refers to R & D acquired in an acquisition.

Going-Concern Value

The term *going-concern value* has two separate and distinct meanings, depending on the context in which it is used.

In one sense, it refers to the premise of the total value of the operations of the company on an ongoing basis. This concept is discussed in more detail in the section on Premises of Value in Chapter 2.

The other concept of going-concern value is that of an intangible asset. In that context, it means the value of having a system of operating assets, systems, and personnel in place, with the ability to operate. It can be thought of as the difference between merely a set of physical assets and a "turnkey" operation ready to do business. For example, some courts in addressing the value of a professional practice for marital dissolution purposes, have distinguished between the personal goodwill of the professional (not part of the marital estate) and the value of having support staff, systems, and other operating systems in place (the "going-concern value," to be valued and included as part of the marital estate). Other courts, however, conceive of "going-concern value" as "the ability to generate income without interruption, even when there has been a change in ownership," and find that goodwill value is a *component* of the going concern value of a business.[24]

Enterprise Value

A term that causes much confusion is *enterprise value*. Frequently it is used to mean the market value of the company's entire capital structure (all equity and long-term debt). Less often it is used to describe market cap plus interest-bearing debt plus preferred stock minus total cash and cash equivalents. At other times, it refers to the total value of the company's common stock on a control basis. When this term is encountered, one should carefully try to interpret its meaning from the context in which it is used.

Liquidation Value

Liquidation value means the net amount that can be realized (after liquidation expenses) in either an orderly or a forced sale of the business assets or some portion of them. Variations of liquidation value are discussed in Chapter 2 under the section on Premises of Value.

Strategic Value (Synergistic Value)

A *strategic* or *synergistic value* reflects added benefits to a particular acquirer because of synergies with the acquiree. That is, it is a price or potential price reflecting all or

24. *See, e.g.*, Gaydos v. Gaydos, 693 A.2d 1368 (Pa. Super. Ct. 1997).

some portion of the value of synergistic benefits created through the combination of the respective entities for which a buyer might be willing to pay. Such benefits could include, for example, increasing market share, adding new strategic alliances, reducing costs by combining operations, particularly in the form of either staff reductions, sale of redundant assets or economies of scale, and/or raising prices by eliminating a competitor, to name a few.

Synergistic value generally reflects some added value above fair market value. Because it reflects the value of benefits available to a particular buyer, it is usually considered to fall within the concept of *investment value*, as discussed previously.

Transaction Value

Transaction value is the price at which an actual transaction occurs. The transaction could be either in the form of an asset sale or a stock sale. The International Business Brokers Association (Business Brokers Glossary) defines the term as follows:

> The total of all consideration passed at any time between the buyer and seller for an ownership interest in a business enterprise and may include, but is not limited to, all remuneration for tangible and intangible assets such as furniture, equipment, supplies, inventory, working capital, non-competition agreements, employment, and/or consultation agreements, licenses, customer lists, franchise fees, assumed liabilities, stock options, stock or stock redemptions, real estate, leases, royalties, earn-outs, and future considerations.

Some definitions exclude the value of non-competition agreements and/or employment agreements on the basis that payments for these intangibles often are contingent on future personal performance.

Transaction value specifically refers to *price* as opposed to *value.* It is empirical (historical) in nature, not a legal standard of value. *Price* is the *face value* (the amount shown on the transaction documents) at which a specific transaction occurred, without any adjustment to cash-equivalent value to reflect special terms. The price may or may not represent arm's-length negotiation. It may be arrived at by negotiation, by contract, by court order, or by some other means. It may or may not comport to any of the definitions of value discussed in the previous section. The use of transaction prices in the market approach to appraisal is further discussed in Chapter 6.

Sources of Authority for Definition of Value

The search for the appropriate definition of value usually proceeds in approximately the following hierarchy:

- Statutory law
- Legally binding rules and regulations
- Contractual definitions of value
- Non–legally binding administrative rules
- Precedential court decisions
- Direction from the court
- Direction from the lawyer
- Use of IRS authority in non-tax situations
- Opinions of other lawyers and appraisers

Statutory Law

Our experience has been that statutes have the advantage of having the greatest force of law and the disadvantage of being the least explicit of all sources in defining value.

The relevant statutes may be either federal or state. For example, federal statutes require that valuations for tax purposes will be at fair market value.[25] Most state statutes governing dissenting stockholders require that valuations will be at fair value and most (if using the Revised Model Business Corporation Act or a close variation of it) add that the valuation date will be the day before the event to which the shareholder dissents, without considering the effect of that event. Most state statutes governing marital dissolution are silent about definitions of value other than some language about valuation dates.

Specifics of statutory law are discussed in considerable detail in the various chapters relating to the purposes of the valuation, such as gift and estate tax, shareholder disputes, marital dissolution, etc. The purpose of this chapter is simply to make the point that statutory law usually is the first stop in the quest for the proper legal definition of value. Some examples of statutory law include:

Federal Statutes

- The Internal Revenue Code (IRC), especially § 2031 on estate taxes, § 2512 for gift taxes, and §§ 2701–04 on intra-family transfers
- ERISA (The Employee Retirement Income Security Act) (29 U.S.C. §1002(26))
- The U.S. Bankruptcy Code (11 U.S.C §522(a)(2) "value" means fair market value as of the date of filing the petition)[26]
- The Securities and Exchange Act

25. I.R.C. § 2031.

26. *See, e.g.,* Active Wear, Inc. v. Parkdale Mills, Inc., 331 B.R. 669 (W.D. Va. 2005), which elaborates on the statutory definition, and defines fair market value as the "value the debtor/bankrupt could receive for the property in a liquidation sale."

State Statutes

- State revenue codes
- State securities codes
- Business Corporations Act (often the Uniform Business Corporation Act), usually addressing dissenting stockholder valuations
- Statutes granting oppressed minority shareholder relief, including an appraisal option (in a growing number of states)
- Marital dissolution statutes, which generally do not address valuation matters

Legally Binding Rules and Regulations

Many legislative bills authorize rules and regulations that have the force of law, with implementation delegated to an administrative authority. Examples include:

- U.S. Treasury regulations
- Federal Rules of Evidence and Civil Procedure
- Various state revenue regulations
- DOL (Department of Labor) proposed regulation 29 CFR Part 2510[27] on Definition of Adequate Consideration for ESOP (Employee Stock Ownership Plan) stock
  - DOL issued the proposed regulation in 1988, it has never been finalized.
  - Despite lack of finalization, it provides guidance, and most ESOP appraisers consider compliance with it important.

Contractual Definitions of Value

Parties sometimes are bound by contractual definitions of value in documents governing certain types of transactions. Such documents may include:

- Articles of organization
- Articles of incorporation or partnership
- Bylaws
- Shareholder, operating or partnership agreements
- Prenuptial agreements
- Agreements entered into specifically for the purpose of settlement of the instant dispute, such as arbitration agreements

27. Prop. DOL Reg. § 2510.3-18(b)(2)(ii) includes a two-part test: (1) The price paid must reflect the fair market value of the asset, and (2) the trustee/fiduciaries must conduct a careful and independent investigation of the circumstances prevailing at the time of the investment.

Such agreements may be very helpful in defining value for the purpose at hand, or they may be the source of another element of controversy.

- **Is the definition of value legally binding in the instant case?** Even if it is not, it *may* be accorded some weight, especially if it has been used in other transactions with some similar characteristics.
- **Is the definition of value clear and unambiguous?** Unfortunately, documents intended to provide guidance all too often are drafted with ambiguous language that leaves the interpretation open to a controversy in itself. We recommend that an appraiser be consulted to review draft language relating to value to be sure that the lawyers and all parties to the agreement understand the value implications in the document.

Non–Legally Binding Administrative Rulings

Many government agencies issue rulings containing their interpretations of definitions of value. Courts usually give consideration to such rulings, but a court will not necessarily accept them if it feels that they are not consistent with the law.

For example, the IRS issued Revenue Ruling 81-253, which said that a minority discount should not be applied to gifts of minority shares of stock if other members of the family controlled the company. IRS Revenue Rulings represent the position of the IRS; they are not the law. The position taken in Revenue Ruling 81-253 lost every time it was challenged in court,[28] and finally (after 12 years) the IRS reversed its position with Revenue Ruling 93-12, recognizing that shares were to be valued on the basis of the size of the block transferred, irrespective of attribution of family control value.

Precedential Court Decisions

By far the richest source of specific guidance as to definitions of value in almost any legal context is interpretation found in precedential case decisions. This book contains many annotations to decisions on valuation issues in many legal contexts (for example, tax, dissent, divorce) and in many jurisdictions. Careful study of precedential case law is a very important step in understanding the relevant legal definition of value.

Having made that point, again, it is also important to examine many challenges and pitfalls inherent in using precedential case law as a source of guidance for definitions of value and understand the context.

28. *See, e.g.,* Estate of Andrews v. Comm'r, 79 T.C. 938 (1982).

- **Lack of precedent.** There are valuation issues for which no precedent exists in many state jurisdictions. In such cases, courts tend to cite precedent from other states that have similar statutes governing the issue. Each lawyer, of course, seeks out precedent in other jurisdictions that support his or her position.
- **Ambiguous language.** Most judges are not experts in financial language, and financial language itself has many ambiguities. For example, an opinion may use the term *fair market value* and then accept valuation methods that reflect factors that are not consistent with most courts' and financial analysts' understanding of the definition.
- **Distinguishable facts and circumstances.** The lawyers, and sometimes the appraisers, may identify facts and circumstances in the case at bar that may lead to an interpretation of the definition of value that is different from that found in a seemingly on-point precedential decision.
- **Sweeping generalizations.** Opinions sometimes contain broad statements that, if read literally, would apply to a broader set of cases or circumstances than the court may have intended. Here the solution would seem to be to carefully distinguish the facts and circumstances of the instant case from those of the case with the oversweeping statement. It usually is preferable that the lawyer, rather than the appraiser, originate the discussion of such distinctions in court.
- **Changing and contradictory precedent.** Precedential positions on issues sometimes change as a result of revisiting an issue. Be sure to rely on the latest case decisions. Precedents within a jurisdiction sometimes seem to contradict each other. In that case, one might look for possible differentiation in facts and circumstances between the seemingly contradictory precedents. When relying on a U.S. Court of Appeals decision, remember that it is only controlling in the circuit that issued the opinion, and it is not uncommon to find different circuits holding contradictory opinions.

Direction from the Court

Sometimes, especially in a case of first impression on an issue, it is possible for the lawyer to request and get a ruling from the court on the definition of value and/or the applicable valuation date before the appraiser prepares the report. This can save a great deal of expense in preparing reports under different definitions of value and/or two or more different valuation dates.

Direction from the Lawyer

Sometimes the lawyer has a clear-cut concept of the legal theory of the case, and that theory dictates a definition of value that the lawyer directs the appraiser to use. If the source of the definition of value is the lawyer rather than some quotable statutory or regulatory language, the appraiser usually will state this in the discussion of the definition of value in the introductory portion of the report.

Use of IRS Authority in Non-Tax Situations

It is not uncommon for appraisers to cite IRS authority, such as Revenue Rulings, when describing the nuances of the definition of fair market value. If this is done for a valuation other than for federal taxes, counsel should make sure that the legal standard of value is fair market value, and that the legal context has not created any nuances of the definition different from those for federal tax purposes.

Opinions of Other Lawyers and Appraisers

From time to time one may gain points of view on definitions of value from experienced lawyers or appraisers. These may come from either writings or discussions.

For example, one leading California corporate lawyer has published clear-cut ideas about the definition of fair value under California Corporations Code 2000. This attorney adds that "the cases provide only a patchwork of insights, only some of which are consistent with the basic purpose of Section 2000."[29]

29. Arthur J. Shartsis, *Dissolution Actions Yield Less than Fair Market Value (Appraising for 'Fair Value' Under California Corporations Code Section 2000)*, BVR's Annual Guide to Fair Value in Shareholder Dissent, Oppression, and Marital Dissolution, chs. 6-1 through 6-13 (Portland, Ore: Business Valuation Resources 2009).

Chapter 2

Value to Whom? Levels and Premises of Value

"Level of value" refers to the degree of control and liquidity of the shares. The greater the control and the more liquid, the higher the value. Discounts for lack of control usually are taken before discounts for lack of marketability (DLOM) and the DLOM usually is applied to whatever level of control is determined. In other words, the discounts for lack of control and lack of marketability are taken sequentially not additively.

"Premise of value" in this context refers to the state of the company at the valuation date, that is, is it a going concern value or a value in liquidation?

Levels of Value

The attorney and the appraiser should decide at the outset what level of value the appraisal will represent. Exhibit 2-1 (page 20) is a schematic depiction of the basic possible levels of value. The relative dollar amounts and percentages used are strictly for illustration purposes. Each situation should be analyzed on a fact-specific basis.

The typical levels of value to be appraised in a closely held company are either control or minority nonmarketable. "Nonmarketable" means that the shares cannot be sold to the general public because they have not been registered with the Securities and Exchange Commission (SEC).

The level above control is the strategic acquisition value. This level reflects the incremental amount over the control value that a strategic buyer might pay recognizing the perceived synergies between the selling company and the buying company. This level could be appropriate if the purpose of the appraisal was to estimate a price that a synergistic buyer might pay. However, unless there are a group of synergistic buyers who create a market, fair market value reflects the value of the company on a stand-alone basis and does not include possible synergies with other companies.

The line below control, "minority marketable," reflects an estimate of what the minority shares might trade for in a public market. If the company is run to its

Exhibit 2-1
"Levels of Value" in Terms of Characteristics of Ownership

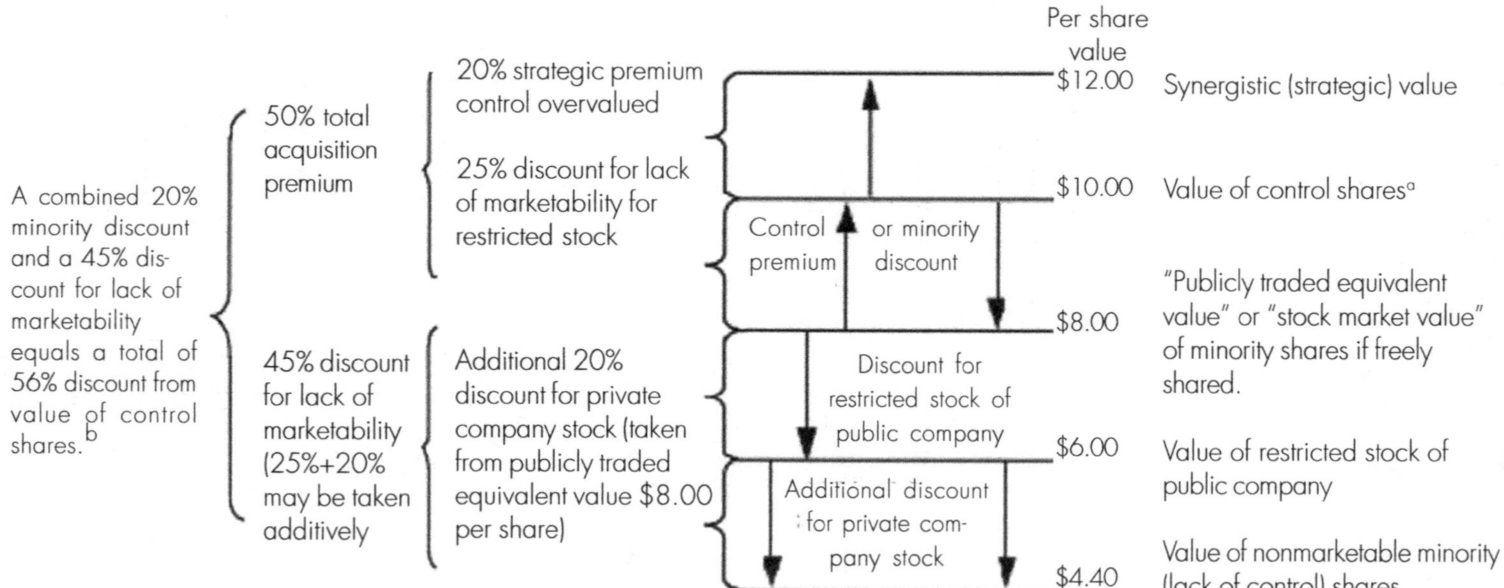

Notes:

a Control shares in a privately held company may also be subject to some discount for lack of marketability, but usually not nearly as much as minority shares.

b Minority and marketability discounts normally are multiplicative rather than additive. That is, they are taken in sequence:

$10.00	Control Value
– 2.00	Less: Minority interest discount (.20 x $10.00)
$ 8.00	Marketable minority value
– 3.60	Less lack of marketability discount (.45 x $8.00)
$ 4.40	Per-share value of nonmarketable minority shares

Source: Jay E. Fishman, et al., *PPC's Guide to Business Valuations*, 19th ed.

maximum efficiency and minority shareholders are treated equally with control shareholders, there may be no basis for a control premium. This is discussed further in Chapter 15 on "Discounts and Premiums."

The next level down is restricted stocks of public companies. Some publicly traded companies may not have all their shares registered for public trading (they might issue unregistered shares for an acquisition, for example), but they can sell blocks of unregistered shares to qualified investors (such as institutional investors). These blocks usually are sold at a discount compared to the same day's public trading price. (See Chapter 15 for more details.) Until the 1990s, these discounts averaged about 35 percent (but a very wide range of discounts existed) and the restricted stock discounts sometimes were used as a proxy for the discount for lack of marketability for closely held stocks.

Around 1990, the SEC started to loosen restrictions on sales of restricted stocks and, accordingly, the discounts started to come down. But the loosening of SEC regulations for restricted stocks of publicly traded companies did nothing to enhance the marketability of closely held stock, for which there is little or no market. So another lower line was added to reflect the fact that minority interests in closely held stocks are much less marketable than restricted stocks of public companies.

Chapter 15 discusses discounts for lack of control and lack of marketability as well as discounts for other attributes.

Premises of Value

A *premise of value* is an assumption about the status of the business under which a transaction would be expected to take place, that is, as a going concern or in liquidation, or some variation or combination of going concern or liquidation value, e.g., some operating assets and some excess assets? The selection among alternative possible premises of value obviously can have a major impact on value.

In some situations, the premise of value is mandated as part of the definition of value by controlling documents or the purpose of the valuation. In other situations, the premise (or premises) of value is left to the appraiser's judgment. For example, it may be left to the appraiser to determine what premise of value represents the highest and best use of the business or property.

Virtually all businesses or interests in businesses may be appraised under any of the following four alternative premises of value:

1. *Value as a going concern.* Value in continued use, as a mass assemblage of income-producing assets, and as a going-concern business enterprise.

2. *Value as an assemblage of assets.* Value in place, as part of a mass assemblage of assets, but not in current use in the production of income and not as a going-concern business enterprise.
3. *Value as an orderly disposition.* Value in exchange, on a piecemeal basis (not part of a mass assemblage of assets), as part of an orderly disposition; this premise contemplates that all the assets of the business enterprise will be sold individually and that they will enjoy normal exposure to their appropriate secondary market.
4. *Value as a forced liquidation.* Value in exchange, on a piecemeal basis (not part of a mass assemblage of assets), as part of a forced liquidation; this premise contemplates that the assets of the business enterprise will be sold individually and that they will experience less than normal exposure to their appropriate secondary market.[1]

Each of these alternative premises of value may apply under the same standard, or definition, of value. For example, the fair market value standard calls for a "willing buyer" and a "willing seller." Yet the willing buyer and seller have to make an informed economic decision about how they will transact with each other with regard to the subject business. In other words, is the subject business worth more to the buyer and the seller as a going concern that will continue to operate as such or as a collection of individual assets to be put to separate uses? In either case, the buyer and seller are still "willing." And in both cases, they have concluded a set of transactional circumstances that will maximize the value of the collective assets of the subject business enterprise.[2]

If left to the judgment of the appraiser, the premise of value selected may depend on whether the interest is being valued on a controlling interest or minority interest basis. In a controlling interest valuation, the selection of the appropriate premise of value typically is a function of the highest and best use of the collective assets of the subject business enterprise. The appraiser might value the operations of the business on a going-concern basis and the assets not necessary to operations on a liquidation basis.

If valuing on a minority interest basis, the appraiser is more likely to value on the assumption of "business as usual," that is, as a going concern. In other words, the appraiser normally would not assume a liquidation of any assets unless there was an indication that such a liquidation was imminent. This treatment has been accepted by the courts.[3]

1. Shannon P. Pratt & Alina V. Niculita, Valuing a Business 47 (5th ed. 2008).
2. *Id.*
3. *See, e.g.,* Foltz v. U.S. News & World Report, Inc., 106 F.R.D. 338 (D.C. Cir. 1984), *appealed and affirmed.*

Chapter 3

Overview of Business Valuation Approaches, Methods, and Procedures

Approaches and Methods Not Totally Discrete

The classification of business appraisal methodology is somewhat arbitrary because the methods are not totally discrete. Nevertheless, classification of methodologies helps bring some organization, which aids in both implementing and reviewing the appraisal process. The classification of methodology as presented in this chapter, while not followed universally, represents a growing consensus on the taxonomy of business appraisal. The organization of the remainder of the book generally follows this classification.

Business appraisers usually try to use two or more appraisal methods to maximize the reliability of the final result. They may give different relative weights to different methods or conclude that one appraisal method is dominant in a given situation. The reconciliation of results from different methods to reach a final conclusion is discussed in Chapter 16.

When business appraisers implement different methods, they generally try to make the data and procedures used in each method as discrete as possible from those used in the other methods to reach the different indications of value as independently as possible. For example, net cash flow usually is used in the income approach, while other income measures, e.g., sales or net income, typically are employed in the market approach.

However, there is necessarily some interrelationship among the methods. All methods are based on some form of economic income and/or asset values, and all depend to some extent on market data. The income approach uses expected economic income, while the market approach may use both historical and expected economic income. The asset approach uses adjusted asset values for all assets, while the income and market approaches may use asset values for excess or nonoperating assets. The income approach derives its discount and capitalization rates from data extracted from the market. The market approach uses market-derived multiples of some form of economic income variables and/or asset values.

Business appraisers capitalize income in both the market and income approaches—they just develop their capitalization rates in different ways. In the market approach, capitalization rates come from direct observation of specific market transactions. In the income approach, on the other hand, capitalization rates are developed through a cost of capital model using broad market data. The asset approach develops its adjusted asset values from market data.

In reviewing descriptions of different appraisal methods used in an appraisal report, the reviewer should think about the extent to which each method is really an indication of value independent of another method, or whether the appraiser is simply presenting the same data in different formats. For instance, the use of a market multiple of book value of equity in the market approach and the use of the book value of equity in the asset approach as separate indications of value are actually one and the same method. Another common misconception is the use of both a single-year capitalization of cash flows method and a multiyear discounted cash flows method. These two methods should not be used to produce two separate value indications within the same valuation assignment. As will be seen later, theoretically these methods produce the same value. Rather, the appraiser should determine if cash flow is sustainable (use a single-year capitalization) or not (use a multiyear forecast for the discounted cash flow).

Hierarchy of Approaches, Methods, and Procedures

The business valuation professional community generally has adopted a hierarchy of the terms *approach, method,* and *procedure:*

- *Approach* is the broadest of the three terms.
- *Method* refers to general ways of implementing the approaches.
- *Procedure* means the specific calculations, data used, and other details involved in a specific method.

Basic Appraisal Approaches

The three approaches recognized in business valuation essentially are analogous to the three approaches used in real estate appraisal:

1. **Income approach**—valuing the business or business interest on the basis of some form of expected economic income stream; in real estate appraisal usually called "capitalization."

2. **Market approach**—valuation of the business or business interest by reference to other transactions; in real estate appraisal usually called the "comparable sales approach."
3. **Asset-based approach**—valuation of the business on the basis of assets and liabilities; somewhat analogous to the "cost approach" in real estate appraisal.

Methods Used within Appraisal Approaches

Within each of the three approaches, there is reasonably wide consensus on the terminology used to denote the methods employed:

Income Approach Methods

Discounting. Projecting the expected economic income over the life of the investment and discounting each increment of that expected income back to a present value at a rate of return known as a *discount rate*. This method also is known as the discounted cash flow (DCF) method. (The procedures are similar to the method known as "yield capitalization" in real estate appraisal.)

Capitalizing. Observing or estimating a single period's economic income and dividing it by a rate of return adjusted for expected growth known as a *capitalization rate*. This method also is known as the capitalization method. (It is analogous to "direct capitalization" in real property appraisal.)

Market Approach Methods

Guideline public company method (sometimes called the "comparable company method"). Derives valuation multiples from prices and financial data of company stocks traded in the public market and applies the multiples to the appropriate financial data of the subject company. No counterpart exists in real estate appraisal because there is no organized market for fractional interests in real estate; any markets that might exist for fractional interests in real estate are likely to be very small and ad hoc.

Guideline transaction method. Derives valuation multiples from prices and financial data of public or private companies that have been sold and applies the multiples to the appropriate financial data of the subject company. This method is analogous to the "comparable sales approach" in real estate appraisal. (Some might further subdivide this method based on whether the guideline company was public or private before the sale.)

Past transactions method. Uses multiples of financial data from the company's own past transactions:

- Past change of ownership of 100 percent or a controlling interest in the subject company
- Past transactions of minority interests in the subject company
- Past acquisitions made by the subject company
- Past offers (but must examine whether bona fide and arm's length)

Buy-sell agreements. Placed arbitrarily under the market approach with the idea that someone negotiated and agreed to the buy-sell terms at some point in the past. Depending on the purpose of the valuation and the terms of the buy-sell agreement, its valuation provisions may range from completely controlling to irrelevant. The weight, if any, to be accorded to the valuation terms of the agreement is often a critical decision. The agreement may be controlling for some valuation purposes and not for others. Sometimes the degree of weight may depend on the extent to which the agreement was arm's length when negotiated. Often the appraiser and/or the court decides that the terms of the buy-sell agreement are a factor to be considered but are not controlling. One reason is because these agreements can be, and often are, changed.

Rules of thumb. Employs "ballpark" ranges of possible values derived from simple formulas used in an industry. Sometimes classified under the market approach, because the rules are allegedly market-derived but generally without support from any body of underlying market data. Rules of thumb are discussed in detail in Chapter 9.

Asset Approach Methods

Adjusted net asset value method. Adjusts all the company's assets (both tangible and intangible) and liabilities to current value, usually fair market value, and subtracts the liabilities from the assets.

- *Going-concern premise:* Adjusts all assets and liabilities to current fair market value in continued use and subtracts the liabilities from the assets.
- *Liquidation premise:* Adjusts all assets and liabilities to fair market value on a liquidation premise of value and subtracts all the liabilities and liquidation costs from the assets.
- *Hybrid premise:* Values assets expected to be in continuing operation on a going-concern basis and nonoperating assets on a liquidation basis. This could involve more than one operating unit of the business, where each operating unit is valued on a going-concern basis and nonoperating assets on a liquidation basis. This latter version sometimes is called a "breakup method" or "disaggregation method."

Excess earnings method. Adjusts only the company's tangible assets to current value—again, usually fair market value in continued use—and subtracts the liabilities to obtain a net tangible asset value. Estimates the amount of income needed to support the net tangible assets. If there is income over and above that amount, the excess income is divided by a capitalization rate to estimate the value of the company's intangible assets. Adds the estimated value of the intangibles to the value of the tangible assets.

This method is classified under the asset approach because, in theory, it adds the values of the tangible and intangible assets. Because it involves the capitalization of excess income, some appraisers prefer to call it a "hybrid method," and some may even classify it under the income approach. In this book, it is treated separately in Chapter 8.

Summary of Business Appraisal Approaches and Methods

A schematic diagram of this classification of business valuation approaches and methods is presented in Exhibit 3-1.

Exhibit 3-1
Schematic Diagram of Business Valuation Approaches and Methods

Approaches	Methods
Income	Discounting (Discounted cash flow—DCF) Capitalizing (Capitalization)
Market	Guideline public companies Guideline transactions Past transactions Buy-sell agreement Rules of thumb
Asset-based	Adjusted net asset value • Going-concern basis • Liquidation basis • Hybrid basis Excess earnings (sometimes classified as "hybrid")

Business Appraisal Procedures

The "procedure" is a more detailed step used in implementing an appraisal method. For example, as we will see in Chapter 5, several accepted procedures can be employed to develop discount and capitalization rates within the discounting and capitalizing methods. These procedures often are referred to as "methods" and can be considered as methods within methods or as the different ways that a method can be carried out.

For example, the "DCF method" is a good example of ambiguous terminology. The discounted cash flow method or the discounting method is a major valuation method within the income approach. However, that same term is commonly used to describe a procedure for estimating the discount or capitalization rate to be used within either the discounting or the capitalization method in the income approach.

Invested Capital versus Equity

Another important example of different procedures is the choice of either valuing the equity directly or valuing the firm's total invested capital (common stock [common equity] plus any preferred stock and long-term debt, including current maturities) and then subtracting the debt to arrive at a value for the common equity.

This choice of procedures can be available within most of the valuation methods. For example, within the market approach, using either the guideline public company or the guideline transaction method, one could value the equity directly by using a price/earnings multiple. Alternatively, one could use the multiple of market value of invested capital to earnings before interest, taxes, and depreciation (MVIC/EBITDA) to estimate the value of the firm's invested capital and then subtract the debt from that value to estimate the value of equity.

Some businesses have more than one class of equity, usually preferred equity and common equity. The preferred equity is senior to the common equity and, from a financial analysis point of view, usually has more of the characteristics of debt than equity. Therefore, the term *equity* typically is used to mean only the common equity, and the value of preferred equity would be subtracted along with the debt in the invested capital procedures to arrive at the common (or residual) equity value. This may require the preferred stock to be valued as well.

Exhibit 3-2 summarizes procedures commonly used within various valuation methods.

Ambiguities of Business Valuation Terminology

Unfortunately, the terminology found in the literature of financial theory and corporate finance is loaded with ambiguities, and these carry over into the literature of

Exhibit 3-2
Value of Invested Capital and Direct Valuation of Equity Procedures

Valuation Method	Valuation Procedures
Income Approach: either discounting or capitalizing	*Invested capital:* Discount or capitalize the expected returns (usually measured as cash flows) available to holders of all components of invested capital and then subtract the debt to obtain value of common equity. *Direct to common equity:* Discount or capitalize only those returns available to common equity.
Market Approach: using either guideline public companies, guideline transactions, or other market approach methods	*Invested capital:* Use market value of invested capital in the numerator of the ratio used to compute the multiple, returns available to all invested capital in the denominator; apply the multiple to the returns available to all invested capital and subtract the debt to obtain the value of common equity. *Direct to common equity:* Use only value of equity in the numerator of the ratio used to compute the multiple, returns available to common equity in the denominator.
Asset Approach: adjusted net asset value	By definition, the assets on which all invested capital has claims are valued and the debt subtracted to obtain net asset value (value of common equity).
Excess Earnings Method	This method values common equity directly, because the method requires subtracting the debt to obtain the net tangible asset value.
Rules of Thumb	Rules of thumb generally are intended to value all the invested capital. An example is the price-to-sales multiple. Therefore, the debt, if any, would have to be subtracted to obtain the common equity value (although the exact procedure may vary from one rule of thumb to another).

business appraisal and business appraisal reports. It is very important for financial analysts to properly define all approaches, methods, and procedures to present a clear understanding of the analysis.

In this book, we have defined terminology within the context of the discussion where it is used, as well as in Chapter 4, and we have also provided a glossary in Appendix A.

Many appraisal reports contain definitions of terms. These definitions should be read carefully, because different appraisers may use the same term differently.[1] If definitions are not included, consult the index of this book or the glossary for common uses. Some appraisers may not always use terms as they are most commonly used, and the reader may have to figure out the intended definition. Reading and trying to interpret court case decisions is also a huge problem when the author of the opinion has not had a technical education in the esoteric terminology of finance.

The following chapter is a primer on terminology commonly found in financial statements and business appraisal.

Summary

While business valuation approaches and methods are not totally discrete, there is broad consensus on three generally accepted approaches: the income approach, the market approach, and the asset-based approach.

Within each approach, there are two or more generally accepted methods. For example, within the income approach, the basic methods are *discounting* and *capitalizing*. Within the market approach, there is the *guideline public company method,* the *guideline transaction method,* the *past transactions and/or offers method, buy-sell agreements,* and *rules of thumb*. Within the asset-based approach, there is the *adjusted net asset method* and the *excess earnings method.*

Within each method there is a variety of accepted procedures for its implementation. Two of the most important are the *invested capital procedure* (valuing the entire capital structure and subtracting the senior obligations to arrive at the residual common equity value) and the *direct equity valuation procedure* (using techniques that value the equity directly); either procedure may be used with most methods.

Business valuation can include some ambiguous terminology. This book defines each term in the context in which it is used, and a general glossary is included in Appendix A. Chapter 4 also discusses common terminology found in business appraisal.

1. Additional guidance may be found in SHANNON P. PRATT, BUSINESS VALUATION BODY OF KNOWLEDGE (2d ed., John Wiley & Sons 2003).

Chapter 4

Financial Statement Terminology Used in Business Appraisal

Because virtually all business appraisal approaches, methods, and procedures use either actual or estimated numbers extracted or computed from financial statements, this chapter provides a road map to the terminology and meanings of those numbers as they are used in business appraisal.

This chapter includes both accounting and financial terms. Many of the numbers represented by the accounting terms can be read directly from financial statements. Numbers representing other accounting terms and numbers for most of the financial terms must be computed. This chapter will define the terms and, where necessary, also illustrate how to compute amounts for each. However, readers should understand that this is only the most perfunctory primer and that they will need to refer to other sources, such as those shown at the end of Chapter 12, for illustrations of more complex financial statements.

With the information shown in Exhibit 4-1 (page 32), it is possible to extract or compute most of the financial variables that typically are used in the various approaches to business valuation. This chapter necessarily involves numbers and computations. However, it would be impossible to simplify it much more without omitting concepts that one is almost certain to encounter within the scope of reviewing valuation reports. Therefore, we suggest that the reader peruse it fairly quickly the first time through and thereafter use it for reference.

The Basic Financial Statements

The two most commonly used financial statements are the *balance sheet* and the *income statement.* The balance sheet presents assets, liabilities, and owner's equity at a point in time, all at *book value.* Book value generally represents original, historical

Exhibit 4-1
Widget Corporation Financial Data

Widget Corporation Balance Sheet

Assets

Current Assets		
Cash		$ 500,000
Accounts Receivable		1,000,000
Inventory		1,500,000
Total Current Assets		$3,000,000
Plant & Equipment		
At Cost	$5,000,000	
Less: Accumulated Depreciation	3,000,000	
Net Plant & Equipment		$2,000,000
Total Assets		$5,000,000

Liabilities and Equity

Current Liabilities	
Accounts Payable	$500,000
Accrued Expenses	$500,000
Total Current Liabilities	$1,000,000
Long-Term Debt	3,000,000
Total Liabilities	$4,000,000
Preferred Stock	0
Common Equity (1,000 shares outstanding)	$1,000,000
Total Liabilities and Equity	$5,000,000

Widget Corporation Income Statement

Sales	$10,000,000
Cost of Goods Sold	6,000,000
Gross Margin	$ 4,000,000
Selling, General and Administrative Expenses	2,700,000
Operating Income, Before Interest and Taxes	$ 1,300,000
Interest Expense	300,000
Income Before Taxes	$ 1,000,000
Income Taxes	300,000
Net Income	$ 700,000

Widget Corporation Other Financial Data

The following data are derived from Statement of Cash Flows, footnotes to financial statements, and company books and records:

1. Interest rate on the long-term debt is 10%.
2. The selling, general and administrative expenses include depreciation of $250,000.
3. The selling, general and administrative expenses include compensation for the president (who owns 100% of the stock and both manages the company and maintains all the key customer contacts) as follows:

Salary	$500,000
Bonus	200,000
Retirement Plan Contribution	100,000
Health and Life Insurance	50,000
Discretionary Entertainment Expenses (golf club, yacht, etc.)	100,000
Total Owner's Compensation	$950,000

4. Capital expenditures average about $300,000 per year.
5. The company's sales are growing at about 10% per year.
6. The company maintains net working capital at about 20% of sales, typical for its industry.
7. No changes in the level of long-term debt are contemplated in the foreseeable future.

cost less depreciation and other noncash charges in accordance with accounting principles. Adjustments to bring these figures to market value are discussed in Chapter 12.

The income statement presents revenues, expenses, and income over a period of time (fiscal period), usually a year. Sometimes, if the valuation date is not close to the end of a company's fiscal year, it may be necessary to use *interim financial statements*, that is, those prepared at a time other than the company's fiscal year-end.

The three levels of preparation of financial statements, in descending order of their degree of detail (and, usually, their reliability) are: audited, reviewed, and compiled. Definitions of each are shown in Exhibit 4-2 (page 34). The appraiser's report should indicate which level of financial statement preparation was used and also who prepared the statements. This may be different for different dates and, if so, the correct information should be listed for each date.

The balance of this chapter merely defines the terms used to describe the most important components of the context of these statements. Analysis of the statements is covered in Chapters 12 and 13.

Exhibit 4-2
Levels of Financial Statement Preparation

- **Audited Statements.** In *audited statements*, the independent auditor expresses an opinion or, if circumstances require, disclaims an opinion, regarding the fairness with which the financial statements present the financial position, the results of operations, and the changes in financial position, in accordance with generally accepted accounting principles.
- **Reviewed Statements.** The independent accountant expresses limited assurance in *reviewed statements* that there are no material modifications that should be made to the statements in order for them to be in conformity with generally accepted accounting principles. A review does not provide assurance that the accountant will become aware of all significant matters that would be disclosed in an audit.
- **Compiled Statements.** Finally, the *compiled statements* are management's representations presented in the form of financial statements, but the accountant has not undertaken any efforts to express assurance on the statements. Sometimes statements are prepared internally by management without the services of an outside accountant.

Balance Sheet Concepts

Common Equity

Common equity (at book value) is paid in capital plus retained earnings. In Widget Corporation, it is:

$1,000,000 from the Balance Sheet

Invested Capital

Invested capital is equity plus interest-bearing debt. For Widget Corporation, invested capital at book value is:

Long-term debt	$3,000,000
Common equity	1,000,000
Book value of invested capital[1]	$4,000,000

1. Some analysts deduct cash when computing invested capital. Also, some deduct cash that they consider to be in excess of the company's cash requirements for operations. The important thing is that the analyst be consistent. For example, if cash is deducted when computing invested capital for the subject company in the market approach, it must be deducted when computing invested capital for the guideline companies as well.

If the company had preferred stock, that would be shown as a separate item in the capital structure and would be included in the market value of invested capital (MVIC).

Capital Structure

Capital structure is the relative proportions of the various elements of invested capital. In this case, at book value:

Long-term debt	$3,000,000	75%
Equity	1,000,000	25%
	$4,000,000	100%

Book Value

With respect to assets, the book value of the plant and equipment is the capitalized cost less the accumulated depreciation. For Widget Corporation, for example:

Plant and equipment	$5,000,000
Less: Depreciation	3,000,000
Net book value of plant and equipment	$2,000,000

With respect to the business as a whole, the book value is the difference between the total assets (net of depreciation, depletion, and amortization) and the total liabilities. This is also the book value of equity. For Widget Corporation, this is:

Total assets	$5,000,000
Total liabilities	4,000,000
Book value of equity	$1,000,000

Book Value per Share

On a per-share basis, the book value is the value of common equity divided by the number of shares outstanding. For Widget Corporation, it is:

$$\frac{\$1{,}000{,}000}{1{,}000 \text{ shares}} = \$1{,}000 \text{ per share}$$

Tangible Book Value versus Total Book Value

Tangible book value reflects only the company's tangible assets. Total book value reflects both tangible and intangible assets, such as copyrights, patents, and many other items. If a company buys its intangible assets, they generally are on the balance sheet and thus are part of the book value. On the other hand, if the company creates its own intangible assets, they usually are expensed and do not appear on the balance sheet. Therefore, for comparative consistency, analysts usually prefer to work with only the tangible book value rather than the total book value. In any case, to completely understand the financial statements being analyzed, the reviewer of the report should know whether or not there are any intangible assets included in the book value and if that figure is used for any computations in the valuation report.

Net Working Capital

Net working capital is the current assets minus the current liabilities. For Widget Corporation, it is:

Current assets	$3,000,000
Less: Current liabilities	1,000,000
Net working capital	$2,000,000

Miscellaneous Expense Concepts

Noncash Charges

Noncash charges are items that are charged as expenses on the income statement but do not require a cash outlay. Examples would include depreciation, depletion, amortization, and deferred taxes.

For Widget Corporation, the only noncash charge is:

Depreciation: $250,000 from Other Financial Data

Noncash charges are added back to the net income to arrive at either the gross or net cash flow, and added back to the operating income to arrive at the earnings before interest, taxes, depreciation, and amortization (EBITDA).

Owner's Compensation (Including Disclosed or Hidden Perks)

Owner's compensation includes all elements of compensation, including salary, bonuses, retirement benefits, life and health insurance benefits, discretionary expenses, and value of stock options. For Widget Corporation, owner's compensation is:

$950,000 from Other Financial Data

Levels of Economic Income

One of the most crucial and yet highly ambiguous concepts used in business valuation is that of income, also sometimes referred to as earnings. It is common to see one or the other of these two terms used without further definition. So many different levels of income are employed in various business valuation methods and procedures that the term *income* is virtually meaningless until the level of income intended is clearly specified.

In recent years, the business appraisal profession has embraced the broad term *economic income* to mean some level of income (any level) that needs further specific definition before it can be used meaningfully in a business valuation method or procedure. All the following levels of economic income are commonly used in business appraisal practice:

- Sales
- Discretionary earnings
- Earnings before interest, taxes, depreciation, and amortization (EBITDA)
- Earnings before interest and taxes (EBIT)
- Gross cash flow (net income plus noncash charges)
- Debt-free net income
- Debt-free cash flow
- Pretax income
- Net income
- Net cash flow to invested capital
- Net cash flow to equity

Sales (Net Revenues)

The terms *sales* and *net revenues* generally are used interchangeably. For Widget Corporation, it is:

$10,000,000 from the Income Statement

A multiple of sales often is used in the market approach when valuing invested capital. It is less frequently used (and potentially very misleading) when valuing equity directly, because sales are based on the assets supported by the entire capital structure.

Discretionary Earnings (Also Called Seller's Discretionary Cash Flow [SDCF] and Owner's Cash Flow [OCF])

Discretionary earnings may be defined, in certain applications, to reflect earnings of a business enterprise prior to the following items: income taxes, nonoperating income and expenses, nonrecurring income and expenses, depreciation and amortization, interest expense or income, and owner's total compensation for those services, which could be provided by a sole owner/manager.[2] For Widget Corporation, it is:

2. American Society of Appraisers Business Valuation Standards.

Pretax operating income (before interest expense) from Income Statement	$1,300,000
Plus: Depreciation	250,000
Plus: Owner's compensation	950,000
Discretionary earnings	$2,500,000

Discretionary earnings are used in the transaction method in the market approach usually only when valuing small companies.

Earnings before Interest, Taxes, Depreciation, and Amortization (EBITDA)

EBITDA is computed as earnings before interest, taxes, and *all* noncash charges, including depreciation, amortization, depletion, and deferred taxes. Widget Corporation's EBITDA is:

EBIT (Operating income)	$1,300,000
Plus: Depreciation	250,000
EBITDA	$1,550,000

EBITDA is one of the most commonly used variables in the market approach *when valuing invested capital.*

Earnings before Interest and Taxes (EBIT) (Also Called Operating Income)

For Widget Corporation, it is:

$1,300,000 from the Income Statement

EBIT is one of the most commonly used variables in the market approach *when valuing invested capital.*

Gross Cash Flow

When the term *gross cash flow* is used, it almost always means *gross cash flow to equity,* sometimes just called *cash flow.* It is defined as net income plus noncash charges. For Widget Corporation, it is:

Net income	$ 700,000
Plus: Depreciation	250,000
Gross cash flow	$ 950,000

Debt-Free Net Income (DFNI)

Debt-free net income means what the net income would be if there were no debt. It is computed by adding the interest expense, net of the tax effect (income taxes saved because the interest is a tax-deductible expense) to the net income. For Widget Corporation, it is:

	Net income	$700,000
+	Interest expense, net of pro forma income taxes $300,000 x (1-.30) (taxes of $300,000 on $1,000,000 pretax income, or 30%)	210,000
	Debt-free net income	$910,000

The same result is obtained by tax-affecting EBIT, or the operating income:

Operating income	$1,300,000
Less income taxes (30% tax rate)	$390,000
Debt-free net income	$910,000

When debt-free net income is used, it is in the context of the market approach *when valuing invested capital.*

Debt-Free Cash Flow (DFCF)

Debt-free cash flow means *gross* debt-free net cash flow. It is debt-free net income plus noncash charges. For Widget Corporation, it is:

Debt-free net income	$910,000
Depreciation	250,000
Debt-free cash flow	$1,160,000

When debt-free cash flow is used, it is in the context of the market approach *when valuing invested capital.* The "debt-free" measures are used to make companies with significantly different capital structures more comparable to each other.

Pretax Income

Pretax income is income after all expenses except income taxes. For Widget Corporation, it is:

$1,000,000 from the Income Statement

Pretax income often is used in the market approach when valuing equity directly. It is sometimes used in the excess earnings method, sometimes as a proxy for net income in a small company, sole proprietorship, limited liability company, or partnership that does not pay any income taxes.

Net Income

Net income is income after all expenses, including interest, owner's compensation, noncash charges, and income taxes. For Widget Corporation it is:

$700,000 from the Income Statement

It is used in the market approach when valuing equity directly. It is sometimes used in the excess earnings method and sometimes used in the income approach, but, more frequently, net cash flow is used in the income approach.

Primary versus Diluted Net Income per Share

On a per-share basis, net income can be stated as either primarily *net income per share* or *diluted net income per share.* "Primary" is computed on the basis of the number of shares actually outstanding. "Diluted" is computed on the assumption of convertible debt being converted to common stock, preferred stock being converted to common stock, and warrants and options to buy stock exercised. When performing comparative analysis, it is important to be sure that any figures used for comparison are computed on the same basis.

Net Cash Flow to Invested Capital

Net cash flow to invested capital is the amount of cash available to distribute to owners and stakeholders of all components of the capital structure (preferred and common equity and interest-bearing debt) after leaving enough for the capital expenditures and working capital necessary to sustain projected operations. The computation is as follows:

Net income (after taxes) to common equity
\+ Noncash charges (depreciation, amortization, deferred taxes, etc.)
\- Capital expenditures[3]
\- Changes in net working capital[4]
\+ Interest expense, net of the income tax effect
(interest expense x [1 - tax rate])
\+ Preferred dividends, if any
= Net cash flow to overall invested capital

3. Assumes that these amounts are those necessary to support projected business operations.
4. *Id.*

For Widget Corporation, it is:

	Net income	$700,000
+	Depreciation	250,000
-	Capital expenditures	300,000
-	Additions to net working capital	200,000
+	Interest expenses, net of pro forma income taxes[5] $300,000 x (1-.30)	210,000
	Net cash flow to invested capital	$ 660,000

This is the measure of economic income that is preferred by the professional financial community when using the income approach to value a company's invested capital. From the valuation of invested capital, the debt and preferred equity are subtracted to obtain the value of common equity.

Net Cash Flow to Equity

Net cash flow to equity (sometimes called "free cash flow to equity" or "net free cash flow to equity") is the amount of cash available to equity owners to withdraw from or distribute from the business after leaving enough for the capital expenditures and working capital necessary to sustain projected operations. The computation is as follows:

	Net income (after taxes)
+	Noncash charges (e.g., depreciation, amortization, deferred income taxes)
-	Capital expenditures[6]
-	Changes in net working capital[7]
+	Net changes in long-term debt
=	Net cash flow to equity

If there are preferred dividends, they must to be subtracted. The objective is to estimate the net cash flow available to common equity holders. For Widget Corporation, it is:

5. Taxes of $300,000 on $1 million pretax income, or 30 percent.
6. Assumes that these amounts are the levels necessary to support projected business operations.
7. *Id.*

	Net income	$ 700,000
+	Depreciation	250,000
-	Capital expenditures	300,000
-	Additions to net working capital	200,000
Net cash flow to equity[8]		$ 450,000

This is the measure of economic income that is most preferred by the corporate financial community when using the income approach to value equity. Sometimes it is also used as the economic income variable in the excess earnings method.

Variables Affecting Net Cash Flow

Capital Expenditures

Capital expenditures are the amounts paid for assets expected to have a long-term economic life (usually more than one year), recorded on the balance sheet at the amount paid, and usually depreciated (or depleted or amortized) over time as expenses on the income statement and reductions to book value on the balance sheet. For Widget Corporation, they are:

Approximately $300,000 per year from Other Financial Data

Expected capital expenditures must be estimated as a component in computing the net cash flow in the income approach, for the capital expenditure requirements represent a portion of the gross cash flow that must remain in the business to support projected operations.

Changes in Net Working Capital

Changes in the net working capital are the amounts added to or subtracted from the net working capital needed to support the operations of the business.

Expected sales growth:		
10% x $10,000,000	=	$1,000,000
Percentage of sales needed as additional net working capital (the percentage of incremental sales, from Other Financial Data)		20%
Expected additions to net working capital		$ 200,000

8. If the company is growing, it may increase long-term debt; if highly leveraged, it may decrease long-term debt. Increases in long-term debt would be increases in net cash flow to equity, and payoffs of long-term debt would decrease net cash flow to equity.

Changes in the net working capital must be estimated as one of the components in computing the net cash flow in the income approach, for it represents an amount of cash flow that must remain in the business to support projected operations. The net cash flow to equity is also increasingly becoming the economic income measure of choice to use in the excess earnings method.

Changes in Debt

If the company increases its long-term debt, the increase is an addition to the net cash flow to equity. Conversely, repayments of the long-term debt are a deduction when calculating the net cash flow to equity.

Cash versus Accrual Basis Accounting

Most companies record their accounting on an accrual basis in accordance with generally accepted accounting principles (GAAP). However, some companies, especially smaller ones, prepare their financial statements on a cash basis. Some companies prepare financial statements on an accrual basis and tax returns on a cash basis. Other companies do not prepare financial statements separate from the tax returns, in which case it should be ascertained whether the tax returns are on a cash or accrual basis.

Accrual Basis Accounting

In *accrual basis accounting,* revenues and expenses are recorded when they are earned or incurred. For example, if a company renders services and bills the customer for later payment, the revenue is shown on the income statement when it is earned and the account receivable becomes an asset on the balance sheet. This is based on the accounting principle of matching costs with related revenues.

Cash Basis Accounting

In *cash basis accounting,* revenues and expenses are recorded when they are received or paid. For example, if a company renders services and bills the customer for later payment, the revenue is shown on the income statement when it is collected and the account receivable is never shown on the balance sheet.

Conversion from Cash to Accrual Basis

Valuations usually are performed on accrual basis data. For example, once a service has been performed, the revenue and profit generally are considered part of the income stream and the related receivable usually is considered an asset of the company.

Therefore, if the subject company accounts on a cash basis, the valuation analyst usually adjusts the financial statements from a cash to an accrual basis for the purpose of valuation. Of course, there can be exceptions, such as when a buy-sell agreement requiring valuation using cash basis accounting data is determined to be controlling for the valuation purpose at hand.

All data that has been presented in this chapter have been assumed to be on an accrual basis.

Summary

This chapter has provided a rudimentary guide to the terms most often encountered with respect to financial statements as they are used in business valuation. It is a handy reference for any term with which the reviewer is unfamiliar or unsure of the definition commonly used in the context of valuation.

Chapter 5

The Income Approach

The income approach is presented first because, in theory, it is the dominant approach in business valuation (although Revenue Ruling 59-60 and many investment bankers also place heavy emphasis on the market approach). The discounted cash flow (DCF) method is the most conceptually correct method because it captures the driving principle of valuation: Value is the present worth of future benefits. Capitalizing is merely a shortcut method that hopes to produce a similar result. A basic corporate finance text articulates this critical point: "Value today always equals future cash flow discounted at the opportunity cost of capital."[1]

Not only is discounted cash flow the most theoretically correct valuation method, it is also the most widely practiced valuation method in the world of corporate finance. Furthermore, the method is increasingly used by valuation experts and increasingly accepted by the courts. For example, in the family law area, the DCF method has been accepted in some cases,[2] but, as in other areas, it has been rejected where the data to support the method were insufficient.[3]

In both *discounting* and *capitalizing,* we are converting an expected stream of income into a present value. In other words, we are estimating what someone would pay today (or as of the effective valuation date) for an expected stream of future economic income.

For those not familiar with the arithmetic formulas and notations used in business valuation, this certainly is the most technical chapter in the book and is not recommended for recreational reading. Exhibit 5-1 (page 46) contains the most commonly used terminology and notations that should be of some assistance.

---

1. Richard A. Brealey & Stewart C. Myers, Principles of Corporate Finance 75 (7th ed. 2003).

2. *See, e.g.,* Guiffre v. Baker, 1996 WL 535254, 1996 Ohio App. LEXIS 3673 (Ohio Ct. App. 1996) and Sergi v. Sergi, 1996 WL 425914, 1996 Ohio App. LEXIS 3241 (Ohio Ct. App. 1996) (the courts in those cases accepted the DCF method over the excess earnings method); Howell v. Howell, 523 S.E.2d 514 (Va. Ct. App. 2000).

3. *See, e.g.,* Shooltz v. Shooltz, 498 S.E.2d 437 (Va. Ct. App. 1998).

Exhibit 5-1
Terms and Notations Commonly Used in the Income Approach

The notation system used in this book is the Pratt notation system, which is used in the courses of the American Society of Appraisers and the American Institute of Certified Public Accountants. No matter what notation system is used in an appraisal report, each term should be defined.

PV	=	**Present Value** In appraisal terms, this is the estimated value as of the specified appraisal date.
D	=	**Dividend** This is usually the expected annual dividend, although it could be the actual dividend for the past 12 months or some other time period.
c	=	**Capitalization rate** A percentage, expressed as a decimal (for example, 20% = .20), which is used as a denominator to divide into some amount of income (for example, dividends, earnings, cash flow) to arrive at an indication of value.
k	=	**Discount rate (Cost of capital)** The total expected rate of return that the market requires to attract investment into the business or securities of the type being valued, reflecting investment risk and other characteristics of the investment.
g	=	**Growth** The average compound annual rate at which a financial variable (for example, dollar amount of dividends, earnings, cash flow) is expected to increase in the future. As used in the income approach formulas, this usually is a long-term rate, technically in perpetuity.
E	=	**Expected economic income** This is a generalized variable used in an income formula without specifying the definition of income. Income in this formula could be dividends, earnings cash flow, or some other income variable.
WACC	=	**Weighted Average Cost of Capital** The weighted discount rate for each type of security in the company's capital structure (for example, common stock, preferred stock, long-term debt), each component weighted by its percentage of the market value of the company's total invested capital that is represented by the respective capital component.
W	=	**Weight** The percentage of each component of the capital structure out of the total, with each measured at market value.
t	=	**Tax rate** The company's combined federal and state corporate tax rate.

Subscripts denoting time periods:

0	=	**The base period** Usually the time period immediately before the effective valuation date (for example, D_0 would be the dividends for the last year).
1,2,3, etc.	=	**Future time periods** Usually the first time period following the valuation date, etc. (For example, D_1 would be expected dividends for the coming year.)
n	=	**The last period** In the income approach, it is usually the last period for which specific projections of expected future benefits are available. (For example, D*n* would be projected dividends in the last year for which a specific dividend projection is available.)

Subscripts denoting type of capital component:

e	=	**Equity** Common stock or partnership interests without any senior priority. (For example, *ke* would be the cost of equity; that is, the discount rate or market-required rate of expected return for an equity investment in the company.)
d	=	**Debt** Borrowed capital. (For example, *kd* would be the cost of the company's borrowing.)
d(pt)	=	**Debt, pretax** Debt, not reflecting the tax deductibility of interest cost. (For example, *kd(pt)* would be the company's gross cost of borrowing, not adjusted for the tax deductibility of the interest.)

The Concept of Discounting

In discounting, we are specifically estimating each future period's expected income and reducing each period's expected amount by a *discount rate,* which is the market's required rate of return for investments of comparable risk and other characteristics.

Discounting is exactly the opposite of *compounding.* In compounding, we invest a certain amount of money at some expected, annually compounded rate of return. Assuming that the expected rate of return is achieved and that each year's return is added to the principal to continue to compound, we can compute what that investment will be worth any number of years into the future. In discounting, we do just the opposite. We start with an expected payment at some specified time in the future. In effect, we discount the value backwards for the length of time until we expect to receive it, at the required rate of return reflecting the risk (degree of uncertainty) of realizing the payment at the time and in the amount expected.

We discount the amount of each individual increment of expected future return to a present value and then add the present values of each increment to obtain the value of the investment. An example is shown schematically in Exhibit 5-2.

Exhibit 5-2
Discounted Present Value of an Annuity

Today's Value (Present Value)	**Amount to be received at end of each year**		
	Year 1	Year 2	Year 3
	$1,000	$1,000	$1,000
$ 925.93	1 year @ 8%		
$ 857.34	2 years @ 8%		
$ 793.83	3 years @ 8%		
$2,577.10	Total present value of 3-year annuity of $1,000 per year with a compound rate of return of 8% per year.		

Note how this is just the opposite of compounding: If you invested $925.93 for a year at 8%, it would be worth $1,000 at the end of the year. If you invested $857.34 for 2 years at 8% compounded annually, it would be worth $1,000 at the end of 2 years, and so forth.

$925.93 x 1.08 = $1,000
$857.34 x 1.08 x 1.08 = $1,000
$793.83 x 1.08 x 1.08 x 1.08 = $1,000

The Concept of Capitalizing

In capitalizing, instead of projecting each future increment of income and dividing it by the discount rate compounded for some number of years into the future, we select a single expected number and simply divide that number by a rate of return adjusted for expected growth that we call a *capitalization rate.* We are really using a procedure that is a shortcut form of discounting. It is still our objective to estimate the present value of an expected future income stream. However, we are making some implicit assumptions to simplify the procedure.

The assumptions that are implicit in the capitalization method in the income approach are that either:

(a) The amount of income being capitalized will remain constant each year in perpetuity, or

(b) The amount of income being capitalized will either increase or decrease at some constant annually compounded rate in perpetuity.

In capitalizing, as in discounting, we are converting expected future income into a value. However, in capitalizing, instead of projecting all the future expected benefits, we are using only a single period's expected benefit—often, for example, next year's expected return. We divide that return by a *capitalization rate.*

As will be explained in more detail, the capitalization rate, as used in the income approach, is a function of the discount rate, that is, it is derived by starting with the discount rate. In the unique situation of assumption (a) above (constant income), the capitalization rate and the discount rate are equal. Under assumption (b) above (reasonably constant growth or decline in the income stream), the capitalization rate equals the discount rate less the long-term sustainable rate of growth or plus the long-term rate of decline.

The capitalization procedure also may be used in the context of the market approach in either the guideline public company or the transaction method. In the market approach, however, capitalization rates are developed by direct observation in the market rather than as a function of the discount rate, and implied assumptions (a) and (b) above do not necessarily apply. Also, for the capitalization method in the income approach, the income variable that is preferred is *net cash flow,* as discussed later. However, in the market approach, net cash flow is rarely used; instead, other economic income measures, such as net income and earnings before interest and taxes, are capitalized.

The Basic Capitalized Cash Flow Model

The Constant Income Capitalization Model

The simplest form of the constant income capitalization model found in the market, and familiar to most people, is the perpetual life (noncallable) preferred stock.

Preferred stock is technically equity, but from a financial viewpoint, in some ways it is much more like debt. The dividends normally are at a fixed-dollar amount for the life of the stock, which in many cases is in perpetuity. Payment of the dividends is senior to any dividends on common stock but junior to debt service requirements. If, as in the case of the perpetual life preferred stock, the expected income stream is the same every year and expected to last forever, the procedure is simply to divide the amount of annual dividend or cash distribution by the capitalization rate.

The constant income capitalization formula is:

Formula 5-1

$$PV = \frac{D}{c}$$

Where:

PV	=	Present Value
D	=	Dividend (or distributions, in case of a partnership)
c	=	Capitalization rate

For example, assume:

Dividend:	$5 per year
Discount rate	13%
Less growth rate	3%
Equals capitalization rate:	10%

Inserting these numbers in Formula 8-1 gives us:

Formula 5-2

$$PV = \frac{\$5}{.10}$$

$$= \$50$$

(The choice of the capitalization rate is just as important as the amount of income being capitalized. Proper procedures for developing capitalization rates are discussed in a later section.)

The Income Capitalization Growth Model (Gordon Growth Model)

In many business enterprises, the cash flow or other income stream is expected to increase over time. If one accepts the assumption that growth in the income stream can be predicted at a reasonably steady rate and for a very long period of time, then the expected rate of growth in the returns can be impounded into a capitalization model that takes account of that expected growth.

The procedure for the capitalization growth model is:

1. In the numerator of the capitalization equation, multiply last year's economic income by a growth factor.
2. In the denominator, subtract the rate of growth from the discount rate.

The capitalized income formula under the assumption of a constant rate of growth is:

Formula 5-3

$$PV = \frac{E_0 (1 + g)}{k - g}$$

Where:

PV	=	Present Value
E_0	=	Economic income in the year immediately preceding the effective valuation date
g	=	Growth rate in expected income level, sustainable into the indefinite future (theoretically in perpetuity)
k	=	Discount rate (cost of capital)

The discount rate represents the *total* required rate of return (dividends or distributions plus capital appreciation). Development of discount rates is presented in a later section.

For an example of the application of the above formula, assume:

Last year's payout	\$10
Expected annually compounded growth in amount of payout	3%
Discount rate	13%

Inserting those numbers in Formula 5-3 gives us:

Formula 5-4

$$PV = \frac{\$10(1+0.03)}{0.13-0.03}$$

$$= \frac{\$10.30}{0.10}$$

$$= \$103$$

Of course, if the starting point were next year's expected return (E_1 instead of E_0), then we would not need to multiply by the growth factor in the numerator. We still would subtract the growth rate from the discount rate (total required rate of return) to obtain the capitalization rate in the denominator.

When using this growth model, it is very important that the long-term sustainable growth rate is realistic. If one uses a long-term growth rate close to the discount rate, then the capitalization rate is extremely low and the calculated indication of value will be materially overstated.

The Basic Discounted Cash Flow Model

The Discounted Cash Flow Model for a Limited Life Investment

The simplest form of a limited life investment model found in the market, and familiar to most people, is a bond with no special features. The bond pays a fixed amount of interest each year and the holder expects to receive a fixed amount when the bond matures.

The discounted cash flow formula for the value of a limited life investment is:

Formula 5-5

$$PV = \frac{E_1}{(1+k)} + \frac{E_2}{(1+k)^2} + \ldots + \frac{E_n}{(1+k)^n}$$

Where:

PV	=	Present value
$E_1 \ldots E_n$	=	Expected economic income in each of periods 1 through n
k	=	Discount rate (cost of capital)

For example, for a bond that matures in three years, assume:

Annual interest payment:[4]	$80
Value at maturity:	$1,080
($1,000 plus the last year's $80 interest payment)	
Yield to maturity on bonds of comparable risk	
as of the effective valuation date:	10%
n, the number of years to maturity:	3

In other words, the yield to maturity available on comparable bonds today (in the above example) is greater than the rate of interest on the face value of the subject bond (8% = $80/$1,000). In this case, the value of the bond is less than its face value.

Inserting these numbers in Formula 5-5 gives us:

4. Most bonds pay interest semiannually, but, for the sake of simplifying the illustration, we will assume that this bond pays interest only at the end of each year.

Formula 5-6

$$PV = \frac{\$80}{(1+.010)} + \frac{\$80}{(1+.010)^2} + \frac{\$1080}{(1+0.10)^3}$$

$$PV = \frac{\$80}{1.100} + \frac{\$80}{1.210} + \frac{\$1080}{1.331}$$

$$= \$72.73 + \$66.12 + \$811.42$$

$$= \$950.27$$

Note that in the above computations, each year's return is reduced to a present value by a calculated divisor. This divisor can easily be converted to a multiplier by dividing each divisor into 1. For example, the divisor for the first year's payment is 1.100. Dividing that into 1 (1÷1.100) equals a multiplier of 0.909. Similarly, the multipliers for years 2 and 3 are 0.826 and 0.751, respectively. It is common to see these multipliers presented as discounting "factors." Such a presentation of the above data would appear as follows:

Year	Amount	PV Factor	Present Value
1	$ 80	0.909	$ 72.72
2	$ 80	0.826	$ 66.08
3	$ 1,080	0.751	$811.08
			$949.88

The small differences between this tabular presentation and the formula presentation above are because of rounding.

The Discounted Cash Flow Model Using a "Terminal Value"

Most businesses are expected to have an indefinite life. However, it is not usually possible to make reasonably accurate forecasts of expected returns on a year-by-year basis for very many years into the future.

Appraisers deal with this dilemma by using specific forecasts as far into the future as reasonably reliable and then assume a value for the business at the end of the specific forecast period. This value is called a "terminal value" or a "residual value."

The procedure preferred by most appraisers for developing the estimate of the terminal value is to use the capitalization model, usually the constant growth capitalization model (Gordon Growth Model). In other words, the implied assumption is that, after the specific forecast period, the business's net cash flow will continue to grow at some average annual compound rate.

The formula for the discounted cash flow model, using a terminal value calculated by the constant growth capitalization model, is:

Formula 5-7

$$PV = \frac{E_1}{(1+k)} + \frac{E_2}{(1+k)^2} + \ldots + \frac{E_n}{(1+k)^n} + \frac{\frac{E_n (1+g)}{k-g}}{(1+k)^n}$$

Where:

PV	=	Present Value
$E_1 \ldots E_n$	=	Expected economic income in each of the periods 1 through n
k	=	Discount rate (cost of capital)
g	=	Growth rate in economic income beyond year n (expected sustainable annually compounded rate)

Note that the above formula is an exact combination of Formula 5-5, the limited life discounted cash flow model, and Formula 5-3, the income capitalization growth model. In Formula 5-7, the terminal value is $E_n (1 + g)/(k - g)$ and is estimated using the Gordon Growth Model.

What projection period should be used (i.e., how many years) before using the terminal value factor? The analytically correct answer is until the company is expected to reach a steady growth state. The specific forecast period typically runs from three to 10 years, with five years being common.

To make our example as simple as possible, we will assume only a three-year specific forecast period. Assume the following forecasts:

Net cash flow Year 1:	$100
Net cash flow Year 2:	$130
Net cash flow Year 3:	$150
Required rate of return (discount rate):	20%
Annually compounded growth in net cash flow beyond Year 3:	5%

Inserting these numbers in Formula 5-7 gives us:

Formula 5-8

$$PV = \frac{\$100}{(1+0.20)} + \frac{\$130}{(1+0.20)^2} + \frac{\$150}{(1+0.20)^3} + \frac{\frac{\$150\ (1 + 0.05)}{0.20 - 0.05}}{(1+0.20)^3}$$

$$= \frac{\$100}{1.200} + \frac{\$130}{1.440} + \frac{\$150}{1.728} + \frac{\frac{\$157.50}{.15}}{1.728}$$

$$= \$83.33 + \$90.28 + \$86.81 + \$607.64$$

$$= \$868.06$$

Each year's expected return, plus the terminal value, has been reduced to a present value by a divisor. Note that the terminal value divisor is based on the same number of years into the future as the expected return in the last year's specific forecast period. That is because the last period's return is expected to be received at the *end* of Year 3 and the capitalized value in the terminal value calculation represents the value as of the *beginning* of Year 4, essentially the same moment as the end of Year 3.

If we were to convert the divisors used in Formula 5-8 to multipliers and present the results in tabular form, we would have the following:

Year	*Amount*	*PV Factor*	*Present Value*
1	$ 100	0.833	$ 83.30
2	$ 130	0.694	$ 90.22
3	$ 150	0.579	$ 86.85
Terminal Value	$ 1,050	0.579	$ 607.95
Total Present Value			$868.32

(The figures differ slightly because of rounding.)

Another important item to note is that the shorter the specific forecast period, the greater the impact of the terminal value on the indicated present value, that is, the shorter the specific forecast period, the more the discounting method approaches the equivalent of the capitalizing method. Because of this, the assumed long-term growth rate following the specific forecast period takes on great significance and the reviewer should consider whether the growth rate into the long-term future seems reasonable.

As a result, the shorter the specific forecast period, the more important the terminal value becomes as a percentage of the total present value. To illustrate this point, assume growth rates in income beyond Year 3 in the above example from zero to 15 percent, still assuming a discount rate (total cost of capital) of 20 percent. These varying assumptions would have the following impact on the figures in the above example:

Assumed Growth Rate after Year 3	*Terminal Value (TV)*	*Present Value of Terminal Value (PVTV)*	*Total Present Value (TPV)*	*PVTV as a % of TPV*
0%	$ 750	$ 434	$ 694	63%
1	$ 797	$ 461	$ 721	64%
2	$ 850	$ 492	$ 752	65%
3	$ 909	$ 526	$ 786	67%
4	$ 975	$ 564	$ 824	68%
5	$ 1,050	$ 608	$ 868	70%
6	$ 1,136	$ 657	$ 917	72%
7	$ 1,235	$ 715	$ 975	73%
8	$ 1,350	$ 781	$ 1,041	75%
9	$ 1,486	$ 860	$ 1,120	77%
10	$ 1,650	$ 955	$ 1,215	79%
11	$ 1,850	$ 1,070	$ 1,330	80%
12	$ 2,100	$ 1,215	$ 1,475	82%
13	$ 2,421	$ 1,401	$ 1,661	84%
14	$ 2,850	$ 1,649	$ 1,909	86%
15	$ 3,450	$ 1,996	$ 2,256	88%

As shown above, the greater the growth rate assumed in the terminal value calculation, all else constant, the greater the present value of the terminal value as a percentage of total present value.

The discounted cash flow model obviously is very sensitive to the amounts of income projected during the discrete projection period and the growth expected beyond the projection period. The reviewer should inquire whether the projections used were prepared during the normal course of business or in connection with a transaction for buyers or lenders (often optimistic) or for justifying the price to be paid (perhaps pessimistic).

If the projections were made in the normal course of business, the reviewer might inquire into the company's "track record" of meeting, failing to meet, or exceeding its projections. The reviewer also might inquire if any "sensitivity analysis" was conducted, that is, computing the impact of changing certain variables in the assumptions.

It is important to consider the reasonableness of the components of a projection. For example, although depreciation can exceed capital expenditures in some years, over the long term, capital expenditures must exceed depreciation in a growing company.[5]

Capitalization Model versus Market Multiples for Estimating Terminal Value

An alternative procedure to estimate the terminal value is to use estimated market multiples applied to some measure of the company's economic income projected for the year following the end of the discrete forecast period. An example would be to estimate net income for the year following the forecast period and use a price/earnings ratio to estimate the terminal value.

If valuing the entire invested capital rather than just the common equity (as discussed in a later section), then one might use a multiple of earnings before interest and taxes (EBIT) or a multiple of earnings before interest, taxes, depreciation, and amortization (EBITDA). This procedure is commonly used by investment bankers.

Although the market multiples procedure may be used to estimate terminal value, many in the business valuation community tend to prefer the income capitalization growth model for the following reasons:

- A frequently used assumption is that market multiples will remain the same as on the effective valuation date. However, they probably would not. Markets change, especially markets for specific industries. For example, if an industry is in a high-growth stage now, that usually is reflected in high market multiples. When the industry reaches more of a steady state, market multiples are not likely to be so high. Even if the analyst assumes that multiples in a high-growth industry will decline, the level of multiples at any future date is hard to predict.
- Using market multiples brings an element of the market approach into the income approach, thus compromising the independence of the two approaches. The greater the impact of the terminal value on the estimated total present value, the greater the impact of the market approach influence on what started as an income approach if market multiples are used to estimate the terminal value.

---

5. M. Mark Lee, *The Ratio of Depreciation and Capital Expenditures in DCF Terminal Values*, Financial Valuation and Litigation Expert 7–8 (Aug.-Sept. 2007); Daniel L. McConaughy & Bordi, Lorena, *The Long-Term Relationships between Capital Expenditures and Depreciation Across Industries: Important Data for Capitalized Income Based Valuations*, Business Valuation Review 14–24 (March 2004); Gilbert E. Matthews, *CapX = Depreciation Is Unrealistic Assumption for Most Terminal Values*, Shannon Pratt's Business Valuation Update (March 2002).

This terminal value issue is critically important in the discounting method, because the terminal value often accounts for more than half the total value in the discounted cash flow method. If the analyst uses the constant growth model to estimate the terminal value, the reviewer can check to see whether the market multiples implied by the terminal value are reasonable. If the analyst uses market multiples to estimate the terminal value, the reviewer can check to see whether the capitalization rate implied by the terminal value is reasonable.

Concept and Estimation of Discount Rates

From the formulas in the preceding sections, it should be apparent that the estimation of the discount rate has a major impact on the indicated present value. One should be suspicious of appraisals that fail to provide detailed attention to the estimation of the discount rate. This section explains the concept of the discount rate and accepted procedures for estimating it.

The Concept of the Discount Rate

The discount rate is the expected *total rate of return* the investor requires to commit funds to the particular investment. It is market-driven for it represents the expected rates of return available in the market on other investments that are comparable in terms of risk.

The expected total rate of return includes two elements:

- Cash payouts
- Capital appreciation (or capital depreciation)

For example, consider a stock market investment opportunity for which the investor has the following expectations:

Stock price	$50
Annual dividend	$2
Expected annual price increase	10%

The expected appreciation would be $5 per share (0.10 x $50). Add that to the dividend of $2 and the total expected return is $7. On an investment of $50, that is a total expected return of 14 percent ($7 total return divided by $50 purchase price = 0.14).

These observed or expected total rates of return for various components of the market provide an empirical basis for estimating market-required total rates of return (discount rates) for various types of investments.

Elements of the Discount Rate: A Risk-Free Rate and a Premium for Risk

From a financial analysis perspective, the discount rate impounds within it the following elements:

- A risk-free rate of return, including:
  - A "real rate of return" for forgoing the use of money for some period of time
  - Expected rate of inflation over the life of the investment

  (The yield to maturity on U.S. Government securities typically is used as a proxy for the risk-free rate, the implied assumption being that the U.S. Government will not default on these obligations and that interest rates reflect inflation.)
- A premium for risk

Risk is defined as *the degree of certainty or uncertainty of actually realizing the expected returns at the times and in the amounts expected.* Because risk lies in the eye of the beholder and is not directly observable in the marketplace, financial analysts have developed various empirical procedures using market data to quantify the element of risk in the discount rate. Arguably, this quantification of the risk element is the single most challenging exercise in the discipline of valuation analysis. The next sections explain procedures used for quantifying risk in the discount rate.

Estimating Discount Rates for Fixed-Income Securities

Unlike discount rates for equities, estimating discount rates for fixed-income securities is relatively easy, because the expected returns (yield to maturity) are specified for each publicly traded bond security in the daily financial press and rating services provide guidelines for categorizing bonds and preferred stocks by their degree of risk.

The difference between the yield to maturity for any given bond and a Treasury bond of the same maturity represents the risk premium impounded into the market's required rate of return for that bond. Rating agencies (for example, Standard & Poor's, Moody's) publish risk ratings for most publicly traded bonds and the general criteria for each level of risk range. If the appraisal requires estimating the risk for the debt or preferred stock of a private company, the analyst compares the private company risk factors with one of the rating service's criteria for risk grades, estimates the risk grade for the private company, and observes the market's required rates of return for that risk grade.[6]

6. For detailed procedures for analyzing and valuing debt instruments and preferred stock, *see* Shannon Pratt & Alina Niculita, Valuing a Business 547–62, 563–84 (5th ed. 2008).

We are presenting the Buildup Model before presenting the Capital Asset Pricing Model (CAPM) only because the Buildup Model is simpler; it is actually a simplified version of the Capital Asset Pricing Model. The Buildup Model implicitly reflects the simplifying assumption that sensitivity of returns for the subject company relative to returns for the market as a whole are about the same as for the typical public company in the market.

Estimating Equity Discount Rates: The Buildup Model

As the name suggests, the Buildup Model for estimating equity discount rates consists of a series of building blocks. Most analysts implement this procedure with four elements:

- The risk-free rate
- A general equity risk premium
- A size premium
- A specific company risk adjustment (usually an addition, but could be a subtraction)

The Risk-Free Rate

As noted earlier, the risk-free rate usually is a yield-to-maturity rate available on U.S. Treasury securities as of the effective valuation date. Analysts usually use one of three maturities: 30-day, five-year, or 20-year. These maturities are used because they are the maturities for which *Morningstar® (Ibbotson Associates®)* has developed matching general equity risk premium series (see next section). Analysts generally prefer the 20-year maturity. They recognize that it has an element of risk called *horizon risk,* or *interest rate risk,* meaning that the value of the principal will fluctuate with changing levels of interest rates, but investors generally accept this risk. The longer rates are preferable partly because they are more stable over time and less subject to short-term influences. Also, the longer maturity more closely matches the assumed long life of most businesses.

The Equity Risk Premium

The next building block is a general equity risk premium. This is the rate of return that investors expect from a portfolio of large public stocks (such as the Standard & Poor's 500) over and above the rate available on U.S. Treasury securities.

As noted earlier, *Morningstar®* publishes three series of general equity risk premium data, based on 30-day, five-year, or 20-year U.S. Treasury yields. If the analyst is using *Morningstar®* data for the equity risk premium, the report should show which of the three maturity series he or she used and the risk-free rate used should be for a maturity that matches the equity risk premium. However, the long horizon equity risk premium is preferable for most business valuation assignments because of the long-term nature of the investment.

The *Morningstar®* risk premium data are based on historical stock market returns compared with historical U.S. Treasury security yields. There are some major controversies about how that data should be used to estimate a general equity risk premium as of any given date, but the technical details of these controversies are beyond the scope of this book.[7]

The other important source of risk premiums is *Duff & Phelps Risk Premium Report* (formerly known as Standard & Poor's Corporate Value Consulting *Risk Premium Report*).

The Size Premium

Extensive empirical studies have shown that smaller companies tend to have higher risk than do larger companies. Although this is controversial, most observers believe this to be true. Because of this higher risk, such companies have a higher cost of capital. The incremental addition to the discount rate to reflect the company size component of risk is called the "size premium."

Morningstar® is also the primary purveyor of data on the historical magnitudes of the size effect in terms of how much should be added to the general equity risk premium to properly reflect the size effect in the discount rate.

Duff & Phelps is another provider of size premium data. *Duff & Phelps*'s risk premium report uses eight different measures of size: market value of common equity, book value of common equity, five-year average net income, market value of invested capital, total assets, five-year average EBITDA, sales, and number of employees.

Specific Company Risk Adjustment

To the extent that the risk of the subject company differs from the average of the companies from which the size adjustment was derived, the last of the four building blocks in the buildup discount rate is a specific company risk adjustment.

Estimating this adjustment necessarily requires some subjective judgment on the part of the appraiser. The more the judgment is based on rigorous financial analysis, the more reliable the result is likely to be.

7. For more detail about these and other *Morningstar®* data and arguments regarding their use, *see* Michael W. Barad & Tara McDowell, *Using Morningstar Cost of Capital Data, in* SHANNON PRATT & ROGER GRABOWSKI, COST OF CAPITAL: APPLICATIONS AND EXAMPLES (3d ed. 2008). *See also* STOCKS, BONDS, BILLS & INFLATION, VALUATION EDITION, published annually by *Morningstar®*.

The subject of financial statement analysis is addressed in Chapter 13. The analyst can use many of the ratios shown in that chapter to compare the subject company to industry averages or to other specific companies, perhaps specific public companies chosen to be guideline companies in the market approach. If a market approach is used, financial ratios for the subject company can be compared with financial ratios for the guideline companies used in the market approach.

There are many qualitative factors that also might have an impact, such as recent actual or potential competition, quality and depth of management, condition of facilities, and countless other possibilities. It is important, however, not to double-count in the specific company risk premium factors that have already been reflected in the size premium.

Industry Risk Premia

Morningstar® introduced an alternative formula for the buildup model in the *SBBI Valuation Edition 2002 Yearbook.* They included in the buildup model one more element: industry risk premium, which reflects the characteristics of the subject company's industry. *Morningstar®* publishes this risk premium in the *SBBI Valuation Edition Yearbook.*

Summary Illustration of the Equity Discount Rate Using the Buildup Model

The following is a typical presentation of the estimation of an equity discount rate by the Buildup Model (using *Morningstar®* data):

Risk-free rate	4.3%[1]
Equity risk premium	7.1[2]
Size premium	2.7[3]
Specific company risk adjustment	2.0[4]
Equity discount rate	16.1%

1. Yield on 20-year U.S. Treasury bonds as of valuation date.
2. *Morningstar®* arithmetic mean equity risk premium for full period 1926–2006, from *Stocks, Bonds, Bills & Inflation,* 2007 Valuation Edition, p. 189.
3. *Morningstar®*, 2007 *SBBI, op. cit.,* p. 137 (9th decile).
4. See pp. xx of analyst's valuation report for supporting analysis.

Here is the other example illustrating the usage of an industry risk premium when calculating an equity discount rate (using *Morningstar®* data):

Risk-free rate	4.3%[1]
Equity risk premium	7.1[2]
Size premium	2.7[3]
Industry risk premium	0.35[4]
Specific company risk adjustment	2.0[5]
Equity discount rate	16.45%

1. Yield on 20-year U.S. Treasury bonds as of valuation date.
2. *Morningstar®* arithmetic mean equity risk premium for full period 1926–2006, from *Stocks, Bonds, Bills & Inflation,* 2007 Valuation Edition, p. 189.
3. *Morningstar®*, 2007 *SBBI, op. cit.,* p. 137 (9th decile).
4. *Morningstar®*, 2007 *SBBI, op. cit.,* p. 45 (Oil and Gas Field Services, SIC 138).
5. See pp. xx of analyst's valuation report for supporting analysis.

The following is a typical presentation of the estimation of an equity discount rate by the Buildup Model (using *Duff & Phelps* data):

Risk-free rate	4.3%[1]
Equity risk premium (including size premium)	10.4[2]
Specific company risk adjustment	2.0[3]
Equity discount rate	16.7%

1. Yield on 20-year U.S. Treasury bonds as of valuation date.
2. *Duff & Phelps, LLC, Risk Premium Report* 2007, smoothed equity risk premium for portfolio 20, Exhibit A-1, p. 26.
3. See pp. xx of analyst's valuation report for supporting analysis.

Estimating Equity Discount Rates: The Capital Asset Pricing Model

The Capital Asset Pricing Model (CAPM) today is considered by many to be the most theoretically correct model for estimating an equity discount rate. It has been theoretically challenged but is still the model most commonly used by corporate finance practitioners.

The only difference between the CAPM and the Buildup Model is a modifier (coefficient) to the general equity risk premium called *beta.*

Definition of Beta

The coefficient called *beta* is a measure of market risk. It measures the sensitivity of returns on an individual security (or portfolio of securities) to returns on the market. The total return (dividends and capital appreciation) on the Standard & Poor's 500-stock composite average (S&P 500) is the most commonly used benchmark for returns on the market.

Beta measures the risk called *systematic risk* because it is the risk of the overall market. The theory is that market risk cannot be removed by holding a fully diversified portfolio of securities and, therefore, is unavoidable if investing in equities. A fundamental assumption of CAPM is that the risk premium portion of a security's expected total return is a function of that security's systematic risk. (The risk that is *not* related to the market is called *unsystematic risk.*)

Computation of Beta

For a publicly traded security (or portfolio), beta is measured from market data, usually for the past three to five years. The computation of beta is a linear regression of the rate of return on a given security (or portfolio of securities) on the market return for a series of time periods. If returns for the subject security or portfolio go up and down about the same degree as the market, then beta equals 1.0. If the returns tend to be more volatile in response to market moves (that is, go up more than the market when the market goes up and down more than the market when the market goes down), then beta is greater than 1.0. Conversely, if the returns tend to be less volatile in response to changes in market returns, then beta is less than 1.0.

Exhibit 5-3 shows schematically how the market-required rate of return increases as beta increases.

Betas for Privately Held Companies

Because a privately held company by definition does not have regular public market trading prices, such volatility in daily, weekly, or monthly returns cannot be measured directly. Therefore, analysts wishing to use the CAPM to estimate an equity discount rate for a private company must develop a proxy for the private company's beta.

The most common way of doing this is to observe betas of public companies in the same industry. The analyst then may use some average of the betas of those companies as a proxy for the beta of the private company. If the analyst also uses a public guideline company valuation method, the companies used in that method very likely would be the ones from which the betas are analyzed. Or the analyst might use industry average betas from *Morningstar®*'s *Cost of Capital Yearbook* or *Quarterly Updates.*

Incorporating Beta into the Equity Risk Premium

To incorporate beta into the equity risk premium, one multiplies the general equity risk premium by the beta. To illustrate, we will use the general equity risk premium of 7.1 that we used in the illustration of the Buildup Model (using *Morningstar®* data).

Exhibit 5-3
Schematic Diagram Illustrating Beta

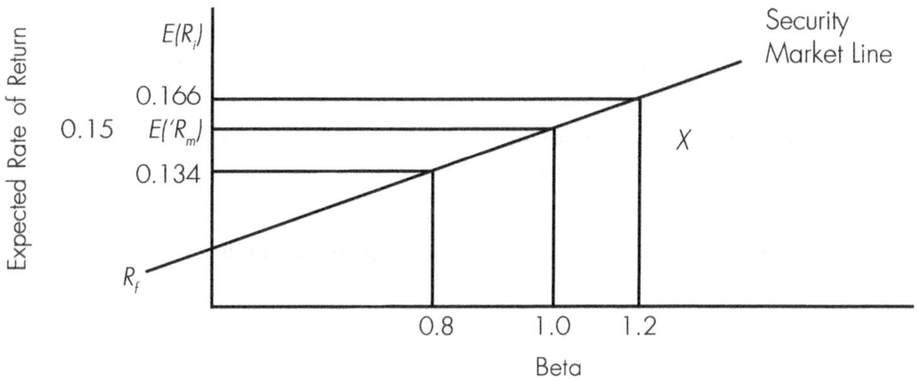

In this diagram:

$E(R_i)$	=	Expected return for the individual security
$E(R_m)$	=	Expected return on the market
R_f	=	Risk-free rate available as of the valuation date
X	=	Risk and return profile for a particular company

In a market in perfect equilibrium, all securities would fall on the security market line. If security *X* has a high beta (as shown in the diagram) and a security analyst expects the returns for that security to be as shown, the analyst would consider the security overpriced.

As this exhibit shows, the beta for the market as a whole is 1.0. Therefore, from a numerical standpoint, the beta has the following interpretations:

Beta > 1.0	When market rates of return move up or down, the rates of return for the subject tend to move in the same direction and with greater magnitude. For example, for a stock with no dividend, if the market is up 10%, the price of a stock with a beta of 1.2 would be expected to be up 12%. If the market is down 10%, the price of the same stock would be expected to be down 12%. Many high-tech companies are good examples of stocks with high betas.
Beta = 1.0	Fluctuations in rates of return for the subject tend to equal fluctuations in rates of return for the market.
Beta < 1.0	When market rates of return move up or down, rates of return for the subject tend to move up or down, but to a lesser extent. For example, for a stock with no dividend, if the market is up 10%, the price of a stock with a beta of .8 would be expected to be up 8%. The classic example of a low-beta stock would be a utility that has not diversified into more risky activities.
Negative beta (Rare)	Rates of return for the subject tend to move in the opposite direction from changes in rates of return for the market. Stocks with negative betas are rare. A few gold-mining companies have had negative betas in the past.

Source: Shannon Pratt and Roger Grabowski, *Cost of Capital: Applications and Examples*, 3d Ed. John Wiley & Sons, Inc., 2008, at 81–82.

First, consider company *i*, whose returns are assumed to be less sensitive to changes in overall market returns than those of the average company and for which we have assigned a beta of 0.75:

0.75 x 7.1 = 5.3 equity risk premium for company *i*.

Next, consider company *j*, whose systematic risk is estimated to be equal to the market as a whole, with a beta of 1.0:

1.0 x 7.1 = 7.1 equity risk premium for company *j*.

Finally, consider company *k*, which is estimated to have 20 percent more volatility in returns in response to the overall market than does the average company and therefore has a beta of 1.2:

1.2 x 7.1 = 8.5 equity risk premium for company *k*.

The Size Premium (Small Stock Premium) in CAPM

The *Morningstar®* studies show that small companies tend to have larger betas on average than do big companies. However, the *Morningstar®* studies also show that only some, not all, of the extra risk of smaller companies is captured by beta. Therefore, *Morningstar®* publishes a series called *Size Premium in Excess of CAPM* for guidance in incorporating the size effect into the equity discount rate when using the CAPM.

Specific Company Risk Adjustment in CAPM

To the extent that the company has risk factors that have not already been reflected in the general equity risk premium as modified by beta and the small company size premium, a further specific company risk adjustment could be warranted. Be careful to ensure that the analyst is not double-counting risk factors already captured by beta and the size premium. For example, are the subject company's weaknesses in management depth, geographical and product diversification, breadth of customer base, and other such elements any more limited than the companies from which the size factor was estimated?

Summary Illustration of the Equity Discount Rate Using CAPM

The following is a typical presentation of the estimation of an equity discount rate using the CAPM (using *Morningstar®* data):

Risk-free rate		4.3[1]
Equity risk premium:		
General equity risk premium	7.1[2]	
Beta	x 1.3[3]	9.2
Size premium in excess of CAPM		2.7[4]
Specific company risk adjustment		1.0[5]
Equity discount rate		17.2%

1. Yield on 20-year U.S. Treasury bonds as of valuation date.
2. *Morningstar®* arithmetic mean equity risk premium for full period 1926–2006, from *Stocks, Bonds, Bills & Inflation,* 2007 Valuation Edition, p. 189.
3. Median beta for the group of guideline public companies as determined for the subject company
4. *Morningstar®*, 2007 *SBBI, op. cit.,* p. 137, 9th decile.
5. See pp. xx of analyst's valuation report for supporting analysis.

Duff & Phelps also publishes data for the CAPM model but take a slightly different approach from *Morningstar®*. The following is a typical presentation of the estimation of an equity discount rate using the CAPM (using *Duff & Phelps* data):

Risk-free rate		4.3[1]
Equity risk premium:		
General equity risk premium	4.9[2]	
Beta	x 1.3[3]	6.4
Size premium in excess of CAPM		4.4[4]
Specific company risk adjustment		1.0[5]
Equity discount rate		16.1%

1. Yield on 20-year U.S. Treasury bonds as of valuation date.
2. *Morningstar®* arithmetic mean equity risk premium for period 1963–2006, from *Stocks, Bonds, Bills & Inflation,* 2007 Valuation Edition, p. 191.
3. Median beta for the group of guideline public companies as determined for the subject company
4. *Duff & Phelps, LLC, Risk Premium Report* 2007, smoothed premium over CAPM for portfolio 20, Exhibit B-1, p. 34.
5. See pp. xx of analyst's valuation report for supporting analysis.

Although the CAPM is probably the most widely used procedure in corporate finance today for estimating the cost of equity capital, there is some controversy about the use of the beta factor. There are alternative models that purport to capture the risk associated with an equity as well or better, although they have not achieved wide usage.

Concept and Estimation of Capitalization Rates

The Concept of a Capitalization Rate

As noted earlier in this chapter, a *capitalization rate* is a divisor applied to a single number representing some type of economic income to derive an estimate of value. As such, unlike a discount rate, it does *not* represent the total annual rate of return expected by the investor over the life of the investment. It represents the *current* return, but it does not reflect the total return.

In the discounting method, all the changes in future expected returns are fully accounted for in the numerator of the discounting formula. In capitalizing, only a single number is used in the numerator and *all future changes in the expected income are impounded into the capitalization rate,* that is, subtracting the growth rate from the discount rate reflects the future changes in expected income.

Elements of the Capitalization Rate

There are two basic elements impounded in a capitalization rate:

1. A discount rate, which represents the total annually compounded rate of return the investor requires over the life of the investment, reflecting the risk of the investment.
2. An annualized expected rate of growth or decline in the amount of the economic income variable being capitalized.

In the context of the income approach, we specifically quantify each of these two elements. In the context of the market approach (see the next chapter), we simply observe the total capitalization rate for each of several possible measures of economic income, but we have no way of knowing for sure what portion of any observed capitalization rate represents the required total rate of return and what portion represents the expected changes in the variable being capitalized.

Estimating Equity Capitalization Rates

As suggested in the section above, the capitalization rate is simply the discount rate plus or minus the expected annually compounded rate of change in the variable being capitalized. In terms of a formula, this computation is:

Formula 5-9

$$c = k - g$$

Where:

c	=	Capitalization rate
k	=	Discount rate (cost of capital or total required rate of return)
g	=	Growth rate (in the variable being capitalized)

For an example, assume:

Discount rate:	20%
Long-term sustainable growth rate:	5%

Inserting these numbers in Formula 5-9 gives us:

Formula 5-10

$$0.20 - 0.05 = 0.15$$

It is important to note that the *growth rate* is assumed to be an *expected annualized rate in perpetuity.* The reasonableness of the rate used must be assessed with this requirement in mind. If this growth rate is overestimated, then the capitalization rate is underestimated, the resulting value is overestimated, and vice versa.

The growth rate normally includes expected inflation. For example, if the company expected to maintain a physical volume increase of 3 percent with constant margins and expected price increases of 2 percent annually in line with expected inflation, the expected growth rate would be 5 percent. The capitalization model reflecting constant growth sometimes is referred to as the Gordon Growth Model.

Valuing Invested Capital versus Valuing Equity

In Chapter 3, we said that an accepted procedure in any of the valuation approaches is to value all the *invested capital* and subtract the debt (and the value of preferred stock, if any) to obtain the value of the common equity.

To use the procedure in the income approach, the numerator of the equation (the dollar amounts of expected returns) must include the returns available to all the invested capital, that is, the debt holders as well as the equity holders. The denominator (the discount or capitalization rate) must reflect a blending of the costs of each of the component costs of capital on the basis of their proportions in the capital structure, measured at market value. This blended rate is called the Weighted Average Cost of Capital (WACC).

The Concept of Weighted Average Cost of Capital

The Weighted Average Cost of Capital (WACC) is the blended discount rate of all the capital structure components, each weighted at its pro rata portion of the total capital structure. It is critical that the weight assigned each component is *at market value not at book value.* (Weighting the components at book value rather than at market value is a common error that can result in a significant misestimation of value.)

The Basic WACC Computation Model

The formula for the weighted average cost of capital is:

Formula 5-11

$$WACC = (k_e \text{ x } W_e) + (k_{d(pt)}[1\text{-}t] \text{ x } W_d)$$

Where:

WACC	=	Weighted Average Cost of Capital
W	=	Weight (the percentage of each component of the company's total capital structure, measured at market value)
k_e	=	Cost of equity capital (equity discount rate)
$k_{d(pt)}$	=	Cost of debt capital before tax (that is, before adjusting the cost for the tax deductibility of interest expense)
t	=	Tax rate

Of course, if there is preferred stock or other components of the capital structure, there would need to be a component in the above formula for each capital structure component.

For an example of application of the above formula, assume:

Equity discount rate:	20%
Percentage of equity in the capital structure (at market value):	60%
Cost of debt (pretax):	10%
Tax rate:	30%
Percentage of debt in the capital structure:	40%

Inserting these numbers in Formula 5-11 gives us:

Formula 5-12

WACC	=	(0.20 x 0.60) + (0.10[1-0.30] x 0.40)
	=	0.12 + (0.07 x 0.40)
	=	0.12 +0.028
	=	0.148 or 14.8%

The above often is presented in tabular form:

Component	*Cost*	*Weight*	*Weighted Cost*
Equity	0.20	0.60	0.12
Debt	0.10(1-0.30)	0.40	0.028
Weighted Average Cost of Capital			0.148

Derivation of Weights for WACC

In the above example, the cost of equity is 20 percent and the net cost of debt (after the tax effect) is only 7 percent. Such a large difference is not uncommon. Consequently, selection of the weights in the WACC can have a large bearing on the invested capital discount rate and thus on the indicated value. This is often a major area of controversy and one source of differences in value between appraisers.

The choice of weights may be different when one is valuing a controlling interest versus a minority interest. They also may be different under different standards of value. We will confine the discussion here to fair market value, but, for example, under investment value (value to a particular investor), that investor could select any weights considered most appropriate.

- **Controlling Interests.** Some would use the company's actual capital structure. However, in estimating the fair market value of controlling interests, a good case can be made for using an industry average capital structure, because one of the prerogatives of control ownership is to change the capital structure.

  One of the few sources that provides industry average capital structures at market value is *Morningstar®*'s *Cost of Capital Yearbook* or *Quarterly Updates.* A common error is to use industry average capital structures at book value. Usually, book values have debt at close to market value but equity (based on depreciated historical costs) at considerably less than market value. This distorts the weights by overstating the debt proportion and understating the equity proportion, thus understating the invested capital discount rate and overstating the value.

The data in *Morningstar®'s Cost of Capital Yearbook* or *Quarterly Updates* is all from public companies. Private companies may have less access to the debt markets than do public companies. Thus, it may be appropriate to assume a little higher proportion of equity for a private company.

Changing the capital structure weights significantly also can change the cost of each component of the capital structure. As leverage (percentage) of debt is increased, risk is increased for both the debt and the equity, thus increasing the cost of each component. A common error is to hypothesize a much greater percentage of debt with no increase in the cost of debt or equity, thus lowering the computed WACC and reaching an unattainably inflated indicated value for the company.

- **Minority Interests.** When valuing a minority interest at fair market value or in a fair value calculation when the legal standard assumes no change in management (such as a Delaware appraisal), the appraiser almost always uses the company's actual capital structure, because the minority interest owner has no power to change the capital structure. At first glance this may seem like a dilemma, because we have to weight the capital structure components at market value—which we do not yet know—because that is what we are trying to determine. However, the dilemma is easily solved with modern computers using an *iterative process,* that is, testing different capital structures until one works out.[8]

Another source of weights for the capital structure, if using the market approach and/or the capital asset pricing model in the income approach, would be the capital structures of the guideline companies used. If the capital structures among the companies vary a great deal, this may be calculated by a procedure called "unlevering and relevering betas," a topic that is beyond the scope of this book.[9]

Preference for Net Cash Flow in Income Approach

The consensus among professional business appraisers and the corporate finance community is that net cash flow is the preferred measure of economic income to use in the income approach. There are good reasons for this:

- Matches with empirical data supporting the discount rate.

8. The iterative process is described in SHANNON PRATT & ROGER GRABOWSKI, COST OF CAPITAL: APPLICATIONS AND EXAMPLES (3d ed. 2008). A shortcut for a reasonable estimate is presented by Frank Evans, *Debt and Equity Weightings in WACC*, CPA EXPERT, at 4–5 (Fall 1998), abstracted in SHANNON PRATT'S BUSINESS VALUATION UPDATE, March 1999, at 11.

9. In Duff & Phelps' LLC Risk Premium Report, published annually and *available at* http://corporate.morningstar.com/ib/html/home.htm and www.bvresources.com.

- Conceptual preference for net cash flow: It represents what the owner can take out and still expect to achieve the projected returns.
- Helps make the income approach discrete from the market approach, because the market approach usually uses other income variables and generally not net cash flow.

Net Cash Flow Matches Empirical Data

Both the *Morningstar®* data and the *Duff & Phelps* data reflect *total return,* that is, dividends plus or minus capital appreciation or depreciation. (The data are based on public stocks, for which the dividends are distributed and the stock is in a liquid market, so the investor can sell the stock and realize the appreciation or depreciation.) This is tantamount to the appraiser's definition of net cash flow.

Net Cash Flow Is What You Get

When defining net cash flow in Chapter 4, we explained that net cash flow is cash flow remaining *after* allowing for necessary capital expenditures and net working capital to support sales growth. In other words, it is what can be taken out of the company (at least by a control owner) without impairing the company's operations. This is the economic income variable that ultimately is of greatest importance to most investors.

Public companies look relatively more to net income than do private companies, but in the long run, net cash flow is the most essential ingredient to the success of public companies as well. This is an important conceptual reason for focusing on net cash flow in estimating value.

Use of Net Cash Flow Keeps Income Approach Discrete

Appraisers like to be able to use two or more approaches to valuation to help increase the reliability of the valuation conclusion. To the extent that components of the different methods do not overlap, this increases the independence of one valuation method compared with another.

Despite the preference for net cash flow in the income approach, it is almost never used in the market approach, because, for the comparative companies, we don't know whether two of the components of net cash flow—capital expenditures and additions to net working capital for any year—represent normalized amounts for those companies, and capitalizing abnormal figures would produce a distorted indication of value. Therefore, in the market approach, we generally use every measure of economic income *except* net cash flow (for example, net income, pretax income, gross cash flow, EBIT, EBITDA, "discretionary earnings," all defined in Chapter 4).

Thus, using net cash flow as the economic income variable in the income approach tends to make the income approach results more independent of the results from other valuation approaches.

Exhibit 5-4
The Midyear Discounting Convention

The income approach procedures shown in previous sections implicitly assume that all the proceeds are received or distributed at the end of each year. Indeed, many businesses wait until the end of the year to assess cash availability and needs before deciding what to distribute to owners. Also, many have seasonal cash flow patterns.

If, however, it is more reasonable to assume that proceeds are received more or less evenly throughout the year, appraisers reflect this assumption with a mathematical procedure called the *midyear discounting convention.*[10]

The idea is that the effect of receiving proceeds more or less evenly throughout the year can be approximated by assuming that all the proceeds are received in the middle of each year, thus the term *midyear convention.* Because the assumption is that the cash flows will be realized earlier, the midyear convention procedure always will produce a higher indication of value than the assumption of receiving cash flows only at the end of each year. The way the mathematics work out, the higher the discount or capitalization rate, the greater the difference will be between the values indicated by the two alternative assumptions.[11]

10. The formulas and examples are described in SHANNON PRATT & ROGER GRABOWSKI, COST OF CAPITAL: APPLICATIONS AND EXAMPLES (3d ed. 2008), Appendix 10A, at 143.

11. It is, of course, appropriate to make calculations adjusting for uneven but predictable cash flow patterns, e.g., a toy retailer at Christmas or H&R Block in April, but such models usually are more complex to create.

Exhibit 5-5
The Midyear Convention in the Capitalization Method

The midyear convention is accomplished in the capitalization method by a minor variation in the capitalization formula presented earlier.

The modification is made in the numerator of the capitalization formula. In **Formula 5-12,** we capitalize next year's economic income as follows:

$$PV = \frac{E_1}{c}$$

Where:

PV	=	Present Value
E_n	=	Expected economic income in the full period immediately following the effective valuation date
c	=	Capitalization rate (as defined previously)

To introduce the midyear convention assumption, we multiply the above by 1 plus the discount rate (k), raised to the power of 0.5 (to reflect a half year). In other words, the expected income is multiplied by $(1 + k)^{0.5}$, resulting in the following formula:[12]

Formula 5-13

$$PV = \frac{E_1(1+k)^{0.5}}{c}$$

Where:

PV	=	Present Value
E_n	=	Expected economic income in the full period immediately following the effective valuation date
k	=	Present value discount rate (cost of capital)
c	=	Capitalization rate (as defined previously)

To illustrate the above with an example, assume:

E_n	=	$105
k	=	20%
c	=	15% (20% less growth rate of 5%)

12. Proof of the accuracy of this method is presented in Todd A. Kaltman, *Capitalization Using a Mid-Year Convention*, Business Valuation Review (Dec. 1995), at 178–82.

Inserting these numbers in Formula 5-13 gives us the following:

Formula 5-14

$$PV = \frac{\$105(1+0.20)^{0.5}}{0.15}$$

$$= \frac{\$105(1.09545)}{0.15}$$

$$= \frac{\$115.02}{0.15}$$

$$= \$766.82$$

Similarly, the Gordon Growth Model (Formula 5-3) can be modified to reflect the mid-year convention by adding the same term in the numerator:

Formula 5-15

$$PV = \frac{E_0(1 + g)(1 + k)^{0.5}}{k-g}$$

Where:

- PV = Present Value
- E_0 = Expected economic income in the full period immediately preceding the effective valuation date
- g = Expected long-term sustainable rate of growth in the economic income from the year immediately preceding the effective valuation date
- k = Present value discount rate (cost of capital)

To illustrate the above with an example, assume:

- E_0 = \$100
- g = 5%
- k = 20%

Inserting these numbers in Formula 5-15 gives us the following:

Formula 5-16

$$PV = \frac{\$100(1+0.05)(1+0.20)0^{0.5}}{0.20 - 0.05}$$

$$= \frac{\$100(1.05)(1.09545)}{0.15}$$

$$= 766.82$$

Exhibit 5-6
The Midyear Convention in the Discounting Method

To reflect the midyear convention in the discounting method, the number of periods by which each year's proceeds is discounted is reduced by a half year. In other words, each exponent in the denominator, n, is reduced by 0.5. The modified formula (modified from Formula 5-7) is as follows:

Formula 5-17

$$PV = \frac{E_1}{(1+k)^{0.5}} + \frac{E_2}{(1+k)^{1.5}} + \ldots + \frac{E_n}{(1+k)^{n-0.5}} + \frac{\dfrac{E_n(1+g)}{k-g}}{(1+k)^{n-0.5}}$$

where the variables are defined the same as in Formula 5-7.

For simplicity in an example, we will use only a three-year specific forecast period and will use the same assumed figures as in Formula 5-8:

Net cash flow Year 1	\$100
Net cash flow Year 2	\$130
Net cash flow Year 3	\$150
Required rate of return (discount rate):	20%
Annually compounded growth in net cash flow beyond Year 3	5%

Inserting these numbers in Formula 5-17 gives us:

Formula 5-18

$$PV = \frac{\$100}{(1+0.20)^{.5}} + \frac{\$130}{(1+0.20)^{1.5}} + \ldots + \frac{\$150}{(1+0.20)^{2.5}} + \frac{\dfrac{\$150(1+0.05)}{0.20-0.05}}{(1+0.20)^{2.5}}$$

$$= \frac{\$100}{1.10} + \frac{\$130}{1.31} + \frac{\$150}{1.58} + \frac{\dfrac{\$157.50}{0.15}}{1.58}$$

$$= \$90.91 + \$99.24 + \$94.94 + \$664.56$$

$$= \$949.65$$

Note that the above value is higher than the value from the year-end assumption—in this case \$949.65 compared with \$868.06 from Formula 5-8.

An alternative procedure is to reflect the midyear convention in the terminal value using the modified Gordon Growth Model (Formula 5-15), in which case the terminal value is discounted by n years instead of n–0.5 years. This formula is written as follows:

Formula 5-19

$$PV = \frac{E_1}{(1+k)^{.5}} + \frac{E_2}{(1+k)^{1.5}} + \ldots + \frac{E_n}{(1+k)^{n-0.5}} + \frac{\frac{E_n(1+g)(1+k)^{0.5}}{k-g}}{(1+k)^n}$$

Where the variables are defined the same as in Formula 5-7.

This will produce exactly the same result as Formula 5-17.

The difference in value between the year-end and the midyear conventions is equal to $(1+k)^{0.5}$.

References

Basic Income Approach References

Fishman, Jay E., Shannon P. Pratt, J. Clifford Griffith, et al. 2008. "Capitalized and Discounted Returns Methods." PPC's *Guide to Business Valuations*, 5-1 to 5-113.

Hitchner, James R. 2006. "Income Approach." In *Financial Valuation: Applications and Models*, 2d Ed., Chap. 4, 97–150.

Pratt, Shannon P. and Alina V. Niculita. 2008. "Income Approach: Discounted Future Economic Income Method." In *Valuing a Business,* 5th Ed., Chap. 9. Includes extensive bibliography and data references.

Pratt, Shannon. 2003. "The Income Approach: Cost of Capital," "The Income Approach: The Discounting Method," and "The Income Approach: The Capitalization Method." In *Business Valuation Body of Knowledge,* 2d Ed., 100–41.

Pratt, Shannon P. and Roger J. Grabowski. 2008. *Cost of Capital: Applications and Examples,* 3d Ed.

Trugman, Gary. 2002. "The Income Approach" and "Discount Rates and Capitalization Rates." In *Understanding Business Valuations,* 2d Ed., 281–322, 323–56.

Cost of Capital Data References

Duff & Phelps LLC, 55 E. 52nd St., 31st Fl., New York, NY 10055, (212) 871-2000. *Risk Premium Report,* published annually and *available at* http://www.bvresources.com and http://corporate.morningstar.com.

Morningstar® (Ibbotson Associates®), 225 N. Michigan Ave., Ste. 700, Chicago, IL 60601, (312) 616-1620. Publishes three series of data dealing with cost of capital:

Stocks, Bonds, Bills & Inflation, Valuation Edition, published annually. Provides equity risk premium series, small stock premium series, and other data to develop cost of equity capital.

Cost of Capital Yearbook or *Quarterly Updates,* published annually with quarterly updates. Contains cost of equity by both CAPM and DCF procedures and Weighted Average Cost of Capital by Industry, as well as capital structure at market value by industry.

Beta Book, published semiannually. Several computations of beta for more than 5,000 publicly traded stocks.

Morningstar® Cost of Capital Center, online service for all of above data on per-inquiry basis, http://corporate.morningstar.com.

Chapter 6

The Market Approach

Market Approach Concept and Overview

The concept of the market approach is that valuation guidance can be found in transactions involving similar companies. In a way, this is like appraising a house by analyzing sales of similar houses. However, "similar" businesses have far more differences among them than do similar houses, and the appraiser must carefully analyze the similarities and differences.

The market approach to business appraisal also has several dimensions that must be considered that are either not found at all or treated differently in the real estate appraisal comparative sales approach:

- Valuing controlling versus minority interests
- Valuing total invested capital versus direct valuation of equity
- Whether guideline transactions are sales of entire businesses or publicly traded minority interest stock market transactions

These possibilities are shown schematically in Exhibit 6-1 (page 82).

Valuing Controlling versus Minority Interests

In real estate appraisal, the valuation is virtually always that of a controlling (fee-simple) interest in the property. After that, if valuing a partial interest, some minority discount may be applied to the fractional interest's pro rata portion of the fee-simple interest value. In business appraisal, minority interests often are valued directly, that is, without ever addressing the question of what the company as a whole, on a controlling interest basis, might be worth. This is possible because thousands of public companies with minority shares are actively traded every day.

As discussed more fully in Chapter 15, the differences between minority and control value usually are considerably greater for businesses than for real estate, be-

Exhibit 6-1
Major Market Approach Business Valuation Scenarios

Valuing Controlling Interest		
	Valuing Total Invested Capital	Using sales of entire companies
		Using publicly traded guideline companies
	Direct Valuation of Equity	Using sales of entire companies
		Using publicly traded guideline companies
Valuing Minority Interest		
	Valuing Total Invested Capital	Using sales of entire companies
		Using publicly traded guideline companies
	Direct Valuation of Equity	Using sales of entire companies
		Using publicly traded guideline companies

cause owners of a fractional interest in real estate usually have the right to demand partition, thus converting their ownership interest to a controlling or fee-simple interest. Owners of stock or partnership interests generally have no such right, leaving them at the mercy of policy decisions of the control owners.

If one starts with guideline sales of entire companies (merger and acquisition transactions) in the market approach (called the *transaction method*), then, if valuing a minority interest, it usually would be appropriate to make both a minority interest and lack of marketability adjustment to the indicated control value. If one starts with publicly traded minority interest transactions in the market approach, then, if valuing a controlling interest, it may be appropriate to apply a control premium to the indicated value, and one might also consider a discount for lack of marketability.

However, as discussed in Chapter 15, control premiums certainly are *not* automatic when using publicly traded minority interest transactions to value a controlling interest. A possible alternative is to make adjustments to the financial statements with respect to various levels of income that a control owner would make, such as an adjustment for reasonable compensation, provided that such adjustments are soundly supportable. Such a procedure is discussed in more detail in Chapter 15.

Valuing Total Invested Capital versus Direct Valuation of Equity

In real estate appraisal, property normally is appraised without regard to how much debt or other claims there may be against it. In business appraisal, if all components of the capital structure are appraised, it usually is called *value of invested capital* or *market value of invested capital* (MVIC). However, in business appraisal, the equity interest sometimes is valued directly without going through the step of estimating the value of the entire company, including debt and equity interests combined.

To obtain a value for the equity, one can use market multiples of various levels of income available to equity owners (for example, price/earnings ratios, etc.). Alternatively, one can value the entire invested capital, including returns available to holders of interest-bearing debt and preferred stock, and then subtract the value of the senior securities to obtain the value of the common equity.

Either procedure can be used for valuing either controlling or minority interests. However, the invested capital procedure tends to be preferred for valuing controlling interests and the direct valuation of equity tends to be preferred for valuing minority interests. The reason for this preference is that a controlling interest holder can change the capital structure if that may enhance the value of the equity, while the minority interest owner does not have that option. If the subject and guideline companies have considerably diverse capital structures, however, eliminating the potential effects of that difference sometimes is a reason (sometimes a compelling reason) to use the invested capital procedure even when valuing minority interests.

Using Sales of Entire Companies or Publicly Traded Guideline Companies

As noted in Chapter 3, there are two commonly used types of market transactions:

- Sales of entire companies or possibly controlling interests in companies. Some would divide this into two subcategories:
  —Companies that were publicly traded before the transaction
  —Companies that were privately owned before the transaction[1]
- Publicly traded company transactions (day-to-day transactions of minority interests in companies in the public stock markets)

Unfortunately, there are virtually no reliable data available on minority interest transactions in privately held companies. Therefore, if the appraiser is using the market approach to value a private company minority interest, he or she is forced to start with the above available data and adjust for the minority and marketability factors. If the standard of value is fair market value, the appraiser may consider eliminating or

1. *See* ch. 26, *The Private Company Discount, in* SHANNON PRATT & ROGER GRABOWSKI, COST OF CAPITAL: APPLICATIONS AND EXAMPLES (3d ed. 2008).

making adjustments for transactions that may have been representative of investment value rather than fair market value.

Fortunately, however, there have been huge improvements in recent years in the amount, quality, and ease of access to both public market transaction data and data on sales of entire companies, both public and private. This makes a good market approach valuation much more feasible today for many companies than it would have been at any time in the past.

Sources of Market Approach Data

As noted above, market data can be classified in two groups: (1) sales of entire companies or controlling interests of companies that were publicly traded or privately owned before the sale and (2) publicly traded company market transactions.

Public company data usually have the advantages of being more complete and more verifiable. On the other hand, if one is valuing a controlling interest, it may be preferable to start with controlling interest guideline transactions and not have to deal with the issue of a control premium. Most appraisers consider a control-adjusted income stream to be "control" when using the publicly traded guideline company method.

Another reason to use private company controlling interest transactions in some cases is because many industries and professional practices have few or no public companies.

Sales of Public Companies

If a public company is sold, required filings with the Securities and Exchange Commission (SEC) provide excellent data for implementing a market approach valuation. Because the transactions are not likely to be on the effective valuation date for the subject, the analyst should either explain adjustments for changes in market conditions between the transaction date and subject valuation effective date or explain why none are necessary.

Valuation analysts use many sources to locate sales of public companies. Unlike with currently traded stocks, however, there is no single source that is totally comprehensive, so analysts often use several sources to search for transactions.

If one is relying on public company sales, it is preferable to use the actual SEC filing data rather than data summarized in secondary sources. Besides eliminating a possible source of error from secondary sources, original company filings often provide more detail than do secondary sources.

Sales of Private Companies

Data on sales of private companies usually are considerably more limited than data on sales of public companies. Unlike real estate transactions, for which data generally are required to be filed at the relevant government agency and made publicly available, there is no requirement for releasing any data on sales of privately owned companies. Therefore, unless the buyer is a public company and the purchase is of a sufficient size to require an SEC filing, the data services that collect private company transaction data usually gather it from the transaction intermediaries rather than directly from the companies sold. This generally means that the data for each individual transaction cannot be independently verified. While this is a limitation, the services have no reason to be biased. Furthermore, if valuing a private company or an interest in a private company, it often is considered more comparable to use private company rather than public company transactions as a starting point.

There are four major private sale transaction databases, all greatly expanded in recent years. These are listed and described briefly in the "References" section at the end of this chapter.

Guideline Public Company Data

More than 12,000 operating companies are required to file financial data with the SEC. The major reports are:

- 10-K—Annual report
- 10-Q—Quarterly report
- 8-K—Special events report
- S-1—Registration statement for initial public offering
- S-4—Registration statement and proxy statement for merger in which securities are issued
- 14D9—Information with respect to company being acquired

There are also thousands of public companies that are not required to file with the SEC, because either their number of stockholders or the amount of their assets falls below the SEC levels that require filing.

Since May of 1996, all companies required to file with the SEC must do so electronically on the Electronic Data Gathering and Retrieval (EDGAR) system. All documents filed on EDGAR are in the public domain and may be retrieved at no charge through the Internet. Commercial systems also are available at reasonable charges that provide enhanced capabilities to manipulate the data. The data provide the information to perform all the market multiple calculations discussed in this chapter.

Because public transactions occur daily, the price information for public companies should be as of the effective date of the subject company valuation. Usually, the public company fundamental data (sales, earnings, etc.) should be as close to the valuation date as possible or as close to the latest date available for the subject company as possible.

Developing Market Multiples for Valuation

As in the market approach in real estate appraisal, the market approach in business appraisal requires some "units of comparison." In real estate, for example, price per square foot is a common unit of comparison. In business valuation, however, physical units of comparison (for example, number of board feet per year of manufacturing capacity) are much less common. The units of comparison usually are in some form of dollar measurement of various levels of income-producing capacity or asset values.

In other words, the objective is to observe the transaction price and compute the multiple of that price times some relevant fundamental variables, such as sales, earnings, gross cash flow, net asset value, etc. The fundamental variables used in the market approach are defined and illustrated in Chapter 4. This chapter will present an example of the market approach using some of the most commonly encountered market multiples.

Invested Capital Multiples

When valuing the entire invested capital of a company (i.e., equity and debt), the numerator of the market multiple is the market value of invested capital (MVIC). This is defined as the market value of all the common and preferred stock and interest-bearing debt. Technically, invested capital would include only long-term debt, including the current portion. However, more often than not, short-term interest-bearing debt also is included. One reason for this is that it often is difficult or even impossible, at least for the guideline companies, to determine how much of the interest expense is attributable to long-term versus short-term debt.

Many valuation analysts and almost all investment bankers subtract out cash and cash equivalents when they are defining and computing market value of invested capital. This is to focus on the valuations of companies' operations without distortions of cash-rich versus cash-poor companies. If this is carried out for the guideline companies, then, of course, cash and equivalents for the subject company must be added back in after the multiples have been applied to estimate the company's value and an appropriate pro forma adjustment must be made for interest.

Because of these two ambiguities in computing market value of invested capital, it is essential that the report or analysis that uses market value of invested capital define how it is computed.

Because the numerator includes the market value of all invested capital, the denominator used to create the multiple must include all the returns available to all the invested capital. Usually, this means adding all the interest paid in addition to all the returns available to common equity. If there is preferred stock, the dividends on the preferred stock also must be included.

To recap from Chapter 4, the denominators typically used for invested capital multiples include the following:

- Sales. This is the only income statement denominator that can logically be used in either invested capital or equity market multiples. It is a more relevant multiple for invested capital than for equity, because the multiples of market value of equity to sales can be significantly distorted by differences in capital structures among the companies.
- Discretionary Earnings. Gross cash flow before interest, taxes, and all compensation to one owner/manager. Typically used only for small businesses and professional practices with one key owner/operator.
- Earnings before Interest, Taxes, Depreciation, and Amortization (EBITDA). A multiple of EBITDA is the market multiple most preferred by acquirers for valuing companies under the market approach. It represents gross cash flow before taxes and eliminates the possibly distorting effect of differing depreciation policies among companies.
- Earnings before Interest and Taxes (EBIT). This is the second most frequently used invested capital market multiple.
- Debt-Free Net Income (DFNI). A multiple based on an estimation of what after-tax net income to invested capital would be if there were no interest-bearing debt.
- Debt-Free Cash Flow (DFCF). A multiple based on an estimate of what after-tax gross cash flow available to invested capital would be if there were no interest-bearing debt.
- Book Value of Invested Capital. When this multiple is used, it may refer to total book value or only include tangible book value. Intangibles usually are eliminated because the different methods of acquiring intangibles and accounting for them can distort comparisons between companies.
- Adjusted Book Value of Invested Capital. In some cases, this multiple can be used if it is possible to adjust values of major assets to market value for both the subject and guideline companies. Ideally, one would adjust all assets and liabilities to market value, but this may be impractical in most cases.

Equity Multiples

When valuing equity directly, the numerator of the market multiple is the market value of common equity, often simply referred to as "price." This may be expressed on either the basis of the aggregate value of common stock outstanding or on a per-share basis. Of course, the financial fundamental in the denominator must be expressed on the same basis.

Because the numerator is the market value of common equity, the denominator used to create the multiple must consist of returns at the common equity level (after deductions for interest and preferred dividends). To recap from Chapter 4, the denominators typically used for equity valuation multiples include:

- Sales. One should be careful using a multiple of sales for an equity valuation because:
  - It may be distorted because of different degrees of leverage among companies.
  - Using sales by itself, there is an implicit assumption that the subject and guideline companies have similar cost structures, which may or may not be true. (If earnings data are available for the guideline companies, the price/sales multiple can, and should be, adjusted to reflect differences in the companies' cost structures.)
  - It may be more appropriate for a control-basis valuation than for a minority valuation on the theory that a control buyer may be able to bring the cost structure into line with industry averages after acquiring the customer base.
  - If sales is used in the denominator of an equity multiple (that is, stock price/sales), the level of the multiple should be justified by references to the relative return on sales between the subject and the guideline companies.
- Gross Cash Flow (often just called Cash Flow). Net income plus noncash charges; particularly helpful if the subject and guideline companies have significantly different depreciation accounting policies.
- Pretax Income (Net Income Before Taxes). Price/earnings ratios for public companies are reported on an after-tax basis. Be careful that the analyst has not used an after-tax P/E ratio and applied it to pretax earnings (a common error).
- Dividends or Withdrawals. When valuing a controlling interest, the focus usually is on the capacity to pay dividends or withdrawals. However, when valuing a minority interest, the focus generally is on actual dividends or withdrawals, for the minority owner cannot cause more to be paid.
- Book Value of Equity. Same comments apply as for book value of invested capital.
- Adjusted Book Value. Same comments apply as for adjusted book value of invested capital.

Time Periods for Company Financial Statement Data

Unless there is some special reason, balance sheet data normally should be the latest available data as of the valuation date. However, if using guideline public company data, there usually are many possible time periods for income data:

- Latest fiscal year
- Latest 12 months
- Some number of years' simple average (such as three, five, seven, or 10 years, with five years the most common)
- Some number of years' weighted average (usually weighting latest years more on the theory that most current results should be most representative of future expectations)
- Estimates for the coming year (available for earnings, but generally not for other income variables, for several thousand public companies)

It is important that the time periods for which the guideline public company data are computed are similar to those used for the subject company. If the subject company had drastic changes in its operations (such as major new or discontinued product lines), it may be appropriate to go back only as far as the latest major change. The reviewer should be satisfied that the rationale for the time period or periods chosen makes sense in terms of developing a reasonable value for the subject by reference to the guideline companies.

If one is using sales of private companies for guideline multiples, usually only the latest year's data prior to the private company sale are available. While this is a limitation, it is often the case that the private companies sold were much more comparable to the subject than any public companies that may exist.

Criteria for Selecting Guideline Companies

One succinct quote summarizes the essence of the key characteristic that should be present in a guideline company: "Do the underlying economics driving this comparable company match those that drive our company?"[2]

In Revenue Ruling 59-60, the Internal Revenue Service, one of the strongest proponents of the guideline public company method, makes the following observation:

> Although the only restrictive requirement as to comparable corporations specified in the statute is that their lines of business be the same or similar, yet it is obvious that consideration must be given to other relevant factors in order that the most valid comparison possible will be obtained.[3]

2. Daniel W. Bielinski, *The Comparable Company Approach: Measuring the True Value of Privately Held Firms*, Corporate Cashflow Magazine 64–66 (Oct. 1990).

3. Rev. Rul. 59-60, 1959-1 C.B. 237, § 4(h).

The most obvious criterion for comparability is line of business. The next most important criterion probably is markets served. For example, in valuing a manufacturer of electrical controls for sawmills, the most important criterion might not be manufacturers of electrical controls but manufacturers of equipment used in the forest products industry. In *Estate of Gallo*[4] (Gallo Wine Co.), in the absence of wine producers, appraisers on both sides expanded the line of business criteria to include brewers, distillers, soft-drink bottlers, and major consumer brand agricultural food producers. The Tax Court accepted this procedure.

Other criteria may include:

- Size
- Comparability of earnings patterns
- Position in industry
- Capital structure
- Maturity of company

One thing that all the selection criteria have in common is that they attempt to identify companies that are subject to the same risk factors as is the subject company.

Once in a while, the analyst has the luxury of many available guideline companies and can narrow the selection down to a few that are the most similar. More often it is necessary to broaden the criteria.

As noted earlier, it is useful to the reader of the valuation report if the appraiser states the criteria used and demonstrates that all companies that met the criteria were used or, if not, why certain ones that would appear to meet the criteria were rejected.

How Many Guideline Companies?

The more detailed and reliable the data for each company and the more similar the guideline companies to the subject company, the fewer companies are needed. With public company data, or with detailed private company data, analysts usually are comfortable with five to seven companies, sometimes as few as three. However, in *Estate of Hall*[5] (Hallmark Greeting Cards), the Tax Court rejected a valuation based entirely on the only other good public company at the time, American Greetings, and accepted the analysis of a broad group of high market share consumer goods, such as Parker Pens. If there is only one excellent guideline company, the analyst certainly should use it but generally should not rely on it entirely.

4. Estate of Gallo v. Comm'r, 50 T.C.M. 470 (1985).
5. Estate of Hall v. Comm'r, 92 T.C. 312 (1989).

Illustration of Developing Guideline Company Market Multiples

Exhibit 6-2 is financial data for Marvel Corporation, selected as a guideline public company, in the same format as the data for Widget Corporation in Exhibit 4-1. Exhibit 6-3 develops four invested capital multiples for Marvel Corporation, using the information from Exhibit 6-2. Exhibit 6-4 develops five equity valuation multiples for Marvel Corporation, also using the information from Exhibit 6-2.

Exhibit 6-2
Marvel Corporation Financial Data

Marvel Corporation Balance Sheet		
Assets		
Current Assets		
Cash		$ 1,500,000
Accounts Receivable		2,500,000
Inventory		5,000,000
Total Current Assets		$ 9,000,000
Plant & Equipment		
At Cost	$24,000,000	
Less: Accumulated Depreciation	$20,000,000	
Net Plant & Equipment		4,000,000
Total Assets		$13,000,000
Liabilities and Equity		
Current Liabilities		
Accounts Payable		$ 3,000,000
Long-Term Debt (including current portion)		6,000,000
Total Liabilities		$ 9,000,000
Common Equity (4,000,000 shares outstanding)		4,000,000
Total Liabilities and Equity		$13,000,000
Marvel Corporation Income Statement		
Sales		$40,000,000
Cost of Goods Sold		26,000,000
Gross Margin		$14,000,000
Selling, General and Administrative Expenses		10,000,000
Operating Income, Before Taxes		$ 4,000,000
Interest Expense		480,000
Income Before Taxes		$ 3,520,000
Income Taxes		1,408,000
Net Income		$ 2,112,000

Marvel Corporation Financial Data

The following data are derived from Statement of Cash Flows, footnotes to financial statements, and other available data:

1. Interest rate on the long-term debt is 8%.
2. The selling, general and administrative expenses include depreciation of $1,000,000.
3. Market value of debt is about the same as book value of debt.
4. Market price of stock as of valuation date is $6 per share.
5. Consensus forecast is that sales and earnings will grow at about 12% per year.

Exhibit 6-3
Marvel Corporation Invested Capital Valuation Multiples

Market Value of Invested Capital (MVIC)

Long-Term Debt:	$6,000,000	20%
Equity: 4,000,000 shares @ $6	24,000,000	80%
Market Value of Invested Capital	$30,000,000	100%

MVIC/Sales:

$$\frac{\text{MVIC}}{\text{Sales}} = \frac{\$30{,}000{,}000}{\$40{,}000{,}000} = .75$$

MVIC/EBITDA:

Operating Income Before Taxes (pretax income plus interest expense)	$4,000,000
Plus: Depreciation	1,000,000
Earnings Before Interest, Taxes, Depreciation and Amortization	$5,000,000

$$\frac{\text{MVIC}}{\text{EBITDA}} = \frac{\$30{,}000{,}000}{\$5{,}000{,}000} = 6.00$$

MVIC/EBIT:

Operating Income Before Taxes (pretax income plus interest expense)	$4,000,000

$$\frac{\text{MVIC}}{\text{EBIT}} = \frac{\$30{,}000{,}000}{\$4{,}000{,}000} = 7.50$$

MVIC/Book Value of Invested Capital:

Book Value of Long-Term Debt	$ 6,000,000
Book Value of Equity	4,000,000
Book Value of Invested Capital	$10,000,000

$$\frac{\text{MVIC}}{\text{BV of Invested Capital}} = \frac{\$30{,}000{,}000}{\$10{,}000{,}000} = 3.00$$

Exhibit 6-4
Marvel Corporation Invested Capital Valuation Multiples

Note: When valuing equity directly, these multiples often are presented on a per-share basis. The multiple should be exactly the same whether computed on a per-share or aggregate common equity basis.

Market Value of Equity ("Price")

4,000,000 shares x $6 per share = $24,000,000

Price/Sales (Price/Revenue)

$$\frac{\text{Price}}{\text{Sales}} = \frac{\$24{,}000{,}000}{\$40{,}000{,}000} = .60$$

Price/Cash Flow (Price/Gross Cash Flow)

	Net Income	$2,112,000
Plus:	Depreciation	1,000,000
	Cash Flow (gross)	$3,112,000

$$\frac{\text{Price}}{\text{Cash Flow}} = \frac{\$24{,}000{,}000}{\$3{,}112{,}000} = 7.71$$

Price/Pretax Income (Price/Pretax Earnings)

$$\frac{\text{Price}}{\text{Pretax Income}} = \frac{\$24{,}000{,}000}{\$3{,}520{,}000} = 6.82$$

Price/Earnings (Price/Net Income)

$$\frac{\text{Price}}{\text{Net Income}} = \frac{\$24{,}000{,}000}{\$2{,}112{,}000} = 11.36$$

Note: The term price/earnings (P/E), as used in the daily financial press, stock reporting services, and corporate finance, means price to net income *after* taxes. A common error is to apply the P/E ratio to pretax income. The only condition under which this is justifiable is where it can be assumed that the effective tax rate is zero.

Price/Book Value

$$\frac{\text{Price}}{\text{Book Value of Equity}} = \frac{\$24{,}000{,}000}{\$4{,}000{,}000} = 6.00$$

Deciding Where Subject Company Multiples Should Fall Relative to Observed Ranges

The appraiser will have developed valuation multiples for several guideline companies in the same manner as illustrated previously for Marvel Corporation. For each variable, the appraiser must select a multiple to apply to the subject company's counterpart financial variable. An important step in evaluating the work of the appraiser is to evaluate how the multiple to be applied to each subject company financial variable was selected.

Relationship Between Market Multiples and Capitalization Rates

A "multiple" in the market approach is like a "capitalization rate" in the income approach. A multiple is actually the reciprocal of a capitalization rate, that is, 1 divided by the multiple equals the capitalization rate. Conversely, 1 divided by the capitalization rate equals the multiple.

To illustrate, assume the following:

Guideline company price:	\$20 per share
Guideline company earnings:	\$ 1 per share

To compute the guideline company price/earnings multiple, one divides the price by the earnings:

Formula 6-1

$$\frac{\text{Price}}{\text{Earnings}} = \frac{\$20}{\$1} = 20$$

To convert the P/E multiple to a capitalization rate applicable to net income, one divides 1 by the P/E multiple:

Formula 6-2

$$\text{Cap Rate} = \frac{1}{20} = 0.05$$

To convert the capitalization rate to a multiple, one divides 1 by the capitalization rate:

$$\text{P/E Multiple} = \frac{1}{0.05} = 20$$

Multiplying by the P/E multiple or dividing by the capitalization rate should lead to the same result. For instance, if earnings equal $10 million, the value of the company will be $10 x 20 = $200 million or $10/0.05 = $200 million.

The level of the multiple depends largely on two factors: expected growth and risk. With the income approach, the respective factors of risk and expected growth were quantified individually. However, in the market approach, multiples for company variables are observed in the market, that is, computed from market transaction data, and it is not possible to determine exactly how much any given company's multiple for any variable was influenced by expected growth and how much by perceived risk. Comparative analysis between the guideline and subject companies cannot separate these factors completely but can give some useful clues.

Multiples Selected Should Be Based on Comparative Analysis

Each multiple selected should be based on comparative analysis between the subject company and the guideline companies. This usually involves some combination of quantitative and qualitative analysis.

- Quantitative Analysis. Exhibit 6-5 is a somewhat abbreviated example of a typical comparative quantitative analysis, using selected ratios discussed in Chapter 13.
- Qualitative Analysis. Most of the qualitative factors that the analyst would consider are those that bear on assessing risk. Just as higher risk requires a higher discount rate or capitalization rate in the income approach, higher risk predicts lower multiples in the market approach. Some of the common comparative qualitative factors to consider include:
  - Depth of management
  - Concentration versus breadth of customer base
  - Concentration versus breadth of product/service base
  - Concentration versus breadth of geographical operations
  - Comparative cost structure (Make sure, however, that the analyst has not double-counted this both here and in the quantitative analysis.)

— Other effects of difference in size, such as buying power, supplier dependence, affordability of advertising, and similar factors[6]

Having conducted a careful comparative analysis, the expert may conclude that the subject company is so comparable to the average of the guideline companies that every multiple for every variable should be the median as observed among the guideline companies. If so, the expert should say so (not just apply median or average multiples without comment). More often than not, however, based on the comparative analysis, the expert will differentiate the subject from the guideline companies, resulting in a departure from the average multiples for one or more variables. Reasons for selection of each multiple should be noted. Many appraisers will remove outlier pricing multiples even before determining the coefficient of variation.

In some cases, the comparative financial analysis may indicate that the subject company is most like one, two, or a few of the guideline companies. In that case, the analyst may choose multiples close to those of the companies that appear to be more comparable to the subject than others. Some try to stay away from saying one guideline company is most like the subject company. They generally show percentiles—ranging from 0 percent, 10 percent, 25 percent median, to 75 percent—and then decide on what percentile to use.

Different Multiples May Be Higher or Lower Relative to Guideline Companies

We noted earlier that expected growth and risk are the two most important determinants of what multiple should be chosen for the subject company relative to the guideline companies, at least with respect to many of the variables. For example, higher leverage and lower coverage of interest obligations would be indications of higher risk.

These differences between subject and guideline companies may lead to reductions of average multiples, the differentials chosen sometimes referred to as a "fundamental discount."

However, criteria for selection of multiples may be influenced by factors other than just expected growth and risk. For example, price to sales multiples are heavily influenced by return on sales. This is logical, for a company that earns more per dollar of sales is likely to sell for more per dollar of sales. Similarly, return on invested capital and return on equity influence the MVIC/book value of invested capital and price/book value of equity valuation multiples. This also is logical, for a

6. In *Bridging the Gap Between Public and Private Market Multiples,* Business Valuation Review 95–101 (Sept. 1998), Richard W. Goeldner II suggests going as far as quantifying all these factors in terms of their impact on risk and potential future growth, and suggests that it is not unreasonable for private company multiples to be half of observed public company multiples, or even less.

Exhibit 6-5
Widget Corporation and Guideline Companies Comparative Financial Analysis

	Company								
Ratio	**Marvel**	**Neon**	**Optimal**	**Premier**	**Quartz**	**Range**	**Median**	**Widget**	**Comment**
Return on Equity	.528	.150	.700	.300	.900	.150–.900	.528	.700	Above median, but range very wide
Return on Invested Capital	.240	.100	.400	.200	.500	.100–.500	.240	.228	Near median, but range very wide
Return on Sales	.053	.030	.080	.090	.040	.030–.090	.053	.070	Above median
Long–Term Debt to Total Capital (at book value)	.60	.67	.32	.40	.50	.32–.67	.50	.75	Highly leveraged, above top of range
Current Ratio	3.0	4.0	3.5	2.5	2.0	2.0–4.0	3.0	3.0	At median
Quick Ratio	1.3	2.0	1.8	1.0	.8	.8–2.0	1.3	1.5	Near median
Times Interest Earned (EBIT/ Interest Expense)	8.3	2.0	9.8	5.0	4.0	2.0–9.8	5.0	2.3	Near bottom of range

company that earns more per dollar of book value is likely to sell for more per dollar of book value. Therefore, for example, a company with a very low return on equity may be operating very conservatively with a low degree of risk and deserve higher than average multiples for some or all income variables, but a below average price/book value ratio. The appraiser should consider the long-term growth performance of guideline companies as compared to the subject company when deciding on what pricing multiples to use.

Relative Weights to Accord Various Multiples

Some valuation multiples are clearly more important for some industries than for others. For example, values of financial assets are very important for valuing financial institutions, while asset values may have very little relevance for most service businesses and professional practices.

One clue to the relative importance of different valuation multiples in any given industry is the degree of central tendency versus dispersion of the multiples observed in the market for that industry. If multiples for a certain variable cluster in a narrow range, that tends to indicate that pricing of companies in that industry tends to depend more on that financial variable than on others. On the other hand, a very wide dispersion among observed multiples suggests that the particular multiple is not very important in that industry.

On the other hand, multiples with wide dispersions can be used if they can be explained. For example, a wide dispersion of price to book value often reflects a wide dispersion of return on equity. In this case, the multiple can be used if it reflects the level of the subject's return on equity relative to the guideline companies.

Another judgmental factor is the available data. If data to compute certain valuation multiples are not available for several companies among those chosen, the analyst may choose to put less weight on that valuation multiple even if it might be considered more important if it were available for more companies.

Also, multiples for certain variables may be accorded little or no weight if they appear to be not very meaningful. For example, if an industry had such a bad year that earnings tended to be minimal, resulting in atypical P/E ratios, the P/E ratio on that year's earnings may be accorded no weight.

Illustration of Valuation by Market Approach

Using the data from Exhibits 6-3 through 6-5, Exhibit 6-6 develops invested capital multiples to apply to Widget Corporation. Exhibit 6-7 develops an indicated value for Widget Corporation using the invested capital procedure. Exhibit 6-8 develops equity multiples to apply to Widget Corporation. Exhibit 6-9 develops an indicated value directly for Widget Corporation's equity. In this illustration, the rationale for the analyst's various choices is indicated briefly in the footnotes to the tables. In most reports, the rationale would be explained more fully in the text, exploring underlying relationships and explaining reasons for the appraiser's judgment. For example, while dispersion of observed multiples for the guideline companies is a useful quantitative observation, the analytical reasoning and judgment applied may be more important in assigning weights to variables in many cases.

The various multiples within each group (invested capital and equity) produced similar results, but the direct equity procedure produced significantly higher values. The reason is that the company has benefited from a considerably higher degree of leverage than the guideline companies have. Perhaps this risk should be reflected by equity multiples having greater discounts from the guideline medians than were actually used. The analyst in this case was cautiously optimistic and valued the equity at $5.7 million on the basis of a continued good outlook for the company. This value was based on an equal weighting of the two indications of value from the equity and the invested capital procedures. Most analysts would use *either* invested capital multiples *or* equity multiples. In any case, when using both, most would consider it only one method.

Variations for Smaller Companies and Professional Practice Valuations

Smaller businesses and professional practices have certain characteristics that generally lead to more emphasis on specific variables than might be inappropriate for larger companies. Among the most important of these characteristics are:

- The involvement of the owner/manager, and
- The availability of good accounting data for comparison for both the subject company and the guideline companies.

Such companies are regularly the subject of valuation disputes in marital dissolution and sometimes also in other legal contexts.

Generally, because of the owner/manager involvement and also because of limited accounting data, the smaller the company and the greater the role of the owner/manager, more emphasis often is appropriately placed on variables toward the "top line" versus the "bottom line" of the income statement. In other words, in valuations of smaller companies and professional practices, price to sales and price to discretionary earnings tend to become relatively more important than in valuations of larger companies.

Exhibit 6-6
Widget Corporation Guideline Company Invested Capital Multiples

	Market Value of Invested Capital (MVIC) to			
	Sales	**EBITDA**	**EBIT**	**Book Value**
Marvel	.75	4.68	5.55	3.00
Neon	.40	5.00	6.20	1.50
Optimal	.80	5.50	6.90	6.00
Premier	.90	6.00	8.00	2.00
Quartz	.60	4.80	5.00	7.00
Mean	.67	5.20	6.33	3.90
Median	.75	4.80	6.20	3.00
Range	.40–.90	4.68–6.00	5.00–8.00	1.50–7.00
Coefficient of Variation	.283	.102	.175	.631
Multiple Selected	.80(a)	5.50(b)	6.90(c)	3.00(d)

(a) Above median because Widget return on sales above median (Exhibit 6-5).
(b) Near median—Widget reasonably comparable to group.
(c) At median—Widget quite comparable to group.
(d) At median because Widget return on invested capital near median (Exhibit 6-5).

Involvement of the Owner/Manager

Typically, owners of small businesses and professional practices withdraw enough in compensation that there are no "earnings" left to capitalize. Therefore, using valuation measures that are before owner's compensation avoids the argument about how much is reasonable compensation. Of course S corporations tend to have the opposite issue—officers' compensation is typically lower than fair market value in order to save payroll taxes.

For marital dissolution valuations, this is fine for states in which any personal goodwill is included in the marital estate. However, in states where only "practice" or "entity" goodwill is included in the marital estate, the issue of reasonable compensation cannot be avoided just by using price/sales and price/discretionary earnings multiples.

Availability of Comparative Accounting Data

For most very small businesses and professional practices, there may be few or no truly comparable public companies to use to develop valuation multiples, but in most cases an investigation should be undertaken to reach this determination. All three data

Exhibit 6-7
Widget Corporation Valuation Using Invested Capital Multiples

	Sales		EBITDA		EBIT	Book Value		Weighted Value of Invested Capital
Widget Corporation Fundamental (as computed for Widget Corporation in Chapter 4)	$10,000,000		$1,550,000		$1,300,000	$4,000,000		
Selected Multiple (from Exhibit 9-6)	x .80		x 5.50		x 6.90	x 3.00		
Indicated Value	$8,000,000		$8,525,000		$8,970,000	$12,000,000		
Weight	x .20 (a)		.50 (b)		.30 (c)	0 (d)		
Weighted Value	$1,600,000	+	$4,262,500	+	$2,691,000		=	$8,553,000
Less: Long-Term Debt								3,000,000
Indicated Value of Common Equity								$5,553,500

(a) Deserves some consideration, but profitability ratios more important.
(b) Lowest coefficient variation (Exhibit 6-6)—the variable the industry considers most important.
(c) Next lowest coefficient (Exhibit 6-6).
(d) No weight. Coefficient of variation very wide, likely because of differences in historical costs and depreciation.

Most analysts would not show computations to which they gave no weight, but we show this for illustration only.

Exhibit 6-8
Widget Corporation Guideline Company Equity Multiples

	Market Value of Equity to				
	Sales	**Cash Flow**	**Pretax Income**	**Net Income**	**Book Value**
Marvel	.60	7.71	6.82	11.36	6.00
Neon	.30	6.20	5.52	7.78	2.50
Optimal	.70	7.29	6.21	8.63	7.21
Premier	.75	8.13	7.04	9.86	2.92
Quartz	.50	6.83	4.55	6.28	7.50
Mean	.57	7.23	6.03	8.78	5.23
Median	.60	7.29	6.03	8.63	6.0
Range	.30–75	6.2–8.13	4.55–7.04	6.28–11.36	2.5–7.5
Coefficient Variation	.314	.104	.169	.221	.453
Multiples Selected	.65(a)	7.0(b)	5.8(b)	7.5(b)	7.0(c)

(a) Above median because Widget return on sales above median (Exhibit 6-5).
(b) Slightly below median because of slightly higher risk (Exhibit 6-5).
(c) Above median because of above-average return on equity (Exhibit 6-5).

sources that provide multiples for such smaller companies and practices *(BIZCOMPS®, IBA Market Database,* and *Pratt's Stats®)* provide price/sales and price/discretionary earnings multiples, but only *Pratt's Stats®* provides any of the other valuation multiples discussed in this chapter.

In any case, it often is somewhere between difficult and impossible to develop reliable income data for such subject entities beyond sales and discretionary earnings, so it may be necessary to limit the market approach multiples to these variables. The three databases that do provide data on such small businesses and professional practices (see "References" at the end of this chapter) have expanded in recent years and now collectively encompass many thousands of transactions, making the market approach for valuing such companies and practices much more feasible than was the case only a few years ago.

Exhibit 6-9
Widget Corporation Valuation Using Equity Multiples

	Sales	Cash Flow	Pretax Income	Net Income	Book Value	Weighted Value
Widget Corporation Fundamental (as computed for Widget in Chapter 4)	$10,000,000	$ 950,000	$1,000,000	$ 700,000	$1,000,000	
Selected Multiple (from Exhibit 6-8)	x .65	x 7.0	x 5.8	x 7.5	x 7.0	
Indicated Value	$ 6,500,000	$6,650,000	$5,800,000	$5,250,000	$7,000,000	
Weight	x .20(a)	x .50(b)	x .15(c)	x .15(d)	x 0(e)	
Weighted Value	$ 1,300,000 +	$3,325,000 +	$ 870,000 +	$ 787,500		= $6,282,500

(a) Deserves some consideration, but profitability ratios more important (also, multiple of sales considered in invested capital ratios, where it may be a more meaningful multiple).

(b) Lowest coefficient of variation, clearly the variable the industry considers most important; similar to EBITDA in invested capital ratios.

(c), (d) Approximately the industry average effective tax rates and equal coefficients of variation, so equal weight to each but combined, less than cash flow

(e) Very wide coefficient of variation reflecting greatly different leverage and historical cost bases—not a good comparison with guideline companies.

Most analysts would not show computations to which they gave no weight, but we show this for illustration only.

Prior Transactions, Offers, and Buy-Sell Agreements

In this chapter, we also discuss the impact of considering prior transactions, offers to buy, and buy-sell agreements on the market approach because they sometimes provide some market evidence of value and, to some extent, may be analyzed using some of the methods in the market approach.

Arm's-Length Negotiations

Whether considering a transaction, an offer, or an agreement, the first question is whether the indication of value it represented was negotiated on an arm's-length basis.

If it was among unrelated parties, it usually is assumed to be arm's length. Even among related parties, investigation may lead to the conclusion that there was an arm's-length negotiation. If the degree of arm's-length negotiation cannot be ascertained, a valuation analyst may make a judgment about whether or not it represented fair market value at the time, in which case one can conclude that the parameters are controlling or at least useful guidance for valuation in the current transaction.

Prior Transactions

If reasonably arm's length, prior transactions may be one of the best guides to market value. Such transactions may include:

- A prior purchase or sale of the entire company
- Sales of minority ownership interests
- Acquisitions of subsidiary companies by the subject company

Any such transactions can be analyzed to determine the valuation multiples discussed in this chapter that the transactions represented at the time. The relevance of the actual transaction should be judged based on the time since the transaction and the changes to the company, industry, and economy. Adjustments to the actual multiples should be made if appropriate based on changes in market conditions.

Offers to Buy

If the company received a bona fide offer to buy, it can be analyzed in the same way as a prior transaction. Such bona fide offers that can be used in this manner do occur and the possibility should be investigated, but they are rare.

Inquiries about buying companies don't often reach the stage of a bona fide offer that is never consummated. Even if an offer appears bona fide on the surface, it should be investigated in terms of escape clauses and prospective price changes based on due diligence and whether the buyer was legitimately willing and able to complete the transaction.

Buy-Sell Agreements

One of the most frequent controversies is the extent to which an existing buy-sell agreement should control or influence the value for any given transaction. This may ultimately be a legal determination, based on the purpose of the appraisal. For example, the buy-sell value may not be controlling for estate taxes if it fails to meet certain criteria (see Chapter 17 on federal tax valuation), even though it is binding on the estate. In marital dissolutions, most courts have great discretion as to how much weight, if any, to accord the buy-sell agreement. One needs to refer to the case law.

Alternative Definition of Market Value in Some Fair Value Cases

In cases determining fair value for dissenting stockholder and minority oppression suits, courts tend to look at income value, asset value, and market value. In some cases, what they consider market value may be based only on past transactions.

If this is the case, then the multiples of income statement variables derived from the guideline public company method would be subsumed under the income value and multiples of asset variables would be considered under asset value.

References

Basic Market Approach References

Crow, Matthew R. "Developing Valuation Multiples Using Guideline Companies." *CPA Litigation Service Counselor,* September 1999, 8–9.

Fishman, Jay, et al. 2008. "Valuation Methods Based on Comparative Company Data." In *PPC's Guide to Business Valuations,* 6–1 to 6–55.

Fowler, Bradley, A. "How Do You Handle It?" *Business Valuation Review,* September 1996, 136–7.

Goeldner, Richard W. "Adjusting Market Multiples of Guideline Companies." Presentation to the 18th Annual Advanced Business Valuation Conference of the American Society of Appraisers, October 29, 1999. Available online at www.BVLibrary.com.

_____. "Bridging the Gap between Public and Private Market Multiples." *Business Valuation Review,* September 1998, 97–101.

Hitchner, James R. *Financial Valuation: Applications and Models*, 2nd Ed. Hoboken, NJ: John Wiley & Sons, 2006.

Matthews, Gilbert E. "When Averaging Multiples, Apply the Harmonic Mean." *Business Valuation Update,* June 2006.

Nath, Eric W. "How Public Guideline Companies Represent 'Control' Value for a Private Company." *Business Valuation Review,* December 1997, 167–71.

Peters, Jerry O. "Adjusting Price/Earnings Ratios for Differences in Company Size." *Business Valuation Review,* June 1999, 71–85.

Pratt, Shannon P. "Controversies Involving the Market Approach to Business Valuation; Raising the Issues, Soliciting Feedback." *Shannon Pratt's Business Valuation Update,* November 2000.

_____, and Alina V. Niculita. 2008. "Market Approach: Guideline Publicly Traded Company Method" and "Market Approach: Guideline Merged and Acquired Company Method." In *Valuing a Business,* 5th Ed., 261–330. Both chapters include some bibliography.

_____. 2003. "Market Approach: Guideline Public Company Method," "Market Approach: Transaction Method," and "Prior Transactions, Offers, and Buy-Sell Agreements." In *Business Valuation Body of Knowledge,* 2nd Ed., 142–62.

_____, and Alina V. Niculita. *The Market Approach to Valuing Businesses Workbook,* 2nd Ed. New York: John Wiley & Sons, 2006.

_____. *The Market Approach to Valuing Business,* 2nd Ed. Hoboken, NJ: John Wiley & Sons, 2005.

Ross, Franz. "'Just One Thing': The Most Reliable Variable for Use in the Market Approach." *Shannon Pratt's Business Valuation Update,* August 2004.

Sheeler, Carl L. "The Market Approach: A Neglected and Misunderstood Aspect of Business Value." *Journal of Financial Planning,* May 2004, Article 7.

_____. "A Misunderstood Aspect of Business Value: The Market Approach." *The CPA Journal,* October 2004.

Slee, Robert T. "Is the Subject Company Similar?" *Valuation Strategies,* May/June 1998, 4–7, 34.

Trugman, Gary. "Guideline Public Company Method-Control or Minority Value?" *Shannon Pratt's Business Valuation Update,* December 2003.

_____. 2002. "The Market Approach" and "The Valuation Reports." In *Understanding Business Valuations,* 2nd Ed., 157–256, 421–48.

_____. "Guideline Public Company Method: Control or Minority? Control Position." *BVPapers,* February 2005. Available online at www.BVLibrary.com.

Wise, Richard. "Application of the Market Approach in Valuing a Canadian Business." *BVPapers,* February 2005. Available online at www.BVLibrary.com.

_____. "Caveats for Market Approach." *CA Magazine,* January-February 2004.

_____. "Multiple-of-Revenues as a Valuation Method." *Business Valuation Digest,* October 1996, 1–4.

Private Company Sale Databases

BIZCOMPS, P.O. Box 97757, Las Vegas, NV 89193, (858) 457-0366. Provides price to sales and price to discretionary earnings ratios, average transactions over $1,000,000. Available online at www.BVResources.com.

Done Deals, Thomson PPC, P.O. Box 966, Fort Worth, TX 76101-0966, (800) 323–8724. Provides price to assets, book value of equity, revenue, net income, and cash from operations, transactions $1 million to $1 billion, about 79 percent of the selling companies being privately owned.

IBA Market Database, Institute of Business Appraisers, P.O. Box 17410, Plantation, FL 33318, (954) 584-1144. Provides price to sales and price to discretionary earnings ratios, mostly small businesses and professional practices.

Pratt's Stats, Business Valuation Resources, 1000 S.W. Broadway, Ste. 1200, Portland, OR 97205, (888) 287-8258. Provides eight invested capital and equity valuation multiples already computed, and information for most companies to compute all market valuation ratios discussed in this chapter, transaction sizes $50,000 to $7,300 million. Available online at www.BVResources.com.

Public Company Transaction and Sale Data

Public company data fall into two categories, each of which has readily available sources of information far too extensive to list here.

- Publicly Traded Securities. There are more than 20,000 publicly traded operating companies, all of which report data electronically to the Securities and Exchange Commission on a system called Electronic Data Gathering and Retrieval (EDGAR). This data is free to the public. In addition, many services publish summaries of the data filed, both electronically and in print.

  Compustat and other Standard & Poor's Products
  Standard & Poor's Corporation
  www.compustat.com
  www.standardandpoors.com
  (800) 523-4534

  Directory of Companies Required to File Annual Reports with the Securities and Exchange Commission under the Securities Exchange Act of 1934
  U.S. Government Printing Office
  www.gpo.gov
  (202) 512-1800

EDGAR Database
Securities and Exchange Commission
www.sec.gov/cgi-bin/srch-edgar
www.sec.gov/edgar/searchedgar/webusers.htm

Factiva
www.factiva.com
(800) 369-0166

Mergent (previously Moody's)
www.mergent.com
(888) 369-0166

OneSource (a division of *InfoUSA*)
www.onesource.com
(978) 318-4300

Thomson Financial
www.thomson.com/solutions/financial
www.dialog.com
(800) 843-7747

- Acquisitions of Public Companies. Several hundred public companies are acquired or "go private" every year. They are required to file details of the transactions with the SEC, which also are available free through EDGAR. In addition, many services publish summaries of such transaction data.

FactSet Mergerstat, FactSet Mergerstat LLC, 2150 Colorado Ave., Ste. 150, Santa Monica, CA 90404, (310) 315-3100. Their database includes Mergerstat Review (annual), Flashwire Monthly, Online Transaction Roster, Flashwire Weekly, Control Premium Study, and M&A Decade Library (CD-ROM).

Mergerstat/BVU's Control Premium Study. A Web-based tool used to quantify minority discounts and control premiums used in the business valuation, business appraisal, venture capital, and merger and acquisition professions. Available online at www.BVResources.com.

SDC Platinum (previously Securities Data Corp.), Thomson Financial, 195 Broadway, New York, NY 10007, (800) 782-5555. Provides financial transactions for the entire global financial marketplace. Provides detailed information on new issues, M&A, syndicated loans, private equity, project finance, poison pills, and more.

Details of the many information sources for publicly traded company data, public company acquisition, and going-private data are available in the *Business Valuation Directory,* published annually by Business Valuation Resources, LLC.

Chapter 7

The Asset-Based Approach

Basic Concept of the Asset-Based Approach

The basic concept of the asset-based approach is that if all the company's assets and liabilities are revalued to current values, then the difference between the assets and the liabilities should equal the value of the equity.

The asset-based approach generally is assumed to produce a control basis value. From this value, if one is valuing a minority interest, it may be appropriate to adjust for factors such as minority interest and lack of marketability, as discussed in Chapter 15, "Discounts and Premiums." If one is valuing a controlling interest, it may or may not be appropriate to deduct a discount for lack of marketability, although it would be a smaller discount than for a minority interest, as discussed in Chapter 15.

Discrete versus Collective Revaluation

If each asset and liability is individually identified and valued, that method may be called, for instance, the *net asset value method, the adjusted net worth method, the adjusted book value method, the asset buildup method, the asset accumulation method,* or some similar method. For the purpose of this chapter, we will refer to the discrete revaluation of all assets as the *adjusted net asset value (ANAV)* method. The premise of value may be either going concern or liquidation.

In collective revaluation of assets, the tangible assets, or at least the preponderance of them, usually are adjusted to current values, as discussed in subsequent sections of this chapter. The intangibles then are valued collectively by capitalizing any amount of return that the company achieves over and above a fair return on the tangible assets at their current values.[1] This method is called the *excess earnings*

1. Conceivably, certain intangibles, such as intellectual property, could be identified and valued separately, but in practice this is rarely done.

method, which assumes a going-concern premise of value and is treated separately as the subject of the next chapter.

In some cases, only a partial revaluation of assets is practical. There are too many variations on this possibility to go into details and the reviewer is left to judge whether the conclusions reached are adequately supported.

Steps in the Adjusted Net Asset Value Method

The six basic steps are as follows:

1. **Obtain or develop an accrual basis balance sheet.** If the entity does its accounting on a generally accepted accounting principles (GAAP) basis, this requires only adjustments necessary to conform to GAAP. If the company does its accounting on a cash basis, then adjustments to the accrual basis are necessary.
2. **Determine which assets and liabilities on the GAAP-basis balance sheet require revaluation.**
   - Assets with no realizable value, such as deferred finance points that were capitalized and are being amortized over the life of the loan.
3. **Identify any off-balance-sheet actual or contingent assets or liabilities.** This could be an unlimited list, but some of the more common items include:
   - Assets fully depreciated but still in service
   - Inventory or accounts receivable written off by accounting policy but still salable or collectible
   - Intellectual property developed internally and therefore expensed instead of capitalized
   - Workforce in place, systems, and similar elements of "going-concern value"
   - Goodwill
   - Expected proceeds or costs related to existing or potential lawsuits
   - Environmental liabilities
   - Liability for corporate capital gains taxes on appreciated assets[2]

2. Tax cases have begun to recognize all or some portion of this liability. *See, e.g.,* Estate of Jelke v. Comm'r, 507 F.3d 1317 (11th Cir. 2007); Estate of Davis v. Comm'r, 110 T.C. 530 (1998); Eisenberg v. Comm'r, T.C.M. 1997-483, 74 T.C.M. (CCH) 1046 (1997); Estate of Simplot v. Comm'r, 112 T.C. No. 13, 1999 WL 152610 (1999). Family law courts have been reluctant to recognize this liability unless sale is imminent. *See, e.g.,* Granger v. Granger, 579 N.E.2d 1319 (Ind. Ct. App. 1991); *In re* Marriage of Hay, 907 P.2d 334 (Wash. Ct. App. 1995); Crooker v. Crooker, 432 A.2d 1293 (Me. 1981).

4. **Value the items identified in Steps 2 and 3.** This may require appraisals by asset appraisers, for appraisal of real estate and/or machinery and equipment would not be a skill possessed by most business appraisers.
5. **Take on a deferred tax liability for appreciated assets that will be liquidated.**
6. **Construct a market value–based balance sheet using the adjusted values.** The net result of this should be the market value of the equity. In other words, the difference between the market value of assets and the market value of liabilities equals the market value of equity.

Valuation Premises for Adjusting Balance Sheet Values

Generally speaking, each item will be valued on one of the following four premises of value:

1. **Value in continued use, as part of a going concern.** This usually means either *used replacement cost,* including installation, or *replacement cost new* less depreciation, amortization, and/or adjustments for obsolescence.
2. **Value in place, as part of a mass assemblage of assets.** This generally would be used for a manufacturing plant in working order but not currently operating because of market conditions, bankruptcy, or any various reasons.
3. **Value in exchange, in an orderly liquidation.** This may be appropriate for all assets if an orderly liquidation is contemplated for the entire company. If the company is being valued as a going concern, an orderly liquidation premise may be appropriate for nonoperating or excess assets.
4. **Value in exchange, in a forced liquidation.** This may be appropriate if, for example, it was assumed that the assets would be sold piecemeal at auction.

Illustrative Adjusted Net Asset Value

Exhibit 7-1 shows an example of an adjusted balance sheet resulting in an adjusted net asset value. There would be an explanation in either the text or footnotes for each item added to the balance sheet or adjusted from its original balance sheet value.

Breakup Value

Some companies may have two or more operating entities and possibly some nonoperating assets. The stock market tends to value such companies at less than the total of the value of each operating company plus the nonoperating assets.

Exhibit 7-1
Alpha Company Adjusted Net Asset Value

Assets	As Reported	Adjustments	As Adjusted
Cash & Marketable Securities	$100,000	$ 30,000(a)	$130,000
Inventory	200,000	50,000(b)	250,000
Total Current Assets	$300,000		$380,000
Property & Equipment	70,000		70,000
Land Held for Expansion	150,000	100,000(c)	250,000
Total Assets	$520,000		$700,000
Liabilities & Equity			
Accounts Payable	$ 50,000		$ 50,000
Long-Term Debt	200,000	−20,000(d)	180,000
Corporate Taxes		30,000(e)	30,000
Total Liabilities	$250,000		$260,000
Stockholders' Equity	270,000		440,000
Total Liabilities & Equity	$520,000		$700,000

(a) To adjust to market prices as of the effective valuation date
(b) To adjust from LIFO to FIFO cost basis as of the effective valuation date
(c) To adjust land to appraised market value as of the effective valuation date
(d) To reduce the value of the long-term debt (with interest rate of 8%) to current market value (in light of current market interest rate of 10% on other comparable debt)
(e) To record the corporate tax liability on the difference between the assets' cost basis and current market value

In considering a possible acquisition of such a company, the acquirer might like to estimate what could be realized by selling each of the operating companies and the nonoperating assets separately. This is called the *breakup value*.

Studies have shown that conglomerates tend to sell at about a 15 percent discount from their breakup values. Investors seem to prefer a "pure play" in an industry over a package of dissimilar companies or assets. One variation on the asset approach is to estimate a company's breakup value.

When Are Asset-Based Methods Used?

The net asset value method is not used very often for valuation of operating entities, particularly in minority interest appraisals. The focus for operating entities tends to be more on the income approach, the market approach, or the excess earnings method.

However, in a number of situations, the courts do reach a valuation conclusion either entirely or partially on valuation by the asset-based approach. These may include but are not limited to:

- Start-up companies
- Holding companies, financial institutions, agricultural businesses, and other asset-intensive businesses
- Marital estate valuations of companies or practices in which all goodwill is personal and the state's case law does not consider personal goodwill a marital asset
- Companies that may not be financially viable as operating companies

In one marital dissolution, for example, the husband owned two start-up companies. The husband's lawyer moved to strike the testimony of the wife's expert, who used the discounted cash flow method, even though the projections had been made by the husband. The trial court granted the motion and was upheld on appeal, "because the expert's projections and opinion were overly speculative and by implication, unreliable," leaving only the testimony on asset value on which the trial court had based its conclusion.[3]

Asset-Based Approach References

Fishman, Jay, et al. 2009. "Underlying Assets Method," "Net Asset Value Method," and "Liquidation Value Method." In *PPC's Guide to Business Valuations,* 7–1 to 7–18.

Hitchner, James R. 2006. "Asset Approach." In *Financial Valuation: Applications and Models,* 2nd Ed., Chap. 7, 317–74.

Pratt, Shannon P., and Alina V. Niculita. 2008. "Asset-Based Approach: Asset Accumulation Method." In *Valuing a Business,* 5th Ed., 349–80.

Trugman, Gary. 2002. "The Asset-Based Approach." In *Understanding Business Valuation,* 2nd Ed., 257–80.

3. Shooltz v. Shooltz, 27 Va. App. 264, 498 S.E.2d 437 (1998).

Chapter 8

The Excess Earnings Method

Even though the excess earnings method is considered the valuation method of last resort by the Internal Revenue Service (Revenue Ruling 68-609) and many in the business appraisal profession, it is one of the most widely used and abused of all business valuation methods because there are many components within its development that are subjective or misunderstood. It is used most often for valuing small businesses and professional practices and is especially popular among appraisers performing valuations for property settlements in marital dissolutions.

In this chapter we will show:

- The background of the excess earnings method
- The basic steps involved in the excess earnings method
- A basic illustration of applying the excess earnings method
- A "sanity check" for the validity of the value developed by the excess earnings method
- A critique of Revenue Ruling 68-609 demonstrating the origin of much of the confusion in applying the excess earnings method
- Common errors in applying the excess earnings method

Background of the Excess Earnings Method

The capitalized excess earnings method is sometimes called the Treasury method, because this valuation method originally appeared in a 1920 publication by the U.S. Treasury Department, *Appeals and Review Memorandum Number 34* (ARM 34). It was adopted to estimate the intangible value of goodwill that breweries and distilleries lost because of the legal imposition of prohibition in the United States. In 1968, the IRS updated and restated ARM 34 into Revenue Ruling 68-609, which is discussed in a subsequent section.

Keep in mind that the excess earnings method originally was created for the purpose of valuing intangible assets, *not* for valuing the company as a whole. Consequently, perhaps the most appropriate application of the excess earnings method is for allocating total value between tangible and intangible assets. Examples of this include:

- Divorce cases in jurisdictions where goodwill value is considered a personal rather than a marital asset and therefore needs to be separated from the value of the business or practice
- Conversions from C corporations to S corporations
- Eminent domain cases, in which the tangible and intangible values need to be recognized separately
- Property tax cases, in which a company's tangible assets are subject to property tax but its intangible assets are not
- Damage cases, such as a breach of a patent or trademark

Basic Steps in the Excess Earnings Method

The basic steps in the excess earnings method are summarized as follows:

Step 1. **Estimate a normalized level of earnings or cash flow.**

Step 2. **Estimate the net tangible asset value for the subject company as of the effective valuation date.** (The net tangible asset value usually is defined as the fair market value of the tangible assets less the liabilities.)

Step 3. **Estimate a rate of return that would be required to support the tangible assets used in the business.**

Step 4. **Multiply the value of net tangible assets (from Step 2) by the required rate of return on net tangible assets (from Step 3).** This is the dollar amount of return required to support the net tangible assets employed in the business.

Step 5. **Subtract the required dollar amount of return on tangible assets (from Step 4) from the estimated normalized earnings (from Step 1).** This is the "excess earnings" or the earnings attributable to the entity's intangible assets.

Step 6. **Select a capitalization rate that is an appropriate required return on intangible assets (excess earnings).**

Step 7. **Divide the excess earnings by the excess earnings capitalization rate (from Step 6).** This is the value of the excess earnings, thus the implied value of the entity's intangible assets.

Step 8. **Add the entity's intangible value (from Step 7) to the entity's net tangible asset value (from Step 2).** This is the total value of the business or practice, generally assumed to represent a 100 percent controlling ownership value. (Thus, in a sense, the excess earnings method is viewed by many as a subset of the net asset value method, that is, adding the derived value of the intangible assets to the value of the net tangible assets. Most of the time, this method is regarded as a hybrid method.)

Applying the Excess Earnings Method

Exhibit 8-1 illustrates the estimation of the value of an entity by the excess earnings method.

Exhibit 8-1
Illustration of Excess Earnings Method

Step 1. Estimated normalized net cash flow		$ 25,000
Step 2. Estimated net tangible asset value	$100,000	
Step 3. Estimated required rate of return to support tangible assets	15%	
Step 4. Dollar amount of required rate of return on tangible assets		$ 15,000
Step 5. Dollar amount of excess earnings (Step 1 minus Step 4)		$ 10,000
Step 6. Capitalization rate applicable to excess earnings		25%
Step 7. Value of intangible assets, estimated as capitalized excess earnings (Step 5 amount divided by Step 6 rate—$10,000 divided by .25)		$ 40,000
Step 8. Total value of entity: Valuation of intangible assets (capitalized excess earnings, from Step 7) plus value of net tangible assets (from Step 2)		100,000
Total value of entity		$140,000

Step 1, estimating normalized earnings, means calculating an earning power that is expected to be sustainable into the future. The analyst's report should show how the normalized earnings were estimated and what definition of earning power was used (for example, net income, net cash flow, etc.).

Step 2, estimating the net tangible asset value, means adjusting each tangible asset and each liability to its current value (as of the valuation date), usually fair market value on a going-concern basis, and subtracting the liabilities from the adjusted asset values. The analyst's report should show each adjustment that was made to the balance sheet and the basis for each adjustment.

Step 3 involves estimating the rate of return that would be required to support the tangible assets. This rate normally would be higher than the company's bank borrowing rate. Banks will almost never lend 100 percent of the value of tangible assets. Therefore, the rate to support assets usually needs to be some blend (weighting) of the company's cost of debt and its higher cost of equity (as discussed in Chapter 5 on the income approach). The analyst's report should show the computations made to estimate the required rate of return on tangible assets. Usually a rate of return for each discrete asset is selected to arrive at a weighted average rate of return for all net tangible assets.

Step 4 is simply a multiplication of the required rate of return on net tangible assets from Step 3 times their value from Step 2.

Step 5 is simply a subtraction of the dollar amount of the required return on net tangible assets from Step 4 from the estimated normalized earning power from Step 1.

Step 6 involves developing a capitalization rate applicable to the excess earnings. This is the most subjective step in the process.

The capitalization rate usually will be at or above the high end of reasonable capitalization rates, as discussed in Chapter 5. To put it in perspective, the reciprocal of the excess earnings capitalization rate is the number of years' worth of expected future excess earnings the buyer can be expected to pay to acquire the business or practice. For example, a capitalization rate of .25 means that a buyer would be willing to pay four years' worth of expected future excess earnings:

$$\frac{1}{0.25} = 4 \text{ years}$$

If a buyer would only be willing to pay for 90 days' worth of expected future excess earnings (perhaps typical for buying something such as a vending route), the capitalization rate would be 400 percent:

$$\frac{1}{.25 \text{ years } (\frac{1}{4} \text{ of a year})} = 4.0 = 400\%$$

An alternative method of estimating the capitalization rate for excess earnings is to use something above the normal equity capitalization rate, recognizing that the "excess" portion of the earnings is the riskiest part.

The analyst's report should explain how the capitalization rate for excess earnings was developed.

Step 7 is simply a division of the estimated dollar amount of excess earnings from Step 5 by the excess earnings capitalization rate from Step 6.

Note: The excess earning method represents the "big pot" theory of intangible value, that is, the values of individual intangible assets are not separately identified; instead, they are lumped into one figure.[1] This figure frequently is referred to as the entity's goodwill. However, more narrowly, goodwill is defined as the propensity of customers to return to the business, that is, the expectation of continued patronage. The value of excess earnings really is a somewhat broader concept, usually including other intangible assets besides goodwill in the more narrowly defined sense. Exhibit 8-2 (pages 122) shows a variety of definitions of goodwill.

Step 8 is simply the addition of both the net tangible asset portion from Step 2 and the intangible asset portion of the value of the entity from Step 7.

A "Sanity Check" for Validity of an Excess Earnings Method Value

The overall company capitalization rate implied by the value reached by the excess earnings method should, theoretically, equal the company's overall capitalization rate as it would be developed by the buildup method or the Capital Asset Pricing Model (CAPM) used in the income approach, as described in Chapter 5. If the implied overall capitalization rate is higher than what would be indicated by conventional income approach methods, the excess earnings method indication of value may be too low. Conversely, if the implied overall capitalization rate is lower than what would be indicated by conventional income approach methods, the excess earnings method indication of value may be too high. An illustration of applying this test for reasonableness is shown in Exhibit 8-3 (page 121).

Alternatively, if one has developed the excess earnings capitalization rate by adding something to the equity capitalization rate developed by the buildup or CAPM procedure, then the payback period might be used as the reasonableness check. (The "payback period" was discussed in conjunction with Step 6 of the excess earnings method.)

1. Normally, this means all intangible assets. It is possible, however, that certain specific intangible assets may be identified and valued separately.

Exhibit 8-2
Definitions of Goodwill

Black's Law Dictionary shows a variety of definitions of goodwill:

Goodwill. The favor which the management of a business wins from the public. The favorable consideration shown by the purchasing public to goods or services known to emanate from a particular source. *White Tower System v. White Castle System of Eating Houses Corporation,* C.C.A. Mich., 90 F 2d 67, 69. Property of an intangible nature, commonly defined as the expectation of continued public patronage. *In re Marriage of Lukens,* 16 Wash App. 481, 558 P.2d 279, 280.

The custom of patronage of any established trade or business; the benefit or advantage of having established a business and secured its patronage by the public. And as property incident to business sold, favor vendor has won from public, and probability that all customers will continue their patronage. It means every positive advantage that has been acquired by a proprietor in carrying on his business, whether connected with the premises in which the business is conducted, or with the name under which it is managed, or with any other matter carrying with it the benefit of the business.

The excess of cost of an acquired firm or operating unit over the current or fair market value of net assets of the acquired unit. Informally used to indicate the value of good customer relations, high employee morale, a well-respected business name, etc., which are expected to result in greater than normal earning power.

The ability of a business to generate income in excess of normal rate on assets, due to superior managerial skills, market position, new product technology, etc. The capacity to earn profits in excess of a normal rate of return due to establishment of favorable community reputation and consumer identification of the business name. *North Clackamas Community Hospital v. Harris,* C.A. Or., 664 F 2d 701, 706.

As applied to law firms, term refers to ability to attract clients as result of firm's name, location, or the reputation of lawyers. *Bump v. Stewart, Wimer & Bump, P.C.,* Iowa, 336 NW 2d 731, 736.

For accounting purposes, goodwill has no basis unless it is purchased. In the purchase of a business, goodwill generally is the difference between the purchase price and the value of the assets acquired.[2]

2. Black's Law Dictionary 694–95 (6th ed. 1990)

Exhibit 8-3
A "Sanity Check" for a Value Indicated by the Excess Earnings Method

Company overall capitalization rate implied by the excess earnings method valuation shown in Exhibit 8-1:

$$\frac{\text{Estimated normalized net cash flow}}{\text{Indicated entity value}} \quad \frac{\$25{,}000}{\$140{,}000} = .179$$

The "sanity check" would be to develop a capitalization rate by the buildup or CAPM procedures shown in Chapter 5. Then, for example, if the capitalization rate were 19.0 percent, this would be only 1.1 percentage points above the rate implied in the excess earnings method valuation. This is very close. If one were to capitalize the company's normalized net cash flow of $25,000 at 19.0 percent, the indicated value would be $131,579, very close to the $140,000 indicated by the excess earnings method. If, however, the results were significantly different (for example, several percentage points difference in the capitalization rate), then the assumptions supporting each step of the process should be examined carefully.

Critique of Revenue Ruling 68-609

In 1968, the Internal Revenue Service updated and restated the ARM 34 valuation method. This occurred with the publication of IRS Revenue Ruling 68-609, which is reproduced as Exhibit 8-4 (page122). Revenue Ruling 68-609 is still in effect today.

Use of Historical Averages Impractical

The ruling refers to using an average of five or more years' values of the tangible assets and average earnings over a similar period. This does not really make economic sense from a valuation viewpoint, recognizing that, as stated in Revenue Ruling 59-60, "Valuation is a prophesy as to the future." What really matters is the fair market value in continued use of tangible assets employed as of the effective valuation date and the best estimate of earning power as of that date. Most appraisers agree with this.

"Required Return on Tangible Assets" Ambiguous

The statement, "The percentage of return on the . . . value of the tangible assets used should be the percentage prevailing in the industry involved at the date of valuation . . . " is ambiguous. It should be made clear that it means the rate of return an investor would have to expect to receive to supply capital for net tangible assets in that industry as of the effective valuation date.

Exhibit 8-4
Revenue Ruling 68-609*

SECTION 1001. - DETERMINATION OF AMOUNT OF AND RECOGNITION OF GAIN OR LOSS

26 CFR 1.1001-1: Computation of gain or loss.

(Also Section 167; 1.167(a)-3.)

1968-2 C.B. 327; 1968 IRB LEXIS 239; REV. RUL. 68-609

July, 1968

The "formula" approach may be used in determining the fair market value of intangible assets of a business only if there is no better basis available for making the determination; A.R.M. 34, A.R.M. 68, O.D. 937, and Revenue Ruling 65-192 superseded.

The purpose of this Revenue Ruling is to update and restate, under the current statute and regulations, the currently outstanding portions of A.R.M. 34, C.B. 2, 31 (1920), A.R.M. 68, C.B. 3, 43 (1920), and O.D. 937, C.B. 4, 43 (1921).

The question presented is whether the "formula" approach, the capitalization of earnings in excess of a fair rate of return on net tangible assets, may be used to determine the fair market value of the intangible assets of a business.

The "formula" approach may be stated as follows:

A percentage return on the average annual value of the tangible assets used in a business is determined, using a period of years (preferably not less than five) immediately prior to the valuation date. The amount of the percentage return on tangible assets, thus determined, is deducted from the average earnings of the business for such period and the remainder, if any, is considered to be the amount of the average annual earnings from the intangible assets of the business for the period. This amount (considered as the average annual earnings from intangibles), capitalized at a percentage of, say, 15 to 20 percent, is the value of the intangible assets of the business determined under the "formula" approach.

The percentage of return on the average annual value of the tangible assets used should be the percentage prevailing in the industry involved at the date of valuation, or (when the industry percentage is not available) a percentage of 8 to 10 percent may be used.

*Prepared pursuant to Rev. Proc. 67-6, C.B. 1967-1, 576

The 8 percent rate of return and the 15 percent rate of capitalization are applied to tangibles and intangibles, respectively, of businesses with a small risk factor and stable and regular earnings; the 10 percent rate of return and 20 percent rate of capitalization are applied to businesses in which the hazards of business are relatively high.

The above rates are used as examples and are not appropriate in all cases. In applying the "formula" approach, the average earnings period and the capitalization rates are dependent upon the facts pertinent thereto in each case.

The past earnings to which the formula is applied should fairly reflect the probable future earnings. Ordinarily, the period should not be less than five years, and abnormal years, whether above or below the average, should be eliminated. If the business is a sole proprietorship or partnership, there should be deducted from the earnings of the business a reasonable amount for services performed by the owner or partners engaged in the business. *See Lloyd B. Sanderson Estate v. Commissioner*, 42 F.2d 160 (1930). Further, only the tangible assets entering into net worth, including accounts and bills receivable in excess of accounts and bills payable, are used for determining earnings on the tangible assets. Factors that influence the capitalization rate include (1) the nature of the business, (2) the risk involved, and (3) the stability or irregularity of earnings.

The "formula" approach should not be used if there is better evidence available from which the value of intangibles can be determined. If the assets of a going business are sold upon the basis of a rate of capitalization that can be substantiated as being realistic, though it is not within the range of figures indicated here as the ones ordinarily to be adopted, the same rate of capitalization should be used in determining the value of intangibles.

Accordingly, the "formula" approach may be used for determining the fair market value of intangible assets of a business only if there is no better basis therefore available.

See also Revenue Ruling 59-60, C.B. 1959-1, 237, as modified by Revenue Ruling 65-193, C.B. 1965-2, 370, which sets forth the proper approach to use in the valuation of closely-held corporate stocks for estate and gift tax purposes. The general approach, methods, and factors, outlined in Revenue Ruling 59-60, as modified, are equally applicable to valuations of corporate stocks for income and other tax purposes as well as for estate and gift tax purposes. They apply also to problems involving the determination of the fair market value of business interests of any type, including partnerships and proprietorships, and of intangible assets for all tax purposes.

A.R.M. 34, A.R.M. 68, and O.D. 937 are superseded, since the positions set forth therein are restated to the extent applicable under current law in this Revenue Ruling. Revenue Ruling 65-192, C.B. 1965-2, 259, which contained restatements of A.R.M. 34 and A.R.M. 68, is also superseded.

No Definition of "Earnings"

Probably the biggest shortfall in the ruling is the lack of a definition of "earnings." Analysts use net income, pretax income, gross cash flow, net cash flow, or a variety of other economic income variables.

The required rates of return on both tangible and intangible assets are quite different from one definition of earnings to another. As discussed in Chapter 5 on the income approach, analysts today tend to lean toward net cash flow as the measure of economic income to be capitalized. However, little, if anything, had been written about the advantage of net cash flow as a measure of economic income for valuation purposes when the ruling was written in 1968.

No Guidance for Intangibles Capitalization Rate

The ruling offers no guidance for developing a capitalization rate applicable to the excess earnings. Furthermore, the financial community has not developed any satisfactory empirical means of supporting such a rate with market data. Therefore, the rate used represents a major subjective judgment on the part of the analyst about the expected rate that an investor would require to obtain the company's expected stream of "excess earnings." This allows for a high level of manipulation in the value and therefore demonstrates the extreme need for some type of a "sanity check," as discussed earlier. It is this lack of an empirically supported basis for the capitalization rate applied to excess earnings that many consider the weakest link in the excess earnings method.

Common Errors in Applying the Excess Earnings Method

This section explores some of the most common errors to look for in a valuation of a business or practice using the excess earnings method. They are:

- Not defining the earnings stream
- Using an unrealistic amount of earnings
- Failing to allow for reasonable owner's compensation
- Not properly arriving at a fair market basis net tangible asset value
- Using an unsupported and/or unrealistic rate of return on net tangible assets
- Using an unsupported or unrealistic capitalization rate for excess earnings
- Using IRS illustrative rates instead of currently applicable rates
- Representing that the IRS claims that excess earnings is a preferred valuation method: "The 'formula' approach should not be used if there is better evidence available from which the value of intangible assets can be determined." See Rev. Rul. 68-609, 4th paragraph from the end.

Undefined Earnings Stream

As noted earlier, there can be many different levels of earnings, such as net income, pretax income, gross cash flow, net cash flow, and others (see Chapter 4, "Financial Statement Terminology Used in Business Appraisals"). The capitalization rate must be one that is appropriate for the level of earnings capitalized. Unless the level of earnings used is defined, it is hard, if not impossible, to evaluate whether the support provided for it is reasonable or whether the capitalization rate applied to it is appropriate.

Unsupported Normalized Earnings Stream

The critical thing about the earnings stream is that it is expected to be sustainable into the foreseeable future. If past earnings are being used as a guide, Revenue Ruling 68-609 states, "The past earnings to which the formula is applied should fairly reflect the probable future earnings." All too often we see mechanistic compilations of past earnings with no analysis to support any judgment about whether the level of earnings capitalized represents reasonable future expectations.

Failure to Allow for Owner's Compensation

Revenue Ruling 68-609 clearly states, and the valuation profession agrees, that "there should be deducted from the earnings of the business a reasonable amount for the services performed by the owner or partners engaged in the business." Yet analysts often capitalize earnings before taking into account any compensation for the services of the owner(s).

Unsupported Net Tangible Asset Value

This is a common problem, because most business appraisers are not appraisers of tangible assets, such as real estate or machinery and equipment. If the company has such assets but does not have appraisals of them, business appraisers often just use book value, which may bear little relationship to current value. If there is no carefully analyzed and supported net tangible asset value, then the validity of the excess earnings method is highly questionable.

Unsupported or Unrealistic Required Rate of Return on Tangible Assets

Employing tangible assets in a business certainly is not without risk. The required return on tangibles must reflect the degree of risk involved. This rate should reflect some blending of the company's cost of debt and cost of equity, and the details of estimating this rate should be disclosed. Misestimation of the required rate of return on tangibles might be brought to light, or at least suspected, after a "sanity check."

Unsupported or Unrealistic Capitalization Rate for Excess Earnings

The appropriate capitalization rate for excess earnings depends on two factors:

- The expected persistence of the excess earnings (how long into the future the excess earnings are reasonably expected to continue) and
- The risk (how certain a reasonable person would be about whether the expected persistence of the excess earnings actually will be achieved and the potential volatility of expected returns).

As noted earlier, the capitalization rate applied to excess earnings implies a number of years' worth of expected future earnings impounded into the value of the business (for example, a 20 percent capitalization rate implies that the buyer would pay for five years of expected future excess earnings [1/.20 = 5 years], as shown earlier in the chapter). This number of years sometimes is called the payback period. This is a very subjective yet crucial element of the excess earnings method and the choice of capitalization rate should have some reasonable basis. No matter how carefully it is supported, however, many still would consider it a "guesstimate."

Using Rates in the Revenue Ruling 68-609 Illustration Instead of Currently Supportable Rates

Revenue Ruling 68-609 uses, for the purpose of illustration, rates of 8 percent to 10 percent on tangible assets and 15 percent to 20 percent for the excess earnings capitalization rate. The ruling states, "The percentage of return . . . should be the percentage prevailing in the industry involved at the date of valuation. . . . The above rates are used as examples. . . ." Despite this, we find reports using the 8 percent to 10 percent on tangibles and 15 percent to 20 percent on excess earnings "because the IRS recommends these rates."

Claiming that the IRS Recommends Use of the Excess Earnings Method

Revenue Ruling 68-609 clearly states: "The 'formula' approach should not be used if there is better guidance available from which the value of intangibles can be determined. . . . Accordingly, the 'formula' approach may be used for determining the fair market value of intangible assets *only if there is no better basis therefore available*." [Emphasis added.] Yet many reports make it sound as if this is the method recommended by the IRS.

Summary

The excess earnings method continues to be a widely used method to derive a value indication, particularly for smaller businesses and professional firms, and also when separating the value of tangible asset and intangible assets. If this method is used, the reviewer of such an appraisal will want to make sure that all the method's components are thoroughly supportable. In the end, the value indication should be based on a reasonable weighted average rate of return that can be reconciled with the income approach method used.

Excess Earnings Method References

Feder, Robert, Ed. 1997. "Excess Earnings Approach." In *Valuation Strategies in Divorce,* 4th Ed., 130–3.

Fishman, Jay, et al. 2009. "Excess Earnings Method." In *PPC's Guide to Business Valuations,* 7–19 to 7–31.

Hitchner, James R. 2006. "Excess Cash Flow Method" In *Financial Valuation: Applications and Models,* 2d Ed., 133–42.

Internal Revenue Service. IRS Appeals Officer Valuation Training Course, 1997 Ed., 7–15 to 7–16.

Pratt, Shannon P., and Alina V. Niculita. 2008. "The Capitalized Excess Earnings Method." In *Valuing a Business,* 5th Ed., 331–48.

_____. 2003. "The Excess Earnings Method." In *Business Valuation Body of Knowledge,* 2d Ed., 174–8.

_____, and Roger J. Grabowski. 2008. "How Cost of Capital Relates to the Excess Earnings Method of Valuation," In *Cost of Capital: Applications and Examples,* 3d Ed.

_____. 1997. "Practitioners disagree strongly on excess earnings methodology" (results of a survey of business appraisers). In *Shannon Pratt's Business Valuation Update,* April, 1–3.

Trugman, Gary. 2002. "The Excess Earnings Method." In *Understanding Business Valuations,* 2d Ed., 310–12, 857–61.

Chapter 9

Rules of Thumb

Transaction Databases with Price/Revenue and Price/ Discretionary Earnings Ratios

The first thing to say about rules of thumb is that they should practically never be relied on as a primary appraisal method. Having said that, if there are valuation rules of thumb for an industry, especially if they are widely recognized, they can be useful to estimate a "ballpark" range of value.

Rules of thumb often are classified within the market approach to business valuation because they are thought to have their origins in transactions in the industry. However, their actual origins can vary from pure folklore to (rarely) actual transaction studies.

Rules of Thumb Disclaimers

Two books provide extensive listings of business valuation rules of thumb. In both, the authors express strong admonitions against relying on rules of thumb for business appraisal.

Tom West, veteran business broker and editor of *The Business Broker* monthly newsletter, says:

> [R]ules of thumb are just that—they are guesses. They can make great sanity checks, "ballparks" for pricing, but they should not be used for valuing or anything that is even close to a valuation or an appraisal.[1]

Longtime appraiser Glenn Desmond offers a variety of caveats about rules of thumb:

> [F]ormula values are not substitutes for careful consideration of other appropriate valuation methods that are applicable to the business being appraised. . . .

1. Tom West, The 2008 Business Reference Guide.

> [M]ultiplier ranges are broad. . . . To maximize the usefulness of this book, . . . multiplier ranges have been narrowed to represent the *typical* ranges found nationally. These might be quite broad in some cases and not broad enough in others. The reader needs to be aware that the appropriate multiplier for a given business type in a particular area may be above or below the ranges shown in this text.[2]

Desmond cautions that valuations change over time in response to changing economic and industry conditions. Furthermore, at any given time, valuations may vary considerably from one locale to another.

General Nature of Rules of Thumb

Rules of thumb usually are expressed as multipliers. The most common is a multiple of revenues, such as "Many accounting practices sell for .75 to 1.25 times annual revenues." The other popular multiple for rules of thumb is a multiple of "discretionary earnings," also called Sellers Discretionary Cash Flow (SDCF) or Owner's Cash Flow (OCF), earnings that may be defined, in certain applications, to reflect earnings of a business enterprise prior to the following items: income taxes, nonoperating income and expenses, nonrecurring income and expenses, depreciation and amortization, interest expense or income, and owner's total compensation for those services, which could be provided by a sole owner/manager.[3]

Occasionally, one finds rules of thumb relating to some measure of physical volume. For example, a rule of thumb for taverns might be so many dollars for each keg of beer sold per month. Both the cable and cellular phone industries have been valued at x dollars per actual and/or potential subscriber. A Delaware decision used dollars per recoverable ton of coal reserves as a valuation method.[4]

To the extent that rules of thumb are used, they usually apply to small businesses and professional practices. They generally assume that the sale of the business would be on an asset basis rather than on a stock basis. It is usually assumed that the rule represents the transfer of the operating tangible and intangible assets but not real estate or current assets or liabilities (for example, cash, accounts receivable, inventory, accounts payable). Often a covenant not to compete is included as is sometimes an employment agreement. A major problem with rules of thumb is that they are not clear about exactly what business assets they purport to represent. Furthermore, they do nothing to deal with the essential valuation factors of relative risk and growth prospects.

---

2. Glenn Desmond, Handbook of Small Business Valuation Formulas 3 (3d ed. 1993).
3. American Society of Appraisers Business Valuation Standards.
4. Neal v. Ala. By-Products Corp., 1990 Del. Ch. LEXIS 127 (Aug. 1, 1990), *aff'd*, Ala. By-Products Corp v. Neal, 588 A.2d 255 (Del 1991).

Rules of Thumb Not Cash-Equivalent Prices

The rule of thumb values are intended to indicate face values of transactions, not necessarily (or even usually) cash-equivalent values; most businesses are sold on terms and not for cash. Normally, the seller receives a note for the balance, usually at a rate of interest below market rates for comparable credits, and sometimes including contingencies. Thus, if such rules or transactions are used to develop fair market value (which assumes cash equivalency, as discussed in Chapter 1), adjustments must be made accordingly.

Rule of Thumb Examples

Tom West's *2010 Business Reference Guide* includes an extensive section on rules of thumb. Some of these rules of thumb, which are stated in terms of multiples of revenue, are shown in Exhibit 9-1. However, West also includes rules based on other parameters, particularly multiples of discretionary earnings (see Chapter 6 on the market approach).

Another source of rules of thumb is *101+ Practical Solutions for the Family Lawyer,* in which Harriet Cohen presents rules of thumb for valuing several types of businesses and professional practices.[5]

Checking Alleged Rules of Thumb Against Actual Transactions

If one wants to check an alleged rule of thumb against actual transactions, three databases report ratios of price to discretionary earnings, as well as price to revenues, for actual completed sales of businesses. These are *BIZCOMPS,®* the *IBA Market Database,* and *Pratt's Stats.®* The latter also indicates whether a covenant not to compete or an employment agreement was involved and, if so, how much value was allocated to it. These databases are listed in the "References and Sources" at the end of this chapter.

Exhibit 9-1 includes data on multiples of revenue derived from actual transactions from the *Pratt's Stats®* and *BIZCOMPS®* databases. As can be seen from the exhibit, the actual multiples diverge quite a bit from the rules of thumb, proving that rules of thumb are not very reliable.

It is important to recognize that these rules of thumb and the transaction prices shown in both *Pratt's Stats®* and *BIZCOMPS®* represent face values of transactions, not cash-equivalent values. They usually include seller financing, which in some

5. GREGG HERMAN, 101+ PRACTICAL SOLUTIONS FOR THE FAMILY LAWYER (2d ed. 2003).

Exhibit 9-1
Rules of Thumb for Valuation

Occupation	2010 Business Reference Guide[1]	Actual Transactions from Pratt's Stats[2]	Actual Transactions from BIZCOMPS[3]
Accounting Firms	75 to 125% of annual revenues	Range: 56–161% m=1.07 me=1.06	Range: 37–132% m=0.93 me=1.00
Auto Repair Shops	25 to 30% of annual sales plus inventory	Range: 14–121% m=0.47 me=0.37	Range: 4–144% m=0.39 me=0.35
Beauty Shops	35% of annual revenues plus inventory, fixtures and equipment.	Range: 12–142% m = 0.44 me = 0.38	Range: 6–202% m=0.40 me=0.33
Dental Practices	60 to 65% of gross annual sales, including inventory.	Range: 13–189% m=0.61 me=0.61	n/a
Drug Stores	18 to 42% of annual sales, depending on profit, including inventory.	Range: 7–93% m=0.35 me=0.34	Range: 8–35% m=0.19 me=0.20
Dry Cleaners	75 to 85% of annual sales plus inventory.	Range: 30–137% m=0.71 me=0.68	n/a
Fast-Food Franchises	35 to 45% of annual sales plus inventory	Range: 7–161% m=0.48 me=0.42	Range: 8–204% m=0.42 me=0.39
Grocery Stores	10 to 15% of annual sales plus inventory.	Range: 1–145% m=0.31 me=0.24	Range: 3–160% m=0.29 me=0.21
Insurance Agencies	150 to 175% of annual sales, including inventory.	Range: 16–247% m=1.31 me=1.14	Range: 8–224% m=0.72 me=0.68

m=mean; me=median; n/a=insufficient transactions for meaningful results

1. Tom West. *The Business Reference Guide 2010.*
2. From *Pratt's Stats*, compiled by Business Valuation Resources, LLC.
3. From *BIZCOMPS*, compiled by Business Valuation Resources, LLC.

Occupation	2008 Business Reference Guide	Actual Transactions from Pratt's Stats	Actual Transactions from BIZCOMPS
Medical Practices (Small Family Practice)	35 to 50% of annual fee revenue; may require earnout	Range: 72–170% m=1.07 me=0.94	Range: 13–98% m=0.55 me=0.55
Restaurants	30 to 35% of annual sales plus inventory.	Range: 3–83% m=0.54 me=0.59	Range: 10–73% m=0.36 me=0.32
Retail Businesses	30 to 35% of annual sales plus inventory.	Range: 17–135% m=0.54 me=0.45	Range: 14–114% m=0.44 me=0.38
Travel Agencies	35 to 40% of annual sales plus inventory.	Range: 3–132% m=0.44 me=0.40	Range: 2–93% m=0.13 me=0.06

m=mean; me=median; n/a=insufficient transactions for meaningful results

cases is at below market rates, and often include future payments that are contingent on future performance, such as retention of existing customers. Perhaps more important, the prices generally *include* values of noncompete covenants and employment agreements, portions that may or may not be considered part of the marital estate, depending on the state of jurisdiction.

If the data are to be used for marital property settlements, we highly recommend that the parties' experts obtain the actual transaction data now widely available to derive multiples based on recent transactions and recompute the ratios after eliminating noncompete and employment agreements in jurisdictions where those agreements would not be considered marital property.

Also, most rules of thumb reflect the assumption that the seller will stay with the business for some period of time to assist in the transaction. To this extent, they implicitly imply some personal goodwill. There is a trend among states to separate personal from enterprise goodwill and exclude personal goodwill from the marital estate. (See Chapter 10, "Personal versus Enterprise Goodwill.")

Court Reaction to Rules of Thumb

Courts generally have been inclined to reject valuation opinions based on rules of thumb. One opinion, for example, contained the following language:

> [These] formulas . . . "are in reality the starting point of negotiation; and should not be confused with a valuation procedure." . . . Formulas based on gross billings are usually converted to a time pay-out of the purchase price and, as such, can be misleading because they are often negotiated more over the terms of payment than over the actual value of the business being acquired. . . . While "rules of thumb may be helpful to accountants or business people to gauge the overall fairness of a particular transaction," i.e., whether it is "in the ballpark," they are not at all helpful to the Court in fixing a specific value on a specific economic enterprise in an ancillary proceeding. . . . A rule of thumb by definition provides no theory. At best it is a guide or points out direction. At worst, it is nothing.[6]

Rules of thumb, however, have been accepted by courts in one form or another. In one case, the husband's expert simply utilized a rule of thumb multiplier of three to five times the husband's salary, then subtracted corporate debt to reach a final value. The trial court adopted this figure as opposed to the asset-based valuation presented by the wife's expert. The decision was appealed and upheld.[7]

References and Sources

Basic Rules of Thumb References

Cohen, Harriet N. 2003. "Using Rules of Thumb in Valuation." In Gregg Herman, *101+ Practical Solutions for the Family Lawyer,* 2d Ed. Chicago: American Bar Association.

Desmond, Glenn M. 1993. *Handbook of Small Business Valuation Formulas and Rules of Thumb*, 3d Ed.

Feder, Robert, Ed. 1997. "Courts' Use of Rules of Thumb to Value Assets." In *Valuation Strategies in Divorce*, 4th Ed., 450-3.

Fishman, Jay, et al. 2008. "Rules of Thumb" and "The Problem with Rules of Thumb in the Valuation of Closely-Held Entities." In *PPC's Guide to Business Valuations*, 7-40, 7-51 to 7-53.

Pratt, Shannon P., and Alina V. Niculita. 2008. "Formulas or Rules of Thumb." In *Valuing a Business,* 5th Ed., 319-20.

West, Tom. "Rules of Thumb." In *The Business Reference Guide 2010,* 20th Ed.

6. Bostwick v. Bostwick, 1991 WL 42628 (Del. Fam. Ct. 1991), *quoted in* Robert D. Feder, Valuation Strategies in Divorce 451 (4th ed. 1997). *See also, e.g.,* Bolan v. Bolan, 32 Ark. App. 65, 796 S.W.2d 358 (1990) and Young v. Young, 600 So. 2d 1140 (Fla. Dist. Ct. App. 1992).

7. Carter v. Carter, 1990 WL 145736 (Ohio App. 11 Dist. 1990).

Transaction Databases with Price/Revenue and Price/Discretionary Earnings Ratios

BIZCOMPS*
Asset Business Appraisal
P.O. Box 97757
Las Vegas, NV 89193
(858) 457-0366

IBA Market Database
Institute of Business Appraisers
P.O. Box 17410
Plantation, FL 33318
(954) 584-1144

Pratt's Stats*
Business Valuation Resources
1000 S.W. Broadway, Ste. 1200
Portland, OR 97205
(888) 287-8258

* These databases can be accessed through *BVResources.com.*

Chapter 10

Personal versus Enterprise Goodwill

The distinction between personal and enterprise goodwill is becoming an increasingly important aspect of business valuation. This is primarily true in conjunction with marital dissolution disputes, where an increasing number of states are requiring a separation of personal versus enterprise goodwill and excluding personal goodwill from the marital estate. The distinction sometimes can be a factor in corporate taxation, where the source of proceeds from a liquidation can be considered personal goodwill and therefore not subject to taxation.

At the last count prior to publication, the latest court cases in 29 states and the District of Columbia now regard enterprise goodwill as part of the marital estate in a dissolution but not personal goodwill. Louisiana has even passed a statute to that effect![1]

The number of states whose latest court cases included both enterprise and personal goodwill as part of the marital estate has shrunk to 13. Four states say neither form of goodwill is marital and two have not yet taken a stand on the issue. The outcome in the remaining states depends on whether the business is a professional practice or whether the professional will continue to practice.[2]

Closely related to personal goodwill is the matter of covenants not to compete, which most, but not all, states have categorized as a personal asset, not subject to distribution, for it restricts the future activities of the spouse.[3]

---

1. LA. REV. STAT. § 9:2801.2 (2009).
2. BUSINESS VALUATION RESOURCES, GOODWILL HUNTING IN DIVORCE (2009).
3. *See, e.g.*, Kricsfeld v. Kricsfeld, 588 N.W.2d 210, 1999 Neb. App. LEXIS 1 (Neb. Ct. App. 1999), in which Nebraska's court of appeals looked to other jurisdictions and concluded that the covenant not to compete is not a marital asset.

Distinction Between Enterprise and Personal Goodwill

Goodwill is that intangible asset that contributes to earnings as a result of name, reputation, customer and employee loyalty, location, products, and similar factors not separately identified.

Enterprise goodwill is that part of goodwill attributable to the entity as opposed to the individual.

Personal goodwill is that part of goodwill attributable to the individual as opposed to the entity.

Enterprise Goodwill Characteristics

The following characteristics would be indicative of enterprise goodwill:

- Company has written contracts with major customers
- Company has written contracts with major suppliers
- Company has written employment and/or noncompete agreements with key employees
- Advantageous location
- Large business with formalized organizational structure, systems, and controls
- Company has formalized production methods and business systems
- Business or practice not heavily dependent on personal service performed by the owner(s)
- Company sales result from company name recognition and/or sales force

Personal Goodwill Characteristics

The following characteristics would be indicative of personal goodwill:

- Small entrepreneurial business highly dependent on owner's personal skills and relationships
- No noncompete or employment agreements
- Personal services provided by the owner(s) an important feature in the company's products or services
- Sales largely dependent on owner's personal relationship with customers
- Product and/or services know-how and supplier relationships rest primarily with the owner(s)

Case Examples

Divorce Cases

In a large neuropsychiatry practice that the authors valued, the doctor, who owned 100 percent of the stock, had largely institutionalized the goodwill. The company had a staff of about 60 doctors and therapists, some as employees and some as independent contractors. It had employment and noncompete agreements with all the department heads and key doctors. It also had contracts with all the hospitals it serviced and most of the doctors had their own patient relationships. The doctor/owner personally saw few patients, but he negotiated the contracts with the hospitals and hired all the key professionals. The court concluded that the goodwill was 70 percent institutional and 30 percent personal.

A specialized niche insurance agency that the authors valued was the opposite. The president had personal relationships with all the underwriters and most of the larger customers. He had developed very loyal relationships with all the largest producing agents. The agency had no contracts with any customers and no employment or noncompete agreements. In this case, most of the goodwill was found to be personal.

Tax Cases

In the *Martin Ice Cream*[4] case, a gentleman named Strassberg was the first distributor of Häagen-Dazs ice cream. He had successfully placed Häagen-Dazs ice cream in a significant number of large grocery chains. When Pillsbury bought out Häagen-Dazs, it bought out all the distributor rights. The IRS determined there was a large enterprise-level intangible asset. The court ruled that most of the value of the distributorship was personal to Pillsbury, which saved a large amount of tax at the corporate level.

In the landmark *Norwalk*[5] case, an accounting firm liquidated and the IRS agent determined there had been a liquidating distribution of enterprise-level intangible assets, so the agent assessed a tax on about $600,000 corporate gain on the distribution. Because there was no noncompete between the shareholders and the accounting firm, the court ruled that all the otherwise enterprise-level intangibles that the IRS had deemed distributed at the time of the liquidation were, in fact, personal goodwill. The court stated, "We find no authority which holds that an individual's ability is part of the assets of a corporation by which he is employed where, as in the instant case, the corporation does not have a right by contract or otherwise to the future services of the individuals."

4. Martin Ice Cream, Co. v. Comm'r, 110 T.C. 189, 1998 U.S. Tax. Ct. LEXIS 17 (1998).
5. Norwalk v. Comm'r, T.C. Memo. 1998-279 (1998).

References

Business Valuation Resources. *Calculating Goodwill: What Is Personal and What Is Professional?* Teleconference, January 18, 2006, with Ron Seigneur, R. James Alerding, Mark Dietrich, and Kevin Yeanoplos, available at BVResources.com (both CD and transcript).

Business Valuation Resources. *Goodwill Hunting in Divorce,* 2009. A state-by-state summary of the leading U.S. court cases deciding the disposition of goodwill in marital dissolution.

Business Valuation Resources' Guide to Personal v. Enterprise Goodwill. 2009. Introduction by David Wood, with contributions by Jay Fishman, Mark Dietrich, James Alerding, Shannon Pratt, Noah Gordon, and Kevin Yeanoplos.

Business Valuation Resources. "Multiattribute Utility Model Accepted in Allocating Personal/Enterprise Goodwill." *Business Valuation Update,* December 2006 (case abstract of *In re Marriage of Alexander,* 2006 Ill. App. LEXIS 836 (Ill. Ct. App. 2006)).

Dietrich, Mark. "Identifying and Measuring Personal Goodwill in a Professional Practice." *CPA Expert,* Part 1 (Spring 2005), Part 2 (Summer 2005).

Wood, David, "'MUM's the Word': A Formal Method to Allocate Blue Sky Value in Divorce." *Business Valuation Update,* March 2007.

Chapter 11

Reasonable Compensation

This chapter was contributed by Kimberly Linebarger, a financial analyst with Shannon Pratt Valuations. She has contributed to various publications concerning business valuation.

Often one of the largest adjustments in a business valuation is reasonable compensation. Reasonable compensation is a normalizing adjustment taken when a key employee or officer is found to be underpaid or overpaid. Some situations where the issue of reasonable compensation may be critical are when the key person is also a shareholder, when there is a family relationship between the payor and payee, and when personal versus enterprise goodwill is a concern.

Reasonable compensation adjustments are most frequently taken when a controlling interest is being valued. The underlying idea behind the adjustment is that a controlling owner would be able to adjust the owner's compensation to reflect current market rates. In the valuation of a noncontrolling position, an adjustment sometimes is not taken because the shareholder would not have the ability to correct any excess compensation unless otherwise stated as part of the equity position. An example where an adjustment might take place in a noncontrolling valuation is if the issue being litigated deals with shareholder oppression of the controlling shareholder over the minority shareholder.

When reasonable compensation is a key issue in a business valuation, a compensation expert often is consulted. More often, however, the business appraiser is responsible for deciding any reasonable compensation adjustments.

Determining Reasonable Compensation

When determining reasonable compensation, the business appraiser must identify the total compensation being paid to the employee in question and compare that to the compensation needed to attract an employee (or in some cases employees) of similar skill. For example, if a company has a bookkeeper who is also the sister of the company's owner and is receiving a wage that appears to be reasonable for a full-time employee, the appraiser should inquire as to whether this employee is actually a full-time bookkeeper. If during interviews it is determined that the employee works only 10 hours per week, an adjustment to the employee's wages to that of a part-time bookkeeper should be made. If the appraiser fails to identify this adjustment, it may be detrimental to the viability of the valuation.

The business appraiser should keep in mind that he or she is not giving an opinion about whether the specific person is overcompensated or undercompensated based on how well the person performs his or her duties. The question the appraiser should ask is *What would it cost the company for a hypothetical replacement for the position in question?* The adjustment is based on the principle of substitution, not on whether the specific individual is worth more or less.

When determining adjustments to compensation, the professional appraiser must identify the following:

- The job position (including all duties performed by the executive and location)
- The total compensation being paid to the executive (including stock option plans, bonuses, pensions, etc.)
- Sources of salary information for the identified job position
- Relevancy of the data
- The shortcomings of the compensation data utilized

Sources of Information

To verify the compensation needed to attract an executive of similar skills, many valuators will consult a database or a trade association survey. The availability of faultless data is scarce; therefore, the business appraiser needs to use common sense and logic when deciding on the information he or she will use. When the data are available, the business appraiser should examine more than one source of data and use his or her best judgment to determine the reasonableness of the data for the position in question. ValuationResources.com provides a comprehensive list of compensation data resources. The following is a list of broad sources often consulted:

- Executive Compensation Assessor, Economic Research Institute (ERI)
- American Salaries and Wages Survey, Gale Research
- America's Career InfoNet, sponsored by the U.S. Department of Labor
- Executive Insight, Equilar

Many of the above sources provide data by company size, industry, and location. While it is easy to simply use a number given by one of the above sources, it is critical that the business appraiser be aware of the assumptions and limitations of the data and, thus, the defensibility of the number utilized. The appraiser should know that he or she is looking at a job position that is equivalent and that all compensation is accounted for so that the adjustment he or she takes is not understated or overstated. Exhibit 11-1 is a checklist of 12 points that valuators should know about the compensation data they utilize.

Exhibit 11-1
12-Point Checklist for Valuation Appraisers

1. Is the data collected on a national or regional basis?
2. Does the data include owner/employees where the amount of compensation reported may also include business profits as compensation (i.e., partners in professions and businesses)?
3. Concerning data from business and professional associations, what are the sampling sizes that relate to the subject valuation?
4. When using SIC codes in identifying comparables, how do the particular characteristics of the subject company compare with the broader range of companies covered by the SIC code?
5. How does the data use/define the job titles, and are the actual duties comparable to the duties/hours of the subject owner/employee?
6. Does the data survey reflect averages? Medians? Quartiles?
7. Does the survey fairly reflect compensation for people with particular niches and sub-specialties; i.e., matrimonial attorneys, forensic accountants, lobbyists, etc.?
8. Does the valuator need to include multiple job titles from the survey data to cover the owner/employee's duties?
9. What is the reliability of the statistics and sources that the survey uses?
10. Where applicable, are stock options, restricted stock, shadow stock compensation as well as other perks reflected in the data survey, and comparable to the owner/employee in question?
11. Were all companies in the database consistent in having/not having retirement plans separate from salary?
12. Is the owner a 'key person' in the business or a top performer/sales generator?

Source: "Reasonable Compensation: Can Your Opinion Survive This 12-point Checklist?" *Business Valuation Update,* July, 2006, 8-10.

Tax Court and Reasonable Compensation

As reasonable compensation has become more of an issue, some guidance has come out of the Tax Court. There are two main tests that the Tax Court has used to determine reasonable compensation: the Multifactor Test and the Hypothetical Independent Investor Test.

The Multifactor Test is essentially a list of factors the Tax Court examines. That analysis produces a conclusion about the reasonableness of the employee's compensation. While the factors looked at are not consistent among courts or cases, many of them follow some of the same underlying ideas. The factors considered in two different Tax Court cases dealing with closely held corporations are shown in Exhibit 11-2. It is not the purpose of this chapter to go into detailed analysis of tax cases. For a thorough examination of these and other cases dealing with reasonable compensation, please see Shannon P. Pratt, *Valuing a Business*, 5th Ed., 771–92.

Exhibit 11-2
Tax Court's Examples of the Factor Test

Five-Factor Test

Introduction

In *LabelGraphics, Inc. v. Commissioner,* * the Tax Court used a five-factor test for assessing the reasonableness of the executive compensation income tax deduction related to employees/owners of closely held corporations.

The Tax Court's Five-Factor Test

The Tax Court's Five-Factor Test is composed of the following factors:

Factor One	The employee's role in the company.
Factor Two	A comparison of the compensation paid to similarly situated employees in similar companies.
Factor Three	The character and condition of the company.
Factor Four	Whether a relationship existed between the company and employee that may permit the company to disguise nondeductible corporate distributions as deductible compensation.
Factor Five	Whether the compensation was paid pursuant to a (1) structured, (2) formal, and (3) consistently applied program.

* *LabelGraphics, Inc. v. Commissioner,* T.C. Memo 1998-343 (Sept. 28, 1998), *aff'd* 221 F.3d 1091 (9th Cir. 2000).

Nine-Factor Test

Introduction

In *Brewer Quality Homes, Inc. v. Commissioner,*** the Tax Court weighed a nine-factor test as set forth in *Owensby & Kritikos, Inc. v. Commissioner* in determining whether compensation was reasonable and therefore deductible.

The Tax Court's Nine-Factor Test

The Tax Court's Nine-Factor Test is composed of the following factors:

Factor One	The employee's qualifications.
Factor Two	The nature, extent, and scope of the employee's work.
Factor Three	Size and complexity of the company.
Factor Four	Comparison of the employee's salary with the company's gross and net income.
Factor Five	Prevailing general economic conditions.
Factor Six	Comparison of salaries with distributions to stockholders.
Factor Seven	Compensation for comparable positions in comparable concern.
Factor Eight	Salary policy of the company as to all employees.
Factor Nine	Amount of compensation paid to the employee in previous years.

** *Brewer Quality Homes, Inc. v. Commissioner,* T.C. Memo 2003-200 (July 10, 2003)
Tax Court's Examples of the Factor Test

Source: Shannon P. Pratt with Alina V. Niculita, *Valuing a Business: The Analysis and Appraisal of Closely Held Companies.* New York: McGraw-Hill, 2007, 771-92.

Criticism concerning the Multifactor Test has lead to an increase in the use of the hypothetical Independent Investor Test. The Independent Investor Test looks at whether, given the company's current dividends and return on equity, a neutral stockholder would approve the employee's level of compensation. This test allows for a more unbiased and quantitative analysis versus the Multifactor Test. Often a Tax Court will use both tests to reach a decision on reasonable compensation.

Summary

Reasonable compensation adjustments sometimes can dramatically impact a valuation. The appraiser should have a thorough understanding of any reasonable compensation adjustments taken in a business valuation. By understanding and identifying key personnel and job responsibilities, the appraiser can determine whether a compensation adjustment is necessary and to what degree. If a compensation adjustment is necessary, the appraiser needs to conduct comprehensive research of relevant data sources for the particular industry and job responsibilities. Knowledge of both the pros and cons of the data utilized will assist in justification of the adjustment.

References

Fannon, Nancy. "Rates of Return: Don't Ignore Public Market or Transactional Data." In *Business Valuation Update,* September 2007, available online at BVResources.com.

Fishman, Jay, et al. 2008. "Business Valuation Discounts and Premia Databases." In *PPC's Guide to Business Valuations.* Fort Worth, Texas: Practitioners Publishing Co., 8–43.

Hitchner, James R. 2006. "Valuation Discounts and Premiums." In *Financial Valuation: Applications and Models,* 2d Ed., Chap. 8.

Ostermueller, Ralph E. "Reasonable Executive Compensation." In *AICPA National Business Valuation Conference,* December 3, 2006.

Pratt, Shannon P., and Alina V. Niculita. 2008. "Gathering Company Data." In *Valuing a Business,* 5th Ed., Chap. 4. New York: McGraw-Hill.

Trugman, Gary. 2002. "Data Analysis." In *Understanding Business Valuation,* 2d Ed., Chap. 5.

Chapter 12

Financial Statement Adjustments

One of the frequent sources of controversy is adjustments to financial statements made for the purpose of valuation. The reviewer faces the following questions:

- Were adjustments made that should not have been made for the purpose of this valuation?
- Are there adjustments that should have been made but were not?
- For the adjustments made, is there adequate support for the amount of each?

Reasons for Financial Statement Adjustments

There are several reasons to make financial statement adjustments, and the reviewer can best assess the propriety of each adjustment with these reasons in mind. A certain adjustment may be appropriate for one valuation but not another.

One of the reasons for financial statement adjustments is to make the statements reflect numbers closer to economic reality for valuation purposes. Another reason, if a market approach is used, is to put the subject company's and guideline companies' figures on a mutually consistent accounting basis for comparative purposes. Similarly, if the subject company's financial ratios are being compared to "industry averages" from some source, the adjustments should put the subject company's figures on a basis consistent with the industry-average figures for comparative purposes.

In a somewhat broad sense, it may be helpful to think of financial statement adjustments in four categories:

- Normalization adjustments. These are adjustments for abnormalities that generally would be made for all valuation purposes. (While this chapter focuses on the subject company, these adjustments should be made to statements of guideline companies used in the market approach as well.)

- Control adjustments. These are adjustments that a typical control stockholder would make, usually to assess the actual economic income that would be available to a control stockholder. These generally would be made if valuing a controlling interest but not a minority interest.
- Separating nonoperating from operating items. In some cases, nonoperating items should be removed from the balance sheet and/or income statement and treated separately for valuation purposes. This normally would be an adjustment for a controlling interest valuation, but in some cases it may be appropriate for a minority interest valuation. The reason for doing this usually is to value the company's operations primarily on an income basis and the nonoperating items on an asset basis. In some cases, these adjustments are highly controversial, as we will discuss later in this chapter.
- Adjusting from cash to accrual basis. The financial statements used in valuations mostly are prepared on an accrual basis.

Some adjustments may affect both the income statement and the balance sheet, while some may affect only one or the other. Destruction of a building by fire, for example, ordinarily would result in a lower-than-normal reported net income and removal of the building from the company's balance sheet. In this circumstance, the income statement might be adjusted to eliminate the effects of this nonrecurring event. However, there would be no need to adjust the balance sheet because the property no longer would be available to the company. If the market approach to valuation has been used, it is appropriate to make similar adjustments to the guideline companies' financial statements, as discussed in Chapter 6 on the market approach.

The potential variety of financial statement adjustments is endless. This chapter specifically discusses those most commonly encountered. References to more extended discussions of financial statement adjustments are included at the end of the chapter.

There is considerable latitude in acceptable accounting policies, even within the rather broad constraints of generally accepted accounting principles (GAAP). To the extent that the subject company's accounting policies differ from typical industry or guideline company policies, it may be appropriate to make adjustments to put accounting data on a comparable basis.

Normalizing Adjustments

The basic idea of normalizing adjustments is to present data so that it represents the economic reality of an ongoing business or of accounting customary in the industry for comparative purposes. If the statements are to be used as guidance for estimating future economic income, then nonrecurring items should be eliminated. If the statements are to be compared with other specific companies or industry averages, they should be put on a comparable accounting basis. This section briefly discusses the most commonly encountered normalizing adjustments and lists several more that are less frequent but not unusual.

It makes no difference whether or not such accounting entries are classified as "extraordinary" under GAAP. There are many items, such as gains/losses on sales of major assets, that are nonrecurring but would not be qualified as extraordinary by GAAP.

Nonrecurring Items

The effect of nonrecurring items should be removed from the subject company financial statements to make them more representative of ongoing operations. Such adjustments also usually make the statements more comparable to industry averages or to other guideline companies. Also note that similar adjustments may be necessary for guideline companies.

Some examples of nonrecurring events include:

- Effect of strikes
- Gains/losses from sale of major assets
- Gains/losses from litigation
- Net casualty losses (after insurance recovery)

While this list is brief, it conveys the general idea. These items are removed so that historical statements are more representative of the company's ongoing operations.

Sometimes an appraiser may regard an item (such as a strike) as infrequent although not totally nonrecurring. A reasonable treatment in that case would be to spread the adjustment over several years of income statements instead of eliminating it entirely. The same may apply to write-downs, which should be charged to a series of prior periods.

When the appraiser adjusts the income or expense, it is important that the adjustment nets out any related income or capital gains tax effect, as discussed later in the chapter.

Discontinued Operations

If a company has discontinued a line of business that had income or losses that have not been or would not be replaced by alternative uses of the company's resources with comparable returns, then the effects of those discontinued operations usually should be removed. If an alternative line of business is being consummated, the financial statements should be adjusted for any abnormalities that might result during the start-up phase.

If it is difficult or impossible to sort out the effects of the discontinued operation(s) in the company data, then a reasonable alternative may be to consider financial statements only for the period since the operations were discontinued. If using a market approach, averages of financial data for the guideline companies should be compared only for periods similar to those used for the subject company.

Inventory Accounting Methods

Two basic categories of inventory adjustments often are encountered: first-in, first-out (FIFO) versus last-in, first-out (LIFO) accounting policies and write-down and write-off policies.

- First-In, First-Out (FIFO) versus Last-in, First-out (LIFO) Accounting Policies. Both GAAP and the IRS (tax law) allow accounting for inventory on either a First-In, First-Out (FIFO) basis or a Last-In, First-Out (LIFO) basis. The FIFO inventory accounting method assumes, for accounting purposes, that the oldest unit of an inventory item purchased is the next unit sold. The LIFO method assumes that the most recently purchased unit of an inventory item purchased is the next unit sold. To the extent that inventory prices go up, LIFO produces lower figures for earnings and inventory than does FIFO.

  If using the market approach, all companies' data should be stated on a comparable basis, either all LIFO or all FIFO (unless the difference is immaterial). If a company accounts on a FIFO basis, the financial statements do not contain the data that would be needed to convert to a LIFO basis. Therefore, if some companies are on LIFO and others are on FIFO, the only practical adjustment available is to convert all companies to a FIFO basis.

  There are also some other methods of inventory accounting that are acceptable under GAAP that should be adjusted for valuation purposes, but they are encountered infrequently and thus beyond the scope of this book.
- Write-down and Write-off Policies. Companies may be very aggressive or very lax in their periodic inventory adjustments. Some companies may write off anything that hasn't sold in a certain number of months, resulting in tens or hundreds of thousands of dollars of salable inventory removed from the balance sheet and expensed as cost of goods sold. Others may hold obsolete inventory that should have been written off the balance sheet and charged to cost of goods sold. This is a subject that appraisers usually address during a field visit and management interviews if they believe it may be a material item.

Depreciation and Depletion Methods and Schedules

There is wide latitude within GAAP regarding methods of accounting for depreciation and depletion. There is also considerable latitude regarding the length of the time period over which various assets may be depreciated.

Again, the general goals of adjustments are to approximate economic reality and to conform to industry practices if comparisons are to be made either to industry averages or to individual guideline companies.

Net Operating Losses Carried Forward

If a company is expensing a prior period's net operating loss (NOL) over time, the effect of that normally would be removed from the income statement, because it would not represent ongoing operations and because guideline companies and industry averages would not be expected to reflect such NOLs.

Whether the present value of such NOLs is a proper addition to the balance sheet for valuation purposes is highly problematical and frequently becomes an issue. The main criterion for deciding whether to recognize NOLs as assets is the degree of certainty and timing of the company's ability to deduct them against future taxable income (or the potential for a buyer of the company to do so). In most sales of companies with NOLs, some compromise about their value is reached if they are transferable, although some buyers may not accord them any value at all. In any event, the value of NOLs projected to be used in the future should be discounted to a present value, with the appropriate discount rate usually being the company's cost of capital.

Reserve and Allowance Accounts

Many reserve and allowance expense items may appear on the income statement and related reserve accounts may appear on the balance sheet.

- *Allowance for Doubtful Accounts*—Accounts Receivable. Many companies carry accounts receivable and deduct some allowance for potentially uncollectible accounts. As with inventory, some companies are very aggressive and others very lax in writing off or establishing valuation reserves for potentially uncollectible accounts. Some companies may have written substantial amounts of receivables off their books that eventually may be collected, while other companies may show no allowance for doubtful accounts and no related bad-debt expense, even though their receivables may include substantial uncollectible accounts. Analysts can vary considerably in their degree of thoroughness in investigating these items and in their aggressiveness or conservatism in making adjustments to the numbers presented on the financial statements.

- *Allowance for Doubtful Accounts*—Notes Receivable. Notes receivable can be ways for a company to attempt to collect on trade account receivables, which may or may not be truly collectible. Notes receivable may be vehicles for stockholders to infuse cash into the company and may act more as long-term loans or capital.
- *Pension Liabilities*—Underfunded or overfunded pension accounts can be other areas of adjustment and sometimes controversy. If a company's pension trust is underfunded, the company typically shows a liability account, which it reduces with annual contributions. Amounts can be highly controversial, depending on actuarial assumptions. If a company's pension benefit plan is overfunded, the company rarely shows the surplus as an asset, but some would argue that the company should do so for valuation purposes. In some cases, if a discounted cash flow method is used, the recognition of overfunding may be reflected through a lower level of contributions in the future.

Other Normalizing Adjustments

Many other adjustments may be encountered either to approximate economic reality or to adjust accounting numbers for comparative purposes. If any of them become a controversy over which the court or the lawyer desires insight beyond what is presented in the evidence or in this book, the references at the end of this chapter should be helpful. Following are some other subjects that sometimes give rise to normalization adjustments:

- Treatment of intangible assets, including leaseholds and other intangibles
- Capitalization versus expensing of various costs
  - Usually, a sizable current expenditure that is expected to produce benefits in future periods is recorded as an asset (capitalized). Later, as the asset is disposed of or used up, its balance is reduced and an expense recorded. If the expenditure is inconsequential or if no future benefits are apparent, the current expenditure might be immediately recorded as an expense. Obviously, judgments regarding the materiality of or the future benefits associated with the current expenditures can differ across entities, resulting in inconsistent accounting treatments.
- Timing of recognition of revenues and expenses
  - Contract work (for example, work in progress, contingent fee work, percentage of completion or completed contract terms)
  - Installment sales
  - Actual or contingent liabilities (for example, guarantees, warranties)
  - Prior-period adjustments
- Deferred maintenance (for example, routine maintenance neglected)

- Treatment of interests in affiliates
- Adequacy or deficiency of liabilities

All these and many others are discussed in the "Financial Statement Adjustment References" at the end of this chapter.

Control Adjustments

Control adjustments reflect changes that a control owner might make in the operation of the company, as opposed to adjustments in the presentation of actual operations or conditions. For the most part, this category of adjustments deals with financial relationships with insiders or members of a control group. To some extent, this category could include adjustments for perceived inefficiencies or excess costs.

Reasonable Compensation

The most frequent financial statement adjustment issue is reasonable compensation to control parties. "Compensation" in this context includes all payments and perquisites—salary, bonuses, stock and stock options, retirement plans, medical benefits, and expenses—that could be construed as personal benefits. Chapter 11 covers in more detail the adjustments for reasonable compensation.

Insider Transactions

Insider transactions that might be adjusted usually are payments for services at other than market rates or of dubious value. The most common of these are:

- Nonmarket rate rents or leases. If the related parties lease premises to the operating company, such leases often are not at market rates. This adjustment would involve restating the expense on the income statement at estimated market rent.
- Employment payments. If relatives or friends are on the payroll at more than the value of services rendered, an adjustment to eliminate or reduce that expense may be warranted.
- Planes, trains, and automobiles (not to mention boats). It is common to question the company's need for one or more airplanes, private passenger train cars, luxury automobiles, yachts, sailboats, condominiums, hunting lodges, and other retreats, although there are situations in which they are legitimate expenses. If these items are adjusted, this usually involves reducing or eliminating the income statement expenses and sometimes reclassifying the assets to other (nonoperating) assets rather than operating assets.

Note: There is a minority (but legitimate) school of thought that considers what we have just classified as control adjustments to be normalizing adjustments, even in a minority interest valuation where the minority holder cannot force the company policy to change. The reason for this is to put the subject company on a basis comparable to the guideline companies. The minority interest factor, if applicable, then is handled as a separate discount at the end of the valuation.[1]

Separating Operating Assets from Nonoperating and Excess Assets

Two primary reasons to separate operating assets from nonoperating and excess assets are:

- To make comparisons with other entities
- To consider adding some value for nonoperating or excess assets to the going-concern value of the company as an operating entity (If valuing on a minority interest basis, there may be little or no adjustment, for the minority owner cannot control disposal of the assets.)

Comparisons with Other Entities

If the analyst is using a market approach to valuation, the guideline companies and the subject company should be as comparable as possible to make the derived valuation ratios as valid as possible. Thus, valuation multiples derived from guideline companies can be applied to the operations of the subject company to derive a value as an operating company.

If the analyst is using an income approach, the operations should be valued separately from the nonoperating assets, using comparative industry data to help develop appropriate discount and/or capitalization rates for a well-defined industry operation comparable to others.

Similarly, if comparing various financial ratios with industry averages and guideline companies, the comparisons are most meaningful if the companies are as purely comparable as possible.

While this separation is very nice for purity in comparisons, it leaves the sticky problem of how to treat the assets separated from the operating assets.

1. David Laro & Shannon Pratt, Business Valuation and Taxes: Procedure, Law and Perspective (John Wiley & Sons, 2005).

Treatment of Nonoperating and Excess Assets

If nonoperating or excess assets are separated, then the controversial question arises about how to treat them for valuation purposes. Even the question about whether something should be classified as a nonoperating or excess asset may be controversial.

It may be possible to find public holding companies whose major assets are similar to the nonoperating assets of the subject firm. In this event, relevant valuation multiples derived from the public companies may be used to value the nonoperating assets of the subject firm.

However, much of the answer to the appropriate treatment of nonoperating or excess assets depends on the question of whether the valuation is carried out on a controlling or minority basis. If the valuation is performed on a controlling basis, each asset may be valued assuming its highest and best use. Therefore, if it is worth more in liquidation than in use, the estimated net proceeds from liquidation may be added to the value as an operating company.

But even on a controlling basis, if valuing as a going concern, some policies that the control owners follow might not be followed by others, and there may be a debate about the existing control owners' policies. Treatment then becomes a matter of negotiation, and there are no hard-and-fast rules.

If valuing on a minority basis, the minority owner can have little or no influence over devoting the assets to their highest and best use, so little or no value usually is added beyond the present value of whatever income the assets may be expected to produce.

Cash versus Accrual Accounting

Cash accounting means that both revenues and expenses are recognized when they are received or paid. Accrual accounting means that revenues are recognized when they are earned and expenses are recognized when they are incurred. For example, under accrual accounting, a legal fee is recorded as revenue when it is earned, even though it may not be collected until a year later. Under cash accounting, the revenue would not be recognized until the cash was in hand.

Valuation is based primarily on accrual accounting, reflecting revenues earned and expenses incurred. Certain private companies, including many professional practices, keep their books on a cash basis. If so, for valuation purposes, it usually is necessary to convert the cash basis financial statements to accrual basis financial statements before proceeding with the valuation process.

If there is a buy-sell agreement tied to cash basis accounting, then there may be an issue about whether or not to convert to an accrual basis for valuation purposes. This dispute often arises in marital dissolutions. In this case, it generally is necessary to consult precedential case law in the relevant jurisdiction to assess whether the court will consider the buy-sell agreement to be controlling, or what impact it might have, if any.

Illustrative Financial Statement Adjustments

Exhibits 12-1 and 12-2 show typical presentations reflecting a few examples of financial statement adjustments discussed in this chapter. In some cases, the text of the report may contain more explanation of each adjustment than the brief footnote in the exhibit, especially if the adjustment is significant. In other cases, it may be necessary to obtain the analyst's working papers or to question the analyst to gain a more complete explanation.

Exhibit 12-1
Meteor Manufacturing, Inc.
Adjustments to Income Statements

	20X3	20X4	20X5	20X6	20X7
Net Income as Reported	$240,000	$250,000	$150,000	$280,000	$300,000
Plus: Loss from Fire[a]			80,000		
Plus (Minus): Adjustment to Cost of Goods Sold to convert from LIFO to FIFO[b]	15,000	(10,000)	10,000	20,000	30,000
Plus: Adjustments to Widget Machines Depreciation[c]	7,000	7,000	8,000	10,000	
Plus: Compensation Adjustment[d]	60,000	70,000	75,000	80,000	100,000
Adjusted Net Income	$322,000	$317,000	$323,000	$390,000	$430,000

a. Physical damage was $250,000 and business interruption loss estimated at $150,000, totaling $400,000, offset by $300,000 insurance. Loss $100,000 less $20,000 tax effect (at 20% effective tax rate) equals $80,000.
b. Convert Meteor and guideline companies from LIFO to FIFO inventory basis, net of related tax effect.
c. To convert Meteor Manufacturing depreciation from five-year straight-line to seven-year straight-line (net of related tax effect) to conform to average industry practice.
d. To adjust CEO compensation to level typical for similar executives, net of 20% effective tax rate.

Exhibit 12-2
Meteor Manufacturing, Inc.
Adjustments to Balance Sheet

	As Reported	Adjustments	As Adjusted
Assets			
Cash	$ 50,000		$ 50,000
Accounts Receivable	30,000		30,000
Inventory[a]	200,000	$100,000	300,000
Total Current Assets	$280,000	$100,000	$380,000
Plant and Equipment	200,000		200,000
Less: Accumulated Depreciation[b]	(100,000)	30,000	(70,000)
Net Plant and Equipment	$100,000		$130,000
Total Assets	$380,000	$130,000	$510,000
Liabilities and Equity			
Accounts Payable	$ 60,000		$ 60,000
Long-term Debt	200,000		
200,000			
Total Liabilities	$260,000		
$260,000			
Stockholders' Equity	120,000	$130,000	250,000
Total Liabilities and Equity	$380,000		$510,000

a. To adjust inventory from LIFO to FIFO basis to put book value on a basis comparable to guideline companies.
b. To convert Meteor portion of accumulated depreciation from a five-year life to a seven-year life to put book value of plant and equipment on an accounting basis comparable to guideline companies.

In the example of income adjustments, the tax effect is accounted for in each individual line item; another acceptable treatment is to adjust the pretax income and take the tax adjustment as an additional line item.

Income Statement Adjustments

- *Nonrecurring Event Adjustment.* Adjustment a for the fire is an example of an adjustment for a nonrecurring event. This adjustment would be made whether valuing a controlling or minority interest, to make the statements more representative of ongoing earning power and more directly comparable to industry averages and guideline companies.

- *Inventory Adjustment.* Adjustment b is to put the subject company on a FIFO inventory basis for direct comparison with guideline companies (those that were on LIFO also were adjusted). This adjustment would be made whether valuing a controlling or minority interest if necessary for comparative purposes.
- *Depreciation Adjustment.* Adjustment c decreases the annual depreciation charged to one-seventh of the purchase cost per year from one-fifth of the purchase cost per year (thus increasing adjusted net income) to conform to industry-average and guideline company depreciation policies for comparative purposes. This adjustment would be made whether valuing a controlling or minority interest if appropriate for comparative purposes.
- *Compensation Adjustment.* Adjustment d removes compensation that is above industry averages for comparable executives from expenses, thus increasing the adjusted net income (net of the income tax effect of the lower expense). This adjustment would be typical if valuing on a controlling interest basis on the assumption that a control owner could replace the CEO with an equally competent executive for the amount of compensation substituted on the income statement. This adjustment normally would not be made if valuing on a minority interest basis because the minority stockholder could not cause this expense reduction to occur, and the expense saving would not, in fact, inure to the corporation, thus overstating income available to the benefit of all stockholders if this adjustment were made.[2]

Balance Sheet Adjustments

- *Inventory Adjustment.* Adjustment a adds the LIFO reserve shown on the company's financial statement footnotes back to the inventory account so that it is reflected as if on a FIFO basis. This adjustment would be made for comparative purposes whether valuing on a controlling or minority interest basis.
- *Depreciation Adjustment.* Adjustment b decreases the accumulated depreciation, thus increasing the net plant and equipment to what it would be on a seven-year depreciation schedule for Meteor Manufacturing. The purpose is to put the book value for comparative purposes on the same basis as guideline companies and industry averages.

Note: Although these adjustments may bring the asset accounts closer to the fair market value, this is *not* their purpose. The assets normally would be further analyzed

2. Some analysts would make this adjustment for comparability even when valuing a minority interest, and then reflect the compensation disparity in a minority interest discount.

if an asset approach to value were to be used. These adjustments are for comparative purposes, to make meaningful financial ratio comparisons between the subject company and guideline companies or industry averages and to make it possible to use meaningful valuation multiples in the market approach.

For example, note that the adjustments more than doubled the book value of the equity. If the industry average price to book value ratio were 2.0, applying that ratio to the unadjusted book value would give a misleading indication of value for the equity of less than half what it should be based on the adjusted balance sheet.

Financial Statement Adjustment References

Fishman, Jay, et al. 2009. "Review and Adjustment of the Financial Statements." In *PPC's Guide to Business Valuations,* 4-18 to 4-31.

Internal Revenue Service. 1994. "Closely Held Corporations—Financial Analysis." In *IRS Valuation Guide for Income, Estate and Gift Taxes,* 6-1 to 6-14.

Penman, Stephen H. 2001. *Financial Statement Analysis & Security Valuation.* New York: McGraw-Hill.

Pratt, Shannon P. 2003. "Adjustments to Financial Statements." In *Business Valuation Body of Knowledge,* 2d Ed., 205–07.

Pratt, Shannon P., and Alina V. Niculita. 2008. "Analyzing Financial Statements" (including bibliography of both books and articles) and "Financial Statement Analysis" (as part of sample case). In *Valuing a Business,* 5th Ed., 129–52, 510–12.

Wild, John J., K. R. Subramanyam, and Robert F. Halsey. 2006. *Financial Statement Analysis,* 9th Ed. New York: McGraw-Hill.

Chapter 13

Comparative Financial Statement Analysis

This chapter originally was contributed by Don Shannon, a professor of accounting at DePaul University and also a practicing business valuation analyst. In the latest edition, this chapter has been updated by Angelina McKedy, a senior analyst with Shannon Pratt Valuations. The chapter provides a useful reference for those seeking some insight into the calculation and interpretation of financial statement analysis techniques commonly used in business valuation.

As Dr. Shannon points out, while financial statement analysis is an exercise based on historical data, it can help in formulating expectations about the future. These expectations are the basis for valuation, and they fall largely into two categories: ***levels of operating performance*** *(for example, various measures of profitability) and* ***risk*** *(the certainty or uncertainty of achieving expected results).*

The valuation report should use financial statement analysis as a guide to formulating these expectations. In the income approach, for example, the financial statement analysis should help formulate both the expected performance results (projections) and the degree of risk that affects the discount or capitalization rate to be applied to those projections. In the market approach, the financial statement analysis should give insight into both expected growth and risk, both of which should have an impact on the choice of multiples to be applied to the subject company's fundamental data.

The reviewer should keep in mind that all financial statement analysis discussed in this chapter is ***based on book values after normalizing adjustments and not on market values.*** *Thus, to the extent that companies in an industry are more homogenous with respect to factors such as the age of their assets and their accounting practices, the more meaningful the comparative financial analysis will be.*

Finally, every financial ratio is not so important as every other financial ratio in any given valuation. The nature of the industry and/or the specific company may make certain ratios particularly relevant to the valuation at hand. Some ratios, although computed in a standardized ratio template, may be irrelevant and require no discussion at all. Hopefully, the analyst identifies those financial analysis factors that are significant to the valuation of the subject company and explains how those factors affect the numbers (for example, projections, discount and capitalization rates, valuation multiples) that lead to the valuation conclusion. If the analysis is not connected, at some point in the report, to the steps leading to the value conclusion, it is a rather empty exercise.

—S.P.

Introduction

Most of us have had the experience of trying to evaluate the bewildering maze of attributes associated with complex products such as homes, automobiles, or major appliances. How can a serious comparison be made? In financial markets, ownership interests are the "products" and the financial reports are the brochures used to describe those products. Financial statement analysis, or ratio analysis, simply provides a means of organizing the relevant financial information to facilitate an orderly comparison.

While a number of useful facts tend to be the natural by-products of this analysis, the analyst is primarily concerned with projecting *future* corporate performance. Hopefully, a close review of a company's past performance will highlight its relevant characteristics, resulting in more insightful forecasts of the company's future.

Financial statement or ratio analysis involves comparison. Seldom is the value of an individual ratio meaningful in its own right. However, the changes in the value of a ratio from one period to another, or over a succession of periods, can be very informative. Likewise, the comparison of one company's ratios to the ratios of its competitors or to industry benchmarks also can be very informative.

The financial information used in this chapter has been taken from three steel companies.

Tools of Financial Statement Analysis

Analysts use several groups of tools to make meaningful comparisons, for the subject company over time and against other specific companies and/or industry averages. These tools are discussed in this chapter in the following order:

- **Horizontal analysis**—Comparison of a company's numbers between one year and the next.
- **Trend analysis**—Description of changes in a company's numbers over several successive years.
- **Vertical analysis**—Comparisons among specific companies and/or between the subject company and industry averages for the same time period. Vertical

analysis employs the tool called *common-size statements*:
  - **Common-size income statements.** Every line item is expressed as a percent of sales.
  - **Common-size balance sheets.** Every line item is expressed as a percent of total assets.
- **Profitability ratios**—Various measures of profitability expressed as a percentage of some financial statement item.
- **Liquidity measures**—Ratios among various financial statement items indicative of the firm's short-term liquidity.
- **Long-term solvency measures**—Ratios indicating a firm's financial risk over the long term.

Various authors and analysts may classify these tools by different groups and different names, but the essence of the ideas is quite consistent from one writer to another.

One caveat is worth mentioning at the outset. There is no single set of ratios, published by reporting services or used by analysts, that establishes a universally accepted convention. Different reporting services furnish different ratios, although they may have the same name, such as "profit divided by total assets." Risk Management Associates provides the ratio "profit *before* taxes divided by total assets," while Dun & Bradstreet provides "profit *after* taxes divided by total assets." Furthermore, a ratio bearing the same name may be calculated in a slightly different way by different services or analysts. Also, the different services may furnish information for different points in time or for different time intervals.

For the comparisons to be meaningful, they must be computed the same way for the subject company as for the companies used for comparison. The report should include a definition of each ratio used, either in the text or in an exhibit or appendix.

Horizontal Analysis

Exhibit 13-1 shows the balance sheets and income statements for Nucor Corporation for two years. No doubt an analyst could spot some interesting shifts in these numbers, as they stand, from 2006 to 2007.

However, Exhibit 13-2 shows that after applying horizontal analysis, the significant shifts in the information become more apparent.

Horizontal analysis involves displaying the amounts and percentages of the changes in the numbers from one year to the next. For example, accounts receivable decreased by $87,108, which represents a decrease of 22.5 percent.

Notice in the balance sheet that total assets increased by $242,162 or 8.1 percent. There was a nearly proportional increase in inventory. However, other current assets and net plant and equipment increased proportionately more than did the total assets.

These increases were partially offset by the significant drop in accounts receivable.

In the income statement, net income dropped by $30,774, or 10.5 percent. This was due in part to the 0.8 percent drop in sales accompanied by the 0.4 percent increase in cost of sales and a 1.8 percent increase in selling, general, and administrative expenses. These three shifts were responsible for a decline in the operating income of $48,671. This decline was partially offset by a significant increase in the nonoperating income and less tax expense.

No doubt the analyst might have gleaned these observations from the presentations in Exhibit 13-1. However, showing the percentages of the change together with the respective dollar amounts (as in Exhibit 13-2) simply makes it easier to establish what has happened over the interval.

Of course these observations, per se, are not answers; they simply raise questions. Why did these shifts take place? What might the underlying causes for these current shifts imply about the future? Are these transient changes or are similar changes likely to persist?

Horizontal analysis does not provide all the answers. However, it does help the analyst identify important questions.

Trend Analysis

Trend analysis is a variation of horizontal analysis. Instead of focusing on changes from one year to the next, trend analysis describes changes over several successive years using one of three popular methods. Trends can be analyzed on the basis of ratios (as in Exhibit 13-4) or as absolute numbers (as in Exhibit 13-5).

Exhibit 13-3 shows the sales figures for Nucor Corporation and Oregon Steel Mills Inc. for four years.

Nucor's sales are 4.5 to 5.5 times greater than Oregon's sales. This difference in size makes it difficult to determine which company has enjoyed the greater sales growth over the entire interval, each year relative to the base year, by simply reviewing the dollar amounts.

The first method is demonstrated in Exhibit 13-4. This exhibit shows the data from Exhibit 13-3 expressed as percentages of the base year, 12/31/04. (For example, Oregon's figure of 125.5 percent for 12/31/07 is calculated by dividing 892,583 by 710,971 and multiplying by 100.)

Once the figures have been converted in this fashion, it becomes apparent that Oregon's sales growth exceeded that of Nucor (although in 2006 the reverse was true).

The second and third methods for describing trends will be illustrated using Oregon's sales figures from 1998 through 2007 as shown in the first three columns of Exhibit 13-5. (The "period" is simply an alternative way to identify the year. Zero is the

Exhibit 13-1
Nucor Corporation Two-Year Balance Sheet and Income Statement

Balance Sheet (000$)	**Nucor Corporation**	
	12/31/07	**12/31/06**
Cash and Marketable Securities	$ 308,696	$ 283,381
Accounts Receivable	299,244	386,352
Inventory	435,884	397,048
Other Current Assets	85,643	58,727
Total Current Assets	$1,129,467	$1,125,508
Net Plant and Equipment	2,097,078	1,858,875
Total Assets	$3,226,545	$2,984,383
Total Current Liabilities	$ 486,897	$ 524,453
Long-Term Debt	215,450	167,950
Other Liabilities	169,250	139,362
Total Liabilities	$ 871,597	$ 831,765
Retained Earnings	$2,016,856	$1,795,276
Other Equity	338,092	357,342
Shareholders Equity	$2,354,948	$2,152,618
Total Liabilities and Equity	$3,226,545	$2,984,383

Income Statement (000$)	**Nucor Corporation**	
	12/31/07	**12/31/06**
Sales	$4,151,232	$4,184,497
Cost of Goods Sold	3,591,783	3,578,941
Gross Margin	$ 559,449	$ 605,556
Selling, General and Administrative Expenses	147,973	145,409
Operating Income	$ 411,476	$ 460,147
Nonoperating Income	3,832	35
Income Before Taxes	$ 415,308	$ 460,182
Income Taxes	151,600	165,700
Net Income	$ 263,708	$ 294,482

Exhibit 13-2
Nucor Corporation Horizontal Analysis of Balance Sheet and Income Statement

Balance Sheet	Nucor Corporation	
	Amount of Change	% Change
Cash and Marketable Securities	$ 25,315	8.9%
Accounts Receivable	(87,108)	−22.5%
Inventory	38,836	9.8%
Other Current Assets	26,916	45.8%
Total Current Assets	$ 3,959	0.4%
Net Plant and Equipment	238,203	12.8%
Total Assets	$242,162	8.1%
Total Current Liabilities	$ (37,556)	-7.2%
Long-Term Debt	47,500	28.3%
Other Liabilities	29,888	21.4%
Total Liabilities	$ 39,832	4.8%
Retained Earnings	$221,580	12.3%
Other Equity	(19,250)	−5.4%
Shareholders Equity	$202,330	9.4%
Total Liabilities and Equity	$242,162	8.1%

Income Statement	Nucor Corporation	
	Amount of Change	% Change
Sales	$ (33,265)	−0.8%
Cost of Goods Sold	12,842	0.4%
Gross Margin	$ (46,107)	−7.6%
Selling, General and Administrative Expenses	2,564	1.8%
Operating Income	$ (48,671)	−10.6%
Nonoperating Income	3,797	10,848.6%
Income Before Taxes	$ (44,874)	−9.8%
Income Taxes	(14,100)	−8.5%
Net Income	$ (30,774)	−10.5%

Exhibit 13-3
Nucor Corporation and Oregon Steel Mills Inc. Sales Figures in Dollars

SALES (000$)	12/31/07	12/31/06	12/31/05	12/31/04
Oregon Steel Mills Inc.	892,583	768,558	772,815	710,971
Nucor Corporation	4,151,232	4,184,497	3,647,030	3,462,045

Exhibit 13-4
Nucor Corporation and Oregon Steel Mills Inc.
Sales Figures in Percentages

SALES (Base = 04)	12/31/07	12/31/06	12/31/05	12/31/04
Oregon Steel Mills Inc.	125.5%	108.1%	108.7%	100.0%
Nucor Corporation	119.9%	120.9%	105.3%	100.0%

earliest year and nine is the most recent.)

The second method is to fit a trend line to the data. The points in Exhibit 13-6 represent Oregon's sales by period. The dotted line has been fitted through these points (using regression analysis, a statistical technique). The numerical values associated with the line are shown in the fourth column of Exhibit 13-5. The important thing to recognize about this method is that it presumes sales are increasing by a constant *amount* each period.

The third method is to calculate a growth rate. In Exhibit 13-5, the initial sales figure (for period zero) is 230,192, and the final figure (for period nine) is 892,583. Mathematically, it is easy to find the percentage increase that, if applied period by period, will cause the initial amount to grow to the final amount. In this example, this percentage, or growth rate, is 16.25 percent.

The fifth column of Exhibit 13-5 shows the numerical values associated with the "smooth" transition from the initial figure to the final figure. Exhibit 13-7 is identical to Exhibit 13-6 with the addition of a solid line representing this "smooth" transition. The important thing to recognize about this method is that it presumes sales are in-

Exhibit 13-5
Oregon Steel Mills Sales Figures

(1)	(2)	(3)	(4)	(5)
Year	**Period**	**Oregon's Sales**	**Adding the Constant Amount of 69,928.9**	**Applying the Growth Rate of 16.25%**
98	0	**230,192**	296,472	**230,192**
99	1	331,234	366,401	267,600
00	2	489,357	436,330	311,086
01	3	397,722	506,259	361,640
02	4	679,823	576,188	420,409
03	5	838,268	646,117	488,728
04	6	710,971	716,046	568,149
05	7	772,815	785,975	660,477
06	8	768,558	855,903	767,809
07	9	**892,583**	925,832	**892,583**

Exhibit 13-6
Trend of Oregon Steel Mills Sales

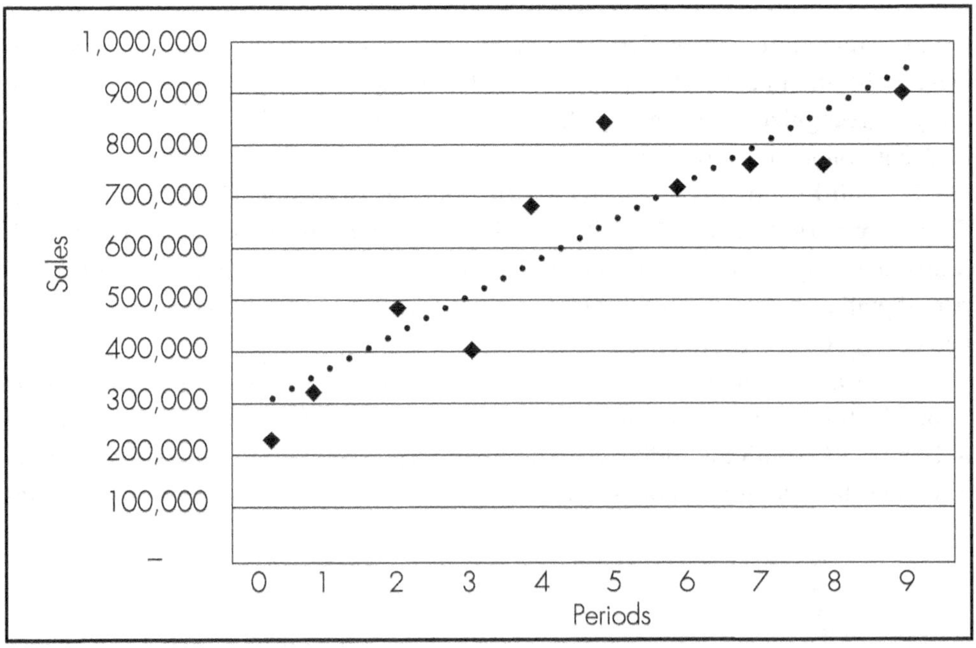

Exhibit 13-7
Growth of Oregon Steel Mills Sales

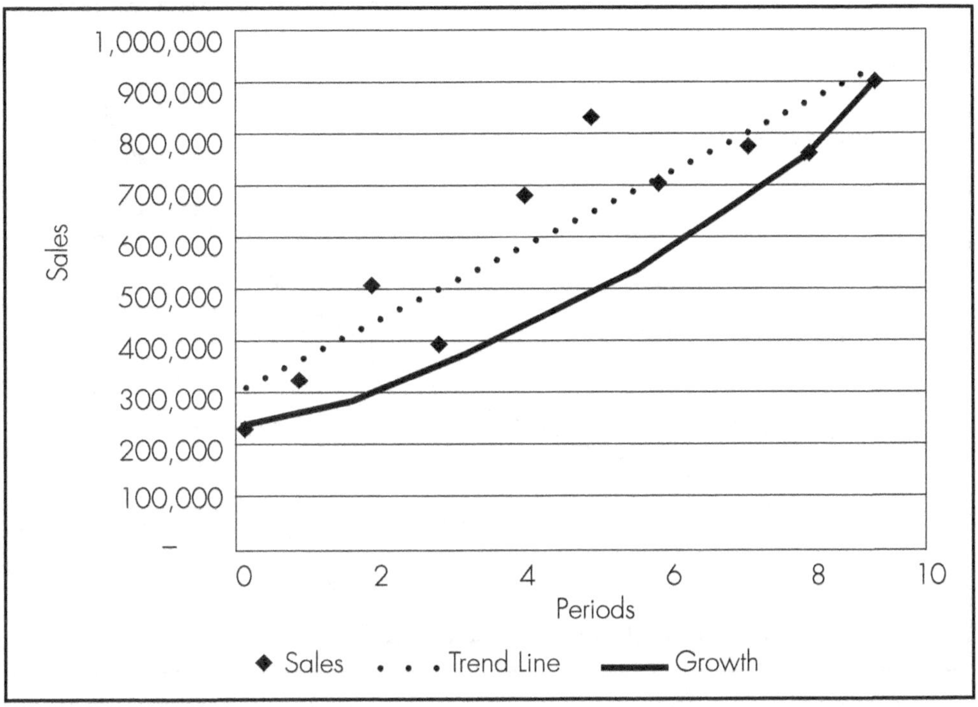

creasing by a constant *percentage* each period.

It is worth noting that trend lines and growth rates are calculated from historical data. Care should be exercised when using these characterizations of historical information to project future performance. Very different inferences can result.

Exhibit 13-8 shows the results of carrying the trend line and the growth path out to the 15th period. Obviously, the pattern of sales after period 10 implied by using the constant percentage growth rate exceeds that implied by using the constant dollar trend line. This trend line technique can be used to analyze changes over time in many different financial variables.

For presentation purposes, trends can be presented either graphically or in tabular form.

Vertical Analysis

Exhibit 13-9 shows the balance sheets and income statements for L.B. Foster, Oregon, and Nucor for 2007. Again, owing to differences in the size of these companies, it is not particularly easy to identify similarities or differences in their financial pro-

Exhibit 13-8
Trend and Growth of Oregon Steel Mills Sales

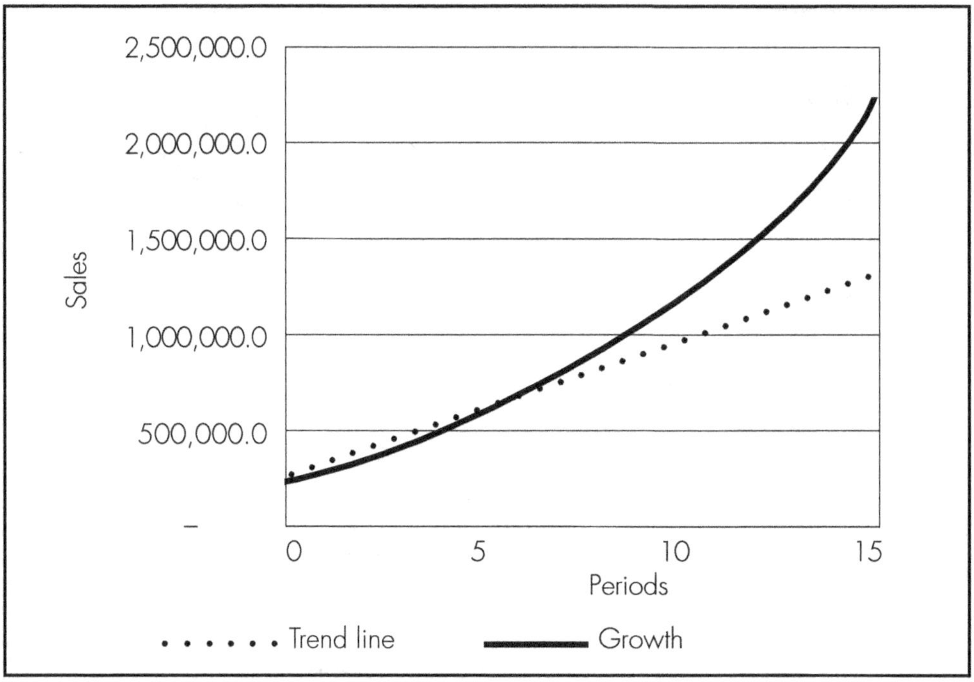

files simply by looking at the dollar amounts.

Vertical analysis involves displaying the amounts as percentages of total assets, or total sales, to eliminate the effects of size. The resulting statements frequently are referred to as "common-sized" statements. Exhibit 13-10 restates the financial statements in terms of these percentages. For example, L.B. Foster's accounts receivable were 39.6 percent of its total assets (= 47,311 ÷ 119,434) and its cost of goods sold was 85.3 percent of its sales (= 187,222 ÷ 219,475).

Given this perspective, one might immediately notice a number of things. In the balance sheets, while plant and equipment make up approximately 65 percent of Oregon's and Nucor's total assets, Foster's plant and equipment represent only 17.6 percent of its total assets. This could indicate that Foster's assets are older and more fully depreciated. (Other explanations might be plausible.) Oregon also relies more heavily on debt financing than do either Foster or Nucor.

In the income statements, the cost of goods sold percentages do vary somewhat across the firms, but the relatively large differences in operating income percentages are explained, for the most part, by selling, general, and administrative expenses.

Exhibit 13-11 is the same as Exhibit 13-10 except that 2007 industry statistics have been added for the Standard Industrial Classification (SIC) code—3312. Foster,

Exhibit 13-9
L.B. Foster, Oregon Steel Mills, and Nucor Corporation
2007 Balance Sheet and Income Statement

Balance Sheet (000$)	L.B. Foster 12/31/07	Oregon 12/31/07	Nucor 12/31/07
Cash and Marketable Securities	$ 874	$ 9,044	$ 308,696
Accounts Receivable	47,311	67,254	299,244
Inventory	36,418	196,279	435,884
Other Current Assets	614	20,188	85,643
Total Current Assets	$ 85,217	$292,765	$1,129,467
Net Plant and Equipment	21,060	638,609	2,097,078
Other Assets	13,157	62,596	–
Total Assets	$119,434	$993,970	$3,226,545
Total Current Liabilities	$ 30,326	$252,516	$ 486,897
Long-Term Debt	13,829	270,440	215,450
Other Liabilities	1,785	89,607	169,250
Total Liabilities	$ 45,940	$612,563	$ 871,597
Retained Earnings	$ 40,002	$125,479	$2,016,856
Other Equity	33,492	255,928	338,092
Shareholders Equity	$ 73,494	$381,407	$2,354,948
Total Liabilities and Equity	$119,434	$993,970	$3,226,545

Income Statement (000$)	L.B. Foster 12/31/07	Oregon 12/31/07	Nucor 12/31/07
Sales	$219,475	$892,583	$4,151,232
Cost of Goods Sold	187,222	781,789	3,591,783
Gross Margin	$ 32,253	$110,794	$ 559,449
Selling, General and Administrative Expenses	24,940	56,189	147,973
Operating Income	$ 7,313	$ 54,605	$ 411,476
Nonoperating Income	1,731	4,196	3,832
Interest Expense	1,631	38,485	–
Income Before Taxes	$ 7,413	$ 20,316	$ 415,308
Income Taxes	3,036	8,387	151,600
Net Income	$ 4,377	$ 11,929	$ 263,708

Exhibit 13-10
L.B. Foster, Oregon Steel Mills, and Nucor Corporation
Common-Size Balance Sheet and Income Statement

Balance Sheet (%)	**L.B. Foster 12/31/07**	**Oregon 12/31/07**	**Nucor 12/31/07**
Cash and Marketable Securities	0.7%	0.9%	9.6%
Accounts Receivable	39.6%	6.8%	9.3%
Inventory	30.5%	19.7%	13.5%
Other Current Assets	0.5%	2.0%	2.7%
Total Current Assets	71.4%	29.5%	35.0%
Net Plant and Equipment	17.6%	64.2%	65.0%
Other Assets	11.0%	6.3%	0.0%
Total Assets	100.0%	100.0%	100.0%
Total Current Liabilities	25.4%	25.4%	15.1%
Long-Term Debt	11.6%	27.2%	6.7%
Other Liabilities	1.5%	9.0%	5.2%
Total Liabilities	38.5%	61.6%	27.0%
Retained Earnings	33.5%	12.6%	62.5%
Other Equity	28.0%	25.7%	10.5%
Shareholders Equity	61.5%	38.4%	73.0%
Total Liabilities and Equity	100.0%	100.0%	100.0%

Income Statement (%)	**L.B. Foster 12/31/07**	**Oregon 12/31/07**	**Nucor 12/31/07**
Sales	100.0%	100.0	100.0%
Cost of Goods Sold	85.3%	87.6	86.5%
Gross Margin	14.7%	12.4%	13.5%
Selling, General and Administrative Expenses	11.4%	6.3%	3.6%
Operating Income	3.3%	6.1%	9.9%
Nonoperating Income	0.8%	0.5%	0.1%
Interest Expense	0.7%	4.3%	0.0%
Income Before Taxes	3.4%	2.3%	10.0%
Income Taxes	1.4%	0.9%	3.7%
Net Income	2.0%	1.3%	6.4%

Exhibit 13-11
L.B. Foster, Oregon Steel Mills, and Nucor Corporation
Common-Size Balance Sheet and Income Statement
with 2007 Industry Statistics

Balance Sheet (%)	L.B. Foster	Oregon	Nucor	RMA	Integra*
Cash and Marketable Securities	0.7%	0.9%	9.6%	6.7%	8.7%
Accounts Receivable	39.6%	6.8%	9.3%	30.9%	23.9%
Inventory	30.5%	19.7%	13.5%	25.1%	16.2%
Other Current Assets	0.5%	2.0%	2.7%	3.3%	3.6%
Total Current Assets	71.4%	29.5%	35.0%	65.9%	52.4%
Net Plant and Equipment	17.6%	64.2%	65.0%	25.6%	33.1%
Other Assets	11.0%	6.3%	0.0%	8.4%	14.5%
Total Assets	100.0%	100.0%	100.0%	100.0%	100.0%
Total Current Liabilities	25.4%	25.4%	15.1%	43.0%	27.1%
Long-Term Debt	11.6%	27.2%	6.7%	17.4%	25.9%
Other Liabilities	1.5%	9.0%	5.2%	7.2%	7.1%
Total Liabilities	38.5%	61.6%	27.0%	67.6%	60.1%
Retained Earnings	33.5%	12.6%	62.5%		
Other Equity	28.0%	25.7%	10.5%		
Shareholders Equity	61.5%	38.4%	73.0%	32.4%	39.9%
Total Liabilities and Equity	100.0%	100.0%	100.0%	100.0%	100.0%

Income Statement (%)	L.B. Foster	Oregon	Nucor	RMA	Integra*
Sales	100.0%	100.0%	100.0%	100.0%	100.0%
Cost of Goods Sold	85.3%	87.6%	86.5%	76.5%	78.2%
Gross Margin	14.7%	12.4%	13.5%	23.5%	21.8%
Selling, General and Administrative Expenses	11.4%	6.3%	3.6%	17.5%	18.9%
Operating Income	3.3%	6.1%	9.9%	6.0%	2.9%
Nonoperating Income	0.8%	0.5%	0.1%		0.1%
Interest Expense	0.7%	4.3%	0.0%		1.7%
Income Before Taxes	3.4%	2.3%	10.0%	4.7%	1.3%
Income Taxes	1.4%	0.9%	3.7%		0.5%
Net Income	2.0%	1.3%	6.4%	____	0.8%

*Most recent industry data available from Integra report is for year 2006.

Oregon, and Nucor all belong to that industry. Risk Management Associates (RMA) and Integra Information (Integra) compile industry statistics. At the end of this section is a brief listing of commonly used industry resources and the strengths and weaknesses of each. This additional information confirms some of the prior observations and mitigates others. For example, Foster's plant and equipment percentage still is low relative to the industry statistics displayed. On the other hand, Oregon's and Nucor's plant and equipment appear to be somewhat excessive. This last fact would not have been evident without the industry comparison.

Oregon's debt and equity proportions seem to be in line with those of the industry aggregates. Both Foster and Nucor appear to rely less heavily on debt and more heavily on equity than the industry does as a whole. Again, this fact would not have been evident without the industry comparison.

In the income statements, all three companies show higher percentages for cost of goods sold than do the industry aggregates.

In addition, all the companies' selling, general, and administrative expenses are lower than the industry's comparable data. Foster's operating income percentage is only about half that of the industry information provided by RMA and in line with the industry information provided by Integra as a whole. Surely an analyst needs to ask some additional questions concerning this state of affairs for Foster and the differences in the industry information being reported.

For Oregon, its operating profits seem to be roughly in line with the RMA statistics (which include only the larger firms) and double the industry average as reported by Integra. Once again an analyst needs to dive deeper into the data being reported and the possible differences. Part of the reason Oregon may be in line with the RMA data may be that Oregon includes some expenses in its cost of goods sold that other firms in the industry tend to include in their selling, general, and administrative expenses.

At this point, we have completed the descriptions of horizontal, trend, and vertical analyses. These are the tools analysts use to make comparisons over time, across firms, or against industry standards. While doing so, we have briefly suggested the types of insights that might result while using these tools in a particular context. The discussion has been purposely kept to a minimum.

Most valuation reports will include some explicit or implicit form of trend analysis of sales, other major expenses, capital expenditures, working capital requirements, and so forth. Also, many reports will include vertical analysis as the analyst attempts to compare the subject company to potential comparable companies of somewhat different size or to industry norms. Horizontal analysis from one year to the next may not be formally presented in the report, but it must be conducted in the analyst's mind or working papers, for the analyst must be cognizant of all significant changes that have taken place in the subject company over the recent past.

Perhaps the "art" of financial statement analysis is becoming apparent. In a practical context, there is no clear stopping point. The analyst can always continue to probe, search for explanation, comment. No doubt the reader could find other issues worthy of comment that were not covered here. There is always more that can be done. Perhaps the ultimate judgment is when to quit.

With this in mind, we will turn to the analysis of a firm's profitability.

Analysis of Profitability

Information from the Nucor Corporation will be used to illustrate the analysis of profitability. Selected information from Exhibit 13-9 is repeated as Exhibit 13-12 for this purpose.

Exhibit 13-12
Selected Nucor Corporation Financial Information

Nucor	**12/31/07**
Total Assets	$3,226,545
Total Liabilities	$ 871,597
Equity	$2,354,948
Sales	$4,151,232
Net Income	$ 263,708

This limited amount of information is sufficient to begin to dissect Nucor's performance.

One popular measure for gauging a company's profitability is its *return on assets* (ROA), the amount of income it generates compared to the amount invested in its

Exhibit 13-13
Nucor Corporation Return on Assets

RETURN ON ASSETS	=	TURNOVER	x	PROFIT MARGIN
$\frac{\text{Net Income}}{\text{Total Assets}}$	=	$\frac{\text{Sales}}{\text{Total Assets}}$	x	$\frac{\text{Net Income}}{\text{Sales}}$
$\frac{263{,}708}{3{,}226{,}545}$	=	$\frac{4{,}151{,}232}{3{,}226{,}545}$	x	$\frac{263{,}708}{4{,}151{,}232}$
8.17%	=	1.29 times	x	6.35%

total assets. As shown in Exhibit 13-13, Nucor's return on assets was 8.17 percent.

Return on assets can easily be decomposed into two separate factors: turnover and profit margin. *Turnover* is simply a measure of how efficiently the company can generate sales with the assets under its stewardship. *Profit margin* is the amount of income or profit per dollar of sales.

Nucor's profit margin per dollar of sales was 6.35 percent. Because Nucor's sales were 1.29 times larger than its total assets, its return on assets was 8.17 percent, which is 1.29 times as large as its profit margin of 6.35 percent.

It is important to note that companies can control the amount of assets they utilize and their profit margin. They cannot control sales. No doubt they can take steps to influence the amount of their sales—for example, modifying their selling, advertising, and promotion strategies. In the final analysis, however, the consumers or the marketplace will determine the level of sales.

The implications of the potential market reaction can easily be illustrated. Assume the starting point shown in Exhibit 13-14, which uses the same structure as

Exhibit 13-14
Hypothetical Return on Assets

RETURN ON ASSETS	=	TURNOVER	x	PROFIT MARGIN
Net Income / Total Assets	=	Sales / Total Assets	x	Net Income / Sales
240 / 2,400	=	3,600 / 2,400	x	240 / 3,600
10.0%	=	1.5 times	x	6.67%

Exhibit 13-13 but simpler, *hypothetical* numbers.

At this point, management might attempt to improve its return on assets by reducing its assets (see Exhibit 13-15, left side). Initially, the return on assets may increase. However, the market may react. The company may have cut its assets by granting less credit and reducing its receivables, or holding less inventory, or cutting back on the number of its delivery trucks, or eliminating a warehouse. All of these could easily produce market dissatisfaction and sales might fall. There are no guarantees.

Alternatively, management might attempt to increase its profit margin (see Exhibit 13-15, right side). Again, the return on assets initially may increase and, again, the market may react. The company may have increased its profit margin by increasing the price of its products or lowering their quality. Sales may well fall.

The purpose of this discussion was to show that the ideal or optimal levels of these

Exhibit 13-15
Effect of Asset Levels

USE FEWER ASSETS MAINTAIN PROFIT MARGIN	MAINTAIN ASSET LEVELS INCREASE PROFIT MARGIN
$\frac{240}{1,800} = \frac{3,600}{1,800} \times \frac{240}{3,600}$	$\frac{320}{2,400} = \frac{3,600}{2,400} \times \frac{320}{3,600}$
13.3% = 2.0 x 6.67%	13.3% = 1.5 x 8.88%
SALES MIGHT FALL	**SALES MIGHT FALL**
$\frac{180}{1,800} = \frac{2,700}{1,800} \times \frac{180}{2,700}$	$\frac{240}{2,400} = \frac{2,700}{2,400} \times \frac{240}{2,700}$
10.0% = 1.5 x 6.67%	10.0% = 1.125 x 8.88%
SALES MIGHT FALL EVEN FURTHER	**SALES MIGHT FALL EVEN FURTHER**
$\frac{160}{1,800} = \frac{2,400}{1,800} \times \frac{160}{2,400}$	$\frac{213.3}{2,400} = \frac{2,400}{2,400} \times \frac{213.3}{2,400}$
8.88% = 1.33 x 6.67%	8.88% = 1.0 x 8.88%

two principal ratios (turnover and profit margin) are not easy to discern. Predicting market reaction is a tricky proposition. For this reason, industry norms or aggregates are frequently referenced. Analysts want to know where a company stands relative to its peers. If the company in question has deviated too far from standard industry practice with respect to either of these two measures, then some explanation is in order. What caused the deviation? What are its likely consequences? Will it persist?

Returning to the Nucor case, recall that its return on assets was 8.17 percent in 2007. How does this compare with Nucor's past experience and how does it compare to industry benchmarks? Exhibit 13-16 summarizes information that can be used to answer these questions.

It appears that Nucor's 2007 return on assets of 8.17 percent is the end result of a gradual deterioration in the firm's profitability. Both its profit margin and its turnover have declined somewhat since 2003. However, Nucor appears to have a much higher return on assets than do current industry benchmarks. Its profit margin also is higher than the industry's and its turnover is in line with industry benchmarks.

The analyst might like to carry the investigation of the return on assets even further. Starting with the profit margin, the analyst might review common-size income statements over a series of years and compare these to industry norms. The

Exhibit 13-16
Nucor Corporation Profit Margin, Turnover, and Return on Assets 2003–2007

	NUCOR						
Return on Assets	**12/31/07**	**12/31/06**	**12/31/05**	**12/31/04**	**12/31/03**	**RMA**	**Integra**
Profit Margin (%)	6.35%	7.04%	6.80%	7.93%	7.62%		0.8%
Turnover (times)	1.29	1.40	1.39	1.51	1.49	1.5	1.54
Return on Assets (%)	8.17%	9.87%	9.47%	11.96%	11.32%		1.2%

Exhibit 13-17
Nucor Corporation Common-Size Income Statement 2003–2007

	NUCOR						
Income Statement (%)	**12/31/07**	**12/31/06**	**12/31/05**	**12/31/04**	**12/31/03**	**RMA**	**Integra**
Sales	100.00%	100.00%	100.00%	100.00%	100.00%	100.0%	100.0%
Cost of Goods Sold	86.52%	85.53%	86.07%	83.77%	83.74%	76.5%	78.2%
Gross Margin	13.48%	14.47%	13.93%	16.23%	16.26%	23.5%	21.8%
Selling, General and Administrative Expenses	3.56%	3.47%	3.30%	3.77%	3.81%	17.5%	28.9%
Operating Income	9.91%	11.00%	10.62%	12.46%	12.45%	6.0%	2.9%
Nonoperating Income	0.09%	0.00%	0.01%	0.03%	(0.45%)		
Income Before Taxes	10.00%	11.00%	10.63%	12.49%	12.00%	4.7%	1.3%
Income Taxes	3.65%	3.96%	3.83%	4.56%	4.38%		0.5%
Net Income	**6.35%**	**7.04%**	**6.80%**	**7.93%**	**7.62%**		**0.8%**

relevant data for such comparisons is given in Exhibit 13-17.

Over the past five years, Nucor's cost of goods sold has increased somewhat. It appears this increase is the principal reason for the decline in the profit margin. Additional effort would be required to ascertain whether this tendency is likely to continue into the future or possibly reverse.

Had there been erratic shifts in the firm's profit margins or any of its components, this type of analysis would have brought them to light.

Comparing Nucor's 2007 experience to the industry benchmarks shows that it is doing quite well, comparatively. Its net income before taxes is a higher percentage of its sales than is true for the industry as a whole. As mentioned previously, the fact that its cost of goods sold is a higher percentage of sales and its selling, general, and administrative expense is a lower percentage of sales for the industry as a whole may simply be partly because of the way Nucor classifies certain expenses. It would require further and perhaps more detailed investigation on the part of the analyst to ascertain why these differences exist.

The purpose of reviewing the common-size balance sheets over a series of years and the relevant industry benchmarks is to begin to ascertain which assets, if any, might be too high or too low. The relevant data for such comparisons is given in Exhibit 13-18.

As was found in the income statements, Nucor's common-size balance sheets have remained fairly stable over time. Just focusing on total current assets and net plant and equipment, it seems that Nucor maintains a smaller percentage of its total assets in current assets and a much larger percentage in net plant and equipment than is true for the rest of the industry. This observation, made for the year 2007 during the initial discussion of vertical analysis, seems to be applicable since at least 2003.

One limitation of the common-size balance sheets is that they simply relate assets to assets, that is, they relate each component asset to total assets. The concern here is with the relationship between assets and sales. Therefore, the analyst may refer to the component turnover measures that relate the component assets to sales, as shown in Exhibit 13-19.

Overall, Nucor is generating lower sales per dollar of total assets than is the rest of the industry. Its sales are 1.3 times its total assets (its total asset turnover is 1.3), which is lower than the RMA and Integra benchmarks. The receivable turnover measures are higher than the industry benchmarks, which indicates that these assets are smaller than assets that might be found for other companies in the industry, relative to their sales.

The opposite is true for the fixed-asset turnover measure. Nucor's fixed-asset turnover of 1.98 is significantly lower than the RMA and Integra industry benchmarks. Again, it would appear that Nucor's fixed assets are excessive. In other words, Nucor appears to be making less-efficient use of its assets than are its competitors.

Exhibit 13-18
Nucor Corporation Common-Size Balance Sheet 2003–2007

	NUCOR						
Balance Sheet (%)	**12/31/07**	**12/31/06**	**12/31/05**	**12/31/04**	**12/31/03**	**RMA**	**Integra**
Cash and Marketable Securities	9.57%	9.50%	3.99%	8.79%	5.09%	6.7%	8.7%
Accounts Receivable	9.27%	12.95%	11.17%	12.33%	12.89%	30.9%	23.9%
Inventory	13.51%	13.30%	14.73%	13.36%	12.14%	25.1%	16.2%
Other Current Assets	2.65%	1.97%	1.74%	1.70%	1.78%	3.3%	3.6%
Total Current Assets	35.01%	37.71%	31.62%	36.18%	31.90%	65.9%	52.4%
Net Plant and Equipment	64.99%	62.29%	68.38%	63.82%	68.10%	25.6%	33.1%
Other Assets	0.00%	0.00%	0.00%	0.00%	0.00%	8.4%	14.5%
Total Assets	100.00%	100.00%	100.00%	100.00%	100.00%	100.0%	100.0%

Exhibit 13-19
Nucor Corporation Turnover Ratios 2003–2007

	NUCOR						
Turnover Ratios (%)	**12/31/07**	**12/31/06**	**12/31/05**	**12/31/04**	**12/31/03**	**RMA**	**Integra**
Sales/Receivables (times)	13.87	10.83	12.46	12.22	11.53	7.1	6.48
Sales/Fixed Assets (times)	1.98	2.25	2.04	2.36	2.18	3.8	4.62
Total Asset Turnover (times)	**1.3**	**1.4**	**1.4**	**1.5**	**1.5**	1.5	1.54

This point has purposely been emphasized to encourage cautious interpretations of the numbers. Nucor's fixed assets indeed are high relative to it sales. Every measure previously discussed has so indicated. However, are these assets excessive? Perhaps not.

There is an alternative explanation. Perhaps Nucor's fixed assets are relatively new. Perhaps its fixed assets are "fresher" and have been used and depreciated less than the fixed assets of other firms in the industry. In this event, the low fixed-asset turnover measure probably should not be interpreted as a sign of too many fixed assets that simply are being used inefficiently, but rather as a potential competitive advantage for Nucor.

To summarize, Nucor's return on assets fell from nearly 12 percent in 2004 to a little more than 8 percent in 2007. This decline in Nucor's profitability for the most part was caused by a rising cost of goods sold and a slight decline in the total asset turnover. Despite this, in 2007 the firm is very much in line with and slightly higher than its industry's profitability benchmarks.

So far, in the discussion of a firm's profitability, the focus has been on the return on total assets. Before leaving the analysis of profitability, some attention should be given to return on equity. A firm's *return on equity* (ROE) is the amount of income it generates relative to its equity. As shown in Exhibit 13-20, Nucor's return on equity

Exhibit 13-20
Return on Equity and Debt to Equity

RETURN ON EQUITY	DEBT TO EQUITY
$\frac{\text{Net Income}}{\text{Equity}}$	$\frac{\text{Total Liabilities}}{\text{Equity}}$
$\frac{263{,}708}{2{,}354{,}948}$	$\frac{871{,}597}{2{,}354{,}948}$
11.20%	**0.37**

was 11.20 percent.

The debt to equity ratio also been calculated. The reason it has been calculated is because this ratio provides an important link between return on equity and return on assets. The simple formula in Exhibit 13-21 shows that for a given return on assets, the larger the debt to equity ratio, the larger the return on equity will be. In Nucor's case, its 2007 return on equity of 11.20 percent can be explained by multiplying its

Exhibit 13-21
Effect of Debt to Equity Ratio

$$\text{Return on Equity} = \text{Return on Assets} \times \left[1 + \frac{\text{Total Liabilities}}{\text{Equity}}\right]$$

$$11.20\% = 8.17\% \times 1.37$$

return on assets of 8.17 percent times one plus its debt-equity ratio of 0.37.

There are several reasons why the analyst should be concerned with the return on equity. First, it is the rate of return relevant to the owners, buyers, and sellers of firms. However, there is another important reason.

A firm's growth rate is determined by how much it earns on its equity and how much it reinvests. Firms with higher returns on equity that reinvest a larger proportion of their earnings will have higher growth rates, other things being equal.

As anyone familiar with valuation understands, a firm's projected future growth is a critical determinant of its value. Here we have suggested that:

- Return on assets is determined by (1) turnover and (2) profit margin,
- Return on equity is determined by the return on assets and (3) the debt to equity ratio, and
- Growth in net income is determined by return on equity (which is affected by many factors) and (4) how much the firm reinvests.

Thus the analyst should have a clear understanding of how these four factors have behaved in the past and the values that are likely to be sustained for these measures over future periods.

Analysis of Liquidity

The analysis of a firm's profitability is most important in determining its value. However, the analyst also should assess the firm's liquidity. Liquidity refers to a firm's ability to pay its bills on a timely basis and to meet unexpected needs for cash. Exhibit 13-22 includes some of the more popular ratios used to make this assessment for Nucor.

As shown in Exhibit 13-22, the numerator of the quick ratio includes cash and marketable securities and accounts receivable. These items are cash or can be converted into cash quickly. These near-cash assets are compared to the firm's current or short-term liabilities. When the value of the ratio is large, more near-cash assets are

Exhibit 13-22
Nucor Corporation Liquidity Ratios 2003–2007

Liquidity Ratios	NUCOR 12/31/07	12/31/06	12/31/05	12/31/04	12/31/03	RMA	Integra
Quick (times)	1.2	1.3	0.9	1.1	0.9	0.8	1.20
Current (times)	2.3	2.1	1.8	1.9	1.7	1.7	1.93
Sales/Inventory (times)	9.5	10.5	9.5	11.3	12.2		
Cost of Sales/Inventory (times)	8.2	9.0	8.1	9.5	10.3	4.7	7.44

QUICK RATIO

$$\frac{\text{Cash \& Securities + Receivables}}{\text{Current Liabilities}}$$

$$\frac{308{,}696 + 299{,}244}{486{,}897}$$

1.2

RECEIVABLE TURNOVER

$$\frac{\text{Sales}}{\text{Accounts Receivable}}$$

$$\frac{4{,}151{,}232}{299{,}244}$$

13.9

CURRENT RATIO

$$\frac{\text{Current Assets}}{\text{Current Liabilities}}$$

$$\frac{1{,}129{,}467}{486{,}897}$$

2.3

available to meet the firm's short-term obligations. By this measure, in 2007 Nucor was slightly more liquid than the RMA benchmark and in line with Integra benchmark measures of other firms in the industry.

The current ratio is similar to the quick ratio except that the numerator includes all current assets. This means inventory is counted as one of the assets that can be converted into cash. Because inventory takes longer to convert into cash than cash and marketable securities or accounts receivable, the current ratio is viewed as a "softer" measure of a firm's ability to meet its short-term obligations. Again, by this measure, in 2007 Nucor was more liquid than benchmark measures of other firms in the industry.

To take the analysis of liquidity a step further, the accounts receivable are analyzed more closely. Small turnover ratios (sales/receivables) indicate large receivable balances. Unduly large balances in this account may signal problems such as uncollectible accounts.

In Exhibit 13-22, another modification of the component turnover measures involves the inventory turnover. Often the inventory turnover measure is calculated with cost of goods sold in the numerator rather than sales. By eliminating the gross profit, which may vary from firm to firm, it is hoped that the modified inventory measure will give a more accurate indication of the number of times inventory is turned over during the year. In Exhibit 13-22, it was shown that Nucor's cost of sales to inventory measure was slightly higher than the industry's.

Analysis of Long-Term Solvency

Long-term solvency refers to a firm's ability to survive over an extended time period. Declining profitability and liquidity measures may be signals of a company's eventual bankruptcy. Analysts often look at two other ratios as well when analyzing solvency. These ratios are the debt to equity ratio and interest coverage. Exhibit 13-23 shows Nucor's values for these ratios.

The debt to equity ratio was described earlier when discussing the link between return on assets and the return on equity. It expresses the relationship between capital contributed by creditors and that contributed by owners. A large value for this ratio signals a firm's increasing principal and interest obligations and a corresponding increasing risk to creditors. A lower ratio generally indicates greater long-term financial safety. Nucor has a much lower debt to equity ratio based on its minimal reliance on debt. This may or may not be ideal and the analyst needs to understand what the optimal capital structure for a company in this industry might be.

The interest coverage ratio shows how many times a firm would be able to make its interest payments. A large value indicates that a borrower should have little difficulty meeting its interest obligations. For 2007 through 2003, Nucor had little or

Exhibit 13-23
Nucor Corporation Solvency Ratios 2003–2007

	NUCOR						
Solvency Ratios	**12/31/07**	**12/31/06**	**12/31/05**	**12/31/04**	**12/31/03**	**RMA**	**Integra**
Debt/Equity (times)	0.37	0.39	0.40	0.43	0.54	1.9	1.5
EBIT/Interest (times)	n/a	n/a	n/a	n/a	27.4	5.7	1.69

Interest Coverage

$$\frac{\text{Earnings Before Interest and Taxes}}{\text{Interest Expense}}$$

$$\frac{370{,}447}{13{,}515}$$

27.4

negligible interest expense. Apparently the bulk of its liabilities were noninterest-bearing. The calculation in Exhibit 13-23 uses information taken from Nucor's 2003 financial statements.

Nucor relies very little on debt financing. Barring some unforeseen deterioration in its profitability or liquidity or a major change in its capital structure, this company is at very little risk of becoming insolvent.

Industry Data Resources

Comparing subject companies and comparable companies to industry statistics is highly useful in analyzing financial statements. The following is a sample of several data resources that appraisers might use to make such comparisons and the strength and weaknesses of each resource:

Almanac of Business and Industrial Financial Ratios. Englewood Cliffs, NJ: Prentice Hall, updated annually.
Strengths: The *Almanac* breaks out industries into two groupings, all companies in Table I and profitable companies in the industry in Table II; this allows for less noise (or outliner) ratios analysis.
Weakness: The *Almanac* is based on corporate tax returns supplied by the IRS and the information typically has a three-year lag time; for example, the 2008 *Almanac* is based on 2004 and 2005 data.

Industry Norms and Key Business Ratios. New York: Dun & Bradstreet, Inc., updated quarterly.
Strengths: Information is based on both public and private companies that covers more than 800 lines of business, broken down into three size ranges by net worth for each SIC.
Weaknesses: Part of the Dun & Bradstreet databases; the cost associated with accessing the information can be high. Only covers 14 key ratios.

Integra Information's Online Industry and Benchmark Reports. Kennesaw, GA: Integra.
Strengths: *Integra* offers benchmarking reports based on five years of data and three years of data. It covers 900 industries and breaks out each industry into 13 different sales size ranges. It also covers more than 70 financial ratios.
Weaknesses: The *Integra* information is based on annual information and at times this information can take several months to be added to these databases.

RMA Annual Statement Studies. Philadelphia: Risk Management Associates, annual.
Strengths: *RMA* data covers more than 700 different industries; its company data includes privately owned company data. RMA also breaks out companies by sales size ranges.
Weaknesses: *RMA* data comes from member institutions (typically banks). Some of the industry groups may report only small or a few companies and one needs to determine if that truly captures an industry. The data also is based on companies applying for credit, which may indicate some financial need or distress.

There is a wide range of industry sources available and it is prudent to recognize the strengths and weaknesses of the resources that an appraiser chooses; it also may be fruitful to explore industry sources that were not utilized by an appraiser.

Summary

In this chapter we have examined horizontal, trend, and vertical analysis. We also have assessed the profitability, liquidity, and long-term solvency of an enterprise. Hopefully, the artful nature of this type of analysis and the judgment required in its execution have been satisfactorily communicated.

Again, the purpose of the analysis of historical financial statements is to call attention, in an organized manner, to questions whose resolution will assist the analyst in making projections about the financial *future* activity of an enterprise. Appraisers analyze the past and present to gain a better understanding of the future. Value is all about future expectancy. The word *future* is used in Revenue Ruling 59-60 15 times!

Comparative Financial Statement Analysis References

Books

Fishman, Jay, et al. 2009. "Financial Statement Analysis." In *PPC's Guide to Business Valuations,* 4-32 to 4-36.

Internal Revenue Service. 1994. "Closely Held Corporations—Financial Analysis." In *IRS Valuation Guide for Income, Estate and Gift Taxes,* 6-1 to 6-14.

Penman, Stephen H. 2001. *Financial Statement Analysis & Security Valuation.* New York: McGraw-Hill.

Pratt, Shannon P. 2003. "Financial Statement Analysis." In *Business Valuation Body of Knowledge,* 2d Ed., 205–14.

Pratt, Shannon P., and Alina V. Niculita. 2008. "Financial Statements Ratio Analysis" and "Financial Statement Analysis" (as part of sample case). In *Valuing a Business,* 5th Ed., 152–70, 510–12.

Wild, John J., K. R. Subramanyam, and Robert F. Halsey, 2006. *Financial Statement Analysis,* 9th Ed. New York: McGraw-Hill.

Databases

Almanac of Business and Industrial Financial Ratios, CCH Inc., 4025 W. Peterson Ave., Chicago, IL 60646, (800) 248-3248, tax.cchgroup.com.

Industry Norms and Key Business Ratios, The D&B Corp., 103 JFK Pkwy., Short Hills, NJ 07078, (973) 921-5500, www.dnb.com.

Integra Data and Report, Integra Information: A Division of MicroBilt Corp., (800) 780-2660, www.integrainfo.com.

RMA Annual Statement Studies, The Risk Management Association, 1801 Market St., Ste. 300, Philadelphia, PA 19103, (215) 446-4000, (Fax) (215) 446-4101, www.rmahq.org.

Chapter 14

Economic and Industry Analysis

This chapter in the first edition was contributed by Don Shannon, professor of accounting at DePaul University. The chapter was updated by Kimberly Linebarger, a financial analyst with Shannon Pratt Valuations. She has contributed to various publications concerning business valuation. The chapter provides useful insight into the issue of economic and industry analysis as it applies to business valuation.

Economic and industry analysis is a vital part of a business valuation, for a company cannot be analyzed in a vacuum. The focus of the economic and industry sections of a business valuation is on the broad context in which the subject company operates and in which it is likely to continue to operate. The Internal Revenue Service recognizes the importance of the broader context. Revenue Ruling 59-60 requires consideration of "the economic outlook in general and the condition and outlook of the specific industry in particular" when the fair market value of a business is being determined.

The purpose of examining the economy and industry is to temper or add to the conclusions that might be reached from the analysis of financial statements alone. The value of a company should benefit from the current perception that the industry or economy will be prosperous and should be impaired if expectations of a decline in the industry or economy are strong. For example, a particular company may have been enjoying increasing sales in an industry that is expected to die off in the near future. The future prospects for the relevant industry, its anticipated growth rate, and current opinions about the factors that might promote or impede this growth need to be understood by the analyst.

As is true with the analysis of financial statements, economic and industry analysis requires the valuation professional to make a vast array of choices about which factors to review, emphasize, pursue in greater detail, and find relevant to the case under consideration. The conventions for economic and industry analysis, if any, are even more loosely defined than they are for financial statement analysis. The valuation professional possesses extra latitude in structuring the economic and industry analysis segment of a valuation report.

The professional must be able to present the relevant factors that will logically impact the subject company. With the analysis of economic and industry conditions, the business valuation professional in most cases will interpret and summarize analyses that have been prepared by others. This chapter will outline some of the basic components found, in some form, in the typical economic and industry analysis.

The sources of information used often in this segment will be broadly described and a few specifically identified. The intent is to be illustrative rather than comprehensive.

From the valuation perspective, it is important to understand first the recent history and current state of the economy and industry, and then the current perception of their probable future prospects.

National Economy—Recent Status

The sales of all firms depend to a greater or lesser extent on the vigor of the overall economy. There is an enormous amount of readily available information concerning the U.S. economy. The Federal Reserve Bank of St. Louis is one of the most comprehensive sources of information. The Bank of St. Louis offers three online databases that provide current and historical data on U.S. economic time series. The information is easily viewed and downloadable into commonly used applications. When used in conjunction, these three databases offer a wealth of information.

- Federal Reserve Economic Data (FRED) offers current and revised historical time series.
- Archival Federal Reserve Economic Data (ALFRED) offers economic time series available as of a specific date in history.
- Federal Reserve Archival System for Economic Research (FRASER) provides links to historical economic statistical publications.

The analyst must be able to identify relevant information that will clearly impact, whether positively or negatively, the subject company. The following is a sampling of key measures that might be referenced.

- **Gross Domestic Product.** Available from the Bureau of Economic Analysis Survey of Current Business. It represents the total output of goods and services produced by labor and property located in the United States.
- **Federal Reserve Board Index of Industrial Production.** This provides the

current amount of industrial production relative to a base-year period. The index is presented for a large number of component parts of the economy, giving the analyst a convenient measure of the relative growth for the specific element of interest.

- **Selected labor, personal income, and population statistics.** These explain the extent to which the nation's citizens are employed and provide the analyst with some insight into consumers' ability to purchase goods and services.
- **Consumer Price Index.** This shows the extent to which the nation's growth is the result of real increases in output rather than higher prices being paid for the same amount of goods.
- **Capacity utilization.** This explains the level of manufacturers' activity and may be used to detect inflationary pressure.
- **Key interest rates.** These provide the costs of borrowing funds for consumption and investment.

The gross domestic product (GDP) is the broadest measure of economic activity used to determine where the economy has been, is, and is likely to go.[1] It is calculated by summing the expenditures of the four major participants in the system—households (personal consumption expenditures), businesses (gross private domestic investment), the foreign sector (net exports of goods and services), and the government (government consumption expenditures and gross investment). These four major participants can be broken down further. Exhibit 14-1 shows GDP in billions of current dollars for the year 2007.

The Consumer Price Index is an often-used measure of inflation. The index represents the goods and services purchased for consumption by a population. A rise in inflation indicates a general rise in the price and costs of a given good over time. For example, with all other things being equal, if the subject company experiences an inflationary increase in its product costs but does not increase its product prices at the general rate of inflation, this will negatively impact the subject company's gross margin and consequently its cash flows. Exhibit 14-2 presents information from the all-urban consumer price index.

Using these and other measures, the analyst should be able to review the economy's recent performance as a helpful introduction to the projections of its future performance.

Exhibit 14-1
2007 GDP in Billions of Current Dollars

	Billions of Dollars	Percentage Change
Personal Consumption Expenditures	9,732.7	2.9%
Gross Private Domestic Investment	2,129.1	–4.8%
Net Exports of Goods and Services	(708.6)	-
Government Consumption Expenditures and Gross Investment	2,690.6	2.0%
Gross Domestic Product	**13,843.8**	2.2%
Personal Consumption Expenditures		
Durable	1,078.4	4.7%
Nondurable	2,833.5	2.4%
Services	5,820.8	2.8%
Gross Private Domestic Investment		
Fixed Investment	2,123.5	–2.9%
Change in Private Inventories	5.6	-
Net Exports of Goods and Services		
Exports	1,641.4	8.0%
Imports	(2,350.0)	1.9%
Government Consumption Expenditures and Gross Investment		
Federal	976.2	1.7%
State and Local	1,714.5	2.2%
Gross Domestic Product*	**13,843.8**	2.2%

*Does not add precisely because of rounding.

Source: Bureau of Economic Analysis, *Survey of Current Business* (March 2008).

Exhibit 14-2
All-Urban Consumer Price Index
1982-84 = 100

			Percent Change	
Year	December	Annual Average	Dec-Dec	Ave-Ave
1997	161.3	160.5	1.7%	2.3%
1998	163.9	163.0	1.6%	1.6%
1999	168.3	166.6	2.7%	2.2%
2000	174.0	172.2	3.4%	3.4%
2001	176.7	177.1	1.6%	2.8%
2002	180.9	179.9	2.4%	1.6%
2003	184.3	184.0	1.9%	2.3%
2004	190.3	188.9	3.3%	2.7%
2005	196.8	195.3	3.4%	3.4%
2006	201.8	201.6	2.5%	3.2%
2007	210.0	207.3	4.1%	2.8%

Source: Bureau of Labor Statistics, "Table Containing History of CPI-U U.S. All Items Indexes and Annual Percent Changes from 1913 to Present."

National Economy—Outlook

What is a reasonable estimate of the magnitude of change in the nation's economic activity that an analyst might expect? Over the relevant past, the GDP, measured in real terms, has expanded at a rate of 2.2 percent to 3 percent per year on average. During strong expansions, the pace of the growth may increase to 5 percent or more for brief periods. During severe recessions, real GDP actually can decline for an extended period.

This range of national economic activity may appear somewhat inconsequential and may seem to have only a relatively small impact on a company's sales. However, even small changes in sales can significantly impact a company's profits. As a preliminary matter, it is important to distinguish between two types of costs or expenses: (1) fixed costs that remain constant over different levels of sales and (2) variable costs that tend to fluctuate, in total, with sales. Firms with larger proportions of fixed costs generally experience larger profit swings. The presence of fixed costs *amplifies* the impact a percentage change in sales will have on the percentage change in profits.

Exhibit 14-3 demonstrates this fact. All three firms initially have profits of $2. From this position the effects of a 1 percent rise or fall in sales is shown. The profits of Firm A, with no fixed costs, also rise or fall by 1 percent. On the other hand, the profits of Firm C, with $25 of fixed costs, rise or fall by 13.5 percent. (Firm B is an intermediate case.)

Exhibit 14-3
Impact from Variable versus Fixed Costs

	Initial	Up	Down
Firm A			
Sales	100.0	101.0	99.0
Variable Costs	98.0	99.0	97.0
Fixed Costs	0.0	0.0	0.0
Profit	2.0	2.0	2.0
Percentage Change		**1.0%**	**–1.0%**
Firm B	Initial	Up	Down
Sales	100.0	101.0	99.0
Variable Costs	90.0	90.9	89.1
Fixed Costs	8.0	8.0	8.0
Profit	2.0	2.1	1.9
Percentage Change		**5.0%**	**–5.0%**
Firm C	Initial	Up	Down
Sales	100.0	101.0	99.0
Variable Costs	73.0	73.7	72.3
Fixed Costs	25.0	25.0	25.0
Profit	2.0	2.3	1.7
Percentage Change		**13.5%**	**–13.5%**

Because most firms have substantial levels of fixed costs, the analyst needs to be alert to any potential change in overall economic activity and aware of the likely impact this change may have on the sales and profits of the subject company. One way to forecast economic fluctuations is to study leading indicators, which are a series of measurements that typically go down or up before the GDP does. Most often, the valuation analyst will defer to the judgment of economic analysts. Several publications provide forecasts for the U.S. economy. Among those are:

- *The Economic Report of the President,* prepared by the U.S. Council of Economic Advisors
- *Economic Indicators,* prepared by the U.S. Council of Economic Advisors
- *National Economic Trends,* prepared by the Federal Reserve Bank of St. Louis
- *Standard & Poor's Trends and Projections,* published by Standard & Poor's
- *Economic Outlook Update,* published by Business Valuation Resources
- *National Economic Review,* published quarterly by Mercer Capital

Also, a number of business periodicals, such as *Business Week, Forbes, Fortune, Barron's,* and *The Wall Street Journal,* are good sources of timely information on the national economy.

After reviewing the aforementioned data (with, of course, selected emphasis) and reading informed forecast reports prepared by economic analysts (taking care to note any issues that are receiving special attention), the valuation analyst should be in a good position to give his or her synopsis of the prevailing assessment of the current state of the economy and its prospects over the near future.

Regional Information

In many cases, a company's operations may be significantly affected by the economies of one or more states or regions. In those instances, the analyst should acquire some knowledge of the economic climate within these areas.

Fortunately, the Bureau of Economic Analysis (BEA) offers access to many regional economic indicators called BEA's Regional FACT Sheets (BEARFACTS) on its Web site. The GDP information shown in Exhibit 14-1 is broken down by state. Exhibit 14-4 shows the gross state product information for 10 of the 50 states in billions of current dollars for the year 2006.

Another potential barometer of the relative well-being of a state is the total personal income earned by its residents. The national measure of personal income also is available by state. Exhibit 14-5 shows the personal income of 10 of the 50 states for the year 2006. Again, the data shown in Exhibits 14-4 and 14-5 are available for many years and can be used by the analyst to detect trends in the state economies of interest.

Banks and universities frequently provide useful regional analyses and outlooks. For example, the Federal Reserve Bank prepares periodic analyses of business and economic trends for each district in its respective region. In many cases, these appear in periodicals, such as the *Regional Review* (Federal Reserve Bank of Boston), the *Quarterly Review* (Federal Reserve Bank of Minneapolis), the *Chicago Fed Letter,* etc.

Exhibit 14-4
Per Capita Real GDP by State, 2006*

	GDP	Rank by State
United States	37,714	
Delaware	59,288	1
Connecticut	50,332	2
Massachusetts	46,721	3
New York	46,617	4
New Jersey	44,885	5
...		
Oklahoma	29,545	46
Montana	27,942	47
Arkansas	27,875	48
West Virginia	24,748	49
Mississippi	24,062	50

*Advance estimate

Source: U.S. Bureau of Economic Analysis

Exhibit 14-5
2006 Personal Income

	Per Capita	Total (Thousands)
United States	$36,794	10,978,053,000
District of Columbia	$58,830	34,440,167
Connecticut	$51,600	179,974,214
New Jersey	$46,813	404,473,847
Massachusetts	$46,305	298,363,148
Maryland	$43,889	245,878,837
...		
New Mexico	$29,346	56,870,351
Utah	$29,243	75,598,342
Arkansas	$28,473	79,845,017
West Virginia	$27,935	50,472,339
Mississippi	$27,072	78,419,024

Source: U.S. Bureau of Economic Analysis

International Information

Often a company will be affected by international economies. Nowadays, even small companies may have some international operations. The amount of information concerning international operations is rapidly growing. The valuation professional should be aware of any international factors that may affect the subject company. The availability and sources of information will depend on the specific country. The following are broad sources of information:

- *International Economic Trends,* prepared by the Federal Reserve Bank of St. Louis
- *International Comparison Program,* prepared by The World Bank
- *The Country Data Gateway,* available from The PRS Group
- *The World Federation of Exchanges Annual Report & Statistics,* available online

The analyst should be able to find more specific information through basic research concerning the precise country. The country's government offices and public firms currently operating within the country often will provide useful information.

Industry—General Data

Having completed their review of the national economy, most analysts will turn their attention to providing an assessment of the recent status of, and forecast for, a particular industry. To obtain a deeper understanding of the factors facing the industry and a clearer sense of its prospects, the analyst will turn to sources designed to provide this type of information. Many of these sources are very extensive and very insightful. They usually provide a review of the industry's recent status before, or in conjunction with, making their forecasts. Some publications that provide industry forecasts are:

- *Standard & Poor's Industry Surveys,* published by Standard & Poor's+
- *Industry Valuation Update,* published by Business Valuation Resources
- *The Cost of Capital Resources, Individual Reports & Statistics,* published by Morningstar
- *Industry Profiles,* published by First Research
- *Industry Growth Outlook Report,* published by Integra Information

The analyst also should review business periodicals (*Business Week, Forbes, Fortune, Barron's,* and *The Wall Street Journal*) for industry-relevant information.

Trade associations are very important sources of information, which should be referenced when studying specific industries. Frequently, these associations collect financial information from their members and publish interesting composite financial data in their periodicals. Also, they publish general information about their industries and provide insiders' views on the issues that might impact their industries' outlook. Descriptions of these associations, their publications, and how to contact them can be found in the *Encyclopedia of Associations,* published by Gale.

Exhibit 14-6 has been included to show the differences in future growth rates that exist across industries. Four sets of industry composite data as well as the GDP and the Personal Consumption Deflator, an inflation indicator, are shown from Integra Information's *Industry Growth Outlook Report* for 2006. A review of this data shows the range of future growth differences that can exist across industries. The forecasted growth rate across the industries presented for 2007 range from -0.50 percent to 2.8 percent.

While studying a particular industry, the analyst should keep in mind the end objective of this effort. The analysis is being conducted to see how the subject company is and will be affected by the various industry trends. For example, how would the subject company be affected by increases in the prices of the raw materials it uses, new technology, changes in population demographics, increased foreign competition, inflation, and so on?

The broader industry perspective should give the analyst a reasonable basis for answering questions of this nature. It should help the analyst see how to modify the conclusions reached from the analysis of the subjective company's financial statements, if any such modification is warranted.

Industry—Composite Company Data

In addition to studying the industry issues, trends, and prospects, the analyst should understand the industry profile. What are the typical patterns found in the financial statements of firms in the industry? What is a characteristic turnover ratio, profit margin, debt to equity ratio, current ratio, etc.? Some major sources of this type of composite data are:

- *Almanac of Business and Industrial Financial Ratios,* published by CCH
- *Annual Statement Studies,* published by The Risk Management Association
- *Industry Norms & Key Business Ratios,* prepared by Dun & Bradstreet
- *Integra Information Industry Reports,* published by Integra Information

Exhibit 14-6
Selected Historical and Forecasted Revenue Growth Rates

	SIC# 4724	SIC# 3716	SIC# 1311	SIC# 3312		
	NAICS# 561510	NAICS# 336213	NAICS# 211111	NAICS # 324199 331111 331221 331112		
	Travel Agencies	Motor Homes Manufacturing	Crude Petroleum and Natural Gas Extraction	Blast Furnaces and Steel Mills	GDP	PCE Deflator
Historical						
2004	3.50%	10.40%	19.00%	53.60%	6.90%	2.70%
2005	4.60%	3.90%	29.30%	6.70%	6.40%	2.90%
2006	4.70%	9.30%	12.90%	-0.50%	6.80%	3.10%
Forecasted						
2007	2.80%	1.00%	–0.50%	0.30%	4.40%	2.70%
2008	3.60%	6.00%	–3.60%	1.70%	4.70%	2.10%
2009	3.70%	4.00%	–4.00%	6.10%	5.20%	2.20%

Notes:

(a) Integra utilizes proprietary econometric models to deliver its industry-specific sales growth data, which is updated every six months. The sales growth rates are developed using: (1) a historical database derived from government and private sources and (2) macroeconomic forecasts of the U.S. economy provided by INFORUM, a leader in forecasting and modeling. Depending on the level of detailed information available, aggregated sales growth rates may be applied to related industries.

(b) Gross Domestic Product (GDP) is a measure of the total production of goods and services in the U.S. economy. The GDP forecast information is provided by INFORUM.

(c) Personal Consumption Expenditure (PCE) Deflator. The PCE Deflator is an index of the prices of goods and services purchased by people resident in the United States. The PCE deflator information is provided by INFORUM.

Source: All Integra Information Reports are owned by Integra Information, a division of MicroBilt Corporation, and are protected by U.S. copyright laws. All rights reserved. Used with permission. Please visit www.integrainfo.com for more information.

Exhibit 14-7 has been included to show the differences that exist across industries. Four sets of industry composite data are shown from Integra Information's *5-year Industry Reports* for 2006. Even a cursory review of the common-size statements reveals major differences across these industry groupings. In the balance sheets, current assets range from 33 percent to 57.6 percent, fixed assets from 14.8 percent to 37.6 percent, and long-term debt from 18.4 percent to 24.7 percent of total assets. In the income statements, the gross margin percentages range from 16.6 percent to 66 percent, and the profit before taxes ranges from 1.1 percent to 13 percent of sales.

After studying one or more reports on the industry outlook, relevant trade association publications, selected commentaries from business periodicals, and the industry composite data described in this section, the analyst should have a clear understanding of the measures that are considered important benchmarks for the particular industry under review.

It is important for the user of industry benchmarks to understand the following:

- The North American Industry Classification System (NAICS) has replaced the Standard Industrial Classification (SIC) system used to determine a company's industry designation. The SIC system had been criticized for having too many dissimilar products grouped together under one industry heading. At this time, most publications present both SIC and NAICS codes.
- Many companies have varied product lines. Companies are sorted into industries according to their primary product lines. In many cases, the primary product line accounts for less than a majority of a company's sales.
- There is no central agency that assigns NAICS codes or SIC codes, but rather they are assigned based on information provided by the company itself.
- The benchmark may have been derived from a small selection of firms.
- The benchmark may include data from companies with extreme characteristics.

For these and similar reasons, composite industry measures should be used with some caution. When provided, statistics that reveal the ranges of these measures should be reviewed. Wide ranges may be the result of including dissimilar operations in the composite. Also, it is desirable (although not always possible) to study the changes in an industry's benchmarks over a full business cycle.

Additionally, to the extent possible, an industry composite should be calculated from the data of companies that are roughly the same size as the subject company.

Exhibit 14-7
Selected Industry Common-size Financial Statements and Ratios

	SIC# 4724	SIC# 3716	SIC# 1311	SIC# 3312
				NAICS# 324199 331111 331221 331112
	NAICS# 561510 Travel Agencies	NAICS# 336213 Motor Homes Manufacturing	NAICS# 211111 Crude Petroleum and Natural Gas Extraction	Blast Furnaces and Steel Mills
Balance Sheet (%)				
Current Assets	45.2%	57.6%	33.0%	51.5%
Fixed Assets	37.0%	37.6%	14.8%	34.9%
Other Assets	3.6%	0.8%	2.9%	3.1%
Total Assets	100.0%	100.0%	100.0%	100.0%
Current Liabilities	36.2%	26.5%	23.7%	29.1%
Long-term Debt	18.4%	20.6%	20.8%	24.7%
Other Liabilities	2.7%	5.2%	9.1%	5.3%
Total Liabilities	59.1%	52.4%	55.5%	59.3%
Equity	40.9%	47.6%	44.5%	40.7%
Income Statement (%)				
Revenue	100.0%	100.0%	100.0%	100.0%
Gross Margin	24.9%	16.6%	66.0%	17.6%
Operating Expenses	23.3%	13.8%	52.5%	15.0%
Operating Income	1.6%	2.8%	13.5%	2.6%
Pretax Income	1.3%	1.5%	13.0%	1.1%
Net Income	0.8%	0.9%	8.0%	0.7%
Selected Ratios				
Return on Equity	4.5%	4.8%	9.8%	2.2%
Return on Assets	1.8%	2.3%	4.4%	0.9%
Current Ratio	1.25	2.17	1.40	1.77
Quick Ratio	0.97	0.96	1.16	0.99
Debt/Equity	1.45	1.10	1.25	1.46
Notes:	Year Ending:	2006		
	Sales Range:	All		

Source: All Integra Information Reports are owned by Integra Information, a division of MicroBilt Corporation, and are protected by U.S. copyright laws. Please visit www.integrainfo.com for more information.

Summary

The analysis of the financial statements of a particular company tends to be somewhat introspective. Economic and industry analysis calls for a more encompassing point of view. Many complex relationships must be assessed simultaneously.

The analyst needs to understand the recent *past* performance of the national, regional, or international economy, how the industry under review has reacted to recent shifts in the economy, and how the subject company has reacted to recent shifts in the performance of that industry. Next, the analyst needs to understand the current perception of the probable future direction of the economy and how the industry will react to any future shifts. Then, the analyst must determine how the subject company may be affected by such industry reactions.

In the process of reviewing the appropriate data and reading relevant reports, the analyst should be able to discern which factors pertaining to the subject industry require emphasis. Focusing on these factors should result in more reliable statements about the outlook for the subject company.

Chapter 15

Discounts and Premiums

Very often the biggest money issue in a valuation of a business or business interest is not the basic value of the entity, but what discounts and/or premiums should or should not be applied, at either the entity or the shareholder level, and in what magnitudes.

Generally, the two biggest issues are:

- *Minority/control.* Should there be a minority (lack of control) discount or a control premium? If so, how much?
- *Lack of marketability.* Should there be a discount for lack of marketability (illiquidity)? If so, how much?

These two factors, taken together, can easily make the value of a minority interest less than half the value of a proportionate share of the value of the business as a whole.

Other discounts or premiums that sometimes come into play at the entity level include:

- Key person discount
- "Portfolio" discount (for unattractive combination of assets or operations; lack of synergy between/among the various components)
- Trapped-in capital gains discount
- Litigation risk
- Environmental risk

Other discounts or premiums at the shareholder level may include:

- Voting versus nonvoting shares
- Blockage discount

Discounts and premiums have no meaning until the base to which they are applied (for example, the level of value) is clearly defined. To assist the reader's conceptual thinking about the various base values to which premiums or discounts might be applied, Exhibit 15-1 presents a business appraiser's traditional view of the levels of value, emphasizing the ownership characteristics of minority/control and marketability. (This is Exhibit 2-1, repeated here for the reader's convenience.)

Distinguishing the Minority Factor from the Marketability Factor

Twenty-five years ago, it was common practice to combine the minority and marketability factors into a single discount.[1] Over the past couple of decades, however, it has become more common to distinguish these two related factors and to quantify the impact of each separately, one in a discount for lack of marketability (DLOM), the other in a discount for lack of control (DLOC).[2] This results in a "multiplicative" rather than "additive" result, which can been seen in Exhibit 15-1 where a 20 percent lack of control and 45 percent marketability discount results in a 56 percent effective discount ($10.00 control share is $4.40 per nonmarketable share) and not 65 percent (20 percent plus 45 percent).

Today, the distinction between the concepts and quantification of the minority and marketability factors is recognized in the courses of all the professional business valuation organizations discussed in Chapter 30, "Business Valuation Standards and Credentials," and has been encouraged by the U.S. Tax Court. A 1982 estate tax decision articulated the distinction very clearly:

> In their arguments, neither petitioner nor respondent clearly focuses on the fact that two conceptually distinct discounts are involved here, one for lack of marketability and the other for lack of control. The minority shareholder discount is designed to reflect the decreased value of shares that do not convey control of a closely held corporation. The lack of marketability discount, on the other hand, is designed to reflect the fact that there is no ready market

1. While not as common today, a combined discount may nonetheless be determined by the courts. *See, e.g.*, Janda v. Comm'r, T.C. Memo. 2001-24 (Feb. 2, 2001) (40% combined discount); Estate of Mitchell v. Comm'r, T.C. Memo. 1997-461 (1997), *vacated by* 250 F.3d 696 (9th Cir. 2001), *reaff'd on remand by* T.C. Memo. 2002-98 (April 9, 2002) (35% combined discount); Estate of Magnin v. Comm'r, T.C. Memo. 2001-31 (Feb. 12, 2001) (60% combined discount); Estate of Deputy v. Comm'r, T.C. Memo. 2003-176 (June 13, 2003) (30% combined discount); Temple v. United States, 2006 U.S. Dist. LEXIS 16171 (E.D. Tex. 2006).

2. *See, e.g.*, Hess v. Comm'r, T.C. Memo. 2003-251 (Aug. 20, 2003) (25% DLOM; 15% DLOC); Estate of Green v. Comm'r, T.C. Memo. 2003-348 (Dec. 29, 2003) (35% DLOM; 17% DLOC); Estate of Thompson v. Comm'r, T.C. Memo. 2004-174 (July 26, 2004) (30% DLOM; 15% DLOC).

Exhibit 15-1
"Levels of Value" in Terms of Characteristics of Ownership

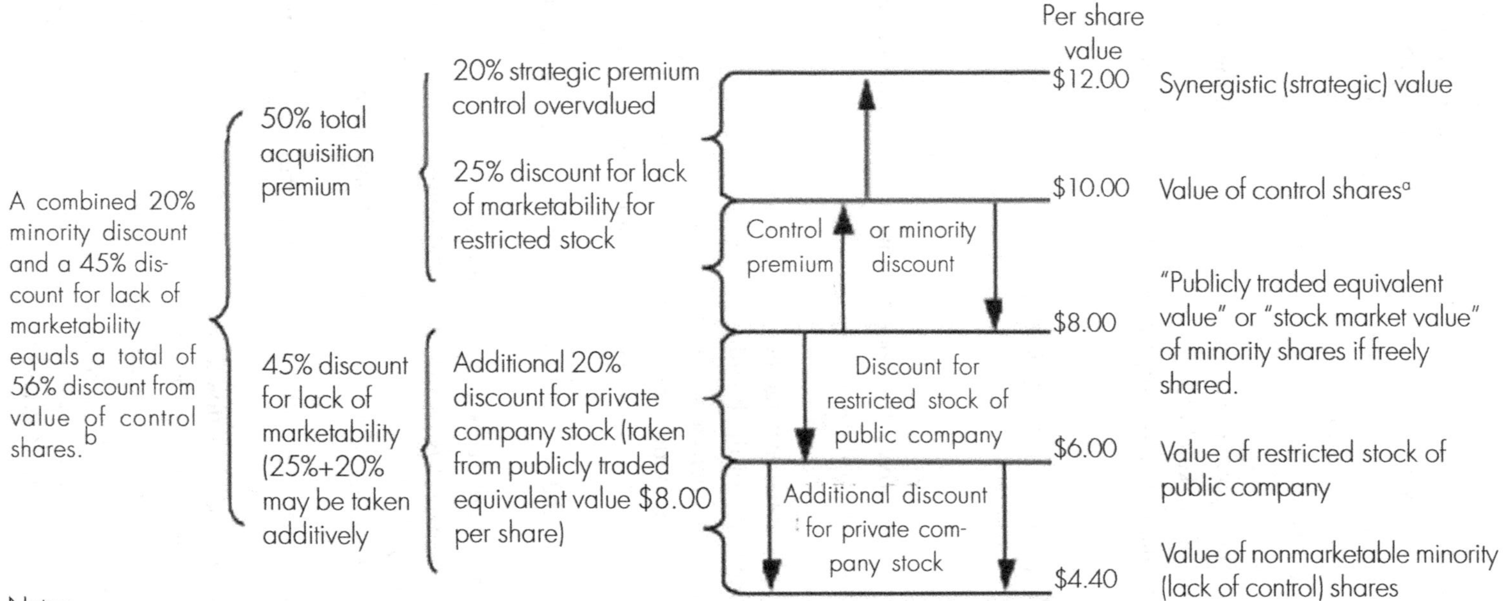

Notes:

a Control shares in a privately held company may also be subject to some discount for lack of marketability, but usually not nearly as much as minority shares.

b Minority and marketability discounts normally are multiplicative rather than additive. That is, they are taken in sequence:

$10.00	Control Value
– 2.00	Less: Minority interest discount (.20 x $10.00)
$ 8.00	Marketable minority value
– 3.60	Less lack of marketability discount (.45 x $8.00)
$ 4.40	Per-share value of nonmarketable minority shares

Source: Jay E. Fishman, et al., *PPC's Guide to Business Valuations*, 19th ed.

> for shares in a closely held corporation. Although there may be some overlap between these two discounts in that lack of control may reduce marketability, it should be borne in mind that even controlling shares in a nonpublic corporation suffer from lack of marketability because of the absence of a ready private placement market and the fact that flotation costs would have to be incurred if the corporation were to publicly offer its stock.[3]

Significantly, the court in this opinion recognized that even controlling interests may have some degree of lack of marketability.

Exhibit 15-1 shows a schematic relationship between the control/minority factor and the marketability factor.

Minority versus Control

The Minority Owner's Situation

Following are some valuable prerogatives of ownership that a control owner enjoys but a minority owner does not. A control owner can:

1. Appoint or change operational management
2. Appoint or change members of the board of directors
3. Determine management compensation and perquisites
4. Set operational and strategic policy and change the course of business
5. Acquire, lease, or liquidate business assets, including plant, property, and equipment
6. Select suppliers, vendors, and subcontractors with whom to do business and award contracts
7. Negotiate and consummate mergers and acquisitions
8. Liquidate, dissolve, sell out, or recapitalize the company
9. Sell or acquire Treasury shares
10. Register the company's equity securities for an initial and secondary public offering
11. Register the company's debt securities for an initial and secondary public offering
12. Declare and pay cash and/or stock dividends
13. Change the articles of incorporation or bylaws
14. Set one's own compensation (and perquisites) and the compensation (and perquisites) of related-party employees

3. Estate of Andrews v. Comm'r, 79 T.C. 938 (1982).

15. Select joint ventures and enter into joint venture and partnership agreements
16. Decide what products and/or services to offer and how to price those products/services
17. Decide what markets and locations to serve, to enter into, and to discontinue serving
18. Decide which customer categories to market to and which not to market to
19. Enter into inbound and outbound license or sharing agreements regarding intellectual properties
20. Block any or all of the above actions[4]

Degrees of Minority versus Control Ownership

As noted earlier, the matter of minority versus control is not simply a "one or the other" matter but rather one of degree. This spectrum can be summarized as follows:

- **100 percent control.**
- **Slightly less than 100 percent control.** Minority might be a nuisance; any shareholder, no matter how small the ownership interest, has shareholder rights that can be exacted on the majority.
- **Less than 80 percent control.** Cannot consolidate financial statements for tax purposes.
- **Less than a supermajority where a supermajority is required for certain corporate actions.** About half the states require a supermajority vote (often two-thirds, but some states have different requirements) to effect certain corporate actions, such as merger or liquidation. Some articles of incorporation and bylaws contain such requirements, even if they are not mandated by state law. Supermajority voting requirements also may be imposed contractually in a stockholders' agreement, debt instrument, or other contract. This can be a very significant factor when valuing either a minority interest large enough to block a corporate action (often referred to as "blocking control") or a majority not large enough to control all corporate actions.
- **50 percent interest of a closely held company.** Has blocking power, but cannot force things to happen (except when one party is accorded certain control prerogatives by contract). It is neither control nor minority, with a very real potential for deadlock. (For a public company, 30 percent to 40 percent often represents working control.)
- **"Swing vote" minority block.** Whether a minority block constitutes a "swing block" depends on the distribution of the other stock. If it is likely that the

4. Shannon P. Pratt & Niculita, Alina V., Valuing a Business 385 (5th ed. 2008).

block can be combined with another block to effect a corporate action, it usually is considered a swing block. Of course, the relationships between the parties owning the other stock may have a bearing on the value of the swing block as a practical matter.

- **Enough votes to elect a director under cumulative voting.** There may be some element of control value to the ability to elect one or more directors. However, the cumulative voting provision has become less frequent in recent years.
- **High enough percentage to bring a minority oppression dissolution action.** As further discussed in Chapter 18, "Shareholder and Partner Disputes," some states have provisions that require a minimum percentage of the outstanding stock to be involved to commence a minority dissolution action under the state's minority oppression statute. Whether such a right adds any value to the stock depends not only on whether the size of the block is sufficient, but also on whether the company has created whatever conditions are required to institute such an action.[5]

Quantifying Minority or Lack of Control Discounts

As seen from the previous section, there may be reason to take some discount from a proportionate value of a 100 percent controlling interest even if the interest is more than strictly a minority. Similarly, a minority interest that involves some elements of control may be accorded something less than the full minority interest discount that it might be accorded absent such factors.

Even apart from these complications, mustering empirical evidence to support a percentage discount for lack of control is not an easy task. Almost certainly some element of subjectivity is involved, because most of the empirical data on which business appraisers rely do not precisely isolate the minority versus control factor from other factors that may influence transaction prices.

Some of the bodies of empirical evidence most commonly used to quantify discounts for lack of control are the following:

- **Differences between market prices and underlying net asset values for publicly traded holding companies.** These could include closed-end investment companies, real estate holding companies, real estate investment trusts (REITs), and other holding companies. Because the stocks are fully market-

5. Under California Corporation Code Section 2000, such an action requires 33-1/3% of the stock. In a suit claiming inadequate consideration paid in buying out a 40% ESOP interest, the court determined that the block size added no value pursuant to this provision because the corporation had not conducted any actions sufficient to trigger a dissolution suit by the minority. Howard v. Shay, 100 F.3d 1484 (9th Cir. 1996).

able minority interests, the implication is that the average discount from underlying net asset value reflects lack of control.[6]

- **Acquisition premiums for publicly traded stocks.** Every year, many companies whose stock has traded in the public markets are acquired in some form of buyout or merger. Studies are published regularly comparing public market trading prices before the announcement of an acquisition or merger to the price paid stockholders (or value received) in the acquisition or merger. The percentage difference between the takeover price and the previous market trading price may be viewed as a proxy for the minority discount. For example, if the takeover price was $10 per share and the public market trading price had been $8 per share, the difference of $2 per share as a percentage of the $10 control acquisition price would suggest a 20 percent minority interest discount. (In this sense, the implied minority interest discount is the "other side of the coin" of the control premium, that is, the control premium would be $2 divided by $8, or 25 percent; the implied minority discount would be $2 divided by $10, or 20 percent.) Valuation analysts have many sources available for such data. A few of the most common are listed in the references at the end of this chapter. No single source is totally comprehensive.

  The strengths of such data are that they are readily available, easily verifiable, and almost always representative of arm's-length negotiated transactions. However, certain caveats also should be recognized:

  — Acquisition prices often reflect elements of strategic or synergistic value and, therefore, the premiums paid may reflect some elements of such value over and above just the value of the elements of control.

  — On the other hand, in the public companies, control stockholders may not have exploited the prerogatives of control at the expense of the minority stockholders to the extent often found in private companies. This argument suggests that the minority discount in any particular private company may be greater.

  The databases consist primarily of companies that buyers believe are worth more than market price. The universe of guideline transactions includes companies that were undervalued in the market but necessarily excludes companies that were overvalued.

6. Closed-end investment companies report underlying asset values daily, published regularly in the financial press. Many real estate holding companies and REITs report estimates of underlying asset values or are followed by stock analysts who publish such estimates. There are various services that publish such estimates.

Out of the tens of thousands of public companies, only a small percentage actually is acquired each year. In recent years, the companies purchased often have been the "best of breed," making them a very unique subset of the market. Statistically, it is unlikely that this small select group is universally representative of the market as a whole.

- **Limited partnership discounts from net asset value.** During the 1960s and 1970s, thousands of limited partnerships were formed, with interests sold to the general public. Most invested in real estate and some in oil and gas and other assets. There was no secondary market for resale of these interests at the time, but during the 1990s many holders were interested in selling and a market for trading such interests developed.

  Data on transaction prices, underlying net asset values, and partnership distributions are collected and published in *Direct Investments Spectrum Newsletter* (see the references at the end of this chapter). The discounts at which transactions take place relative to underlying net asset values provide some evidence about minority interest discounts. However, it should be recognized that the limited partnership secondary trading market is a relatively thin market compared to an organized stock exchange and, thus, the discounts, to some extent, may reflect an element of lack of marketability.
- **Trust and estate sales studies.** Two studies were conducted by H. Calvin Coolidge, a bank trust officer responsible for administering trusts that owned all or portions of closely held businesses. Although the Coolidge Studies are somewhat dated, they remain interesting and relevant today.

In his first study (1975), Coolidge compiled data on 30 actual sales of minority interests. He found that the average transaction price was 36 percent below book value and concluded with the following observations:

> Only 20 percent of the sales were made at discounts less than 20 percent. A little more than half the sales (53⅓ percent) were made at discounts that ranged from 22 percent to 48 percent, and 23⅓ percent of the sales were made at discounts of from 54.4 percent to 78 percent.
>
> It would be dangerous to draw too many generalizations from the survey, but those sales where the discounts were below 20 percent involved, with one exception, purchases from close relatives where friendly relations existed. The exception was the sale by a holder of swing shares who used his leverage well, but still took a 4.3 percent discount. At the other end of the spectrum was the settlement of a three-year bitter dispute between two families; the majority family raised its token offer only after threat of a lawsuit, but the

price the minority interest took nonetheless represented a 78 percent discount.[7]

Coolidge's second study (1983) indicated a trend toward even higher discounts when disposing of minority interests in closely held corporations. That study found a much higher concentration of discounts from book value at the high end of the range, and the average discount for the two studies combined was approximately 40 percent. The second study concludes as follows:

> Each of the sales used in the survey involved a combination of factors that made it somewhat unique. To use any of the data, or any classification of the data, as definitive proof of the discount to be applied in a prospective valuation would be dangerous. This should not, however, obscure the true significance of the data, which is that in the actual marketplace, the typical discount is not of token size, but of substantial magnitude.
>
> It should be recognized that the discounts are from book value, not from the market value of the business. Since "book value" represents historical cost less depreciation, it is likely that the total values of the businesses were above book value in most cases, so the total discounts from the values of the businesses would be greater. Also, these figures represent total discounts, reflecting marketability as well as minority factors.[8]

While none of these bodies of empirical data are totally satisfactory to quantify the minority interest discount for any particular situation, they do demonstrate that minority interest discounts are a very real factor in the marketplace. Some would argue there is an element of marketability discount embedded in these discounts. For evidence in trying to quantify discounts for lack of control, analysts usually seek data on securities or companies as comparable to their subject as possible. Because there are virtually no data currently available on transactions of minority interests in closely held companies, analysts can only do the best they can with what is available. Beyond that, the analyst usually is left to present a narrative description of the minority status of the subject being appraised to support a final estimate of the impact of the lack of control factor.

7. H. Calvin Coolidge, *Fixing Value of Minority Interest in Business; Actual Sales Suggest Discount as High as 70%, reprinted with permission* from ESTATE PLANNING, Spring 1975, at 141.

8. H. Calvin Coolidge, *Survey Shows Trend Toward Larger Minority Discounts*, ESTATE PLANNING 282 (September 1983).

Discounts for Lack of Marketability

The Concept of Marketability

The concept of *marketability* means the liquidity of the interest, that is, how quickly and certainly it can be converted to cash at the owner's discretion. A good working definition of marketability is "the ability to convert the property to cash quickly, with minimum transaction and administrative costs, and with a high degree of certainty of receiving the expected amount of net proceeds."[9]

This definition is consistent with the definition of marketability in the *Encyclopedia of Banking and Finance:*

> MARKETABILITY. The relative ease and promptness with which a security or commodity may be sold when desired, at a representative current price, without material concession in price merely because of the necessity of sale. Marketability connotes the existence of current buying interest as well as selling interest and is usually indicated by the volume of current transactions and the spread between the bid and asked price for a security—the closer the spread, the closer are the buying and selling interests to agreement on price resulting in actual transactions. To look at it from the standpoint of a dealer maintaining the MARKET, the closer his bid to current transactions and the smaller his markup as to asking prices, the larger the volume will be. By contrast, inactive securities that rarely trade or for which buyers have to be located or sales negotiated are characterized by large spreads between the bid and asked prices.[10]

Some authors attempt to draw fine distinctions between the terms *marketability* and *liquidity,* but most authorities use the two terms interchangeably, as indicated by the definition of liquidity from the same source:

> LIQUIDITY. The amount of time required to convert an asset into cash or pay a liability. For noncurrent assets, liquidity generally refers to marketability. . . .[11]

To the extent that some do distinguish the term *marketability* from *liquidity,* they may think of marketability as the ability to make the sale and liquidity as the timing and certainty of realizing cash proceeds.

9. Pratt, *supra* note 4, at 332.
10. Charles J. Woelfel, Encyclopedia of Banking & Finance 729 (10th ed. 1994).
11. *Id.* at 703.

It is apparent from these definitions that marketability means much more than just lack of restrictions against a sale; it means, in a very positive sense, the existence of an efficient market mechanism to convert the interest into cash.

Conversely, then, the lack of marketability means the lack of an established, efficient market. The Internal Revenue Service states, "Lack of marketability is defined as the absence of a ready or existing market for the sale or purchase of the securities being valued."[12]

Degrees of Marketability or Lack Thereof

As with the minority versus control factor, an interest is not necessarily fully marketable or nonmarketable. The marketability or lack thereof usually is a matter of degree. Without attempting to address every conceivable situation, the following gives a general idea of the spectrum of marketability or lack thereof:

- **Registered with the Securities and Exchange Commission (SEC) and with an active trading market** (the benchmark from which some lack of marketability discount usually is indicated)
- **Registered with the SEC and fully reporting, but with a somewhat thin trading market**
- **A stock with contractual "put" rights** (right of the owner to sell, usually to the issuing company, under specified circumstances and terms). The most common example is Employee Stock Ownership Plan (ESOP) stock, where the plan includes a "put" option to sell the stock at the employee's retirement or certain other times.
- **Registered with the SEC, but not required to file 10-K and other reports**[13] (a "nonreporting company")
- **Private company with an imminent (or likely) public offering**
- **Private company with frequent private transactions**
- **Private company with few or no transactions**
- **Private company with interests subject to restrictive transfer provisions**
- **Private company with ownership interests absolutely prohibited from transfer** (for example, tied up in a trust for some period of time)

12. IRS VALUATION GUIDE FOR INCOME, ESTATE AND GIFT TAXES, May 1997, at 9–3.

13. Many companies are registered with the SEC for public trading of their stock, but are exempt from filing 10-K, 10-Q, 8-K, and similar reports because of either a small asset size or a limited number of stockholders. Details of such exemptions are beyond the scope of this book, but such companies usually have very limited trading markets.

Other Factors Affecting Discounts for Lack of Marketability

Besides the factors implied in the "Degrees of Marketability" section, certain other factors influence the size of the discount for lack of marketability:

- **Dividends or partner distributions.** These probably are most important. This makes sense, because stockholders or partners who receive a good cash return on their investment on a regular basis do not depend so much on their ability to sell to realize cash proceeds.
- **Pool of potential buyers.** The more potential buyers there are, the greater the likelihood of being able to sell; the fewer the potential buyers, usually the harder it is to sell.
- **Information access and reliability.** The degree to which information is or is not made available to minority owners and the reliability of that information affects the discount for lack of marketability. For example, an article on partnership interest valuations states, "An important basis for illiquidity discounts is the difficulty faced by prospective purchasers in obtaining information."[14] One private company discount study concluded that companies with audited financial statements have lower marketability discounts than do companies with unaudited financial statements.

Benchmark for Marketability

As noted earlier, for a discount to have a precise meaning, there must be a precise definition of the benchmark to which the discount is to be applied.

In the U.S. public markets, a security holder is able to sell a security over the telephone (or Internet) in seconds, usually at or within a small fraction of a percent of the last price at which the security traded, with a very small commission cost, and receive the cash proceeds within three working days.

This market for securities in the United States is the most liquid market for any kind of property anywhere in the world. This is one of the major reasons companies are able to raise investment capital from both institutional and individual investors—the ability to liquidate the investment immediately, at little cost, and with virtual certainty about the realization of the widely publicized market price.

14. Mark S. Thompson & Eric S. Spunt, *The Widespread Overvaluation of Fractional Ownership Positions,* TRUSTS & ESTATES 62–66 (June 1993). *See also* Michael J. Bolotsky, *Adjustments for Differences in Ownership Rights, Liquidity, Information Access, and Information Reliability: An Assessment of 'Prevailing Wisdom' versus the 'Nath Hypotheses,'* BUSINESS VALUATION REVIEW 94–110 (Sept. 1991). Bolotsky's position is that conceptually, this is a factor separate from marketability, but he recognizes the reality that we have no good way to measure this factor separately.

By contrast, the universe of realistically potential buyers for most closely held minority ownership securities is an infinitesimally small fraction of the universe of potential buyers for publicly traded securities. In any case, in the United States, it is *illegal* for a person or company to sell privately held securities to the general public without registering with either the SEC or the state corporation commission, which is an expensive and time-consuming process. Furthermore, *a minority stockholder cannot register stock for public trading;* only the company can register its stock for public trading.

Besides the problems of actually trying to sell the stock (and because of them), the liquidity of closely held stock is further impaired by banks and other lending institutions' unwillingness to accept it as loan collateral, as they would accept public stock.

The "cash in three days" benchmark for marketability is commonly referred to by business appraisers as the "publicly traded equivalent value" or the "value as if publicly traded." Investors are willing to pay a high premium for this level of marketability. Conversely, however, they extract a high discount relative to actively traded securities for stocks or other investment interests that lack this high degree of marketability.

Because of these extreme contrasts in the ability to sell or hypothecate closely held minority stock compared with publicly traded stock, empirical evidence suggests that discounts for lack of marketability for minority interest closely held stocks tend to cluster in the range of 35 percent to 50 percent from their publicly traded counterparts, although the total range is quite wide. Naturally, each situation must be analyzed on the basis of its individual facts and circumstances, which may, in some cases, justify a discount for lack of marketability above or below this typical range.

Fortunately, although certainly not perfect, the empirical evidence available for guidance in quantifying discounts for lack of marketability is much stronger and more clear-cut than the evidence for quantifying discounts for lack of control (minority interests). As we will see in the next two sections, there are two distinct, extensively researched, and widely recognized series of empirical studies that help to quantify discounts for lack of marketability:

- **Restricted stock studies** (studies of transactions in restricted stock of publicly traded companies) and
- **Pre-IPO studies** (studies of private transactions in stocks of companies that subsequently went public).

Evidence Quantifying Lack of Marketability Discounts: Restricted Stock Studies

Many companies that have publicly traded stock also have otherwise identical shares of stock that are not registered for public trading or that are restricted from public trading for some period of time. These shares are called "restricted stock" or "letter stock" (the latter term because sometimes a legend is attached to the stock certificate explaining the limitations on its transferability). The unregistered or restricted shares may be founders' or insiders' stock that has never been registered or may be stock issued in an acquisition or to raise capital.

Although such shares may not be sold on the open market to the general public, they may be sold to qualified purchasers in private transactions with institutions or other sophisticated investors. Following such a private sale, the restrictions continue.

Primarily because of the restrictions on marketability, such transactions usually are at a discounted price compared to the same day's public market price. Because the restricted stocks are identical to the stocks sold in the public market in every respect except for their marketability, differences in the prices of these restricted stock transactions and the same day's public market price pretty well isolate the discount attributable to lack of marketability.

To help quantify the marketability factor, studies of differences between restricted stock transaction prices have been conducted for almost 40 years. These studies have been conducted by many different independent parties and encompass hundreds of transactions. Until the SEC lowered the required holding period from two years to one year in 1997, the average discounts ranged from 22 percent to 45 percent, with the majority clustering around 35 percent. Exhibit 15-2 presents a summary of the results of these studies. The holding period since has been reduced to six months, but there have been no studies published since then.

Analysts have tried to identify factors that affect the percentage of discount for lack of marketability. Apart from the amount of dividends or withdrawals, the factor that seems to stand out most clearly is the size of the company. The Management Planning[15] study found the following differences in average discounts based on the size of the company as measured by revenues:

Revenues	**Average Discount**
Under $10 million	32.9%
$10 million to $30 million	30.8%
$30 million to $50 million	25.2%
$50 million to $100 million	19.4%
Over $100 million	14.9%

Both the Securities and Exchange Commission[16] and the Johnson[17] studies also show that the marketability discounts are higher, on average, for smaller companies.

15. *See* Exhibit 15-2.
16. *Id.*
17. *See* Bruce Johnson, ***Restricted stock discounts, 1991-95***, SHANNON PRATT'S BUSINESS VALUATION UPDATE, March 1999, at 1–3.

Exhibit 15-2
Summary of Restricted Stock Studies

Empirical Study	Years Covered in Study	Average Price Discount (%)
SEC overall average [a]	1966–1969	25.8
SEC nonreporting OTC companies [a]	1966–1969	32.6
Gelman [b]	1968–1970	33.0
Trout [c]	1968–1972	33.5
Moroney [d]	[k]	35.6
Maher [e]	1969–1973	35.4
Standard Research Consultants [f]	1978–1982	45.0 [l]
Willamette Management Associates [g]	1981–1984	31.2 [l]
Silber [h]	1981–1988	33.8
FMV Opinions, Inc. [i]	1979–April 1992	23.0
Management Planning, Inc. [j]	1980–1996	27.1
Johnson (m)	1991–1995	20.0
Columbia Financial Advisors	1996–April 1997 (n)	21.0
Columbia Financial Advisors	May 1997–1998 (n)	13.0

a. "Discounts Involved in Purchases of Common Stock (1966–1969)." *Institutional Investor Study Report of the Securities and Exchange Commission,* H.R. Doc. No. 64, Part 5, 92nd Congress, 1st Session, 1971, 2,444–56.
b. Gelman, Milton. "An Economist-Financial Analyst's Approach to Valuing Stock in a Closely Held Company." *Journal of Taxation,* June 1972, 353.
c. Trout, Robert R. "Estimation of the Discount Associated with the Transfer of Restricted Securities." *Taxes,* June 1977, 381–85.
d. Moroney, Robert E. "Most Courts Overvalue Closely Held Stocks." *Taxes,* March 1973, 144–55.
e. Maher, J. Michael. "Discounts for Lack of Marketability for Closely Held Business Interests." *Taxes,* September 1976, 562–71.
f. Pittock, William F., and Charles H. Stryker. "Revenue Ruling 77-276 Revisited." *SRC Quarterly Reports,* Spring 1983, 1–3.
g. Willamette Management Associates study (unpublished).
h. Silber, William L. "Discounts on Restricted Stock: The Impact of Illiquidity on Stock Prices." *Financial Analysts Journal,* July-August 1991, 60–64.

i. Hall, Lance S., and Timothy C. Polacek. "Strategies for Obtaining the Largest Valuation Discounts." *Estate Planning,* January/February 1994, 38–44.
j. Oliver, Robert P., and Roy H. Meyers. "Discounts Seen in Private Placements of Restricted Stock: The Management Planning, Inc., Long-Term Study (1980–1996)." In Robert F. Reilly and Robert P. Schweihs, Eds., *The Handbook of Advanced Business Valuation,* Chap. 5. New York: McGraw-Hill, 2000.
k. Although the years covered in this study are likely to be 1969–1972, no specific years were given in the published account.
l. Median discounts.
m. Johnson, Bruce. "Restricted Stock Discounts, 1991–95," *Shannon Pratt's Business Valuation Update,* March 1999, 1–3; "Quantitative Support for Discounts for Lack of Marketability."
n. Aschwald, Kathryn, F. "Restricted Stock Discounts Decline as Result of 1-Year Holding Period." *Shannon Pratt's Business Valuation Update,* May 2000, 1–5.

In 1977, the Internal Revenue Service issued Revenue Ruling 77-287, which specifically recognizes the restricted stock transaction data as relevant evidence for quantification of the discount for lack of marketability.

Restricted stocks generally are restricted only for some period of time, usually two years or less, after which they can be sold in an active public market, which already exists.[18] The studies discussed above did not seek to determine whether the discount would be greater if the stock were of a private company, which has no public market and may not ever have a public market. That issue is addressed in another line of empirical lack of marketability studies, the pre-IPO studies.

As of this writing, the only restricted stock study undertaken since the Rule 144 holding period was reduced to one year in 1997 is the one headed by Kathryn Aschwald at Columbia Financial Advisors, Inc. (CFA).[19]

That study was divided into two parts: January 1, 1996, through April 30, 1997 (before the reduction in the Rule 144 holding period), and May 1, 1997, through December 31, 1998 (after the one-year holding period became effective, April 29, 1997). As noted earlier, the required holding period is now six months.

The study identified 23 transactions for the 1996 to April 1997 period, with discounts ranging from .8 percent to 67.5 percent, with a mean of 21 percent. For the May 1997 to December 1998 period, the study identified 15 transactions, with a range of 0 percent to 30 percent, and a mean of 13 percent and a median of 9 percent.

18. In 1995 the SEC amended its Rule 144 (establishing holding periods for restricted stocks) to reduce the required holding period for restricted stocks from two years to one year.

19. Kathryn F. Aschwald, *Restricted Stock Discounts Decline as Result of 1-Year Holding Period*, SHANNON PRATT'S BUSINESS VALUATION UPDATE, May 2000, at 1–5.

As explained by Kathryn Aschwald, author of the CFA study:

> Many "rumblings" in the appraisal community have centered around the fact that discounts for restricted stock have been declining, and many appear to be concerned about what this might mean in valuing privately held securities. It makes perfect sense that the discounts for restricted securities have generally declined since 1990 as the market (and liquidity) for theses [sic] securities has increased due to Rule 144A and the shortening of restricted stock holding periods beginning April 29, 1997. Thus, while the newer studies are specifically relevant for determining the appropriate discounts for restricted securities, the studies conducted after 1990 are not relevant for purposes of determining discounts for lack of marketability for privately held stock, because they reflect the increased liquidity in the market for restricted securities. Such increased liquidity is not present in privately held securities.[20]

There are two sets of restricted stock transactions accessible online. Studies on both of these indicate that an important factor in the magnitude of the discount for lack of marketability is the size of the block relative to the total number of shares outstanding. Therefore, when using restricted stock studies to assist in quantifying the discount for lack of marketability for a minority interest in a private company, those transactions that represent the highest percentage of the shares outstanding are the most relevant.

FMV Opinions Database

The FMV Opinions database contains details on more than 400 restricted stock transactions. The details provide more than 40 pieces of information on each transaction, so anyone searching the database can select transactions with characteristics as closely matching the subject company as possible. The FMV Opinions database is available at www.bvmarketdata.com.

LiquiStat Database

The LiquiStat database, a study by Espen Robak at Pluris Valuation Advisors LLC, is a continuously updated database of transactions in the secondary market for illiquid securities.[21] Different from other studies, the LiquiStat database specializes in the analysis of discounts taken when investors not affiliated with the issuing company sell

20. *Id.* at 4–5.

21. The transactions in the LiquiStat database are made on the Restricted Securities Trading Network (RSTN), an online trading platform managed by Restricted Stock Partners of New York. More information on this trading market for restricted securities is *available at* www.restrictedsecurities.net.

restricted stock in private transactions to other investors. See Exhibit 15-3 for the LiquiStat discounts for restricted stock. The LiquiStat database is available at www.PlurisValuation.com.

Evidence Quantifying Lack of Marketability Discounts: Pre-IPO Studies

Exhibit 15-3
LiquiStat™ Discounts for Restricted Stocks

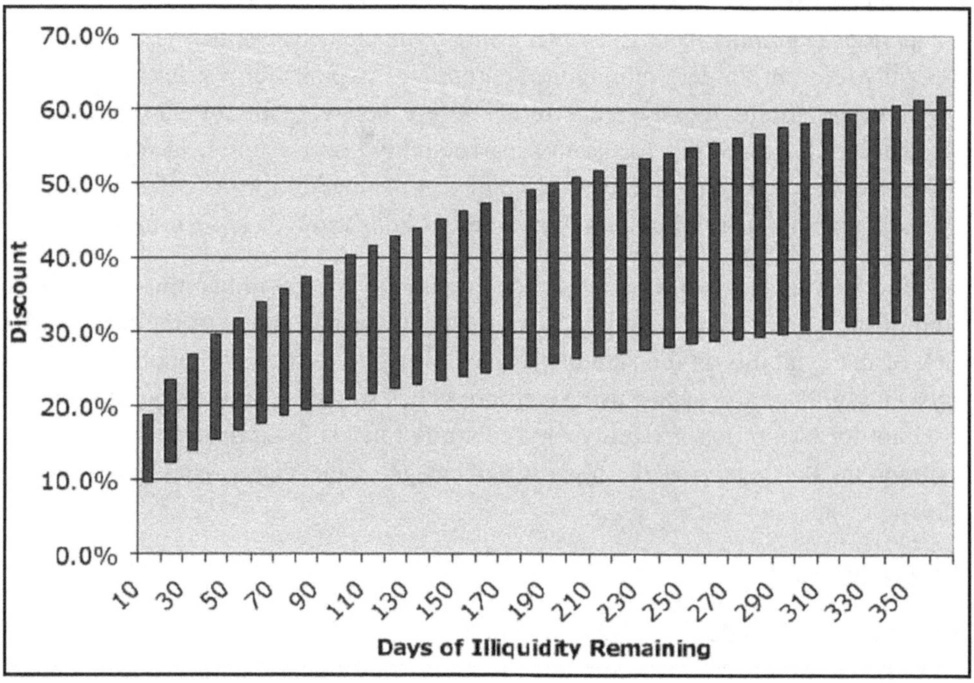

Source: Espen Robak. *Fair Value of Illiquid Securities: Restricted Securities and Auction-Rate Securities, Handbook on FAS 157 and Fair Value—How Do We Get from Here to There?* March 2008. Used with permission. Available at www.PlurisValuation.com.

When a company goes public for the first time, that is, undertakes an initial public offering (IPO), it is required to file a registration statement with the Securities and Exchange Commission. One of the disclosures required, along with financial statement information, is details of all transactions in the company's stock during the three years prior to filing. These details include transaction date, transaction price, number of shares, and identities of buyers and sellers. From these and the financial statement data, it is possible to compute price/earnings ratios, transaction size as a percent of shares outstanding, and other analytical details.

There are two publicly available databases that track pre-IPO transactions relative to public offering prices:

- Emory & Co. Pre-IPO Studies (formerly Baird & Co. Pre-IPO Studies)
- Valuation Advisors Discount for Lack of Marketability Studies

Emory & Co. Pre-IPO Studies (formerly Baird & Co. Pre-IPO Studies)

The Emory & Co. studies go back five months prior to the IPO. If a company had more than one private transaction, only the latest is included. Option and insider transactions were not eliminated from the Emory & Co. studies, because it was felt that the prices could reasonably have been expected to be at fair market value and should be able to withstand Securities and Exchange Commission, Internal Revenue Service, or judicial review, particularly in light of the closeness in time to the subsequent public offering.

A summary of the results from the eight Emory & Co. studies is shown as Exhibit 15-4. Details and discussion of each of the studies can be found in issues of the Ameri-

Exhibit 15-4
The Value of Marketability as Illustrated in Initial Public Offerings of Common Stock

Study	Number of IPO Prospectuses Reviewed	Number of Qualifying Transactions	Discount Mean	Discount Median
1997–2000		92	54	54
1995–1997	732	91	43	42
1994–1995	318	46	45	45
1991–1993	443	54	45	44
1990–1992	266	35	42	40
1989–1990	157	23	45	40
1987–1989	98	27	45	45
1985–1986	130	21	43	43
1980–1981	97	13	60	66
All 8 studies	2,241	310	44%	43%

Source: John D. Emory. "The Value of Marketability as Illustrated in Initial Public Offerings of Common Stock, November 1995 through April 1997." *Business Valuation Review,* Sept. 1997, 125. The latest version was published in 2000, including study from 1997 to 2000.

can Society of Appraisers quarterly journal, *Business Valuation Review*,[22] as well as in BVResearch™ at www.bvlibrary.com. This information also is available online at www.emorybizval.com. The Emory studies have not been updated since 2000.

Valuation Advisors Discount for Lack of Marketability Studies

The Valuation Advisors database records transactions within two years prior to the IPO. For retrospective valuations, its data goes back to 1999. At this writing, there are about 3,000 transactions in the database, which is accessible at www.bvmarketdata.com.

Transactions can be searched and compiled by date, length of time prior to IPO, revenues, industry code, profitability, and several other parameters. Results are summarized by the length of time intervening between the private transaction and the IPO. The summary results are shown in Exhibit 15-5.

Court Recognition of Marketability Discount Studies

Court decisions often rely on the restricted stock and pre-IPO studies as empirical evidence to assist in quantifying discounts for lack of marketability when valuing minority interests.

The pre-IPO studies were first used in the *Estate of Mark Gallo*. In that case, the taxpayer claimed a lack of marketability discount of 36 percent. The Internal Revenue Service claimed a discount for lack of marketability of only 10 percent. Relying on a pre-IPO study conducted specifically for that case, the court determined that the discount for lack of marketability was 36 percent, the highest discount *purely* for marketability (not a discount combining any other factors) determined by the Tax Court up to that time.[23]

---

22. John D. Emory, *The Value of Marketability as Illustrated in Initial Public Offering of Common Stock—January 1980 through June 1981*, BUSINESS VALUATION NEWS, Sept. 1981, at 21–24, also in ASA VALUATION, June 1986, at 62–66; *The Value of Marketability as Illustrated in Initial Public Offering of Common Stock, January 1985 through June 1986*, BUSINESS VALUATION REVIEW, Dec. 1986, at 12–15; *The Value of Marketability as Illustrated in Initial Public Offering of Common Stock, August 1987–January 1989*, BUSINESS VALUATION REVIEW, June 1989, at 55–57; *The Value of Marketability as Illustrated in Initial Public Offering of Common Stock, February 1989–July 1990*, BUSINESS VALUATION REVIEW, Dec. 1990, at 114–16; *The Value of Marketability as Illustrated in Initial Public Offering of Common Stock, August 1990 through January 1992*, BUSINESS VALUATION REVIEW, Dec. 1992, at 208–12; *The Value of Marketability as Illustrated in Initial Public Offering of Common Stock, February 1992 through July 1993*, BUSINESS VALUATION REVIEW, Mar. 1994, at 3–5; *The Value of Marketability as Illustrated in Initial Public Offering of Common Stock, January 1994 through June 1995*, BUSINESS VALUATION REVIEW, Dec. 1995, at 155–60; *The Value of Marketability as Illustrated in Initial Public Offering of Common Stock, November 1995 through April 1997*, BUSINESS VALUATION REVIEW, Sept. 1997, at 128–31.

23. Estate of Gallo v. Comm'r, T.C. Memo. 1985-363 (1985). Presented with similar data but for a later period, the Tax Court also concluded a 36% discount for lack of marketability in *Estate of Hall v. Comm'r*, 92 T.C. 312 (1989).

Exhibit 15-5
Valuation Advisors' Lack of Marketability Discount Study™
Transaction Summary Results by Year from 1999–2007

Time of Transaction Before IPO	1–90 Days	91–180 Days	181–270 Days	271–365 Days	1–2 Years
1999					
Number of Transactions	148	174	103	91	174
Median Discount	30.8%	54.2%	75.0%	76.9%	82.2%
2000					
Number of Transactions	129	176	116	91	141
Median Discount	28.7%	45.1%	61.5%	68.9%	76.6%
2001					
Number of Transactions	15	17	18	17	48
Median Discount	14.7%	33.2%	33.4%	52.1%	51.6%
2002					
Number of Transactions	9	13	7	16	36
Median Discount	6.2%	17.3%	21.9%	39.5%	55.0%
2003					
Number of Transactions	12	22	24	21	44
Median Discount	28.8%	22.3%	38.4%	39.7%	61.4%
2004					
Number of Transactions	37	74	63	59	101
Median Discount	16.7%	22.7%	40.0%	56.3%	57.9%
2005					
Number of Transactions	18	59	58	62	99
Median Discount	14.8%	26.1%	41.7%	46.1%	45.5%
2006					
Number of Transactions	25	76	69	72	106
Median Discount	20.7%	20.8%	40.2%	46.9%	57.2%
2007					
Number of Transactions	46	76	92	79	124
Median Discount	11.1%	29.4%	36.3%	47.5%	53.1%
1999–2007					
Number of Transactions	439	687	550	508	873
Median Discount	25.3%	36.1%	49.4%	60.8%	65.8%

Source: Valuation Advisors. *Discount for Lack of Marketability Database.* Database access is available at www.bvmarketdata.com. Used with permission.

In *Estate of Mandelbaum,* the only issue before the court was the discount for lack of marketability. The expert for the Internal Revenue Service cited three restricted stock studies. The expert for the taxpayer cited seven restricted stock studies and two series of pre-IPO studies. The court used the studies cited by the taxpayer's expert as a starting point, noting a 35 percent average discount for restricted stock studies and a 45 percent average discount for private transactions prior to IPOs. The court then identified nine factors that might cause the marketability discount in a given case to be higher or lower than the benchmark averages, on balance. The court concluded that the facts and circumstances of the particular company led to a discount lower than the benchmark averages and determined a marketability discount of 30 percent.[24] The nine factors were:

1. Financial statement analysis
2. Dividend policy
3. Nature of the company, its history, its position in the industry, and its economical outlook
4. Management
5. Amount of control in the transferred shares
6. Restrictions on transferability
7. Holding period for the stock
8. Company redemption policy
9. Costs associated with a public offering

In a 1998 Tax Court case specifically addressing the issue of the magnitude of the discount for lack of marketability, the expert for the Internal Revenue Service cited only restricted stock studies, while experts for the taxpayer cited both restricted stock and pre-IPO studies. The opinion of the court stated:

> We found those (the taxpayer's experts) reports and the additional testimony of (one of the taxpayer's experts) at trial to be quite helpful in ascertaining the lack-of-marketability discount that we shall apply in this case. . . . (The IRS's expert) should have considered the . . . data reflected in those pre-IPO studies because they, together with the restricted stock studies, would have provided a more accurate base range and starting point for determining the appropriate lack-of-marketability discount. . . .[25]

24. Mandelbaum v. Comm'r, T.C. Memo. 1995-255 (1995), *aff'd,* 78 AFTR 2d Par. 96-5037.
25. Estate of Davis v. Comm'r, 110 T.C. 530 (1998).

Up to this writing, 50 percent is the highest discount for lack of marketability found by the U.S. Tax Court unless other factors also were reflected in the discount.[26] However, in a class-action suit over the fair market value of a block of Employee Stock Ownership Plan stock constituting just under 40 percent of the company's outstanding shares, the court also upheld a 50 percent discount for lack of marketability. One of the plaintiff's arguments, not supported by any empirical evidence, was that the marketability discount should be lower because of the large size of the block as a percentage of the shares outstanding. One of the experts for the defendants presented specific transactions covering transactions involving blocks of 25 percent to 50 percent of the outstanding stock. The data showed that most of the discounts in those transactions were *not* below the overall averages shown in the studies but actually tended to be very close to the 50 percent discount used in the appraiser's original report.[27]

There have been some cases that have questioned or rejected the restricted stock and pre-IPO studies as a source of marketability discount data.[28]

Trend Away from "Benchmarking"

As the above case illustrates, the evidence is much more powerful if it isolates transactions with characteristics chosen to be as similar as possible to the subject, rather than merely citing the average of the various studies. A good example is a case in which the senior author of this book testified. The subject company was Schwan Ice Cream Company, which at the time had about $1 billion revenues and was quite profitable. As noted earlier, the studies show that larger companies tend to have lower discounts for lack of marketability than do smaller companies.

My testimony used both the FMV Opinions restricted stock database and the Valuation Advisors pre-IPO database; I selected only companies that were profitable

---

26. Huber v. Comm'r, T.C. Memo. 2006-96, 2006 Tax Ct. Memo. LEXIS 97 (May 9, 2006).

27. Howard v. Shay, 100 F.3d 1484 (9th Cir. 1996).

28. *See, e.g.*, McCord v. Comm'r, 120 T.C. No. 13, 2003 U.S. Tax Ct. LEXIS 16 (U.S. Tax Ct. May 14, 2003), *rev'd on other grounds*, 461 F.3d 614, 2006 U.S. App. LEXIS 21473 (5th Cir. 2006). In this case, the taxpayer's expert opined that a 35% DLOM was appropriate based on his analysis of restricted stock studies, and testified that pre-IPO studies supported this discount. The IRS expert determined a 7% discount based on the expert's own study of 88 private placements (the "Bajaj study"). The Tax Court found that of the 88 private placements, only the 29 middle placements were useful. Using these, the court concluded a 20% DLOM. There was no rebuttal to the IRS DLOM evidence in this case. Although the court rejected the pre-IPO studies, the court did review the taxpayer's expert's restricted stock study analysis and found a number of flaws in his reasoning and methodology. Expressly because of these errors, the court rejected his restricted stock analysis. Nonetheless, the court did not completely reject the restricted stock studies as a source of marketability discount data, but concluded that the expert had not adequately analyzed the data from the studies in reaching a 35% discount.

and had $100 million revenues. In the opinion concluding 45 percent discount for lack of marketability for one date (the amount to which I opined) and 40 percent for the other date, the court said:[29]

> Dr. Pratt's expert reports contain a far more detailed analysis of the empirical studies of trading prices of restricted shares and pre-initial public offering transactions than the AVG Report. . . . According to Dr. Pratt, the discounts observed in restricted stock studies reflect the existence of a public market for the stock once the temporary restrictions lapse. For a variety of reasons, . . purchasers of restricted stock "generally expect to be able to resell the stock in the public market in the foreseeable future." Pre-IPO discounts, on the other hand, are based on purely private transactions before a company enters the public market, a situation more comparable to closely held companies.

Discounts for Lack of Marketability for Controlling Interests

If the standard of value is fair market value, then a cash-equivalent value as of a certain date must be estimated. The choice of date may be one over which the owner has little or no control (for example, either date of death or the six-months-later alternative date for estate tax valuations or the date a transaction closed).

It usually takes months, even years, to prepare a business for a planned change in control ownership. There typically are significant accounting, legal, and management costs. There is a considerable degree of risk regarding whether the eventual sale of the business actually will result in the expected proceeds. For these and other reasons, it may be appropriate to apply a discount for lack of marketability when valuing a controlling interest.

Discounts for lack of marketability for controlling interests, if appropriate, are justified on the basis of a qualitative analysis of the costs and other factors enumerated above (time and risk) and *not* on the basis of the empirical studies used to quantify discounts for lack of marketability for minority interests. They tend to be much less than the discounts for lack of marketability for minority interests, usually in the range of 10 percent to 25 percent.

The U.S. Tax Court has been inconsistent about discounts for lack of marketability for controlling interests. Some cases have allowed up to 30 percent, while others have denied the discount entirely.[30]

29. Okerlund v. United States, 53 Fed. Cl. 341 (Fed. Ct. 2002), *motion for new trial denied,* 2003 U.S. Claims LEXIS 42 (Fed. Cl. 2003), *aff'd,* 365 F.3d 1044 (Fed. Cir. 2004).

30. *See, e.g.,* Estate of Dunn v. Comm'r, T.C. Memo. 2000-12 (Jan. 12, 2000), *rev'd on other grounds,* 301 F.3d 339 (5th Cir. 2002) (7.5% discount); Estate of Hendrickson v. Comm'r, T.C. Memo. 1999-278 (Aug. 23, 1999) (30% discount); Estate of Maggos v. Comm'r, T.C. Memo. 2000-129 (April 11, 2000), *aff'd in part and remanded in part on other grounds,* 32 Fed. Appx. 305, 2002 U.S. App.

In the marital dissolution situation, the spouse most actively involved in the business usually retains the controlling ownership interest in the business, and the nonoperating spouse generally retains much more liquid assets, such as cash, marketable securities, and real estate. A rational argument can be made that the same factors discussed above should be reflected in the value of the illiquid controlling ownership interest in the business or professional practice for marital dissolution valuation purposes.

Three recent empirical studies (one in 2000 and two in 2007) have shown that closely held companies tend to sell for lower multiples of underlying financial variables than do public companies. This is after controlling for other explanatory variables such as size and industry.[31]

The most comprehensive of these studies showed a surprising 37 percent discount in price to EBITDA multiples for acquisitions of private versus public firms.[32] Another study indicated an average 18 percent discount for enterprise value to EBITDA multiples.[33] Another study broke down the acquisitions between those that were for cash versus those that were for stock, finding that the cash acquisition reflected a 22 percent discount while the acquisition for stock reflected only a 12 percent discount, averaging a 17 percent overall discount.

How the Applicable Definition of Value Affects the Minority/Control and Discount for Lack of Marketability Adjustments

Fair Market Value

As discussed in Chapter 1, the fair market value standard implies the most likely price at which an arm's-length transaction would be expected to take place between normally motivated investors in open market conditions. In cases of minority interests, the value usually would fully reflect both minority and marketability discounts com-

LEXIS 3629 (9th Cir. 2002) (25% discount); Estate of Doughtery v. Comm'r, T.C. Memo. 1990-274 (May 31, 2000) (25% discount); Estate of Jameson v. Comm'r, T.C. Memo. 1999-43 (Feb. 9, 1999) (3% discount); Estate of Cloutier v. Comm'r, T.C. Memo. 1996-49 (Feb. 13, 1996) (no discount permitted).

31. These studies are described more fully in chapter 26, *The Private Company Discount*, *in* Cost of Capital: Applications and Examples 429-35 (3d ed. 2008).

32. Gus De Franco et al., "The Existence and Explanations for the Private Company Discount," Working paper, April 27, 2007.

33. John Koeplin, Atulya Sarin & Alan C. Shapiro, *The Private Company Discount*, 12:4 Bank of America Journal of Applied Corporate Finance 94–101 (Winter 2000).

pared with the value of a 100 percent interest. When valuing controlling interests, discounts for lack of marketability sometimes are applied.

Fair Value

Under the standard of fair value, which is the statutory standard of value for most dissenting stockholder and minority oppression actions, court decisions vary widely on the application of minority and/or marketability discounts. There are even instances of control premiums. Treatment of discounts and premiums under the fair value standard is discussed in some detail in Chapter 18, "Shareholder and Partner Disputes." Although never statutorily mandated and rarely found in case opinions, it is conceivable that fair value may be considered as a standard of value in marital dissolutions. Indeed, New Jersey courts have applied the fair value standard in at least one divorce case.[34]

Investment Value

Chapter 1 pointed out that investment value reflects value to a *particular* buyer or owner. When valuing minority ownership interests under the standard of investment value, the analyst may be taking into account one owner's relationships with other owners. Family law courts, in particular, often take into consideration the value to the specific owner, thus ameliorating or even eliminating discounts that would apply under the fair market value standard. (Watch out! Family law courts often do this even when they *say* that they are using the fair market value standard.)

How the Valuation Method Used Affects Premiums and Discounts

Income Approach

When using the income approach, the minority/control question generally revolves around the assumptions used in estimating the amount of income to be discounted or capitalized. If the income estimates reflect "business as usual," the value implied usually would be a minority value, and little or no minority discount would be warranted. (There could be some discount for the lack of prerogatives of control discussed earlier.) If valuing a controlling interest, a control premium may be appropriate if a control owner might achieve enhanced returns. (However, if valuing for a con-

34. Brown v. Brown, 348 N.J. Super. 466, 792 A.2d 463 (N.J. App. Div. 2002); *see also* Piscopo v. Piscopo, 232 N.J. Super. 559, 557 A.2d 1040 (N.J. Super. 1989), applying a value to the owner standard, which closely resembles the fair value standard in the marital dissolution context.

trolling interest, rather than assume business as usual and add a control premium, most analysts would prefer to adjust the income stream to what the control owner would expect and then use the income approach to directly estimate a control value.)

If the buildup or capital asset pricing model or discounted cash flow method is used to develop the discount or capitalization rate (as is usually the case in the income approach), the discount or capitalization rates are developed from public market transactions and the assumption of full marketability usually is appropriate, so a discount for lack of marketability should be considered.

Market Approach

Because there are virtually no data on transactions of minority interests in privately held companies, the market approach usually relies on either publicly traded guideline company trades in the day-to-day stock market or transactions involving changes of control ownership.

If public guideline company transactions are used, they clearly are fully marketable, and a discount for lack of marketability should be applied if valuing a closely held minority interest. The matter of a minority interest discount is not so clear. There is no question that the transactions used are minority transactions, so conventional wisdom would suggest that a minority interest discount would not be appropriate. However, one school of thought says that those in control of public companies normally don't use their prerogatives of control to exploit their own advantage as control owners of closely held companies might do, and therefore a minority interest discount is appropriate when valuing minority interests using the publicly traded guideline company method. One should inspect the guideline public companies to see if there is room for a control premium.

In some cases this issue can be handled by adjustments, or lack of them, to the financial statements (and thus to the financial variables to which the market multiples are applied). For a minority interest valuation, adjustments that only a control owner could make would not be considered. Other differences might be accounted for in the discount for lack of marketability.

If merger and acquisition data are used, then the indication of value would be for a control transaction; if valuing on a minority interest basis, both a minority interest discount and a discount for lack of marketability usually would be appropriate. If valuing a controlling interest, some discount for lack of marketability may be appropriate.

Rules of thumb are intended to represent control transactions. Therefore, the same adjustments as if using mergers and acquisitions would be appropriate.

Asset Approach and Excess Earnings Method

The asset approach and the excess earnings method develop control basis estimates of value. Therefore, the same adjustments as if using the merger and acquisition method are appropriate if valuing on a minority interest basis (both minority and lack of marketability discounts). If valuing on a control basis, a discount for lack of marketability may be appropriate.

Other Discounts at the Entity Level

Key Person Discount

Some businesses are so dependent on a few key people or a single key person that a discount is warranted to reflect the potential impact of the loss of their services. This may be the case in an estate where the key person has died or when there is cause for concern about a key person's health or continued availability for whatever reasons.

The appropriate amount of a key person discount is not something that can be estimated with precision. Some factors to consider are:

- **Services rendered** and the cost to the company of losing those services
- **Potential for replacement,** including the ability of others to take over and the costs of replacement
- **Risks** associated with disruption and replacement

There are two potential offsets to the possible costs:

- **Compensation saved** (after any continuing obligations)
- **Key person insurance**

The U.S. Tax Court frequently has recognized key person discounts. Amounts usually have ranged from 10 percent to 25 percent of the value of the business before other adjustments such as minority and marketability.[35] Alternatively, a key person risk can be included in the company specific premium of the discount rate.

Portfolio Discount

A "portfolio" discount is a discount for a company that owns dissimilar operations and/or assets that do not necessarily fit well together. Many private companies have

35. *See, e.g.*, Estate of Furman v. Comm'r, T.C. Memo. 1998-157 (1998); Estate of Mitchell v. Comm'r, T.C. Memo. 1997-461 (1997), *vacated*, 250 F.3d 696 (9th Cir. 2001); Estate of Feldmar v. Comm'r, T.C. Memo. 1988-429 (1988).

accumulated such a package of disparate operations or assets over the years, the combination of which probably would not be particularly attractive to a buyer seeking a position in any one of the industries, necessitating a discount to sell the entire company as a package.

The best empirical evidence supporting quantification of a portfolio discount is found in conglomerate public companies, which tend to sell at a discount of 10 percent to 15 percent from their breakup value.

Trapped-in Capital Gains Discount

"Trapped-in capital gains" means that the entity holds assets with a fair market value substantially greater than the amounts at which they are carried on the books, and thus there would be a liability for capital gains tax when and if the assets were to be sold.

Until 1986, tax law embraced what was called the General Utilities Doctrine, which allowed a C corporation to liquidate and distribute proceeds to shareholders within one year and by so doing avoid paying capital gains tax at the corporate level. Changes brought about by the Tax Reform Act of 1986 eliminated the General Utilities Doctrine, thus leaving no practical method to avoid paying a corporate-level capital gains tax on the sale of appreciated assets.

Nevertheless, despite a strong consensus by the business valuation professional community that the capital gains tax liability should be recognized, the Internal Revenue Service continued to resist allowing any discount for trapped-in capital gains tax liability unless a sale of the assets was clearly imminent. In 1998, however, two landmark cases brought recognition of the discount for trapped-in capital gains.[36]

In *Estate of Davis,* the Tax Court clearly articulated that a discount for the trapped-in capital gains tax should be recognized. The following are brief excerpts from the court's opinion:

> We reject respondent's position that as a matter of law, no discount or adjustment attributable to ADDI&C's built-in capital gains tax is allowable in the instant case. . . . Although [the taxpayer's expert] recognized in his expert report that as of the valuation date it would have been possible for ADDI&C to convert to an S corporation, he did not consider conversion to S corporation status to be likely. . . . [w]e agree that as of the valuation date it was unlikely that ADDI&C would have converted to an S corporation. Based on the record before us, we reject respondent's unwarranted assumptions that

36. For articles explaining the reasoning as to why the trapped-in capital gains factor should be recognized, see Shannon Pratt, *Trapped-in capital gains affect real-world value,* SHANNON PRATT'S BUSINESS VALUATION UPDATE, Feb. 1996, at 1, 3; and John R. Gilbert, *Built-in Gain Valuation Adjustment: No Longer 'If'—But 'How' and 'How Much,'* CPA EXPERT, Winter 1999, at 7–10.

> ADDI&C could have avoided all of ADDI&C's built-in capital gains tax by having it elect S corporation status and by not permitting it to sell any of its assets for 10 years thereafter, and the record does not establish that there was any other way as of the valuation date by which ADDI&C could have avoided all of such tax. We are convinced on the record in this case, and we find that, even though no liquidation of ADDI&C of sale of the assets was planned or contemplated on the valuation date, a hypothetical willing seller and a hypothetical willing buyer would not have agreed on that date on a price for each of the blocks of stock in question that took no account of ADDI&C's built-in capital gains tax. We are also persuaded on that record, and we find, that such a willing seller and such a willing buyer of each of the two blocks of ADDI&C stock at issue would have agreed on a price on the valuation date at which each such block could have changed hands that was less than the price that they would have agreed upon if there had been no ADDI&C's built-in capital gains taxes of that date.[37]

In late 1997, the Tax Court had rejected a discount for trapped-in capital gains on real estate holding in a gift tax case, citing pre-1986 cases as precedent, and the taxpayer appealed. Shortly following the *Davis* decision, the Second Circuit Court of Appeals reversed, citing favorably *Estate of Davis.* The Second Circuit's decision explained:

> Our concern . . . is not whether or when the donees will sell, distribute or liquidate the property at issue, but what a hypothetical buyer would take into account in computing fair market value of the stock.
>
> The issue is not what a hypothetical willing buyer plans to do with the property, but what considerations affect the fair market value of the property he considers buying. While prior to the TRA any buyer of a corporation's stock could avoid potential built-in capital gains tax, there is simply no evidence to dispute the fact that a hypothetical willing buyer today would likely pay less for the shares of a corporation because of the buyer's inability to eliminate the contingent tax liability.[38]

The case was subsequently settled with a discount of about half the capital gains tax, about the same as *Davis*. Then in *Estate of Simplot,*[39] a dollar-for-dollar discount for the tax on imbedded capital gains was accepted without discussion. Close to a

37. Estate of Davis, *supra* note 25.
38. Eisenberg v. Comm'r, T.C. Memo. 1997-483 (1997), *vacated,* 82 AFTR 2d Par. 98-5173 (Aug. 18, 1998).
39. Estate of Simplot v. Comm'r, 112 T.C. 130 (1999).

decade later, overturning the Tax Court, the Eleventh Circuit held in *Estate of Frazier Jelke III v. Comm'r*[40] that dollar-for-dollar discounts for trapped-in capital gains should be granted.

Family law courts generally have denied any adjustments to values to recognize potential trapped-in capital gains tax liability unless sale of the assets is imminent, and the operating spouse usually is left with no adjustment to the value of the company for this contingent liability. Of course, as with most rules, there are some exceptions.[41]

Litigation Risk

Actual or potential risk of litigation can be a very difficult issue to deal with in valuing a business. In a market transaction, litigation risk normally would be handled by a reserve, either withheld by the buyer or put into a trust account, to be liquidated when the matter is settled. This sometimes can be done in dissolutions or other legal proceedings, but in other cases an exact valuation must be determined as of the valuation date.

Ideally, the appraiser would deal with litigation risk by estimating the probability of various outcomes, including both litigation costs and possible judgments, and the amount of the discount would be the probability-weighted amount of the possible outcomes. However, this is a very chancy process, because it is unlikely that lawyers on either side of the litigation matter will give candid opinions of probabilities of outcomes.

Because of the lack of precision in this exercise, appraisers usually tend to be conservative in their estimates and give fairly heavy weight to the more negative possible outcomes. There certainly is an element of fairness in this bias, for the party left with the ownership interest bears all the risk if it is not possible to handle it by a contingency reserve.

The same problem and basically the same solutions tend to apply when the company is the potential beneficiary of the outcome of a lawsuit.

Environmental Risk

Like litigation risk, environmental risk often is difficult to quantify with any degree of precision. Indeed, environmental risk may be even more difficult to quantify than litigation risk is. At times, the cost of the environmental studies needed to quantify the risk can be prohibitive. A company can be put out of business completely as a result of

40. Estate of Frazier Jelke III v. Comm'r, 507 F.3d 1317; 2007-2 U.S. Tax Cas. (CCH) ¶ 60,552; 21 (11th Cir. 2007).

41. *See, e.g.,* Hamilton v. Hamilton, 2002 Ohio 2417 (Ohio Ct. App. 2002) (the court permitted a deduction for capital gains taxes, even though a sale was not imminent, where the husband would effectively have been forced to purchase the wife's shares in a company).

property condemnation or costs of environmental remedies. But both the ultimate outcome and the length of time until something has to be done often are unknown. Where this is a serious potential problem, the appraiser is left to make the best possible estimate, with all parties recognizing the wide potential for error. In light of the high degree of uncertainty, this is a situation in which parties should be open to reasonable compromise.[42] Courts have granted discounts for such risk, especially where there is a detailed, fact-specific analysis that supports the discount.[43]

Other Discounts or Premiums at the Shareholder Level

Voting versus Nonvoting Shares

The difference in value between voting and nonvoting minority shares depends largely on the size of the block and the distribution of ownership. In general, the greater the extent to which control is involved, the greater the impact of voting rights on the stock's value. If one stockholder has total control and there is no cumulative voting, the question of whether the minority shares are voting or nonvoting is academic unless a split of the control block is foreseeable. As noted earlier, when swing votes are involved, the value impact can be considerable.

Empirical studies on the price differentials between voting and nonvoting publicly traded stocks indicate that for small minority interests, the market generally accords very little or no value to voting rights. Where differentials in favor of voting stock exist, they generally have been under 5 percent, and no study of U.S. markets has indicated a differential of more than 10 percent.

Restrictive agreements also can have a bearing. Some voting stocks are subject to an agreement that causes them to be converted to nonvoting stock in the event of transfer. Such a provision can render voting rights virtually impotent for valuation purposes.

If there are "supervoting" shares—a very small proportion of all the stock has all the voting power—the value of those voting shares can be very significant. There are

42. The senior author had an estate tax valuation where there was a high probability of the company being put completely out of business because of known contamination in its waterfront location. The problem had been known and studied for 10 years, and the company was still in business. The author proposed a 50% discount from the going-concern value, and the parties accepted it.

43. *See, e.g.*, Estate of Klauss v. Comm'r, T.C. Memo. 2000-191 (June 27, 2000) (the court accepted an 8.15% discount for environmental and product liability claims where the taxpayer's analysis was detailed and enumerated specific items); Estate of Desmond v. Comm'r, T.C. Memo. 1999-76 (Mar. 10, 1999), *reaff'd*, T.C. Memo. 2002-98 (April 9, 2002) (a 25% discount for environmental liability was permitted, but only for values based on asset and income approaches, since the market approach already accounted for such liability).

only a limited number of actual market transactions for guidance in this situation, and each must be analyzed on a case-by-case basis.

Blockage

The concept of blockage is that the quantity of individual units of something held would take a long time for the market to absorb under normal market conditions without a significant discount. Therefore, to sell all the units as one block, one would have to accept a discount from the aggregate value of the units if sold separately. The concept often is applied to real estate, where it might take a long time to sell off the individual lots in a subdivision.

A blockage discount often is applied to blocks of public stock when the size of the block might represent several weeks or more of normal trading. The concept is well recognized by the courts,[44] but careful empirical evidence of trading must be presented to support it in each case. Most blockage discounts are relatively small, typically 3 percent to 7 percent.

The concept of blockage usually is not applied directly in the case of closely held stocks, for there is no record of average trading volume with which to compare the size of the block.

References

Basic Discount and Premiums References

Bishop, David. 1999. "Trapped-in Capital Gains: Where Do We Go From Here?" *Business Valuation Review,* June, 64-68.

Feder, Robert D., Ed. "Discounts and Premiums." In *Valuation Strategies in Divorce,* 4th Ed., Vol. 1, 156-76.

Fishman, Jay, et al. 2009. "Application of Premiums and/or Discounts." In *PPC's Guide to Business Valuations,* 8-13 to 8-32.

Internal Revenue Service. *IRS Appeals Officer Valuation Training Course,* 9-1 to 9-60.

44. *See, e.g.,* Gallun v. Comm'r, T.C. Memo. 1974-284, 33 T.C. Memo. (CCH) 1316 (1974), in which the experts agreed that blockage reduced the value of an investment portfolio from $18,087,263 to $16,204,439, a difference of over 10%. *See also, e.g.,* Estate of Foote v. Comm'r, T.C. Memo. 1999-37 (3.3% blockage discount permitted where the block constituted 2.2.% of the stock outstanding and was equal to 29 days of trading volume); Estate of Mellinger v. Comm'r, 112 T.C. 26 (1999) (25% blockage discount permitted); Estate of Gimbel v. Comm'r, 2006 Tax Ct. Memo. LEXIS 274 (Dec. 19, 2006) (effective 14.2% discount permitted on both restricted (14.4%) and nonrestricted stock (13.9%)).

Lee, M. Mark. "Control Premiums and Minority Discounts: the Need for Economic Analysis." *Shannon Pratt's Business Valuation Update,* August 2001.

Lee, M. Mark. "The Discount for Lack of Control and the Ownership Control Premium." In R. Reilly and R. Schweihs, Eds., *The Handbook of Business Valuation and Intellectual Property Analysis.* McGraw-Hill, 2004.

Matthews, Gilbert E. "Fairness Opinions: Common Errors and Omissions." In R. Reilly and R. Schweihs, Ed., *The Handbook of Business Valuation and Intellectual Property Analysis*. McGraw-Hill, 2004.

Mercer, Z. Christopher, and Travis W. Harms. *Business Valuation: An Integrated Theory,* 2d Ed. Wiley, 2007.

Mercer, Z. Christopher. *Valuing Shareholder Cash Flows: Quantifying Marketability Discounts*. E-Book. Memphis: Peabody Publishing, 2005.

Pratt, Shannon P., and Alina V. Niculita. 2007. "Control and Acquisition Premiums," "Discount for Lack of Control," "Discounts for Illiquidity and Lack of Marketability," and "Other Valuation Discounts." In *Valuing a Business,* 5th Ed., 383–470 (these chapters include extensive bibliographies of articles). McGraw-Hill, 2008.

Pratt, Shannon P. *Business Valuation Discounts and Premiums,* 2d Ed., Wiley, 2009.

Pratt, Shannon P. 2003. "Discounts and Premiums." In *Business Valuation Body of Knowledge,* 2d Ed., 179–97.

Trugman, Gary. 2002. "Premiums and Discounts." In *Understanding Business Valuation,* 2nd Ed., 357–408.

References for Premium and Discount Court Cases

BVUpdate,™ *Deluxe BVUpdate,*™ and *BVLaw*™ are available online at www.BVLibrary.com. Portland, OR: Business Valuation Resources, LLC. The online service can be searched by key word, such as marketability, minority, key person, etc.

Hamilton, Janet. "Marketability Discounts in the Courts, 1991–1996." Published as a supplement to the March 1997 issue of *Shannon Pratt's Business Valuation Update*. Covers cases of all types.

Howitt, Idelle A., Ed. *Federal Tax Valuation Digest.* New York: Warren, Gorham & Lamont. Updated annually.

Mercer, Z. Christopher. 1997. "Overview of Tax Court Decisions" and "Tax Court Case Summary." In *Quantifying Marketability Discounts,* 95-154, 465–82.

Widely Used Premium and Discount Data References

Control Premium Study. FactSet Mergerstat, LLC, 2950 31st St., Bldg. T, Ste. 130, Santa Monica, CA 90405, (800) 455-8871, www.mergerstat.com. Published quarterly.

Direct Investments Spectrum Newsletter. Partnership Profiles, Inc., 1300 Lakeside Ct., Argyle, TX 76226-6393, (940) 455-2173, www.partnershipprofiles.com. The May/June issue each year is a compilation of empirical data concerning discounts from net asset value at which minority interests in real estate partnerships trade in the *informal resale market.*

Emory & Co. Pre-IPO Studies. Emory & Co., 611 N. Broadway, Ste. 210, Milwaukee, WI 53202, 800) 252-5984, www.emorybizval.com. It also is available from www.bvlibrary.com.

Mergerstat®/BVR Control Premium Study.™ Business Valuation Resources, LLC, 1000 S.W. Broadway, Ste. 1200, Portland, OR 97205, (888) 287-8258, www.bvmarketdata.com.

Mergerstat Review. FactSet Mergerstat, LLC, 2950 31st St., Bldg. T, Ste. 130, Santa Monica, CA 90405, 800) 455-8871, www.mergerstat.com. Published annually.

The FMV Restricted Stock Study.™ Business Valuation Resources, LLC, 1000 S.W. Broadway, Ste. 1200, Portland, OR 97205, (888) 287-8258, www.bvmarketdata.com.

The LiquiStat™ *Database.* Pluris Valuation Advisors LLC, 17 Battery Pl., Ste. 1343, New York, NY 10004, (212) 248-4500, www.plurisvaluation.com.

Valuation Advisors' Lack of Marketability Discount Study.™ Business Valuation Resources, LLC, 1000 S.W. Broadway, Ste. 1200, Portland, OR 97205, (888) 287-8258, www.bvmarketdata.com.

Chapter 16

Reconciliation of Value Indications

As we discussed in previous chapters, there are three generally accepted approaches to the valuation of businesses and professional practices: the income approach, the market approach, and the asset-based approach. Within each approach are a number of generally accepted valuation methods. And within each method are a number of generally accepted procedures. Accordingly, valuation analyses progress from the more general to the more specific. First, the analyst selects the appropriate approaches. Second, within each approach, the analyst applies the appropriate methods. And, finally, within each method, the analyst performs the appropriate procedures.

Overview of the Reconciliation Process

The first step in reaching the business valuation synthesis and conclusion is to perform the reconciliation process. During the reconciliation process, it is important for the analyst to review all the steps of the business valuation. The first procedure is to review the business valuation assignment. At this point, the reviewer should answer the following two questions:

- Did the analyst appraise the right thing?
- Did the analyst appraise the right thing the right way?

In other words, from an overall engagement perspective, the reviewer should consider the question, "Did the appraiser accomplish what he or she set out to accomplish?"

A review of the business valuation assignment should consider the following:

- The purpose and objective of the appraisal
- The business enterprise ownership interest subject to appraisal
- The bundle of legal rights subject to appraisal

Does the Conclusion Appraise the Right Property?

It is surprising how often we see appraisals of something other than the specific property at issue. The nature of the property has a bearing on appraisal methods and also on premiums and/or discounts.

A common error is to ignore the existence of a corporate or partnership entity and simply appraise the assets owned by the entity. This can result in an entirely asset-based appraisal, when an appraisal of a going-concern with the weight primarily (or even entirely) on an income approach would be more appropriate. The error also can result in ignoring valuable intangible assets, including goodwill.

A classic example of this occurred in *Sommers Drug Stores Co. v. Corrigan Enterprises, Inc.*,[1] an ESOP valuation case, in which the plaintiff's expert used an asset liquidation method to determine fair market value. The court soundly rejected this approach, indicating that the "other relevant factors" that the expert should have considered included:

> The goodwill of the business; the economic outlook in the particular industry; the company's position in the industry and its management; the degree of control of the business represented by the block of stock to be valued; and the values of securities of corporations engaged in the same or similar lines of business which are listed on a stock exchange.

The court summed up its disapproval by saying, "[the expert's] utter failure to consider other relevant factors, or to explain his reasons for disregarding them, renders his testimony unworthy of credit."

In the same vein, courts have observed that an asset approach alone usually is inappropriate to value operating companies, which generally are valued on earnings because an asset valuation tends to undervalue such companies,[2] and that in a minority valuation, assets may or may not play an important role in arriving at a per-share figure because owners of minority interests cannot reach those assets.[3] Courts also have ruled that the exclusive use of an asset approach in a fair value appraisal action is erroneous because it is akin to determining the company's theoretical liquidation value.[4]

1. Sommers Drug Stores Co. v. Corrigan Enters., Inc., 793 F.2d 1456 (5th Cir. 1986).
2. BTR Dunlop Holdings, Inc. v. Comm'r, T.C. Memo. 1999-377, 1999 Tax Ct. Memo. LEXIS 432 (Nov. 15, 1999); Foltz v. U.S. News & World Report, Inc., 663 F. Supp. 1494, 1987 U.S. Dist. LEXIS 5592 (D.D.C. 1987).
3. Foltz v. U.S. News & World Report, Inc., 663 F. Supp. 1494, 1987 U.S. Dist. LEXIS 5592 (D.D.C. 1987); Gibbons v. Gibbons, 94 P.3d 879, 194 Or. App. 257 (Or. Ct. App. 2004).
4. *See, e.g.*, Paskill Corp. v. Algoma Corp., 747 A.2d 549 (Del. 2000) (under Delaware law, the company's fair value must be determined on a going-concern basis, and a determination on a theoretical liquidation basis is proscribed).

More important, a corporate or partnership structure standing between the owner and the assets usually calls for some discounts from the total fair market value of net assets. If valuing on a control basis, discounts to consider would include, for example, trapped-in capital gains (if not already recognized as a deferred liability), contingent liabilities, and discount for lack of marketability. If valuing on a minority interest basis, typically there would be discounts for both lack of control and lack of marketability.

Another problem regarding valuing the right property can arise when there are two or more classes of stock. The analyst must identify which class is being valued and how its features differ from the other.[5] If valuing a minority interest, discounts may differ among classes. Indeed, even within a class, some shares may be subject to transfer restrictions that affect value. Hopefully, throughout the report and at the point of reaching the final conclusion, the analyst has provided clear explanations supporting the choice of approaches and methods and the weight accorded to each. The reviewer must consider whether the methods used (and the weights accorded each) are consistent with the appropriate definition of value in the specific legal context and are supported by the data available.

Still another problem related to valuing the right property may arise when the appraiser has not inquired into the purpose of the valuation. In *Chao v. Hall Holding Co., Inc.,*[6] the appraiser was hired to value a subsidiary of a holding company, but was never informed and never knew that the purpose of the valuation was to determine how much an ESOP should pay for the holding company's stock. The court concluded that the appraiser had valued the wrong company and should have valued the holding company. Accordingly, the court concluded that the valuation could not be relied on.

Major Considerations in the Reconciliation Process

After the appraiser has developed different indications of values from the methods used, he or she must reconcile these into a final opinion of value, assuming it is the appraiser's intent to conclude with a single estimate of value rather than the sometimes permitted, but infrequently exercised, option of a range of values.

The reconciliation process is one in which the appraiser reconsiders each of the methods employed in the context of his or her level of confidence in each method. Questions to consider in the reconciliation include:

---

5. For example, in rejecting an expert's report, "[the expert] did not address the nature of the two classes of stock issued by the corporation, whether they had cumulative voting rights or what differences existed between the two classes of stock." Estate of Kaufman v. Comm'r, T.C. Memo. 1999-119 (1999).

6. Chao v. Hall Holding Co. Inc., 285 F.3d 415, 2002 U.S. App. LEXIS 5929 (6th Cir. 2002).

- What was the degree of reliability of the data in each of the methods?
- How appropriate was each of the methods for the specific valuation purpose?
- What was the spread (dispersion) of the value indications by the employed methods?

It is reasonable to expect the various methods will produce different values, as each approach takes a different perspective—income, market, and asset. At the same time, the company being valued under each method is the same company. Its degree of risk, competence of management, degree of competition, financial structure, etc., remain the same. This suggests that if all the methods developed were appropriate, each used reasonably reliable data, and each was developed correctly, the differences in the values should be reasonable in relation to one another.

Values should be compared after they are on a like basis, that is, after premiums or discounts to reach the level of value being sought. In other words, the values to be reconciled should all be on the same basis—a control basis, a minority nonmarketable basis, or whatever is appropriate.

A common error is the application of a single premium or discount to an indication of value developed from two or more valuation methods that imply dissimilar ownership characteristics. This can produce a conclusion that is not clearly fish or fowl, that is, not clearly a minority or control value, nor clearly a fully marketable or nonmarketable value. In each situation, any discount or premium applied must be appropriate to adjust from the definition of value implied in the valuation method to the definition of value being sought in the appraisal.

A good way to ensure the appropriateness of any control premium or discount to a particular valuation method (or "indication of value") is to ask: "What type of value does this valuation method produce?"

- Control marketable?
- Control nonmarketable?
- Marketable minority interest?
- Nonmarketable minority interest?

By answering this question, you then will know whether a control premium or discount is appropriate.

Reconciling Divergent Results Among Business Valuation Methods

Ideally, the appraiser will use two or more approaches in the subject business valuation and these approaches all will yield virtually identical value conclusions. In practice, this rarely happens.

Appraisers expect to estimate a range of valuation conclusions when several alternative valuation approaches are used. The normal situation occurs when several approaches result in a reasonably narrow dispersion of conclusions. These alternative conclusions, then, indicate the reasonable range of values for the subject business. They also provide mutually supportive evidence regarding the final valuation synthesis and conclusion.

Occasionally, two or three valuation methods produce value indications within a reasonable range and then one method, which we often call an outlier, produces a clear and obvious value estimate far outside the range of the others. For example, the value indication of the asset accumulation method may be a clear and obvious outlier compared to three other value estimates. Accordingly, the appraisal requires further analysis and consideration before a valuation conclusion can be reached.

What should the appraiser do regarding such an outlier value estimate? The appraiser could discard the valuation method that yields the outlier value estimate. This action is based on the rationale that the outlier valuation method simply does not work given the subject set of facts and circumstances or that, on careful consideration, the method is not appropriate for the type of company being valued (for example, the asset value of a high-tech company is very unlikely to be a meaningful measure of the company's fair market value).

If, after careful review, one of the appraisal methods that appears to have merit still produces an outlier, then it becomes a matter of appraisal judgment as to the extent to which the factors reflected in the valuation method actually contribute to the value of the business or interest being appraised, with weight accorded commensurately to the method in the final value estimate.

Weighting of Valuation Method Results

As with the selection of valuation methods, there are no scientific formulas or specific rules with regard to the weighting of the results of two or more business valuation methods. In fact, the same factors or guidelines that affect the selection of the valuation methods will influence the appraiser with regard to weighting the conclusions of these methods.

The chapters on the various approaches and methods contain more extensive discussion of the circumstances when each is most useful, and the reader is encouraged to read those chapters for guidance in weighting approaches and methods.

Keep in mind that different approaches to value are not discrete but have considerable overlap. For example, within the market approach, heavy emphasis may appropriately be placed on a multiple of an economic income figure, such as a price/earnings multiple. It could be argued that this is an alternate form of an income approach, thus lessening the need for separate weight on an income approach per se.

Similarly, income approaches depend on information about market conditions to estimate appropriate discount and capitalization rates. Thus, the better the job an income approach does on capturing and documenting market-required discount and/or capitalization rates, the less the need for separate weight on a market approach per se.

The appraiser must ask, "What attributes of ownership of this business or business interest give rise to the value of owning it?" If the income available for distribution to the owner is the primary value driver, then it may be appropriate that one or more methods within the income approach dominate the value conclusion. Of course, a capitalization of dividends (for a minority interest) or dividend-paying capacity (for a controlling interest) within the market approach based on public companies could very well also capture the income-related value.

If the ability to sell the business or interest in the business is the primary value driver, then it may be appropriate that one or more methods within the market approach dominate the value conclusion.

If the value derives primarily from ownership of assets, then an asset approach may dominate. However, a market approach using a multiple of the market price of stock to underlying net asset value also may be a satisfactory way to capture asset-driven value (for example, in industries where asset value is correlated with fair market value of the stock, such as financial institutions). Generally, if asset value is high relative to other approaches, an asset approach tends to be more appropriate in valuing a controlling interest than a minority interest, for one of the important things that a control owner controls—and a minority owner does not—is utilization of the assets.

Through all of this, the reviewer must keep in mind the operative standard of value and court interpretations of the standard of value, if applicable. For example, family law courts in some states adhere to a strict definition of *fair market value* as "value in exchange." In such cases, personal goodwill that could not be transferred would not be considered a marital asset, even though it may represent considerable value to the owner, but it would be considered if *investment value* (value to the owner) were the applicable standard of value. (See Chapter 10, "Personal versus Enterprise Goodwill.")

The final estimate typically should be a number within the final range of values indicated by the various business valuation methods used in the analysis. The final value estimate may be a number indicated by one of the valuation methods; it may be heavily weighted to the result of the valuation method relied on most or it may be another number within the indicated range.

It is generally inappropriate to calculate a simple, unweighted arithmetic average to arrive at a final value estimate. A simple arithmetic mean implies that all the valuation methods have equal validity and equal weight. While this may occur in certain instances, this is usually not the case.

Explicit Weighting

An intuitively appealing method of presenting the value conclusion is for the analyst (1) to use subjective but informed judgment and decide on a percentage weight to assign the results of each relevant valuation approach or method used and (2) to base the final valuation on a weighted average of the results of the various methods.

Suppose, for example, the analyst is valuing a minority ownership in a closely held manufacturing company and ultimately relies on three value measures developed through the guideline public company method. Because it is an operating company but it has a substantial asset base, the analyst thinks the appropriate price/earnings multiple should be accorded 60 percent of the total weight, the price dividends 10 percent, and the price/asset value multiple 30 percent. We will assume in this case that the company has been unable to generate a good rate of return on its asset base; thus, the result would be as presented in the following table:

Multiple Name	Multiple Amount	Subject Company Fundamental	Value per Share	Weight	Total
Price/Earnings	5	$2.00/share	$10.00	0.6	$6.00
Price/Dividends	20	$0.60/share	$12.00	0.1	$1.20
Price/Net Asset Value	0.8	$20.00/share	$16.00	0.3	$4.80
					$12.00
Less discount for lack of marketability: 0.35 x 12.00					4.20
Indicated value per share					$7.80

In this case, although companies in the same industry generally are selling below book value, the subject company is valued at a larger discount from book value than the average in its industry because of poorer earnings. However, the asset base is accorded some weight, and the company is valued at a lower discount from book value ($16 versus $20, a 20 percent discount) than it would be if it were valued strictly on a multiple of earnings basis ($10 versus $20, a 50 percent discount). As it turns out, in this case the effect of the capitalization of dividends is neutral.

The main weakness of the above valuation synthesis procedure is that no generally accepted mathematical model is available for use in deriving the weights to assign to the results of each valuation procedure. The relative weights to assign each pricing multiple depends on the analyst's judgment; however, this forces the analyst to present his or her thinking in clearly quantified terms. The above narrative, coupled with the explicit weighting, provides important information about the appraiser's thought process. The procedure also has the appeal of being clear and easy to understand. If someone evaluating the results disagrees with some aspect of the analyst's judgment, the point of departure is readily identifiable and it is easy to apply an alternate set of numbers and quickly recompute the result.

The above example applies the weights to several variables within the market approach. It also is possible to apply specific weightings to the results of different approaches.

Court cases in which values of stock must be estimated under dissenting stockholders' appraisal rights have tended to rely on this weighting procedure. However, the wording of Revenue Ruling 59-60 does not embrace the method. The ruling states:

> Because the valuations cannot be made on the basis of a prescribed formula, there is no means whereby the various applicable factors in a particular case can be assigned mathematical weights in deriving the fair market value. For this reason, no useful purpose is served by taking an average of several factors (for example, book value, capitalized earnings, and capitalized dividends) and basing the valuation on the result. Such a process excludes active consideration of other pertinent factors, and the end result cannot be supported by a realistic application of the significant facts in the case except by mere chance.[7]

Implicit Weighting

Some appraisers use an implicit weighting scheme in their final valuation synthesis and conclusion, that is, they present the valuation indications for each method performed and then simply present a final value estimate. They do not document or justify the valuation synthesis process.

An example of this implicit weighting scheme is provided in the following table:

Illustrative Business Enterprise, Inc.
Business Valuation Methods and Value Estimates
Valuation Synthesis and Conclusion

Valuation Method	Value Estimate
Guideline public company method	$18,000,000
Discounted economic income method	$20,000,000
Adjusted net asset value method	$24,000,000
Valuation synthesis and conclusion	$22,000,000

7. Rev. Rul. 59–60, 1959-1 C.B. 237.

This analysis presents the final valuation conclusion. However, it is incomplete unless the appraiser explains and justifies the final value estimate concluded from this synthesis. The explanation can cover both the conceptual preferability among the methods used and also the degree of confidence in each method based on the relative quantity and quality of data available. When each method is performed properly, there probably will be little or no difference in the result between using an explicit or implicit weighting of value indications.

Final Value Estimate

Any of the following types of final value estimates may be appropriate, given the purpose and objective of the business valuation:

- **A point estimate.** Usually the business valuation final value estimate is stated as a single figure or point estimate.
- **A range of value.** In this conclusion, the business valuation indicated value falls somewhere within a range of values. This may be reported solely, as the conclusion of value, or in conjunction with a point estimate.
- **A relationship value.** In this conclusion, the business valuation estimate is expressed as a relationship to a given value. For example, the value estimate is indicated to be "no less than $X million" or "no more than $Y million."

References for Reconciliation of Value Indications

Bishop, David M. 1998. "Reconciling the Indicated Values." In *Business Valuation Review (*March), 13–15.

Fishman, Jay, et al. 2008. "Selecting a Value from a Range of Values." In *PPC's Guide to Business Valuations,* 8-2 to 8-10.

Pratt, Shannon P., and Alina V. Niculita. 2008. "Valuation Synthesis and Conclusion." In *Valuing a Business,* 5th Ed., 471–82.

______, 2003. "Reconciliation and Value Conclusion." In *Business Valuation Body of Knowledge,* 2d Ed., 198–202.

Chapter 17

Valuations for Federal Tax Matters

This chapter was updated from the first edition by Noah J. Gordon, legal counsel for Shannon Pratt Valuations, Inc. Mr. Gordon is a regular contributor to valuation and legal publications.

There is more definitive precedential case law in the general area of valuations for federal tax purposes than for any other business valuation purpose. Some issues are well settled, but decisions on other issues continue to evolve. This chapter attempts to distinguish which issues are well settled, nearly settled, or still in some stage of evolution.

There also are issues about which decisions seem to be conflicting (for example, discounts for lack of marketability for controlling interests). However, as Judge David Laro has explained:

> Each valuation case is unique. Although guidance can be obtained from earlier cases, one case is rarely on point with another, and a significant differentiation of the facts can usually be made.[1]

Even among issues that are well settled in principle, there still is a lot of room for argument about magnitudes, especially in such areas as discounts for minority interest and lack of marketability. Chapter 15, "Discounts and Premiums," addresses empirical data to support quantification of such discounts, and this chapter will discuss principles articulated by the courts regarding quantification of these factors and also magnitudes of discounts ultimately decided.

---

1. Hon. David Laro, *Judge Laro's views on "fair market value,"* Judges & Lawyers Business Valuation Update, May 1999, at 1–3. Full text of address before the AICPA National Business Valuation Conference (Nov. 17, 1998) *available at* www.BVLibrary.com.

An understanding of valuations for federal tax purposes is also very important for valuations for many other purposes. Because of the extensive case law, Internal Revenue Service (IRS) Revenue Rulings, and other literature, valuation principles and decisions for tax purposes often are cited in valuation reports and court decisions for other purposes, especially marital dissolution, and also in bankruptcy courts.

Federal tax cases involving business valuations fall primarily into the following categories:

- Estate taxes
- Gift taxes
- Ordinary income and capital gains taxes
- Charitable contributions
- Transfer pricing

Although the standard of fair market value applies equally in all cases, the manner in which it applies can have extreme consequences for estate planning. Most important, for gift tax purposes each transfer is valued individually, while for estate tax purposes the entire amount in the estate is aggregated, regardless of how many different beneficiaries there may be. For example, if a 100 percent interest in a company is in an estate, it will be valued as a 100 percent control interest, even if it is willed equally to three beneficiaries. But if three gifts of one-third interests are made, each will be valued as a minority interest, benefiting from the well-settled principle that the minority interest is discounted compared to a pro rata portion of the value as a whole.

Also, if the estate holds more than one class of security, the combined effect of all may be aggregated for the purpose of valuation,[2] but in some cases it is more appropriate to value only the subject voting shares, rather than valuing all voting shares of the company and deriving a pro rata value from that.[3]

Fair Market Value[4]

The standard of value for all federal tax cases is *fair market value,* defined by the Internal Revenue Service as:

> the price at which the property would change hands between a willing buyer and a willing seller, when the former is not under any compulsion to buy and

2. Ahmanson Found. v. United States, 674 F.2d 761 (9th Cir. 1981).
3. Estate of Simplot v. Comm'r, 249 F.3d 1191 (9th Cir. 2001).
4. For an extensive discussion available on the nuances of fair market value in the federal tax valuation context, see Jay E. Fishman, Shannon P. Pratt & William J. Morrison, Standards of Value: Theory and Applications 35–85 (John Wiley & Sons 2007).

the latter is not under any compulsion to sell, both parties having reasonable knowledge of the relevant facts.[5]

There are many nuances to this definition, as discussed in a subsequent section. However, over several decades, the federal courts have developed seven standards that must be considered in determining fair market value. These are:

1. Both the buyer and seller must be "willing."
2. Neither buyer nor seller is under a compulsion to buy or sell the item in question.
3. Both the buyer and seller are hypothetical persons.
4. Both the buyer and seller are aware of all facts and circumstances involving the item in question.
5. The item in question is valued at its highest and best use, regardless of its current use (in the business valuation context, this usually means that investor value is maximized).
6. The item is valued without regard to an event subsequent to the valuation date, unless such an event was reasonably foreseeable as of the valuation date or was relevant to the valuation.
7. The transaction is for cash and will be consummated within a reasonable commercial time frame.[6]

To this day, one of the most instructive cases on fair market value of closely held stock for federal tax purposes is *Central Trust Company v. United States*,[7] a lengthy, detailed discussion of valuation issues written more than 40 years ago. Although the reader must recognize that the structure of markets and financial theory and evidence have advanced in quantum leaps since that decision, it is still the most comprehensive tax case discussion of basic valuation issues and well worth reading today. One other case of comparable instructive detail and quality on valuation under the fair market value standard is *Foltz v. U.S. News and World Report*.[8] It involves a class-action suit alleging undervaluation of retiring employee stock under the fair market value standard. Both these lengthy cases are available for downloading at www.BVLibrary.com.

One of the more lengthy discussions of the Tax Court's posture in determining fair market value is contained at the beginning of the opinion in *Estate of Furman*, which case we suggest is instructive reading in general.[9]

---

5. Rev. Rul. 59-60.
6. Hon. David Laro & Shannon P. Pratt, Business Valuation and Taxes: Procedure, Law, and Perspective 9 (John Wiley & Sons 2005).
7. Central Trust Co. v. United States, 305 F.2d 393 (Ct. Cl. 1962).
8. Foltz v. U.S. News and World Report, Inc., 106 F.R.D. 338 (D.C. Cir. 1984).
9. Estate of Furman v. Comm'r, T.C. Memo. 1998-157 (1998).

Another case that is a good source for the modern history of fair market value is *Bank One Corporation v. Comm'r.*[10]

Fair Market Value Assumes Adequate Knowledge

Central Trust makes the point that "[F]air market value presupposes not only hypothetical willing buyers and sellers, but buyers and sellers who are informed and have adequate knowledge of the material facts affecting value."[11] In a 1999 case, for an example of this principle, Judge Laro rejected two sales proffered as evidence of fair market value, noting, "Neither seller was reasonably informed regarding the value of their stock. . . . Both took the offer . . . because it sounded like a good amount of money. Their testimony revealed that they were not knowledgeable sellers who aimed to realize the fair market value of their stock."[12]

Must Consider *Both* Buyer and Seller—and Both Must Be Hypothetical

Quite a few Tax Court decisions have either modified or rejected an expert's opinion of value because the expert focused solely, or unduly, on the *buyer,* with no or inadequate consideration given to whether the value would be acceptable to a hypothetical willing seller. For example:

> (Petitioner's expert) seems to have focused too much on the willing buyer portion of the fair market value definition. He failed to consider whether a seller, under no compulsion to sell, would discount the pro rata value of his interest by 40 or 50 percent in order to consummate the sale. [FN: we note that petitioner . . , a minority-interest holder under no compulsion to sell, testified that he would not sell his interest at the discount advocated by (petitioner's expert).][13]

Similarly, in another case:

> (Taxpayer's expert) focuses exclusively on the hypothetical willing buyer. (He) failed to consider whether a hypothetical seller would sell his or her interest in the partnership for $399,000. . . . Ignoring the views of the willing seller is contrary to this well-established rule.[14]

10. Bank One Corp. v. Comm'r, 120 T.C. 174, 2003 U.S. Tax Ct. LEXIS 13, 120 T.C. No. 11 (2003), *rev'd and remanded,* 2006 U.S. App. LEXIS 20430 (7th Cir. 2006).
11. Central Trust Co. v. United States, 305 F.2d 393 (Ct. Cl. 1962).
12. Estate of Kaufman v. Comm'r, T.C. Memo. 1999-119 (1999).
13. Moore v. Comm'r, T.C. Memo. 1991-546 (1991).
14. Estate of Lehmann v. Comm'r, T.C. Memo. 1997-392 (1997).

Of course, a transaction cannot take place at more than the highest price that some willing buyer will pay. Fair market value assumes market conditions as they exist at the date of valuation. Therefore, if the seller is really willing, the implication would seem to be that he or she must accept what the market will bear at the valuation date. The existence of a market implies both buyers and sellers,[15] but it can be difficult to determine the market for a closely held company. For example, some buyers might be interested in continuing the business as their own, while others might be interested in the business as an investment. There also might be other buyers who see the business as offering synergies with other acquisitions or assets.[16] Addressing this issue, some tax regulations require that the value of the property at issue be measured in the market where it would most likely be sold.[17] To comply with this requirement, the attorney should instruct the business appraiser to analyze the marketplace to identify the most likely pool(s) of buyers. In any event, the "[s]election of the proper market for valuation purposes is a question of fact."[18]

In any case, the lawyer would be well advised to be sure, in reviewing the report, that the willing seller part of the hypothetical willing buyer/willing seller combination is not ignored.

Finally, both the seller and the buyer must be hypothetical. In one case, the Tax Court' decision was reversed because, according to the Court of Appeals, it based its ruling on speculation and imaginary scenarios that identified particular buyers, rather than hypothetical buyers.[19]

Qualifications of Appraisers

While the quality of evidence is of primary importance, the Tax Court also is very interested in appraisers' qualifications when deciding on the relative weight to accord the respective experts' testimony. For example, in *Estate of Berg,* the court's opinion included lengthy discussions of the experts' qualifications.

> (Taxpayer's first expert) is an experienced certified public accountant who has served on the faculty of several universities. He has also served as an expert witness in several cases that involved the determination of the effect of

15. *See, e.g.,* Walter v. Duffy, 287 F.41 (3d Cir. 1923).

16. Roger J. Grabowski, *Identifying Pool of Willing Buyers may Introduce Synergy to Fair Market Value*, SHANNON PRATT'S BUSINESS VALUATION UPDATE, BUSINESS VALUATION RESOURCES 7, NO. 4 (April 2001).

17. *See, e.g.,* IRS Treas. Regs., Estate Tax Reg. § 20.2031-1; IRS Treas. Regs., Gift Tax Reg. § 25.2512-1.

18. Leibowitz v. Comm'r, T.C. Memo. 1997-243 (1997).

19. Estate of Simplot v. Comm'r, 249 F.3d 1191 (9th Cir. 2001).

> minority interest discount and lack of marketability discount. However, (he) has no formal education as an appraiser.
>
> (Taxpayer's second expert) is an experienced certified public accountant who has served as a professor at a university. (He) has no formal training as an appraiser, but has provided advisory services related to valuation of equity interest, mergers, acquisitions, leveraged buyouts, employee stock ownership plans, and litigation.
>
> (IRS's first expert), a professional appraiser, has completed courses sponsored by the American Society of Appraisers in research and analysis of business valuations, advanced valuation, and closely held business valuation. He is an associate member of the American Society of Appraisers, Business Valuation Section.
>
> (IRS's second expert), a professional appraiser, has completed an advanced business valuation seminar, a closely held corporations valuation seminar, four business valuation courses, and a business valuation strategy seminar. He is an associate member of the American Society of Appraisers, Business Valuation Section, and is a member of the Institute of Business Appraisers.
>
> (IRS's third expert), a professional appraiser, has completed courses in eminent domain valuation, going-concern valuation, and two courses in valuation of businesses and professional practices. He is a member of the American Institute of Real Estate Appraisers, an associate member in the American Society of Appraisers, Business Enterprise Section, and a member in the Institute of Business Appraisers.[20]

The Tax Court not only sustained the IRS's position, but also invoked the underpayment penalty:

> In addition, the expert reports submitted by petitioner were lacking in substance and analysis. The authors of the reports were not professional appraisers, had no formal education in the valuation of business enterprises, and were not members of any professional associations involved in the education and certification of appraisers.
>
> Petitioner has failed to carry its burden of showing that respondent abused his discretion in determining that petitioner failed to show a reasonable basis existed for the valuation on petitioner's 1986 estate tax return or that the claim was made in good faith. We therefore sustain respondent's determination with respect to the addition to tax pursuant to Section 6660.[21]

20. Estate of Berg v. Comm'r, T.C. Memo. 1991-279 (1991).
21. *Id.*

In other cases, however, even though the reported amounts could trigger the Section 6660 undervaluation penalty, the Tax Court has refused to impose the penalty on the grounds that the taxpayer retained a qualified appraiser and submitted the amount shown on the return in good faith.

With thousands of well-qualified business appraisers available and with recognized business valuation standards in place, as discussed in Chapter 2 on business valuation professional credentials and professional standards, it seems amazing that lawyers present so many unqualified "experts" with inadequate evidence and methodology before the U.S. Tax Court (or any court, for that matter). All too typical is this U.S. Court of Appeals opinion:

> The Tax Court rejected (taxpayer's expert's) entire opinion, emphasizing his lack of qualifications and the deficiencies in his methodology. We do not find the Tax Court clearly erred in rejecting (taxpayer's expert's) opinion.[22]

In *Kohler v. Comm'r,*[23] the Tax Court gave no weight to the opinions of the IRS's expert who, although a chartered financial analyst (CFA) with a doctorate, was not credentialed in business valuation and did not provide USPAP certification. The court also looked unfavorably at the expert's innovative, but unsupported, financial model. In *Estate of Thompson v. Comm'r,*[24] the Tax Court criticized the experts for both parties, finding that they were inexperienced and that their valuations generally lacked credibility. Conversely, in *Caracci v. Comm'r,*[25] the court rejected the taxpayer's attempt to challenge the IRS's expert's qualifications as "nonsensical and border[ing] on the frivolous" where the expert was a certified public accountant and a principal in a business valuation firm who had conducted numerous business valuations.

In *Estate of Josephine Thompson v. Comm'r,*[26] the Tax Court rejected both parties' valuations and, while declining to impose an underpayment penalty, criticized the estate's decision to hire an accountant and lawyer from Alaska (the estate was in New York) with relatively little valuation experience.

Burden of Proof

For examinations commencing before July 22, 1998, if the IRS issued a Notice of Deficiency, the burden of proof was on the taxpayer to prove that the value claimed

22. Estate of Ford v. Comm'r, 53 F.3d 924 (8th Cir. 1995).

23. Kohler v. Comm'r, T.C. Memo. 2006-152 (2006).

24. Estate of Thompson v. Comm'r, T.C. Memo. 2004-174 (2004).

25. Caracci v. Comm'r, 118 T.C. 379, 118 T.C. No. 25, 2002 U.S. Tax Ct. LEXIS 25 (2002).

26. Estate of Josephine Thompson v. Comm'r, T.C. Memo. 2004-174 (2004), *aff'd*, 499 F.3d 129 (2d Cir. 2007).

by the IRS was wrong.[27] For example, in *Estate of Kaufman,* the Tax Court rejected as unpersuasive the petitioner's expert's report, which valued the estate's stock at $30.85 per share. The court also rejected the petitioner's evidence of prior sales at $29.77 per share because they were not made at arm's length. The court then concluded:

> Where, as is the case here, the record falls short of the standard which we require, we are left to decide the case against the party who has the burden of proof. Because petitioners bear the burden here, we sustain respondent's determination, as modified by concessions in brief. We hold that the fair market value of the estate's stock was $56.50 per share on the applicable valuation date.[28]

For examinations commenced after July 22, 1998 (or, if no examination, court proceedings arising in connection with taxable periods beginning or occurring after July 22, 1998), the burden shifts to the IRS, "[i]f, in any court proceeding, the taxpayer introduces credible evidence with respect to any factual issue relevant to ascertaining the liability of the taxpayer. . . ." In *Kohler v. Comm'r,*[29] the estate/taxpayer successfully shifted the burden of proof to the IRS. In that case, at issue was a determination of the fair market value of stock of the company owned by the estate of Frederic C. Kohler on the alternate valuation date. The estate elected the alternate valuation date and filed its return with a $47.01 million appraisal. The IRS determined the fair market value of the Kohler holdings on the alternate valuation date was $144.5 million. The parties stipulated that the value of the Kohler stock at issue in related gift tax cases would be calculated by reference to the value of the Kohler stock determined in the estate tax case. The parties also agreed that the per-share value for the different classes of Kohler stock in each case would be determined by reference to an agreed-on formula that would take into account the value of the Kohler stock determined in the estate tax case.

The Tax Court ruled that all the requirements for shifting the burden of proof were met. Although the IRS argued that the estate did not cooperate fully because it filed a motion to quash certain discovery requests, the court determined that the estate had legitimate concerns about providing confidential and proprietary business information that was possibly irrelevant absent a court order. Once the Tax Court denied the estate's motion to quash the summons, the estate provided the requested documents the respondent requested. Accordingly, the court found that the numerous exhibits that were part of the record belied the IRS argument. Accordingly, the burden shifted to the IRS.

27. Tax Ct. Rule 142.
28. Estate of Kaufman v. Comm'r, T.C. Memo. 1999-119 (1999).
29. Kohler v. Comm'r, T.C. Memo. 2006-152, 2006 Tax Ct. Memo. LEXIS 156 (2006).

In *Estate of Josephine Thompson v. Comm'r,*[30] one issue the Second Circuit confronted was whether, once the taxpayer submitted a credible appraisal, the burden shifted to the IRS to prove valuation after the Tax Court rejected the IRS's values, and whether, as a result, the Tax Court should have adopted the taxpayer's values.

The taxpayer estate had included approximately 20 percent of the common shares of a closely held corporation. The estate calculated the value of the decedent's share of the company at $1.75 million, using the capitalization of income method. The IRS valued the estate's interest in the company at $32 million, using the comparable public company method and the discounted cash flow method.

The Second Circuit determined that the allocation of the burden of proof does not require the Tax Court to adopt the taxpayer's valuation, however erroneous, whenever the court rejects the IRS's proposed value; the burden of disproving the taxpayer's valuation can be satisfied by evidence in the record that impeaches, undermines, or indicates error in the taxpayer's valuation. In this case, the IRS not only presented evidence in support of its valuation, but also successfully rebutted the estate's valuation by identifying its errors and inconsistencies. The court reasoned that notwithstanding the allocation of the burden of proof in IRC Section 7491, the "Tax Court is not bound by the formulas and opinions proffered by expert witnesses. It may reach a determination of value based upon its own analysis of all the evidence in the record."

Adequate Disclosure of Gifts

A gift and its value must be adequately disclosed on a gift tax return to start the three-year statute of limitations on the assessment of gift tax.[31] On December 3, 1999, the Internal Revenue Service published final regulations pertaining to the adequate disclosure of gifts.[32] The regulations contain a list of what information may be included with the gift tax return to ensure the gift will be deemed adequately disclosed. In response to extensive comments and concerns about the regulations as previously proposed, the IRS added a section to the regulations providing that a "qualified appraisal" may be submitted "in lieu of the information required" under one of the items in the list.[33]

30. Estate of Josephine Thompson v. Comm'r, 499 F.3d 129 (2d Cir. 2007).

31. I.R.C. § 6501(c)(9).

32. 64 Fed. Reg. 67,767 (Dec. 3, 1999).

33. For a full discussion of the final regulations, see *IRS adequate disclosure final regulations respond to extensive comments,* JUDGES & LAWYERS BUSINESS VALUATION UPDATE, January 2000, 1, 4–5.

Access to Sites, Management, and Records

Clearly, the Tax Court expects experts to have access to site visits, management interviews, and company records to the extent necessary for a thorough appraisal. For example, a gift tax decision stated:

> It is also noted that petitioner's counsel refused to allow respondent's expert an opportunity to visit PCBCED's warehouse and bottling plant. To the extent that this reflects counsel's attitude and approach towards Tax Court litigation, the Court suggests that this is not the way we conduct proceedings.[34]

In *Kohler v. Comm'r,*[35] the court discredited an opinion based on a site visit that lasted less than three hours because it did not provide the expert with adequate knowledge of the subject company, and the court lauded the opposing party's expert's detailed knowledge of the firm. In *Polack v. Comm'r,*[36] the court credited the expert's appraisal because it was based on a thorough site visit, with interviews of individuals at the company who were key to an understanding of the company's value.

Arm's-Length Transactions

The Tax Court will accord some weight to arm's-length sales of businesses or business interests, defined by *Black's Law Dictionary* as "a transaction negotiated by unrelated parties, each acting in his or her self-interest; the basis for fair market value determination."[37]

For example, in *Estate of Bennett,* the court said, "Usually, in determining the value of untraded stock, one would look at actual arm's-length sales of such stock in the normal course of business within a reasonable time before or after the valuation date."[38] (Although the decision clearly articulated the principle, there were no such transactions in the *Bennett* case.) In *Morrissey v. Comm'r,*[39] the Ninth Circuit reversed the Tax Court's rejection of the taxpayer's evidence of actual sales near the valuation date. The appellate court concluded that because those actual sales had been arm's-length transactions, they presented the best evidence of fair market value.

34. Estate of Bruce v. Comm'r, T.C. Memo. 1993-244 (1993).
35. Kohler v. Comm'r , T.C. Memo. 2006-152, 2006 Tax Ct. Memo. LEXIS 156 (2006).
36. Polack v. Comm'r , T.C. Memo. 2002-145, *aff'd*, 366 F.3d 608 (8th Cir. 2004).
37. Black's Law Dictionary 71 (6th ed. 1990).
38. Estate of Bennett v. Comm'r, T.C. Memo. 1993-34 (1993).
39. Morrissey v. Comm'r, 243 F.3d 1145 (9th Cir. 2001).

Approaches to Value

The Tax Court expects all approaches to value to be considered. The relative weight it will accord to the various valuation approaches and methods generally depends on three factors:

1. The type of company,
2. The quality of available evidence, and
3. Whether the company might be liquidated or continue as a going concern.

The Tax Court tends to rely more on an asset approach for holding companies and on an income or market approach for operating companies. For hybrid companies, the court may weight the approaches to correspond to the degree to which the company has assets and earnings.[40]

A Tax Court opinion was even critical of an expert for not considering an asset approach for a company for which most appraisers would have been very unlikely to have accorded the asset approach any weight.[41]

In *Hess v. Comm'r,*[42] the court split the difference between the taxpayer's discounted cash flow (DCF) and the guideline publicly traded company approach and the IRS's DCF, net asset value, prior transaction, and guideline publicly traded company approaches.

In *Estate of Leichter v. Comm'r,*[43] the issue of liquidation versus going concern was key. There, the expert opined that the company was worth less on a going-concern basis than in liquidation, but the court criticized the expert for not explaining why a hypothetical seller would choose not to liquidate under such circumstances.

The Tax Court's ultimate decisions, however, often are based on a single approach (in effect, a weight of 100 percent to one approach)—more often than not the market approach—or a blending of the results of two approaches.

Market Approach

The IRS and the Tax Court look very favorably on the market approach, which is heavily emphasized in Revenue Ruling 59-60. However, it is not uncommon for the court to reject an expert's utilization of the market approach if the court is not satisfied that the companies selected are comparable to the subject company.

40. Shannon P. Pratt & Alina Niculita, Valuing a Business: The Analysis and Appraisal of Closely Held Companies 663 (5th ed., McGraw-Hill, 2008).

41. Estate of Kaufman v. Comm'r, T.C. Memo. 1999-119 (1999).

42. Hess v. Comm'r, T.C. Memo. 2003-251 (2003).

43. Estate of Leichter v. Comm'r, T.C. Memo. 2003-66 (2003).

For example, in *Estate of Brookshire,* two experts for the taxpayer and the IRS's expert all used the guideline public company method, among others. However, the court rejected the IRS's version of the guideline company method:

> Respondent's expert overstates the value of the Brookshire common stock because of his use of three companies as comparable companies that have significant sales in markets other than retail grocery and that are not comparable to Brookshire. The use of these companies distorts each of the valuation methods used by respondent's expert.[44]

Note that this is *not* a rejection of the guideline company method; the court accepted the guideline companies used by the taxpayer's experts.

It should be borne in mind that Revenue Ruling 59-60 uses the language "the same or similar." Companies may be accepted as similar for reasons other than product or service line—for example, the markets into which they sell or their degree of brand dominance.

To illustrate, in both *Estate of Gallo*[45] and *Estate of Hall*[46] (Hallmark Greeting Cards), the court relied entirely on the guideline publicly traded company method, even though there were no good public wine companies to use for *Gallo* and only one public greeting card company to use for *Hall.* In *Gallo,* the experts used breweries, distilleries, soft-drink bottlers, and high brand recognition and market share food producers. In *Hall,* they used high brand recognition and market share consumer nondurable products companies, such as Parker Pen. In both cases, the court arrived at a value as if the stock were publicly traded, then applied a 36 percent discount for lack of marketability based on restricted stock and pre-IPO transaction study data. However, in *Estate of Heck v. Comm'r,*[47] the court rejected the use of a single comparable company where it was insufficiently similar to the subject company. The court said, "As similarity to the company to be valued decreases, the number of required comparables increases. . . ."

In *Hess v. Comm'r,*[48] the court upheld the comparison of the subject company to guideline companies solely on the basis of price/earnings ratios where the guideline companies were similar to the subject company and the guideline companies were properly adjusted.

Estate of Watts was a classic clash of opposing opinions on appropriate approaches to value—in that case, the taxpayer's reliance on the market approach and the IRS's

44. Estate of Brookshire v. Comm'r, T.C. Memo. 1998-365 (1998).
45. Estate of Gallo v. Comm'r, T.C. Memo. 1985-363 (1985).
46. Estate of Hall v. Comm'r, 92 T.C. 312 (1989).
47. Estate of Heck v. Comm'r, T.C. Memo. 2002-34 (2002).
48. Hess v. Comm'r, T.C. Memo. 2003-251 (2003).

reliance on the asset approach. Decedent's estate filed a valuation of $2,550,000 for a 15 percent interest in a timber-growing and timber-processing partnership. The notice of deficiency valued the interest at $20,006,000, based primarily on the liquidation value of the assets.

At trial, the taxpayers' experts based their valuations on publicly traded companies that processed timber and held timberlands. Based on these companies, they presented valuation parameters such as price/earnings multiples, multiples of partnership interest value to book value and to adjusted net asset value, and capitalization of partnership withdrawals. Because the Tax Court did not accept the respondent's liquidation value approach, it relied on values provided by the business valuation experts, including a 35 percent discount for lack of marketability, and ultimately concluded the estate's value as originally filed at $2,550,000.[49]

Income Approach[50]

Both the IRS and the U.S. Tax Court have traditionally leaned more toward the market approach than the income approach. This is partly because of language in Revenue Ruling 59-60, written before the development of modern capital market theory, which evolved particularly in the 1960s. It also is partly because of concern about possible manipulation of both cash flow forecasts and discount rates in the discounted cash flow (DCF) method. Nonetheless, as the DCF method has achieved greater utilization in the professional financial community, it also has achieved greater acceptance in the Tax Court.

In a 1985 case, the IRS challenged income tax returns reflecting deductions for a company's contributions to the employee stock ownership trust at $61.35 per share, based on the fair market value arrived at by an independent appraisal firm. The IRS asserted that the value was between $5.36 and $8.00 per share. The independent appraisal gave heavy emphasis to earning power and dividend-paying capacity, while the IRS stressed net asset value (book value was $7.05 per share).

The court found itself in agreement with the emphasis placed on the earning power and dividend-paying capacity. The court was somewhat concerned "that the appraisal took into account a 20-year earnings projection" but thought it was "not unreasonable in light of past earnings increases." The court concluded that "the only reasonable appraisal presented to it was the one at $61.35 per share."[51]

Yet the Tax Court has *rejected* the DCF method in cases where it believed that the model used by the expert was far too sensitive to minor changes in assumptions, such

49. Estate of Watts v. Comm'r, T.C. Memo. 1985-595 (1985), *aff'd,* 823 F.3d 483 (11th Cir. 1987).

50. Shannon Pratt, Cost of Capital 157 (1998).

51. Las Vegas Dodge v. United States, No. CV LV 79-7, RDF, 1985 WL 6366 (D. Nev. Mar. 20, 1985).

as the discount rate and/or the growth rate.[52] The court also rejected the income approach where the CAPM was used to value a small closely held company, as pure CAPM does not address unsystematic risk.[53]

The Tax Court also has been known to reach its conclusion by giving partial weight to a DCF method and partial weight to a market approach method. For example, one case gave 70 percent weight to the market method and 30 percent weight to the DCF method.[54]

In *Estate of Jung,* the Tax Court relied on the DCF approach because the publicly traded guideline companies available were not very good comparables. The court stated:

> In the instant case, we believe the DCF approach to valuing Jung Corp. is more reliable than the market comparable approach. The market comparable approach does not work well in the instant case because the comparable corporations do not have the same product mix (health and elastic textile) as Jung Corp. None of the experts relied exclusively on the market comparable approach. . . .[55]

The Tax Court accepted the DCF method for valuing an interest in a real estate partnership that owned a property with a hotel. The court said:

> The value of any interest in real property that has an income stream can be estimated by the DCF method. See *Estate of Bennett v. Commissioner.*[56] The evidence before the Court shows that the property had a determinable income stream.[57]

The court then took into consideration the minority, nonmarketable status of the partnership interest.

In another case, the Tax Court accepted the DCF method over the market approach and applied a 31 percent discount for lack of control.[58]

52. Morton v. Comm'r, T.C. Memo. 1997-166 (1997).

53. Estate of Hendrickson v. Comm'r, T.C. Memo. 1999-278, 1999 Tax Ct. Memo. LEXIS 318 (1999).

54. Estate of Freeman v. Comm'r, T.C. Memo. 1996-372, 1996 WL 453872 (1996).

55. Estate of Jung v. Comm'r, 101 T.C. 412 (1993).

56. Estate of Bennett v. Comm'r, T.C. Memo. 1993-34 (1993); Estate of Hatchett v. Comm'r, T.C. Memo. 1989-637 (1989).

57. Estate of Lehmann v. Comm'r, T.C. Memo. 1997-392 (1997).

58. Rakow v. Comm'r, T.C. Memo. 1999-177.

Asset-Based Approach

Revenue Ruling 59-60 suggests that the asset approach should be accorded more weight for holding companies, while earnings-related methods should be accorded more weight for operating companies. For example, in *Estate of Jameson v. Comm'r,*[59] which involved the valuation of a controlling interest in a holding company the primary asset of which was timber, the Tax Court determined the asset approach was appropriate because earnings were relatively low as compared to the fair market value of the assets. The IRS has tended to push this notion to the ultimate in the case of family limited partnerships, where they often have used the asset approach exclusively.[60]

Until 1998, the IRS had been intransigent in its refusal to consider trapped-in capital gains liabilities. This would seem to be an internal contradiction. Insistence on the asset approach to value an interest implies that value arises from potential proceeds from sale, which necessarily would be net of capital gains taxes. If one is not willing to recognize tax consequences in case of a sale, then it seems that one should value by other approaches, that is, the income and market approaches. As we will see in a subsequent section, the Tax Court has insisted on recognizing trapped-in capital gains liability as a valuation factor and the IRS has acquiesced.

Discounts[61]

Discounts for Lack of Marketability (Minority Blocks)

The principle that minority blocks of closely held stock are worth less, because of the lack of a ready market, than otherwise similar publicly held stock is thoroughly entrenched in Tax Court rulings. The argument is not whether, but how much?

There appears to be two long-term trends:

- The size of marketability discounts concluded has gradually increased.
- The court has increasingly emphasized reliance on empirical data in deciding on the size of the lack of marketability discount.

59. Estate of Jameson v. Comm'r, T.C. Memo. 1999-43 (1999), *vacated and remanded,* 267 F.3d 366 (5th Cir. 2001).

60. For a discussion of valuation and tax issues related to family limited partnerships, see Shannon P. Pratt & Alina Niculita, Valuing a Business: The Analysis and Appraisal of Closely Held Companies 689-99 (5th ed., McGraw-Hill 2008).

61. For the most extensive sets of case citations and discussions of discounts and premiums in federal tax cases, see John A. Bodganski, Federal Tax Valuation 4–1 to 4–121, together with the 2000 Cumulative Supplement No. 1, 54–1 to 54–63. (1996).

Gradually Increasing Marketability Discounts

In the 1980s, discounts purely for marketability reached 36 percent, the highest up to that time.[62] In the late 1990s, there were several conclusions of a 40 percent lack of marketability discount.[63] In 2006, a 50 percent discount for lack of marketability (DLOM) was recognized.[64]

Increasing Reliance on Empirical Data

To some extent, the gradually increasing level of marketability discounts is attributable to the growing body of empirical data available to assist in quantifying such discounts and the Tax Court's increasing emphasis on that data. As discussed in more detail in Chapter 15 on premiums and discounts, the relevant empirical data for a long time have been the Restricted Stock Studies (sales of blocks of nonregistered or restricted stock of public companies) and the Pre-IPO Studies (transactions in stock of private companies that subsequently had successful initial public offerings (IPOs)). With time, these studies have been criticized for various deficiencies, and other ways of arriving at discounts for lack of marketability have been employed, including the use of put options, put-call collars, regression analysis of the restricted stock studies, private placement studies, the Quantitative Marketability Discount Model (QMDM), and even analyses of stock illiquidity versus lack of marketability. All these alternatives have their own weaknesses and flaws.

The Restricted Stock Studies were first published in the early 1970s and include data going back to the late 1960s. They were recognized as valid evidence supporting discounts for lack of marketability in Revenue Ruling 77-287. The Pre-IPO Studies first appeared in the early 1980s, with data back to 1975. They were first introduced in *Estate of Gallo*[65] and also used in *Estate of Hall.*[66]

In the late 1990s, the Tax Court explicitly directed attention to *both* these lines of studies in reaching discount for lack of marketability conclusions.[67] However, the court has not always accepted these data. Some criticisms of these studies are that they are dated, have limited sample sizes, are spread out over long periods of time, and may have substantial standard errors in their estimates. In *Estate of Jelke v. Comm'r*[68]

62. *See, e.g.,* Estate of Gallo v. Comm'r, T.C. Memo. 1985-363 (1985) (36%); Estate of Hall v. Comm'r, 92 T.C. 312 (1989) (36%).

63. *See, e.g.,* Brookshire v. Comm'r, T.C. Memo. 1998-365 (1998) (40%).

64. Huber v. Comm'r, T.C. Memo. 2006-96 (2006).

65. Estate of Gallo v. Comm'r, T.C. Memo. 1985-363 (1985).

66. Estate of Hall v. Comm'r, 92 T.C. 312 (1989).

67. *See, e.g.,* Mandelbaum v. Comm'r, T.C. Memo. 1995-255 (1995); Estate of Davis v. Comm'r, 110 T.C. 530 (1998); Estate of Williams v. Comm'r, T.C. Memo. 1998-59 (1998); Estate of Brookshire, T.C. Memo. 1998-365 (1998); Okerlund v. United States, 53 Fed. Cl. 341 (Fed. Ct. Cl. 2002), *aff'd,* 365 F.3d 1044 (Fed. Cir. 2004).

68. Estate of Jelke v. Comm'r, T.C. Memo. 2005-131 (2005).

(affirmed as to the discount issue by 507 F.3d 1317 (11th Cir. 2007)), for example, the court rejected the use of restricted stock studies, determining they were insufficiently similar to the subject company as to size. In *McCord v. Comm'r*,[69] the Tax Court preferred the data from a study of private placements (the "Bajaj" study) instead of data from pre-IPO studies (on appeal, the Fifth Circuit reversed on other grounds and did not address the DLOM issue). In *Estate of Kelly v. Comm'r*,[70] where interests in an investment limited partnership were being valued, the court rejected the use of restricted stock studies, finding that such studies examine mostly operating companies and that "there are fundamental differences between an investment company . . . and operating companies." Instead, it used the Bajaj private placement study and adjusted the discount derived from this analysis by 3 percent to account for characteristics specific to the partnership. The court in *Lappo v. Comm'r*[71] had similarly preferred the private placement approach to what it characterized as the more "narrow" restricted study approach in valuing an interest in a family limited partnership whose assets were marketable securities and real estate. The court in that case had also adjusted the discount by 3 percent to account for partnership-specific characteristics, such as the fact that it was closely held, relatively small, and unknown; there was no market for the interests; and the partnership had a right of first refusal to purchase the interests. In *Peracchio v. Comm'r*,[72] rather than criticizing the restricted stock studies themselves, the court criticized the taxpayer's expert for failing to analyze and apply the data from these studies to the particular partnership interests being valued. In *Estate of Deputy v. Comm'r*,[73] the IRS relied on restricted stock studies, while the taxpayer's expert applied a matrix his company had created to replicate an investor's decision process. The Tax Court preferred the taxpayer's matrix because it focused on the subject company's unique attributes. In *Janda v. Comm'r*,[74] the court rejected the IRS's use of restricted stock studies as being too general, because it did not present evidence on the subject company's industry or companies with similar characteristics. However, the court also had "grave doubts" about the taxpayer's use of the QMDM, which the court found could produce dramatically different results based on slight variations in assumption inputs. Although *Litman v. United States*[75] rejected a generalized use of restricted stock studies, the Claims Court expressed a preference for using individual transactions from the restricted stock studies rather than averages, a procedure that Shannon Pratt, one of the authors of this book, advocates and has used

69. McCord v. Comm'r, 120 T.C. 358 (2003), *rev'd*, 461 F.3d 614 (5th Cir. 2006).
70. Estate of Kelly v. Comm'r, T.C. Memo. 2005-235 (2005).
71. Lappo v. Comm'r, T.C. Memo. 2003-258 (2003).
72. Peracchio v. Comm'r, T.C. Memo. 2003-280 (2003).
73. Estate of Deputy v. Comm'r, T.C. Memo. 2003-176 (2003).
74. Janda v. Comm'r, T.C. Memo. 2001-24 (2001).
75. Litman v. United States, 78 Fed. Cl. 90 (Cl. Ct. 2007).

effectively many times. In *Temple v. United States,*[76] the court rejected the taxpayer's exclusive reliance on restricted stock studies in preference for the IRS's "fuller" analysis that included academic research, the cost of going public, secondary market transactions, asset liquidity, partnership interest transferability, and historic distributions. Similarly, the court in *Robertson v. United States*[77] rejected a discount based on restricted stock studies that used subjective factors in favor of a discount that also relied on restricted stock studies but supplemented the data from the studies with academic research. In *Estate of Green v. Comm'r,*[78] the court accepted discount values from restricted stock studies, but indicated that while pre-IPO studies were "entitled to some consideration," they did not justify a discount greater than 35 percent.

A brief description of some of the other sources of empirical data supporting discounts for lack of marketability (or lack of liquidity) follows.[79]

Put Options

The put-option method calculates a discount for lack of marketability by calculating the cost of locking in the current price to protect the downside risk of price movements while the security is illiquid. The price of the put provides market evidence of the price investors will pay to ensure marketability. The formula for this model, as well as its key inputs (such as the risk-free rate and volatility) can be audited. The term of this model is more subjective. Potential criticisms of using this model are that it is a short-term, theoretical pricing model designed for liquid securities that is being applied to an illiquid security and that put options protect only against downside price movements, although the Black-Scholes model can be used to estimate the price of a theoretical put for stock that is not publicly traded. In *Estate of Gimbel v. Comm'r,*[80] the court rejected the use of this method where the block was large and restricted, concluding that such options would have been unavailable for the estate's sizable block of restricted stock, which lacked both liquidity and marketability.

Put-Call Collars

A put-call collar locks in a security's price by selling away the upside while protecting against the downward price movements. This is done by buying a put option and

---

76. Temple v. United States, 2006 U.S. Dist. LEXIS 16171 (E.D. Tex. 2006).

77. Robertson v. United States, 2006 U.S. Dist. LEXIS 1167 (N.D. Tex. 2006).

78. Estate of Green v. Comm'r, T.C. Memo. 2003-384.

79. For a discussion of these sources of empirical data supporting a discount for lack of marketability, see Scott Beauchene & Robert Duffy, *Getting Ready for 409A: Some Practical Considerations*, Business Valuation Update, May 2007, at 1-5; AICPA National Business Valuation Conference, Dec. 2-4, 2007, Discounts for Lack of Marketability Panel—*Who's on First, What's on Second, I Don't Know's on Third,* Linda Trugman, Moderator, Mel H. Abraham, Z. Christopher Mercer, and Ronald L. Seigneur, Session No. 10.

80. Estate of Gimbel v. Comm'r, 2006 Tax Ct. Memo. LEXIS 274 (2006).

selling a call option. Potential criticisms of this type of analysis to determining discounts for lack of marketability are that the lack of a derivatives market in the subject security results in significantly understating the cost to execute this strategy for a privately held security and that cost information is not available and can result in significant subjective judgment. Where this analysis is feasible, it can be used to establish a floor for the discount. In *Litman v. United States,*[81] involving the valuation of a large block of restricted shares of stock, the court rejected the IRS's use of an option collar approach, finding that the size of the subject company's restricted stock, as compared to the public float, would render such a transaction impossible as a practical, real-world matter. Similarly, in *Estate of Gimbel v. Comm'r,*[82] the court rejected the use of this method where the block was large and restricted, saying that "[c]ashless collars and prepaid variable forward contracts generally are used with blocks of stock that are highly liquid and marketable"; the court concluded that there would not have been a market for such hedging contracts in this instance.

Regression Analysis

Francis Longstaff and others use regression analyses of restricted stock studies to provide a quantitative indication of the DLOM. This is, therefore, a mathematical method that can be audited and, similar to the other approaches listed here, the inputs also can be audited. The key drivers of this approach are duration and volatility. Potential criticisms are that a key assumption—that an investor could perfectly time the market—may not be realistic. However, a test of the Longstaff model shows that it is very sensitive to volatility; in fact, it results in DLOMs greater than 100 percent at a relatively short holding period. The author of the study concludes that the Longstaff model "seems to have limited usefulness in most situations."[83]

Liquidity versus Marketability

Ashok Abbott differentiates between marketability and liquidity, defining marketability as relating to a security's registration (ease of transfer or salability) and liquidity as relating to the actual sale of the security (converting the asset to cash). Abbott postulates that the cost to trade becomes a critical factor, which most trading models overlook, but "where the difference between marketability and liquidity become even more pronounced." According to Abbott, large blocks of stock are illiquid, so he uses the Black-Scholes or Longstaff models to calculate "look back put" data to reveal discounts from liquidity-related issues. He finds that for the largest publicly traded

81. Litman v. United States, 78 Fed. Cl. 90 (Claims Ct. 2007).

82. Estate of Gimbel v. Comm'r, 2006 Tax Ct. Memo. LEXIS 274 (2006).

83. John J. Stockdale, *A Test of DLOM Computational Models*, Business Valuation Review 131–37 (Fall 2008).

companies (more than $100 billion), the liquidity discounts range from 4 percent for the smaller blocks of stock up to 12 percent for the larger blocks. But for smaller companies, a 25 percent block creates a discount of around 35 percent. Still, these companies are bigger than most in a valuation pool.[84]

Combined Minority and Lack of Marketability Discounts

As discussed in Chapter 15, minority interest and marketability discounts are two different concepts, although there may be some overlap. The Tax Court has clearly articulated this distinction:

> In their arguments, neither petitioner nor respondent clearly focuses on the fact that two conceptually distinct discounts are involved here, one for lack of marketability and the other for lack of control. The minority shareholder discount is designed to reflect the decreased value of shares that do not convey control of a closely held corporation. The lack of marketability discount, on the other hand, is designed to reflect the fact that there is no ready market for shares in a closely held corporation.[85]

In the majority of Tax Court cases in the 1980s and 1990s, minority and marketability factors were treated separately. However, more recent cases have combined the two factors in the final decision.[86]

Discounts for 50 Percent Interest

A 50 percent interest is neither controlling nor minority. In most cases, the court will allow some discount for lack of control and also some discount for lack of marketability. For example, in one case of valuation of a 50 percent interest, the court stated, "We conclude that, in addition to a minority discount, some amount of lack of marketability discount should be applied. . . ."[87] In that case, the court was very critical of the evidence offered by experts on both sides. The final value concluded by the court represented almost exactly a combined discount of 27 percent from the value arrived

84. *See* Ashok Abbott, *Calculating the Cost of Liquidity in Current Markets*, Business Valuation Update, Vol. 14, No. 5 (May 2008); Ashok Abbott, *New Abbott Analysis Aids Valuators in Assessing Liquidity Discounts*, Business Valuation Update, Vol. 13, No. 11 (November 2007).

85. Estate of Andrews v. Comm'r, 79 T.C. 938 (1982).

86. Estate of Furman v. Comm'r, T.C. Memo. 1998-157 (1998); Estate of Magnin v. Comm'r, T.C. Memo. 2001-31 (2001); Estate of Mitchell v. Comm'r, 250 F.3d 696 (9th Cir. 2001); Estate of Janda v. Comm'r, T.C. Memo. 2001-24 (2001); Estate of Deputy v. Comm'r, T.C. Memo. 2003-176 (2003); Temple v. United States, 2006 U.S. Dist. LEXIS 16171 (E.D. Tex. 2006).

87. Estate of Fleming v. Comm'r, T.C. Memo. 1997-484 (1997).

at by the comparative transaction method, although the court did not describe exactly how the final value was reached.

Discounts for Lack of Marketability (Controlling Interests)

In many reported decisions, the Tax Court has recognized that discounts for lack of marketability for controlling interests in closely held companies are appropriate. The courts have used language such as the following:

> Even controlling shares in a nonpublic corporation suffer from lack of marketability because of the absence of a ready private placement market and the fact that flotation costs would have to be incurred if the corporation were to publicly offer its stock.[88]

The Tax Court has allowed discounts for lack of marketability for controlling interests up to 30 percent.[89]

In *Estate of Cloutier,* the only issue was whether or not a discount for lack of marketability should be applied to a 100 percent interest in a company whose primary asset was a television station. The taxpayer's expert argued for a 25 percent discount based on restricted stock and pre-IPO data, which apply to minority interests. The Tax Court disallowed the discount entirely. The opinion concluded, "Because the stipulated value has not been shown to be representative of CGT's freely traded value, no discount for marketability is allowable."[90]

The foregoing case is in sharp contrast to other cases. For example, in *Estate of Dougherty,*[91] the court found a 25 percent discount for lack of marketability applicable to a 100 percent interest in the stock of an investment company where the base value was the value of the underlying assets. Another case that permitted a 25 percent discount for a controlling interest was *Estate of Maggos v. Comm'r.*[92]

In a 1999 case, the Tax Court determined a 20 percent discount for lack of marketability for an 81.93 percent interest in an S corporation that sells industrial coatings.[93] There are many cases in the 10 percent to 15 percent range for discounts for lack of marketability for controlling interests.[94] A typical example is *Estate of Bennett,*

88. Estate of Andrews v. Comm'r, 79 T.C. 938 (1982).

89. Estate of Hendrickson v. Comm'r, T.C. Memo. 1999-278, 1999 Tax Ct. Memo. LEXIS 318 (1999).

90. Estate of Cloutier v. Comm'r, T.C. Memo. 1996-049 (1996).

91. Estate of Dougherty v. Comm'r, 59 T.C. 772 (1990).

92. Estate of Maggos v. Comm'r, T.C. Memo. 2000-129 (2000).

93. Estate of Desmond v. Comm'r, T.C. Memo. 1999-76 (1999).

94. *See, e.g.,* Estate of Dunn v. Comm'r, T.C. Memo. 2000-12 (2000), *rev'd on other grounds,* 201 F.3d 339 (5th Cir. 2002) (15 percent); Temple v. United States, 2006 U.S. Dist. LEXIS 16171 (E.D. Tex. 2006) (12.5 percent).

where the Tax Court determined a 15 percent discount for a 100 percent interest in a real estate management and development company.[95]

Discounts for Lack of Control (Minority Discount)

As indicated in Chapter 15, discounts are applied to noncontrolling ownership interests. These discounts sometimes are referred to as discounts for lack of control (DLOCs) or minority discounts. This discount may be granted independently of, or in addition to, the discount for lack of marketability.

In *Estate of Jelke v. Commissioner,*[96] the taxpayer's expert discounted the subject minority interest by 25 percent for lack of control, while the IRS's expert discounted it by 5 percent. The taxpayer's expert assumed that the company was most like a closed-end and not widely traded investment fund holding publicly traded securities. Applying this assumption, the expert arrived at a 20 percent discount base and added an additional 5 percent discount because the subject company had fewer assets, paid fewer dividends, and posted lower short-term returns than did the comparable funds. The IRS expert's analysis began with an average discount (8.61 percent) for closed-end funds and reduced this on the basis that the company outperformed the comparables used by the estate. The court adopted a 10 percent lack of control discount, finding that although the company was smaller than some of the comparables presented, it was well diversified, which reduced investment risk, and that investors in the company would base their investments on the company's history of good performance.

In *Estate of Green v. Commissioner,*[97] the Tax Court concluded a 17 percent DLOC for a minority interest in a bank, rejecting a poorly explained 20 percent discount asserted by the taxpayer, but also not accepting the IRS's 15 percent discount, which it also found was not well supported.

In *Estate of Thompson v. Commissioner,*[98] after adjusting the estate's expert's capitalization rate, the court applied a 15 percent minority discount to a 20 percent interest in a publishing company. The experts for both sides in *Hess v. Commissioner*[99] agreed that a 15 percent DLOC applied, but the court criticized the taxpayer's expert for using a discount under the guideline public company method, concluding that such a discount is already included and inherent in that method. The court in *Adams v. United States*[100] applied a 20 percent DLOC to a 25 percent interest in a partnership because the taxpayer's expert provided "the lone specific analysis of the issues." In

95. Estate of Bennett v. Comm'r, T.C. Memo. 1993-34 (1993).

96. Estate of Jelke v. Comm'r, T.C. Memo. 2005-131 (2005), *rev'd,* 503 F.3d 1317 (11th Cir. 2007).

97. Estate of Green v. Comm'r, T.C. Memo. 2003-384 (2003).

98. Estate of Thompson v. Comm'r, T.C. Memo. 2004-174 (2004).

99. Hess v. Comm'r, T.C. Memo. 2003-251 (2003).

100. Adams v. United States, 2001 U.S. Dist. LEXIS 13092 (N.D. Tex. 2001).

Temple v. United States,[101] the court determined minority discounts in a range of 3.3 percent to 10.1 percent for limited partnerships holding publicly held marketable securities. The court arrived at this range by using closed-end funds data. The IRS's expert used all reporting closed-end funds and calculated the discount based on the mean of the reported discounts and premiums from net asset value. The taxpayer's expert used a limited universe of funds and computed the discount using the 75th percentile of the limited universe. The court preferred the IRS's expert's approach, finding it was more comprehensive.

Robertson v. United States[102] involved the valuation of limited partnership interests in determining a Generation Skipping Tax (GST). The taxpayer's expert arrived at a 22 percent minority discount based on 8 percent median discounts in closed-end funds, plus 11 percent based on "structural differences" between closed-end funds and the subject limited partnership, plus 3 percent for other factors. The court rejected the 3 percent discount for other factors, finding it was unwarranted, for this was based on six factors unique to the partnership, none of which was empirically quantifiable—and many of which had already been factored into the closed-end fund analysis. The IRS's expert arrived at a 6 percent minority discount, based on an average discount for closed-end funds. The court not only found that the taxpayer's expert's analysis was more thorough, but also commented that use of the median was more appropriate than the average, which could be unduly influenced by outliers. Thus, a 19 percent discount for lack of control was allowed.

Blockage

Blockage is a term used primarily in conjunction with publicly traded stock. It denotes a block of stock so large relative to typical daily or weekly trading volume that it would require a long time to release it into the public market slowly enough to avoid depressing the price of the stock.

Blockage discounts tend to be relatively modest, often in the 3 percent to 10 percent range. However, sometimes the Tax Court denies the discount totally, sometimes even inexplicably.[103] At the other extreme, the Tax Court allowed a 25 percent blockage discount on a block of thinly traded public stock of Frederick's of Hollywood.[104] More typical is *Estate of Foote,* where the Tax Court concluded a 3.3 percent

101. Temple v. United States, 2006 U.S. Dist. LEXIS 16171 (E.D. Tex. 2006).

102. Robertson v. United States, 2006 U.S. Dist. LEXIS 1167 (N.D. Tex. 2006).

103. *See, e.g.,* Estate of Davis v. Comm'r, 110 T.C. 530 (1998), where the court recognized in its decision that it probably would have taken five to six months to sell the stock without depressing the price, yet concluded that petitioner failed to satisfy the burden of proof that a blockage discount should be applied.

104. Estate of Mellinger v. Comm'r, 112 T.C. 26 (1999).

discount for blockage.[105] Nonetheless, unique facts and circumstances can lead to a higher discount.[106] In *Estate of Adams v. Comm'r,*[107] the court applied both a discount for lack of marketability and a blockage discount on the same block of stock.

Key Person Discount

Dependence on a key person introduces a risk of the consequences of the loss of that person's services in case of death, disability, or resignation. This risk sometimes is recognized through a separate discount for the key person factor.

Typical of the Tax Court's position on this issue is the following:

> Where a corporation is substantially dependent upon the services of one person, and where that person would no longer be able to perform services for the corporation by reason of death or incapacity, an investor would expect some form of discount below fair market value when purchasing stock in the corporation to compensate for the loss of that key employee. See *Estate of Huntsman v. Commissioner,* 66 T.C. 861, 1976 WL 3635 (1976); *Estate of Mitchell v. Commissioner,* supra; *Estate of Feldmar v. Commissioner,* T.C. Memo. 1988-429; *Estate of Yeager v. Commissioner,* T.C. Memo. 1986-448. Although FIC could have purchased key-person life insurance on Robert's life, a minority shareholder could not compel FIC to purchase such insurance, and FIC had no such insurance in effect.
>
> We have found as facts that Robert was a key person in the management of FIC, that FIC had no second layer of management, and that Robert's contacts, experience, and managerial expertise were critically important to the success of FIC. We therefore agree with petitioners and find that a key-person discount of 10 percent was appropriate in determining the value of FIC stock as of February 1980 and August 1981.[108]

In *Estate of Mitchell v. Comm'r,*[109] the Tax Court applied a 10 percent key person discount, but rejected a key person discount in *Estate of Renier v. Comm'r*[110] where factual reasons supporting such a discount were absent from the valuation report.

---

105. Estate of Foote v. Comm'r, T.C. Memo. 1999-37 (1999).

106. *See, e.g.,* Estate of Gimbel v. Comm'r, 2006 Tax Ct. Memo. LEXIS 274 (2006) (14.2% net discount rate for restricted and nonrestricted stock).

107. Estate of Adams v. Comm'r, T.C. Memo. 2002-80 (2002).

108. Estate of Furman v. Comm'r, T.C. Memo. 1998-157 (1998).

109. Estate of Mitchell v. Comm'r, T.C. Memo. 1997-461 (1997), *vacated,* 250 F.3d 696 (9th Cir. 2001),

110. Estate of Renier v. Comm'r, T.C. Memo. 2000-298 (2000).

Nonvoting versus Voting Stock

If a company has nonvoting as well as voting stock outstanding, the nonvoting stock may be discounted compared to the value of the voting stock. For public companies that have both voting and nonvoting stock, the discount for nonvoting in most cases is quite small, often less than 5 percent, and that level of discount often is used for private companies and accepted by the IRS and the Tax Court.

In the unusual situation where the voting stock that controls the company is only a tiny percentage of the total stock outstanding, voting control may be quite valuable, and it might be meaningless to measure the difference in value on the basis of a percentage discount. In the case of *Estate of Simplot,*[111] a tiny percentage of all the stock was voting, but it was owned by four parties, each a minority. The Tax Court placed a superpremium on the voting stock. On appeal, however, the Ninth Circuit reversed, finding that the Tax Court had based its ruling on speculation by creating a scenario in which a buyer would purchase a minority share of the voting stock, but with time would be able to play a role in the company.[112]

Premiums

Premiums may be added to value for factors such as control, industry risk, or a swing vote. In *Estate of Deputy v. Commissioner,*[113] the Tax Court accepted a negative industry risk premium. In determining the capitalization rate to apply, the industry risk premium represents the difference between the general industry risk premium for the market and the risk premium for the particular industry. The taxpayer's expert concluded a 17.5 percent capitalization rate, including a 3 percent industry adjustment. The IRS concluded a negative 5.2 percent industry risk premium, which resulted in a lower capitalization rate of around 10 percent. The court determined that the negative industry risk premium was supported by the fact that the company tended to outperform the industry and the economy.

In *Estate of Simplot v. Commissioner,*[114] the decedent owned a minority interest in a small control block of stock. The Tax Court, adopting the IRS's position, attributed a 3 percent premium to the swing vote block and then took a 35 percent discount for lack of control from the decedent's pro rata share in that block. This resulted in a multimillion-dollar control premium on the noncontrolling interest in the control block. On appeal, the Ninth Circuit reversed, finding that a buyer of the block never

111. Estate of Simplot v. Comm'r, 112 T.C. 130 (1999).
112. Estate of Simplot v. Comm'r, 249 F.3d 1191 (9th Cir. 2001).
113. Estate of Deputy v. Comm'r, T.C. Memo. 2003-176 (2003).
114. Estate of Simplot v. Comm'r, 112 T.C. 13 (1999), *rev'd*, 249 F.3d 1191 (9th Cir. 2001).

could recover the premium. In accepting the taxpayer's application of a zero premium, the court decided that a controlling block of stock is not to be valued at a premium for estate tax purposes unless it can be shown that a purchaser of the block would be able to use it "in such a way to assure an increased economic advantage worth paying a premium for."

In *Estate of Maggos v. Commissioner,*[115] the decedent's controlling block of stock in a company was repurchased by the company without the benefit of a formal valuation. After applying a 25 percent DLOM, the court applied a 25 percent control premium based on average premiums paid in the industry at the time of purchase.

In *Estate of Wright v. Commissioner,*[116] the court refused to apply a control premium asserted by the IRS's expert that was based on a hypothetical scenario in which other investors might purchase decedent's block of stock.

Trapped-in Capital Gains Taxes

One of the most dramatic developments in Tax Court decisions, starting in 1998, was explicit recognition of liability for capital gains taxes on significantly appreciated property.

In cases arising before 1987, a corporation could liquidate its assets, distribute the proceeds, and dissolve within 12 months, and by so doing eliminate the payment of capital gains taxes at the corporate level. The Tax Reform Act of 1986 eliminated that option.

Before 1986, at least partially relying on the tax-free liquidation option (known as the General Utilities Doctrine, named after a case that exercised the option), the Tax Court had steadfastly denied recognition of any trapped-in capital gains tax liability unless liquidation of the appreciated assets was clearly imminent.

After 1986, there were no C corporation gift or estate tax valuation cases clearly isolating this issue until the *Eisenberg*[117] case in 1997, when the Tax Court again denied recognition of capital gains liability as a factor diminishing value, citing several pre-1987 cases as precedent. Then in 1998, in *Estate of Davis,* the Tax Court decided as follows:

> We reject respondent's position that, as a matter of law, no discount or adjustment attributable to ADDI&C's built-in capital gains tax is allowable in the instant case. . . .
>
> We are convinced on the record in this case, and we find that, even though no liquidation of ADDI&C or sale of its assets was planned or con-

115. Estate of Maggos v. Comm'r, T.C. Memo. 2000-129 (2000).
116. Estate of Wright v. Comm'r, T.C. Memo. 1997-53 (1997).
117. Eisenberg v. Comm'r, T.C. Memo. 1997-483 (1997).

> templated on the valuation date, a hypothetical willing seller and a hypothetical willing buyer would not have agreed on that date on a price for each of the blocks of stock in question that took no account of ADDI&C's built-in capital gains tax.[118]

The court ultimately recognized a diminution in value equal to approximately half the trapped-in capital gains tax liability. Shortly following the *Davis* decision, the Second Circuit Court of Appeals, citing favorably *Estate of Davis,* reversed *Eisenberg:*

> In the past, the denial of a reduction for potential capital gains tax liability was based, in part, on the possibility that the taxes could be avoided by liquidating the corporation. . . . These tax-favorable options ended with the Tax Reform Act of 1986 (TRA). . . .
>
> Now that the TRA has effectively closed the option to avoid capital gains tax at the corporate level, reliance on these cases in the post-TRA environment should, in our view, no longer continue.[119]

The Second Circuit concluded by vacating the Tax Court opinion and remanding the case to the Tax Court to determine the gift tax based on a valuation taking into consideration the capital gains tax liability. The case was settled with a discount of about the same percentage of the trapped-in gains tax as was decided by the court in *Davis.*

Then in 1999, in *Estate of Simplot,* the Tax Court reached a decision that reflected a valuation deduction of 100 percent of the trapped-in capital gains tax on a block of stock owned by the company being valued.[120]

Another 1999 case, citing *Davis,* recognized the trapped-in capital gains tax liability of a company's timber. The court estimated the rate of growth, the rate of inflation, the capital gains tax rate, and the time period over which the timber would be cut. It discounted the estimated capital gains tax for each year to a present value, using an estimated equity cost of capital (discount rate). It then deducted the full present value of the capital gains liability thus estimated.[121]

The majority of cases that have followed, either at the Tax Court level or on appeal, have permitted discounts for trapped-in capital gains. The Tax Court in *Estate of Welch v. Comm'r*[122] denied such a discount, but was reversed by the Sixth Circuit,

118. Estate of Davis v. Comm'r, 110 T.C. 530 (1998).
119. Eisenberg v. Comm'r, 155 F.3d 50 (2d Cir. 1998).
120. Estate of Simplot v. Comm'r, 112 T.C. 130 (1999).
121. Estate of Jameson v. Comm'r, T.C. Memo. 1999-43 (1999).
122. Estate of Welch v. Comm'r, T.C. Memo. 1998-167 (1998), *rev'd,* 208 F.3d 213 (6th Cir. 2000).

which found that even though the company was eligible to defer the tax under IRC Section 1033, such eligibility—or even the exercise of such deferral rights—did not automatically preclude application of the discount. In *Estate of Borgatello v. Comm'r,*[123] the Tax Court allowed a 24 percent discount for trapped-in capital gains on a controlling interest in a real estate holding company. The Tax Court in *Estate of Dunn v. Comm'r*[124] permitted only a 5 percent discount, but on appeal, the Fifth Circuit ruled that a dollar-for-dollar reduction, amounting to a 34 percent discount, had to be applied to the company's asset-based value. In *Estate of Jelke v. Comm'r,*[125] the Tax Court had rejected a dollar-for-dollar reduction for trapped-in capital gains on a minority interest, reasoning that a hypothetical willing buyer of a minority interest would not adjust the purchase price to reflect the entire amount of the company's built-in capital gains tax liability, and that a hypothetical seller would not accept that was reduced for such liability. Finding the Fifth Circuit's approach in *Dunn* persuasive, the Eleventh Circuit reversed, essentially assuming that all company assets were sold in liquidation on the valuation date and that 100 percent of the trapped-in tax liability would be offset against the fair market value of the stock, dollar-for-dollar. The court thus rejected the Tax Court's distinction between a minority and controlling interest for purposes of the discount, noting that "whether or not a majority or minority interest is present is of no moment in an assumption of liquidation setting."

Cases that have rejected the discount for trapped-in capital gains have involved partnership interests, where the capital gains tax could have been avoided by an IRC Section 754 election. The courts in those cases have reasoned that a hypothetical buyer and seller would negotiate with the understanding that such an election would be made.[126]

Charitable Contributions

Regulation Section 1.170A-13 (c) requires a summary appraisal by a qualified appraiser in conjunction with any charitable contribution in the form of a closely held business interest valued at more than $5,000. The section defines a qualified appraiser as an individual who:

1. Holds himself or herself out to the public as an appraiser or who regularly performs appraisals

123. Estate of Borgatello v. Comm'r, T.C. Memo. 2000-264 (2000).

124. Estate of Dunn v. Comm'r, T.C. Memo. 2000-12 (2000), *rev'd and remanded*, 301 F.3d 339 (5th Cir. 2002).

125. Estate of Jelke v. Comm'r, T.C. Memo. 2005-131 (2005), *rev'd,* 503 F.3d 1317 (11th Cir. 2007).

126. Estate of Jones v. Comm'r, 116 T.C. 121 (2001); Temple v. United States, 2006 U.S. Dist. LEXIS 16171 (E.D. Tex. 2006).

2. Is qualified to appraise property because of his or her qualifications
3. Is aware of the appraiser penalties associated with the overvaluation of charitable contributions under IRC Section 6701

Certain individuals, however, may not act as qualified appraisers, including:

1. The property's donor (or the taxpayer who claims the deduction)
2. The property's donee
3. A party to the property transfer transaction (with certain very specific exceptions)
4. Any person employed by, married to, or related to any of the above persons
5. An appraiser who regularly appraises for the donor, donee, or party to the transaction and does not perform a majority of his or her appraisals for other persons
6. An individual who would otherwise be a qualified appraiser, but the donor has knowledge of facts that would cause a reasonable person to expect the appraiser falsely to overstate the value of the donated property (e.g., the donor and the appraiser make an agreement concerning the amount at which the property will be valued and the donor knows that such amount exceeds the fair market value of the property)

The IRS and the Tax Court enforce this requirement. For example, in one case, the IRS completely disallowed charitable deductions claimed in two years because the donor failed to comply with the appraisal requirement, even though the commissioner conceded that the values claimed as deductions were the same as the fair market value of the stock contributed. The Tax Court upheld the commissioner's determination. The Court of Appeals found that "Congress intended the qualified appraisal requirement to be mandatory." Accordingly, the taxpayer's failure to obtain an appraisal was fatal to any claim of deduction for his charitable contributions.[127]

In addition, other valuation issues arise in the charitable deduction context, such as the appropriate discounts to apply. For example, where shareholders owned a 45 percent interest in a corporation and simultaneously donated their interest "in lockstep" with the corporation's other minority shareholders, as part of a prearranged plan, the Tax Court reduced the IRS's proposed 22 percent minority discount to 10 percent, but failed to explain why any minority discount was justified, because collectively 100 percent of the company was being transferred.[128]

127. Hewitt v. Comm'r, 166 F.3d 332 (4th Cir. 1998).
128. Koblick v. Comm'r, 2006 Tax Ct. Memo. LEXIS 63 (2006).

With regard to contributions of qualified appreciated stock, an issue that can arise is whether on the transfer date market quotations with respect to the shares are readily available on an established securities market. In *Todd v. Comm'r,*[129] the stock at issue had not been listed on any exchange and the taxpayer based the claimed deductions on subsequent sales of stock that occurred shortly after the contributions were made. The Tax Court disallowed the deductions, holding that the shares were not qualified appreciated stock on the transfer date. Therefore, the taxpayer was subject to substantiation requirements, which the taxpayer failed to provide. The case thus illustrates the importance of obtaining a formal appraisal when shares are not traded on an exchange.

Contingent Liabilities

The most common contingent liabilities are environmental liabilities (discovered or potential) and outcomes of lawsuits. The uncertainty, of course, makes it very difficult to quantify the impact on value of these contingencies at a moment in time. In a true market setting, the solution normally would be to create a reserve account in escrow pending resolution of the uncertainties, but in a tax setting one must arrive at a specific number as of the effective valuation date.

A 1999 case involved a paint company that was considered a hazardous-waste producer with potential environmental liability. The court allowed a 10 percent discount from the value indicated by the discounted cash flow method but no discount from the value indicated by the guideline public company method, on the theory that the guideline company stock market prices probably already reflected the potential environmental liability.[130] In *Estate of Mitchell v. Comm'r,*[131] the Tax Court took a $1.5 million discount for a pending compensation lawsuit. In *Estate of Klauss v. Comm'r,*[132] the court permitted a 10 percent discount for product liability and environmental claims.

Subsequent Events and Information

The principle is clear that only events or information that were known or foreseeable as of the valuation date may be taken into consideration. Clear as the principle may be, the admissibility and relevance of postvaluation date information is often a major controversy.

129. Todd v. Comm'r, 118 T.C. 354 (2002).

130. Estate of Desmond v. Comm'r, T.C. Memo. 1999-76 (1999).

131. Estate of Mitchell v. Comm'r, T.C. Memo. 1997-461 (1997), *vacated*, 250 F.3d 696 (9th Cir. 2001).

132. Estate of Klauss v. Comm'r, T.C. Memo. 2000-191 (2000).

Proximity of Financial Information to Valuation Date

If valuing stock late in a fiscal period, it usually is acceptable to use financial data as of the end of that period. The philosophy is that late in a fiscal period, the performance for the period would be reasonably foreseeable in most cases.

For example, for a valuation date of December 12, 1988, the court stated:

> [we] agree with respondent that it makes more sense to value a gift of stock made in December 1988 using financial data as of December 31, 1988, rather than December 31, 1987. . . .[133]

In *Central Trust v. Commissioner,* the subject company prepared financial statements quarterly. Gifts were made on August 3 and October 25. For the August 3 gifts, the court used earnings for the 12 months ended June 30 for the fifth year of a five-year weighted average for both the subject and guideline public companies. For the October 25 gifts, the court used earnings for the 12 months ended September 30 for the fifth year of a five-year weighted average for both the subject and guideline public companies. This is a commonly used procedure, avoiding any subsequent information dispute.[134]

On appeal in *Polack v. Comm'r,*[135] the taxpayer used unaudited financials for years subsequent to the valuation date to argue that actual results were significantly lower than projections provided by the IRS at trial. The Eighth Circuit did not admit these, saying that "post-transaction earnings would not have been known to a prospective purchaser" as of the valuation date.

In *Okerlund v. United States,*[136] the Federal Circuit affirmed the Court of Federal Claims' ruling that estate plan provisions requiring the purchase of stock upon decedent's death should not have been included in valuing the stock when decedent's death was untimely and unexpected. The court said that valuation must always be made as of the donative date relying primarily on ex ante information; ex post data should be used sparingly. As with all evidentiary submissions, however, the critical question is relevance. The closer the profile of the later-date company to that of the valuation-date company, the more likely ex post data are to be relevant (though even in some cases, they may not be). The greater the significance of exogenous or unforeseen events occurring between the valuation date and the date of the proffered evidence, the less likely ex post evidence is to be relevant—even as a sanity check on the assumptions underlying a valuation model.

133. Rabenhorst v. Comm'r, T.C. Memo. 1996-92 (1996).
134. Central Trust v. United States, 305 F.2d 393 (Ct. Cl. 1962).
135. Polack v. Comm'r, T.C. Memo. 2002-145 (2002), *aff'd*, 366 F.3d 608 (8th Cir. 2004).
136. Okerlund v. United States, 365 F.3d 1044 (Fed. Cir. 2004).

In *Estate of Noble v. Comm'r,*[137] the court permitted the use of a postdeath event to value minority shares in a bank. The estate presented as evidence of value an offer by the controlling shareholder to purchase the decedent's shares for $878,004 a few months after the date of death. However, the IRS presented evidence of the estate's sale of the shares to the bank for $1.1 million 10 months later. The court noted that there had not been any material change in circumstances between the sale date and the date of death. The court reasoned that "An event occurring after a valuation date, even if unforeseeable as of the valuation date, also may be probative of the earlier valuation to the extent that it is relevant to establishing the amount that a hypothetical willing buyer would have paid a hypothetical willing seller for the subject property as of the valuation date. . . . . Unforeseeable subsequent events which fall within this latter category include evidence, such as we have here."[138]

Subsequent Sales

Readers should be put on notice that the Tax Court frequently relies on subsequent sales as evidence of value. The court distinguishes between subsequent sales that *affected* the value and those that are merely *evidence of value.*

A subsequent sale surfaced as an issue in *Estate of Jung* in an opinion released in November of 1993. The matter involved the fair market value of a 20 percent interest in an operating company as of October 9, 1984. In mid-1986, the company was approached about selling its major operating assets, a transaction was completed on December 29, 1986, and the company was liquidated. The Tax Court explained its position as follows:

> Respondent contends that, in valuing Jung Corp. stock, this Court should consider the sale to Kendall, the other sales, and the ensuing liquidation of Jung Corp. Petitioner contends the 1986 sales and the liquidation are irrelevant because the sales and liquidation were unforeseeable at the valuation date.
>
> We agree in part with respondent and in part with petitioner.
>
> A distinction may usefully be drawn between later-occurring events which affect fair market value as of the valuation date, and later-occurring events which may be taken into account as evidence of fair market value as of the valuation date.

137. Estate of Noble v. Comm'r, T.C. Memo. 2005-2 (2005).

138. For an extensive list of notable susbsequent events court cases, see exhibit 28-1 in Shannon P. Pratt & Alina Niculita, Valuing a Business: The Analysis and Appraisal of Closely Held Companies 672 (5th ed., McGraw-Hill 2008).

> If a prospective October 9, 1984, buyer and seller were likely to have foreseen the 1986 sale to Kendall, and the other activities leading to the liquidation, then those later-occurring events could affect what a willing buyer would pay and what a willing seller would demand as of October 9, 1984. We conclude, and we have found that, on October 9, 1984, Jung Corp. was not for sale, the sale to Kendall was not foreseeable, and the liquidation was not foreseeable. Accordingly, we conclude that those later-occurring events did not affect the October 9, 1984, fair market of decedent's stock. *Estate of Gilford v. Commissioner,* 88 T.C. 38, 51-55 (1987).
>
> However, we have stated that "for purposes of determining fair market value, we believe it appropriate to consider sales of properties occurring subsequent to the valuation date if the properties involved are indeed comparable to the subject properties." *Estate of Thompson v. Commissioner,* 89 T.C. 619, 628-629 n. 7 (1987), *rev'd.* on other grounds 864 F.2d 1128 (4th Cir. 1989). To the same effect are e.g., *Krapf v. United States,* 977 F.2d 1454, 1458-1460 (Fed. Cir. 1992); *Estate of Kaplin v. Commissioner,* 748 F.2d 1109, 1111 (6th Cir. 1984), *rev'g.* T.C. Memo. 1982-440 (1982); *Estate of Brown v. Commissioner,* 425 F.2d 1406, 1407 (5th Cir. 1970), *aff'g.* T.C. Memo. 1969-91 (1969). See *Estate of Jung v. Commissioner,* T.C. Memo. 1990-5 and cases cited therein.
>
> Of course, appropriate adjustments must be made to take account of differences between the valuation date and the dates of the later-occurring events. . . . Although any such changes must be accounted for in determining the evidentiary weight to be given to the later-occurring events, those changes ordinarily are not justification for ignoring the later-occurring events (unless other comparables offer significantly better matches to the property being valued).
>
> When viewed in this light—as evidence of value rather than as something that affects value—later-occurring events are no more to be ignored than earlier-occurring events.
>
> Accordingly, we do not consider the sales and eventual liquidation as affecting the October 9, 1984, value of Jung Corp., but we do consider these events as evidence of the October 9, 1984, value.[139]

Ultimately, the Tax Court determined that some of the petitioner's higher indications of value were reconcilable with the subsequent sale.

In *Saltzman v. Commissioner,*[140] a holding company sold its major asset, film rights, seven months after the valuation date at a much higher price than the taxpayer's

139. Estate of Jung v. Comm'r, 101 T.C. 412 (1993).

140. Saltzman v. Comm'r, T.C. Memo. 1994-641, 68 T.C. Memo. (CCH) 1544 (1994).

expert had appraised the rights as of the valuation date. The court relied on the sale value, discounted for the time value back to the effective valuation date. The court explained its position as follows:

> Generally, a sale of the property close in time to the valuation date is the best evidence of fair market value. *Estate of Spruill v. Commissioner,* 88 T.C. 1197, 1229, 1233 (1987); sec. 20.2031-1(b) Estate Tax Regs. A sale of the property after the valuation date is highly relevant evidence of value if there are no material changes in the interim. *Estate of Kaplin v. Commissioner,* 748 F.2d 1109, 1111 (6th Cir. 1984), *rev'g.* T.C. Memo. 1982-440 (sale 2 years after the valuation date). In contrast, material market changes following the valuation date may make a later sale price less probative or irrelevant in deciding the value on the valuation date. *Estate of Spruill v. Commissioner,* supra at 1233.
>
> Petitioners argue that the RKO sale should not be considered in deciding the value of the film library because the sale was not foreseeable. We disagree. The test used to decide whether we may consider a later sale is not whether the sale was foreseeable, but whether later events have materially changed the value of the property. See *Estate of Kaplin v. Commissioner* supra. Petitioners argue that *Estate of Gilford v. Commissioner,* 88 T.C. 38, 52-55 (1987), holds that the test is whether the subsequent sale was foreseeable at the valuation date. We disagree. In *Estate of Gilford,* we found that a merger 6 months after the valuation date was a major unforeseen change in circumstances that effected the value of the property at issue. ID. at 54-55. Thus, we did not consider the later sale.

Here, there were no major changes in circumstances between the recapitalization and the RKO sale that affected the value of MBI stock.[141]

The most extreme case of the Tax Court relying on a sale long after the effective valuation date is found in *Estate of Cidulka.*[142] The effective valuation date was January 25, 1982. Four years later (January of 1986), the company, an outdoor advertising sign company, sold its assets to a major competitor for 2.89 times its gross revenue. The Tax Court used this sale to conclude that the value of the stock should be 2.5 times the company's gross revenue for 1981 (the year prior to the effective valuation date).

In one case, the Tax Court relied on a January 1994 sale to value minority stock in an estate as of July 16, 1991. The estate tax return valued the stock at $35.20 per share, based on an update of an appraisal conducted in 1989. The 1994 sale took place

141. *Id.*
142. Estate of Cidulka v. Comm'r, T.C. Memo. 1996-149, 71 T.C. Memo. (CCH) 2555 (1996).

at $75.15 per share. The Tax Court reduced the sale price by 30 percent, resulting in a value of $50.51 per share. The reason for the reduction was because the IRS offered no expert testimony and the court rejected the taxpayer's expert's opinion for several reasons:

- He was unable to explain certain parts of the analysis contained in the reports.
- He arbitrarily applied a 35 percent marketability discount.
- He made no mention of a hypothetical seller.
- While the 1989 report states that (taxpayer's expert) toured the facilities, there is nothing in his testimony or the 1991 report to suggest that he did likewise before preparing the 1991 report.
- The 1991 report does not adequately account for the fact that the company's 1991 earnings increased dramatically over the years covered by the 1989 report.
- The 1991 report does not adequately take into account that the company began paying dividends after the time covered by the 1989 report.
- The 1991 report refers to the financial data of publicly traded companies, yet never explains how those companies were selected or in what respects their lines of business were similar to that of the subject company.[143]

The estate tax value filed might well have held up in court had it been adequately supported. In some other valuation context, such as family law, the case may have been remanded because of lack of adequate valuation evidence, but the Tax Court goes ahead and reaches a conclusion based on whatever it has before it.

In another case, the Tax Court relied on a redemption 16 months following the valuation date. Again the IRS offered no expert testimony and the court rejected the taxpayer's expert's opinion as unpersuasive, noting, among other shortcomings, reliance on companies that were not comparable. The final determination of value was the redemption amount of $1,947,845, compared to $15,335 filed on the decedent's federal estate tax return. The court also upheld the fraud penalty under Section 6663(a).[144]

Buy-Sell Agreements

The value established by a buy-sell agreement may be controlling, may be ignored, or may be a factor to consider.

143. Estate of Scanlan v. Comm'r, T.C. Memo. 1996-331 (1996).
144. Estate of Trompeter v. Comm'r, T.C. Memo. 1998-35 (1998).

For buy-sell agreements entered into after October 8, 1990, a buy-sell price is binding for federal estate tax purposes if it meets all the following criteria:[145]

- The price must be fixed or determinable as of a determinable date.
- The agreement must be binding on the parties both during life and after death.
- The agreement must have been entered into for a bona fide business reason.
- It must not be a substitute for testamentary disposition.
- The agreement must result in a fair market value for the subject business interest at the time the agreement is executed.
- Its terms must be comparable to similar arrangements entered into by persons in arm's-length transactions.

The Tax Court, in *Estate of Lauder v. Commissioner* (*Lauder II*),[146] adopted this test and ruled that the test's elements are conjunctive, meaning that all of them must be independently satisfied to give the buy-sell price dispositive effect.

Regulations Section 20.2031-2(h) provides:

> Such price will be disregarded in determining the value of the securities unless it is determined under the circumstances of the particular case that the agreement represents a *bona fide* business arrangement and not a device to pass the decedent's shares to the natural objects of his bounty for less than full and adequate consideration in money or money's worth.

In *Estate of Blount v. Commissioner,*[147] the Tax Court disregarded a buy-sell agreement in determining decedent's interest in a closely held company on the date of his death because decedent had the unilateral ability to modify it, thus failing to satisfy the requirement that it be binding during life. The court also disregarded the agreement under IRC Section 2703, which requires that to be included in a valuation, a buy-sell agreement's terms must be "comparable to similar arrangements entered into by persons in an arm's length transaction." Here, the court concluded that the parties were "related" and had not engaged in arm's-length bargaining. The Eleventh Circuit affirmed.

145. IRC § 2703. For a discussion of Section 2703's treatment of buy-sell agreements, see Howard M. Zaritsky & Ronald D. Aucutt, Structuring Estate Freezes, chs. 4 and 8 (Warren Gorham Lamont 1996).

146. Estate of Lauder v. Comm'r (*Lauder II*), T.C. Memo. 1992-736 (1992).

147. Estate of Blount v. Comm'r, T.C. Memo. 2004-116 (2004), *aff'd,* 428 F.3d 1338 (11th Cir. 2005).

Interestingly in this case, there was a life insurance policy owned by the company that provided $3.1 million to pay off the mandated buyout of the shares. The Tax Court included the full amount of the insurance proceeds as nonoperating assets and also concluded that because the buy-sell agreement had been disregarded, the issue of whether the company's obligation under that agreement to redeem decedent's stock should offset the proceeds was not before the court. As to the insurance proceeds, the Eleventh Circuit ruled that the Tax Court had erred because those proceeds had already been taken into account in the determination of net worth. The court noted that even when a buy-sell agreement is inoperative for purposes of establishing the value of the company for tax purposes, the agreement remains an enforceable liability against the valued company, if state law fixes such an obligation—which it had in this case. Here, the insurance proceeds were offset dollar-for-dollar by the company's obligation to satisfy its contract with the decedent's estate. The court thus concluded that such nonoperating "assets" should not be included in the fair market valuation of a company where, as here, there was an enforceable contractual obligation that offset such assets.

In *Estate of True v. Commissioner,*[148] one issue was whether the book value price specified in the buy-sell agreements controlled estate and gift tax values of the subject interests in several family companies gifted and deeded to children. The analysis focused on the *Lauder II* factors. The court found that the fact that the children did not have independent legal or accounting advice, while not dispositive, reasonably suggested less than arm's-length dealings. The court was critical that the companies' buy-sell agreements did not provide a mechanism for periodic review or adjustment to the tax book value formula. The court also considered an analysis under the adequacy of consideration test. This test requires that the formula price (1) be comparable to what persons with adverse interests dealing at arm's length would accept and (2) bear a reasonable relationship to fair market value. As the court said, "[T]hese standards must be applied with the heightened scrutiny imposed on intrafamily agreements restricting transfers of closely held businesses." The court concluded that "[t]he True family buy-sell agreements do not satisfy the *Lauder II* test, because they are substitutes for testamentary dispositions. As a result, under Section 2031 and the related regulations, the tax book value buy-sell agreement price does not control estate tax values of interests in the True companies at issue in the estate tax case." The court also determined that the buy-sell agreements were not controlling for the gift tax case. The Tenth Circuit affirmed.

An example of a case where the buy-sell agreement price was controlling is *Hutchens Non-Marital Trust v. Commissioner.*[149] The court upheld the buy-sell price

148. Estate of True v. Comm'r, T.C. Memo. 2001 167 (2001), *aff'd,* 390 F.3d 1210 (10th Cir. 2004).

149. Hutchens Non-Marital Trust v. Comm'r, T.C. Memo. 1993-600 (1993).

because it found that the negotiations had been at arm's length and in the ordinary course of business. In arriving at this decision, the court noted that a formal appraisal had been conducted and that each of the parties to the agreement had been individually represented by attorneys during negotiations. This case demonstrates the benefit of having an appraisal conducted not only after the buy-sell agreement has been entered into but also to aid in setting a buy-sell price or formula.

Weighting of Valuation Method Results

As discussed in Chapter 16, "Reconciliation of Value Indications," Revenue Ruling 59-60 is opposed to the idea of reconciling two or more indications of value by applying mathematical weights to each. Judge Laro discusses the issue as follows:

> In spite of this, some valuation practitioners apply weights to various factors in reaching their valuation conclusions because this allows them to clearly demonstrate the importance that they attach to various valuation considerations. This approach was used by the Tax Court in *Estate of Feldmar v. Comm'r,* T.C. Memo. 1988-429; *Estate of Titus v. Comm'r,* T.C. Memo. 1989-466; *Estate of Campbell v. Comm'r*, T.C. Memo. 1991-615. The weighing of various methods, however, was squarely rejected by the Court in *Estate of Mueller v. Comm'r*, T.C. Memo. 1992-284.
>
> With what appears to be conflicting judicial positions on this issue, there is some concern about whether the weighing of factors is a proper method of appraisal.
>
> I believe that one should consider carefully all relevant factors but should not assign weights to each factor. However, practitioners may emphasize a few factors that could influence the ultimate valuation.[150]

Another case in which the court ultimately utilized an explicit percentage weighting of factors was the oft-quoted *Central Trust v. United States* in the U.S. Court of Claims. In this case, the court relied entirely on the guideline public company method and applied 50 percent of the weight to the price/earnings multiples, 30 percent to the dividend yield, and 20 percent to the price/book value multiple.[151] In *Hess v. Comm'r,*[152] the IRS's expert did not assign any weight to the discounted cash flow method because the company's future income was difficult to predict and because valuation conclusions were highly sensitive to small changes in assumptions. The Tax Court

150. Laro, *supra* note 1.
151. Central Trust v. United States, 305 F.2d 393 (Ct. Cl. 1962).
152. Hess v. Comm'r, T.C. Memo. 2003-251 (2003).

indicated that while less weight should be accorded to this method under such circumstances, it nonetheless should be considered in the valuation process. The court did not, however, specify an exact percentage of weight to be accorded to the method. In *Estate of Dunn v. Comm'r,*[153] the court indicated that weighting was a key issue. The IRS's expert accorded the asset approach a 100 percent weight, while the taxpayer's expert weighted the income and asset approaches equally given that no liquidation was planned. The Tax Court decided the appropriate weight was 65 percent for the asset approach and 35 percent for the income approach, based on various factors, such as the depressed nature of the industry and the company's low profitability and high debt. On appeal, the Fifth Circuit determined that the likelihood of liquidation was a relevant factor for weighting and ruled that the earnings-based method should be weighted at 85 percent to reflect the low likelihood of liquidation.[154]

If the expert says, "I accorded more weight to x factor," the judge may ask, "Well, how *much* weight?" My colleagues and I have previously opined on this dilemma as follows:

> Despite this wording, the method has been used successfully in many gift and estate tax cases both in dealing with the IRS and in cases decided in court. The wording of Revenue Ruling 59-60 indicates concern that the averaging or weighted average method leaves room for omission of pertinent factors. However, it is possible to use the basic weighted average of factors procedure and still, at one stage or another, incorporate consideration of all the pertinent factors mentioned in Revenue Ruling 59-60. Of course, it is important to be careful to demonstrate in each case that all other pertinent factors were actively considered and reflected in the result to the appropriate extent.[155]

All this discussion would seem to lead to the conclusion that neither explicit nor implicit weighting of varying indications of value is clearly superior. If an explicit weighting is used, we suggest a disclaimer to the effect that there is no empirical basis for the weighting; it is presented only to help the reader understand the analyst's thinking regarding relative importance.[156]

---

153. Estate of Dunn v. Comm'r, T.C. Memo. 2000-12 (2000), *rev'd on other grounds*, 201 F.3d 339 (5th Cir. 2002).

154. Other examples of express weighting are Estate of Freeman v. Comm'r, T.C. Memo. 1996-372 (1996) (court accepts IRS's 70% weighting of market approach and 30% of income approach, but accords no weight to taxpayer's value); Estate of Smith v. Comm'r, T.C. Memo. 1999-368 (1999) (court accepts a 70/30% weighting to asset/income approaches, respectively).

155. SHANNON PRATT ET AL., VALUING A BUSINESS 374 (3d ed. 1996).

156. For further discussion of this issue, see ch. 20, *Weighting of Approaches*, *in* DAVID LARO & SHANNON P. PRATT, BUSINESS VALUATION AND TAXES: PROCEDURE, LAW, AND PERSPECTIVE (John Wiley & Sons, 2005).

Pressure to Settle

The Tax Court has consistently urged taxpayers and the IRS to attempt to settle valuation disputes rather than bring them to trial. For example:

> Once again we must advise counsel that valuation cases such as this are better suited for the give and take of the settlement process than adjudication. See *Buffalo Tool & Die Manufacturing Co. v. Commissioner,* 74 T.C. 441, 451 (1980); *Messing v. Commissioner,* 48 T.C. 502, 512 (1967). It is quite clear from the record that the experts have not been permitted to meet to discuss their reports and attempt to resolve their differences. Furthermore, the Court concludes that counsel have failed to meaningfully confer with each other regarding settlement and stipulation as required by the Court's Standing Pretrial Order. The result of this "Rambo" approach to Tax Court litigation is that the parties and the Court have had to spend considerable time and effort in trial, on briefs, and in opinion writing to resolve a question which clearly should have been settled.[157]

In another example:

> Because valuation may not be reduced to the rote application of formulas, and because of the imprecision inherent in determining fair market value of stock that lacks a public market (and the Solomon-like pronouncements that often follow), we again remind the parties that these matters are better resolved by agreement rather than trial by ordeal in which conflicting opinions of the experts are pitted against each other. See *Estate of Hall v. Commissioner,* supra; *Messing v. Commissioner,* 48 T.C. 502, 512, 1967 WL 960 (1967).[158]

References for Valuations for Federal Tax Matters

Articles and Books

Bellatti, Robert M., and Shari L. West. 1999. *Estate Planning for Farms and Other Qualified Family-Owned Businesses*. Boston: Warren, Gorham & Lamont. Covers Section 2032A and Section 2057 special-use valuations.

157. Estate of Bruce v. Comm'r, T.C. Memo. 1993-244 (1993).
158. Estate of Furman v. Comm'r, T.C. Memo. 1998-157 (1998). *See also* Estate of Fleming v. Comm'r, T.C. Memo. 1997-484 (1997); Buffalo Tool & Die Mfg. Co. v. Comm'r, 74 T.C. 441, 1980 WL 4569 (1980).

Bogdanski, John. 1996. *Federal Tax Valuation*. Plus annual supplements. Includes thousands of case citations with discussions.

Feld, Daniel E. 2002. *Estate and Gift Tax Digest*, 4th Ed. Boston: Warren, Gorham & Lamont. Cites and digests, cases and rulings.

Fishman, Jay, et al. 2008. "Estate and Gift Tax Valuations." In *PPC's Guide to Business Valuations*, 10–1 to 10–75. Fort Worth, TX: Practitioners Publishing Co.

Howitt, Idelle A. 2002/2003. *Federal Tax Valuation Digest: Business Enterprise and Business Interests*. Boston: Warren, Gorham & Lamont. Summarizes most federal cases involving valuations of businesses and business interests from 1945 through the present. Each annual edition is cumulative.

Kasper, Larry J. 1997. "Federal Tax Valuations." In *Business Valuations, Advanced Topics*, 211–58. Westport, CN: Greenwood Publishing.

Pratt, Shannon. 2003. "Tax Related Valuations." In *Business Valuation Body of Knowledge*, 2nd Ed., 309–14. New York: John Wiley & Sons.

Pratt, Shannon P., and Alina V. Niculita. 2008. "Valuation for Estate and Gift Tax Purposes" and "Valuation for Income Tax Purposes." In *Valuing a Business*, 5th Ed., 627–60, 723–52. New York: McGraw-Hill.

Saltzman, Michael J. 2006. *IRS Practice and Procedure*, Rev. 2nd Ed. Warren, Gorham & Lamont. Covers the complete range of IRS procedures from rulings to collection of taxes.

Solomon, Lewis D., and Lewis J. Saret. 1998. "General Rules of Valuation: Tax Perspective." In *Valuation of Closely Held Businesses,* 67–104. New York: Panel Publishers.

Stockdale, John J. "A Test of DLOM Computational Models." *Business Valuation Review,* Fall 2008, 131–37.

Trugman, Gary. 2002. "Revenue Ruling 59–60." In *Understanding Business Valuations,* 2nd Ed., 409–48. New York: American Institute of Certified Public Accountants.

Zaritsky, Howard M., and Ronald D. Aucutt, 1996. *Structuring Estate Freezes,* Chaps. 4 and 8. New York: Warren, Gorham & Lamont.

Web Sites

Www.BVResources.com contains BVLibrary.com. Contains full text of all case opinions in this chapter, all searchable by key word.

Www.ustaxcourt.gov contains all appealable Tax Court opinions from January 3, 1999, to the present.

Chapter 18

Shareholder and Partner Disputes

Virtually all states have dissenting stockholder statutes. Dissenters' rights are triggered by major corporate actions, such as mergers, acquisitions, or liquidations, the criteria for which vary from state to state. Stockholders who dissent may not reverse the corporate action but are entitled to be paid the *fair value* of the shares immediately before the action has been put into effect, excluding any anticipatory appreciation or depreciation.

A growing number of states also have minority oppression statutes, many of which are based on the Model Business Corporation Act (MBCA), as revised.[1] Significantly, Delaware, considered a bellwether of corporate law, does not have a minority oppression statute, and the Delaware Supreme Court has refused to impose a remedy for minority shareholder oppression absent a pronouncement from the state's legislature.[2] Nonetheless, it is clear that a majority of states provide some form of relief for oppressed minority shareholders.[3]

Some states require that the collective minority seeking oppression relief own some minimum percentage of the total stock; others have no such requirement. Criteria required to trigger a finding of oppression or irreconcilable differences vary. In

---

1. *See* Model Bus. Corp. Act § 14.30(2)(ii) (2002), *available at* http://www.abanet.org/buslaw/library/onlinepublications/mbca2002.pdf (providing that a shareholder may petition for dissolution when "the directors or those in control of the corporation have acted, are acting, or will act in a manner that is illegal, oppressive, or fraudulent").

2. Nixon v. Blackwell, 626 A.2d 1366, 1377 (Del. 1993).

3. *See* John H. Matheson & R. Kevin Maler, *A Simple Statutory Solution to Minority Oppression in the Closely Held Business*, 91 MINN. L. REV. 657, February 2007. (Based on its survey of the law in all 50 states, the article indicates that 20 states apply the reasonable expectations standard, one state uses reasonable expectations as a factor, and 12 states have adopted a fiduciary duty approach that, for the most part, is expansive and could be employed to reach the same result as the reasonable expectations standard.)

most states, oppressed owners may seek dissolution of the entity. Most states also provide for alternative remedies, particularly a compulsory buyout of the minority by the majority or the company at fair value.[4]

One line of cases requires a finding of wrongdoing by the controlling shareholder, such as self-dealing or repudiation of going-in corporate governance arrangements.[5] In such jurisdictions, the judicial scrutiny ordinarily takes the doctrinal form of an inquiry into whether the majority shareholder has breached a duty of "utmost good faith and loyalty" that is owed to the minority investor. Another line of cases defines oppression with reference to what a court determines to be the reasonable expectations of the minority shareholders. This "reasonable expectations" test is normally applicable only to founding shareholders and is based on expectations at formation.[6] Some states, such as Illinois, define oppression as heavy-handed and overbearing or arbitrary conduct.[7] Especially in states that do not have an oppression dissolution statute, some courts have imposed a fiduciary duty between close corporation shareholders and have permitted a minority shareholder to bring a direct cause of action for breach of this duty. In the seminal decision of *Donahue v. Rodd Electrotype Co.*, the Massachusetts Supreme Judicial Court adopted such a standard:

> We hold that stockholders in the close corporation owe one another substantially the same fiduciary duty in the operation of the enterprise that partners owe to one another. In our previous decisions, we have defined the standard of duty owed by partners to one another as the "utmost good faith and loyalty." Stockholders in close corporations must discharge their management and stockholder responsibilities in conformity with this strict good faith standard. They may not act out of avarice, expediency or self-interest in derogation of their duty of loyalty to the other stockholders and to the corporation.[8]

Other courts have imposed a similar duty.[9] It is arguable that such a duty should

4. *Id.* at fn. 32 (indicating that about 40 states provide this remedy by statute or through case law).

5. *See, e.g.*, Baker v. Commercial Body Builders, 264 Ore. 614, 507 P.2d 387 (1973); Alaska Plastics, Inc. v. Coppock, 621 P.2d 270 (Alaska 1980).

6. *See, e.g.*, Landstrom v. Shaver, 561 N.W.2d 1 (S.D. 1997); Meiselman v. Meiselman, 307 S.E.2d 551 (N.C. 1983); Fox v. 7-L Bar Ranch Co., 645 P.2d 929 (Mont. 1982); Mulenberg v. Bicon Corp., 669 A.2d 1382 (N.J. 1996); *In re* Kemp & Beatley, Inc., 473 N.E.2d 1173 (N.Y. 1984).

7. Compton v. Paul K. Harding Realty Co., 285 N.E.2d 574 (Ill. Ct. App. 1972).

8. Donahue v. Rodd Electrotype Co., 328 N.E.2d 505, 515 (Mass. 1975).

9. *See, e.g.*, Guy v. Duff & Phelps, Inc., 672 F. Supp. 1086, 1090 (N.D. Ill. 1987); Orchard v. Covelli, 590 F. Supp. 1548, 1556-59 (W.D. Pa. 1984); W & W Equip. Co. v. Mink, 568 N.E.2d 564, 570–71 (Ind. Ct. App. 1991); Evans v. Blesi, 345 N.W.2d 775, 779 (Minn. Ct. App. 1984); Fought v. Morris, 543 So. 2d 167, 170–71 (Miss. 1989); Crosby v. Beam, 548 N.E.2d 217, 220–21 (Ohio 1989); Estate of Schroer v. Stamco Supply, Inc., 482 N.E.2d 975, 981 (Ohio Ct. App. 1984).

be imposed in limited liability companies as well.[10]

Shareholder, limited liability company member, and partnership suits involving valuation of interests arise in a variety of situations. The most common are:

- Dissenting stockholder actions
- Suits for dissolution of a corporation, limited liability company, or partnership, usually based on a claim of minority oppression
- Breach of fiduciary duty (often coupled with minority oppression)

Although shareholder actions in all these categories are on the rise throughout the country, several states do not have precedential case law on many valuation issues. In deciding on issues, it is very common for states to quote case law from several different states.

"Fair Value" Standard in Most Dissent and Dissolution Suits

Stockholder appraisal rights are defined by state statute. The state statutes also designate the standard of value to be applied. A recent review of the state statutes relating to dissenting stockholder rights indicates that all states except California designate *fair value* or *fair cash value* as the standard of value (California's statute specifies *fair market value*). Most states have modeled their dissenting stockholder statutes after the Model Business Corporation Act. This act was revised in 1984 and became known as the Revised Model Business Corporation Act (RMBCA), which has had revisions through 2002. Until 1999, the RMBCA defined fair value as follows:

> The value of the shares immediately before the effectuation of the corporate action to which the shareholder objects, excluding any appreciation or depreciations in anticipation of the corporate action unless exclusion would be inequitable.

10. *See* Douglas K. Moll, *Minority Oppression & The Limited Liability Company: Learning (Or Not) From Close Corporation History*, 40 WAKE FOREST L REV. 883, 925–40 (2005), which shows that the limitations imposed on limited liability companies by the new default withdrawal and dissolution provisions enacted after promulgation in late 1996 of the IRS "check the box" regulations (Treas. Reg. [26 C.F.R.] §§ 301.7701-1 to 301.7701-3) were intentional and designed for estate and gift tax purposes "[t]o minimize the tax value of an ownership interest" in an LLC "to reflect (1) that the interest is difficult to liquidate, and (2) that purchasers will generally pay less for illiquid positions." (40 WAKE FOREST L REV. at 936 [collecting authorities at 937–39].) "While perhaps accomplishing an estate tax goal, the elimination of default withdrawal and dissolution rights leaves minority members vulnerable to oppressive majority actions since the minority can no longer easily exit the venture with the value of its investment."

In 1999, the definition changed to:

> "Fair value" means the value of the corporation's shares determined:
> (i) immediately before the effectuation of the corporate action to which the shareholder objects;
> (ii) using customary and current valuation concepts and techniques generally employed for similar businesses in the context of the transaction requiring appraisal; and
> (iii) without discounting for lack of marketability or minority status except, if appropriate, for amendments to the articles pursuant to section 13.02(a)(5).[11]

The majority of states[12] use the pre-1999 definition and only a handful have adopted the 1999 version. A minority of states uses the pre-1999 definition without the "unless exclusion would be inequitable" phrase, and some states omit this phrase but add a clause that states that all relevant factors should be considered in determining value. Florida and Illinois use a hybrid of the pre-1999 and 1999 definitions.[13]

According to the official comment of the RMBCA, the definition of fair value leaves to the parties (and, ultimately, to the courts) the details by which fair value is to be determined within the broad outlines of the definition. As a result, interpretations of fair value vary considerably from state to state.

A typical and frequently quoted interpretation of the philosophy of fair value in a dissenting stockholder situation is the following:

> Fair value, in an appraisal context, measures "that which has been taken from [the shareholder], viz., his proportionate interest in a going concern." *Tri-Continental Corp. v. Battye,* Del. Supr. 74 A.2d 71, 72 (1950).[14]

"Delaware Block Rule" Expanded

There is far more shareholder dispute litigation in Delaware than in any other state, primarily because so many corporations are incorporated in Delaware. This is particularly true of dissenting stockholder litigation. One of the results is that Delaware dissenting stockholder cases are quoted more than cases from any other state.

11. Model Business Corporation Act § 13.01(4) (2002 ed.).

12. For a review of the standard of value for dissenters' rights and oppression actions in the 50 states, see Jay E. Fishman, Shannon P. Pratt & William J. Morrison, Standards of Value: Theory and Applications 115–19 (John Wiley & Sons 2007).

13. For a listing of states that have adopted some version of the RMBCA definition of fair value, see Jay E. Fishman, Shannon P. Pratt et al., PPC's Guide to Business Valuations (19th ed., Thomson Tax & Accounting 2009), Ex. 15-1, "States That Have Adopted the RMBCA Definition of Fair Value," at 15-5.

14. In Matter of Shell Oil Co., 607 A.2d 1213 (Del. Sup. Ct. 1992).

Before 1983, dissenting stockholder cases primarily used the "Delaware Block Method." This method develops values in each of three categories: investment value, market value, and asset value.

Mathematical weightings then are assigned to the indications of value from each of the three approaches (although the weight to one, or even two in extreme cases, could be zero) and the resulting weighted average is the concluded value.

The definitions of investment value and market value in this context are a little different from those discussed in the three basic approaches to value in Chapter 3.

"Investment value" in the context of the Delaware Block Method means value based on expected earnings and/or dividends. It is akin to the value based on the income approach in the three basic approaches to value. It may be arrived at by discounted cash flow, capitalization of earnings, or capitalization of dividends. In this sense, it mixes the traditional income approach and market approach for it may derive capitalization rates by methods under either (see Chapter 5, "The Income Approach," and Chapter 6, "The Market Approach").

"Market value," on the other hand, has historically been based on prior transactions in the subject company's securities. This contrasts with the traditional appraisal concept of market value as discussed in Chapter 6, where multiples of both income statement and balance sheet parameters based on comparable transactions are used.

The summary of a typical Delaware Block Method appraisal might look something like the following:

	Indicated Value per Share	**Weight**	**Weighted Value**
Capitalization of earnings	$10.00	30%	$3.00
Capitalization of dividends	$ 6.00	20%	1.20
Market value	$ 8.00	30%	2.40
Asset value	$15.00	20%	3.00
Weighted value per share			$9.60

However, a landmark case in 1983 said that the traditional factors considered under the Delaware Block Rule alone were not necessarily sufficient; instead, all relevant factors must be considered. In that particular case, the court specifically made the point that projections of future earnings were available and should be considered. The court also made the point that a determination of fair value "must include proof of value by any techniques or methods which are generally considered acceptable in the financial community."[15]

15. Weinberger v. UOP, Inc., 457 A.2d 701 (Del. 1983).

All Relevant Factors Must be Considered

The interpretation of fair value is a subject of continued debate and is difficult to generalize. However, most states have embraced the notion that "all relevant factors should be considered."

Courts have treated investment value (defined in this context as value based on earning capacity) as the most important of the three elements. In fact, in one case, the Delaware Court of Chancery stated that the discounted cash flow (DCF) model is "increasingly the model of choice for valuations in this court."[16] However, as noted earlier, one landmark case pointed out that *all* relevant factors must be considered,[17] and the Delaware Court of Chancery has rejected the DCF method where it finds that the projections or data underpinning the DCF analysis are inadequate.[18] Some courts also have indicated that a fair market value analysis may be a "relevant factor" that should be considered in determining fair value.[19]

Courts tend to rely heavily on expert reports and testimony in resolving fair value cases. In one Delaware case, however, Vice Chancellor Steele observed:

> Reading petitioner's submissions, one might easily conclude that MPM was poised to become the Microsoft of the SMT industry. By contrast, respondent's submissions give the impression that a more likely comparison given MPM's myriad management, technical and legal problems, is Apple [Computer]. In sum, one report is submitted by Dr. Pangloss, and the other by Mr. Scrooge.[20]

---

16. Grimes v. Vitalink Commc'ns Corp., 1997 Del. Ch. LEXIS 124, 1997 WL 538676 (Del. Ch. 1997). *See also* Gholl v. eMachines, Inc., 2004 Del. Ch. LEXIS 171 (Del. Ch. 2004) ("This method is widely accepted in the financial community and has frequently been relied upon by this Court in appraisal actions.);" Andaloro v. PFPC Worldwide, Inc., 2005 Del. Ch. LEXIS 125 (Del. Ch. 2005) ("The DCF model of valuation is a standard one that gives life to the finance principle that firms should be valued based on the expected value of their future cash flows, discounted to present value in a manner that accounts for risk. The DCF method is frequently used in this court and I, like many others, prefer to give it great, and sometimes even exclusive, weight when it may be used responsibly."); *In re* U.S. Cellular Operating Co., 2005 Del. Ch. LEXIS 1 (Del. Ch. 2005) ("While DCF analyses have become the dominant approach in appraisal proceedings . . . the ultimate selection of a valuation framework remains within the court's discretion."); *In re* PNB Holding Co., 2006 Del. Ch. LEXIS 158 (Del. Ch. 2006) (the court focused exclusively on the experts' DCF analyses); Crescent/Mach I Partnership, L.P. v. Turner, 2007 Del. Ch. LEXIS 63 (Del. Ch. 2007) (citing prior Delaware decisions, the court reiterated its preference for the DCF method and its general opinion that "other methodologies—all based on comparables of one form or another—are of limited value").
17. Weinberger v. UOP, Inc., 457 A.2d 701, 710 (Del. 1983).
18. *See, e.g.,* The Union Illinois 1995 Inv. Ltd. P'ship v. Union Fin. Group, Ltd., 847 A.2d 340 (Del. Ch. Dec. 19, 2003); Doft & Co. v. Travelocity.com Inc., 2004 Del. Ch. LEXIS 75 (Del. Ch. 2004); Finkelstein v. Liberty Digital, Inc., 2005 Del Ch. LEXIS 53 (Del. Ch. 2005); Highfields Capital, Ltd. v. AXA Fin., Inc., 2007 Del. Ch. LEXIS 126 (Del. Ch. 2007).
19. *See* Bair v. Purcell, 2008 U.S. Dist. LEXIS 6518 (M.D. Pa. 2008).
20. Gilbert v. MPM Enters., 709 A.2d 663, 667 (Del. Ch. 1997).

Despite its cynicism (which has continued unabated given the continued divergence of values concluded by opposing experts[21]—in fact, in a recent case, the values were apart by more than $200 million[22]), the court went on to accept certain portions of each expert's DCF valuation and fashioned its own conclusion using a DCF model.

It is also noteworthy that throughout the opinion in the above case, the court rejected various valuation procedures that reflected any value not only from the actual merger but also *in anticipation of* the merger. The opinion repeatedly made the point that, under Delaware law, *fair value* means the value as a going concern and on a stand-alone basis.

Strategic Value

The question frequently arises whether a "relevant factor" is what a company might be sold for if it were put "in play." The most likely buyer of many companies is another industry participant, who may be expected to pay more because of operational synergies or competitive advantages obtainable from the purchase. One difficulty is that any attempt to apply this standard requires some assumptions regarding the prospective buyer and is not limited to the operating characteristics of the company on a stand-alone basis. Strategic buyer valuation also would seem to be in conflict with the language contained in most dissenters' rights statutes that appreciation in anticipation of the corporate action is not to be included. While the Delaware courts

21. The court's skepticism of appraiser independence has not changed significantly. For example, *see* Lane v. Cancer Treatment Centers of America, Inc., 2004 Del. Ch. LEXIS 108 (Del. Ch. July 30, 2004) ("All too often in appraisal actions, the Court is presented with two competing experts espousing 'wildly divergent' interpretations of the circumstances confronting the corporation. This case is no exception."); Henke v. Trilithic, Inc., 2005 Del. Ch. LEXIS 170 (Del. Ch. 2005) ("The parties' experts have presented remarkably divergent valuations. As is often the case in an appraisal action, the Court does not find either party to have fully satisfied its burden of persuasion regarding its valuation. The Court therefore must conduct its own independent valuation.);" Finkelstein v. Liberty Digital, Inc., 2005 Del Ch. LEXIS 53 (Del. Ch. 2005) ("This appraisal case is unusual in one respect that is refreshing . . . what is less typical is that the parties were able to stipulate to the value of all but one of [the corporation's] assets. . . . Men and women who purport to be applying sound, academically-validated valuation techniques come to this court and, through the neutral application of their expertise to the facts, come to widely disparate results, even when applying the same methodology. These starkly contrasting presentations have, given the duties required of this court, imposed upon trial judges the responsibility to forge a responsible valuation from what is often ridiculously biased 'expert' input."); *In re* PNB Holding Co., 2006 Del. Ch. LEXIS 158 (Del. Ch. 2006) ("The 'experts' . . . drew the depressingly familiar parentheses [of value] within whose capacious bounds I am to identify a single estimate of [the company's] value."); Highfields Capital, Ltd. v. AXA Fin., Inc., 2007 Del. Ch. LEXIS 126 (Del. Ch. 2007) (the Chancery Court found that the two experts' divergent valuations were like "two ships passing in the night").

22. Cox Enters., Inc. v. News-Journal Corp., 2007 U.S. App. LEXIS 29533 (11th Cir. 2007).

appear to have rejected this standard,[23] language in opinions from other states may be construed to permit consideration of strategic buyer values.[24] (In Canada, courts routinely include strategic value as an element of fair value in dissenting stockholder cases.) Some commentators also contend that not all synergies should be disregarded, because only those synergies not available to a particular buyer may be indicative of investment value.[25]

Discounts or Premiums Often Major Issue

The largest single issue in most shareholder and partner valuation disputes is whether discounts and/or premiums are applicable and, if so, what is the magnitude of such discounts and/or premiums? The most common issues involve minority discounts or control premiums and discounts for lack of marketability. Positions on these issues vary from state to state and sometimes state case precedents change, so it is necessary to be aware of the latest precedential case law. For example, not many states have adopted the RMBCA, but even some of those that have not have refused minority and marketability discounts, citing the revision. Furthermore, case precedent often is different for dissenting stockholder actions than it is for dissolution actions.

Discounts for Lack of Marketability and Lack of Control

Discounts Left to Court's Discretion

Some states leave the question of applicability of both minority and marketability discounts to the court's or a jury's discretion.[26] For example, the Illinois Court of

23. *See, e.g.,* Bell v. Kirby Lumber Corp., 413 A.2d 137 (Del. 1980); The Union Illinois 1995 Inv. Ltd. P'ship v. Union Fin. Group, Ltd., 847 A.2d 340 (Del. Ch. Dec. 19, 2003) (the fair value of the company's shares as of the merger date was the merger price minus any synergies).

24. *See, e.g., In re* Valuation of Common Stock of McLoon Oil Co., 565 A.2d 997 (Me. 1989) ("Especially in fixing the appraisal remedy in a close corporation, the relevant inquiry is what is the highest price a single buyer would reasonably pay for the whole enterprise."); BNE Mass. Corp. v. Simms, 588 N.E.2d 14 (Mass. App. Ct. 1992) (the task assigned under the appraisal statute was "not to reconstruct an 'intrinsic value' of each share of the enterprise but, rather, to determine what a willing buyer realistically would pay for the enterprise as a whole on the statutory valuation date. . . . [O]nly in this fashion can minority stockholders be assured that insiders in control of a company, burdened by conflicting interests, may not purchase the enterprise at a price less than that obtainable in the marketplace of qualified buyers and avoid paying a full and fair price to the minority.").

25. Jay E. Fishman, Shannon P. Pratt & William J. Morrison, Standards of Value: Theory and Applications 122 (John Wiley & Sons 2007).

26. These states include *Alabama—Ex parte* Baron Service, Inc., 874 So. 2d 545 (Ala. 2003); *California*—Thompson v. Miller, 2003 Cal. App. LEXIS 1489 (Cal. Ct. App. 2003); *Illinois*—Jahn v. Kinderman, 814 N.E.2d 116 (Ill. Ct. App. 2004); *Missouri*—King v. F.T.J., Inc., 765 S.W.2d 301 (Mo. Ct. App. 1988); *Nevada*—Steiner v. Benninghoff, 5 F. Supp. 2d 1117 (1998); *New Mexico*—McCauley

Appeals in *Jahn v. Kinderman* said with regard to such discounts that "the application of a discount was a matter for the discretion of the trial court."[27] These courts are reluctant to set a bright-line rule in the event that circumstances or justice require the application of a discount. For example, in *Advanced Communication Design, Inc. v. Follett,*[28] the Minnesota Supreme Court indicated that it would only be fair and equitable to apply a marketability discount to the value of the company because there was no possibility that the company could achieve the liquidity necessary to compensate the departing shareholder. This was viewed as an extraordinary circumstance warranting the application of the discount. The American Law Institute (ALI) recognizes such extraordinary circumstances in the definition of fair value it includes in its *Principles of Corporate Governance.*[29] It defines fair value as:

> The value of the eligible holder's proportionate interest in the corporation, without any discount for minority status or, absent extraordinary circumstances, lack of marketability.

Extraordinary Circumstances

Other states also find the applicability of minority and marketability discounts a discretionary matter, but require the court to consider whether extraordinary circumstances warrant the application of a discount for lack of marketability.[30] For example, the primary issue in two cases, decided the same day by the New Jersey Supreme Court,[31] was whether a marketability discount should be applied in determining the fair value to be paid in shareholder suits.

In *Wheaton,* a statutory appraisal action, the court found:

> The history and policy behind dissenters' right and appraisal statutes lead us to conclude that marketability discounts generally should not be applied when determining the "fair value" of dissenters' shares in a statutory appraisal ac-

v. Tom McCauley & Son, Inc., 724 P.2d 232 (N.M. Ct. App. 1986); and *North Carolina*—Garlock v. Southeastern Gas & Power, 2001 NCBC 10, 2001 NCBC LEXIS 9 (N.C. Super. 2001).

27. Jahn v. Kinderman, 814 N.E.2d 116 (Ill. Ct. App. 2004).

28. 615 N.W.2d 285, 292 (Minn. 2000).

29. American Law Institute, Principles of Corporate Governance: Analysis and Recommendations (1992).

30. *Arizona*—Pro Finish USA, Ltd. v. Johnson, 63 P.3d 288 (Ariz. Ct. App. 2003); *Minnesota*—Rain Forest Café, Inc. v. State of Wis. Inv. Bd., 677 N.W.2d 443 (Minn. Ct. App. 2004); Advanced Commc'n Design, Inc. v. Follett, 615 N.W.2d 285 (Minn. 2000); *New Jersey*—Balsamides v. Protameen Chemicals, Inc., 734 A.2d 721 (N.J. 1999); Lawson Mardon Wheaton, Inc. v. Smith, 734 A.2d 738 (N.J. 1999); and *Utah*—Hogle v. Zinetics Med., Inc., 63 P.3d 80 (Utah 2002).

31. Lawson Mardon Wheaton, Inc. v. Smith, 734 A.2d 738 (N.J. 1999); Balsamides v. Protameen Chemicals Inc., 734 A.2d 721 (N.J. 1999).

tion. Of course, there may be situations where equity compels another result. Those situations are best resolved by resort to the "extraordinary circumstances" exception in 2 ALI Principles, 7.22(a).

In *Balsamides,* a breach of fiduciary duty action, the court found:

To secure "fair value" for Perle's stock, a marketability discount should be applied. To do otherwise would be unfair, particularly since Perle was the oppressor and Balsamides was the oppressed shareholder.

Rejection of Shareholder-Level Discounts

Delaware has consistently rejected the application of discounts. In *Cavalier Oil v. Harnett,*[32] the Delaware Supreme Court indicated that the objective of the appraisal outlined by the state's appraisal statute was to value the corporation itself rather than a specific fraction of shares in the hands of one shareholder and, therefore, no shareholder-level discounts should be applied.

Of the states that have declared themselves on the issue of discounts in dissenters' rights actions, several follow the lead of Delaware and reject discounts for either minority interest or lack or marketability, either by statute[33] and/or case law.[34] For example, the Iowa Supreme Court affirmed a lower court valuation that rejected a discount for lack of marketability.[35] Another example is *Pueblo Bancorporation v. Lindoe, Inc.,*[36] where a divided Colorado Supreme Court affirmed a decision denying a lack of marketability discount when determining fair value under Colorado's dissenters' rights statute. The court noted that the trial court must first determine the value of the corporation as a going concern and the pro rata value of each outstanding share, and that discounts should not be applied, except under extraordinary circumstances.

In *Brown v. Arp and Hammond Hardware Co.,*[37] the Wyoming Supreme Court, finding that the clear majority of courts have held that minority discounts do not

32. Cavalier Oil v. Harnett, 564 A.2d 1137; 1989 Del. LEXIS 325 (Del. 1989).

33. Connecticut—CONN. GEN. STAT. § 33-855(4) (enacted 2002); Florida—FLA. STAT. § 607.1301(4) (enacted 2006) (applies to corporations with 10 or fewer shareholders); Idaho—IDAHO CODE § 30-1-1301 (enacted 2004); Iowa—IOWA CODE § 490.1301(4) (enacted 2002); Maine—13-C MAINE REV. STAT. § 1301(4) (enacted 2003); Mississippi—MISS. CODE ANN. § 79-4-13.01(4) (enacted 2007); South Dakota—S.D. CODIFIED LAWS § 47-1A-1301 (enacted 2005); Virginia—VA. CODE ANN. § 13.1-729 (enacted 2005); West Virginia—W. VA. CODE § 31D-13-1301(4) (enacted 2002).

34. For a list of states and cases that reject discounts, see exhibit 3.7, Cases Rejecting Discounts, *in* JAY E. FISHMAN, SHANNON P. PRATT & WILLIAM J. MORRISON, STANDARDS OF VALUE: THEORY AND APPLICATIONS 139–42 (John Wiley & Sons 2007)

35. Sieg Co. v. Kelly, 568 N.W.2d 794 (Iowa 1997).

36. Pueblo Bancorporation v. Lindoe, Inc., 37 P.3d 492 (Colo. 2003).

37. Brown v. Arp and Hammond Hardware Co., 141 P.3d 673 (Wyo. 2006).

apply when determining fair value in the appraisal context, ruled that it would join the majority and not permit such discounts.

The Supreme Court of Kansas overruled a previous decision that allowed a minority discount in an action for appraisal, *Moore v. New Ammest, Inc.*[38] The court held that:

> In answering the certified question before us, we hold that minority and marketability discounts should not be applied when the fractional share resulted from a reverse stock split intended to eliminate a minority shareholder's interest in the corporation.[39]

We believe it is important to recognize that this decision's applicability is limited to the narrow circumstances of the question put to the court: "when the fractional share resulted from a reverse stock split intended to eliminate a minority shareholder's interest in the corporation." There are many other actions where dissenters' rights are triggered even though the stockholders are not forced to be cashed out, a fact set that would seem to be very distinguishable from this case.

In Oregon, a marketability discount may be applied in a dissenters' case, but a minority discount may not (*Columbia Management Co. v. Wyss,* 94 Ore. App. 195, 765 P.2d 207 (1988)). However, in a minority oppression case (*Hayes v. Omstead & Associates, Inc.,* 21 P.3d 178 (Or. Ct. App. 2001)), neither discount is to be applied for the minority shareholder is entitled to recover his pro rata interest without regard to discounts applicable in other settings.

It is important to keep up on the current case law, because states sometimes change their positions or take different positions from one case to another depending on the facts and circumstances of each. For example, a 1998 Montana Supreme Court dissenting stockholder case reversed a lower court decision that had accepted a 30 percent minority interest discount. Under the Montana Business Corporation Act, the Supreme Court prohibited the consideration of a minority interest discount when establishing fair value.[40] This was despite the fact that a 1996 Montana Supreme Court minority oppression case allowed a 25 percent minority discount, stating that the stockholder "has not demonstrated to the satisfaction of this court that 'fair value' necessarily excluded an application of a minority discount."[41]

38. 630 P.2d 167 (Kan. 1981).

39. Arnaud v. Stockgrowers State Bank of Ashland, 992 P.2d 216, 1999 Kan. LEXIS 645 (1999).

40. Hansen v. 75 Ranch Co., 957 P.2d 32 (Mont. 1998).

41. McCann Ranch, Inc. v. Quigley-McCann, 915 P.2d 239 (Mont. 1996).

Discounts Permitted

Some states permit the application of shareholder-level discounts in determining fair value (or "fair cash value") in shareholder dissent and oppression cases. Some permit only the lack of marketability discount,[42] some permit only the lack of control discount,[43] and some permit both.[44]

Control Premiums

One of the most commonly cited cases regarding the use of a control premium is the Delaware Supreme Court case of *Rapid-American Corp. v. Harris*.[45] This case involved a statutory appraisal action contesting a merger. The state Supreme Court held that the trial court was required to add a control premium to the publicly traded equity value of a corporation's shares for each of the corporation's operating subsidiaries.

In *Hintmann v. Weber*,[46] a case decided by the Delaware Court of Chancery after *Rapid-American*, the corporation was a holding company whose primary asset was 100 percent of Fred Weber, Inc.'s class A common stock, which represented approximately 90 percent of Fred Weber's value. Based on *Rapid-American*, the court decided that a control premium should be added to the value of Fred Weber's as a subsidiary of Weber Industries, Inc. The mean premium for publicly held companies in the 12 months ended June 30, 1992, was approximately 45 percent and the median premium was about 55 percent. Because a portion of those premiums reflected postmerger values expected from synergies, the appraiser arbitrarily adjusted the premium down to 20 percent, which the court accepted.

Gilbert Matthews, currently an investment broker with Sutter Securities, Inc., in San Francisco, has commented that although this decision is well reasoned in accordance with case law, there are several errors of logic with respect to the control premium:

1. Discounted cash flow (DCF) value should represent the full value of the future cash flows of the business. Excluding synergies, a company cannot be

---

42. *See, e.g.*, Ford v. Courier-Journal Job Printing Co., 639 S.W.2d 553, (Ky. Ct. App. 1982); *In re* Brooklyn Home Dialysis Training Center, Inc., 741 N.Y.S.2d 280 (N.Y. App. Div. 2002).

43. *See, e.g.*, Shopf v. Marina Del Ray P'ship, 549 So. 2d 833 (La. 1989) (in determining fair cash value, the "fair value" equivalent in Louisiana, the court permitted the application of a discount for lack of control to a 12% minority interest).

44. *See, e.g.*, English v. Atromick Int'l Inc., 2000 Ohio App. LEXIS 3580 (Ohio Ct. App. 2000) (in determining fair cash value, the "fair value" equivalent in Ohio, the court applied the willing buyer–willing seller approach and determined that both marketability and minority discounts were appropriate).

45. Rapid-America Corp. v. Harris, 603 A.2d 796 (Del. 1992).

46. Hintmann v. Fred Weber, Inc.,1998 Del. Ch. LEXIS 26 1998 WL 853052 (Del. Ch. 1998).

worth a premium over the value of its future cash flows. Thus, it is improper and illogical to add a control premium to a DCF valuation.

2. The average premium in other transactions is not a relevant standard. It is biased upward by the fact that it includes purchases of companies that are undervalued in the market but excludes those that are overpriced.
3. Even if the average premium were relevant, it is calculated in relation to unaffected market value. Market price may include a minority discount, particularly for acquisition targets. Delaware courts have added premiums to offset minority discounts in appraisals using the guideline company method.[47]
4. The value of Industries to any third party would not have been affected by its corporate structure. If Industries had not been a holding company but had owned Fred Weber, Inc., as a division, *Rapid-American* would not have applied and there would have been no control premium added. This elevates form over substance.[48]

In a subsequent Delaware case, *Borruso v. Communications Telesystems International,*[49] the issue before the Court of Chancery was not whether a control premium should be applied, but when it should be applied during the calculations. The court accepted one expert's methodology on this issue over the other expert's:

> I am persuaded that Petitioners' approach to the control premium is wrong. The observation that the comparable company method of analysis produces a minority equity value does not require that I change the methodology of that analysis. Rather, it requires only that I adjust the result derived from it to eliminate the implicit minority discount. Instead of adjusting the result, Huck undertook to alter, in a significant way, the methodology itself. Doing so, in my view, introduced an analytical distortion that, in this case, significantly overstates the value of the WXL equity. Neither Petitioners nor Huck has supplied authority in the valuation literature justifying this change in the accepted methodology. Because Huck's methodology is inconsistent with the methodology followed in *Harris v. Rapid-American Corp.,* 1992 Del. Ch.

47. Some commentators have criticized the Delaware courts' assumption that market prices of most public companies include a minority discount. *See* Lawrence A. Hamermesh & Michael L. Wachter, *The Short and Puzzling Life of the 'Implicit Minority Discount' in Delaware Appraisal Law*, 156 U. Pa. L. Rev. 1 (2007); Gilbert E. Matthews, *Misuse of Control Premiums in Delaware Appraisals*, Business Valuation Review, Summer 2008.

48. Gilbert E. Matthews, *Delaware court adds control premium to subsidiary value*, Shannon Pratt's Business Valuation Update, May 1998, at 9–10; *A Review of Valuations in Delaware Appraisal Cases, 2004-2005*, Business Valuation Review, Vol. 25, No. 2 (Summer 2006).

49. Borruso v. Communications Telesystems Int'l, 1999 Del. Ch. LEXIS 197 (1999).

LEXIS 75, *9, Del. Ch., C.A. No. 6462, Chandler, V.C. (April 1, 1992), and because it is otherwise hard to square with the comparable company method, I will not adopt it.

In *Doft & Co. v. Travelocity.com, Inc.,*[50] the court, sua sponte, added a 30 percent control premium, saying, "The equity valuation produced in a comparable company analysis does not accurately reflect the intrinsic worth of a corporation on a going concern basis. Therefore, the Court, in appraising the fair value of the equity, 'must correct this minority trading discount by adding back a premium designed to correct it.'"

In a Maine dissenters' rights action involving a small closely held business, the court permitted a control premium adjustment, concluding that the control premium could properly be used as an upward adjustment of the value of the subject company's shares when compared to similar companies in the industry.[51] Iowa's Supreme Court also has held that in an appraisal action a control premium may be considered in determining fair value if it is supported by the evidence.[52]

Other Discount Issues

Discounts for Trapped-in Capital Gains

Another frequently encountered issue is whether the value of a company with low-basis assets should be discounted because of the risk of tax liability if some or all of these assets are later sold. As discussed in Chapter 17, the Tax Court recently has reversed its prior position and approved a discount for such built-in capital gains.[53] The Washington Court of Appeals in *Matthew G. Norton Co. v. Smyth,*[54] rejected a bright-line rule rejecting a discount for trapped-in capital gains, reasoning that while discounts for such gains are not generally appropriate in dissenters' rights appraisal cases where no liquidation of the corporation is contemplated, such discounts might be appropriate, at the corporate level, if the business of the company is such that appreciated property is scheduled to be sold in the foreseeable future, in the normal course of business. The Wyoming Supreme Court ruled that under the state's ap-

50. Doft & Co. v. Travelocity.com, Inc, 2004 Del. Ch. LEXIS 75 (Del. Ch. 2004).

51. *In re* Valuation of Common Stock of Penobscot Shoe Co., 2003 Me. Super. LEXIS 140 (Me. Super. 2003).

52. Northwest Inv. Corp. v. Wallace, 2007 Iowa Sup. LEXIS 87 (Iowa 2007).

53. *See* Estate of Davis v. Comm'r, 110 TC 530 (T.C. 1998); Estate of Jameson v. Comm'r, T.C. Memo. 1999-43, 77 T.C.M. (CCH) 1383 (T.C. 1999); Estate of Eisenberg v. Comm'r, T.C. Memo. 1997-483, 74 T.C.M. (CCH) 1046 (T.C. 1997).

54. Matthew G. Norton Co. v. Smyth, 112 Wash. App. 865, 51 P.3d 159 (Wash. Ct. App. 2002).

praisal statute (pre-1999 RMBCA version), absent clear evidence that the company was undergoing liquidation, a discount for trapped-in capital gains would violate the purpose of the statute: to compensate dissenting shareholders for the "fair value" of their shares in a going concern.[55] The Delaware Supreme Court did not permit the deduction of deferred taxes on investment assets that a company had no intent to sell at the time of the transaction triggering the appraisal.[56]

Lack of Combinatorial Value Discount

In *Dobler v. Montgomery Cellular Holding Company, Inc.*,[57] which involved a telecommunications holding company, the company's valuation expert argued that cellular companies are significantly more valuable in specific combinations, and because the subject company was a stand-alone cellular company, it had a lack of combinatorial value as part of a network. Accordingly, the expert proposed applying a 48 percent discount for lack of combinatorial value. The Delaware Court of Chancery rejected the discount, finding that the company was already in combination with other cellular companies owned by the company's parent and reasoning that permitting the proposed discount would deprive the minority shareholders of existing value. The Delaware Supreme Court affirmed, finding that the contractual relationships with other cellular providers represented value to which the minority shareholders were entitled.[58]

Lack of "Entire Fairness" May Broaden Remedies

The Delaware courts employ the concept of "entire fairness." This means *procedural fairness* as well as *substantive fairness* or *fair value*. If the transaction fails in terms of procedural fairness (fair dealing), the relief to the plaintiffs may go beyond just the fair value as adjudicated pursuant to dissenting stockholder statutes.

Procedural fairness generally is measured by two criteria: (1) independence and (2) competence and thoroughness.

Substantive fairness (fair price) also has two elements: absolute fairness and relative fairness.

Violations of these criteria caused Delaware Vice Chancellor Jacobs to deny a motion for summary judgment to dismiss a class-action suit that allowed plaintiffs only the appraisal remedy. Among the facts cited by Judge Jacobs:

55. Brown v. Arp and Hammond Hardware Co., 141 P.3d 673 (Wyo. 2006).

56. Paskill Corp. v. Alcoma Corp., 747 A.2d 549 (Del. 2000) at 552.

57. Dobler v. Montgomery Cellular Holding Co., Inc., 2004 Del. Ch. LEXIS 139 (Del. Ch. 2004).

58. Montgomery Cellular Holding Co. v. Dobler, 880 A.2d 206, 2005 Del. LEXIS 295 (Del. 2005).

- The company obtained no fairness opinion at the time of the cash-out merger.
- The board did not establish an independent committee to safeguard the interests of the minority stockholders.
- There had been a series of private purchases at prices higher than the cash-out price, a fact that was undisclosed.

Judge Jacobs concluded that because there was evidence that the entire fairness test was not met, "the Court must reject the defendants' argument that appraisal is the exclusive remedy."[59]

In another case, the Delaware Supreme Court found that "the Special Committee [of the board] chose as its financial advisor a bank which had lucrative past dealings with . . . related companies." Furthermore, the special committee's legal advisor was previously retained by two related companies. The court concluded that the special committee did not act in an independent and informed manner. Therefore, the case was remanded for a new fairness determination, with the burden of proof shifted to the defendants.[60]

A classic example of lack of fairness is found in *Ryan v. Tad's Enterprises.* First, the controlling stockholders arranged an asset sale of the corporation's major holding, a six-store New York restaurant chain, with employment and noncompete contracts of $1 million each. It then did a squeeze-out merger. One lawyer acted as a board member, represented the corporation in the transactions, and represented the controlling stockholders personally in negotiating their employment and noncompete agreements. The board did not retain any unaffiliated law firm, financial advisor, or other independent representative to represent or negotiate the merger on behalf of Tad's minority shareholders.

The opinion states, "Normally this court will defer to a decision involving the business judgment of a corporation's directors. . . . However, that presumption vanishes in cases where the minority shareholders are compelled to forfeit their shares in return for a value that is determined as a result of a bargaining process in which the controlling shareholder is in a position to influence both bargaining parties."[61] The dissenters ultimately were awarded $23.86 per share versus $13.36 originally offered.

Another Delaware case finding a lack of entire fairness was *M.G. Bancorporation v. Le Beau,*[62] which found that the directors' failure to establish an independent committee of directors to represent the minority shareholders' interests, while on its own did

59. Seagraves v. Urstadt Prop. Co., 1996 Del. Ch. LEXIS 36, 1996 WL 159626 (Del. Ch. 1996).

60. Kahn v. Tremont Corp., 694 A.2d 422, 429 (Del. 1997).

61. Ryan v. Tad's Enters., 709 A.2d 682 (Del. Ch. 1996).

62. M.G. Bancorporation v. Le Beau, 737 A.2d 513 (Del. 1999).

not constitute evidence of unfair dealing, when combined with other pleaded facts could support a claim of unfair dealing. The court also found that the difference between the stock's $85 per share fair value and the $41 per share merger price, combined with the other pleaded unfairness claims, created an inference that the merger was the product of unfair dealing.

Lack of entire fairness usually occurs when control stockholders cause transactions that benefit them at the expense of other stockholders without independent oversight. The most common scenario is a transaction without an independent appraisal, often coupled with not having an independent committee of the board of directors to evaluate the transaction from the perspective of fairness to minority stockholders. Directors or controlling shareholders who stand on both sides of a transaction have the burden of establishing the transaction's entire fairness.[63]

In *Gesoff v. IIC Industries, Inc.*,[64] the class of minority shareholders argued that a going-private merger, intended by a foreign parent corporation to remove the minority shareholders of its U.S. subsidiary, was a product of unfair dealing, producing an unfair price for the subsidiary. Notwithstanding the defendants' argument that the merger was fair because any irregularities in the merger dealings did not affect the fairness of the merger price, the Delaware Court of Chancery found that the merger process was marked with grave examples of unfairness and led to a plainly unfair price for the going-private transaction. Consequently, the court awarded damages to the class and to those stockholders seeking appraisal based on the court's determination of fair value at the time of the merger—a figure significantly in excess of the consideration offered in the going-private transaction. In reaching its conclusion, the court determined that the process established by the defendants unilaterally imposed on the minority a price of the parent's own choosing, established a deceptive negotiation between the parties, and left the minority's putative special committee almost entirely powerless against its parent.

Fair Value Is Not Fair Market Value

One thing that is clear is that virtually no court equates fair value with fair market value.[65] In a New York case, the expert retained by the company based his valuation on a fair market value. The court stated, "The Standard on which (the expert's) valuation was based was Market value. . . . The statutory standard is much broader. . . . The Court *may give no weight* [emphasis added] to market value if the facts of the case so require."

The court also decided that the company's appraiser "was not independent in its evaluation and was unduly controlled and influenced by the petitioner to arrive at a

63. Weinberger v. UOP, Inc., 457 A.2d 701 (Del. 1983).

64. Gesoff v. IIC Indus., Inc. 902 A.2d 1130 (Del. Ch. 2006).

65. An exception is Ohio. *See* Armstrong v. Marathon Oil Co., 513 N.E.2d 776, 787–90 (Ohio 1987)

low value."[66] Ultimately, the court rejected any minority and marketability discounts and awarded the dissenter $99 per share, as compared with the $32 per share originally offered.

In another example, the Colorado Supreme Court in *Pueblo Bancorporation v. Lindoe, Inc.*, said, "We are convinced that 'fair value' does not mean 'fair market value.'"[67] The New Jersey Supreme Court has expressed a similar sentiment,[68] as has a majority of courts in other jurisdictions.[69]

Other courts, however, have indicated that use of a fair market value analysis may inform the fair value standard of value where such an analysis is a "relevant factor," and that although the market value may be accorded little or no weight by a fact finder, the fair market value analysis may not be excluded and must be permitted at trial.[70] The Eleventh Circuit, while acknowledging that "fair value" and "fair market value" are not synonymous, also has indicated that they are not "mutually exclusive," so that when dealing with "potentially distorting corporate actions" such as a merger or a sale, fair market value may serve as an estimate of fair value.[71]

States Borrow Other States' Precedents

When states lack precedential case law on an issue, they often look to other states for guidance. Thus, appraisers and lawyers often research cases in other states, especially states with similar statutory wording.

For example, in Utah's case of first impression under its dissenting stockholder statute, the appellate court cited case law from other states with similar statutes, including Iowa, Maryland, Maine, Delaware, and Massachusetts. Among its conclusions, it stated: "We agree with the courts cited above that a dissenting stockholder disclaims both the burden and the benefit of the disfavored corporate action. . . . Any effect of the sale must be excluded. . . . Fair value is not measured by any unique benefits that will accrue to the acquiring corporation."[72]

---

66. *In re* Slant/Fin Corp., 236 A.D.2d 547, 654 N.Y.S.2d 627 (N.Y. App. Div. 1997).

67. Pueblo Bancorporation v. Lindoe, Inc., 63 P.3d 353 (Colo. 2003).

68. *See* Lawson Mardon Wheaton, Inc. v. Smith, 716 A.2d 550, 558 (N.J. Super. App. Div. 1998), *aff'd,* 734 A.2d 738 (N.J. 1999) ("Fair Value carries with it the statutory purposes that shareholders be fairly compensated, which may or may not equate with the market's judgment about the stock's value. This is particularly appropriate in the close corporation setting where there is no ready market for the shares and consequently no Fair Market Value.").

69. *See, e.g.,* Swope v. Seigel-Robert, Inc., 243 F.3d 486, 2001 U.S. App. LEXIS 2760 (8th Cir. 2001); Wenzel v. Hopper & Galliher, P.C., 779 N.E.2d 30 (Ind. Ct. App. 2002); First W. Bank Wall v. Olsen, 2001 SD 16, 621 N.W.2d 611 (S.D. 2001); Matthew G. Norton Co. v. Smyth, 112 Wn. App. 865, 51 P.3d 159 (Wash. Ct. App. 2002); HMO-W, Inc. v. SSM Health Care Sys., 2000 WI 46, 234 Wis. 2d 707, 611 N.W.2d 250 (Wis. 2000).

70. Bair v. Purcell, 2008 U.S. Dist. LEXIS 6518 (M.D. Pa. 2008).

71. Cox Enters., Inc. v. News-Journal Corp., 2007 U.S. App. LEXIS 29533 (11th Cir. 2007).

72. Oakridge Energy Inc. v. Clifton, 937 P.2d 130 (Utah 1997).

Before determining that "fair value" does not mean "fair market value," the Colorado Supreme Court conducted an extensive review of the law in other jurisdictions on this issue.[73]

Apparent inconsistencies are common in the field of fair value cases, often as a result of less than fully informed expert testimony. In a North Dakota case, it was alleged (and unrebutted) that an appraisal followed Delaware case law. However, it was apparent after reading what was done that the appraisal did not interpret the appraisal methodology as it is actually applied in Delaware.[74]

Timely Actions Essential

Courts usually hold assiduously to requirements for timeliness of filings and other procedural matters in dissenting stockholder actions. If the dissent is not filed within the statutory period, dissenters' rights are almost always considered waived.

When dissenters' rights actions are filed, most state statutes then require the corporation to commence a proceeding to determine the fair value of the shares within 60 days after receiving the demand. If it doesn't commence the proceeding within the 60 days, it must pay the dissenters the amount demanded.

In a Georgia case, for example (where the statute was based on the Model Business Corporations Act), the trial court awarded the dissenters the amount demanded because the corporation failed to initiate the valuation proceeding within the statutory period. The corporation appealed and the trial court's judgment was affirmed.[75]

References for Shareholder and Partner Disputes

Brewer, Wilbur, Jr. "Minority Shareholder Rights." A 17-page paper on rights of minority shareholders in closely held corporations, available at www. BVLibrary.com.

BVR's Guide to Fair Value in Shareholder Dissent, Oppression, and Marital Dissolution, 2009 Ed., Portland, OR: Business Valuation Resources, 2009.

Cory, Jacques. *Business Ethics: The Ethical Revolution of Minority Shareholders*. New York: Springer, 2004.

Eggart, James. "Replacing the Sword with a Scalpel: The Case for a Bright-Line Rule Disallowing Application of Lack of Marketability Discounts in Shareholder Oppression Cases." *Arizona Law Review* 44:1 (2002): 213–46.

Emory, Jr., John D. 1996. "The Role of Discounts in Determining 'Fair Value' Under Wisconsin's Dissenters' Rights Statutes: The Case for Discounts." *Wisconsin Law Review, 1995* 5 (March 1996): 1,155-75. Although specifically oriented to Wisconsin, the article references statutes and cases throughout the United States.

73. Pueblo Bancorporation v. Lindoe, Inc., 63 P.3d 353 (Colo. 2003).
74. Berens v. Ludwig, 160 F.3d 1144 (7th Cir. 1998).
75. Riddle-Bradley, Inc. v. Riddle, 459 S.E.2d 576 (Ga. Ct. App. 1995).

Fishman, Jay E., Shannon P. Pratt, et al. "Fair Value under Shareholder Dissent and Minority Oppression Actions." In *PPC's Guide to Business Valuations*, 19th Ed., Chap. 5. Fort Worth, TX: Practitioners Publishing Company, 2009.

Gordon, Noah, J. "The Non-Delaware View of Fair Value in Shareholded Dissent and Oppression Cases." In *BVR's Guide to Fair Value in Shareholder Dissent, Oppression, and Marital Dissolution,* 2009 Ed., Ch. 3, Portland, OR: Business Valuation Resources, 2009.

Hamermesh, Lawrence A., and Michael L. Wachter. "The Fair Value of Cornfields in Delaware Appraisal Law." 31 *J. Corp. Law* 119 (2005).

Hamermesh, Lawrence A., and Michael L. Wachter. "The Short and Puzzling Life of the 'Implicit Minority Discount' in Delaware Appraisal Law." 156 *U. Pa. L. Rev.* 1 (2007).

Jacobs, Jack B. 1999. "Adjudicating Statutory Appraisal and Breach of Fiduciary Duty Valuations in the Delaware Court of Chancery" (interview with Shannon Pratt). *Judges & Lawyers Business Valuation Update* (September): 1, 3–4.

Malick, S. A. *Oppression of and Relief for Minority Shareholders: Cases and Commentaries.* Golden Books Centre, 2000.

Mantese, Gerard V., and Ian Williamson. "Minority Shareholder Oppression: From Estes to Franchino." *Michigan Bar Journal* (August 2005): 16–20.

Matthews, Gilbert E. "A Review of Valuations in Delaware Appraisal Cases, 2004–2005." *Business Valuation Review,* Summer 2006.

Matthews, Gilbert E. "Misuse of Control Premiums in Delaware Appraisals." *Business Valuation Review,* Summer 2008.

Minnesota Institute of Legal Education, Minneapolis. "Minority Shareholder Disputes." Several hundred pages of conference papers in three-ring binder. Although primarily oriented to Minnesota, the papers reflect national research on the issues.

Moll, Douglas K. "Minority Oppression and the Limited Liability Company: Learning (or Not) from Close Corporation History." *Wake Forest Law Review* 40 (2005): 883.

O'Neal, F. Hodge, and Robert B. Thompson. 1998. *O'Neal's Oppression of Minority Shareholders: Protecting Minority Rights in Squeeze-Outs, and Other Intracorporate Conflicts,* 2d Ed. St. Paul, Minn.: West Group.

Pratt, Shannon. 1999. "Shareholder Suit Valuation Criteria Vary from State to State." *Valuation Strategies* (January/February): 12–15.

Pratt, Shannon. 2003. "Shareholder Buyouts and Disputes." In *Business Valuation Body of Knowledge,* 2d Ed., 321–24. New York: John Wiley & Sons.

Shartsis, Jr., Arthur. 1999. "Dissolution Actions Yield Less Than Fair Market Enterprise Value." *Judges & Lawyers Business Valuation Update* (January): 5.

Chapter 19

Marital Dissolution Valuations

This chapter was updated from the first edition by Noah J. Gordon, legal counsel for Shannon Pratt Valuations, Inc. Mr. Gordon is a regular contributor to valuation and legal publications.

While business valuations are performed for many reasons, the various courts' positions on how a valuation should be performed are least settled in the area of marital dissolution. This is especially true in terms of different approaches from one state to another, but there also are inconsistencies within states. Even when there is general agreement on broad approaches, the courts still take contradictory positions on many issues. Courts have a very high degree of discretion, into which appellate courts are reluctant to intrude.

This chapter is not intended to provide appraisal guidance for any particular state but to provide an overview of the business valuation issues that frequently arise and a sampling of how various states have treated them. The lawyer assigning a business valuation case for marital dissolution purposes should be sure that the appraiser possesses a good working knowledge of all the case law that would affect that appraisal and support his or her ability to handle cross-examination. As will be seen in this chapter, states borrow widely from decisions in other states in ruling on valuation issues. Therefore, relevant case law may be found in states other than the state in which the case will be tried.

Standard of Value for Marital Dissolutions

At the core of the differences among jurisdictions on how to value businesses or practices for marital dissolution is the appropriate standard of value. By "standard of value," we mean the definition of value as discussed in Chapter 1.

The purpose of this section is to focus the courts' and the lawyers' attention on the fact that there can be many definitions (and interpretations of definitions) of value. Unfortunately, in most states, the definition of value for marital dissolution purposes is not clearly spelled out, leaving much room for interpretation. The lack of clear definitions and interpretations challenges appraisers and lawyers to work together to assist the courts in creating sound precedential case law that will clear up much of the existing confusion.

Family law courts sometimes use a *fair value* standard of value that can be inferred from the language and rulings in the case. When this standard is used, it usually is not intended to be synonymous with "fair value" as used in dissenting stockholder actions, although some marital dissolution decisions have expressly referred to the fair value standard used in shareholder oppression and appraisal actions.[1] Rather, it usually means something akin to the fair market value with some (usually not-well-defined) modification(s). Some traits characteristic of fair value cases are that distributions are made on a pro rata share of enterprise value with no discounts;[2] there are no "shareholder level" discounts, such as discounts for lack of marketability or lack of control; some element of goodwill is included, but discounts are disallowed; the case emphasizes that the spouses are unwilling sellers (or buyers);[3] or the case emphasizes that the distribution must be "fair."

This section discusses the most common standards of value and some of their implications and interpretations. It also addresses arguments in favor of and opposed to different definitions of value.

Several states, such as Florida, Hawaii, Illinois, Missouri, Pennsylvania, South Carolina, Texas, and Wisconsin, adhere quite strictly to the standard of *fair market value,* the price at which the property would change hands between well-informed, willing buyers and sellers on an arm's-length basis. Some states, such as Arkansas[4] and Louisiana,[5] mandate this standard by statute for the valuation of certain types of marital property. Those espousing the fair market value standard say that it is unfair to value the property that one spouse will receive at more than that spouse could actually realize in a sale. Other states adhere to the concept of *value to the owner,* reflecting whatever special circumstances may make the property more valuable to

1. *See, e.g.,* Brown v. Brown, 792 A.2d 463, 2002 N.J. Super. LEXIS 105 (N.J. App. Div. 2002); Piscopo v. Piscopo, 557 A.2d 1040 (N.J. Super. 1989) (indicating that since both shareholder oppression and marital dissolution cases are brought in equity, it would be unreasonable to treat them differently).

2. *See, e.g.,* Bobrow v. Bobrow, State of Indiana, Hamilton Superior Court Cause No. 29D01-0003-DR-166; Howell v. Howell, 1998 WL 972312 (Va. Cir. Ct. Sept. 4, 1998), *aff'd,* 523 S.E.2d 514 (Va. Ct. App. 2000).

3. Ellington v. Ellington, 842 So. 2d 1160 (La. Ct. App. 2003).

4. A.C.A. § 9-12-315(4) (2008).

5. LA. REV. STAT. § 9:2801-(1)(a) (2008).

that owner than to someone else. Although the courts are not consistent in what they call this value, both business appraisers and real estate appraisers call it *investment value.*[6] States that have used an investment value standard of value include Arizona, California, Colorado, Kentucky, Michigan, Montana, Nevada, New Mexico, North Carolina, and Washington (however, such use has not precluded the application of other standards in these states). Depending on the owner's special circumstances, this value could be much higher than the value to other investors.[7] The rationale for this position is that if a sale is not imminent, the question of how much the property would bring is irrelevant. States do not have totally consistent positions on this critical issue.

The court, the lawyer, and the appraiser all should be wary that many case decisions in family law that use the term *fair market value* actually take positions that are not consistent with fair market value as defined in Chapter 1 and in the Tax Court case law. Therefore, when seeking precedential case law guidance, it is necessary to read the entire opinion to see what valuation procedures actually were accepted.

Business appraisers who have been active in valuations for marital dissolution have debated the issue of the appropriate standard of value. Alan Zipp advocates that the value should be the "current value to the marital community in the hands of the present owner."[8] David Bishop and Steven Schroeder counter:

> The relevant point to the court should be the amount the business assets could bring in cash or cash equivalent at the appropriate date. The point of whether or not the business or any other asset will actually be sold is beside the point. In fact, there is a sale of sorts which occurs within the dissolution. The net effect of the separation of marital assets is that each spouse purchases a (let's assume) 50% interest in certain assets from their spouse and pays for the purchase by selling back their 50% interest in other assets. The transfers occur and the marital assets are separated. The end result is not substantially different than when both spouses agree jointly to each sell a marital asset and divide the funds received. The primary difference is they are the buyers and

6. *See, e.g.,* Golden v. Golden, 270 Cal. App. 2d 401, 1969 Cal. App. LEXIS 1538 (Cal. Ct. App. 1969) (in a community property state, the spouse's contribution to the intangible value of the other spouse's business is treated as an investment in stock).

7. For definitions and discussion of various standards of value, see Shannon Pratt & Alina V. Niculita, Valuing a Business 29–54 (5th ed. 2008), and Jay Fishman et al., Standards of Value: Theory and Applications (2007).

8. Alan S. Zipp, *Business Valuation Standard for Divorce Is Different from Fair Market Value*, Am. J. Fam. L., Fall 1997, at 167–72; Alan S. Zipp, *Fair Value as a Basis for Business Valution in Divorce,* in ch. 5, *Fair Value in Marital Dissolution*, BVR's Guide to Fair Value in Shareholder Dissent, Oppression, and Marital Dissolution, 2009 Ed. (Business Valuation Resources 2009).

sellers, there are no outside parties involved, and the mode of payment is the exchange of interests in the marital assets.[9]

Bishop and Schroeder make the point that marketability discounts should be recognized, as in Tax Court, because one spouse usually gets liquid assets while the other lacks the flexibility and safety of being able to "cash out" readily. They also make the point that "underlying principles are much more consistent and broadly accepted" under the fair market value standard than they are in marital dissolutions not using fair market value. This sentiment has been echoed by others.[10]

If the standard of value is fair market value, then goodwill should be a marital asset only to the extent that it is transferable. Furthermore, if the state does not allow proceeds from future activities of the spouse (or restrictions on future activities) to be a factor in property division, then goodwill should have to be transferable without requiring either an employment agreement or a noncompete agreement in order for it to be given value for marital asset purposes. Most state statutes contain language to this effect, but case decisions often ignore it.

Typical of language among states using the fair market value standard is the following:

> When dividing and distributing the value of the property of the parties in a divorce case, the relevant value is, as a general rule, the fair market value (FMV) of the parties' interest therein on the relevant date. We define the FMV as being the amount at which an item would change hands from a willing seller to a willing buyer, neither being under any compulsion to buy or sell and both having reasonable knowledge of the relevant facts.
>
> We disagree with the position advanced by Wife, and In re *Marriage of Fleege,* 91 Wash. 2d 324, 588 P.2d 1136 (1979), that the relevant value of a sole professional business is its value to the professional who operates it. Other assets are, as a general rule, valued at their FMV. We know of no valid reason why sole professional businesses should not be valued at their FMVs.[11]

One of the states claiming fair market value as the standard of value in marital property distributions is Wisconsin.[12] Nevertheless, at least one Wisconsin case in-

9. David M. Bishop & Steven F. Schroeder, *Business Valuation Standard of Value for Divorce Should Be Fair Market Value,* Am. J. Fam. L., Spring 1999, at 48–52.

10. *See, e.g.,* Robert Kleeman, Jr., *Fair Value versus Fair Market Value: Is There a Place for Fair Value in Marital Dissolution?,* ch. 5 *in* BVR's Guide to Fair Value in Shareholder Dissent, Oppression, and Marital Dissolution, 2009 Ed. (Business Valuation Resources 2009).

11. Antolik v. Harvey, 761 P.2d 305 (Haw. Ct. App. 1988).

12. Liddle v. Liddle, 410 N.W.2d 196, 199 (Wis. Ct. App. 1987), *cited* in Sommerfield v. Sommerfield, 454 N.W.2d 55 (Wis. Ct. App. 1990).

cluded goodwill in the value of an accounting practice, even clearly recognizing that the spouse would have to execute a noncompete covenant to realize that goodwill in a sale.[13] If the standard were strictly fair market value of the practice, the value of the noncompete covenant should be separate property and carved out of the total value.

Premise of Value

A key issue regarding the premise of value is whether the business should be valued on a going-concern basis or on a liquidation basis. In *Sommers v. Sommers,*[14] the wife's expert valued the husband's orthodontic practice on a going-concern basis, while the husband's expert used a liquidation value. The trial court accepted the husband's valuation, but, on appeal, the North Dakota Supreme Court reversed, finding no evidence that the husband intended to sell the practice. In *Bausano v. Bausano,*[15] the husband's expert claimed liquidation value was the appropriate premise of value because the company had operated at a loss in recent years. The court rejected this approach and found the valuation of the wife's expert more credible because it used replacement value and valued the business as a going concern. The court found that the business had potential, especially since the husband indicated he planned to focus his efforts on the business once the divorce was final. In *Hoverson v. Hoverson,*[16] the court rejected liquidation value for valuing a farm that had losses of about $1 million, finding that the assets had value to the farm as long as it continued in business. The court indicated that the business had to be valued as a going concern despite its current financial condition.

Appreciation—Active versus Passive

Some states consider appreciation in a premarital asset a marital asset, while others do not. Of the many states that consider such appreciation a marital asset, some hold that this depends on whether the increase resulted from the natural growth of the business (separate property) or from an individual's management skills (marital property).[17] In some, the appreciation is marital if it results from either spouse's efforts.[18] Sometimes it is not clear whether appreciation has resulted from "active" efforts or merely market forces; if the latter, the appreciation is not held not as a marital asset.[19] Also, courts

13. Liddle v. Liddle, *id.*
14. Sommers v. Sommers, 660 N.W.2d 586, 2003 N.D. 77 (N.D. 2003).
15. Bausano v. Bausano, 632 N.W.2d 123, 246 Wis. 2d 987 (Wis. Ct. App. 2001).
16. Hoverson v. Hoverson, 629 N.W.2d 573, 2001 N.D. 124 (N.D. 2001).
17. *See, e.g.,* Baum v. Baum, 584 P.2d 604 (Ariz. Ct. App. 1978).
18. *See, e.g.,* Brown v. Brown, 913 S.W.2d 163 (Tenn. Ct. App. 1994).
19. *See, e.g.,* Scottson v. Scottson, 1995 WL 550925 (Minn. Ct. App. 1995).

have held that the party seeking to characterize appreciation as "active" must prove that marital efforts have resulted in the appreciation.[20]

Valuation Date

Many possible dates can be used for the valuation date in marital dissolutions. Many courts use the date of trial as the valuation date.[21] Some use a date as near as possible to the final divorce decree.[22] The effective date in some cases is the date the complaint was filed.[23] Some use date of separation.[24] Also, trial courts may exercise discretion in

20. In *Conway v. Conway*, 1998 WL 865157 (N.C. Ct. App. 1998), the court ruled that to demonstrate active appreciation of separate property, there must be a showing of the value of the asset at the time of the acquisition; value of the asset at the time of separation; and the difference between the two values. Applying these criteria, the court determined that whereas marital efforts had led to the acquisition of a medical license, it did not result in the appreciation of the license's value. In *Deffenbaugh v. Deffenbaugh*, 877 S.W.2d 186 (Mo. Ct. App. 1994), the Missouri court held that where the husband failed to prove that his acumen and effort contributed to the appreciation in the wife's separate mutual fund shares, the appreciation was nonmarital property.

21. *See, e.g.,* Hargrave v. Hargrave, 209 Cal. Rptr. 764, 769 (Cal. Ct. App. 1985); Aufmuth v. Aufmuth, 152 Cal. Rptr. 668, 670 (Cal. Ct. App. 1979); Moffitt v. Moffitt, 813 P.2d 674, 678 (Alaska 1991); Ogard v. Ogard, 808 P.2d 815, 818–19 (Alaska 1991); Taylor v. Taylor, 736 S.W.2d 388, 391 (Mo. 1987); Butler v. Butler, No. 82077, 1998 WL 933354, at *2 (N.Y. App. Div. Dec. 30, 1998).

22. For example, *In re* Marriage of Olinger, 707 P.2d 64, 68 (Or. Ct. App. 1985); Koch v. Koch, 874 S.W.2d 571, 576 (Tenn. Ct. App. 1993); Wilson v. Wilson, 741 S.W.2d 640, 643 (Ark. 1987); *In re* Marriage of Talty, 623 N.E.2d 1041, 1046 (Ill. App. Ct. 1993); *In re* Marriage of Thomas, 608 N.E.2d 585, 587 (Ill. App. Ct. 1993); *In re* Marriage of Lopez, 841 P.2d 1122, 1125 (Mont. 1992); *In re* Marriage of Swanson, 716 P.2d 219, 222 (Mont. 1986); Vivian v. Vivian, 583 P.2d 1072, 1074 (Mont. 1978); *In re* Marriage of Wagner, 679 P.2d 753, 758 (Mont. 1984); Dunn v. Dunn, 802 P.2d 1314, 1320 (Utah Ct. App. 1990); *Sommerfield*, 454 N.W.2d at 60; Skokos v. Skokos, 40 S.W.3d 768 (Ark. 2001).

23. Mallett v. Mallett, 473 S.E.2d 804, 810 (S.C. Ct. App. 1996); Hickum v. Hickum, 463 S.E.2d 321, 323 (S.C. Ct. App. 1995); Hillebrand v. Hillebrand, 546 A.2d 1047, 1049 (N.H. 1988); Rosenberg v. Rosenberg, 510 N.Y.S.2d 659, 662 (App. Div. 1987); Muller v. Muller, 456 N.Y.S.2d 918, 922 (Sup. Ct. 1982); Siegel v. Siegel, 523 N.Y.S.2d 517, 520 (App. Div. 1987) (because possibility of dissipation of corporate assets existed). *But see* Scharfman v. Scharfman, 2005 N.Y. App. Div. LEXIS 6584 (N.Y. App. Div. 2005) (appellate court rejected trial court's acceptance of the date of filing as the valuation date over the trial date where there was no evidence that the husband's efforts caused the appreciation in value of the marital property).

24. Kilbourne v. Kilbourne, 284 Cal. Rptr. 201, 204 (Cal. Ct. App. 1991); Moffitt, 813 P.2d at 678; Ogard, 808 P.2d at 818–19; Richmond v. Richmond, 779 P.2d 1211, 1214 (Alaska 1989); Carlson v. Carlson, 487 S.E.2d 784, 786 (N.C. Ct. App. 1997); Bergeland v. Bergeland, 2000 Minn. App. LEXIS 952, 2000 WL 1239754 (Minn. Ct. App. 2000); *In re* Marriage of Rubens, 2003 Wash. App. LEXIS 1544 (Wash. Ct. App. 2003); Morton v. Morton, 2005 Mich. Ch. App. LEXIS 1406 (Mich. Ct. App. 2005). *But see, e.g.*, Washington v. Washington, 2005 Va. App. LEXIS 177 (Va. App. 2005) (court rejected date of separation, instead of date of evidentiary hearing, which occurred two years after the separation, where the husband's business increased in value over the two years but husband did not present evidence that this increase was the result of his extraordinary efforts).

determining valuation dates,[25] and, when selecting a valuation date for marital dissolution purposes, the date can be different for different assets.[26]

Courts in some states have considerable discretion in choosing the valuation date. Where the valuation date is not set by law or not declared by the court, the valuation expert may need to be prepared to testify to a value as of two or more valuation dates.

Goodwill[27]

As discussed at greater length in Chapter 10, the classic concept of goodwill is the propensity of customers to return. If this propensity is because of the practitioner, it often is called *personal goodwill* or *professional goodwill.* If it is because of other factors (such as location) not dependent on the individual practitioners, it often is called *practice goodwill* or *enterprise goodwill.* Some definitions of goodwill include all intangible value not just the persistence of the customer base.

A key issue in marital dissolution cases involving goodwill valuation is whether it is necessary to distinguish between personal goodwill and enterprise goodwill, and, if such a distinction is necessary, which type of goodwill is a marital or distributable asset. A number of courts, but not a majority, make no distinction between personal and enterprise goodwill. These jurisdictions have taken the position that both personal and enterprise goodwill in a professional practice constitute marital property. A minority of courts have taken the position that neither personal nor enterprise goodwill in a professional practice constitutes marital property. The majority of states differentiate between enterprise goodwill and personal goodwill. Courts in these states take the position that personal goodwill is not marital property, but that enterprise goodwill is marital property. In many states, professional goodwill is an element of marital property value even if it is not transferable. Some states have not issued a decision on whether types of goodwill must be distinguished. For a comprehensive state-by-state guide of the treatment of goodwill in marital dissolution cases, see "Goodwill Hunting in Divorce."[28]

This section explores representative positions taken in various decisions on this issue. The decisions sometimes seem to be inconsistent with the stated definition of

25. Scalero v. Scalero, 1998 WL 23845, at *3 (Ohio Ct. App. 1998); Wallace v. Wallace, 733 S.W.2d 102, 106 (Tenn. Ct. App. 1987); Reese v. Reese, 671 N.E.2d 187, 191 (Ind. Ct. App. 1996); Favell v. Favell, 957 P.2d 556, 462 (Okla. Ct. App. 1997).

26. Green v. Green, 1998 WL 363840, at *3 (Ohio Ct. App. 1998); Quillen v. Quillen, 671 N.E.2d 98 (Ind. 1996).

27. For an extensive discussion of goodwill valuation issues, see Noah J. Gordon, *Goodwill Valuation in the Courts*, ch. 2, BVR's Guide to Personal v. Enterprise Goodwill (Business Valuation Resources 2009).

28. Available from Business Valuation Resources at www.bvlibrary.com.

value. This presents a challenge to the appraisers, lawyers, and courts to make the treatment of goodwill consistent with the espoused definition of value.

A case widely cited that details the factors to consider when calculating the value of professional goodwill in a divorce is the California case *Lopez v. Lopez*.[29] These factors are:

1. The age and health of the professional
2. The professional's demonstrated past earning power
3. The professional's reputation in the community for judgment, skill, and knowledge
4. The professional's comparative professional success
5. The nature and duration of the professional's practice, either as a sole proprietor or as a contributing member of a partnership or professional corporation[30]

An excellent summary and analysis of the extremes of various states' positions on goodwill in a professional practice as a marital asset is found in a decision by the Supreme Court of Missouri, sitting en banc and issuing the decision without dissent:

> The husbands in the consolidated cases are the sole partners in an oral surgery partnership. In *Hanson v. Hanson,* the Circuit Court of Boone County valued the partnership at $324,862, including $233,727, an amount characterized as "goodwill" by the parties. In *Graham v. Graham,* the Circuit Court of Cole County, hearing virtually identical evidence, valued the same partnership at $90,280. . . .
>
> In addressing the question of the existence and value of goodwill in a professional context as marital property, the courts have not spoken with a uniform voice.
>
> In *Dugan v. Dugan,* 92 NJ 423, 457 A.2d 1 (1983), the New Jersey Supreme Court found that goodwill in the law practice of a sole practitioner is property subject to distribution in a dissolution action. The court recognized that reputation is "at the core" of any consideration of professional goodwill. 457 A.2d at 6. While acknowledging that future earning capacity is not per se goodwill, the New Jersey justices noted that when "future earning capacity has been enhanced because reputation leads to probable future pa-

29. Lopez v. Lopez, 38 Cal. App. 3d 93, 113 Cal. Rptr. 58 (Cal. Ct. App. 1974).

30. For cases using similar factors, *see, e.g., In re* Marriage of Fleege, 91 Wash. 2d 324, 588 P.2d 1136 (Wash. 1979); Crosetto v. Crosetto, 1996 WL 389337 (Wash. Ct. App. 1996).

tronage from existing and potential clients, goodwill may exist and have value." *Id.* Dugan has been criticized, and properly so in our view, for its failure to distinguish between the reputation of the professional as an individual and the reputation of the professional practice as a business entity.

In the Matter of the Marriage of Fleege, 91 Wash. 2d 324, 588 P.2d 1136 (en banc 1979), the Washington Supreme Court defined the critical question as "not whether the goodwill of the practice could be sold . . . but whether it [the goodwill] has value to [the practitioner]." 588 P.2d at 1138–39. In determining the value of such goodwill, *Fleege* outlined several factors for consideration: "The practitioner's age, health, past earning power, reputation in the community for judgment, skill and knowledge, and his comparative professional success." 588 P.2d at 1138. Each of these factors is, in our view, directly attributable to the professional as a person. For this reason, we find that the *Fleege* analysis is mired in the same mixture of personal reputation and entity reputation as is found in *Dugan.*

Several courts have refused to acknowledge professional goodwill as property. A leading case is *Holbrook v. Holbrook,* 103 Wis. 2d 327, 309 N.W.2d 343 (App. 1981). There the court refused to follow "the twisted and illogical path that other jurisdictions have made in dealing with the concept of professional goodwill in the context of divorce." The court continued, "If the concept of professional goodwill evanesces when one attempts to distinguish it from future earning capacity . . . the goodwill or reputation of such a business accrues to the benefit of the owners only through increased salary." 309 N.W.2d at 354. See also *Powell v. Powell,* 231 Kan. 456 646 P.2d 218, 223 (1982). ("We are not persuaded that a professional practice such as Dr. Powell's has a goodwill value. The practice is personal to the practitioner. . . . It is totally dependent upon the professional.") *Nail v. Nail,* 486 S.W.2d 761 (Tex. 1972), reaches a similar result.

Between the opposing results reached in *Dugan* and *Holbrook,* several courts have attempted to chart a course which recognizes that goodwill is marital property, but only insofar as it exists independently of the individual professional's reputation. Characteristic of these cases is *Taylor v. Taylor,* 222 Neb. 721, 386 N.W.2d 851 (1986). There the Nebraska Supreme Court concluded that "goodwill must be a business asset with value independent of the presence or reputation of a particular individual, an asset which may be sold, transferred, conveyed, or pledged. . . . If a party produces appropriate evidence establishing salability or marketability of goodwill as a business asset of a professional practice, professional goodwill may be considered in determining the value of property in a marital estate to be divided in a dissolution proceeding." *Taylor,* 386 N.W.2d at 858–59. . . .

As we have said, goodwill is recognized as property in this state; that recognition is not dependent on a traditional mercantile setting. Goodwill may exist in both commercial and professional entities. Irrespective of the setting in which it is found, the meaning of goodwill does not change. It is property which attaches to and is dependent upon an existing business entity; the reputation and skill of an individual entrepreneur—be he a professional or a traditional businessman—is not a component of the intangible asset we identify generally as goodwill.

With the caveats which follow, we hold that goodwill in a professional practice acquired during a marriage is marital property subject to division in a dissolution of marriage proceeding. We define goodwill within a professional setting to mean the value of the practice which exceeds its tangible assets and which is the result of the tendency of clients/patients to return to and recommend the practice irrespective of the reputation of the individual practitioner.

Professional goodwill may not be confused with future earning capacity. We have not declared future earning capacity to be marital property.

Proof of the existence of goodwill is particularly troublesome in a professional context. This difficulty is a product of the fact that the reputation of the individual practitioner and the goodwill of his enterprise are often inextricably interwoven. Because of the difficulties inherent in separating the reputation of the professional from that of his enterprise, evidence that other professionals are willing to pay for goodwill when acquiring a practice is, in our view, the only acceptable evidence of the existence of goodwill. Thus, as a matter of proof, the existence of goodwill is shown only when there is evidence of a recent actual sale of a similarly situated professional practice, an offer to purchase such a practice, or expert testimony and testimony of members of the subject profession as to the existence of goodwill in a similar practice in the relevant geographic and professional market. Absent such evidence, one can only speculate as to the existence of goodwill. Divisions of marital property may not be based on speculation as to the very existence of the property being divided. . . .

The fair market value method is most likely to avoid the "disturbing inequity in compelling a professional practitioner to pay a judicially determined value that could not be realized by a sale or another method of liquidating value." *Holbrook,* 309 N.W.2d at 355. We therefore reject the notion advanced by some courts that goodwill may exist and be subject to division in a dissolution proceeding even though it may not be sold.[31]

31. Hanson v. Hanson, 738 S.W.2d 429 (Mo. 1987).

A case representative of the majority position is *May v. May.*[32] In that case, the Virginia Supreme Court, ruling on an issue of first impression in that state, held that trial courts in marital dissolution cases must distinguish between personal and enterprise goodwill in a professional practice, and that personal goodwill is not a marital asset but enterprise goodwill is. The court specifically noted that enterprise goodwill can exist in a professional practice that is operated as a sole proprietorship. The court also stated that this holding was consistent with its prior ruling that a professional degree or license is not marital property because it represents the future earning capacity of the professional spouse. Likewise, personal goodwill represents the future earning capacity of the professional spouse.

A case representative of the position that either personal goodwill or enterprise goodwill is a marital asset is *Stewart v. Stewart,*[33] in which the Idaho Supreme Court held that "where a professional business is an independent entity . . . goodwill is calculable and divisible in divorce just as goodwill in any other business." In doing so, the court declined to enter the "morass" of trying to distinguish between the values attributable to a professional practice by virtue of the individual attributes of the professional and the value of the goodwill not attributable to those personal assets, valuing each separately and then dividing the latter but not the former. A strong dissent argued that because the majority had held that a professional's personal attributes—including knowledge, skill, reputation, etc.—are not divisible community property, the court should have required the parties to distinguish whether the husband's ability to earn above-average income was based upon his personal attributes or "some other factor."[34]

Once a court had determined whether to distinguish between personal and enterprise goodwill, the issue becomes how to do so. Indiana's *Yoon v. Yoon*[35] exemplifies a case where a court attempted to distinguish personal and enterprise goodwill in a professional corporation. The court ruled that to determine if any goodwill should be included in a marital estate, there must be a determination about what portion of it is attributable to the individual and the value of that portion must be excluded from the estate. In its decision, the court made the following statement to explain that enter-

---

32. May v. May, 2003 W. Va. LEXIS 118 (W. Va. 2003). *See also* Nowzaradan v. Nowzaradan, 2007 Tex. App. LEXIS 1021 (Tex. Ct. App. 2007); Thompson v. Thompson, 576 So. 2d 267 (Fla. 1991).

33. Stewart v. Stewart, 2007 Idaho LEXIS 17 (Idaho 2007).

34. *See also* Gaskill v. Robbins, 2006 Ky. App. LEXIS 364 (Ky. Ct. App. 2006) (court ruled that it would be inequitable to hold that the form of the business enterprise can defeat the community's interest in professional goodwill, since such a result ignores the contribution made by the nonprofessional spouse to the success of the professional); Bunkers v. Bunkers, 2007 Ohio App. LEXIS 523 (Ohio Ct. App. 2007) (court rules that all goodwill of a solo practitioner is subject to equitable division in divorce).

35. Yoon v. Yoon, 711 N.E.2d 1265 (Ind. 1999).

prise goodwill is subject to equitable distribution, while personal goodwill can only affect the relative distribution of property.

> Before including the goodwill of a self-employed business or professional practice in a marital estate, a court must determine that the goodwill is attributable to the business as opposed to the owner as an individual. If attributable to the individual, it is not a divisible asset and is properly considered only as future earning capacity that may affect the relative property division. In this respect, the future earning capacity of a self-employed person (or an owner of a business primarily dependent on the owner's services) is to be treated the same as the future earning capability and reputation of an employee.

On the basis of *Yoon, Bobrow v. Bobrow*[36] discussed the enterprise goodwill of the accounting firm, Ernst & Young (E&Y). The husband, E&Y's global CEO, had a partnership interest in a division of the accounting firm. Although there was a partnership agreement limiting the owner's interest to the value of the capital account, thus excluding goodwill, the husband conceded that the agreement only applied to a transaction of his partnership interest (resignation, retirement, or death). The court recognized that the assets of E&Y were not personal to the partner but belonged to the institution of which each partner had a share. These institutional assets included such intangible assets as E&Y's trade name, the entity's favorable business reputation and name recognition, methods and tools for conducting its business, and its relationships with suppliers. All these items were transferable to an outside purchaser. This case, therefore, contrasted with Yoon, where all these assets were associated with the doctor himself rather than the entity and the court found that they could not be transferred to another individual. Ultimately, the court included the value of enterprise goodwill in valuing E&Y and awarded the wife a share of the value of the husband's partnership interest in E&Y based on his pro rata share of the value of the enterprise.

A method developed by David Wood that has been accepted in some courts to calculate the enterprise and personal components of goodwill in the valuation of a professional practice is called the multiattribute utility model (MUM). This model involves several steps. First, the valuator sets forth an objective. Next, the valuator establishes "alternatives." An alternative is a "range of percentages" that will define the choices "in which the method will result." Each alternative is then assigned a "range." After the objective and the alternatives are set, the valuator then must define the "attributes," which are elements of goodwill to which the valuator must assign a value. Examples of attributes are personal reputation and business location.[37]

36. State of Indiana, Hamilton Superior Court Cause No. 29D01-0003-DR-166.

37. *In re* Marriage of Alexander, 2006 Ill. App. LEXIS 836 (Ill. Ct. App. 2006); Neary v. Neary, Case No. 06-DR-3254 (18th Cir., Seminole, Fla.).

Another issue that may arise in valuing goodwill is the best method to do so. There are five major formulas that are used in valuing goodwill:

1. The straight capitalization accounting method,
2. The capitalization of excess earnings method,
3. The IRS variation of capitalized excess earnings method (based on Rev. Rul. 68-609—the full text of this rule can be found in Chapter 8 of this book),
4. The market value approach, and
5. The buy-sell agreement method.[38]

Of these, the excess earnings method is the most commonly used; some courts find that the market value approach and buy-sell agreement methods are easily manipulated by the professional spouse. The excess earnings method is discussed at greater length in Chapter 8. The capitalization of excess earnings method focuses on the earning power of the business to determine what rate of return the predicted earnings will yield in light of the risks involved to attain them. Broadly put, the excess earnings approach is predicated on a comparison of the earnings of the professional in question with that of a peer whose performance is average. To make this comparison, courts may, among other things, determine the annual salary of a typical salaried employee who has had experience commensurate with the spouse who is the sole practitioner or sole owner/employee. Alternatively, courts may apply the similarly situated professional standard, under which reasonable compensation is based on the cost of hiring a nonowner outsider to perform the same average amount that other people normally are compensated for performing similar services. Although not binding, professional compensation surveys may be used by experts and trial courts as guidelines for determining reasonable compensation of a practitioner's peers. To be relevant, however, the surveys must account for similarly situated professional practices and practitioners.[39]

Other cases have clarified that personal goodwill and enterprise goodwill can be a part of a going-concern value, but that going-concern value and goodwill cannot be the same, for the latter is subsumed within the former. Going-concern value is the intangible value attached to the physical assets of the business, including the business's fixtures, equipment, and its assemblage of personnel, as well as its goodwill.[40]

Several courts, in attempting to determine what constitutes goodwill, have ruled that goodwill is indistinguishable from earning capacity, which is not a distributable

38. *See, e.g.,* May v. May, 2003 W. Va. LEXIS 118 (W. Va. 2003).
39. *See, e.g., In re* Marriage of Ackerman, 2006 Cal. App. LEXIS 2056 (Cal. Ct. App. 2006).
40. Gaydos v. Gaydos, 693 A.2d 1368 (Pa. Super. Ct. 1997).

asset.[41] These courts view goodwill in a professional practice as merely assuring the continuation of earnings in the future. This view has been criticized on the grounds that, at least when it comes to equitable distribution in marital dissolutions, the contributions of each spouse to specific assets must be recognized. Others, however, take the opposite view and argue that goodwill is just not a product of a marital partnership. Other courts have ruled that goodwill is separate from earning capacity where the professional's interest in a practice is transferable and separable from reputation.[42] In such instances, it must be proved that goodwill is separate from earning capacity to avoid double counting the same asset. Still, other courts view goodwill as supplementing earning capacity rather than merging with it.[43]

A related issue is whether enhanced earning capacity, which is an individual's ability to earn over and above what would be earned following a "normal" career path that results from enhancements, such as a degree, license, training, specialized knowledge, unique talent, etc., should be considered goodwill that is a marital asset. Some states, such as New York[44] and New Jersey,[45] recognize celebrity status or celebrity goodwill as marital property. This concept of goodwill is based on the enhanced earnings capacity of a celebrity. Only New York recognizes licenses or degrees as marital assets the value of which must be distributed.[46] In New York, a doctrine developed that holds that where the licensed professional has maintained a professional practice over a long period of time, the license is deemed to have merged with the practice itself and has no value separate from the practice. This doctrine is called the "merger doctrine." Some courts have rejected this doctrine, finding that it generally favors a nonlicensed spouse in a shorter marriage over a nonlicensed spouse in a longer marriage. These courts caution that care must be taken to ensure that the monetary value assigned to the license does not overlap with the value assigned to other marital assets that are derived from the license such as the licensed spouse's professional practice.[47]

---

41. *See* Holbrook v. Holbrook, 103 Wis. 2d 327, 309 N.W.2d 343, 1981 Wis. App. LEXIS 3322 (Wis. Ct. App. 1981) ("The concept of professional goodwill evanesces when one attempts to distinguish it from future earning capacity."); Donahue v. Donahue, 299 S.C. 353, 384 S.E.2d 741 (S.C. 1989); and Hickum v. Hickum, 463 S.E.2d 321 (S.C. Ct. App. 1995).

42. Peerenboom v. Peerenboom, 433 N.W.2d 282 (Wis. Ct. App. 1988).

43. *See, e.g., In re* Bookout, 833 P.2d 800 (Colo. Ct. App. 1991), *cert. denied*, 846 P.2d 189 (Colo. 1993); *In re* Hall, 103 Wash.2d 236, 692 P.2d 175 (Wash. 1984).

44. Golub v. Golub, 139 Misc. 2d 440, 527 N.Y.S.2d 946 (N.Y. Sup. Ct. 1988); Elkus v. Elkus, 169 A.D.2d 134, 572 N.Y.S.2d 901 (N.Y. App. Div. 1991).

45. Piscopo v. Piscopo, 232 N.J. Super. 559, 557 A.2d 1040 (N.J. Super. Ct. 1989).

46. O'Brien v. O'Brien, 489 N.E.2d 712, 66 N.Y.2d 576, 498 N.Y.S.2d 743 (N.Y. 1985).

47. *See, e.g.,* McSparron v. McSparron, 662 N.E.2d 745, 87 N.Y.2d 275, 639 N.Y.S.2d 265 (N.Y. App. Div. 1995). *McSparron* considered factors such as a change in circumstances and location of a practicing professional and decided that no matter how far along one's career is, the license has a value outside of one's career.

Another goodwill valuation issue is to what degree goodwill inheres in a noncompete agreement. It is sometimes difficult to determine the value that should be assigned to a practice's goodwill and the value that should be assigned to a noncompete agreement.[48]

Yet another issue, discussed at greater length in a section that follows, is that of double counting or "double-dipping." This issue arises when a court in a matrimonial dispute considers excess earnings (or other factors that assume continued involvement by the operating spouse) in determining the value of a business as well as in setting alimony. This issue arises more frequently in those jurisdictions that hold that personal goodwill is a marital asset.

The California Business and Professions Code Section 14100 defines goodwill as "the expectation of continued public patronage." However:

> The philosophy of the community property system is that a community interest can be acquired only during the time of the marriage. It would then be inconsistent with that philosophy to assign to any community interest the value of the post-marital efforts of either spouse (*In re Marriage of Fortier* (1973) 34 Cal. App. 3d 384, 109 Cal. Rptr. 915). Since a community interest can only be acquired during the time of the marriage, the value of the goodwill must exist at the time of the dissolution and that value must be established without dependence on the potential or continuing net income of the professional spouse. (*In re Marriage of Fortier*, supra; *In re Marriage of Foster* (1974) 42 Cal. App. 3d 577 at 582, 117 Cal. Rptr. 49.)[49]

The wording in a frequently quoted California case states:

> We believe . . . the good will of the husband's professional practice as a sole practitioner should be taken into consideration . . . [I]n a matrimonial matter, the practice of the sole practitioner will continue, with the same intangible value as it had during the marriage.[50]

48. *See, e.g., In re* the Marriage of Monaghan, 899 P.2d 841 (Wash. Ct. App. 1995) (covenant not to compete is personal property of the practitioner); Kricsfeld v. Kricsfeld, 588 N.W.2d 210, 8 Neb. App. 1 (Neb. Ct. App. 1999) (noncompete agreement is personal to the practitioner and can never be a marital asset); Held v. Held, 2005 Fla. App. LEXIS 14138 (Fla. Ct. App. 2005) (for the purpose of distinguishing enterprise goodwill from personal goodwill in the valuation of a business, there is no distinction between a "non-solicitation/non-piracy agreement" and a covenant not to compete, which is attributable to the personal reputation of the seller/spouse and not to the enterprise goodwill of the business); Sweere v. Gilbert-Sweere, 534 N.W.2d 294, 1995 Minn. App. LEXIS 912 (Minn. Ct. App. 1995) (to the extent that the purpose of a noncompete agreement is to prevent the spouse from interfering with the transfer of goodwill, the agreement is representative of marital goodwill).

49. *In re* Marriage of King, 197 Cal. Rptr. 716 (Cal. Ct. App. 1983).

50. Golden v. Golden, 75 Cal. Rptr. 735 (Cal. Ct. App. 1965).

Considering these quotes, one might think that on the one hand, value can't be based on the spouse's postmarital efforts, and on the other hand, value is based on the assumption that the practicing spouse will continue to practice. California courts' attempts to reconcile these positions are embodied in a long and confusing series of decisions.

This seeming internal contradiction, which also has been referred to as the "market value of goodwill" paradox,[51] is prevalent in family law case decisions. Courts espouse the position that valuation of a business or practice should not depend on future efforts (or restrictions on future efforts) of the operating spouse. Having said this, the same courts often go on to accept appraisal methodology that, in fact, reflects earnings that could only be achieved if the operating spouse continues in the business or practice.[52]

Buy-Sell Agreements

A *buy-sell agreement* is a contract between an owner and the company, or between two or more owners, describing the conditions under which one party may (or must) sell his or her interest to the other. The valuation issues relating to buy-sell agreements are discussed in greater length in Chapter 28. The agreement normally incorporates a price, or a mechanism for determining the price, for such a sale. As such, the buy-sell agreement price is the price that the spouse could realize on withdrawal from the partnership or corporation.

From the company's viewpoint, the agreement provides control over who will be involved in ownership. From the owner's viewpoint, the agreement usually provides liquidity if he or she leaves the company or for the owner's estate in the event of death.

A frequent issue is whether a buy-sell agreement price is controlling for marital property valuation. Some courts hold that the price is controlling.[53] Others, especially in states where professional (personal) goodwill is a marital asset, find that the buy-

51. Shannon Pratt & Alina Niculita, Valuing a Business: The Analysis and Appraisal of Closely Held Companies 971–72 (McGraw-Hill 2008).

52. *See* Shannon Pratt, *Contradictions in family law cases,* Judges & Lawyers Business Valuation Update, Dec. 1999, at 1, 4–5. *See also, e.g.*, Poore v. Poore, 75 N.C. App. 414, 331 S.E.2d 266 (N.C. Ct. App. 1985), which lists as acceptable methods the following:

- The price a willing buyer would pay
- Capitalization of excess earnings
- One year's average gross income
- Evidence of sales of comparable practices.

All of these imply continued participation to some degree, or a noncompete agreement.

53. *See, e.g.,* Rosenberg v. Rosenberg, 510 N.Y.S.2d 659, 662 (App. Div. 1987); Hertz v. Hertz, 657 P.2d 1169, 1174–75 (N.M. 1983); Johnson v. Johnson, 771 P.2d 696, 698 (Utah Ct. App. 1989).

sell agreement price generally is not binding. A Washington case is typical of this position:

> Professional goodwill has been recognized in Washington as intangible property subject to division in a marital dissolution. *Hall* at 238-39, 692 P.2d 175. The important consideration is not whether the goodwill could be sold without the personal services of the professional, but whether it has value to him. *In re Marriage of Fleege,* 91 Wash. 2d 324, 327, 588 P.2d 1136 (1979) (goodwill of husband's solo dental practice was a community asset).
>
> Both parties cite cases from other jurisdictions as authority. Some cases hold the nonshareholder spouse should be bound by the buy-sell agreement or that the buy-sell agreement should at least be considered. *Hertz v. Hertz,* 99 N.M. 320, 657 P.2d 1169, 1174 (1983) (a nonshareholder spouse was bound by the goodwill valuation clause in corporate bylaws for purposes of establishing the valuation of corporate goodwill in a dissolution action. This ensured that the nonshareholder spouse did not receive a greater value than the shareholder.). See also *In re Marriage of Ondrasek,* 126 Wis. 2d 469, 377 NW2d 190, 192 (Ct. App. 1985) (in a dissolution, value of a partner's interest in a professional partnership is determined by the monetary consequences of that partner withdrawing from the business); *Holbrook v. Holbrook,* 103 Wis. 2d 327, 309 NW2d 343, 355 (Ct. App. 1981) (capital account was the only value that should be assigned to a lawyer's partnership as an asset where lawyer was entitled to receive only his capital account value on withdrawal and any goodwill is reflected in his salary which can be considered in setting the family support award); and *Hanson v. Hanson,* 738 SW2d 429, 436 (Mo. 1987) (value of goodwill of professional practice, subject to division in dissolution proceeding, is determined by the price the practice would bring if sold on open, relevant market to qualified professional; under certain circumstances value may be established by buy-sell agreement).
>
> Other courts have held the nonshareholder spouse is not bound by the terms of the withdrawal agreement and, in some cases, even where the nonshareholder spouse cosigned the withdrawal agreement. *In re Marriage of Slater,* 100 Cal. App. 3d 241, 160 Cal. Rptr. 686 (1979) (on theory withdrawal agreement was not signed for dissolution purposes); *Mitchell v. Mitchell,* 152 Ariz. 317, 732 P.2d 208, 210 (1987) (partnership agreement provided that no value was to be placed on goodwill of the firm; however, it did contain provisions for payments to a partner upon retirement or death which were not limited to the firm's tangible assets and accounts receivable, but included a share of net profits for a limited period. A buy-sell agreement had been considered in establishing the valuation of goodwill, but was not dis-

positive. At best it created a presumptive value which either spouse could rebut); *Stern v. Stern,* 66 N.J. 340, 331 A.2d 257, 260, 74 L.R.3d 613 (1975) (of the four payment plans found in the partnership agreement applicable to a partner who withdraws from a firm, becomes disabled, dies or retires, the formula applicable on a partner's death is presumptively the value to be used in dissolution; here, the partner was entitled to the value of his capital account plus a fixed sum appended to the partnership agreement which was revised quarterly). But cf. *Rogers v. Rogers,* 296 NW2d 849, 852-53 (Minn. 1980) (it was reversible error not to consider the terms of the buy-sell agreement which create contingencies that affect the value, such as the possibility the shareholder might die or be disabled before he realizes the full value of his interest).

Our state has not considered whether a buy-sell agreement not made in close proximity to a divorce is binding on the nonshareholder spouse in a dissolution action. *Hall* did not reach this issue but held that, at least in some circumstances, buy-sell agreements are not binding in a dissolution action. In light of *Hall* and *Fleege* (that it makes no difference whether the goodwill can be sold) we hold the court did not err in valuing goodwill even though it was assigned no value in the Brooks & Larson, P.S. corporation bylaws.[54]

In the above case, the spouse had practiced law for four years before the marriage and 13 years since. The court decided that the interest in the practice that the husband bought (and that was subject to the buy-sell agreement) was separate property and that his goodwill (valued at $93,115 by the excess earnings method) was community property.

Sometimes a buy-sell price may be a factor to be considered but not completely controlling.[55] In one case, the husband purchased stock, subject to a buy-sell agreement, for $65,567 from funds borrowed from his mother. In three years, the stock paid $251,000 in dividends, and the buy-sell formula price increased to $82,000. In rejecting the trial court's valuation at the buy-sell price, the court of appeals explained:

54. *In re* Marriage of Brooks, 756 P.2d 161 (Wash. Ct. App. 1988). *See also* In the Matter of Overbey, 2007 Wash App. LEXIS 1651 (Wash. Ct. App. 2007), which continued this state's approach and indicated that a buy-sell agreement was not a binding separation contract, and that while the formula contained therein was relevant, it was not determinative of the company's value.

55. *See, e.g., In re* Marriage of Herlitzke, 2006 Wis. App. LEXIS 972 (Wis. Ct. App. 2006) (buy-sell agreement may establish fair market value of partnership or S corporation, but does not do so as a matter of law); Herron v. Herron, 2004 Ohio App. LEXIS 5209 (Ohio Ct. App. 2004) (court gave weight to the closely held company's buy-sell agreement because "[a]ny willing buyer would certainly take into account the buy/sell agreement before making any offer on the stock"); R.V.K. v. L.L.K, 2002 WL 31421572 (Tex. Ct. App. 2002); Harmon v. Harmon, 2000 WL 286718 (Tenn. Ct. App. 2000); Howell v. Howell, 46 Va. Cir. 339; 1998 Va. Cir. LEXIS 256 (Va. Cir. Ct. 1998), *aff'd,* 31 Va. App. 332, 523 S.E.2d 514 (Va. Ct. App. 2000).

> It is unreasonable to assume the value of the stock to Darrell was only what he could sell it to the company for, in light of the fact it was producing such generous dividends. It stretches the bounds of reasonableness to value a goose for slaughter price when it lays golden eggs.[56]

The appellate court declined to value the stock at $1.6 million, as claimed by the wife's expert based on capitalization of earnings, but did award the wife an additional $40,000 representing her interest during the marriage.

One case that rejected a buy-sell agreement price as controlling the value of a minority interest noted the following:

- There was evidence that another family member had been bought out at a price that exceeded the value set by the buy-sell agreement.
- The buy-sell agreement was taken into consideration to some extent by the expert's reduction of 35 percent in value for minority interest and lack of marketability.[57]

Similarly, in another case where stock was subject to a buy-sell agreement at book value, the court "decreased the unrestricted fair market value substantially more than it increased the book value to arrive at a valuation for purposes of the marriage dissolution."[58]

Another case summarized the most typical position:

> A majority of courts which have considered a buy-sell agreement in a closely held corporation setting the stock value for equitable distribution purposes has determined that such agreement should not be considered as binding, but rather should be weighed along with other factors in making a determination as to the value of such stock. E.g., *In re Marriage of Melnick,* 127 Ill. App. 3d 102, 82 Ill. Dec. 228, 468 N.E.2d 490 (1984); *In re Marriage of Moffatt,* 279 N.W.2d 15 (Iowa 1979); *Rogers v. Rogers,* 296 N.W.2d 849 (Minn. 1980); *Bowen v. Bowen,* 96 N.J. 36, 473 A.2d 73 (1984); *Amodio v. Amodio,* 70 N.Y.2d 5, 516 N.Y.S. 2d 923, 509 N.E.2d 936 (1987); *In the Matter of the Marriage of Belt,* 65 Ore. App. 606, 672 P.2d 1205 (1983); *Bosserman v. Bosserman*, 9 Va. App. 1, 384 S.E.2d 104 (1989); *Arneson v. Arneson,* 120 Wis. 2d 236, 355 N.W.2d 16 (Wis. Ct. App. 1984). It is apparent that buy-sell

56. *In re* Marriage of Dieger, 584 N.W.2d 567 (Iowa Ct. App. 1998).
57. Berenberg v. Berenberg, 474 N.W.2d 843 (Minn. Ct. App. 1991).
58. Lyon v. Lyon, 439 N.W.2d 18 (Minn. 1989).

> agreements in a closely held corporation can be manipulated by the shareholders to reflect an artificially low value. This is why caution should be exercised in accepting their value for equitable distribution purposes.[59]

A New Mexico court found the buy-sell price in a law firm's stockholder's agreement controlling, even though it was computed completely on a cash basis, and even though the court had found goodwill using a capitalization of excess earnings method in a medical practice that had no buy-sell agreement.[60]

In a Washington case involving a minority interest in an insurance agency, the court did find the buy-sell agreement price controlling. The court noted that the minority status was not likely to change, there was no evidence that the company was likely to be sold, and it was reasonable to conclude that if the husband were to sell his stock, he would do so subject to the buy-sell agreement formula.[61]

The most-quoted case in favor of the buy-sell agreement being controlling is from Wisconsin:

> There is a disturbing inequity in compelling a professional practitioner to pay a spouse a share of intangible assets at a judicially determined value that could not be realized by a sale or another method of liquidating value.[62]

Buy-sell agreements involving key persons often are funded with life insurance benefits payable to the designated purchaser under the agreement, providing liquidity to exercise the buy-sell agreement in the case of the death of the owner of the interest. The amount of the "key man" insurance sometimes is presented as evidence of the partners' idea of the value of the interest. Such evidence could be supportive of an appraised value, at best, but certainly no substitute for an appraisal.

In almost any situation where a buy-sell agreement is taken into consideration, the extent to which the agreement was entered into on an arm's-length basis also should be considered.

---

59. Bettinger v. Bettinger, 396 S.E.2d 709 (W. Va 1990). *See also* Barton v. Barton, 2007 Ga. LEXIS 21 (Ga. 2007), where the Georgia Supreme Court joined the clear majority of states on this issue and held that the value of stock set forth in a buy-sell agreement for a closely held corporation is not binding for purposes of property division in divorce proceedings. The court reasoned that "[t]he buy-sell price in a closely-held corporation can be manipulated and does not necessarily reflect true market value."

60. Hertz v. Hertz, 657 P.2d 1169 (N.M. 1983).

61. *In re* Marriage of Gillespie, 948 P.2d 1338 (Wash. Ct. App. 1997).

62. Holbrook v. Holbrook, 309 N.W.2d 343 (Wis. Ct. App. 1981).

Covenants Not to Compete

A *covenant not to compete* or *noncompete agreement* is a contract preventing an individual (or group of individuals) from competing with a given entity or person. For example, a dentist selling a practice may agree not to practice dentistry for a certain amount of time in the metropolitan area of the buyer of the practice. In other cases, some partnerships or corporations require entering into a covenant not to compete as a condition of ownership. The covenant usually enhances the value of the entity by reducing the risk of certain individuals taking away business.

Treatment of an actual or prospective covenant not to compete is controversial. Most courts take the position that such a covenant restricts the postmarital activities of the spouse and therefore is separate rather than marital property.[63] Others find that such covenants are marital property.[64] Others take the position that sales of most small businesses and professional practices require covenants not to compete, and the court may value the enterprise assuming a covenant, or even order the spouse to execute a covenant, with no separate compensation to the spouse.[65] Still others hold that adjustments for hypothetical noncompete agreements are impermissible, even though comparable transactions include such agreements of similar duration, where the appraiser does not present evidence on the nature of such agreements or their impact on value.[66]

A covenant not to compete, by definition, restricts the postmarital efforts of the spouse. In most jurisdictions, this would be considered a nonmarital asset. If the

63. *See, e.g., In re* Marriage of Monaghan, 899 P.2d 841 (Wash. Ct. App. 1995) (the portion of sale price attributable to covenant is husband's separate property); Kricsfeld v. Kricsfeld, 588 N.W.2d 210, 1999 Neb. App. LEXIS 1 (Neb. Ct. App. 1999); Ellerbe v. Ellerbe, 323 S.C. 283, 473 S.E.2d 881 (S.C. Ct. App. 1996); Cutsinger v. Cutsinger, 917 S.W.2d 238 (Tenn. Ct. App. 1995) (court excluded monetary amounts for covenant not to compete from purchase price of chiropractic practice); Hoeft v. Hoeft, 74 Ohio App. 3d 809, 600 N.E.2d 746 (Ohio Ct. App. 1991) (court determined that while proceeds received for the sale of the husband's dental practice were marital property, monies received from a covenant not to compete were nonmarital); Johnston v. Johnston, 778 S.W.2d 674 (Mo. Ct. App. 1989) (covenant not to compete properly excluded in the valuation of dental practice); Donahue v. Donahue, 299 S.C. 353, 384 S.E.2d 741 (1989) (goodwill of a professional practice is not subject to equitable distribution); Lucas v. Lucas, 621 P.2d 500 (N.M. 1980) (the right to compete is a personal right and the separate property of its owner).

64. Reese v. Reese, 671 N.E.2d 187 (Ind. Ct. App. 1996); Sweere v. Gilbert-Sweere, 534 N.W.2d 294, 1995 Minn. App. LEXIS 912 (Minn. Ct. App. 1995) (to the extent that the purpose of a noncompete agreement is to prevent the spouse from interfering with the transfer of goodwill, the agreement is representative of marital goodwill).

65. *See, e.g.,* Carr v. Carr, 701 P.2d 304 (Idaho Ct. App. 1985) (court ordered husband to enter into sales agreement including covenant not to compete, with no allowance to husband for the covenant). *But see In re* Marriage of Mally, 2001 WL 539669 (Iowa Ct. App. 2001) (court accepted that a noncompete agreement was essential to the sale of the practice and reduced the practice's value by $329,000).

66. Duncan v. Duncan, 90 Cal. App. 4th 617 (Cal. Ct. App. 2001).

analyst uses the market approach to value thc business or practice, and the comparable sales include covenants not to compete, it could be argued that the value of the covenants should be deducted from the comparable company or practice sales before they are used for comparison. However, most family law courts seem to ignore this factor.[67]

Minority and Marketability Discounts

As discussed in Chapter 15, a minority interest usually is worth significantly less than a pro rata share of the value of the entity as a whole. This is because a control owner can make many decisions that a minority owner can't—decisions that can affect both the value of the company as a whole and also the relative values of the controlling versus the minority interests.

Therefore, if the valuation methodology produces a controlling interest value, and the interest being valued is minority, a minority interest discount, also known as a discount for lack of control (DLOC), usually would be applied. Also, because minority interests usually are harder to sell than are controlling interests, the minority interest discount might be compounded by also subtracting a discount for lack of marketability (DLOM) (see Chapter 15).

A frequent issue is whether a minority discount should be applied (and if so, how much) if the interest owned is less than controlling.

In one case, an expert for the husband testified that a 15 percent minority discount was appropriate for a 50 percent interest. An expert for the wife testified that no minority discount was appropriate in a divorce settlement context because generally there is no change of ownership. The court rejected the wife's expert's opinion, with several references to decisions in other states:

> We reject (wife's expert's) view as a matter of law. The concept of value is keyed to the price that a prospective buyer would pay. *Moffitt v. Moffitt,* 813 P.2d 674 (Alaska 1991). Sherwin's testimony runs counter to this concept. We also note that courts in many jurisdictions have recognized that a minority discount is frequently appropriate in divorce proceedings. See *Arneson v. Arneson,* 120 Wis. 2d 236, 355 N.W.2d 16, 22 (App. 1984) (not clearly erroneous for trial court to apply minority discount); *In re Marriage of Jorgensen,* 180 Mont. 294, 590 P.2d 606, 610 (1979) (not an abuse of discretion to apply minority discount); *In re Marriage of Belt,* 65 Ore. App. 606, 672 P.2d 1205, 1207-08 (1983) (trial court's valuation modified to include

67. The database *Pratt's Stats* (see Chapter 3) shows how much was allocated to a covenant not to compete when one was involved in the sale of a business or practice.

minority discount where the only credible evidence produced at trial favored discount); *In re Marriage of Reiling,* 66 Ore. App. 284, 673 P.2d 1360, 1364, 1365 (1983) (same); *In re Marriage of Hoak,* 364 N.W.2d 185, 192-93 (Iowa 1985) (not error to apply minority discount, but discount allowed by the trial court was too large and must be reduced); *Bowen v. Bowen,* 96 N.J. 36, 473 A.2d 73, 76-77, 81 (1984) (trial court should appoint independent expert to advise it in deciding whether to apply minority discount).[68]

In one case, the minority interest discount was eliminated because the minority owner had a purchase right that would enable him to obtain control of the corporation sometime within the next seven to 10 years.[69] There have been many marital dissolution cases that have accepted discounts for lack of control[70] and many that have not.[71]

As with discounts for lack of control, many courts in marital dissolution cases have accepted discounts for lack of marketability,[72] while many have not.[73] In one

68. Hayes v. Hayes, 756 P.2d 298 (Alaska 1988).

69. *In re* Marriage of Harrington, 935 P.2d 1357 (Wash. Ct. App. 1997).

70. *See, e.g.,* Priebe v. Priebe, 556 N.W.2d 78 (S.D. 1996) (40%); *In re* Marriage of DeCosse, 936 P.2d 821, 1997 WL 19374 (Mont. 1997) (20%); Arneson v. Arneson, 355 N.W. 2d 16 (Wis. Ct. App. 1984) (25%); Rattee v. Rattee, 767 A. 2d 415, 146 N.H. 44 (N.H. 2001); L.R.M. v. R.K.M., 46 S.W.3d 24 (Mo. Ct. App. 2001) (32% combined discount); Anderson v. Anderson, 2006 Tenn. App. LEXIS 592 (Tenn. App. 2006) (38.3%).

71. *See, e.g.,* Howell v. Howell, 46 Va. Cir. 339, 1998 Va. Cir. LEXIS 256 (Va. Cir. Ct. 1998), *aff'd,* 31 Va. App. 332, 523 S.E.2d 514 (Va. Ct. App. 2000); Oatey v. Oatey, No. 67809, 67973 Ohio Ct. App., 1996 WL 200273 at *22 (Apr. 25, 1996); Nardini v. Nardini, 414 N.W. 2d 184, 189 (Minn. 1987); Cross v. Cross, 586 P.2d 547, 549 (Wyo. 1978); Ferraro v. Ferraro, 2000 WL 251678 (Va. Ct. App. 2000); Brown v. Brown, 348 N.J. Super. 466, 792 A.2d 463, 2002 N.J. Super. LEXIS 105 (N.J. Super. 2002) (discounts disallowed absent extraordinary circumstances); Baltrusis v. Baltrusis, 113 Wash. App. 1037 (Wash. Ct. App. 2002); Hanson v. Hanson, 2005 Alaska LEXIS 166 (Alaska 2005) (no discount where majority spouse acquires the minority spouse's interest).

72. *See, e.g., In re* Marriage of Tofte, 895 P.2d 1387, 1392 (Or. Ct. App. 1995) (35%); Ellis v. Ellis, No. 77407 N.Y. App. Div., 1997 WL 35218 at *2 (Jan. 30, 1997) (25%); Michael v. Michael, 469 S.E.2d 14, 17 (W. Va. 1996) (25%); Kapp v. Kapp, 2005 Ohio App. LEXIS 6144 (Ohio App. 2005) (litigation contingency discount accepted where proof of a pending lawsuit was presented); Rattee v. Rattee, 767 A.2d 415, 146 N.H. 44 (N.H. 2001); L.R.M. v. R.K.M., 46 S.W.3d 24 (Mo. Ct. App. 2001) (32% combined discount); Collier v. Collier, 790 So. 2d 759 (La. Ct. App. 2001) (25% combined discount for lack of marketability and contingent liabilities).

73. *See, e.g.,* Howell v. Howell (no amount specified); Neuman v. Neuman, 842 P.2d 575, 579 (Wyo. 1992) (35%); Hanson v. Hanson, 86 P.3d 94, 192 Or. App. 422 (Or. Ct. App. 2004) (25%); Brown v. Brown, 348 N.J. Super. 466, 792 A.2d 463, 2002 N.J. Super. LEXIS 105 (N.J. Super. 2002); Baltrusis v. Baltrusis, 113 Wash. App. 1037 (Wash. Ct. App. 2002) (25%); Ferraro v. Ferraro, 2000 WL 251678 (Va. Ct. App. 2000); Anderson v. Anderson, 2006 Tenn. App. LEXIS 592 (Tenn. App. 2006) (10% for marketing costs associated with only a hypothetical sale of minority interest); Hanson v. Hanson, 2005 Alaska LEXIS 166 (Alaska 2005); Kapp v. Kapp, 2005 Ohio App. LEXIS 6144 (Ohio App. 2005) (no discount for contingent transaction costs—broker, legal, accounting fees—where no sale is being contemplated); Bertuca v. Bertuca, 2007 Tenn. App. LEXIS 690 (Tenn. Ct. App. 2007) (discount disallowed where a sale of the husband's interest was not "necessary or desirable").

case, the court ruled that discounts for lack of marketability are not precluded as a matter of law in marital dissolution cases.[74]

Trapped-in Capital Gains Taxes[75]

In many cases, the marital estate owns property that is worth more than its cost basis. In this case, if the marital estate (or one of the spouses) were to sell the property, it would be subject to paying federal capital gains taxes. This is a liability called *trapped-in capital gains.*

Whether to consider tax liabilities that would be triggered by the sale of assets is one of the most common issues in marital property divisions. For the most part, family law courts have been unwilling to make any allowance for trapped-in capital gains on appreciated property unless a sale of the property is imminent.[76] Because family law courts often take Tax Court positions into consideration, perhaps the Tax Court's sharp turnaround on this issue in 1998, directing reflection of trapped-in capital gains taxes in valuation (see "Trapped-in Capital Gains Taxes" section in Chapter 17 on valuation for federal tax matters) will lead family law courts to give some consideration to this issue.

A Washington case is typical. The trial court adjusted the gross value of the parties' interest in a real estate partnership from $119,049 to $101,000 to reflect the capital gains tax that would be paid if it were sold. The Court of Appeals reversed. The court noted, "There is no Washington case specifically addressing whether capital gains tax consequences should be a factor in determining the value of marital assets." Thus, the court looked to other states for precedent, citing cases in seven other states. The court then concluded:

> Courts have generally found that consideration of tax consequences is either required or at least appropriate where the consequences are immediate and specific and/or arise directly from the court's decree, but find they are not an appropriate consideration where speculation as to a party's future dealings

74. Erp v. Erp, 2007 Fla. App. LEXIS 18726 (Fla. Ct. App. 2007).

75. Extensive references to treatment of tax consequences can be found in Tracy A. Bateman, Divorce and Separation: Consideration of Tax Consequences in Distribution of Marital Property 9, A.L.R. 5th 568, 2000 Lawyers Cooperative Publishing Co.

76. *See, e.g.*, Buzanell v. Miller, 590 S.E.2d 332, 162 N.C. App. 180, 2004 WL 26524 (N.C. Ct. App. 2004) (consideration of taxes too speculative); *In re* Marriage of Black, 2001 WL 57999 (Iowa Ct. App. 2001); Guill v. Guill, 2001 WL 770942 (Neb. Ct. App. 2001); Skokos v. Skokos, 40 S.W.3d 768, 344 Ark. 420 (Ark. 2001); Kaiser v. Kaiser, 555 N.W.2d 585 (N.D. 1996) (the deduction of hypothetical tax liabilities rejected); *In re* Marriage of Czapar, 232 Cal. App. 3d 1308, 284 Cal. Rptr. 41 (1991) (It is improper to take into consideration the tax consequences of an order dividing a community asset unless the tax liability is immediate and specific and will arise in connection with the division of the community property.).

> with property awarded to him or her would be required. . . . We agree with the rule adopted by most jurisdictions. . . . Mr. Hay testified at trial that he had no plans to sell his partnership interest . . . we remand to enable the trial court to consider the property division without regard to the capital gains tax consequences of a hypothetical sale of H&L Investments.[77]

The practice of reviewing decisions from other states is very common. Typical of a decision reached after doing this is that the court should consider potential tax consequences in valuing marital assets only if:

1. The recognition of a tax liability is required by dissolution or will occur within a short time,
2. The party's future dealings with the assets are definite enough that the court need not speculate, and
3. The future consequences are definite enough that the court need not speculate, and the tax liability can be reasonably predicted.[78]

The courts usually factor in the tax consequences when it is clear that they will be triggered as part of the divorce action. However, a trial court ordered the husband to pay a mortgage, a car loan, and a cash judgment to the wife from the sale of at least one of two laundromats owned. The trial court reduced the marital estate by $53,200 tax liability to be incurred on the sale of the laundromats. The trial court explained that although it did not specifically order the sale of the laundromats, sale was the only way that the husband could comply with the orders of the court. Nevertheless, the appellate court found that the sale of both laundromats was not an immediate consequence of the property disposition and that the trial court erred in reducing the marital estate by the amount of the tax liability.[79]

In an extreme denial of consideration of tax consequences, the property division mandated by the trial court had the effect of requiring the husband to liquidate his closely held business and turn the proceeds over to the wife to satisfy a cash award. Nevertheless, the court rejected the husband's argument that the stock should have been valued at its liquidation value rather than its going-concern value because of the tax consequences, reasoning that to follow this argument would universally prevent a court from valuing property at more than cost because of tax consequences.[80]

---

77. *In re* Marriage of Hay, 907 P.2d 334 (Wash. Ct. App. 1995).

78. Kaiser v. Kaiser, 474 N.W.2d 63 (N.D. 1991).

79. Granger v. Granger, 579 N.E.2d 1319 (Ind. Ct. App. 1991).

80. Bohl v. Bohl, 657 P.2d 1106 (Kan. 1983). The court's reasoning seems flawed in that there is nothing inherent in valuing something at expected net liquidation proceeds that would always necessarily reduce that amount to or below cost. In any case, cost is historical and (except for its effect on taxes) irrelevant to the matter of monies available now or in the future.

There are, however, cases where the tax consequences on sale have been deducted in valuing the marital estate, even when no immediate sale was contemplated. For example, in one case, it was concluded that it was proper to deduct the amount of capital gains tax that the husband would have to pay on the anticipated sale of limited partnership interests. The wife objected to reducing the value by the impounded taxes, claiming that they were "hypothetical, speculative, imaginary, unfair, and arbitrary." Evidence was introduced to show that the partnership was a tax shelter that would have lost its desirability in five to seven years and probably would be sold. The court concluded that the date of sale was not imaginary or hypothetical.

The court then offered an interesting broader statement that *"partnerships ought to be reduced by future capital gains taxes"* where the partnerships were investments that *"were only valuable as long as other investments were not more desirable,"* and the husband *"was more likely to sell his interest in the partnerships than die owning them,"* and would, therefore, incur a capital gains tax from the sale of the partnerships.[81] (Emphasis added.) From the viewpoint of a financial analyst, it is reasonable to think that this reasoning should apply to *any* investment asset.

Another interesting decision upholding subtraction of capital gains tax involved a commercial building. The appellate court held that the trial court did not abuse its discretion in subtracting the capital gains tax that would be incurred on the sale, even though there was no evidence that the property was going to be sold. The court found that experts for both parties attested to the property's fair market value and that the concept of fair market value assumes the sale of the property to an interested buyer. Thus, the court was reluctant to find any error by the trial court in presuming a sale of the real estate with its attendant tax consequences in order to value that marital asset.[82] In another case, where the husband would effectively have been forced to purchase the wife's shares in a company, the court permitted a credit for capital gains taxes, even though there was no evidence of an imminent sale.[83]

Some courts hold that tax consequences may be considered if the court determines that the property division award will force a party to sell the business to generate the cash needed to pay the court-imposed obligations.[84]

The holdings in these and similar cases suggest that if the sale of the assets is so remote a possibility as to eliminate consideration of the capital gains tax liability, the asset approach should not be the only primary valuation approach used; that perhaps an income approach would be more appropriate or maybe an income approach blended with an asset-based approach.[85]

---

81. Liddle v. Liddle, 410 N.W.2d 196 (Wis. Ct. App. 1987).
82. Hogan v. Hogan, 796 S.W.2d 400 (Mo. Ct. App. 1990).
83. Hamilton v. Hamilton, 2002 Ohio 2417 (Ohio Ct. App. 2002).
84. *See, e.g.,* Schuman v. Schuman, 658 N.W.2d 30, 265 Neb. 459 (Neb. 2003).
85. *See* Shannon P. Pratt, *Trapped-in Capital Gains Affects Real-World Value*, SHANNON PRATT'S BUSINESS VALUATION UPDATE 1, 3 (February 1996).

Adequacy of Evidence

Trial courts have wide discretion in deciding factual matters, such as value, but appellate courts expect trial courts to have an adequate evidentiary basis for reaching their conclusions of fact.[86] There is a considerable incidence of "expert" evidence at the trial court level being so inadequate that the appellate court remands the case for new hearings and evidence on the value of a business or practice.[87] This usually means that all the money and time spent on "experts" and the related lawyer fees have been wasted. This can be avoided if competent business valuation experts are retained to begin with, and the lawyer and expert work together to make a good record at trial—especially because courts tend to give significantly greater weight to the valuations of qualified, independent business appraisers.[88] This also means that the attorney must obtain the full cooperation of, and disclosure from, the client.[89]

Access to Records

It is common for an operating spouse to resist access to the records necessary for the nonoperating spouse's expert to conduct a thorough valuation. Because the nonoperating spouse has a financial interest in the property, the lawyer almost always can

86. *See, e.g.,* Zerbe v. Zerbe, 2005 Ohio 1180 (Ohio Ct. App. 2005) ("A finding of value must be supported by competent, credible evidence. The court cannot take the two extremes presented by the evidence and choose a value somewhere between those two extremes."); Augoshe v. Lehman. 2007 Fla. App. LEXIS 6367 (Fla. Ct. App. 2007) ("simply splitting the difference" between two divergent appraisals is an "improper method of valuation"); *In re* Marriage of Keener, 2007 Iowa Sup. LEXIS 13 (Iowa 2007) ("anecdotal evidence is simply an insufficient basis upon which to determine fair market value"); Pickard v. Pickard, 2006 N.Y. App. Div. LEXIS 9961 (N.Y. App. Div. 2006) (discount rate was rejected where the rate was selected arbitrarily without support for it).

87. *See, e.g.,* Crosetto v. Crosetto, 918 P.2d 954 (Wash. App. Ct. 1996) ("Because the trial court here did not state how it reached the valuation figure, we remand . . .").

88. *See, e.g., In re* Marriage of Bidwell, 12 P.3d 76, 170 Or. App. 239 (Or. Ct. App. 2000) (the court accepted the wife's expert's opinion over the husband's since husband had not presented expert evidence); *In re* Marriage of Gabriel, 2005 Cal. App. Unpub. LEXIS 8101 (Cal. Ct. App. 2005); Miller v. Miller, 14 S.W.3d 903, 70 Ark. App. 64 (Ark. Ct. App. 2000); Ballas v. Ballas, 2004 Ohio 5128, 2004 WL 2334329 (Ohio App. 7 Dist. 2004) (expert's opinion given greater weight than that of business manager); Dunn v. Dunn, 2005 Miss. App. LEXIS 637 (Miss. Ct. App. 2005) (appeals by both spouses were unavailing where neither had hired a business valuation expert); Mace v. Mace, 818 So. 2d 1130 (Miss. 2002) (where neither spouse hired a business valuation expert, the court recommended that they provide expert valuation evidence on remand).

89. *See, e.g.,* Weinstein v. Weinstein, 2005 Conn. LEXIS 348 (Conn. 2005) (husband's failure to disclose the true value of his company's intellectual property resulted in a finding of blatant and deliberate misrepresentation and reversal); Stribling v. Stribling, 2005 Miss. App. LEXIS 58 (Miss. Ct. App. 2005) (where "a party fails to provide accurate information, or cooperate in the valuation of assets," the trial court is "entitled to proceed on the best information available").

obtain a court order compelling production of the information needed by the expert to carry on a thorough valuation. (See Chapter 27 on discovery.)

In a case that went all the way to the Supreme Court of Connecticut, a radiologist filed a motion to exclude the wife's expert's report and testimony because the report had not been produced prior to trial. The expert testified that the delay in preparing his report was attributable to a lack of cooperation on the part of the husband in failing to make the pertinent financial records available. In denying the motion, the court declared:

> If anybody is playing cat and mouse, it's the [husband]. . . . It is virtually frivolous for the husband to suggest that the court abused its broad discretion by failing to impose the sanction of excluding testimony because of delay in furnishing the report of an expert witness, after concluding that the delay was largely attributable to the husband's failure to comply with the order for disclosure of his financial records.[90]

The Persistent Problem of "Double-Dipping"

One of the most prevalent problems in family law cases involving a business or professional practice valuation is "double-dipping." Double-dipping means computing a value based, at least in part, on the spouse's future earnings for property division and then using the future earnings capacity as a basis for determining spousal support or alimony payments.

The potential for this problem arises when an income approach, an excess earnings method, or a market approach is used for the valuation. If these methods reflect an implication that the operating spouse will continue to operate, the value of that spouse's future efforts is impounded, at least to some extent, in the distributive value. If payments then are ordered out of the earnings from that spouse's efforts, double counting is the potential result.

This problem is exacerbated in those jurisdictions that consider *personal goodwill* a marital asset. Personal goodwill is a function of future earning power resulting from persistence of patronage of the individual. If this value is fully reflected in the distributive asset, then this earning power is being used twice if it is the basis for future payments to the nonoperating spouse.

This problem can be avoided if the valuation methodology truly follows the philosophy of not depending on future efforts (or restrictions on efforts) of the operating spouse. However, as noted earlier, many court decisions espouse this philosophy

90. Eslami v. Eslami, 591 A.2d 411 (Conn. 1991).

but then accept valuation methodology that actually incorporates an assumption of the operating spouse's continuing efforts or restrictions on those efforts.

In *Steneken v. Steneken,*[91] the trial court determined that the husband's annual compensation was excessive and normalized the compensation in determining the value of his company using the excess earnings method. The court then determined alimony using the husband's actual annual compensation—which was $50,000 more. The husband argued that distributing his excess earnings as the goodwill portion of the value of his business, and also considering it for alimony purposes, was impermissible double counting.

The New Jersey intermediate appellate court ruled that the value of the business was as of the date of dissolution and was based on past excess earnings, while the alimony determination was based on future income. The court also noted that even if this was double counting, it was not banned by New Jersey law, which bans only the double counting of pensions.

The New Jersey Supreme Court expressly rejected the premise that because alimony and equitable distribution are interrelated, a credit on one side of the ledger mandates a debit on the other side. Instead, the court focused on the "bedrock proposition" that all alimony awards and equitable distribution determinations must satisfy basic concepts of fairness, and that, although clearly interrelated, the structural purposes of alimony and equitable distribution are different.

Accordingly, the court rejected the husband's assertions of double counting, saying that the husband "mistakenly equates the statutory and decisional methodology applied in the calculation of alimony with a valuation methodology applied for equitable distribution purposes that requires that revenues and expenses, including salaries, be normalized so as to present a fair valuation of a going concern." The court concluded that it is not inequitable to use a valuation method that normalizes salary in an ongoing closely held corporation for equitable distribution purposes and to use actual salary received in calculating alimony—the valuation methodology chosen for equitable distribution purposes should not alter the alimony award. According to the court, the "interplay of those two calculations does not constitute 'double counting.'" The ultimate judicial inquiry must be whether the ultimate result, both in toto as well as in its constituent parts, is fair under the circumstances and congruent with the standards set forth in the alimony and equitable distribution statutes. The court also rejected the distinction made by the appellate court between the fact that "valuation of the corporate asset was based on [the husband's] past earnings, not his future earnings," while "[the husband's] actual current and future compensation may be treated as income for alimony purposes."

91. Steneken v. Steneken, 843 A.2d 344 (N.J. App. Div. 2004), *aff'd*, 873 A.2d 501, 183 N.J. 290 (N.J. 2005).

Justice Long, in a dissenting opinion, agreed with the husband that the majority's holding would allow the impermissible double counting of income (albeit not dollar for dollar). Justice Long's position was that the majority converted a certain amount of the husband's projected future income stream into an asset and then calculated the amount of alimony based on that asset. According to Justice Long, this was improper, as "[o]nce a court converts a specific stream of income into an asset, that income may no longer be calculated into the maintenance formula and payout." Instead, Justice Long's solution would have used the appellate court's approach, which neither allows the unfettered dual use of a single income stream, nor requires the use of the same figure for both calculations. "Rather, judges should be able to use the 'real' income for alimony and the 'normalized' income for the corporate valuation so long as the ultimate outcome recognizes that a single income source (the difference between the real and normalized income) played a part in both."

It is arguable that to the extent the court used excess compensation as the basis for alimony, the court used that money twice: once to value the distributed value of the business and again to determine the amount of alimony—a classic case of double-dipping.

In *Sampson v. Sampson,*[92] the value of the wife's insurance agency was offset in the husband's property distribution and then was counted as credit towards his alimony support obligations. The wife argued that this was double counting. Because there were inconsistencies in the experts' reports concerning owner salary, the court was unable to determine whether double counting had occurred and it remanded the case for further factual determinations on this issue.

The court in *Champion v. Champion,*[93] noting that there is a split among jurisdictions on the issues of what constitutes double-dipping and whether it ought to be prohibited as a matter of law, rejected a claim of double-dipping and found the business to be both a marital asset and a source of income.

In *Keane v. Keane,*[94] New York's highest court held that the prohibition against double counting applies only to intangible assets, such as professional licenses or goodwill, or the value of a service business, not income-producing tangible assets such as rental property.

In *Sander v. Sander,*[95] the court ruled that it is not double counting to assign a value to a business, as well as to attribute gross income from that business to the spouse, without adjusting either. Where the trial court, in its discretion, valued the

92. Sampson v. Sampson, 2004 Mass. App. LEXIS 1223 (Mass. App. Ct. 2004).

93. Champion v. Champion, 54 Mass. App. Ct. 215, 764 N.E.2d 898, 2002 Mass. App. LEXIS 363 (Mass. App. Ct. 2002).

94. Keane v. Keane, 2006 N.Y. LEXIS 3751 (N.Y. 2006).

95. Sander v. Sander, 2006 Conn. App. LEXIS 280 (Conn. Ct. App. 2006).

company at a value it would have to a buyer who would pay a manager's salary, the court's decision was upheld as both logical and supported by the record.

References for Marital Dissolution

Bateman, Tracy A. *Divorce and Separation: Consideration of Tax Consequences in Distribution of Marital Property.* 9 A.L.R. 5th 568, 2000 Lawyers Cooperative Publishing Co. Contains an exhaustive listing and discussion of cases involving consideration or lack of consideration of tax consequences in marital property settlements.

Business Valuation Resources, www.BVLibrary.com. Contains the complete text of all major state appellate decisions involving business valuation decisions, searchable by case name, key word, and state. Also contains full texts of relevant laws and regulations and unpublished conference presentations.

Business Valuation Resources. 2009. *BVR's Guide to Fair Value in Shareholder Dissent, Oppression, and Marital Dissolution.* Portland, OR.

Business Valuation Resources. 2009. *BVR's Guide to Personal v. Enterprise Goodwill.* Portland, OR.

Feder, Robert D., Ed. 1997. *Valuation Strategies in Divorce*, 4th Ed. New York: Aspen Law & Business.

Fishman, Jay, et al. 2008. "Valuations for Divorce Engagements." In *PPC's Guide to Business Valuations,* 12-1 to 12-49. Fort Worth, TX: Practitioners Publishing Co.

Goldberg, Barth, and Barry A. Schatz. *Valuation of Divorce Assets.* 1984. Plus 1999 Supplement. Pages 335–552 of the 1999 supplement and pages 443–85 of the 1984 volume are case summaries on valuation of closely held corporations and partnerships; pages 176–217 of 1999 supplement and pages 198–227 of the 1984 volume are on valuation of professional entities, goodwill, and license agreements.

Gold-Biken, Lynne Z., Steven A. Kolodny, Adam R. Koritzinsky, and Barbara A. Stark. 1994. *Divorce Practice Handbook.* Charlottesville, VA: Michie Co.

Kleeman, Jr., Robert E., James R. Alerding, and Benjamin D. Miller. 1999. *The Handbook for Divorce Valuations.* New York: John F. Wiley & Sons.

Oldham, L. Thomas. "The Closely Held Business." In *Divorce, Separation and the Distribution of Property.* 1999 Ed., 10–1 to 10–5.

Pratt, Shannon. 2003. "Marital Dissolutions." In *Business Valuation Body of Knowledge.* 2nd Ed., 325–28. New York: John F. Wiley & Sons.

______, and Alina V. Niculita. 2008. "Valuation for Marital Dissolution Purposes" and "Marital Dissolution Court Cases." In *Valuing a Business*, 5th Ed., Chaps. 37 and 38. New York: McGraw-Hill.

Chapter 20

Fair Value for Financial Reporting

This chapter was contributed by Chad P. Phillips, Mr. Phillips provides valuation consulting services for business planning, transfer, estate planning, and dispute resolution purposes, He is a Chartered Financial Analyst (CFA) and a frequent presenter on valuation-related topics to industry groups and business service providers alike.

The Statement on Financial Accounting Standards (SFAS) 157 "Fair Value Measurements" is effective for financial statements issued for fiscal years beginning after November 15, 2007, and for interim periods within those fiscal years. It provides a definition of value for all public companies reporting to the Securities Exchange Commission (SEC). As this chapter explains, it is intended to increase the consistency of fair value requirements in financial reporting and to expand the disclosure public companies provide about their fair value measurements.

According to the Summary of Statement No. 157 issued by the Financial Accounting Standards Board (FASB):

> Prior to [Statement 157], there were different definitions of fair value and limited guidance for applying those definitions in GAAP. Moreover, that guidance was dispersed among the many accounting pronouncements that require fair value measurements. Differences in that guidance created inconsistencies that added to the complexity in applying GAAP.

SFAS 157 supersedes and nullifies contrary guidance in earlier accounting pronouncements. As such, it is intended to increase the consistency and comparability in fair value requirements and to expand the disclosures about fair value measurements.

Definition of Fair Value

The definition of fair value in SFAS 157 applies to all prior FASB pronouncements that require or permit fair value measurements. A list of Accounting Principles Board (APB) and FASB pronouncements that are amended by SFAS 157 is presented in Exhibit 20-1. (The FASB is the successor organization to the APB.) Per SFAS 157, fair value is defined as follows:

> The price that would be received to sell an asset or paid to transfer a liability in an orderly transaction between market participants at the measurement date.

Exhibit 20-1
APB and FASB Pronouncements Amended By SFAS 157

APB and FASB pronouncements amended by SFAS 157 include:

Pronouncement	Title
Opinion 21	Interest on Receivables and Payables
Opinion 28	Interim Financial Reporting
Opinion 29	Accounting for Nonmonetary Transactions
Statement 13	Accounting for Losses
Statement 15	Accounting for Debtors and Creditors for Troubled Debt Restructurings
Statement 19	Financial Accounting and Reporting by Oil and Gas Producing Companies
Statement 35	Accounting for Reporting by Defined Benefit Pension Plans
Statement 60	Accounting for Reporting by Insurance Enterprises
Statement 63	Financial Reporting by Broadcasters
Statement 65	Accounting for Certain Mortgage Banking Activities
Statement 67	Accounting for Costs and Initial Rental Operations of Real Estate Projects
Statement 87	Employers' Accounting for Pensions
Statement 106	Employers' Accounting for Postretirement Benefits Other Than Pensions
Statement 107	Disclosures about Fair Value of Financial Instruments
Statement 115	Accounting for Certain Investments in Debt and Equity Securities

Statement 116	Accounting for Contributions Received and Contributions Made
Statement 124	Accounting for Certain Investments Held by Not-for-profit Organizations
Statement 133	Accounting for Derivative Instruments and Hedging Activities
Statement 136	Transfers of Assets to a Not-for-profit Organization or Charitable Trust that Raises or Holds Contributions for Others
Statement 140	Accounting for Transfers and Servicing of Financial Assets and Extinguishments of Liabilities
Statement 141	Business Combinations
Statement 142	Goodwill and Other Intangible Assets
Statement 143	Accounting for Asset Retirement Obligations
Statement 144	Accounting for the Impairment or Disposal of Long-lived Assets
Statement 146	Accounting for Costs Associated with Exit or Disposal Activities
Statement 150	Accounting for Certain Financial Instruments with Characteristics of Both Liabilities and Equity
Statement 156	Accounting for Servicing of Financial Assets
Interpretation 45	Guarantor's Accounting and Disclosure Requirements for Guarantees, Including Indirect Guarantees of Indebtedness of Others

It is important to note that the "price" specified in the definition is an *exit* price, *not* the price that would be paid to acquire the asset or to assume the liability (an *entry* price). SFAS 157 emphasizes that the subject asset or liability should not be valued at cost (an *entry* price) unless the reporting entity can dispose of the asset or liability at cost. Moreover, fair value per SFAS 157 assumes that the asset or liability will be exchanged in an orderly transaction, including adequate market exposure and time for usual and customary marketing activities, as opposed to a forced transaction, e.g., a forced liquidation or distress sale.

The "market" is referred to as "the market in which the reporting entity would transact for the asset or liability, that is, the principal or most advantageous market for the asset or liability." It specifies an orderly transaction in the most advantageous market. Market participants are buyers and sellers in the principal (or the most advantageous) market for the asset or liability. These market participants are (i) unrelated, (ii) knowledgeable about factors relevant to the asset or liability and the transaction, (iii) able to transact, i.e., have the legal and financial ability to do so, and (iv) willing to transact, i.e., motivated but not forced or otherwise compelled to transact.

SFAS 157 clarifies that the term *fair value* is intended to mean a market-based measure, not an entity-specific measure. The fair value premise for an asset is the asset's highest and best use from the perspective of market participants considering the use of the asset that is physically possible, legally permissible, and financially feasible at the measurement date. The company's intended use of an asset is not necessarily indicative of the highest and best use as determined by a market participant; the fair value measure is *not* an entity-specific measure that reflects that entity's expectations for the asset. SFAS 157 requires that fair value measures consider the perspectives of market participants and the inputs and assumptions about risk they would use to price the subject asset.

Similarly, the fair value premise for a liability is the liability's highest and best use from the perspective of market participants given inputs and assumptions regarding risk, including nonperformance risk related to the reporting entity's own creditworthiness.

Inputs are broadly categorized as *observable* and *unobservable*. Observable inputs generally are defined as inputs that are based on market data obtained from sources independent of the reporting entity. Unobservable inputs include inputs that reflect the reporting entity's own assumptions about market pricing for the subject asset or liability given available information and circumstances. Valuation techniques that maximize the use of observable inputs are preferred vis-à-vis those that utilize unobservable inputs.

SFAS 157 further sets forth that fair value should consider, document, and disclose assumptions regarding risk, including the risk inherent in a particular valuation technique and the risk inherent in the inputs to the valuation technique. To that end, SFAS 157 identifies three levels in the hierarchy of inputs utilized to quantify fair value as follows:

- **Level 1** inputs are quoted prices in active markets for identical assets or liabilities;
- **Level 2** inputs are those inputs other than quoted prices included within Level 1 that are directly or indirectly observable, including: quoted prices for similar assets or liabilities in active markets; quoted prices for identical or similar assets or liabilities in thinly traded or inactive markets; inputs other than quoted prices, e.g., interest rates and yield curves, volatilities, repayment speeds, loss severities, credit risks, and default rates; and market-corroborated inputs, i.e., inputs that are derived from, and corroborated by, observable market data;
- **Level 3** inputs include unobservable inputs and reflect assumptions about what market participants would use in their pricing analyses.

If available, Level 1 inputs are to be used, followed by Level 2 and Level 3 inputs, respectively. If there is an active market for the subject asset or liability, the quoted price on the measurement date would apply. For those assets or liabilities for which there is no active market, the prices of closely comparable assets and liabilities for which there is an active market may be considered, provided appropriate adjustments for differences between the two are considered and accounted for.

The standard clearly favors a mark-to-market approach among the valuation techniques identified by SFAS 157, i.e., market, income, and cost approaches, and, in particular, a mark-to-market approach that utilizes prices generated in active markets. SFAS 157 further states that in those cases where *observable* quoted prices in an active market for identical assets and liabilities exists, a single valuation technique is appropriate; in other cases, multiple valuation techniques will be appropriate and should be evaluated and weighted based on the reasonableness of the range of indicated values.

To be clear, SFAS 157 does not prioritize valuation techniques but rather the inputs to those valuation techniques. Consequently, whether a particular fair value measurement produced by a given valuation technique falls within Level 2 or Level 3 depends on the lowest level input used that is significant to the fair value measurement indicated by the given valuation technique.

Disclosures

SFAS 157 also expands disclosure requirements for reporting entities regarding the assumptions and inputs used when ascertaining the fair value of assets and liabilities. In particular, reporting entities must disclose for interim and annual reporting periods separately for each major category of assets and liabilities:

- The fair value measurements at the reporting date;
- The level within the fair value hierarchy in which the fair value measurements in their entirety fall;
- For fair value measurements using significant unobservable inputs a reconciliation of beginning and ending balances, accounting for changes attributable to (i) total gains or losses for the period whether realized or unrealized, (ii) purchases, sales, issuances, and settlements (net), and (iii) transfers in and/or out of Level 3, e.g., transfers because of changes in the observability of significant inputs;
- The amount of the total gains or losses for the period above; and
- In annual periods, the valuation technique(s) used and a discussion of changes associated therewith.

For assets and liabilities measured on a nonrecurring basis in periods subsequent to the initial recognition:

- The fair value measurements recorded during the period and the reasons for the measurement;
- The level within the fair value hierarchy in which the fair value measurements in their entirety fall;
- For fair value measurements using significant unobservable inputs, a description of the inputs and the information used to develop the inputs; and
- In annual periods, the valuation technique(s) used and a discussion of changes associated therewith.

Adjustments should be made to valuations made in accordance with prior practices that conflict with SFAS 157. The differences should be booked as an adjustment to retained earnings on the opening balance sheet for the period in which the statement is applied.

Differences from Fair Market Value

While the inputs and assumptions utilized in reaching a fair value determination for financial reporting purposes under SFAS 157 and a "fair market value" determination according to generally accepted business valuation practices may be similar, there nevertheless are significant differences between the two standards, and, as a result, the value of a given asset or liability may differ based on the standard applied. In particular, fair value defines "price" as an *exit* price given an orderly liquidation of an asset or liability; fair market value, on the other hand, does not. Furthermore, SFAS 157 prescribes a framework for selecting and/or weighting the results of identified valuation techniques based on a defined hierarchy of inputs; conversely, the selection and weighting of valuation techniques under the fair market value standard is largely at the discretion of the appraiser. Likewise, the assumption of highest and best use to market participants implied by the fair value standard as defined by SFAS 157 is antithetical to the "hypothetical" willing buyer and seller assumption espoused by the fair market value standard. Finally, while fair market value considers all forms of law-based and market-based restrictions on the sale of assets and/or liabilities, SFAS 157 limits its exposure to the latter, as evidenced by its specific rejection of blockage discounts.

The differences between the two standards was intentional, as FASB conceded that it did not adopt the definition of fair market value because it did not want the definition of fair value to be saddled with perceived shortcomings of fair market value for the purpose of financial reporting and the burden of court interpretations of the fair market value standard. As a result, consumers of business valuation work products must be cognizant of the differences between the two standards, critical of the inputs used, and aware of reporting and professional standards related to asset and liability valuation under each standard.

Chapter 21

Employee Stock Ownership Plans

This chapter is updated by the author from the chapter in the first edition contributed by Kim Abello, an Accredited Senior Appraiser at Duff & Phelps.

> ESOPs are one of the most specialized and demanding areas of business valuation, and companies with or contemplating an ESOP are well advised to consult an appraiser with considerable experience in ESOP valuation.
>
> —S.P. and A.N.

General Principles

An employee stock ownership plan (ESOP) is a qualified employee benefit plan that invests primarily in the common stock of the sponsoring corporation. ESOPs provide a means for employers to incentivize employees and provide liquidity to controlling shareholders, who, in turn, are able, in certain instances, to defer taxation on the gain from the sale to the ESOP.

Effective for years beginning after December 31, 1997, the Internal Revenue Code was amended to allow ESOPs to be shareholders in S corporations and to exempt the flow-through earnings to the ESOP from the unrelated business income tax. (Section 1523 of the Tax Relief Act of 1997.) Therefore, effective 1998, the income of an S corporation can pass through to an ESOP, and because the ESOP is tax-exempt, no tax is paid on the income.

Presently, ESOPs are available only to C and S corporations. While important operational differences exist between the two, it is significant to note that ESOPs provide controlling shareholders with an alternative means of creating a liquidity event, other than an outright sale of assets or stock to strategic or financial buyers or an IPO.

Valuation Principles

As a general rule, professional appraisers involved in valuations for purposes of stock held by an ESOP follow many of the principles discussed in other parts of this book.

However, certain valuation considerations specific to ESOPs require a modification of the general valuation theories. A complete understanding of ESOPs requires knowledge of the valuation theory, the Employee Retirement Income Security Act of 1974 (ERISA), trust and fiduciary law, tax law, finance, and accounting issues. The discussion here will focus on the specific valuation factors affecting ESOPs.

Adequate Consideration

An ESOP is a qualified defined contribution plan under Section 401(a) of the Internal Revenue Code. ESOPs are subject to the requirements of ERISA, as amended, and pursuant to IRC Section 4975(e)(7), also subject to regulations issued by the Treasury Secretary. Treas. Reg. 54.4975-11 of the Excise Tax Regulations. Section 3(18) of ERISA generally states that an ESOP cannot pay more than "adequate consideration" when investing in qualifying employer securities. In the case of a stock that is publicly traded, the price in the public market represents adequate consideration.

Responsibility for the interpretation and enforcement of ERISA is divided among the Department of Labor (DOL), the Department of the Treasury (particularly the Internal Revenue Service), and the Pension Benefit Guarantee Corporation (PBGC). With respect to adequate consideration, the DOL issued the "Proposed Regulation Relating to the Definition of Adequate Consideration" on May 17, 1988.[1] Despite the passage of time, this regulation has not been finalized, yet it remains the most authoritative source of guidance on adequate consideration. The DOL's proposed regulations largely adopted the concepts of Revenue Ruling 59-60 for stock that is not publicly traded.

Internal and external ESOP plan trustees and fiduciaries must determine, in good faith pursuant to the terms of the plan, the fair market value of the stock. It is not enough for a fiduciary to rely in good faith on a third-party valuation to establish that adequate consideration was paid. A fiduciary must make his or her own prudent investigation of value and understand the underlying assumptions on which the valuation is made at the time the ESOP purchases the shares.[2] (Lawyers should inform the fiduciaries of this requirement. See *Howard v. Shay* and *Reich v. Valley National Bank of Arizona* later in this chapter.) This process establishes adequate consideration. The aforementioned DOL proposed regulation also defines fair market value as the price

1. Prop. DOL Reg. § 2510.3-18(b)(1)(ii).

2. Donovan v. Cunningham, 716 F.2d 1455 (5th Cir. 1983). *See also* Barker v. American Mobil Power Corp., 64 F.3d 1397 (9th Cir. 1995), and Pugh v. Tribune Co., 521 F.3d 686 (7th Cir. 2008).

at which property would change hands between a willing buyer and a willing seller, when the former is not under any compulsion to buy and the latter is not under any compulsion to sell, and both parties are able, as well as willing, to trade and are well informed about the asset and the market for such asset.

When Appraisals Are Required

Pursuant to the Tax Reform Act of 1986, companies sponsoring ESOPs now are required to have the ESOP stock valued by an independent appraiser at least annually for stock acquired after December 31, 1986. Valuation by an independent appraiser is not required in the case of employer securities that are readily tradable on an established securities market. An appraisal of ESOP stock is required:

1. When the ESOP makes its first acquisition of employer corporation stock;
2. At least annually thereafter (although some companies routinely have their stock appraisals updated semiannually or quarterly);
3. Whenever there is a stock sale transaction with a controlling stockholder or member of a control group, that is, a transaction between the plan and a party-in-interest; and
4. If the ESOP sells out of its stock position.[3]

Independence of Appraiser

Under Internal Revenue Code (IRC) Section 401(a)(28)(C), the ESOP fiduciaries must employ an independent appraiser that meets the requirements of IRC Regulation Section 1.170A-13(c)(5), which defines independence with respect to appraisers for the valuation of donations to charities. The qualified independent appraiser, according to these regulations, meets the following qualifications, among others:

- Is not a party to the transaction, is not related to any party to the transaction, is not married to any person with a relationship to the transaction, is not regularly used by any of the parties to the transaction, and does not perform a majority of appraisals for these persons.
- Holds himself or herself out to the public as an appraiser or performs appraisals on a regular basis.
- Is qualified by background, experience, education, and memberships in professional associations to make appraisals of the type of property being valued.

3. Shannon P. Pratt & Niculita, Alina V., Valuing a Business 814 (5th ed. 2008).

- Understands that an intentionally false or fraudulent overstatement of value may subject the valuation practitioner to a civil penalty.
- Receives an appraisal fee that is not based on a percentage of the appraised value of the property.

This independence requirement is specific to ESOP appraisals. It is intuitive that the appraiser needs to be independent, in this context, because the ESOP transaction typically involves a purchase by the ESOP of stock from a shareholder who may have the ability to control the selection of the appraiser. Internal Revenue Manual (IRM) 4.72.8.7.1, Employee Plans Technical Guidance, Valuation of Assets, Independent Appraiser Rules (September 1, 2006), addresses these independence requirements for audit purposes and lists the examination steps to be taken by IRS examiners. The appraiser should be familiar with these guidelines.

IRS Audit Guidelines

Internal Revenue Manual (IRM) 4.72.4, Employee Plans Technical Guidance, Employee Stock Ownership Plans (ESOPs) (April 1, 2006), contains the IRS's examination guidelines for audits of leveraged ESOPs.[4] Therefore, these guidelines can assist the appraiser in protecting an ESOP from attack by the IRS. The following are the salient ESOP valuation issues covered in these guidelines.

- The balance sheet on Form 5500 provides information such as whether investments are in employer securities, acquisition indebtedness and/or other liabilities (indicates leverage), and party-in-interest transactions. In smaller plans, determine whether a valuation was made by adding the assets at the beginning of the year to the contributions and receipts less the disbursements during the year and comparing the total to the assets at the end of the year. If the total equals the assets at the end of the year, a valuation probably has not been made because the total only reflects the receipts and disbursements.
- When reviewing the income statement, note any noncash contributions for these also may indicate the acquisition of employer securities.
- Where stock is publicly traded, examine stock confirmation slips, trust receipt and disbursement accounts, and market records to verify the fair market value of security transactions.

4. This guideline considers changes enacted under the Small Business Job Protection Act of 1996 (SBJPA), P.L. 104-188 (see 4.4.2), the Taxpayer Relief Act of 1997 (TRA '97), P. L. 105-34 (see 4.2.7), the Economic Growth and Tax Relief Reconciliation Act of 2001 (EGTRRA), P.L. 107-16, and the American Job Creation Act of 2004 (AJCA) P.L. 108-173 (see 4.2.4). Additional guidance pertaining to the examination of both leveraged and nonleveraged ESOPs, including IRC § 1042 transfers, the partial interest exclusion, and special rules pertaining to Sub S ESOPs, can be found at http://www.irs.gov/ustreas/pub/irs-tege/epche80.

- Where stock is not publicly traded, and the transaction does not involve a disqualified person, the fair market value must be determined as of the plan's most recent valuation date. Examine the records used to value the stock at the last valuation date in order to determine whether the assigned value is comparable to the value of comparable nonpublicly traded companies. See Reg. 54.4975–11(d)(5).
- Where stock is not publicly traded and the transaction involves a disqualified person, the fair market value must be determined as of the transaction date. Secure the appraisal report, if any, and use it as a basis for verifying the adequate consideration rules. If possible, request both the prior and subsequent appraisals for comparison purposes. If the appraisal method is not consistently applied, inquire as to the reason for the change. In addition, determine whether any projections used were reasonable estimates of what actually has occurred.

  Note: Particular attention should be given to subsequent events that could have been foreseen and have an impact on value. See Rev. Rul. 59-60, 1959-1 C.B. 237. The independent appraisal will not in itself be a good-faith determination. Also, examine the capital stock accounts of the employer to substantiate transactions of similar stock.
- Determine whether fair market value was paid for the stock. Look at the valuation report on the company's shares. See if the company that makes products has share prices that rise and fall with its earnings. If the company's earnings have fallen but the report says the price per share has risen, this may indicate an incorrect valuation. Also check the correlation between earnings and stock price if there is no valuation report.
- Check the employer's audit report to see if the company's earnings have fallen after the valuation report was written. If they have, it is likely the shares' value also should have fallen. The plan fiduciary no longer can rely on the price per share from the valuation report because the facts on which it was based have changed.
- Ask to see documentation of the fiduciary's prudent investigation to ensure the underlying assumptions have not changed since the last valuation.

Other issues discussed in the examination guidelines affect the review of the ESOP-exempt loan, the IRC Section 1042 rollover, the IRC Section 415 limitations, the Section 404(k) deduction for dividends paid on employer stock, the ESOP put option, voting rights, and other related issues. The appraiser also should be familiar with these guidelines if involved in the structuring of an ESOP transaction.[5]

5. *See* The ESOP Ass'n, Valuing ESOP Shares (2005).

Control versus Minority Interest

Control premiums and minority interest discounts are discussed in detail in Chapter 15. In the ESOP context, there is some controversy over whether an ESOP that owns a controlling interest—more than 50 percent—is really in control. Because the ultimate shareholder is the ESOP participant, it could be argued that the participant really owns the stock and is, therefore, typically a minority interest. Even though there is some controversy, the appraiser should remain consistent in the appraisals for a specific ESOP company.

The DOL proposed regulation provides some guidance on the ESOP's ability to pay a control premium. The regulation generally restricts the ESOP's payment of a control premium unless: (1) a third-party investor would pay a premium and (2) the ESOP receives voting control and control in fact (although the latter phrase is not defined). In addition, if the ESOP plans to purchase control over a period of time, the proposed regulation does allow the ESOP to pay the control price if there is an actual binding agreement obligating the employer to pass control within a reasonable time.

Lack of Marketability Discount

An ESOP company is required to provide a "put option" for distributions from the ESOP of employer stock that is not "readily tradable on an established market."[6] This put option is not binding on the ESOP.[7] The shares, however, may be put to the employer and in such instances it creates what is referred to as the "repurchase obligation," a future obligation on the part of the company to repurchase the shares from departing ESOP participants. Although some commentators suggest otherwise, current practice among a great majority of valuation professionals recognizes the fact that the ESOP's put option enhances the liquidity of the ESOP's stock and thus reduces, or in some cases even eliminates, the lack of marketability discount associated with the price the ESOP can pay.[8]

The marketability discount in general is discussed in detail in Chapter 15.

With respect to ESOP valuations, the proposed regulations state that the appraiser should consider the extent to which the put rights are enforceable, as well as the company's ability to meet its obligation with respect to these put rights (taking into account the company's financial strength and liquidity). To summarize, the following

6. I.R.C. § 409(h)(1)(A) and (B).

7. Rev. Proc. 2004-14.

8. In *Armstrong v. LaSalle Bank Nat'l Ass'n*, 446 F.3d 728 (7th Cir. 2006), Judge Posner reversed the trial court's award of summary judgment in favor of defendant trustee's decision to accept a stock valuation that did not include a discount for lack of marketability. The decision appears to confirm the need to consider this discount, but not the extent.

factors should be considered by the appraiser when selecting the magnitude of the lack of marketability discount:

- The provisions of the ESOP documents, including put rights
- The financial strength and solvency of the company
- The size of the block owned by the ESOP
- The company's liquidity from a balance sheet perspective
- The borrowing capacity of the business
- The repurchase liability and funding thereof
- The company's past repurchase of ESOP shares
- The form and timing of payment by the company to selling shareholders
- The overall priority of acknowledged and contingent financial claims that may conflict with achieving liquidity for the participants over time

Some commentators suggest that because the put option and marketability enhancement do not exist until after the ESOP purchase, the ESOP cannot pay for the put in the initial ESOP purchase. Because marketability is less of an issue for a controlling interest shareholder, this controversy is limited to minority ESOPs. This issue has not been litigated or resolved as of the date of this writing. However, in actual transactions, most minority interest investors, recognizing the marketability limitations of their ownership, negotiate their exit vehicle at the time the investment is made. Thus, a marketability discount is not considered in the estimate of fair market value either before or after the minority investment.

ESOP Financial Statement Adjustments

There are two specific financial statement adjustments typically made in the context of ESOP valuations. The first is recognition that ESOP contributions may be in excess of normal employee benefit plan expenses. The second includes recognition of the additional tax benefits and leverage from any ESOP debt incurred as part of the initial purchase.

Because, in the case of leveraged ESOPs, the magnitude of the ESOP contributions is tied to the amount of ESOP debt, this contribution may not be commensurate with normal employee benefit expense. The appraiser needs to have an understanding of the level of normal employer contributions both before the ESOP and once the ESOP debt is repaid. The typical income statement adjustment would eliminate the ESOP contribution as an expense (that is, add the amount back to earnings) and subtract the expected level of employee benefit expense. If the ESOP contributions were equivalent to the normal level of employee benefit expense, this adjustment would not be necessary. The objective is to arrive at a normalized level of earnings for the company's operations.

The second adjustment gives consideration to the tax benefits associated with the deductibility of the ESOP contributions used to pay ESOP debt. The treatment of this item may vary from one case to another based on the valuation method employed. For example, debt-free methods provide for a subtraction of the ESOP debt from the market value of invested capital. However, as the ESOP debt payments are deductible, this debt is tax-advantaged. Recognition of this can be quantified by calculating the present value of the tax savings created by this debt instrument and adding it back to the equity value.

In addition, the appraiser should consider the effect of the additional financial risk placed on the company after the ESOP transaction in subsequent annual valuations when deciding on discount or capitalization rates in the income approach to value (discusssed in Chapter 5) and on valuation multiples in the market approach to value (discussed in Chapter 6).

Repurchase Liability: Redemption or Recirculation

As previously mentioned, the put option received by the ESOP participants creates a repurchase obligation on the part of the company. The ESOP sponsor must decide whether to "redeem" or "recirculate" shares; this is a strategic decision.[9] A redemption is a direct acquisition by the company from the participant. Recirculation "involves the company repurchasing the shares from the participant and contributing those shares to the ESOP for redistribution to the remaining employees as part of a continuing benefit."[10] Because participant account balances grow over time, the repurchase liability becomes a more significant issue in more mature ESOPs. *Management of the repurchase obligation* by the company is the key concept. Repurchase liability studies help management to quantify and plan for the obligation so that major repurchases do not surprise management at a time when the company cannot afford the payment. In addition, plan design can help the company finance the obligation by establishing methods of distribution that provide flexibility.

The two primary variables affecting the obligation are the number of shares put to the company by participants in a year and the per-share value at the time of the repurchase. This is an annual computation. However, management of an ESOP company needs to understand all the variables that affect this contribution now and in the future to manage the obligation effectively. Other factors affecting this obligation include:

- The amount of existing liquidity in the ESOP trust
- The percentage of stock held by the ESOP

9. ESOP VALUATION 74 (3d ed. 2005).
10. *Id.*

- The demographics of the employee base (age, turnover, and actuarial determinations on life and disability)
- The ESOP plan provisions (vesting, eligibility, etc.)
- The ESOP plan distribution and diversification policy
- Structure of past and future ESOP transactions
- The company's borrowing limitations
- The growth in the value of the company's stock

The interaction of these factors is complex. However, a company must manage this obligation to protect future participants from dilution.

Relevant Case Law

Many issues involved in the valuation of ESOP shares are not settled. Also, the number of potential litigants that can contest the ESOP appraisal is significant.[11] Both the IRS and the DOL are the enforcement agencies that monitor ESOPs in general and thus the appraisal. In addition, each participant (and often participants' spouses and/or beneficiaries) has rights with respect to the appraisal and valuation of his or her ESOP account.

The following is a discussion of some of the most significant cases affecting ESOP valuations today.

Charles S. Foltz v. U.S. News & World Report, Inc.[12]

This case involved the amount of distributions received from 1973 through 1981 by the retirees of U.S. News & World Report, Inc. (U.S. News) from their profit-sharing plan (the Plan), which owned employer stock. Although not technically an ESOP, 100 percent of the stock was owned by the employees. The initial purchase by the Plan was in 1962. The defendants in the case were U.S. News, certain company representatives, the Plan, and the appraiser. The stock value appreciated substantially from the 1975 price of $69 per share to $200 per share in 1980. The company was sold in 1984 for $2,842 per share. The court's decision involved the following valuation positions:

- A series of minority interest transactions did not mandate that the appraiser add a *control premium* for valuation purposes even if the ESOP eventually

11. *See* LaRue v. DeWolff, Boberg & Assoc., 552 U.S. 248 (2008).

12. Foltz v. U.S. News & World Report, Inc., 106 F.R.D. 338 (D.C. Cir. 1984), *aff'd in part* and *vacated in part, remanded*, 760 F.2d 1300 (D.C. Cir. 1985), *on remand*, 613 F. Supp. 634 (D.D.C. 1985) (distributions for 1973 through 1980); and Richardson v. U.S. News & World Report, Inc., 623 F. Supp. 350 (D.C. Cir. 1985) (1981 distributions). (Note: This 80+ page opinion is highly instructive reading on both ESOP valuation issues and minority stock valuation issues in general.)

gained control. The court emphasized the fact that while the participants' combined interests represented a majority position, this did not entitle them to a pro rata percent of a control value.

- The 10 percent *discount for lack of marketability* applied by the appraiser was accepted in light of the fact that the company was under no obligation to repurchase the stock (there was no put option) and the company exercised the stock's call provision from time to time.
- U.S. News held some additional value in *nonoperating assets* that could not be reached by a minority shareholder. The court recognized that appraisals should give primary consideration to the earnings of the company and the shareholder's return on investment. Thus, no additional emphasis was placed on the value of real estate.
- It was appropriate for the annual appraisals to consider the facts and circumstances known or perceived as of the appraisal date and not consider *subsequent events* that could not have been anticipated. The issue here was that employees who separated from the company before its sale did not participate in the appreciation realized upon the sale.

The Court of Appeals for the District of Columbia affirmed the *U.S. News* case on appeal, on all counts, on January 13, 1989.

Las Vegas Dodge, Inc. v. United States[13]

The IRS relied heavily on an asset-based method—that is, book value—in *Las Vegas Dodge, Inc. v. United States* The independent appraisal gave heavy emphasis to the earning power and dividend capacity of the company. The court found that the earnings-based method was more relevant, even though the appraisal considered a 20-year projection period, using the discounted cash flow valuation method. The projections seemed reasonable in light of historical performance.

Howard v. Shay[14]

The *Howard v. Shay* case involved the ESOP of Pacific Architects and Engineers, Inc. (PAE). On November 9, 1988, the administrative committee of the PAE ESOP sold all the shares the ESOP held (about 37 percent of the total) to an irrevocable trust in connection with a termination of the plan. The stock value upon the sale was the

13. Las Vegas Dodge v. United States, 1985 U.S. Dist. LEXIS 21577, 1985 WL 6366 (D. Nev. 1985).

14. Howard v. Shay, 1993 U.S. Dist. LEXIS 20153 (C.D. Cal. 1993), *rev'd and remanded* by 100 F.3d 1484 (9th Cir. Cal. 1996), *cert. denied*, 520 U.S. 1237 (1997).

highest it had ever been. Because the irrevocable trust was created by the controlling shareholder of PAE, some of the former ESOP participants alleged that the administrative committee engaged in self-dealing and sold the stock to the trust for less than fair market value. The following is a summary of the court's findings.

- The original court decision held that independent or neutral fiduciaries were not necessary in light of the fact that Arthur Young was retained to render an independent appraisal and fairness opinion. However, in reversing the trial court, the Ninth Circuit Court of Appeals held that the mere fact that an independent appraisal was performed is an incomplete defense to a charge of imprudence, especially in cases where there is a strong possibility of self-dealing. They found liability in the degree of care exercised by the ESOP trustees.
- There was nothing wrong with the appraisal procedures. In addition, the minority interest discount of 40 percent to 50 percent and marketability discount of 50 percent taken into account were reasonable under the circumstances. The ESOP participants did not have a put option (because all stock was acquired before 1986), and there was some concern over the company's ability to honor the repurchase obligation in the future. Support for these discounts in the form of market evidence in similar facts and circumstances was the overriding reason why the court accepted them.
- The Ninth Circuit court decision added a fiduciary issue to the PAE case. It stated that "the fiduciary is required to make an honest, objective effort to read the valuation, understand it, and question the methods and assumptions that do not make sense." The court even suggested a second appraisal opinion if uncertainties remained.

On remand, the U.S. District Court reaffirmed its original decision concerning the valuation issues. However, based on the Ninth Circuit's decision finding a breach of fiduciary duty, the court granted the ESOP and/or any of the participants the right to buy back the original PAE shares at the tendered price. More important, the plaintiffs were awarded attorneys' fees and costs, which amounted to about $4 million!

Reich v. Valley National Bank of Arizona[15]

Reich v. Valley National Bank of Arizona involves an action brought by the Department of Labor against Valley National Bank of Arizona for its participation as trustee in the Kroy, Inc., ESOP. The case could be characterized primarily as a trustee's

15. Reich v. Valley Nat'l Bank of Ariz., 837 F. Supp. 1259, 1993 U.S. Dist. LEXIS 11837 (S.D.N.Y. 1993).

fiduciary duty case rather than as a valuation case. The Kroy ESOP transaction involved an ESOP and other equity investors, that is, a multiinvestor ESOP. The non-ESOP investor paid a per-share price that was significantly less than the per-share price paid by the ESOP. This involved a 1986 transaction in which Kroy, Inc., was taken private in a management-led leveraged ESOP transaction. Some major points of the case were as follows:

- The fiduciary *must* be an active participant in the *negotiations* regarding the transaction price and terms.
- The *independent financial advisor* should be retained directly by the fiduciary.
- The *due diligence* of the company and security being purchased should be thorough and the fiduciary should not rely on its advisor's due diligence.

The central issues were:

- The bank trustee approved the ESOP's investment without any due diligence or investigation of its own.
- The bank loan department had previously turned down its own investment in the ESOP debt of the leveraged buyout after its own diligence.
- The bank failed to disclose its reasons or documentation for the rejection of its participation in the leveraged buyout debt to its legal or financial advisor.
- The bank could not simply rely on the appraiser's report as a matter of law. In any event, the appraiser's report on its face raised questions that needed to be answered.

On September 20, 1994, the U.S. District Court for the Southern District of New York entered the settlement in the lawsuit against Valley National Bank of Arizona. The settlement consisted of a reimbursement of principal and interest payments on the debt incurred in the ESOP's purchase to the Kroy ESOP.

Gary L. Eyler v. Commissioner[16]

In the *Eyler* case, Gary L. Eyler, the sole or majority shareholder of Continental Training Services (CTS), Inc., disputed the IRS's determination that he had engaged in a "prohibited transaction" with the CTS ESOP because the ESOP paid more than fair market value. Eyler was seeking to sell CTS and had decided to take the company public. The investment banker established a price for the initial public offering (IPO)

16. Eyler v. Comm'r, T.C. Memo. 1995-123 (T.C. 1995), *aff'd,* 88 F.3d 445 (7th Cir. 1996).

of $13 to $16 per share in mid-1986, but failed to attract participants at this price. One month after the IPO failed in December of 1986, Eyler sold stock to the ESOP at $14.50 per share. Seven of CTS's board members also purchased shares at $14.50 per share. In September of 1986, two unrelated investigations for fraudulent practices were pending involving CTS.

The Tax Court's findings in the case were as follows:

- Eyler failed to establish that $14.50 was the fair market value of the CTS stock on the date of the transaction.
- The Tax Court agreed that a lack of marketability discount should be applied to the value of CTS to reflect the hypothetical buyer's concern that there will not be a ready market available when the buyer, in turn, decides to sell.
- The purchases by the directors were related-party sales and did not reflect fair market value.
- Because the board members who approved the ESOP's purchase knew that many of the assumptions underlying the investment banker's IPO price had changed, and they did not conduct any further investigation of the suggested price and did not obtain an independent appraisal, their actions did not rise to the level of prudence imposed on ERISA fiduciaries.

The Appeals Court affirmed the Tax Court and added that the fact that the IPO failed indicated that it did not reflect fair market value. In addition, the Appeals Court noted that the IPO would bring additional cash flow that would enhance market value that would not occur in an ESOP purchase. In fact, the ESOP required additional cash outlays in the form of employer contributions.

The Appeals Court also agreed with the Tax Court on the issue of marketability. It rejected the notion that the ESOP's put option reduces the lack of marketability discount because (1) the put option did not have a fixed price and (2) it could be paid out over five years under the terms of the ESOP. This aspect of the case has drawn attention to the lack of marketability discount in the ESOP context. Because it has been acceptable among ESOP valuation professionals to lower or even eliminate the marketability discount because of the ESOP's "put" right, this case raises some questions. This decision seems to be a situation (with respect to the marketability discount) of bad facts and thus a controversial result. (See the "Lack of Marketability Discount" section earlier in this chapter.)

The conclusion regarding the related-party sales and the prudence of the fiduciaries also was affirmed by the Appeals Court.

Henry v. Champlain Enterprises[17]

The court in *Henry v. Champlain Enterprises* rejected the valuation by a nationally recognized appraisal firm of convertible preferred stock contributed to an ESOP on grounds that the valuation was biased. In addition, because the trustee failed to document that it had challenged some aspects of the valuation, the court found the trustee failed to prove it had not breached its fiduciary duties.

In 1994, the three owners of CommutAir, a closely held regional airline, wanted to establish an ESOP with a contribution of 30 percent of CommutAir's stock. CommutAir had been approached by two investment banking firms who provided CommutAir with written materials indicating CommutAir had an equity value of between $140 million and $225 million. These offers were not pursued, but the CommutAir owners came to the conclusion, based on the offers, that their equity was worth $200 million. Accordingly, they wanted to sell their 30 percent stake for $60 million in a seller-financed transaction.

When they were ready to establish the ESOP, the owners hired U.S. Trust Co. (U.S. Trust), which routinely served as an ESOP trustee. U.S. Trust stressed the need for due diligence and an appraisal of the company, and Houlihan, Lokey, Howard, & Zukin (Houlihan) was retained for this purpose.

Based on a comparable company analysis and a discounted cash flow analysis, Houlihan initially determined that CommutAir was worth $180 million. Subsequently, it still concluded the ESOP was receiving "value in excess" as a result of the features of the convertible preferred stock. Ultimately, the stock sold for $60 million.

ESOP participants brought suit against CommutAir and U.S. Trust over the issue of whether the sale constituted a prohibited transaction under ERISA Section 406 and, if so, whether it qualified under the adequate consideration exception set forth by ERISA.

Both sides agreed that the primary component of the valuation would be to determine CommutAir's total equity value by employing the discounted cash flow (DCF) method and the comparable guideline public company method. The plaintiff's expert concluded a total equity value of just under $106 million and opined that the convertible preferred stock should have been valued at $41.5 million. The expert criticized Houlihan's terminal growth rate, the use of certain financial measures, and the selection of above-the-median multiples used in the comparable company method (finding CommutAir to be at or below the comparable companies while Houlihan found them to be at or above the comparable companies).

The court found that while Houlihan and the plaintiff's expert were correct and in agreement on many issues, there was serious doubt about the overall credibility of

17. Henry v. Champlain Enters., 334 F. Supp. 2d 252, 2004 U.S. Dist. LEXIS 18140 (N.D.N.Y. Sept. 3, 2004).

both. The court determined that Houlihan was not independent because it did not start with an open mind or independent approach to valuation. The court determined that the plaintiff's expert was hired to provide the lowest valuation conclusion possible to maximize the potential damages sustained by the ESOP. Based on their testimony, however, the Trial Court determined that the equity value of CommutAir in 1994 was $145 million, and that, therefore, the fair market value of the stock purchased by the ESOP was $52.5 million.

As to the adequate consideration exception, the court found that U.S. Trust failed to prove that it had made a good-faith, independent determination of fair market value. Specifically, the court questioned the reliability of management projections and the terminal value calculation and, with respect to the comparable companies method, questioned the propriety of the selection of the comparable companies, the financial measures, and the multiples, and whether the most current information was used. The court concluded that U.S. Trust failed to address these areas of concern, noting that U.S. Trust "barely produced a shred of evidence that shows what Goldberg and Shea did." Accordingly, the court awarded the plaintiffs $7.75 million.

This case should serve as a warning to ESOP trustees to document their conduct and decision-making process. In this case, the trustee's failure to create such documentation seems to have given the court no choice but to find that the trustee failed to prove that it engaged in a good-faith investigation of the merits of the transaction at issue. The court also found the appraisals in this case suspect, again serving as a reminder of how crucial it is for valuation experts to remain independent throughout the appraisal. In quoting from another case, the court emphasized that "Little case law exists on valuation, so often a court's conclusion is determined by its evaluation of the credibility and background of the witnesses who performed the valuation."

Chao v. Hall Holding Co., Inc.[18]

In *Chao v. Hall Holding Co., Inc.*, the U.S. Department of Labor brought suit against Hall Holding Co. and others on the grounds, among others, that they breached their fiduciary duty by purchasing Hall Holding stock for the employee stock ownership plan (ESOP) without conducting a prudent and independent investigation to determine the stock's fair market value.

Goldman Financial Group, Inc. (GFGI), purchased Hall Chemical Co. through Hall Holding Co. (Hall Holding). Hall Chemical was Hall Holding's primary asset, with Hall Holding owning 95 percent of Hall Chemical. The decision was made to create a Hall Chemical ESOP and a valuation expert was hired to value Hall Chemical. However, the expert was not informed and never knew that the purpose of the

18. Chao v. Hall Holding Co., Inc., 285 F.3d 415, 2002 U.S. App. LEXIS 5929 (6th Cir. Apr. 3, 2002).

valuation was to determine how much an ESOP should pay for Hall Chemical stock. The expert concluded that Hall Chemical was worth between $32.4 million and $37.4 million, exclusive of debt.

Based on this valuation, Hall Chemical's president and vice president, who also were trustees of the ESOP, offered to and did purchase for Hall Chemical ESOP 110 shares, or 9.9 percent, of Hall Holding stock for $3.5 million (the appraiser had not valued Hall Holding, however).

The District Court, finding that Hall Holding stock should have been valued, conducted its own valuation. The court concluded that the fair market value of Hall Holding stock was $2,450,451. It arrived at this value by using the valuation expert's range of value for the Hall Chemical stock, subtracting a $13.6 million debt of Hall Holding, and applying a 13 percent minority discount to account for the fact that the ESOP purchased only a minority interest (9.96 percent) in Hall Holding. The court also took into account the negative accounts receivable and liabilities of Hall Holding, applied a 5 percent marketability discount, and applied a 5 percent discount to reflect the president's 5 percent interest in Hall Chemical stock.

The court concluded that the trustees did not conduct a prudent and independent investigation to determine the fair market value of Hall Holding stock purchased by the Hall Chemical ESOP. The court also held that the ESOP was entitled to an award of $1,049,549, which represented the difference between the amount originally paid for the stock and the fair market value of the stock as determined by the court.

The Sixth Circuit affirmed the decision, concluding that the plan trustees had failed to prove that they had made a good-faith inquiry into fair market value when: (1) the trustees relied on a valuation by an individual who had valued the wrong company and who testified that if had he been told that the valuation would be used for an employee stock ownership plan transaction, he would have conducted a different valuation; (2) the trustees generally were "unaware of what was going on"; (3) the trustees were not consulted on major decisions, such as the price to pay for the stock; (4) the trustees did not engage in any negotiation as to the price of the stock; (5) the trustees were more concerned with the return on the investment for the trust that had financed the stock purchase than for the plan; and (6) the trustees caused the plan to be charged several thousands of dollars simply to enable the trustees to communicate using round numbers.

This case serves as a valuable reminder that valuation professionals should make a detailed inquiry into the purpose of their valuations. Such inquiry in this case might have led the appraiser to discover that the valuation was for the purpose of establishing an ESOP and might have led the appraiser to value the correct company for that purpose.

Keach v. U.S. Trust Co.

Keach v. U.S. Trust Co. has spawned more than 20 reported decisions. Those of primary concern to valuators are a U.S. District Court case that decided whether a valuation firm hired by a company's board of directors has fiduciary liability to the company's ESOP[19] and a U.S. Court of Appeals case that decided the liability of an ESOP's trustee in relying on a valuator's due diligence.[20]

The F&G ESOP began in 1988, when it purchased about 30 percent of F&G's stock from the company's founders. F&G's largest subsidiary conducted direct-mail sweepstakes promotions to its customers. In 1995, a leveraged purchase of a large number of F&G shares by the ESOP was proposed. At that time, F&G had been enjoying record profitability for several years and was forecasted to continue this trend into the future.

On December 20, 1995, the ESOP, with U.S. Trust Company (U.S. Trust) acting as its trustee, purchased 3,589,743 shares of F&G stock from several F&G officers and directors at a price of $19.50 per share (ESOP II transaction). F&G had retained Valuemetrics, Inc. (Valuemetrics) as its financial advisor. On September 30, 1995, Valuemetrics issued its first transaction memorandum to the F&G board of directors describing a proposed offer to sell 2,916,667 shares to the ESOP at $24 per share. U.S. Trust served as an independent trustee for the ESOP to consider the merits of the proposed transaction.

U.S. Trust, in turn, engaged Houlihan, Lokey, Howard, & Zukin (Houlihan) to assist in valuing the transaction and to render a written opinion to U.S. Trust as to whether the transaction was fair to the ESOP from a financial perspective.

Based on Houlihan's analysis, U.S. Trust determined that Valuemetrics' analysis was too optimistic in some respects. Houlihan prepared a new analysis reflecting a lower valuation range for the price of the F&G shares. U.S. Trust suggested a share price of $18.50; the final price of the transaction was $19.50.

For the next two years, F&G did enjoy record business; however, in 1998, in the wake of significantly increased sweepstakes regulation, its profits began to decline steadily until F&G declared bankruptcy in 2001. ESOP participants sued after the value of F&G shares had reached less than 50 percent of their original purchase price.

In the district court case, the plaintiffs asserted that Valuemetrics was a fiduciary to the ESOP plan because it (1) exercised control over plan assets and (2) rendered investment advice with respect to the property of the plan. Valumetrics moved for summary judgment, countering that it was not a fiduciary to the ESOP plan.

19. 239 F. Supp. 2d 820, 2002 U.S. Dist. LEXIS 24829 (C.D. Ill. Dec. 30, 2002).
20. 419 F.3d 626, 2005 U.S. App. LEXIS 17355 (7th Cir. Aug. 17, 2005).

The district court agreed with Valumetrics. The court first observed that a showing of authority or control requires actual decision-making power rather than the type of influence a professional advisor may have with respect to decisions made by trustees.

It was U.S. Trust, not Valuemetrics, that made the final decision and caused the ESOP to purchase the shares of stock and that had hired Houlihan as its own independent financial advisor for the transaction.

With regard to investment advice, the court stated that the record did not support a finding that Valuemetrics gave any investment advice to the ESOP regarding the transaction. In light of a Department of Labor advisory opinion indicating that appraising the value of closely held stock for an ESOP does not constitute the rendering of investment advice, the court held that Valuemetrics should not be a party to the action.

In the court of appeals case, one of the issues was whether Houlihan should have foreseen that within two years of its due diligence, the government would crack down on the company's sweepstakes promotions, and within three years, F&G would be bankrupt. The plaintiffs alleged that U.S. Trust had breached its fiduciary duty in relying on Houlihan's report. The district court had found that, rather than blindly accept the forecasts of F&G officers as to F&G's financial future, "U.S. Trust and Houlihan probed and challenged a number of assumptions in Valuemetrics' evaluation before developing their own independent evaluation that formed the basis for a price per share at closing that was almost 20 percent less than the selling shareholders' offering price."

The Seventh Circuit Court of Appeals agreed, saying that "When the record establishes that the overlooked matter was one that no one perceived to be a material concern at the time or to be outcome determinative, it cannot be said that the overall investigation was imprudent or in bad faith. ERISA's fiduciary duty of care 'requires prudence, not prescience.'" The court distinguished this case from that in *Chao v. Hall Holding Co.* (see the summary of the *Chao* case, above), saying that in the Chao case, the trustees failed to show they made a good-faith inquiry into fair market value because, in part, they relied on a clearly inadequate valuation.

This case demonstrates that a thorough independent valuation, conducted in light of all known facts at the time, will withstand ERISA's bad-faith or breach of the duty of care claims. The case also is consistent with the principle that valuation professionals do not need to be "fortune-tellers" to provide defensible valuations.

Armstrong v. LaSalle Bank National Association[21]

The U.S. Court of Appeals for the Seventh Circuit reversed the U.S. District Court's grant of summary judgment in favor of LaSalle, serving as ESOP trustee.

21. 446 F.3d 728 (7th Cir. 2006).

Issue: Whether the ESOP trustee breached its fiduciary duty when the valuation of the company stock led to heavy losses to remaining ESOP participants.

Facts: LaSalle National Bank served as ESOP trustee for Amstead Industries, Inc., a closely held manufacturer of railroad and other transportation equipment. Amstead's ESOP provided that it would redeem the shares of participants leaving the company in full and at once. In accordance with the terms of the plan, the price of Amstead ESOP shares was reset every September 30; an employee had until June 30 of the following year to decide whether to leave Amstead to redeem the vested shares at the September 30 value.

In August of 1999, Amstead acquired Varlen Corporation for $800 million. Amstead financed the acquisition by borrowing $1 billion; the loan was unsecured and also enabled Amstead to refinance its previous debt. On September 30, 1999, a month after the acquisition, LaSalle hired a prominent valuation consulting firm to value the ESOP shares. This firm valued Amstead's stock at $184/share, 32 percent higher than the previous September 30 value. This increase matched the amount by which the Dow Jones Index of 30 industrials had increased. LaSalle accepted this valuation report, apparently assuming that Amstead was as a good a performer as the average company in the index. At this juncture in time, Amstead's unused credit line was limited.

In the ensuing year, 2000, redemptions turned out to be not 10 percent—the expected percentage—but 32 percent. The cost to Amstead to redeem the shares was $330 million. This created a liquidity problem and prompted Amstead to eliminate a departing employee's right to a lump-sum distribution and make other changes adverse to the plaintiff class. In subsequent years, Amstead's stock was valued at a far lower amount. The facts revealed that the prominent valuation firm had failed to discount the shares for lack of marketability.

Held: The U.S. Court of Appeals, Seventh Circuit, acknowledged that judicial review of decisions of an ERISA trustee is deferential, unless there is a conflict of interest. Yet, the court stated that "there are rules as to how much deference a court should give non-adjudicators, a pertinent example being the business-judgment rule, which decreases a light hand for a court asked to invalidate a business decision." Here, the court held that "a discretionary judgment cannot be upheld when discretion has not been exercised. [W]e cannot find in the record as now constituted [] any indication that LaSalle considered how best to balance the interests of the various participants in the ESOP in the novel circumstances created by Amstead's acquisition of Varlen . . . A trustee who simply ignores changed circumstances [increases] the risk of loss to trust's beneficiaries is imprudent."

Summary

ESOP valuations are subject to more scrutiny than appraisals for other purposes, mostly because they affect more people. There are more than 10,000 ESOP companies in the United States covering about 20 million employees. Each of these employees has a personal stake in the valuation conclusions that are estimated at least annually. However, the subjective nature of valuation always leaves an opening for controversy and dispute.

The formal legal status of ESOPs was first established with the enactment in 1974 of the Employee Retirement Income Security Act. However, ESOPs did not grow in popularity until the Tax Reduction Act of 1984, which enacted new, tax-favored positions for ESOPs. Thus, the evolution of the issues involved in ESOP valuation is relatively young. As discussed, many issues are well settled, but continually growing case law still plays an important part in formation of ESOP valuation practices.

References

Articles

Ackerman, David. "Technical Issues under the New S Corporation ESOP Laws." *Journal of Employee Ownership Law and Finance* (Winter 1999): 3–19.

Austin, Douglas V. "Beware of Your ESOP." *Hoosier Banker* 84:4 (April 30, 2000): 9–10.

Berka, Jack W. "An ESOP Update Review of Current Issues." Presentation to the International Conference of the American Society of Appraisers, June 1997, *available at* www.BVLibrary.com.

Buckley, Allen, Lynda M. Crouse, and Greg Kniesel. "S Corporation ESOPs in Dispositive Sales and Reorganization Transactions." *Valuation Strategies* (January/February 2001): 20–29, 46–48.

Etkind, Steven M., and Joseph E. Godfrey III. "ESOPs Rediscovered: Tax Advantages and Recyclable Refunding." *The CPA Journal* 72:4 (April 30, 2002): 60–61.

Hirschfeld, Christopher. "ESOPs as an Estate Planning Vehicle for Business Owners." *Journal of Financial Planning* 15:11 (November 30, 2002): 92–97.

Julius, J. Michael. "ESOP Appraisals and Non-ESOP Shareholders." *CPA Litigation Service Counselor* (July 1998): 9–10.

Kober, John A. "A Tool for Shareholder Liquidity, Estate Planning and Management

Succession Planning." White paper (1999), *available at* www.BVLibrary.com.

Korschot, John. "Valuation Issues." *BV Papers* (December 2001), *available at* www.BVLibrary.com.

Kubersky, Andrew S. "Marketability Discounts and ESOP Acquisitions of Minority Share Interests." *Journal of Employee Ownership Law and Finance* (Fall 1998): 97–103.

Lannon, Allan L. R. "Valuing Non-ESOP Shares in ESOP Companies—Some Empirical Evidence." *Business Valuation Review* (March 1994): 19–21.

Lippert-Gray, Carol. "An ESOP's Tale." *Financial Executive* 16:1 (February 28, 2000): 40–42.

May, Richard C., Robert L. McDonald, and Brad Van Horn. "Valuation Issues in Leveraged ESOPs." *Journal of Employee Ownership Law and Finance* (Summer 1994): 61–82.

Miller, Karren L. "Using an ESOP to Let Go." *Central Penn Business Journal* 16:23 (June 9, 2000): 3.

Mueller, Susan L. "An Introduction to ESOP Appraisal Controversies." *Journal of Employee Ownership Law and Finance* (Winter 1998): 89–96.

Mueller, Susan L., and Judith C. Gehr. "Valuation Issues in Multi-Investor ESOP LBOs." In Scott S. Rodrick, Ed., *ESOP Valuation,* Chap. 2. Oakland, Cal.: The National Center for Employee Ownership, 1999.

Pratt, Shannon P., and Noah J. Gordon. "Trustee and Appraiser Duties in ESOP Valuations—Recent Judicial Decisions." *ESOP Report Magazine* (June/July 2007): 65–67.

Regnitz, Timothy J. "Understanding the ESOP Repurchase Obligation." *The Journal of Employee Ownership Law and Finance* (Winter 1999): 21–34.

Suhre, Karen K. "Should the ESOP-Owned Company Elect to Become an S Corporation?" *Benefits Law Journal* (Spring 1998).

"To ESOP or Not to ESOP?" *The Tax Adviser* (May 2004).

Torolopoulos, Sam G. "Valuation of ESOP Shares: Opportunities and Challenges." *CPA Expert* (Fall 2005): 9–12.

Books

An Introduction to ESOP Valuations. Washington, DC: The ESOP Association, 2005.

Ash, Merri E., Virginia J. Bartlett, et al. *The ESOP Association Administration Handbook.* Washington, D.C.: The ESOP Association, 1996.

Bernstein, Ron, David Binns, Marshal Hyman, and Martin Staubus. *Transitioning Ownership in the Private Company: The ESOP Solution.* La Jolla, Cal.: Foundation for Enterprise Development, 2001.

Brown, Karen W. "Payment of Control Premiums by ESOPs." *ESOP Report* (November/December 1993): 6–8.

Cook, Larry R. *Financial Valuation of Employee Stock Ownership Plan Shares.* Hoboken, N.J.: John Wiley & Sons, 2005.

ESOP Accounting Standards. Washington, D.C.: The ESOP Association, 2005.

ESOP Repurchase Obligations. Washington, D.C.: The ESOP Association, 2004.

Frisch, Robert A. *ESOP: The Ultimate Instrument in Succession Planning,* 2d Ed. Hoboken, N.J.: John Wiley & Sons, 2001.

_____. *ESOP Workbook: The Ultimate Instrument in Succession Planning.* Hoboken, N.J.: John Wiley & Sons, 2002.

How the ESOP Really Works. Washington, DC: The ESOP Association, 1997.

Phillips, Perry. *Employee Share Ownership Plans: How to Design and Implement an ESOP in Canada.* Mississauga, Ontario: John Wiley & Sons Canada, 2001.

Pratt, Shannon. "Employee Stock Ownership Plans." In *Business Valuation Body of Knowledge,* 2d Ed., 315–20. New York: John Wiley & Sons, 2003.

Pratt, Shannon P., and Alina V. Niculita. "Valuations for Employee Stock Ownership Plans." In *Valuing a Business,* 5th Ed., 809–36. New York: McGraw-Hill, 2007.

Report on Valuation Considerations for Leveraged ESOPs. Washington, D.C.: The ESOP Association, 1998.

Rodrick, Scott S., Ed. *Leveraged ESOPs and Employee Buyouts.* Oakland, Cal.: The National Center for Employee Ownership, 2005.

_____. *ESOP Valuation.* Oakland, Cal.: The National Center for Employee Ownership, 1999.

Rosen, Corey. *Understanding ESOP Valuation.* Oakland, Cal.: The National Center for Employee Ownership, 2000.

Rosen, Corey, John Case, and Martin Staubus. *Equity: Why Employee Ownership Is Good for Business.* Cambridge, Mass.: Harvard Business School Press, 2005.

Smiley, Robert W., Ronald J. Gilbert, and David M. Binns. *Employee Stock Ownership Plans, 1998 Yearbook.* Boston: Warren, Gorham & Lamont of the RIA Group, 1998.

Smiley, Jr., Robert W., and Ronald J. Gilbert, Eds. *Employee Stock Ownership Plans: Business Planning, Implementation, and Law and Taxation.* New York: Warren, Gorham & Lamont, 1991, supplemented annually.

Staubus, Martin, David Binns, and Ron Bernstein. *Transitioning Ownership in the Private Company: The ESOP Solution,* 2d Ed. La Jolla, Cal.: The Beyster Institute, 2005.

Structuring Leveraged ESOP Transactions. Washington, D.C.: The ESOP Association, 1999.

The Ownership Advantage. Washington, D.C.: The ESOP Association, 2005.

Valuing ESOP Shares. Washington, D.C.: The ESOP Association, 2005.

Valuing ESOP Shares, Rev. Ed. Washington, D.C.: The ESOP Association, 1994.

Associations

The ESOP Association
1726 M St. N.W., Ste. 501
Washington, DC 20036
(202) 293-2971 or (866) 366-3832
www.esopassociation.org

The National Center for Employee Ownership
1736 Franklin St., 8th Fl.
Oakland, CA 94612
(510) 208-1300
www.nceo.org

Chapter 22

Valuing Professional Practices and Small Service Businesses

The primary attribute that distinguishes professional practices and small service businesses from larger businesses is the personal involvement of the owner(s) in day-to-day operations. This impacts both the way that they are bought and sold and the mechanics of the valuation.

Small businesses and professional practices usually are sold either in private transactions among acquaintances or through "main street business brokers." There are brokers who specialize in certain type of businesses, such as restaurants, or certain types of practices, such as dental practices.

Fair market value is a cash or cash equivalent concept. Therefore, when the standard of value is fair market value, when using the market approach (there are abundant data to use the market approach), it usually is necessary to convert the "price" from whatever the terms are to a cash-equivalent value. Obviously, the more lenient the terms, the higher the face amount of the price is relative to the cash-equivalent value. (The most common contract rate is 8 percent.)

Trade-off between Cash and Terms

In reality, the smaller the business or practice, the more likely it is to sell on terms rather than for cash. This is because the market for such businesses or practices consists largely of individuals, most of whom are not cash rich.

There are two common departures from all cash transactions:

1. Easy Terms
2. Earnouts

Easy Terms

It is common for small businesses and practices to sell for low down payments (the usual range is 20 percent to 40 percent of the intended purchase price) with the balance paid over an extended period (usually two to five years, with monthly, quarterly, or annual installments) mostly at a rate of interest that is below what could be attained in a market rate loan, if such a loan could be attained at all. Generally, the only collateral is the business or practice itself.

To convert these extended payments to a cash equivalent value, it is necessary to discount the payments at a market rate. To illustrate with a simple example, assuming annual payments of $10,000 at the end of each year including principal and interest at 6 percent and a market rate of 15 percent, the computation would be as follows:

$$PV = \frac{\$10{,}000}{1.15} + \frac{\$10{,}000}{(1.15)^2} + \frac{\$10{,}000}{(1.15)^3}$$

$$PV = \frac{\$10{,}000}{1.15} + \frac{\$10{,}000}{1.32} + \frac{\$10{,}000}{1.52}$$

$$= \$8{,}696 + \$7{,}561 + \$6{,}575$$

$$= \underline{\underline{\$22{,}832}}$$

If we assume that the down payment was $20,000, the cash-equivalent value would be $42,832 ($20,000 + $22,832).

Exhibit 22-1 is a table of the present value of each $1,000 at various market interest rates over 60 months.

Earnouts

An *earnout* is a contingency payment based on achieving some level of performance, such as sales or profitability. We advise our clients when selling on an earnout contract to base the performance on sales rather than profits because the buyer has more opportunity to manipulate profit than sales. The sales figure may be based on total sales or on "retained" sales (that is revenue from customers existing prior to the sale).

When an earnout is in place, the conversion to a cash-equivalent value requires an estimate of the amount to be received before discounting it to a present value. In the previous simple example, we will assume that the estimated amounts to be received are $8,000 at the end of the first year, $7,000 at the end of the second year, and $6,000 at the end of the third year. Again, assuming the 15 percent market rate of interest, the computation would be as follows:

Exhibit 22-1
Present Value of $1,000 at Various Market Rates of Interest

Market Rate /Month Received	10%	11%	12%	13%	14%	15%	16%
1	991.74	990.92	990.10	989.28	988.47	987.65	986.8
2	983.54	981.92	980.30	978.68	977.07	975.46	973.8
3	975.41	973.00	970.59	968.19	965.80	963.42	961.0
4	967.35	964.16	960.98	957.82	954.66	951.52	948.4
5	959.36	955.40	951.47	947.55	943.65	939.78	935.9
6	951.43	946.72	942.05	937.40	932.77	928.17	923.6
7	943.56	938.12	932.72	927.35	922.01	916.72	911.4
8	935.77	929.60	923.48	917.41	911.38	905.40	899.4
9	928.03	921.16	914.34	907.58	900.87	894.22	887.6
10	920.36	912.79	905.29	897.85	890.48	883.18	875.9
11	912.76	904.50	896.32	888.23	880.21	872.28	864.4
12	905.21	896.28	887.45	878.71	870.06	861.51	853.0
13	897.73	888.14	878.66	869.29	860.03	850.87	841.8
14	890.31	880.07	869.96	859.98	850.11	840.37	830.7
15	882.95	872.08	861.35	850.76	840.31	829.99	819.8
16	875.66	864.16	852.82	841.64	830.62	819.75	809.0
17	868.42	856.31	844.38	832.62	821.04	809.63	798.3
18	861.24	848.53	836.02	823.70	811.57	799.63	787.8
19	854.13	840.82	827.74	814.87	802.21	789.76	777.5
20	847.07	833.19	819.54	806.14	792.96	780.01	767.2
21	840.07	825.62	811.43	797.50	783.82	770.38	757.1
22	833.12	818.12	803.40	788.95	774.78	760.87	747.2
23	826.24	810.69	795.44	780.50	765.84	751.47	737.3
24	819.41	803.32	787.57	772.13	757.01	742.20	727.6
25	812.64	796.03	779.77	763.86	748.28	733.03	718.1
26	805.92	788.80	772.05	755.67	739.65	723.98	708.6
27	799.26	781.63	764.40	747.57	731.12	715.05	699.3
28	792.66	774.53	756.84	739.56	722.69	706.22	690.1
29	786.10	767.50	749.34	731.63	714.36	697.50	681.0
30	779.61	760.52	741.92	723.79	706.12	688.89	672.0
31	773.16	753.62	734.58	716.03	697.97	680.38	663.2
32	766.78	746.77	727.30	708.36	689.93	671.98	654.5
33	760.44	739.99	720.10	700.77	681.97	663.69	645.9
34	754.15	733.27	712.97	693.26	674.10	655.49	637.4
35	747.92	726.61	705.91	685.83	666.33	647.40	629.0
36	741.74	720.01	698.92	678.48	658.65	639.41	620.7
37	735.61	713.47	692.00	671.21	651.05	631.52	612.5
38	729.53	706.98	685.15	664.01	643.54	623.72	604.5
39	723.50	700.56	678.37	656.90	636.12	616.02	596.5
40	717.52	694.20	671.65	649.86	628.79	608.41	588.7
41	711.59	687.89	665.00	642.89	621.53	600.90	580.9
42	705.71	681.65	658.42	636.00	614.37	593.48	573.3
43	699.88	675.45	651.90	629.19	607.28	586.16	565.7

$$PV = \frac{\$8{,}000}{1.15} + \frac{\$7{,}000}{1.15^2} + \frac{\$6{,}000}{1.15^3}$$

$$PV = \frac{\$8{,}000}{1.15} + \frac{\$7{,}000}{1.32} + \frac{\$6{,}000}{1.52}$$

$$= \$6{,}957 + \$5{,}293 + \$3{,}945$$

$$= \underline{\$16{,}195}$$

Adding this amount to the $20,000 down payment would give us a cash-equivalent value of $36,195 ($20,000 + $16,195).

Valuation Approaches and Methods

When valuing a small business or practice, it is important to know exactly what is being sold. Most sellers take out all the cash from the business before the transaction takes place. Most transactions do not include receivables; the seller usually collects the receivables himself or herself. The transaction may or may not include inventory. The IBA Market Database does not include inventory. Pratt's Stats and BIZCOMPS show the amount of the inventory. The transaction prices almost never include real estate.

Income Approach

It is not common to use the discounted cash flow method because most small businesses and practices do not have multiyear projections (or reliable enough multiyear projections to provide a basis for valuation).

If the income approach is used, the method usually is a capitalization of the cash flow or earnings. Capitalization of net cash flow generally is preferred, for reasons given in Chapter 5, "The Income Approach." However, frequently, it does not make much difference which variable is used, because many small businesses do not have significant capital expenditures, depreciation, or working capital needs that would cause net cash flow to differ very much from net income.

Market Approach

As noted earlier, there is an abundance of data to make the market approach a very feasible way to value most small businesses and practices. Among the available databases, Pratt's Stats, BIZCOMPS, and IBA Market Database, there are literally tens of thousands of sales of small businesses and practices.

When the market approach is used, the underlying variables for the valuation multiples usually are sales and/or owner's discretionary earnings (all compensation, benefits, and discretionary expenses to one owner/operator, as discussed in Chapter 6, "The Market Approach").

There are four reasons for this:

1. These are the only two operational variables in either BIZCOMPS or the IBA Market Database.
2. Frequently, these are the only two reliable variables on the financial statements of these small businesses and practices.
3. Owner's discretionary cash flow is "what you get" (what the owner can take out of the business).
4. Frequently, when owner's compensation is taken out, there are no remaining earnings available to capitalize. In other words, rather that buying the business for a return on investment, the buyer is just buying a job.

Excess Earnings Method

Many valuations of small businesses and professional practices are based on the excess earnings method, especially for marital dissolution litigation. This method has many variations and pitfalls, as discussed in Chapter 8.

Asset-Based Methods

Sometimes small businesses and practices are based on an adjusted asset value method, as discussed in Chapter 7.

Rules of Thumb

Small businesses and professional practices prices sometimes are arrived at by loose application of rules of thumb. These rules can be in the form of a range of multiples of sales or owner's discretionary income to "assets plus something."[1] Rules of thumb for a variety of industries are contained in Chapter 9.

Rules of thumb tend to become part of the folklore of an industry. Frequently, they represent what owners *hope* to get when they sell. Moreover, they frequently represent prices on typical terms with seller financing and/or earnouts. If rules of thumb are widely used in an industry, they should not be ignored. A rule of thumb can be used as a check for reasonableness but should not be used as the only method in an appraisal.

---

1. For an extensive list of rules of thumb, see Tom West, *Rules of Thumb*, in The Business Reference Guide, 20th ed. (2010).

Chapter 23

Valuing S Corporations and Other Pass-through Entities[1]

Value and Taxes

"Fair market value," the construct under which valuation analysts most frequently determine value, is viewed from the perspective of a hypothetical investor. Corporations generally need individuals to invest in them, and individual investment for real, and therefore, hypothetical, investors are affected by the relevant tax consequences.[2]

We know this phenomenon is true in our personal investing patterns. *In addition to general investment risk considerations,* whether you're considering investing in a public stock, a state municipal ("muni") bond, or a U.S. Government bond, you consider your *after-personal-tax returns*—the amount of money that eventually will end up in your pocket. For instance, hypothetical investors are willing to earn a different (lower) rate of return on the muni than they are on the public stock, in part, because a municipal bond bears no federal income taxes and likely no state tax.[3] Investors look for the highest rate of return on publicly traded stocks, in part because they bear both federal and state income taxes (again, risk is a key consideration as well).

---

1. This chapter was abstracted from Chapter 2, *Cost of Capital Fundamentals and the Effect of Income Taxes, in* FANNON'S GUIDE TO THE VALUATION OF SUBCHAPTER S CORPORATIONS (Business Valuation Resources, www.bvresources.com, 2008), authored by Nancy J. Fannon, ASA, MCBA, CPA, ABV, BVAL. Fannon is president of Fannon Valuation Group (Portland, Maine); nancy@fannonval.com. Previously published versions of this chapter have appeared in FANNON'S GUIDE TO THE VALUATION OF SUBCHAPTER S CORPORATIONS (Business Valuation Resources, www.bvresources.com, 2008), CPA EXPERT (Spring 2007), VALUATION EXAMINER (March/April, 2007), and BUSINESS VALUATION REVIEW (Spring 2007).

2. Merton H. Miller, *Debt and Taxes*, JOURNAL OF TAXATION (May 1977). In 1977, Merton Miller introduced the effects of personal taxes on investment returns and capital structure in his seminal work, *Debt and Taxes*. Miller argued that investors base their returns on the *after-personal-tax returns* of different investments.

3. Internal Revenue Code (IRC) § 103(a).

An investor wants a publicly traded stock to pay a higher rate of return than a municipal bond, in part because the municipal bond will be tax-free. An investor will accept the 4 percent or 5 percent rate of return on the muni because he or she won't have to pay any taxes on it when the investor receives that return. All other considerations aside, if the total return on the public stock was at that rate, however, an investor would sell it pretty quickly, because the net, after paying taxes, would be next to nothing.

Anyone who has done any amount of investing understands this fairly simple concept: If you have to pay taxes on the income you receive from an investment, you end up with less in your pocket than if you didn't have to pay taxes. Therefore, all things being equal, if one investment has taxes levied on it and another does not, an investor will choose the one that does not.

To recap, we know this about investments and taxes:

All things being equal, if you don't have to pay taxes on an investment, you end up with more money in your pocket compared to an investment that pays out the same amount on which you do have to pay taxes.

The concept is no different with an investment in a closely held business. Investors invest in closely held businesses because they expect they will end up with a certain amount of money in their pockets *after payment of all taxes.* This issue has formed the heart of the S corporation debate: An investment in an S corporation must be worth more than an investment in a publicly traded C corporation simply because investors in an S corporation avoid a level of taxes.[4] To understand what tax the S corporation shareholder avoids, a brief review of the legislative history of Subchapter S is in order.[5]

Legislative Intent: Understanding the Tax Avoided by the S Corporation

From 1945 to 1950, the highest marginal tax rate for corporations ranged from 42 percent to 53 percent, while the highest rate at which individuals were taxed ranged

4. The "S corporation debate" refers to the debate in the valuation profession brought about by the controversial court decisions in *Gross, Heck, Wall,* and *Adams*. The debate initially centered on the issue of whether or not to tax-affect S corporation earnings, after the Tax Court rejected the tax-affecting of S corporation earnings in those cases.

5. *See* Zev Landau, *Recent Reform and Simplications for S Corporations*, CPA Journal OnLine, www.nysscpa.org/cpajournal/2005/1105/essentials/p46.htm. *See also* the Statement of the Honorable Donald C. Alexander (Akin, Gump Strauss Hauer & Feld, LLP), testimony before the Subcommittee on Select Revenue Measures, House Committee on Ways and Means (June 19, 2003); http://waysandmeans.house.gov/hearings.asp?formmode=view&id=540.

from 82 percent to 91 percent. The double taxation system put a particular strain on small businesses. A corporation making a profit of $1,000,000 could end up paying $420,000 in corporate income taxes and another $400,000 to $500,000 in individual taxes if all were distributed, leaving precious little for the investor's efforts.

Recognizing this, in 1954, President Dwight Eisenhower proposed that new closely held corporations with a small number of active shareholders would have the option of being taxed in the same manner as partnerships, *in order to avoid the second level of tax on dividends*. While the Senate adopted this proposal, it did not pass the Congressional Conference Committee.

In 1958, President Eisenhower once again made his proposal to Congress. These recommendations, along with Treasury-drafted provisions, developed into the Subchapter S legislation. All corporate earnings from the Subchapter S corporation would be treated as if they were distributed and taxed only once. In explaining the rationale, the legislative committee wrote:

> [T]he enactment of a provision of this type is desirable because it permits businesses to select the form of business organization desired, without the necessity of taking into account major differences in tax consequence . . . Where the earnings are distributed (and are in excess of what may properly be classified as salary payments), the benefit will extend to individuals with somewhat higher rates *since in this case a "double" tax is removed.*[6]

Neither Eisenhower in his proposal nor Congress in its adoption had any intention of removing taxes on corporate income. Rather, their collective intent was to tax small corporations in the same manner as partnerships and eliminate the dividend tax that hampered the corporate form. Thus we can conclude:

The tax avoided under the S corporation is the dividend tax that the individual shareholder has to pay.

The recent direction of the IRS and the federal Tax Court on this issue is inconsistent with the specific intention of Subchapter S legislation. In five decisions[7] (the *Gross, Heck, Wall, Adams,* and *Dallas* cases), the Tax Court eliminated *any* deduction for corporate income taxes. Clearly, if Congress intended the shareholders to avoid taxes on corporate income, it would both delight those owners and break our federal (and state) budgets. While this may be wishful thinking to many, it is flawed, as any investor in an S corporation knows.

6. U.S. Code, CONG. AND ADMIN. NEWS 4876 (1959) (emphasis added).

7. *Gross v. Comm'r*, T.C. Memo. 1999-254, *aff'd*, 272 F.3d 333 F.3d (6th Cir. 2001); *Wall v. Comm'r*, T.C. Memo. 2001-75; *Adams v. Comm'r*, T.C. Memo. 2002-80; *Heck v. Comm'r*, T.C. Memo. 2002-34; *Dallas v. Comm'r*, T.C. Memo. 2006-212.

So how do our investors—who are looking for the amount of cash that will end up in their pockets—view the S corporation in reality? At the time of this publication, federal personal and corporate income tax rates are nearly equal, and investors must pay taxes on the entire corporate income, whether it is distributed or not. No corporate income taxes are being avoided by the S corporation investment. *However, investors will not have to pay dividend tax on any amount that is distributed to them—the precise result Congress intended.* Therein lies the benefit of investing in an S corporation.

Valuing S Corporations by the Income Approach Requires Usage of Market Return Rates Derived from Public C Corporations

In a perfect world, we would not have to go to the public markets to get a rate of return to value the S corporation; instead, we would have rates of return that were appropriate for S corporation investors. Why do we need a rate of return to value an S corporation? Because, as shown in Chapter 5, value under the discounted cash flow method of the income approach is estimated using the following formula:

$$PV = \frac{E_1}{(1+k)} + \frac{E_2}{(1+k)^2} + \ldots + \frac{E_n}{(1+k)^n}$$

Where:

PV	=	Present value
$E_1 \ldots E_n$	=	Expected economic income in each of periods 1 through n
k	=	Discount rate (cost of capital)

In the above formula, the future cash flows usually are available from management's forecasts or budgets for the future and the discount rate or cost of capital are estimated by the business valuation analyst using empirical data on observed returns in the public market (i.e., risk-free rates, equity risk premium, size premium, industry risk premium). The observed returns in the public market are returns of public C corporations and a mismatch occurs when applying these returns to estimate discount rates for valuing private S corporations. The mismatch is that although the observed returns from public C corporations are returns after corporate taxes, but before personal taxes on dividends, they still reflect the individual investor's expectation that he or she will have to pay the taxes on dividends. In other words, it is the return that the investor accepts, fully knowing that he or she will have to pay another layer of taxes on dividends at the personal level. As we saw in the previous section of this chapter, an investor in an S corporation does not have to pay a second level of tax on dividends.

If we had such a rate of return empirically available from S corporations, we could use it to value the S corporation income directly. At present, analysts do not have such a rate of return available; they only have the rates obtained from the public markets. (Note that even if such rates of return were available, they would be questionable given the quality of reported small company earnings.) Rates of return in the marketplace are set using investors' expectations of paying a dividend tax, but the S corporation investor avoids those taxes. In using the rates of investors in publicly traded stocks to value the S corporation, we must adjust for the different tax expectations of the S corporation investor.

Public C Corporation versus S Corporation Pricing under the Income Approach—an Example

Expressed in its simplest form, value is a function of two things:

1. How much cash flow a company produces and
2. How much an investor will require for a rate of return to invest in that cash flow.[8]

Let's compare how that analysis applies to two companies: Publico, a company whose stock is publicly traded, and SubSco, a private S corporation.

Let's assume you invest $1,000 in Publico stock. You become an owner of Publico, just like the other hundreds (or thousands) of owners, yet you don't have to pay income taxes on the earnings of Publico because as a publicly traded C corporation, the company pays taxes at the corporate level. Assume further that in a given year, your share of Publico has $217 of pretax earnings, pays $87 of taxes (40.1 percent), and reports net income of $130, which it pays to you as a dividend.[9] Therefore, the $130 comes to you after payment of corporate taxes—a 13 percent ($130/$1,000) return on your investment. You only have to pay taxes on the $130 dividend that you received, at your individual tax rate, let's assume 20 percent. Accordingly, after paying $26 (20 percent of $130) in dividend tax, you pocket $104 ($130 – $26). Publico reports a 13 percent rate of return[10] (the $130 dividend it paid out divided by $1,000 you invested).

8. Richard A. Brealey & Stewart C. Myers, Capital Investment and Valuation (McGraw-Hill, Inc. 2003).

9. This is just for illustration purposes, since it is widely acknowledged that public companies rarely pay out 100% of their earnings as dividends.

10. For simplicity's sake, this analysis focuses only on dividend returns assuming that (1) all earnings are distributed and (2) net income equals cash flow (note public and private returns are actually made up of dividends and capital gains). The S corporation valuation models available in practice distinguish between current returns and retained net income.

Now let's say that instead of investing in Publico, you want to consider investing in SubSco, a private Subchapter S company. It is identical to Publico, except that it is privately held. The CFO predicts that your share of the company's pretax earnings for that year will be $217, which you will report as taxable income on your personal tax return and which you will receive in cash. As an S corporation shareholder, you will have to pay income tax on the corporate income allocated to you from SubSco. At your rate, you will pay $87 (40.1 percent) in federal and state income tax, leaving you with a net $130. Because it is an S corporation, you won't have to pay any dividend tax, so you will pocket the entire $130—$26 more than if you had invested in Publico.

How do we value SubSco? If one is using a public market-derived rate of return, value in the public markets is determined by looking into the future and trying to figure out how much cash will be produced *after taxes on corporate income have been satisfied, but before shareholder dividend taxes are assessed,* that is, before the "second level" of tax.[11] In the case of Publico, the cash flow we would measure is $130, and this would be the same cash flow if Publico were a private C corporation.[12] When it comes to SubSco, *the impact of taxes on its corporate earnings is no different, because those taxes on earnings must be paid; where they are paid from makes no difference to the investor.*[13] Therefore, when we value the S corporation, we would similarly measure the $130 of income available to the investor. However, SubSco's shareholder will not have to pay the dividend tax.

Once we predict how much cash we believe the investment will produce before shareholder-level (dividend) taxes, we then have to determine an appropriate rate of return for the investment. This rate of return is the second part of the value equation.

In our calculations for Publico, we determined the return to the shareholder as follows:

Amount Invested	$1,000
Times Publico Rate of Return	x 13%
Equals dividend to investor in Publico	$ 130

The most basic way to calculate value is to reverse this calculation and use a capitalization of dividends method, as follows:

11. We ignore, for this discussion, the impact of capital gains on the rate of return. However, both the public rates and the S corporation models have a capital gain component. For S corporations, we recognize this as the buildup in basis component, which will be discussed in a later section.

12. For the moment, this discussion sets aside the differences in how investors typically receive their returns from publicly traded C corporations versus private C corporations.

13. This statement sets minority and control issues aside, which may affect control over payment of distributions.

Dividend to investor in Publico	\$ 130
Publico rate of return	÷ 13%
Equals value of investment in Publico	\$1,000

If you know the dividend you expect to receive and the company's rate of return, you can calculate how much you should be willing to invest. These calculations for Publico confirm that value, rate of return, and the cash dividend to the investor are in sync with each other. Note that in deciding to accept the investment in Publico at a 13 percent rate of return, the investor expects to pay a dividend tax on the \$130 dividend he or she receives.

When we value an S corporation, we obtain information about its future cash flow from the company, factoring in the current industry and economic outlook. We reduce that cash flow by the taxes on corporate income that the individual investor will bear. Again, these taxes will be paid, and who pays them makes no difference to the investor. This is because the investor only cares about the amount that will end up in his or her pocket. The net (after-tax) amount is the amount that will be available as a dividend (the same as a "distribution" when we're talking about an S corporation) to the investor.[14] Thus, it is the net, after-tax cash flow that we will value. *We will set aside for the moment (but will not forget) the avoided dividend tax—a benefit that we will come back to later.* For now, we need to find information that helps us predict an investor's rate of return for the S corporation's net cash flow.

For this, the only place we can go for meaningful, substantive guidance is the public stock markets. In our example, the rate of return from the public stock markets is 13 percent.[15] Remember, this is a rate of return after corporate income taxes and before the investor's dividend taxes. From an investor in the public market's point of view, this rate is acceptable and is one that would induce a \$1,000 investment in Publico, knowing that after payment of dividend taxes, \$104 will end up in the investor's pocket.

Returning to our example, if we use this same rate of return to value SubSco's after-corporate tax income, we would get the same answer—that the investment is worth \$1,000. However, we know that the cash that would end up in your pocket is more for your investment in SubSco than for one in Publico—so all things being

14. The degree to which the company pays out the available cash flow as current dividends influences the valuation in terms of (1) current recognition versus retained net income (basis), which may be deferred, and (2) control versus minority issues.

15. Returns in the public markets are made up of dividends and capital appreciation; in valuing the S corporation, we recognize the corresponding benefits as (1) the avoided dividend tax and (2) retained net income, which the models assume equals (dollar-for-dollar) capital appreciation. The example in this chapter focuses solely on the avoided dividend portion of the valuation model. Once understood, the concept (and the discussion) extends to the benefit of the retained net income.

equal, you should be willing to pay more than $1,000. Why? Because you get to keep $26 more than if you invested in Publico.

This is the benefit of the avoided dividend tax. But how much more should you be willing to pay? And how do you measure that in terms of value? Understanding the two-part answer to these questions is the foundation for the value differential between the publicly traded C corporation shareholder and the S corporation shareholder.

Value of the Avoided Dividend Tax

In simple terms, the additional cash in the investor's pocket leads to additional value.

For SubSco, we calculate the additional value the same way we always do: additional cash flow divided by rate of return. In this simple example, we have:

Dividend tax avoided (equals additional cash to investor compared to publicly traded C corporation)	$ 26
Divided by rate of return from public markets	÷ 13%
Equals value of dividend tax avoided	$200

Adding this to the value determined for Publico tells us that you should be willing to invest $1,200 in SubSco—the $1,000 that you would be willing to invest in Publico plus $200 for the value of the avoided dividend tax.[16]

This calculation results in a premium for the S corporation of 20 percent, relative to the publicly traded C corporation, for the value of the avoided dividend.[17]

In conclusion, when we value an S corporation using the income approach, the only rate of return we have available comes from C corporations in the publicly traded stock markets. Immediately, we find the rate of return does not match the cash flows. The public stock market investors set their rate of return requirements based on an expectation of having to pay a dividend tax when they receive their cash returns.

16. Another issue that is part of the S corporation valuation method is the value derived from the ability to build up retained net income. The calculations presented so far assume that the company pays out 100% of its profits to the investor. It gets a little more complicated when the company retains some of the earnings, increasing the investors' basis in the stock. In that case, the benefit of the avoided dividend tax is balanced by the avoidance of a portion of capital gains taxes when the investor sells the S corporation stock in the future. While this discussion is beyond the scope of this text, more details can be found in Nancy Fannon's book (*see supra* note 1).

17. This is a simple example of a capitalization model, as opposed to a discounted cash flow model. As such, it assumes perpetual S corporation benefits. This important and material built-in assumption in a capitalization model is one the analyst should make only after understanding the facts and circumstances of the subject company and assessing its implications on the valuation.

We use this same rate of return to value the S corporation cash returns, yet investors pay no dividend tax. Thus, for the income approach, we have to account for this benefit.

Specific S Corporation Issues under Other Valuation Approaches and Methods

When applying a guideline public company method, it is appropriate to consider a benefit of a similar magnitude as we already discussed for the income approach, for the multiples are derived from the public marketplace, where, once again, investors pay a dividend tax.

What about the transaction method? Essentially, when we value an S corporation using the transaction method, particularly when compared directly to other S corporations, we have already valued the entity by comparison to other, similar private corporations, which are most likely subject to the same or similar benefits. This is unlike an income approach valuation, where the purpose of the S corporation adjustment is to measure the difference in cash flow expectations inherent in the rate of return from the public marketplace (which does not include data from S corporations, but this is what analysts typically use in the income approach) compared to the cash flow expectations of an investor in an S corporation. Therefore, when using a transaction method, because we have already valued the company by comparison to other companies like it, we need not take any additional premium or detriments into account. (About half the transactions in the Pratt's Stats database are S corporation.)

Similarly, in the net asset value (NAV) method, one is accounting for the fair market value of the company's assets and liabilities. Because we are not valuing the net assets by reference to a publicly traded stock, we need add no premium.

References

Fannon, Nancy. "Valuing Controlling Versus Minority Interests in S Corporations." *Business Valuation Review* 26:4 (March 2008).

Kasper, Larry. "S Corporation Valuations—An Analysis in Search of a Solution." *Business Valuation Review* 26:4 (March 2008).

Laro, David, and Shannon P. Pratt. "Valuation of S Corporations and Other Pass-Through Tax Entities: Minority and Controlling Interests." In *Business Valuation and Taxes: Procedure, Law and Perspective*. New York: John Wiley & Sons, 2005.

Pratt, Shannon P., and Roger J. Grabowski. "Cost of Capital of Interests in Pass-Through Entities." In *Cost of Capital: Applications and Examples,* 3rd ed. New York: John Wiley & Sons, 2008.

Chapter 24

Valuation Reports

This chapter was contributed by Nicholas J. Mastracchio, Jr., Ph.D., CPA. Dr. Mastracchio practices business valuation from Marco Island, Florida, and Adirondack, New York. He wrote his first book on valuations in the mid-1980s and the AICPA used it to instruct CPAs in business valuation procedures. His testimony has established case law in New York in an oppressed minority shareholder action. In this chapter, Dr. Mastracchio points out the type of valuation reports you may receive and what the content of the reports should be.

There are several types of valuation reports. The most common is the full comprehensive report that discloses sufficient information for the reader to understand the data gathered, the analysis and rationale used, and how the estimate of value was determined. There is also a summary report that is a condensed version of the comprehensive report. It is also possible for the valuation analyst to perform a calculation requested by a client, which may include hypothetical assumptions. An oral report also may be rendered. The valuation analyst generally is allowed to vary the content of the report for a valuation to be used in a trial, arbitration, or similar proceeding or in a government administrative proceeding.

Appraisal Report

This is a comprehensive report. The USPAP refers to it as an "Appraisal Report." The ASA refers to it as an "Appraisal." The AICPA refers to it as a "Detailed Report."

This report should include the following data:

Introduction

This section should provide sufficient information to enable the reader to understand the engagement and includes:

Who the Client Is
The report probably will contain some type of cover letter or letter of transmittal that will be addressed to the client. However, the introduction usually includes an identification of the client and intended users.

The Intended Use of the Valuation
The reader needs to know the intended use of the valuation to understand the standard of value used and other decisions made by the valuation analyst.

What Is Being Valued
This section identifies whether an entire company or a partial interest is being valued.

Effective Valuation Date
The date of the valuation is identified. Generally, the valuation analyst only can use information that was available or could have become known at the date of the valuation. Statistical information released after this date that compiles information prior to this date usually is allowed.

The Degree of Control
If the valuation is of a partial interest, the degree of control is important in normalization decisions, lack of control discounts, and/or control premium considerations. The interest being valued and the distribution of the remaining interests are disclosed to allow the reader to appreciate the governance environment.

The Marketability of the Interest
The size of the company and its ability to go public, along with any restrictions by government regulation, supplier restrictions, or shareholder agreements is provided for the reader to understand the valuation analyst's consideration of any lack of marketability discount.

The Standard of Value Being Utilized
The standard of value used in the report must be stated and the source of that standard cited.

Scope of Work

Any scope limitations experienced in conducting the valuation and the valuation analyst's assessment of the consequences of the opinion are disclosed.

Specialists

A description of any specialists used by the valuation analyst and to what extent they have incorporated their work in the report is explained.

Hypothetical Conditions Used

If the valuation analyst relied upon hypothetical conditions, they should be disclosed.

Professional Standards Followed

For example, the USPAP was the guideline.

Any other information that assists in understanding the engagement should be included.

Sources of Information

This section, which allows assessing the extent of the valuation analyst's research, should include:

Extent to Which the Facilities Were Visited and Persons Interviewed

The valuation analyst normally will have visited the company's facilities or if there are multiple locations the report will identify which facilities were visited. The report also will identify the names and positions of those who were interviewed.

Financial Information

The financial statements should be discussed. If a CPA has a cover letter with the statement, it should be noted whether the statements were compiled, reviewed, or audited. If the valuation firm was associated with the financial statement preparation, that also should be noted. The information may have been acquired from or reconciled with tax returns. If so, the tax returns, and whether they were prepared internally or by an outside professional, should be noted.

Economic Conditions
The valuation analyst will report on general economic conditions that affect the risks associated with the company being valued. The sources, both government and private, should be identified in the report.

Industry Data
The specific attributes of the company's industry should be researched by the valuation analyst to assess the forecasts and risks that are inherent in the industry. The data obtained and its relevance will be discussed here.

Other Empirical Data
There may be information available regarding the segment of the industry that the company specializes in, for instance, information on the specific products and possible substitute products or other empirical information the valuation analyst found meaningful.

Qualitative Analysis of the Company

The valuation analyst should describe the company in qualitative terms. The valuation analyst needs to assess the strengths, weaknesses, opportunities, and threats of the company to determine the appropriate discount rate. This section provides the reader with the qualitative aspects of the analysis and includes:

Background and History
The history of the company including the operational changes over the years and the ownership description and changes should be discussed. The organizational structure of the company and management depth also will be disclosed.

Product and Services
The main activities that generate the primary revenues should be described.

Demographics
The geographical markets and their economic status also should be disclosed in the report.

Customers and Suppliers
To the extent that it can be accomplished without compromising trade secrets, the bargaining power of customers and suppliers should be disclosed. This may include the risk of reliance on a small number of either group.

Threat of New Entrants

The ability of new companies to enter the field is a factor of risk and the assessment should be disclosed.

Technological Risk

The analysis of the technological risk that the company is facing may be discussed if it is significant to the operations.

Environmental Risks

Although the report will have a disclaimer on environmental compliance, the environmental risks will be considered and should be disclosed.

Regulatory Risks

The current and potential regulatory environment should be disclosed.

Sociocultural Risk

Trends in products may have an impact for the company and, if so, should be discussed.

Global Risk

Imports of products and outsourcing of services may have an impact on the company and need to be assessed and disclosed if necessary.

Strategic Plans

The company's plans for the future, including critical success factors, need to be disclosed to fully understand the forecast and risks.

Staff

The intellectual value of the workforce skills established in the company in many cases is a factor that affects risk and may need discussion.

Ownership Interest

If the valuation is of a partial interest in the company, the capital structure is important and a description of the ownership interest and the impact on the interest being valued will be discussed along with any restriction on the sale of the security.

Quantitative Analysis

The historical financial data of the company is analyzed in a valuation to determine trends in profitability, financial health, and comparison with industry statistics. The report should include the following:

Liquidity Ratios
These ratios measure the ability of the company to meet current obligations with cash or assets that can quickly be turned into cash.

Profitability Ratios
These ratios measure the ability of the company to generate net income.

Activity Ratios
These ratios measure how efficiently the company manages its resources.

Leverage Ratios
These ratios measure the degree the company relies on debt financing and the ability to survive a downturn in profitability.

Sales and Profit Trends
The trends in the performance of the company should be presented that should reconcile with any forecasts used in the valuation.

Normalization and Control Adjustments

Based upon the financial analysis and consideration of the ownership interest being valued, any normalization adjustments to the financial statements that make them more predictive of future results under new ownership are explained in this section. These adjustments may include adjustments in the following categories:

Related-Party Transactions
Many possible transactions between the owners and the company are not arm's length. To the extent that they are not and can be changed by the interest being valued, they will be explained here.

Nonrecurring Items
The purpose of the adjusted financial statements is to reflect future operations. The valuation analyst would explain any unusual items that occurred in the past that were eliminated because they were not likely to reoccur.

Multioperations and Nonoperating Assets and Liabilities
The valuation analyst would explain any adjustment for company assets, liabilities, or income-producing items that are not relevant to operations and how they were treated.

Adjustments to Generally Accepted Accounting Principles (GAAP)
In some cases, the valuation analyst may feel that an adjustment of the statements' application of GAAP needs adjustment and should be explained.

Valuation Approaches and Methods Considered

The reader should be able to determine what valuation methodology was considered by the valuation analyst, including those that were rejected. The basic categories of methodology discussed would include:

Income Approach
The basic principle is that a business is worth the present value of its future benefits. One of the two following methods usually is used:

Capitalization of Cash Flow
Usually uses net cash flow rather than income. It is a single (usually normalized) number divided by a capitalization rate.

Discounted Cash Flow
This method projects annual cash flow for a number of years and then determines a value at the end of the projection period.

Market Approach
Another approach that can be persuasive compares the valuation subject at hand with other known transactions. Data would include:

Sales of Ownership Interest in the Same Company
The valuation analyst's explanation of the circumstances of any recent transactions in sales of the subject company stock is included here.

Sale of Ownership Interest in Similar Companies
In some cases, the valuation analyst may have been able to obtain data on similar company transactions.

Guideline Companies
Often the company is large enough and in an industry where there are publicly traded companies. If so, the valuation analyst will discuss the possibility of utilizing the publicly traded company data to interpolate the value of the closely held company.

Asset Approach

The asset approach should be considered, particularly when there is significant capital investment. The asset methods are:

Assets in Use

This method considers the value of the assets in a going operation.

Liquidating Value

This method considers the liquidation of the assets in either a forced or orderly manner.

Valuation Approaches and Methods Used

This section will provide the detail of the valuation methods used in coming to a conclusion of value.

Income Approach

The selection of which method to use under the income approach is explained here. The income approach can be on an invested capital basis, an equity basis, or both.

Definition of Income or Cash Flow Used

The valuation analyst will explain what was used as a measure of future benefits. This may be pretax or after-tax net income or net cash flow or some other measure the valuation analyst deems appropriate.

Appropriate Discount and Cash Flow Rates

The valuation analyst also will explain the discount and capitalization rates used. This may be an explanation of the buildup method, the capital asset pricing model, the weighted average cost of capital, or some combination of rates. The valuation analyst would explain how the data were obtained and how the discount and capitalization rates were determined.

Market Approach

Sales of Ownership Interest in the Same Company

The similarity of ownership percentage, the timing of the transactions, the extent that the transactions were utilizing the same standard of value, and the changes in the company since the transactions occurred all will influence the relevance of the transactions.

Sale of Ownership Interest in Similar Companies

If the valuation analyst decides that the data is worth consideration, it will be discussed here.

Guideline Companies

If guideline companies are used, the following will be presented:

Value Being Estimated—Depending on the comparison of the subject company with the guideline company, and the nature of the valuation, the valuation analyst will select either the total invested capital value of the firm, including debt, or the equity value, or both.

Profile of the Companies—A description of the companies will be provided in to judge the similarity of the company in risk, size, and diversity. Financial data and ratios will be provided and compared with the company being valued.

Multiples Considered—The valuation analyst will consider a number of multiples in determining what the indicators of value are. These include sales, book value, net income, net income before tax, cash flow, earnings before interest and taxes and earnings before interest, taxes, depreciation, and amortization. The valuation analyst will discuss which indicators were selected and why.

Adjustment of the Multiples—When the valuation analyst decides that the multiples should be adjusted to reflect the differences between the subject and the guideline companies, an explanation of the adjustments will be provided.

Asset Approach

Assets in Use

The use of the asset value is typically not very persuasive for it does not consider the fair value of any goodwill of the company. It may be provided by the valuation analyst to indicate a minimum floor value or be a value used if, in fact, there is no goodwill.

Liquidating Value

If the company is in or expected to be in liquidation, the value will be the liquidating value of the assets and the valuation analyst will explain the values determined in this section.

Valuation Adjustments

Often the valuation to this point is of the entity without adjustment for the specifics of the particular ownership interest being valued. At this point, the valuation analyst will discuss any adjustments. This may include:

Lack of Marketability Discount

The valuation analyst will decide the extent the value should be reduced because the interest is not readily marketable.

Lack of Control Discount

If the interest being valued is a minority interest, the valuation analyst will discuss the discount for this fact.

Key Man Discount

In some circumstances, the loss of an owner who is vital to the business may produce a discount. If so, the valuation analyst will discuss the discount taken.

Trapped in Capital Gains

If the valuation analyst determines that a reduction needs to be made because of a lower basis in assets than their fair market value, the calculation of the reduction will be provided here.

Control Premium

If the interest is a controlling interest, the valuation analyst may decide that a premium exists. If so, it would be discussed in this section.

Nonoperating Items

If there are assets or liabilities that are not necessary to the operations, the valuation analyst would have taken them out of consideration in the normalization process. At this point, the valuation analyst would explain how they would now affect the value of the company.

Excess or Deficient Operating Assets

If there are excess operating assets, the valuation analyst will discuss additions to the value. Conversely, if there are deficiencies that need to be corrected, the valuation analyst will discuss reductions to the value.

Representations of the Valuation Analyst

The report should include the representations of the valuation analyst and the signature of the person taking responsibility. This may be accomplished in this section or in other places in the report. It should include:

Assumptions and Limiting Conditions
The report should provide what assumptions and limitations exist. This may appear in an appendix with a reference in the main report.

Reliability of the Sources
The report should acknowledge the fact that the sources used are deemed reliable but that no independent validation was performed.

Restricted Use
Any restrictions on the use of the report should be noted.

Fee
The report should disclose whether the fee is independent of the conclusions or is contingency-based.

Outside Specialist
If the valuation analyst used an outside specialist, this should be disclosed along with the degree of responsibility the valuation analyst is taking for the work.

Updates
Unless agreed to otherwise, the valuation analyst will state that there is no responsibility to update the report.

Qualifications of the Valuation Analyst

A summary of the background and qualifications of the valuation analyst should be provided.

Conclusion of Value

The report will have a section either near the front or at the back that will provide a conclusion of value.

Summary Report

An abridged report also may be given. It will contain less detail than a comprehensive report and the valuation analyst may decide to restrict the report to those who commissioned it. The USPAP calls this a "Restricted Use Report" and the ASA calls it a "Limited Appraisal." The report would include the following portions of a comprehensive report:

Introduction
- Who the client is
- The purpose of the valuation
- What is being valued
- Effective valuation date
- Report date
- The intended users
- The degree of control
- The marketability of the interest
- The standard of value being utilized
- Scope limitations
- Specialists

Sources of Information
- Financial information
- Economic
- Industry data
- Other empirical data

Valuation Approaches and Methods Used
- Income approach
- Market approach
- Asset approach

Representations of the Valuation Analyst

Professional Standards Followed

Assumptions and Limiting Conditions

Restricted Use Solely for the Purpose Intended

Conclusion of Value

Agreed-upon Calculation Report

The valuation analyst can be engaged to perform specific calculations for a client. Because the engagement is limited to the calculations requested, the results do not form an opinion of value. Rather, they report the results of the calculations. The report may include the following:

Introduction
- Who the client is
- The nature of the calculations
- Any hypothetical conditions
- Report date
- The intended users
- Specialists

Summary of Calculated Value
Scope of Work
Representations of the Valuation Analyst
Professional Standards Followed
Assumptions and Limiting Conditions
Any Restricted Use

Oral Report

A report can be given orally. However, care should be taken to minimize the risk of misunderstanding. The presentation should include all the information the valuation analyst believes necessary to adequately provide information regarding the scope, assumptions, limitations, and results of the engagement.

Exceptions to the Report Contents

The valuation analyst generally is allowed to vary the content of the report from the one presented here for a valuation expected to be used in a trial, arbitration, or similar proceeding or in a government administrative proceeding. However, the scope of the work should remain the same.

Chapter 25

Checklist for Reviewing a Business Valuation Report

This chapter is free from copyright restrictions. Readers are free to make copies of it to use as worksheets when reviewing reports of their own appraisers and/or opposing appraisers. Copies also may be distributed to others—attorneys, clients, judges, etc.

Each line item has a box to the left that can be used for an "x," "o," etc. Space is available beneath the lines to include figures, notes, etc. For example, under the heading "Financial Statement Adjustments" in the Income Approach, line item "compensation," one might enter $120,000.

When comparing your analyst's report with an opposing analyst's report, it might be convenient to place these sheets side by side for an item-by-item comparison. This checklist is applicable to a comprehensive level of report but also may be used for a summary report.

This checklist was prepared by Shannon Pratt, CEO, and Alina Niculita, President, Shannon Pratt Valuations, Inc., 6443 S.W. Beaverton Hillsdale Hwy., Ste. 432, Portland, OR 97221, shannon@shannonpratt.com, alina@shannonpratt.com, (503) 459-4700, www.shannonpratt.com.

Credentials of Report Preparer(s)

Even though this usually is in an appendix in the back of the report, most attorneys like to review it first so that they know whose work product it is as they examine the report.

Academic Degrees (Location in report page, exhibit, appendix, etc.)

- ❑ PhD — Doctor of Philosophy
- ❑ DBA — Doctor of Business Administration

- ❑ MS — Master of Science
- ❑ MBA — Master of Business Administration

- ❑ BS — Bachelor of Science
- ❑ BA — Bachelor of Arts

- ❑ Other: ____

Professional Designations (Chapter 30 for explanations of these and others)

- ❑ CFA — Chartered Financial Analyst
- ❑ FASA — Fellow of the American Society of Appraisers
- ❑ ASA — Accredited Senior Appraiser
- ❑ AM — Accredited Member
- ❑ MCBA — Master Certified Business Appraiser
- ❑ ABAR — Accredited in Business Appraisal Review
- ❑ CBA — Certified Business Appraiser
- ❑ CPA/ABV — Certified Public Accountant/Accredited in Business Valuation
- ❑ CVA — Certified Valuation Analyst
- ❑ AVA — Accredited Valuation Analyst (a CVA who is not also a CPA)
- ❑ CBV — Certified Business Valuer (Canada)
- ❑ ARM — Appraisal Review and Management

Other: ____

Introduction (Chapters 1 and 2)

Effective valuation date(s)?

____

Standard (definition) of value?

____

Sources of authority for the standard of value?

Federal or state statute (specify)?

Revenue ruling (specify)?

Articles/bylaws?

Buy-sell agreement?

Other agreement (e.g., arbitration agreement)?

Was the stated standard of value appropriate for the situation?

Level of value (e.g., control, marketable minority, nonmarketable minority)?

Name of entity?

State of incorporation or registration?

Type of entity (e.g., corporation, S corporation, general partnership, limited partnership, etc.)?

Proportion of entity (if less than 100 percent, specify exact percentage or number of shares; if more than one class of ownership, e.g., common/preferred, voting/nonvoting, should have a diagram showing the capitalization)?

Purpose of valuation?

____

Who is the client for the appraisal?

____

Who (what entity) performed the appraisal?

____

Date appraisal completed?

____

Economic Analysis (Chapter 14)

Is it relevant?

____

Does it tie in with and support other parts of the valuation report?

____

Industry Analysis (Chapter 14)

Is it relevant?

____

Does it tie in with and support other parts of the valuation report?

____

Financial Statement Adjustment (Chapter 12)

Were there any adjustments to the subject company's financial statements?

___ No ___Yes

If yes, state year, item adjusted, amount, and reason.

____

If no, was there a statement that the statements were analyzed and no adjustments were necessary?

____

Were there any adjustments to guideline company statements?

___ No ___Yes

If yes, state company, year, item adjusted, amount, and reason.

____

If no, was there a statement that the statements were analyzed and no adjustments necessary?

____

Financial Statement Analysis (Chapter 13)

Is it performed on adjusted or preadjusted statements? (It normally should be performed on statements after adjustments.)

____

If the guideline company method was used, was there a comparative analysis table?

____

Were the subject's strengths and weaknesses compared to the guideline companies reflected in the valuation multiples used?

____

Was there a table comparing the subject company to industry averages?

____

If so, what source was used for the comparison?

____

Were the relative strengths and weaknesses reflected in the valuation multiples and/or discount rates?

____

Reasonable Compensation (Chapter 11)

Was a reasonable compensation adjustment made?

___ No ___Yes

If yes, how much (state for each year if multiple years)?

____

Whether a compensation adjustment was made or not, was it addressed adequately?

___ No ___Yes

Source of information for compensation adjustment (name of source, issue, category)

____

Discounts and Premiums (Chapter 15)

Was there a control premium?

___ No ___Yes

If so, how much?

____

Was there a discount for lack of control (sometimes called a minority discount)?

___ No ___Yes

If so, how much?

____

What data and/or rationale was used to quantify the control premium or discount for lack of control?

____

Was there a discount for lack of marketability?

___ No ___Yes

If so, how much?

____

What database(s) was used in support for the amount of the discount for lack of marketability?

____

Did they apply any other premiums or discounts?

___ No ___Yes

If so, which one(s)?

____

Amount of each?

____

Method(s) Used (Chapter 3)

Income Approach (Chapter 5)

- ❑ Discounted cash flow
- ❑ Capitalization of cash flow
- ❑ Other ______________________________

Market Approach (Chapter 6)

- ❑ Publicly traded guideline companies
- ❑ Transaction method (sales of entire companies)
- ❑ Past transactions in the subject company
- ❑ Rules of thumb
- ❑ Other ______________________________

Asset Approach

- ❑ Adjusted net asset value (Chapter 7)
- ❑ Excess earnings method (Chapter 8)
- ❑ Other ______________________________

Income Approach (Chapter 5)

Discounted Cash Flow Method

- ❑ Source of projections
- ❑ Date projections prepared
- ❑ Adjustments to projections (Chapter 12)
  - ❑ Compensation
  - ❑ Source of compensation adjustment
  - ❑ Rent
  - ❑ Nonrecurring items
  - ❑ Discontinued items
  - ❑ Inventory accounting
  - ❑ Depreciation/amortization/depletion
  - ❑ Net operating loss carryforwards
  - ❑ Excess assets (excess cash or nonoperating assets)

- ❑ Taxes
  ____
- ❑ Other
  ____

Discount/Capitalization Rate for Equity (Chapter 5)

- ❑ Buildup method
  - ❑ Risk-free rate
    ____
  - ❑ Source of risk-free rate
    ____
  - ❑ Equity risk premium
    ____
  - ❑ Source of equity risk premium
    ____
  - ❑ Size premium
    ____
  - ❑ Source of size premium
    (Note: When Morningstar is used, the equity risk premium and size premium are separate numbers; when Duff & Phelps is used, the equity risk premium and size premium are combined into a single number. Many analysts today use both Morningstar and Duff & Phelps.)
    ____
  - ❑ Industry adjustment
    ____
  - ❑ Source of industry adjustment
    ____

- ❑ Specific company adjustment
  ____
- ❑ Was there adequate explanation for the company specific adjustment?
  ____
- ❑ Growth rate
  ____
- ❑ Explanation for growth rate
  ____

❑ Capital asset pricing method

- ❑ Risk-free rate
  ____
- ❑ Source of risk-free rate
  ____
- ❑ Equity risk premium
  ____
- ❑ Source of equity risk premium
  ____
  - ❑ Beta
    ____
  - ❑ Source of beta
    ____

❑ Size premium

❑ Source of size premium

(*Note:* When Morningstar is used, the equity risk premium and size premium are separate numbers; when Duff & Phelps is used, the equity risk premium and size premium are combined into a single number. Many analysts today use both Morningstar and Duff & Phelps.)

- ❑ Industry adjustment

  ____

- ❑ Source of industry adjustment

  ____

- ❑ Specific company adjustment

  ____

- ❑ Was there adequate explanation for the company specific adjustment?

  ____

- ❑ Growth rate

  ____

- ❑ Explanation for growth rate

  ____

❑ Weighted Average Cost of Capital (WACC) (Chapter 5)

- ❑ Equity rate (see previous pages)

  ____

- ❑ Debt rate (pretax)

  ____

- ❑ Source of debt rate

  ____

- ❑ Tax rate

  ____

- ❑ Source of tax rate

  ____

- ❑ Weight of equity
  ____
- ❑ At market
  ____
- ❑ At book
  ____
- ❑ Other
  ____
- ❑ Weight of debt
  ____
- ❑ At market
  ____
- ❑ At book
  ____
- ❑ Other
  ____

- ❑ Other components in capital structure
  - ❑ Is the midyear convention used?
    ____
  - ❑ Year-end convention?
    ____
  - ❑ Other
    ____
  - ❑ Is the terminal value discounted by the proper number of years?
    ____
  - ❑ Total value $__________________
  - ❑ Amount of total value accounted for by terminal value $__________________
  - ❑ Method of arriving at terminal value
    - ❑ Gordon growth model
      ____
    - ❑ Multiple of financial variable (specify which variable)
      ____
    - ❑ Other (e.g., liquidation value)
      ____

Guideline Public Company Method (Chapter 6)

Criteria for Selection

- ❑ Population(s) or database(s) searched ______________________
- ❑ Line of business ______________________
- ❑ SIC code ______________________
- ❑ NAICS code ______________________
- ❑ Size ______________________
- ❑ Position in industry ______________________
- ❑ Profitability ______________________
- ❑ Capital structure ______________________
- ❑ Territory ______________________
- ❑ Maturity of company ______________________
- ❑ Type(s) of customers served ______________________
- ❑ Date of prices ______________________

- ❑ Valuation date for subject company

  ____

- ❑ Dates of financial information

  ____

- ❑ List of companies

  ____

❑ List of rejects	❑ Reasons for rejection
______________	______________________
______________	______________________
______________	______________________

Financial Metrics

(For each metric used, the time frame, e.g., latest 12 months, latest fiscal year, five-year average, five-year weighted average, next 12 months forecast, etc.)

- ❑ MVIC/sales

  ____

- ❑ MVIC/gross profit

  ____

- ❑ MVIC/EBITDA

  ____

- ❑ MVIC/EBIT

  ____

- ❑ MVIC/book value of invested capital

  ____

- ❑ MVIC/adjusted book value of invested capital

  ____

- ❑ MVIC/discretionary earnings

  ____

- ❑ MVIC/other

  ____

- ❑ Price/sales

  ____

- ❑ Price/gross profit

  ____

- ❑ Price/earnings before taxes

  ____

- ❑ Price/earnings (net income)

  ____

- ❑ Price/book value

  ____

- ❑ Price/adjusted book value

  ____

- ❑ Price/other

  ____

Statistics Used

- ❑ Mean

  ____

- ❑ Median (The median generally is considered the preferable measure of central tendency among ratios, because the mean can be unduly influenced by extreme observations, especially on the upside. Sometimes analysts avoid this bias by eliminating ratios they consider not meaningful.)

- ❑ Standard deviation

  ____

- ❑ Coefficient of variation (Generally, the metrics with the lowest coefficient of variation are accorded the most weight because a low coefficient of variation indicates a tight clustering, implying that the market puts the most weight on those variables.)

- ❑ Does the analyst adequately justify where each multiple applied to the subject company falls relative to the range of observed multiples?

Weightings

- ❑ Does the analyst adequately justify which variable is accorded the most weight?

  ____

Transaction (Merger and Acquisition) Method (Chapter 6)

Criteria for Selection

- ❑ Population(s) or database(s) searched

  ____

- ❑ Line of business

  ____

- ❑ SIC code

  ____

- ❑ NAICS code

  ____

- ❑ Size

  ____

- ❑ Position in industry

  ____

- ❑ Profitability
- ❑ Capital structure
- ❑ Territory
- ❑ Maturity of company
- ❑ Type(s) of customers served
- ❑ Date of prices
- ❑ Valuation date for subject company
- ❑ Dates of financial information

❑ List of companies	Date of transaction	Acquirer	Special items

❑ List of rejects	❑ Reasons for rejection

Financial Metrics
(For each metric used, the time frame, e.g., latest 12 months, latest fiscal year, five-year average, five-year weighted average, next 12 months forecast, etc.)

❑ MVIC/sales
____

❑ MVIC/gross profit
____

❑ MVIC/EBITDA
____

❑ MVIC/EBIT
____

❑ MVIC/book value of invested capital
____

❑ MVIC/adjusted book value of invested capital
____

❑ MVIC/discretionary earnings
____

❑ MVIC/other
____

❑ Price/sales
____

❑ Price/gross profit
____

❑ Price/earnings before taxes
____

❑ Price/earnings (net income)

- ❑ Price/book value

- ❑ Price/adjusted book value

- ❑ Price/other

Past Transaction Method (Chapter 6)
This may be a good method for acquisitions made *by* the subject company as well as transactions in interests in the subject company.

Criteria for Selection

- ❑ Date of transaction

- ❑ Percentage of company

- ❑ Any special terms (specify)

- ❑ Value indicated $ ____________________

Financial Metrics
(For each metric used, the time frame, e.g., latest 12 months, latest fiscal year, five-year average, five-year weighted average, next 12 months forecast, etc.)

- ❑ MVIC/sales

- ❑ MVIC/gross profit

- ❑ MVIC/EBITDA

- ❑ MVIC/EBIT
  ____
- ❑ MVIC/book value of invested capital
  ____
- ❑ MVIC/adjusted book value of invested capital
  ____
- ❑ MVIC/discretionary earnings
  ____
- ❑ MVIC/other
  ____
- ❑ Price/sales
  ____
- ❑ Price/gross profit
  ____
- ❑ Price/earnings before taxes
  ____
- ❑ Price/earnings (net income)
  ____
- ❑ Price/book value
  ____
- ❑ Price/adjusted book value
  ____
- ❑ Price/other
  ____
- ❑ Weightings among methods in market approach
  ____
- ❑ Rationale for weightings

Excess Earnings Method (Chapter 8)

- ❑ Basis for adjusting or reclassifying line items to fair market value
  - ❑ Accounts receivable
  - ❑ Inventory
  - ❑ Plant and equipment
  - ❑ Land
  - ❑ Notes payable
- ❑ Off-balance sheet assets and/or liabilities brought onto balance sheet (list, with amounts and explanations)
- ❑ Rate of return on tangible assets
- ❑ Explanation for rate of return on tangible assets
- ❑ Rate of return on intangibles
- ❑ Explanation for rate of return on intangibles

Variable Capitalized

- ❑ Net cash flow
  ____
- ❑ Net income
  ____
- ❑ Other
  ____

- ❑ Adjustments to normalized past financial statements to make them, as realistically as possible, representations of future expected returns (see financial statement adjustment earlier in this chapter).
- ❑ Reconciliation of blended rate of return with capitalization rate derived from buildup method or CAPM?

  ___ No ___Yes

Rules of Thumb (Chapter 9)

- ❑ Source(s) (Cite which edition)
  ____
- ❑ Rule(s) used
  ____

Goodwill (Chapter 10)

- ❑ Amount of goodwill

  $________________

- ❑ How derived?

  ____

- ❑ Distinguished personal goodwill from enterprise goodwill?

  ___ No ___Yes

- ❑ If yes to above question,

  - ❑ How much (either $ or percent) to personal ________________
  - ❑ How much (either $ or percent) to enterprise ________________

- ❑ How justified?

Reconciliation of Indicated Values (Chapter 16)

- ❑ If a single method dominated the conclusion, did the analyst make a convincing case that that was the best method?

  ____

- ❑ If multiple methods were used, did the analyst use mathematical weighting ___ or subjective weighting ___?

- ❑ Were the weights convincingly supported?

  ___ No ___Yes

Overall Assessment

- ❑ Were the steps taken in the report consistent with the stated standard of value?

  ___ No ___Yes

- ❑ If not, where did they diverge?

  ____

- ❑ Were there any contradictions (e.g., industry section not supporting valuation section)?

  ___ No ___Yes

- ❑ If so, what were they?

  ____

- ❑ Did you notice any biases (e.g., tendency toward unsupported high or low valuation multiples and/or discount rate)?

  ___ No ___Yes

- ❑ If so, explain.

  ____

- ❑ Were there any mathematical errors?

  ___ No ___Yes

- ❑ If so, list:

  ____

- ❑ Was the report well documented (e.g., could another analyst find the source materials and replicate it)?

  ___ No ___Yes

❏ If no, note areas where documentation was lacking.

____

❏ Was the report fully defensible?

___ No ___Yes

❏ If no, list errors/areas of weakness.

____

Chapter 26

Admissibility and Impact of Expert Business Valuation Evidence

This chapter was updated from the First Edition by Noah J. Gordon, legal counsel for Shannon Pratt Valuations, Inc. Mr. Gordon is a regular contributor to publications on business valuation and law. The original chapter was contributed by Michele G. Miles, who serves as the Executive Director of the Institute of Business Appraisers. The chapter offers suggestions on selecting appraisers and provides numerous cases that have addressed the admissibility and weight accorded to expert business valuation evidence.
—S.P.

As the chapter title suggests, there are two critical hurdles regarding expert business valuation reports and testimony:

- Will the report and/or testimony be admitted into evidence?
- If so, what weight will it be accorded?

Two threshold questions determine the outcome of the first of these hurdles and affect the second one:

- Is the expert qualified on the subject for which he or she is presented?
- Is the basis for the expert opinion reliable?

Courts also may exercise discretion in determining whether or not the proffered expert evidence is relevant to the question(s) at bar.

Supreme Court Affirms Courts' "Gatekeeper" Role

Daubert v. Merrell Dow Pharmaceuticals

Perhaps the most quoted case of the 1990s is *Daubert v. Merrell Dow Pharmaceuticals Inc.*,[1] in which the U.S. Supreme Court affirmed the trial court's decision not to admit expert evidence regarding causation of a medical problem on grounds of lack of reliability.

The Court in *Daubert* explained:

> Faced with a proffer of expert scientific testimony, then, the trial judge must determine at the outset, pursuant to Rule 104(a), [FN10] whether the expert is proposing to testify to (1) scientific knowledge that (2) will assist the trier of fact to understand or determine a fact in issue. This entails a preliminary assessment of whether the reasoning or methodology underlying the testimony is scientifically valid and of whether that reasoning or methodology properly can be applied to the facts in issue. We are confident that federal judges possess the capacity to undertake this review. Many factors will bear on the inquiry, and we do not presume to set out a definitive checklist or test. But some general observations are appropriate.
>
> FN10. Rule 104(a) provides:
>
> "Preliminary questions concerning the qualification of a person to be a witness, the existence of a privilege, or the admissibility of evidence shall be determined by the court, subject to the provisions of subdivision (b) [pertaining to conditional admissions]. In making its determination it is not bound by rules of evidence except those with respect to privileges." These matters should be established by a preponderance of proof.

The Court then went on to list four factors to consider:

1. Whether the theory or technique can be (or has been) tested
2. Whether the theory or technique has been subjected to peer review and publication
3. Whether there is a known potential rate of error

1. 509 U.S. 579 (1993).

4. Whether the theory or technique enjoys general acceptance within the relevant professional community[2]

Since this decision was rendered, numerous trial courts have applied the *Daubert* factors, and several appeals court decisions have sustained, expanded, and interpreted them. The cases make it clear that the *Daubert* factors apply not only to scientific testimony, but to valuation and economic analysis testimony as well. In 2000, Federal Rule of Evidence 702 was amended in response to *Daubert*. The amendment affirmed the trial court's role as gatekeeper and provided some general standards that trial courts must use to assess the reliability and helpfulness of proffered expert testimony. The rule as amended provided that all types of expert testimony present questions of admissibility for the trial court in deciding whether the evidence is reliable and helpful (this is consistent with the result in *Kumho Tire Co. v. Carmichael,* discussed below). Consequently, the admissibility of all expert testimony is governed by the principles of Rule 104(a). Under that rule, the proponent has the burden of establishing that the pertinent admissibility requirements are met by a preponderance of the evidence.

The number of challenges to the admissibility of experts has dramatically increased since *Daubert* was decided, to the point where business valuation experts should expect to be challenged, almost as a matter of course.[3]

A great majority of courts have admitted the testimony and report evidence presented by proffered business valuation witnesses who have demonstrated their expertise in compliance with *Daubert.* There are, nonetheless, maverick courts that have ruled that business valuation is "junk science." The federal bankruptcy court in *In re Med Diversified, Inc.,*[4] which had previously qualified one of the more recognized authorities in the health-care valuation field, not only retracted its prior ruling on the

2. *Id.* While the *Daubert* standard focuses on a Federal Rule of Evidence, those states whose rules of evidence are modeled upon or have similar language to Rule 702 are allowing trial courts discretion in applying these criteria. *See, e.g.,* Leaf v. Goodyear Tire & Rubber Co., 590 N.W.2d 525 (Iowa 1999), which stated that the observations in *Daubert* will be helpful to a court in assessing reliability of evidence in complex cases, and Iowa trial courts accordingly may use the criteria at their discretion.

3. Deloitte & Touche LLP, The Financial Expert Testimony—Admissibility Standards Database. This database, launched in 2003, shows a steady increase in expert challenges in federal cases since 1993, the year *Daubert* was decided; according to the database, almost half of the challenges resulted in a partial or total exclusion of the expert's testimony.

See also Carol Krafka, Meghan A. Dunn et al., *Judge and Attorney Experiences, Practices, and Concerns Regarding Expert Testimony in Federal Civil Trials*, 8:3 Psychology, Public Policy, and Law 309–32 (2002). This article, based on surveys of judges and lawyers, indicates that judges are much more likely to scrutinize expert evidence in the wake of *Daubert*—and that the rate of exclusion has correspondingly increased.

4. *In re* Med Diversified, Inc., 2006 Bankr. LEXIS 1677 (Bankr. E.D.N.Y. 2006).

basis that the expert's report was biased, but took the opportunity to seemingly discredit the entire business valuation profession as based on "junk science." The court expressed "fundamental skepticism" about certain business valuation methodologies such as the comparison of data from public companies with that of a closely held business, the discounted cash flow method, control premiums, marketability discounts, and other generally accepted methods and data. The court also slighted the entire business valuation profession by characterizing it as a small coterie of self-certifying and self-validating individuals: "The dominant citations are to the writings of two or three consulting firms which hold themselves out as valuation experts either by self designation or by designation through the very small professional valuation societies they have formed for themselves."[5]

Other courts have not followed this line of reasoning. Another federal bankruptcy court, faced with the admissibility of one of the experts who had been excluded in *Med Diversified,* referred to *Med Diversified* as an "isolated" case and as not having any impact on the admissibility of the expert; that court also in no way questioned accepted business valuation methodologies.[6]

General Electric Co. v. Joiner

In *General Electric Co. v. Joiner,*[7] the Supreme Court concluded that courts of appeals must apply an abuse-of-discretion standard when they review a trial court's decision to admit or exclude expert testimony. That standard applies as much to the trial court's decisions about how to determine reliability as to its ultimate conclusion, the Supreme Court ruled. The Court also held that whether the specific *Daubert* factors are appropriate measures of reliability in a particular case is a matter the law grants the trial judge broad latitude to determine—the same broad latitude that the trial judge enjoys with respect to his or her ultimate reliability determination. In other words, "The permissible scope of expert testimony is quite broad, and district courts are vested broad discretion in making admissibility determinations."[8]

Kumho Tire Co. v. Carmichael

In *Kumho Tire Co. v. Carmichael,*[9] the U.S. Supreme Court clearly ruled that the *Daubert* factors and the trial court's "gatekeeping" function regarding the admission of expert testimony do not apply only to scientific experts. Rather, they apply to all technical or other specialized experts.

5. *Id.* at **23.
6. *In re* Doctors Hospital of Hyde Park, 2007 Bankr. LEXIS 605 (Bankr. N.D. Ill. 2007).
7. 522 U.S. 136 (1997).
8. Hill v. Reederei F. Laeisz G.M.B.H. Rostock, 435 F.3d 404, 423 (3d Cir. 2006).
9. 526 U.S. 137 (1999).

Writing for the Supreme Court in the *Kumho Tire* opinion, Justice Breyer made the following unambiguous statement:

> The Daubert "gatekeeping" obligation applies not only to "scientific" testimony, but to all expert testimony. Rule 702 does not distinguish between "scientific" knowledge and "technical" and "other specialized" knowledge, but makes it clear that any such knowledge might be the subject of expert testimony. It is the Rule's word "knowledge," not the words (like "scientific") that modify that word, that establishes a standard of evidentiary reliability.

Explaining the Court's agreement with the trial court's decision, Justice Breyer concluded:

> In *Daubert,* this Court held that Federal Rule of Evidence 702 imposes a special obligation upon a trial judge to "ensure that any and all scientific testimony . . . is not only relevant, but reliable." The initial question before us is whether this basic gatekeeping obligation applies only to "scientific" testimony or to all expert testimony. We, like the parties, believe that it applies to all expert testimony.

Two lawyers who also are business appraisers commented on the implications of *Daubert* for appraisal experts:

> The *Kumho* decision holds good news for business appraisal experts. The trial court, at least in cases where Federal Rules of Evidence apply, has wide latitude to apply whatever criteria it needs to fulfill its duty to make the threshold determination that the appraisal expert's opinion will be reliable. The underlying standard seems to be the same level of intellectual rigor that characterizes practice as a competent business appraiser.
>
> This suggests strongly that, instead of focusing efforts on meeting the four very specific criteria applied to the scientific testimony in *Daubert,* the business appraisal expert should concentrate his efforts on maintaining a degree of professional competence. The appraisal expert should be prepared to offer evidence that his appraisal has employed the same level of intellectual rigor that characterizes the practice of an expert in business valuation.
>
> Certainly there is no single rubric which will meet this evidentiary requirement in every single case, but evidence that the appraisal expert has performed his analysis and formed his opinion in conformance with the *Uniform Standards of Professional Appraisal Practice,* the *Business Appraisal Standards* of the Institute of Business Appraisers, and the *Business Valuation*

Standards of the American Society of Appraisers must be viewed by anyone as probative.[10]

The authors went on to suggest several suitable areas for inquiry by the Court:

- **Lack of bias,** or objectivity, is indicated by adherence to the type of independence mandated by the appraisal and ethical standards of principal professional appraisal societies.
- **Adequacy of inquiry,** which refers to the completeness of the appraisal expert investigation of the business and its financial condition.
- **Consideration of accepted methods.** The appraisal expert should be able to show that he or she has considered every appraisal method that is applicable and appropriate to the subject company.[11]
- **Logical support for analysis.** Appraisal procedures and techniques in accord with fundamental financial theory have evolved over the years and are reflected in the authoritative publications of professional appraisers. Unless otherwise supported, the expert's analysis should fall within the framework of this current body of knowledge.[12]

In addition to the standards cited by these authors, the standards of other organizations that accredit business valuation professionals, such as the AICPA's *Professional Standards* and *Statement on Standards for Valuation Services* (SSVS) or the National Association of Certified Valuation Analysts' professional standards, also might support a claim that an expert who adheres to them is professionally competent.[13]

Generally, *Daubert* challenges are made *in limine* after experts have been disclosed, but sometimes the *Daubert* hearing may occur as late as at trial.[14] A successful

10. Deirdre Russell & Steven F. Schroeder, *Implications of* Kumho *for Business Appraisal Experts*, Apr. 11, 2001, *available at* www.bvlibrary.com/bvresearch.

11. For an outline of the relevant body of knowledge, with references to where all aspects are discussed in detail, *see* SHANNON P. PRATT, BUSINESS VALUATION BODY OF KNOWLEDGE (2d ed., John Wiley & Sons 2003).

12. *Id.* at 3.

13. For a discussion of the professional organizations that offer accreditation in business valuation, *see* Chapter 1 in SHANNON P. PRATT & ALINA V. NICULITA, VALUING A BUSINESS: THE ANALYSIS AND APPRAISAL OF CLOSELY HELD COMPANIES (5th ed., McGraw-Hill 2008).

14. *See, e.g.,* Club Car, Inc. v. Club Car (Quebec) Import, Inc., 362 F.3d 775 (11th Cir 2004), where the court of appeals upheld the district court's holding of the *Daubert* hearing at trial, rejecting the argument that the hearing had been untimely and late. *Compare* FMS Inc. v. Volvo Constr. Equipment North America Inc., 2007 U.S. Dist. LEXIS 19517 (N.D. Ill. 2007) (the court rejected an attempt to resurrect a *Daubert* challenge post-trial as "sandbagging" and, quoting from another case (Alfred v. Caterpillar, Inc., 262 F.3d 1083, 1087 (10th Cir. 2001)), said "*Daubert* generally contemplates a 'gatekeeping' function, not a 'gotcha' junction."); CADCO Inc. v. Fleetwood Enters., 2007 Mo. App. LEXIS 458 (Mo. Ct. App. 2007) (appellate court, finding no plain error, rejected the attempt to review an expert's admissibility on appeal, noting that the party seeking review had ample opportunities below to challenge the expert's admissibility, but failed to do so).

challenge could hurt a case—or even derail it entirely—if the case rests primarily on the appraiser's theory or opinion.[15] To avoid the expert's disqualification, it is essential that an appropriate expert be carefully selected well in advance of disclosure deadlines and that the expert be directed to provide comprehensive and detailed support for his or her position as well as professional competence. The expert should emphasize that the methods he or she used were peer reviewed and are widely accepted in the financial and business valuation community. In responding to a *Daubert* challenge, the expert should detail the data and assumptions used, rather than focusing on the results.

Selecting and Evaluating the Appraiser

Business appraisers can have a range of backgrounds, including finance, accounting, academic, brokerage, and consulting experience. However, when hiring a business appraiser who will likely testify in a litigated (or arbitrated) matter, it is vital to concentrate on qualifications, training, experience in business appraisal, and the ability to communicate effectively. Detailed inquiry must be made into the following:

- As a preliminary matter, whether the appraiser has an interest in the subject company and is independent of the parties. The expert may not have a conflict of interest.
- Efforts made by the appraiser to gain formal training in the theory and application of business appraisal methodology, including continuing education.
- Active participation in professional activities and organizations, such as presenting at or attending professional seminars, authoring articles for professional publications, or authoring professional treatises and books. Such activities help the valuation expert keep up with the latest developments in the profession and also subject the appraiser's positions and methods to constant review by peers. Engaging in such activities will bolster the professional's standing as an expert and credibility for litigation purposes.
- Reports that have been prepared by the appraiser. While not every assignment calls for a written report, formal work product is a palpable demonstration of competence and evidence of the appraiser's ability to present a credible and organized conclusion. For example, in *In re Med Diversified, Inc.*,[16] although

15. *See, e.g.*, Zenith Electronics Corp. v. WH-TV Broadcasting Corp., 395 F.3d 416 (7th Cir. 2005), where the plaintiff's appraisal expert was disqualified because the trial court found that the expert was unable to adequately explain the theory supporting his testimony. The expert's testimony was key to the case, and without it, the plaintiff lost. The Seventh Circuit affirmed, concluding that the expert was not truly an expert where he relied on his own theory rather than on widely accepted analytic strategies that he could have deployed.

16. *In re* Med Diversified, Inc., 2005 Bankr. LEXIS 2236 (Bankr. E.D.N.Y. 2005).

the offered expert averred that his expert report was not to be read as a certified business valuation, and indicated that his support staff were certified business valuators who provided input into the report, the court precluded his testimony, among other reasons, because those valuators were not available for cross-examination. The court indicated it was not prepared to admit an expert report submitted by a corporate entity, saying that "the person who signs the report has to testify until the admission of his Report for all evidentiary purposes has been stipulated to."[17]

- Knowledge of the appraiser in the subject type of business. Regulatory, statutory, and geographic factors can dramatically affect business values, and the appraiser must have sufficient expertise to identify these factors and apply appropriate adjustments to value. However, be cautious with the business appraiser whose background is extensive within one industry if his or her main qualification is as an owner, chief executive officer, or other officer of a business within the industry.[18] Such "industry" people may perform appraisals by substituting their own judgment for that of the market and lack the needed objectivity. The essential element is knowledge of business appraisal. A good business appraiser can get the necessary industry knowledge, but an industry person without knowledge of the business appraisal discipline probably will not be able to do a comprehensive job.[19]
- Whether the appraiser relies on "canned" business appraisal software or software he or she personally developed.[20] While some of the appraisal software commercially available is of high quality, some programs lack flexibility and cannot be manipulated at the discretion of the user. The appraiser who relies

17. *Id.* at *17.

18. *See, e.g.,* KW Plastics v. United States Can Co., 131 F. Supp. 2d 1289, 2001 U.S. Dist. LEXIS 1630 (M.D. Ala. 2001) (company's CFO excluded from testifying because his testimony was not based with any degree of certainty in sound economic principles used in a reliable way—the court noted that it was not unilaterally prohibiting an in-house employee serving as an expert from relying upon his own experience, but that an employee serving as an expert must exercise the same professionalism and thoroughness as any other expert in the field); LifeWise Master Funding v. Telebank, 374 F.3d 917, 2004 U.S. App. LEXIS 13398 (10th Cir. 2004) (CEO was excluded from testifying because the court determined that he was not an expert in damage calculations and could not explain the model he used; the model was not regularly used for projecting future profits, was not peer reviewed, was not uniformly used in any industry, and was capable of manipulation).

19. *See, e.g.,* Guang Dong v. ACI Int'l, Inc., 2008 U.S. Dist. LEXIS 3881 (D. Kan. 2008), where the court admitted the expert, saying that the expert did not need "firsthand knowledge about [the defendant's] business structure" for his opinions to be admissible.

20. A distinction must be made between software written specifically for the performance of business appraisals and common spreadsheet software, such as Excel. Statistical software and graphics programs are a normal and appropriate tool for organization and evaluation of financial data, although their utility, like that of business appraisal software, depends on the skill of the user.

on canned software may substitute the programmer's judgment for his own or rely on a cookie-cutter approach to business appraisal.

Business appraisers who have developed their own appraisal software present different problems for counsel. Unless the appraiser is willing to divulge all the details of the software (and even provide a copy to the opposing appraiser), the valuation conclusion may not be sufficiently replicable to pass scrutiny under professional standards governing business appraisal.[21] The appraiser should thoroughly understand and be able to replicate and defend any of the component processes the computer has performed in determining the value of the subject firm.

- The professional standards adhered to by the business appraiser. Some appraisers apply different standards for "advocacy appraisals," that is, appraisals intended for use in litigation. The use of such differing standards is not appropriate. The expert should employ the same methods and standards whether or not the opinion is intended for courtroom presentation.[22]
- Whether the expert can communicate effectively. This is a key consideration for litigated (or arbitrated) matters. "No matter how brilliant the expert is or how impressive the resume, an expert is of little value if an average juror cannot understand the testimony."[23] Ask a potential expert about his or her track record as an expert witness. Inquire about his or her reputation and litigation experience. Pay attention to whether the individual is articulate, communicates without using excessively technical jargon, and is likable, rather than condescending, arrogant, or patronizing.

Professional Certifications and the Case for Peer Review

Whatever the background of the business appraiser, he or she should possess or be working toward one or more of the professional certifications available. Business appraisal designations are available to all appraisers, and counsel should note the substantial differences among these designations. For example, one difference is the requirement of peer review. It is possible for a business appraiser to be granted a professional designation without having to author a single report in an actual client assignment. It's also possible that, even though the designation requires demonstrated experience with appraisal assignments, the business appraisals performed may have

21. *See* the Appraisal Standards Board's Advisory Opinion 18 on the Use of an Automated Valuation Module (AVM) *in* The Appraisal Found., Uniform Standards of Professional Appraisal Practice (2008-2009).

22. *See* Kumho Tire Co., Ltd. v. Carmichael, 526 U.S. 137 (1999).

23. Robert A. Zupkus, *Using Experts Expertly*, GPSolo (ABA), July/August 2004, at 48–50.

involved flawed methodology. For these reasons, designations that involve peer review offer some assurance that the business appraiser's work product has passed juried scrutiny.

The CPA as Business Appraiser

While there are peculiar advantages to hiring someone with specific training in financial statement review as an appraiser, it is important to note that not all Certified Public Accountants are created equal, or are equally qualified. There are approximately 360,000 CPAs in the United States. Of this number, as of early 2010, around 2,800 have earned the Accredited in Business Valuation (ABV) designation awarded by the American Institute of Certified Public Accountants and only about 5,000 have the Certified Valuation Analyst designation of the National Association of Certified Valuation Analysts. It defies logic to assume that the remaining 327,507 CPAs are just as qualified.

Advantages

- The general practitioner's typical client list generally has a number of businesses whose financial statements are reviewed on a regular basis. Where the client list contains similar businesses, the accountant may have accumulated industry expertise. For example, in *Rossi v. Mobil Oil Corp.,*[24] the appellate court upheld the trial court's admission of expert testimony on profitability figures offered by the bookkeeper. The bookkeeper's client list included 200 service stations, which was a factor in the determination that he was "skilled" in the area. In *Floorgraphics, Inc. v. News America Marketing In-Store Services, Inc.,*[25] the court denied a motion to exclude the proposed testimony of a CPA and Certified Valuation Analyst (CVA), finding that these accreditations, along with his many years of experience, rendered him an expert who could testify on business damages and lost profits. Similarly, in *Guang Dong v. ACI International, Inc.,*[26] *the court admitted the testimony of an expert* who was a CPA with an ABV and who had provided expert testimony in a number of previous lawsuits and had worked in the field of "forensic accounting litigation" for approximately seven years. Based on the expert's experience and education, the court found the expert more than qualified to

24. 710 F.2d 821, 830 (Temp. Emer. Ct. App. 1983).

25. Floorgraphics, Inc v. News America Mktg. In-Store Servs., Inc., 2008 U.S. Dist. LEXIS 8263 (D.N.J. 2008).

26. Guang Dong v. ACI Int'l, Inc., 2008 U.S. Dist. LEXIS 3881 (D. Kan. 2008).

testify regarding lost profits, even though he did not have prior experience with the industry involved.[27]

- The full-time involvement with numbers, balance sheets, profit and loss statements, and tax laws.
- The availability of resources on the topic from membership organizations such as the American Institute of Certified Public Accountants.
- A good CPA is likely to have a general understanding of the operations of closely held businesses, their style of management, and financing needs and sources.
- Some CPAs are active in industry trade associations, which may offer extra insight for that particular industry.

Disadvantages

- The likelihood that the accountant (except for those who specialize in business appraisal) spends only a small percentage of time on business appraisal (a possible qualifications issue in court).[28]
- The nature of most accounting training emphasizes the objective historical perspective of compliance reporting. Business appraisal, on the other hand, typically involves, either directly or indirectly, the analysis of more subjec-

27. *See also* Trugreen Cos., LLC, Inc. v. Scotts Lawn Serv., 2007 U.S. Dist. LEXIS 10916 (N.D. Utah 2007) (Expert who was a CPA, certified fraud examiner, and certified insolvency advisor with 25 years' experience, while not possessing the "ideal" background to opine on lost profits and damages, nonetheless was qualified. The court said that "his lack of certain training or certification does not necessarily mean that he does not have the required expertise.").

28. *See, e.g., In re* Med Diversified, Inc., 2005 Bankr. LEXIS 2236 (Bankr. E.D.N.Y. 2005) (The court, excluding an offered expert, rejected the argument that substantive experience over 20-plus years as an accountant and as a liquidating agent or bankruptcy trustee in bringing avoidance actions in the bankruptcy court added up to a satisfactory substitute for formal education and training in business valuations and in peer recognition in business valuations, especially in the unique and highly regulated business of in-home health care services.). However, *see also In re* Doctors Hospital of Hyde Park, 2007 Bankr. LEXIS 605 (Bankr. N.D. Ill. 2007), where the court admitted the same expert who had been excluded by the Med Diversified court as an insolvency expert (but not a business valuation expert per se), noting that he had been qualified as an expert in insolvency in numerous other cases.

See also, e.g., Acker v. Burlington N. & Santa Fe Ry. Co., 347 F. Supp. 2d 1025 (D. Kan. 2004) (CPA admitted he was not qualified as an expert in lost profit projections); Sun Ins. Mktg. Network, Inc. v. AIG Life Ins. Co., 254 F. Supp. 2d 1239, 1245 (M.D. Fla. 2003) (testimony of expert as to the value of a business stricken because he "is a forensic accountant, not a business appraiser"); Beverly Hills Concepts, Inc. v. Schatz & Schatz, 717 A.2d 724, 732 (Conn. 1998) ("[A]n accounting degree alone should not qualify a witness to testify that a given volume of sales, for example, will continue in the future.") (internal quotations omitted); Santa Monica Picture, L.L.C. v. Comm'r, T.C. Memo. 2005-104 (2005) (CPA with national firm and with extensive experience with corporate NOLs excluded as to valuation of NOLs because "[this expert] . . . has no specific background in valuation; nothing in his testimony or report indicates that he is qualified to value the NOLs. . . ."

tive future projections. CPAs who have earned the ABV designation should be amply sensitive to these different orientations. CPAs without this designation may or may not have a background that supports the type of analysis required in most valuation assignments. There is nothing in the typical college accounting curriculum that addresses business appraisal.

- The possible current involvement of the accountant with the subject business. While economy and familiarity with the business might argue in favor of retaining the business's regular accountant to perform the appraisal, business appraisal standards could be construed to define the accountant's continued relationship with the client as "a contemplated future benefit," which might disqualify the appraisal opinion. A second reason against the use of the regular accountant in the role of business appraiser arises when the appraisal involves the interests of parties that, though joint when the accounting work was performed, may, for purposes of the business appraisal, now be adverse. Consider, for example, the accountant who has compiled the financial statements and prepared the tax returns for a corporation that is now the subject of a shareholder oppression action. Representing the minority shareholder, the accountant as business appraiser would scrutinize the corporate financial statements and might recast expenses charged to the business (such as travel, promotion, and entertainment expenses) as income that should be imputed to the shareholders—and in such a situation, it's possible that the majority shareholders would have more income imputed to them. The accountant-as-business-appraiser situation may create the impression that the accountant will cast the financial statements in favor of whomever is cutting the check for services. Although this impression may be completely wrong, the risk of raising such a red flag should be weighed carefully against the benefit of having a business appraiser who is familiar with the financials of the business. This scenario also may arise when the accountant prepares not only the tax returns for the business but also the personal returns of husband and wife. When the parties decide to separate and the accountant is asked to serve as business appraiser for only one spouse, the question of divided loyalties must inevitably arise. It's also likely that the accountant knows where too many skeletons are buried in both the business and personal financial profiles to be truly objective in the appraisal assignment.

The Financial Analyst as Business Appraiser

By a financial analyst in this context, we mean a securities analyst or someone schooled or experienced in corporate finance, not someone who has performed some type of clerical analysis of various records. For example, about 80,000 individuals worldwide possess the professional designation Chartered Financial Analyst (CFA), awarded by the CFA Institute, but of these only several hundred also have experience in closely held company valuation. Many of these also have one or more of the business valuation professional designations.

Advantages

- The discipline of business valuation is, in fact, an exercise in financial analysis. While business appraisal uses the tools of accounting (much as an engineer uses the tools of mathematics), it is the financial analysis of the accounting, industry, and economic data that leads to a conclusion of value.
- The CFA designation requirements are extremely rigorous. In terms of examinations, they are much more rigorous than any of the professional business valuation designations, including the equivalent of two years of academic accounting courses. You can be sure that the CFA is well schooled in the analysis of public company securities.
- If the person also has an academic degree with a major in finance, he or she should have a good grasp of what drives value. Many economists and corporate finance gurus take the position that the major objective of any firm should be to maximize shareholder value. Financial analysts are well steeped in the analysis of shareholder value.
- If the person is an investment banker with specific valuation experience and has testimony experience, e.g., someone active in mergers and acquisitions and/or with extensive experience in rendering and defending fairness opinions, that person can be a well-qualified expert with respect to valuations of public companies or large private companies.

Disadvantages

- Both the business school courses in finance and CFA study materials tend to be oriented to large companies, especially publicly traded companies. Some people with large-company orientations have trouble relating to smaller companies that often are the subjects of business appraisals. Small companies do not have finance departments, they might not have projections, there can be a lack of sophisticated accounting and other systems, even the owners can be less sophisticated. This transitioning can be difficult for the CFA and usually takes some time to occur.
- Financial analysts oriented to larger companies are proficient in the use of public company databases for market transactions, but often are not proficient with private company transaction databases, such as the *IBA Market Database, BIZCOMPS,® Pratt's Stats,™* and *Done Deals*.

- Financial analysts and investment bankers often are not attuned to being testifying experts and may not be familiar with valuation literature.

The Broker as Business Appraiser

If the business recently has been offered for sale, a broker already may be involved, and the client may be interested in using the broker as the business appraiser. Brokers in the community may offer appraisal services as an outgrowth of their practice. Many brokers who perform business appraisal have substantial experience and additional training and may have earned one or more professional accreditations in business appraisal; however, many have no formal training and a "shoot from the hip" approach may not match the assignment, especially for tax or litigation assignments.

Before agreeing to use a broker, ask if the person has the Certified Business Intermediary (CBI) designation offered by the International Business Brokers Association. Requirements for this designation include two days of recasting financial statements for business pricing and two days of business valuation.

Advantages

- The broker may have a "nose" for discerning the actual earnings of the business (as contrasted with the reported earnings). In many closely held businesses that depend on cash payments—including restaurants, retail stores, service businesses such as auto repair shops, and even professional practices where some patients pay in cash—the reported income may have only a tangential relation to actual revenues. By spotting those issues early, counsel can evaluate not only the real value of the business but also the ramifications of going forward with a valuation when the client may not have reported (and paid taxes) on all the income.
- Brokers deal in the world of "comparables"—similar sales—and may have internal sources of information for the application of the market approach, in addition to the sources mentioned above.

Disadvantages

- Many "business brokers" have practices that include business brokerage as part of larger real estate brokerage practices, and business sales may not constitute the majority of their traffic. Not only may their expertise in business sales be limited, but the broker who does mostly real estate sales or appraisals may not properly apply the market approach in the context of a business appraisal.

- Unless the broker has made a concerted effort to become educated by taking courses from the International Business Brokers Association, the American Society of Appraisers, the Institute of Business Appraisers, or other professional organizations, he or she may have little formal training in the review and adjustment of financial statements or other issues beyond the normal experience of business brokerage. This places the opinion at risk for errors and means the expert may not be able to replicate the appraisal process credibly for the trier of fact.
- If the broker is—or has been—involved in listing the business, or hopes to list the business in the future, there is a conflict of interest that may discredit or disqualify the valuation conclusion.

The Academic as Business Appraiser

Universities with schools of business, economics, or finance may have Ph.D.s or other faculty members who perform business appraisals in addition to their academic load. These academics may have backgrounds that include statistics or a focus on a particular industry that will suit the appraisal assignment. Even a small local college may have adjunct faculty members for whom teaching is only part of a day-to-day practice that includes financial, appraisal, and consulting services.

Advantages

- The academic may be published on business appraisal issues or may have performed academic studies in the particular industry that includes the subject business. This enhances his or her credibility.
- The academic typically will have resources readily available for research and analysis. He or she will be exposed to the latest writings on the topic and may have more time to follow trends in the development of appraisal methodology.
- Some academics (and not only those who are adjunct faculty members) perform "real-world" business consulting assignments as part of their academic role. For example, if the university has a Small-Business Development Center, the academic may have daily interaction with business start-ups and acquisitions as a counselor. Many graduate schools reach out to the local business community and offer continuing education to established professionals or targeted education to the lending industry or other professional groups. These real-life interactions can produce an expert who is simultaneously versed in the latest theory and grounded in the pragmatic world of business.

- Some academics' education, combined with the courses they teach and their work history, may qualify them as business valuation experts.[29]

Disadvantages

- The academic can be well versed in theory but have little practical experience in its application. This may be particularly true of the "career academic" who may have impressive credentials and a long list of writing credits but never may have actually completed an appraisal assignment.
- The academic appraiser may have natural teaching abilities that *should* enable him or her, as an expert witness, to communicate effectively and credibly to the trier of fact. However, academics may not possess the necessary translation ability to make important points in simple terms. Even an undergraduate business student will have a grasp of the terms that is far above the technical vocabulary of many jurors. Unless the academic can abandon jargon to state facts and opinions in simple language (and without giving the impression that the testimony is "dumbed down" for the audience), little will be gained from his or her impressive credentials.
- If the academic appraiser goes through life steeped in academia, there may be a tendency to apply radical or cutting-edge methodology rather than the tried-and-true business appraisal approaches with which the court has some comfort. Developing theories may merit close monitoring and eventually may be adopted into the conventional body of knowledge, but those who pioneer such methods in court without considering established approaches put the client at risk.
- An academic appraiser may be subject to challenge if he or she has no real-world transaction or business valuation experience.

Court Cases Involving Appraiser Challenge

Sometimes proferred appraisers are allowed to testify; then the court accords little or no weight to the testimony. This is often the case with industry experts or academics with-

29. *See, e.g.,* Tidwell Indus., Inc. v. Diversified Home Products, Inc., 2007 U.S. Dist. LEXIS 78227 (W.D. Tex. 2007), where the court admitted as an expert to value lost profits of a cabinet distribution company a finance professor whose master's program included courses relevant to corporate valuation—specifically, managerial accounting, accounting for financial decision-making, and financial management; whose doctorate program included courses in advanced financial management, the theory of finance, and a seminar in corporate finance; who taught finance and corporate valuation at the university level; and who, prior to teaching, had been a bank's senior vice president, served on the bank's loan committee, and assessed the capacities of businesses and individuals to repay loans. The court said, "Even though [the expert] has not previously done a valuation of a cabinet distribution business, he has the knowledge, skill, experience, training, or education to enable him to conduct such a valuation."

out business valuation credentials. A person with business valuation expertise is trained to gain familiarity with a new industry, but the industry expert or academic without business valuation credentials is not trained to gain business appraisal expertise.

The opinion of the Third Circuit in *Unisys Savings Plan Litigation*[30] illustrates the pitfalls of unwise appraiser selection. In an action brought by Unisys employees who participated in individual account pension plans maintained by their employer, the trial court excluded the testimony of the plaintiff's expert witness. The appellate court held that the witness was properly excluded. In its rationale, the court cited the criteria in *In re Paoli R.R. Yard Litigation*[31]: the court must find that the witness must be qualified to opine, that testimony of the expert will be reliable, and that the testimony will assist the trier of fact. The *Unisys* court applied this test to the credibility of the expert and decided that the witness's testimony did not "fit" for the following reasons:

1. The "education credentials were not of the highest caliber." (The expert witness in *Unisys* received his Ph.D. from a correspondence school.)
2. The witness's credential statements during voir dire were not consistent with prior deposition testimony.
3. The witness's expertise was in a related but not identical field. Life insurance was the subject of the proffered testimony, but the witness's expertise was in property and casualty insurance. Furthermore, substantial differences between the two were admitted by the witness. Industry specialists are particularly vulnerable on this issue. Often, the desire to continue to build an appraisal practice will tempt the industry specialist or general consultant to accept assignments beyond his or her expertise. Consider, for example, the dental industry specialist (whose credentials may be mainly a life career as a dentist) who appraises the practice of an orthopedic surgeon. A similar pitfall awaits the accountant with no formal business appraisal training, as any reasonable accountant would admit that not all accounting work involves appraisal. The broker who does few business appraisals is also at risk, as any reasonable broker should admit that there are substantial differences between brokerage and appraisals. The academic economist, statistician, or analyst may fare no better.

These "substantial differences" can even exist within a particular industry. Much has been written, for example, on the differences between publicly traded companies of moderate size and smaller privately held businesses within the same industry. For

30. 173 F.3d 145 (3d Cir. 1999).
31. 35 F.3d 717 (3d Cir. 1994).

example, in *Trustees of the University of Pennsylvania v. Lexington Insurance Co.*,[32] the appellate court upheld the trial court's disqualification of a claims examiner who offered expert testimony on the reasonableness of a $7 million settlement in a medical malpractice action. The court found that the witness had several years' experience as a claims adjuster but insufficient experience in claims of this magnitude.

Notwithstanding the need in some cases for appraisers to have knowledge of, or experience with, a particular industry or even with certain aspects of a specific industry, often such industry-specific knowledge or experience is not necessary if the appraiser has significant experience in business valuation and has peer-reviewed professional certifications. For example, in *Physicians Dialysis Ventures, Inc. v. Griffith*,[33] the business being valued was a dialysis center. Although the challenged expert had no experience with the dialysis business, the court did not hesitate to admit the expert, who in addition to being an author on lost profits calculations, was actively involved in the preparation of business valuations for more than seven years, was certified by both the American Society of Appraisers and the National Association of Certified Valuation Analysts, and held the CPA/ABV credential from the American Institute of Certified Public Accountants. Prior employers included "Big 4" accounting firms and at the time of trial, she was senior manager of her firm's Business Litigation Group. In addition, she had appraised a distributor, manufacturer, professional practice, physician's practice, outpatient surgical center, car dealership, restaurant, photofinisher, specialized metallurgical manufacturer, foreign sales corporation, and minority interest in a family limited partnership. Throughout her career, she formulated opinions in 60 valuation engagements, signed 17 reports, and made "significant contributions" to others. Thus, the court easily concluded that the expert "has developed specific expertise in the appraisal of business damages both in the form of lost profits and lost business value."[34] This reasoning also applies to the valuation of technology, i.e., the expert does not need to have technical know-how provided he or she has business valuation know-how.[35]

32. 815 F.2d 890 (3d Cir. 1987).

33. Physicians Dialysis Ventures, Inc. v. Griffith, 2007 U.S. Dist. LEXIS 78879 (D.N.J. 2007).

34. *See also, e.g.*, Popovich v. Sony Music Entm't, Inc., 2007 U.S. App. LEXIS 26863 (6th Cir. 2007) (the court admitted an expert who had minimal experience valuing certain intangible assets, but had extensive experience as a business valuation professional "sufficient to qualify him as an expert on the value of the contract right in this case"); Henry v. Champlain Enters., Inc., 2003 U.S. Dist. LEXIS 19138 (N.D.N.Y. 2003) (in an ESOP valuation case, the court stated, "While some measure of wariness is indeed expressed as to . . . [this expert]'s qualifications, it is here found, certainly at this stage of the proceedings, that his experience in the financial/securities field is sufficient. . . . As noted, the fact that his experience is not exclusively or largely devoted to valuing stock on behalf of a purchasing ESOP is not enough to exclude his testimony.").

35. *See, e.g.*, Tharo Sys., Inc. v. cab Produckttechnick GmbH & Co. KG, 2006 U.S. App. LEXIS 21895 (6th Cir. 2006) (valuation expert who lacked technical expertise on thermal transfer printers was qualified to testify on the value of the technology).

In contrast, business experience alone may not qualify an individual as a business appraisal expert. In *Rosvold v. LSM Systems Engineering, Inc.*,[36] the court did not admit as an expert an MBA graduate of the Wharton School of Business, one of the country's leading business schools, and a business executive to value a minority corporate interest. The court indicated that the proposed expert lacked any professional experience or credentialing in business valuation.

Even extensive experience in a particular industry may not suffice to qualify an individual to value an entity in that industry. For example, in *24/7 Records, Inc. v. Sony Music Entertainment, Inc.*,[37] the proposed expert had more than 40 years of experience as a consultant in the music industry and, in particular, in creating and developing start-up music companies. Nonetheless, the court found that the music consultant was "not licensed by any organization as a qualified appraiser, has no formal training in valuation, accounting, or finance, and has never read any scholarly treatises or materials on valuation." The court excluded this expert as well as an attorney who practiced in the music industry and had experience in the valuation, negotiation, and sale of assets similar to the subject record company's, finding that he, too, was neither licensed by an accredited appraisal organization nor specifically educated in business valuation.

Ultimately, the court usually will base its decision largely on the proposed expert's education and experience.[38]

The diverse backgrounds of business appraisers all have merits and demerits; often these qualities are not apparent until too late in the appraisal process. For these reasons, there is no real substitute for professional certification, particularly those certifications that include peer review. Proper planning and supervision are essential because an appraiser generally does not perform every aspect of a valuation. Also staff who have different skill sets and different education, training, and experience also can provide a breadth of quality control not available to small "solo" appraisers. Having a staff that works cooperatively as a "team" yet considers each person's perspective (even challenging other team members views) can provide new and important insights that can produce a more objective value conclusion.

36. Rosvold v. LSM Sys. Eng'g, Inc., 2007 U.S. Dist. LEXIS 82061 (E.D. Mich. 2007).

37. 24/7 Records, Inc. v. Sony Music Entm't, Inc., 2007 U.S. Dist. LEXIS 70374 (S.D.N.Y. 2007).

38. *See, e.g.,* Rogers v. Alexander, 2007 Tex. App. LEXIS 5105 (Tex. Ct. App. 2007) (court qualifies a CPA and certified managing accountant (CMA) as an expert in valuing home-health agencies where he has had experience with strategic planning, budgeting, cash management, book value, market value, and economics, and has specialized in Medicare matters and advised clients on buying/selling home-health agencies).

The Appraisal Opinion Must Stay within Expertise

Business appraisers are not a source of "one-stop shopping" for expert opinions. Areas on which the appraiser should *not* be asked to render an opinion include:

- The standard of value appropriate to the claim. For example, the issue of whether fair value or fair market value is the standard in dissenting shareholder cases is a legal call for which information should be provided to the business appraiser.[39] It is not the appraiser's job—nor within the appraiser's expertise—to determine these standards. Failure to provide the business appraiser with the correct standard of value (which should be cited in the report) may render the appraisal conclusion useless. Of course, a professional appraiser probably has a good idea of the appropriate standard of value. This is an issue that the lawyer and the appraiser should agree on at the outset of the assignment and should be included in the engagement letter.
- Interpretation of contractual rights of parties that may give them a right to buyout, first refusal, or appraisal, or that determine liabilities or ultimate facts. For example, in *Morse/Diesel v. Trinity Industries,*[40] a Certified Public Accountant attempted to testify regarding which party was responsible for construction delays and impact of various change orders. The trial court excluded the testimony under Federal Rule of Evidence 703, for there was no foundation for the CPA to have such an opinion. The appellate court agreed with the trial court's statement that:

> [I]n each and every one of the four examples given . . . the proffered testimony is qualitative testimony relating to the reasonableness of including certain work with [Morse/Diesel's construction expert's] calculation. We find that this witness is not qualified by knowledge, skill, experience, training, or education to render these sorts of qualitative opinions under *Daubert.*[41]

---

39. A scathing commentary on the overstepping of an economic expert can be read in *City of Tuscaloosa v. Harcross Chemicals*, 158 F.3d, 548, 567 (11th Cir. 1998). Although the testimony of this particular expert was not even challenged on these grounds, the court noted that the "testimony does indeed appear to warrant exclusion: specifically, [the expert's] opinions regarding the legal standards applicable to the case are outside of his competence as an economist and should be excluded. The same is true of [his] characterizations of pieces of documentary evidence as tending to show collusion; such judgments are for the court to make at summary judgment and for the trier of fact to make at trial. Furthermore, we point out that [his] professed market definition is clearly wrong." The court also noted that the expert's opinion may have been "one with an apparent eye toward litigation," perhaps explaining their pains to critique the expert unasked.

40. 67 F.3d 435 (2d Cir. 1995).

41. 67 F.3d at 444.

The attempt to use the CPA to bootstrap the construction expert's calculations on damages, or to add testimony lacking from another expert, was unavailing.

In *Dering v. Service Experts Alliance, LLC,*[42] the court struck the expert's opinion on punitive damages, indicating that it is the jury's role to set the amount of punitive damages and that to have an expert opine on these would invade the jury's "sacrosanct" role.

The structuring of an appraisal report to follow the organization of a statute, and that incorporates language from the statute, does not necessarily go beyond the scope of an appraiser's expertise. In *In re Joy Recovery Tech. Corp.*,[43] the business appraisal expert had referred to the Illinois Fraudulent Transfer Act (IUFTA) in his written report and lifted language directly from the statute. The court concluded that although the expert organized the disputed section of his report to correspond to subsections of the IUFTA, the actual analysis was consistent with principles of accountancy and therefore did not render it an impermissible legal conclusion.

Source Documents Must Be Those "Typically Relied Upon" by Appraisal Experts

The initial phases of a business appraisal assignment include the review of financial records on the subject business. Throughout the assignment, the appraiser continues to analyze and apply information gleaned from these records. When the appraiser relies on inappropriate or incomplete information, the entire opinion can fail for lack of a credible basis. If the appraiser is aware that the information is incomplete, this should be noted in the limiting conditions.

The risk of relying on the wrong type of documents is illustrated in *Target Market Publishing, Inc. v. ADVO, Inc.*[44] In that case, the parties entered into a joint venture to produce and market direct-mail advertising for auto dealers. The venture failed within six months, never made it beyond the first initial market, and never attracted more than 15 advertisers. In establishing lost profits, the plaintiffs' expert used, as a forecasting tool, a marketing plan that was not a market projection but rather was used only to establish target revenues. The expert projected that had the contract term continued, the venture would have made $1.4 million in first-year profits.

In attempting to bootstrap their expert's opinion, the plaintiffs pointed to "the long experience and voluminous credentials of the report's author." In rejecting the expert's opinions as "completely untenable," the court noted the expert's extraordinary assumptions that, contrary to its actual six-month history, the venture (as it was hoped in the market projections) "would penetrate into a total of forty-nine marketing

42. Dering v. Service Experts Alliance, LLC, 2007 U.S. Dist. LEXIS 89972 (N.D. Ga. 2007).
43. *In re* Joy Recovery Tech. Corp., 2002 Bankr. LEXIS 1307 (Bankr. N.D. Ill. 2002).
44. 136 F.3d 1139 (7th Cir. 1998).

zones, that each zone would generate fourteen advertisers per monthly issue, and that virtually all of those advertisers would pay the full price for their ads." Reviewing the facts against the assumptions, the appellate court agreed with the trial court's assessment that the opinion "relies upon mere assumptions—from which no reasonable inference of lost profits could be drawn," leading the court to reject the testimony under *Daubert.* The marketing department's motivation document was not a reliable basis for the forecasting of the appraiser.

Some categories of documents, however, although they may not be completely representative of the conditions of the business, are nonetheless reliable bases for appraisal projections. For example, in *Rossi v. Mobil Oil Corp.,*[45] the expert used monthly financial statements he prepared for the business that contained expense estimates based on industry averages and also included data on a combination of businesses, some of which were not involved in the suit. The testimony that relied upon these documents was admitted, even though they were not compilations of "regularly maintained business records."

Experts are entitled to rely on this evidence, which would otherwise be inadmissible, and the court found that the documents met the requirements of Federal Rules 703 and 704. This case makes an interesting contrast with the trial court's Memorandum Opinion in *Whelan v. Abell.*[46] The financial expert in that case was found not qualified to testify on damage issues when he attempted to rely on financial statements prepared for the purpose of a public offering. Flaws in that document rendered it noncompliant with Securities and Exchange Commission requirements. A credibility problem was certainly created for the witness when he testified that this type of document (a noncompliant one!) was "typically relied upon" by experts.

Courts also have permitted otherwise qualified business appraisers to rely on the reports of other business valuation professionals. In *In re Greater Southeast Community Hospital Corp.,*[47] the court admitted the net asset valuation and insolvency opinion of a business appraiser who had an extensive background in business valuation and who had relied on third-party appraisals, indicating that all he needed to show was the "requisite knowledge, skill, experience, training, or education to competently render a net asset valuation opinion based on the opinions of others." It is permissible for business valuation analysts to rely on third-party reports, the court said, "so long as those appraisals are of the type experts in the field of business valuation would reasonably rely on."[48]

45. 710 F.2d 821 (Temp. Emer. Ct. App. 1983).

46. 1997 U.S. Dist. LEXIS 9794, 1997 WL 392526 (D.C. Cir. 1997).

47. *In re* Greater Southeast Cmty. Hosp. Corp., 2007 Bankr. LEXIS 1 (Bankr. D.D.C. 2007).

48. *See also* Southwire Co. v. JP Morgan Chase & Co., 2007 U.S. Dist. LEXIS 30294 (W.D. Wis. 2007), where the challenged expert's work was a continuation of data collection and compilation initiated by a third-party accounting firm. The court declined to exclude her testimony, saying, "Analyzing data assembled by another is neither illicit nor unusual, even if the data were prepared for litigation by an interested party."

Subjective Statements Must Be Documented

Discussing the trial court's rejection of the expert opinion, the Court in *Kumho* focused on the expert's fallback position, that his subjective analysis (that is, personal opinion) was the basis for his conclusions. Note that neither the Supreme Court nor the trial court doubted the expert's qualifications. However, they had no comfort level with the expert's repeated subjective judgments.

> [T]hese concerns might have been augmented by [the expert]'s repeated reliance on the "subjectiveness" of his mode of analysis in response to questions seeking specific information regarding how he could differentiate between a tire that had actually been overdeflected and a tire that merely looked as though it had been.[49]
>
> [N]othing in either *Daubert* or the Federal Rules of Evidence requires a district court to admit opinion evidence that is connected to existing data only by the *ipse dixit* of the expert.[50]

In *City of Tuscaloosa v. Harcross Chemicals, Inc.*,[51] the appellate court upheld the exclusion of a CPA's testimony on a bid-rigging conspiracy based on his subjective analysis of bids that were signals to coconspirators. Not only was the judgment of the witness solely his personal conclusion, it also fell beyond the realm of expertise normally possessed by an accountant.[52] However, testimony within the accountant's competency, particularly his statistical testimony, was allowed to stand where it used "well-established and reliable methodologies."[53]

Prediction of future events also calls the subjective judgment of the business appraiser into question. Any number of future contingencies can be created to affect the value of the business interest; however, the appraiser must be able to show that those contingencies are somewhat likely to occur. In *Eisenberg v. Commissioner*,[54] the court rejected a valuation that took into account the ability of a subchapter C corporation to convert to a subchapter S corporation, finding no evidence of such intent and, where such an election could produce other consequences, causing the court to characterize such a choice as "practically remote."

---

49. 526 U.S. 137.

50. 526 U.S. 137 (quoting General Electric Co. v. Joiner, 118 S. Ct. 136, 512 (1997)).

51. 158 F.3d 548 (11th Cir. 1998).

52. *See also* Santa Monica Picture, L.L.C. v. Comm'r, T.C. Memo. 2005-104 (2005) (expert excluded because his analysis was infected with speculation, advocated his client's position, addressed issues beyond the scope of his valuation engagement, and testified to the ultimate legal issue).

53. 158 F.3d at 565.

54. 155 F.3d 50 (2d Cir. 1998).

Weighting methods to arrive at a conclusion (the averaging of values gained through the various methods) is another sore spot for subjective challenge.[55] In assigning the weights, the appraiser must be prepared with clear reasoning and as much related factual material as possible to substantiate the choice or risk having the weight assignment appear as expert advocacy or client direction. Either one will taint the conclusion beyond acceptable limits.

An expert's failure to adequately explain the business valuation theory used also can lead a court to conclude that the opinion is subjective. In *Zenith Electronics Corp. v. WH-TV Broadcasting Corp.*,[56] the appraisal expert was disqualified because the trial court found that he was unable to adequately explain the theory supporting his testimony, and concluded that his opinion was subjective. The court of appeals affirmed, concluding that the expert was not truly an expert where he relied on his own theory.

Superficial Treatment of Issues: The "Down and Dirty" Appraisal

Economic and time factors also can play a part in choices of methodology, which can result in the appraisal expert's testimony being excluded for failure to meet *Daubert* and *Kumho* criteria. A "down and dirty" appraisal used for initial case analysis should not become the opinion that the expert renders at trial. Such initial work (often substituted for final work product when money runs short) rarely will employ the methodology that experts in valuation find essential or the "intellectual rigor" discussed in *Kumho*.

Incomplete work cloaked in technical jargon will not pass a savvy opposing expert. In *Frymire-Brinati v. KPMG Peat Marwick*,[57] the appellees (plaintiffs), claiming to be bilked investors in a limited partnership, alleged that the appellant's certification of partnership financial statements failed to disclose that the investments were worth less than represented on the books. The defendant's "star witness," using a discounted cash flow analysis, valued the projects at 10 times annual cash flow. However, because the historical cash flow of many projects was minimal or even negative, the expert assigned them a value of zero.

The appellate court determined that the expert testimony was inadmissible because it failed to meet *Daubert*'s requirement that the testimony be "not only relevant, but

55. It is also true that appraisers can be criticized for failing to use all the approaches to valuation. *See, e.g.*, Estate of Bennett v. Comm'r, T.C. Memo. 1993-34 (1993); Estate of Campbell, T.C. Memo. 1991-615 (1991); and Estate of Andrews v. Comm'r, 79 T.C. 938 (1982). However, these criticisms are generally not for failure to use a weighted approach, but rather for failure to consider the applicability of all available approaches—a different abuse of subjectivity.

56. Zenith Electronics Corp. v. WH-TV Broad. Corp., 395 F.3d 416 (7th Cir. 2005).

57. 2 F.3d 183 (7th Cir. 1993).

reliable." The trial judge did not conduct any preliminary assessment of the reasoning or methodology used by the expert. The appellate court noted that had such a preliminary assessment been undertaken, the trial court could not properly have admitted the valuation testimony, for it failed to satisfy the requirements of Federal Rule of Evidence 702.

The specific shortcomings of the expert's method lay in the admittedly surface treatment given to the assignment. Normally, to determine market value using a discounted cash flow analysis, the expert considers the *potential* cash flows of the asset not merely the historical cash flow. Commenting on the view of the defendant's expert's scenario as explained by the plaintiff's expert, the court noted that "raw land would be worthless and that a large office building in the final stages of construction also has no value even though it is fully leased out and could be sold for a hundred million dollars."[58] Even the defendant's expert conceded that his valuation was not an attempt to determine the market value of the asset (a fundamental necessity of the plaintiff's claims) but merely "a fairly simple pass at what the magnitude of the problem was."[59]

Often, testimony that may be flawed in method or that may lack credibility can be admitted with proper instruction to the trier of fact. However, the *Frymire* appellate court was reluctant to admit the testimony and allow the trier of fact to assign it an appropriate weight, finding it problematic to admit this "fairly simple pass" into evidence simply because it was offered by an expert witness qualified in accounting matters. Ultimately, it was the lack of conventional methodology that persuaded the appellate court that the testimony was not reliable, for the expert "conceded that he did not employ the methodology that experts in valuation find essential."[60] Such a concession prevented the testimony from meeting the criteria for reliability and relevancy set forth in *Daubert.*

Another aspect of the "down and dirty" business appraisal is the assignment that heavily relies on off-the-shelf or personally developed business appraisal software. Can the business appraiser discuss the software in a manner that will satisfy the requirements of *Daubert?* Who tested the software? Who has peer reviewed it? What has been published on it? Are there standards governing its use? What are the default presets and how were they determined? Is the software generally accepted? How many people use it and what are their credentials? Who developed the software and what are their credentials? If the appraiser cannot answer these questions, the conclusion of value may have no real basis.

It also may fail to comply with the USPAP and its competency requirement. The Appraisal Standards Board's *Advisory Opinion on the Use of an Automated Valuation Model (AVM)* provides specific guidelines on AVM use:

58. 2 F.3d at 186, *citing Daubert,* 113 S. Ct. at 2786.
59. *Id.*
60. *Id.*

In an appraisal assignment, an appraiser must have a basic understanding of how the AVM works in order to reasonably determine that:

1. use of the AVM is appropriate for the assignment;
2. the output of the AVM is credible for use in the assignment; and
3. the AVM does not exclude relevant market measures or factual information necessary for a credible calculation.[61]

Inaccurate or Inadequate Use of Accepted Methodologies—the Expert Must Be Reliable

The expert not only must use accepted or supportable methodologies, but also must do so in a way that evinces a comprehensive understanding of them or that correctly applies them. One study has shown that 85 percent of expert challenges are directed at the expert's reliability.[62] For example, in *In re Med Diversified, Inc.*,[63] the court said that even if the proposed expert were otherwise qualified, it nonetheless would exclude his testimony because the expert "showed a discernible measure of negligence in purportedly applying the alleged professional standards and techniques found in the published practical treatises, including the standards and techniques published in the writings of Dr. Shannon Pratt and his co-authors, which were repeatedly propounded by both the Defendants and the Plaintiffs."[64] The court concluded that it could not accept the testimony of an alleged expert in business valuations when he failed to employ the necessary peer-reviewed methods of business valuation, when he based his analysis on inadequate data, and when he thoroughly mixed up the discreetly different concepts of gross cash flow and net cash flow from operations. The court also concluded that his failure to use the discounted cash flow method—and to offer a satisfactory explanation as to why he omitted this method—amounted to a material flaw in his methodology sufficient to bar his testimony as an expert witness, because his conclusions lacked "good grounds."

61. The Appraisal Found., Uniform Standards of Professional Appraisal Practice, Adv. Op. 18 (2010–2011).

62. Deloitte & Touche LLP, The Financial Expert Testimony—Admissibility Standards Database. This database indicates that federal courts have focused on the following criteria in evaluating financial expert testimony: methodology; assumptions; intellectual rigor and standard of care; research independent of litigation process; consideration of alternative data, explanations, and hypotheses; compliance with legal standards; testing or verification of facts, data, and results; consistency with facts and data of the case; sufficiency of facts and data used; accuracy of facts and data used; ability to define the market; testability of methodology; peer review of methodology; rate of error attributable to methodology; general acceptance of methodology.

63. *In re* Med Diversified, Inc., 2005 Bankr. LEXIS 2236 (Bankr. E.D.N.Y. 2005).

64. *Id.* at **23.

Moreover, the court found that the data on which his conclusions were based were inadequate because he did not conduct any independent analysis as part of a comparable companies approach and did not independently analyze the data from the databases from which he derived his figures in choosing the comparable companies and transactions upon which his analysis was based; the expert admittedly never had considered the nature or products of the businesses or the market in which these businesses operated.

In *Club Car, Inc. v. Club Car (Quebec) Import, Inc.*,[65] the 11th Circuit upheld the exclusion of an expert because he based his opinion on gross figures without reducing them to net figures, which, the court found, did not comport with state law requirements that lost profits be calculated net of expenses. The court stated, "The trial court reasonably concluded his lost profit calculation was based on flawed methodology that was not accepted in the accounting community."

In a case involving the Disney corporation, *Children's Broadcasting Corporation v. The Walt Disney Company,*[66] the court initially admitted the expert, but after the expert made highly unrealistic assumptions, the court changed its mind on a motion for judgment as a matter of law, saying that the expert's "damages projections went so far beyond realistic optimism as to be 'fairy-tale-like.'" The court concluded that it erred by admitting the testimony of the expert and should have excluded it under *Daubert,* for his "testimony 'tainted' the trial by exposing the jury to an 'exaggerated sum' of damages." On appeal, the Eighth Circuit agreed that the expert should not have been permitted to testify because his opinion was speculative and based on conjecture.

In another Eight Circuit decision, *Eckelkamp v. Beste,*[67] the court again upheld the trial court's decision to exclude expert evidence where the trial court found several methodological flaws, including the expert's use of comparable companies that were not, in fact, comparable; the expert's failure to conduct a site visit and employee interviews; the expert's failure to consider certain market factors; double counting in arriving at a control premium; and other flaws.

Another case where faulty assumptions and data resulted in exclusion of the expert evidence is *Fisherman Surgical Instruments, LLC v. Tri-Anim Health Services, Inc.*[68] In this case, the court concluded that there was no factual support for the expert's key assumptions and that this "hole" in his models rendered all his damage calculations unreliable. Similarly, in *Heary Bros. Lightning Protection Co., Inc. v. Lightning*

65. Club Car, Inc. v. Club Car (Quebec) Import, Inc., 362 F.3d 775 (11th Cir 2004).

66. Children's Broad. Corp. v. The Walt Disney Co., 245 F.3d 1008 (8th Cir. 2001).

67. Eckelkamp v. Beste, 315 F.3d 863 (8th Cir. 2002).

68. Fisherman Surgical Instruments, LLC v. Tri-Anim Health Servs., Inc., 2007 U.S. Dist. LEXIS 61222 (D. Kan. 2007).

Protection Institute,[69] the expert's lost damages conclusions were excluded because the expert had made faulty assumptions about market conditions as of the valuation period. In this antitrust case, the expert assumed there were only two market participants at the time, but, in fact, there were many more. The court ruled that this failure of the initial market share assumption rendered the rest of the calculations unreliable and, therefore, inadmissible.

The valuation experts' "numerous outright . . . errors" lost the plaintiffs' case in *Richard A. Lippe v. Bairnco Corporation.*[70] The court found significant deficiencies in the analyses of two experts, including the failure to explain why a discounted cash flow valuation was not performed as a check against a comparable company valuation; failure to explain the assumptions used in the valuation including the selection of p/e multiples, the selection of comparable companies, and income projections; failure to account for differences between the comparables and the subject companies; failure to independently select comparables (instead utilizing comparables suggested by counsel); and failure to explain the selection of control premiums, among others.[71]

Original and Personally Developed Appraisal Methods Create Risk

Viewing the expert's opinion as presented to the *Kumho* trial court, the Supreme Court noted there was:

> [n]o indication in the record that other experts in the industry use [the expert]'s particular approach or that [other experts] normally make the very fine distinctions necessary to support his conclusions, nor are there references to articles or papers that validate his approach.[72]

Appraisers, weary of searching among the proven approaches for one best suited to an assignment, may be tempted to combine approaches or create an untried approach or method to cure what they perceive as deficiencies in the currently sanctioned methodology. Authors, wanting to sell books, may invent new theories. Over time, some of these methods may be evaluated and accepted by the technical community. Until that time, however, the business appraiser uses them at his or her own risk.

69. Heary Bros. Lightning Prot. Co., Inc. v. Lightning Prot. Inst., 287 F. Supp. 2d 1038 (D. Ariz. 2003).

70. Richard A. Lippe v. Bairnco Corp., 2004 U.S. App. LEXIS 7027 (2d Cir. 2004).

71. *See also* Trugreen Cos., LLC, Inc. v. Scotts Lawn Serv., 2007 U.S. Dist. LEXIS 10916 (N.D. Utah 2007) (expert's report was not sufficiently reliable where there was "an impermissible analytical gap . . . between the premises and conclusions" and "this methodology does nothing more than assume the conclusion").

72. 526 U.S. 137.

In *Moore v. Ashland Chemical,*[73] the court discussed that "[u]nder Rule 702 the 'knowledge' of each discipline is both its principles and methodology, and the theories, techniques or inferences produced through its methodology. Thus, the proffered opinion of any expert in a field of knowledge, in order to be evidentially reliable, must either be based soundly on the current knowledge, principles and methodology of the expert's discipline or be soundly inferred or derived therefrom . . . [Moreover,] the focus must be on the principles and methodology upon which the expert's opinion is based, not on the merits of the expert's conclusion."[74] Experts who depart from known principles and methodology, therefore, may develop an incredible conclusion, regardless of its apparent merit.

One of the cardinal rules enunciated in the standards of appraisal organizations is that a valuation conclusion should be replicable. If the method has not been validated and studied, it may not be a replicable method. It certainly won't pass the "indicia of reliability" criteria set forth in *Daubert*. "Simple pass" methods, individual or brand-name methods, or software appraisals are no substitute for the developed body of appraisal knowledge.[75]

In *In re Nellson Nutraceutical,*[76] one of the experts essentially invented the methodology of using EBITDA minus Cap Ex to determine a company's terminal value under a discounted cash flow analysis. The expert admitted that he had never used such a method before and could point to no professional source that validated it. Because the expert's conclusion of terminal value constituted the bulk of his ultimate conclusions regarding value—and was, in fact, "inseparable" from his ultimate conclusion—the court struck the entirety of his testimony and report from the record. In *Haupt v. Heaps,*[77] a state case interpreting a state analogue of *Daubert* standards, the court found the method relied on by the expert was "too novel" for valuation purposes. The method, known as the Straight-Line Ramp-up (SLR) method, had been used by the company's auditors, but the expert admitted that despite his many years as an economics expert, his extensive training, and his experience in business valuation, he had never seen the SLR method of valuation prior to reviewing the audit documents and that he had not been able to verify it independently or investigate the auditors' intent in utilizing it. Thus, the court held that SLR was not "an accepted method of business valuations" and excluded it; this conclusion was affirmed on appeal.

---

73. 126 F.3d 679 (5th Cir. 1997); *appeal after remand,* 151 F.3d 269 (5th Cir. 1998).

74. 126 F.3d at 687, 688.

75. The body of knowledge for business appraisal, reflecting the Uniform Standards of Professional Appraisal Practice and the core courses of all four of the U.S. professional business appraisal organizations, is contained in SHANNON PRATT, BUSINESS VALUATION BODY OF KNOWLEDGE (2d ed., John Wiley & Sons 2003).

76. *In re* Nellson Nutraceutical, 2006 Bankr. LEXIS 3186 (Bankr. D. Del. 2006).

77. Haupt v. Heaps, 2005 Utah App. LEXIS 423 (Utah Ct. App. 2005).

Admissible Expert Evidence versus the Weight Accorded to It

Despite the court's role as gatekeeper, "the rejection of expert testimony is the exception rather than the rule."[78] Often, challenged expert testimony will be admitted on the basis that the proffered expert qualifies as an expert and the methods used by the expert are recognized by other experts in the field, even if the challenge to admissibility is made on the grounds that the expert has omitted relevant factors or has made wrong assumptions that are essential to the methodology. In such a case, the court may decide that what is called for is an adjustment to the expert's result and will leave the decision of how much weight to accord to the expert's opinion to the jury. Because the court's gatekeeper role "is not intended to serve as a replacement for the adversary system,"[79] the challenging party has the burden of providing expert evidence that counters or adjusts the faulty results, and the challenging party's attorney must take the expert to task on cross-examination. Merely because the evidence can be critiqued as a matter of fact does not mean it should be stricken entirely as a matter of law if it otherwise satisfies the requirements of *Daubert* and Federal Rule 702.

For example, in *Floorgraphics, Inc v. News America Marketing In-Store Services, Inc.,*[80] the plaintiff had alleged that the defendants had engaged in various business torts that resulted in plaintiff's damages and lost profits. The plaintiff offered six witnesses as experts, and the defendants moved to exclude the trial testimony of all six. Of these, two were to quantify damages using business valuation methodologies.

The first offered expert used a "before and after" methodology. The defendants claimed that the expert's use of this methodology was fatally flawed because it omitted a fundamental step and failed to account for key factors. The defendants contended that the expert's testimony should, accordingly, be excluded because it rested on flawed assumptions and did not reflect real-world conditions. The court rejected this contention. The court found that the "before and after" method is recognized by experts in the field as an acceptable method to calculate lost profits (citing Shannon Pratt, the coauthor of this book) and it agreed with the plaintiffs that to the extent the expert failed to account for certain factors, it was up to the defendants to demonstrate that those factors mattered. The court said, "When challenging the admissibility of Plaintiff's expert testimony, a party must move beyond empty criticisms and demonstrate that a proposed alternative approach would yield different results."[81] The court

78. Fed. R. Evid. 702, 2000 Amendments.

79. United States v. 14.38 Acres of Land Situated in Leflore County, Miss., 80 F.3d 1074, 1078 (5th Cir. 1995).

80. Floorgraphics, Inc v. News America Mktg. In-Store Servs., Inc., 2008 U.S. Dist. LEXIS 8263 (D.N.J. 2008).

81. *Id.* at *45.

concluded that even assuming the defendants' objections were material and relevant, at most, the expert's testimony could be critiqued by the defendants' expert and should not be stricken. The expert's results would have to be adjusted if his key assumptions were wrong, but not excluded entirely, because in the end the expert's testimony would assist the trier of facts. The court said, "Under Rule 702, it is not the Court's province to determine who is the best expert or the most qualified. Defendants will have an opportunity to vigorously cross-exam [the expert] in addition to presenting their own expert witness at trial."[82]

The defendants also sought to exclude the second business appraisal expert on the ground that his methodologies suffered from flaws. Again citing Shannon Pratt, the court disagreed that the expert's use of business valuation methodologies was flawed and concluded that, in fact, it comported with accepted business valuation methodologies. Finding that not only did the expert have a reliable methodology, but that his testimony would assist the trier of fact, the court declined to preclude his testimony.

In *Guang Dong v. ACI International, Inc.*,[83] the court ruled that the expert's discount of 50 percent, based on a pricing e-mail, and the expert's reliance on "ballpark" sales estimates from deposition testimony, did not render his report unreliable. Instead, the court indicated that these issues went to weight and not admissibility, and that a jury would be able to evaluate whether the expert properly used the e-mail and sales data in reaching his opinion of damages.

In *Southwire Co. v. JPMorgan Chase & Co.*,[84] the defendants challenged defects to the plaintiffs' expert's multiple regression model, but did not challenge the model itself. The court declined to exclude the expert, finding it more significant that the defendants had questioned neither the model nor the expert's credentials. The court said, "Although [the expert's] judgment may not be correct, his errors are fodder for cross-examination, not summary judgment."

> In another case, the business appraisal expert was challenged because he was a de facto contingent witness, that is, the party that retained him ran out of money to pay his fees and owed him an undisclosed sum. The expert admitted that he would not be paid unless the trustee prevailed. The court, however, admitted the expert, finding that this issue went to credibility and the weight of the evidence. The court distinguished between state ethics rules, which prohibit attorneys from using contingent fee experts, and evidentiary rules, which say nothing about contingent witnesses. The court concluded

82. *Id.* at *50–51.

83. Guang Dong v. ACI Int'l, Inc., 2008 U.S. Dist. LEXIS 3881 (D. Kan. 2008).

84. Southwire Co. v. JPMorgan Chase & Co., 2007 U.S. Dist. LEXIS 30294 (W.D. Wis. 2007).

> that there was no authority for the proposition that contingent fee experts are incompetent to testify in federal court or that evidence obtained from such witnesses is inadmissible. Merely showing that the expert may have an incentive to exaggerate his testimony is insufficient to bar that testimony. Instead, this is a nondispositive consideration in the assessment of his credibility.[85]

Echoing the sentiments of many courts that decline to exclude expert testimony, the court in *Humetrix, Inc. v. Gemplus, S.C.A.*[86] said, "To the extent Gemplus sought to challenge the correctness of Humetrix's experts' testimony, its recourse is not exclusion of the testimony, but, rather, refutation of it by cross-examination and by the testimony of its own expert witnesses. Gemplus availed itself of both of these opportunities." Similarly, in *KSP Investments, Inc. v. United States,*[87] where the challenged expert had used the same generally accepted methodologies as the challenging party's expert, but had merely pointed out problematic assumptions and substituted different data in the same formulas, the court indicated that issues with the expert's testimony could be resolved through cross-examination. Likewise, in *ProtoComm Corp. v. Novell Advanced Services, Inc.,*[88] the court rejected challenges to each party's experts, saying, "It appears to this Court that [the parties] are really arguing that . . . [the] opinions are inaccurate in light of the facts. In other words, they focus not on whether the reasoning is valid and the methodology reliable, but rather on whether the conclusions themselves are *correct.* That is not the proper inquiry in a test for admissibility." (Emphasis in original.) The court added that any perceived weakness in the experts' opinions should be challenged through traditional trial tactics.

The defendants in *Tharo Systems, Inc. v. cab Producktechnick GmbH & Co. KG*[89] first challenged the plaintiffs' expert qualifications, claiming that the international auditor (with nearly 100 trial appearances) wasn't familiar with German accounting principles. However, they failed to rebut his assertion that there were no material differences between German and typical U.S. financial statements. And even though the expert had made a translation error, which caused him to exclude 80 percent of

---

85. *In re* Joy Recovery Tech. Corp., 2002 Bankr. LEXIS 1307 (Bankr. N.D. Ill. 2002). *See also* Physicians Dialysis Ventures, Inc. v. Griffith, 2007 U.S. Dist. LEXIS 78879 (D.N.J. 2007), where the expert's references to businesses not in existence as of the valuation date did not render her methodologies or opinions unreliable, but went to the weight, not the admissibility, of her opinion.

86. Humetrix, Inc. v. Gemplus, S.C.A., 268 F.3d 910, 2001 U.S. App. LEXIS 21458 (9th Cir. 2001).

87. KSP Invs., Inc. v. United States, 2008 U.S. Dist. LEXIS 7383 (N.D. Ohio 2008).

88. ProtoComm Corp. v. Novell Advanced Servs., Inc., 171 F. Supp. 2d 473, 2001 U.S. Dist. LEXIS 15811 (E.D. Penn. 2001).

89. Tharo Sys., Inc. v. cab Producktechnick GmbH & Co. KG, 2006 U.S. App. LEXIS 21895 (6th Cir. 2006).

certain salaries from his calculations, he had admitted the error on cross-examination, and the jury had resolved the fact question in its damages award. In the end, his error or lack of familiarity with German accounting statements went to the "weight" of his testimony, according to the court of appeals, not to its admissibility.

Conclusion

This chapter has revealed a sample of the hundreds of cases where an expert either was not allowed to testify or was allowed to testify but the court disallowed or gave little weight to the expert's testimony. Hopefully, these examples and the related discussion will provide lawyers guidance so that they will select appropriate experts and not fall into the same trap.

Chapter 27

Discovery and the Business Valuation Expert

This chapter was updated from the First Edition by Noah J. Gordon, legal counsel for Shannon Pratt Valuations, Inc. Mr. Gordon is a regular contributor to publications on business valuation and law. The original chapter was contributed by Linda L. Kruschke, an attorney with the Oregon State Bar. This chapter addresses discovery as it applies to business valuation cases under the Federal Rules of Civil Procedure, provides details on states' adherence to or deviation from the Federal Rules, and presents practical advice on the business valuation expert's role in the discovery process.

—S.P.

This chapter discusses discovery rules in cases where business valuation expert testimony is presented. It also discusses the business valuation expert's role in the discovery process. The discovery devices discussed include the following:

- Disclosure and written report requirements
- Requests for production of documents and for entry upon land or premises
- Subpoenas served on third parties
- Interrogatories
- Depositions

With respect to each discovery device, this chapter covers the relevant Federal Rule of Civil Procedure (FRCP), jurisdictions that follow the Federal Rules, and jurisdictions that have a discovery rule that differs from the Federal Rules. A table summarizing all federal, state, and territorial rules relating to the discovery devices discussed here is included as Exhibit 27-1.

Exhibit 27-1
Summary of Discovery Rules

Jurisdiction	Written Report Required	Interrogatories Allowed Re: Expert	Limit on Number of Interrogatories	Deposition of Expert Allowed	Limit on Number of Depositions
Federal Rules	Yes	Yes	25	Yes	10
Alabama	No	Yes	40	With court order only	No
Alaska	Yes	Yes	30	Yes	No
Arizona	No	Yes	40	Yes	No
Arkansas	No	Yes	No	With court order only	No
California	On demand	Yes	35	Yes	No
Colorado	Yes	Yes	30	Yes	No
Connecticut	Summary	Yes	No	Yes	No
Delaware	No	Yes	No order only	With court	No
District of Columbia	No	Yes	40	With court order only	10
Florida	No	Yes	30	Yes	No
Georgia	No	Yes	50	Yes	No
Guam	No	Yes	No	With court order only	No
Hawaii	No	Yes	60	Yes	10
Idaho	No	Yes	40	Yes	No
Illinois	If interrogatory served	Yes	30	Yes	No
Indiana	No	Yes	No	With court order only	No
Iowa	If requested	Yes	30	Yes	No
Kansas	Summary	Yes	No (30 in damage actions)	Yes	No
Kentucky	No	Yes	30	Must serve interrogatories first	No

Jurisdiction	Written Report Required	Interrogatories Allowed Re: Expert	Limit on Number of Interrogatories	Deposition of Expert Allowed	Limit on Number of Depositions
Louisiana	No	Yes	35	Yes	No
Maine	No	Yes	30	With court order only	No
Maryland	If interrogatory served	Yes	30	Yes	No
Massachusetts	No	Yes	30	With court order only	No
Michigan	No	Yes	No	Yes	No
Minnesota	No	Yes	50	With court order only	No
Mississippi	No	Yes	30	With court order only	No
Missouri	No	Yes	No	Yes	No
Montana	No	Yes	50	With court order only	No
Nebraska	No	Yes	50	With court order only	No
Nevada	Yes	Yes	40	Yes	No
New Hampshire	Yes	Yes	50	Yes	No
New Jersey	If interrogatory served	Yes	No	Yes	No
New Mexico	No	Yes	50	With court order only	No
New York	No	Yes	No	With court order only	No
North Carolina	No	Yes	50	With court order only	No
North Dakota	No	Yes	No	Yes	No
Ohio	No	Yes	40	Must show exceptional circumstances	No

Jurisdiction	Written Report Required	Interrogatories Allowed Re: Expert	Limit on Number of Interrogatories	Deposition of Expert Allowed	Limit on Number of Depositions
Oklahoma	No	Yes	30	Must serve interrogatories first	No
Oregon	No	No	-	No	No
Pennsylvania	If interrogatory served, discretionary with answering party	Yes	No	With court order only	No
Puerto Rico	No	Yes	No	With court order only	No
Rhode Island	No	Yes	30	Must serve interrogatories first	No
South Carolina	No	Yes	50	Yes	No
South Dakota	No	Yes	No	With court order only	No
Tennessee	No	Yes	No	Yes	No
Texas	If requested	No	-	Yes	No
Utah	Yes	Yes	25	Yes	10
Vermont	No	Yes	No	Yes	No
Virginia	No	Yes	30	Yes	No
Virgin Islands	Yes	Yes	25	Yes	No
Washington	No	Yes	No	Yes	No
West Virginia	No	Yes	40	Yes	No
Wisconsin	No	Yes	No	Yes	No
Wyoming	No	Yes	30	Yes	10

Expert Witnesses: Disclosure Requirements and Written Appraisal Reports

Generally, business valuation experts should provide a written report explaining their opinion of the value of the intangible asset or business interest that is the subject of litigation. The general content and points to be covered in the report should be discussed with the business appraiser before he or she prepares the report. The procedural rules of the jurisdiction that governs the disclosure of expert witnesses and the requirements relating to written appraisal reports should be reviewed to ensure that all the information required is covered by the appraiser. These rules also should be reviewed to ensure that the expert is timely disclosed so he or she may testify at trial, if that is desired. Finally, the expert should be thoroughly prepared before he or she testifies.

Federal Rule of Civil Procedure 26(a)(2)

FRCP 26(a)(2) requires each party to disclose the identity of any expert witness the party intends to call to testify at trial under Federal Rule of Evidence (FRE) 702. As discussed in Chapter 3, the opinion of value of a business appraiser or other valuation expert falls into this category.

This disclosure requirement includes disclosure of a written report "prepared and signed by the witness" unless otherwise stipulated or ordered by the court. (FRCP 26(a)(2)(B)) The required content of the written report as specified in the rule includes:

- A complete statement of the expert's opinion
- The basis and reasons for the opinion
- The data and other information considered in forming the opinion
- The qualifications of the witness
- A list of all publications authored within the past 10 years
- The compensation to be paid
- A list of all cases the expert has testified in at trial or by deposition within the past four years

Absent a stipulation or a court order, the identity of the expert and his or her written report must be provided to opposing counsel and filed with the court within 90 days before trial. This time frame is shortened, however, in the case of expert testimony intended only to rebut expert evidence that was disclosed by the other party. In this instance, the identity and written report of the rebuttal expert must be provided within 30 days of the other party's disclosure of the expert to be rebutted.

Under FRCP 37(c)(1), a party who fails to disclose the identity and written report of an expert witness "is not allowed to use that information or witness to supply evidence on a motion, at a hearing, or at a trial, unless the failure was substantially justified or is harmless." Other appropriate sanctions may be imposed at the discretion of the court. For example, in *U.S. v. Batchelor-Robjohns,*[1] the United States had sued transferees of assets from a corporate taxpayer, alleging that the transfers rendered the taxpayer insolvent and that, therefore, the transferees were liable for the corporation's unpaid taxes. The government's valuation expert had valued the taxpayer's assets and rendered an opinion concerning the corporation's income-generating capacity, but the government refused to disclose information concerning allegedly proprietary computer models used to value the assets. The transferees accordingly moved to strike the expert's report and to exclude witnesses under FRCP 37 for the expert's failure to disclose underlying data as required by FRCP 26(a)(2)(B). The court agreed with the transferees and excluded the expert's opinion for neither the court nor the transferees were able to test the reliability of the opinion in the absence of the data and methodology upon which the opinion was based. In addition, because the transferees had made good-faith efforts to resolve the dispute before seeking court intervention and because admission of the expert's opinion would clearly have prejudiced the transferees' ability to cross-examine the expert and rebut his opinion, the court excluded the testimony of other experts whose opinions concerning the solvency and foreseeable tax liability of the taxpayer relied upon the conclusions of the valuation expert, as well as any testimony to the extent that it relied on the expert's opinion.

However, the court also has significant discretion to permit the expert's testimony notwithstanding a failure to substantially comply with the requirements of FRCP 26(a)(2)(B). For example, in *Audubon Veterinary Hospital, Inc. v. U.S. Fidelity & Guarantee Co.,*[2] *the* defendant submitted a report that was not signed by the expert. The report contained columns of figures without any conclusions or defined sources, it was missing exhibits and a list of the expert's qualifications, and it was not even certain that the expert had written the report. Accordingly, the plaintiff moved to strike the report for failing to comply with FRCP 26. Although the district court found that the plaintiff had made a strong argument for striking the report, given that the suit was "purely about the value of the plaintiff's business interruption insurance claim" and the expert's report was "crucial," the court declined to preclude the expert from providing evidence in the case. It gave the defendant 10 days to comply fully with FRCP 26 and ordered it to pay the plaintiffs' costs of deposing the expert.

Jurisdictions That Follow or Deviate from FRCP 26(a)(2)

Only six jurisdictions—Alaska, Colorado, Nevada, New Hampshire, Utah, and the Virgin Islands—require a written report of an expert witness under rules similar or

1. United States v. Batchelor-Robjohns, 2005 U.S. Dist. LEXIS 13552 (S.D. Fla. June 3, 2005).
2. Audubon Veterinary Hosp., Inc. v. U.S. Fidelity & Guarantee Co., 2007 U.S. Dist. LEXIS 46301 (E.D. La. June 25, 2007).

identical to FRCP 26(a)(2). Other jurisdictions require a written report of an expert witness:

- If demand is made (California),
- If requested in discovery (Iowa and Texas),
- If an interrogatory is directed to the party who will call the witness (Illinois (only for controlled, i.e., retained experts), Maryland, New Jersey), or
- Upon contradictory motion of any party or on the court's own motion (Louisiana).

All these jurisdictions provide for the sanction of not being able to use the expert's testimony at trial, at a hearing, or on a motion if the party does not comply with the written report or summary requirements.

Pennsylvania provides that the party answering an interrogatory may provide the expert's report in response or have the expert answer the interrogatory.

The remaining jurisdictions do not require a written report or summary by an expert witness to be served upon or provided to other parties. However, each jurisdiction, with the exception of Oregon, provides parties with some discovery device to learn about an expert's opinion.

Requests for Production of Documents and Entry for Inspection and Interviews

To perform a thorough business valuation, it is necessary for the business appraiser to review corporate and financial documents of the business to be valued, usually including articles of incorporation, bylaws, buy-sell agreements, financial statements, tax returns, and so on. Depending upon the nature of the business, it often is important for the business appraiser to view the business premises and interview management.

Documents

Exhibit 27-2 is a typical documents and information request list. It should be modified to fit the specific situation.

Exhibit 27-2
Preliminary Documents and Information Checklist for Business Valuation of Typical Corporation

Financial Statements for Typical Corporation

- Balance sheets, income statements, statements of changes in cash flow, and statements of stockholders' equity for the past five fiscal years or economic cycle
- Income tax returns for the same years
- Latest interim statements and interim statements for comparable period(s) of previous year

Other Financial Data

- Summary property, plant, and equipment list, depreciation schedule, and capital budget
- Aged accounts receivable summary
- Aged accounts payable summary
- List of marketable securities and prepaid expenses
- Inventory summary, with any necessary information on inventory accounting policies
- Synopsis of leases for facilities or equipment
- Any other existing contracts (employment agreements, covenants not to compete, supplier agreements, customer agreements, royalty agreements, equipment lease or rental contracts, loan agreements, labor contracts, employee benefit plans, and so on)
- List of stockholders, with number of shares owned by each
- Schedule of insurance in force (key person, life, property and casualty, liability)
- Budgets or projections, for a minimum of five years, business or strategic plan, if available
- List of subsidiaries and/or financial interests in other companies
- Key personnel compensation schedule, including benefits and personal expenses
- Details of any transactions with related parties

Company Documents

- Articles of incorporation, bylaws, and any amendments to either
- Any existing buy-sell agreements, options to purchase stock, or rights of first refusal
- Franchise or operating agreements, if any

Other Information

- Brief history, including how long in business and details of any changes in ownership and/or any bona fide offers recently received
- Brief description of the business, including position relative to competition and any factors that make the business unique
- Marketing literature (catalogs, brochures, advertisements, and so on)
- List of locations where company operates, with size and recent appraisals
- List of competitors, with location, relative size, and any relevant factors
- Organization chart
- Résumés of key personnel, with age, position, compensation, length of service, education, and prior experience
- Personnel profile: number of employees by functional groupings, such as production, sales, engineering/R & D, personnel and accounting, customer service/field support, and so forth
- Trade associations to which the company belongs or would be eligible for membership
- Relevant trade or government publications (especially market forecasts)
- Any existing indicators of asset values, including latest property tax assessments and any appraisals that have been performed
- List of customer relationships, supplier relationships, contracts, patents, copyrights, trademarks, and other intangible assets
- Any contingent or off-balance-sheet liabilities (pending lawsuits, compliance requirements, warranty or other product liabilities, estimate of medical benefits for retirees, and so on)
- Any filings or correspondence with regulatory agencies
- Information on prior transactions in the stock or any related-party transactions

Site Visit and Interviews[3]

Whenever practical, the appraiser should visit a company's operating location(s) and conduct interviews with key personnel and those affiliated with or providing services to the company. The principal objective of such a visit is to gain a broader perspective of the business and its operations than is possible from only a study of documents and telephone interviews. A site visit usually provides an opportunity for the appraiser to fill in details missing from an analysis of the written material, and the appraiser's physical presence may trigger relevant questions and lines of inquiry that would not have been brought up by a mere review of the documents. This in-person site visit

3. This section was adapted with permission from SHANNON P. PRATT & ALINA V. NICULITA, VALUING A BUSINESS: THE ANALYSIS AND APPRAISAL OF CLOSELY HELD COMPANIES (5th ed., McGraw-Hill 2008), ch. 5, and SHANNON P. PRATT ET AL., VALUING SMALL BUSINESSES AND PROFESSIONAL PRACTICES 787–89 (3d ed., McGraw-Hill, 1998).

ideally should be conducted fairly early in the valuation process—after obtaining and reviewing enough preliminary information provided by the client and through discovery and research to create an overview of the company. If the valuation expert is to provide testimony, the expert's credibility will be enhanced by having conducted a site visit, for courts tend to give more credibility to experts who have visited the premises of the company to be valued and have interviewed personnel and individuals who are key to the valuation.

Lawyer's Role

Most appraisers prefer to do interviews without lawyers present, because this usually results in more candid information gathering. However, appraisers are accustomed to having lawyers present when they insist on it. It often is desirable (albeit uncommon) for appraisers on both sides of a case to do site visits and management interviews together, for a combined visit will be less disruptive to operations and personnel, and both sides will have access to the same information on which to base an independent valuation.

Preparation

Generally, the appraiser will want to prepare a thorough list of questions in advance of the site visit. By studying the written materials, including financial statements and other basic information, the appraiser can gain an overview of the company and prepare a list of specific questions that will make the fieldwork more meaningful, productive, and efficient—and also minimize the inconvenience to the company that might be associated with the management interviews.

Mission

The site visit and interviews should focus on establishing the relationship between the data gathered and the existing and prospective company situation and economic environment. The appraiser also will want to lay the groundwork for future communication with company personnel and related individuals. Developing a level of comfort with these personnel and individuals is an important objective of the site visit, so that if additional information is required after the fieldwork is complete, it can be more readily obtained.

Information to Be Gathered

The kinds of information the appraiser will want to gather through the field visit are discussed in previous chapters, but usually include information related to the company's strengths, weaknesses, operations, history, customers, and products. The actual topics and sequence of coverage will vary considerably from one situation to the next, but regardless of which topics are most pertinent to a particular valuation, the appraiser's goal will be to gather as much information as possible to maximize his or her understanding of all major factors that affect the value of the subject company. Additionally, the field trip can be a convenient time to review some of the documents that would be cumbersome or inconvenient to supply to the appraiser away from the premises. However, with the advent of scanning technology that enables the scanning and electronic transmission of very large documents, this is less of a consideration now than it has been previously.

Individuals to Be Interviewed

The title of the person to be interviewed is not as important as the categories of the topics to be probed. Typically, the appraiser may need to interview a company's owner(s), president, chief operating officer, marketing or sales manager, or chief financial officer. In some companies, these job titles are all the responsibility of one person. In other companies, these responsibilities are carried out by individuals who are not employees of the subject company (e.g., an outside accountant serves in the capacity of the CFO). Ultimately, the appraiser will want to work with the client to determine exactly who should be interviewed to gain an understanding of the important information that affects the company's value.

Confidentiality

Confidentiality is one problem that the appraiser frequently must handle carefully on field trips. There can be many good reasons for confidentiality. Experienced appraisers have learned to work around this problem. They can dress and act unobtrusively. If they have to be introduced or identified to someone who is not a confidant in the situation, they are "consultants," which is an accurate and adequately abstruse label.

As a last resort, the appraiser might visit the premises after working hours, when employees are not present. However, this will not give the appraiser as good a picture as would seeing the facility in operation.

All professional business appraisal organizations have provisions in their respective codes of ethics prohibiting dissemination of confidential information obtained during an appraisal assignment. Also, it is common for appraisers to sign confidentiality agreements. If it is necessary to use confidential material at trial, most courts are accommodating to requests to put that portion of the record under seal.

Adversarial Proceedings

Another problem that the appraiser sometimes faces is opposition to an adequate facilities visit (or sometimes any facilities visit at all) in the case of an adversarial proceeding. Undoubtedly, this problem most commonly occurs in appraisals being made for the purpose of property settlements in divorces. Some lawyers and clients will try to stonewall the appraisers retained by the "outside" party (for example, nonoperating spouse, minority stockholder, damage plaintiff) from interviewing the "inside" party and management. However, this is the opportunity for "inside" parties to present their side of the story. To the extent that their story is credible, a good appraiser will take it into account.

In these circumstances, it is the responsibility of the client's lawyer to make the necessary arrangements for the appraiser to visit the facilities and interview the appropriate people. Case law generally supports site visits as essential to do the job properly.[4] The parties should understand that the site visit is a standard part of the appraiser's work. They should understand that the appraiser is neither an adverse party nor an advocate for either party. Rather, the appraiser has been retained to render an independent opinion about value. When using a reputable professional appraiser, the parties should not have to be concerned with confidentiality. Furthermore, the party who is in the adversarial position to the appraiser's client should welcome the opportunity to tell his or her side of the story to the appraiser.

If all discovery has to proceed through interrogatories and court orders, the process will be much more time-consuming, costly, and disruptive to the business operation. It is usually a good business decision for parties on both sides of a dispute to cooperate with independent appraisers.

Federal Rule of Civil Procedure 34

A request for production of documents and electronically stored information (ESI) and for entry upon the premises for inspection under FRCP 34 or the corresponding rule of the appropriate jurisdiction is the proper method of obtaining this vital information for the expert's use. The documents or ESI requested or the premises to be inspected must be in the possession or control of a party to the litigation. (If the needed material is not in the possession of a party to the litigation, see the section on subpoenas below.)

Limitations on the Scope of Discovery

The scope of available discovery under FRCP 34 is limited by FRCP 26 to:

> any nonprivileged matter that is relevant to any party's claim or defense—including the existence, description, nature, custody, condition, and location of any documents or other tangible things and the identity and location of

4. This issue is discussed in Barth Goldberg & Joseph N. DuCanto, Valuation of Divorce Assets (supplement 2004).

> persons who know of any discoverable matter. For good cause, the court may order discovery of any matter relevant to the subject matter involved in the action. Relevant information need not be admissible at the trial if the discovery appears reasonably calculated to lead to the discovery of admissible evidence.

All jurisdictions have a similar limitation on the scope of documents that can be obtained or purposes for which premises may be entered and inspected.

Before drafting a request for production of documents or ESI, discuss with the business appraiser the specific documents or ESI he or she will need to perform the valuation analysis. Request only those documents or ESI that are relevant to a determination of value or to proof of an element of one of your claims or defenses. FRCP 34(b)(E) provides, regarding ESI, that if a request does not specify a form of production, a party must produce it in a form or forms in which it is ordinarily maintained or in a reasonably usable form or forms, but a party is not required to produce the same ESI in more than one form. Keep in mind that under FRCP 26(b)(1), parties are allowed to obtain discovery on any matter, not privileged, that is relevant to the claim or defense of any party. Relevance within the meaning of Fed. R. Civ. P. 26(b)(1) is considerably broader than relevance for trial purposes. For discovery purposes, relevance means only that the materials sought are reasonably calculated to lead to the discovery of admissible evidence.

Nonetheless, the other party will likely be able to resist a request that is overbroad[5] and obtain a protective order regarding documents that are not relevant to the issues presented in the case[6] or that must be kept confidential by the appraiser.[7]

In *Lane v. Cancer Treatment Centers of America,*[8] a dissenting shareholder appraisal suit, the issue was the value of the plaintiffs' interest in Cancer Care Centers. The plaintiffs served a request for production of documents that read:

> All financial statements, stock valuations, asset appraisals, and all documents relating to financial data, concerning any of [Cancer Treatment Centers, RJS, Cancer Care Centers] and/or any of their Affiliated Corporations, including

5. Lane v. Cancer Treatment Centers of Am., 1994 Del. Ch. LEXIS 67, 1994 WL 263558 (Del. Ch. May 25, 1994).

6. Picerne Dev. v. Tasca and Rotelli, 635 So. 2d 149 (Fla. Dist. Ct. App. 1994); Perry v. Perry, 1995 Minn. App. LEXIS 1207, 1995 WL 550902 (Minn. Ct. App. Sept. 19, 1995).

7. Oliver v. Stone, 940 So. 2d 526; 2006 Fla. App. LEXIS 17631 (Fla. Ct. App. 2006) (appraiser could not reveal discovered materials underlying the valuation report even to the party that retained and paid him).

8. *Lane,* 1994 Del. Ch. LEXIS 67, 1994 WL 263558 (Del. Ch. May 25, 1994).

without limitation all financial models, budgets (proposed or otherwise) and pro formas.

The Delaware Chancery Court agreed with the defendants' objection that the request was overbroad and was not limited to the narrow issue of valuation of Cancer Care Centers. The court required the plaintiffs to rewrite the requests so that they did not include financial documents and information on companies other than Cancer Care Centers unless they related specifically to business dealings with Cancer Care Centers.

In *Perry v. Perry,*[9] one of the issues was whether the defendants had received unfair distributions from the corporation. The plaintiff's request for production of documents sought the defendant's individual income tax returns and personal financial statements. The trial court's denial of the plaintiff's motion to compel was upheld by the Minnesota Court of Appeals on the ground that the information sought could be obtained from the corporate books and records, to which the plaintiff had full access.

Sanctions for Failure to Comply with a Discovery Order

If a party fails to respond to a request for production of documents or ESI or for entry upon premises for inspection, the other party may move for an order compelling discovery. Before filing such a motion, however, the party must make a good-faith effort to confer with opposing counsel to resolve the problem.

Trial courts have broad discretion to impose sanctions for failure to comply with discovery orders, especially where the other party is prejudiced by the failure to comply. Motions and orders to compel discovery and sanctions for failure to comply are governed by FRCP 37. All U.S. jurisdictions have a similar provision. Under these rules, sanctions can include:

- An award of lawyers' fees and costs to the party that made the request and obtained the discovery order[10]
- An order "directing that the matters embraced in the order or other designated facts be taken as established for purposes of the action, as the prevailing party claims"[11]
- An order "prohibiting the disobedient party from supporting or opposing designated claims or defenses, or from introducing designated matters in evidence"[12]

---

9. *Perry,* 1995 Minn. App. LEXIS 1207, 1995 WL 550902 (Minn. Ct. App. Sept. 19, 1995).
10. § 37(b)(2)(C).
11. Fed. R. Civ. P. § 37(b)(2)(A)(i).
12. *Id.*

- Striking a pleading or portion of a pleading
- Dismissing the suit or one or more claims or counterclaims
- Rendering a default judgment against the noncomplying party
- Treatment of the failure as contempt of court[13]

However, absent exceptional circumstances, a court may not impose such sanctions on a party for failing to provide ESI lost as a result of the routine, good-faith operation of an electronic information system.[14]

Before one of the harsher sanctions, such as dismissal, may be imposed, the trial court must weigh the following factors:

1. The public's interest in the expeditious resolution of litigation
2. The court's need to manage its docket
3. The risk of prejudice to the party seeking sanctions
4. The public policy favoring disposition of cases on their merits
5. The availability of less-drastic sanctions[15]

In *Anheuser-Busch Inc. v. Natural Beverage Distributors,*[16] the defendant failed to produce business records, claiming that they were destroyed in a fire. After many months of stonewalling, the defendant produced the legible documents that had survived the fire. Nonetheless, the trial court dismissed the defendant's counterclaim as a sanction for its conduct, and the Ninth Circuit upheld the dismissal, stating:

> This court has squarely rejected the notion that a failure to comply with the rules of discovery is purged by belated compliance.

Subpoena for Production of Documents, Electronically Stored Information, or Tangible Things, or to Permit the Inspection of Premises

Often a business appraiser will need to review documents, ESI, or tangible things, or inspect business premises that are in the possession or control of someone who is not a party to the action. Under the Federal Rules, this can be accomplished with a subpoena.[17] As with a request for production or entry upon premises directed at a party, the request must pertain to relevant nonprivileged information. All U.S. jurisdictions similarly provide for the issuance of a subpoena to nonparties.

---

13. Fed. R. Civ. P. § 37(b)(2)(A).
14. Fed. R. Civ. P. § 37(e)
15. Anheuser-Busch, Inc. v. Natural Beverage Distribs., 69 F.3d 337 (9th Cir. 1995).
16. *Supra.*
17. Fed. R. Civ. P. § 45.

With respect to ESI, the subpoena can designate a form or forms for production of electronic data,[18] but the person served with the subpoena may object to the requested form or forms. In addition, if the subpoena does not specify the form or forms for ESI, the person served with the subpoena must produce ESI in a form or forms in which it is usually maintained or in a form or forms that are reasonably usable.[19] However, the person producing ESI does not have to produce the same information in more than one form unless so ordered by the court for good cause.[20] New Jersey, for example, provides that a party need not provide discovery of ESI from sources that the party identifies as not reasonably accessible because of undue burden or cost.[21]

A nonparty upon whom a subpoena is served may object to the subpoena and have it quashed or modified if:

- It doesn't allow a reasonable time for the nonparty to comply.
- It requires the nonparty to travel more than 100 miles.
- It requires the nonparty to disclose privileged or protected matter, including trade secrets, confidential research, development or commercial matter, if no exception or waiver applies.
- It subjects the nonparty to undue burden, including financial burden.
- It is overbroad or not related to a claim or defense of the party serving the subpoena.
- It requires disclosure of "an unretained expert's opinion or information that does not describe specific occurrences in dispute and results from the expert's study that was not requested by a party."[22]

Subpoena of Expert's Work Papers

Although a business valuation expert may be directly involved in litigation, the expert is, of course, not a party. Nonetheless, it is important to obtain the work papers that the expert created and used in preparing a final valuation report. Frequently, a party's own valuation expert will find significant errors in the opposing expert's calculations or assumptions that are not apparent on the face of the valuation report and could only be discovered through a review of the work papers. Detection of these errors can bring the opposing valuations much closer and lead to settlement of the case.

18. Fed. R. Civ. P. § 45(a)(1).
19. Fed. R. Civ. P. § 45(c)(2).
20. Fed. R. Civ. P. § 45(d)(1)(B).
21. Fed. R. Civ. P. § 45(d)(1)(C).
22. Fed. R. Civ. P. § 45(c)(3)(A) & (B).

Because the expert is not a party, the appropriate means of obtaining the work papers is a subpoena,[23] sometimes called a subpoena duces tecum. The same reasons for objecting to any other subpoena of a nonparty apply when serving a subpoena on an expert witness.

Interrogatories: Timing of Service and Limitations

Interrogatories are inferior to depositions as a means of finding out what an appraiser has done because they are not interactive, that is, one question cannot be followed up by a series of other questions depending on the answer. However, interrogatories can be a useful discovery tool to obtain information about a business appraisal expert. This is especially true in those jurisdictions that do not require a written report of the expert to be served on other parties or that do not allow a party to depose an expert witness without a court order.[24] Only two jurisdictions—Oregon and Texas—do not allow interrogatories to be used as a discovery device on expert witnesses.

Interrogatories Depend upon Written Report Requirement

In jurisdictions where the parties are required to provide the written report of an expert witness to all other parties, interrogatories can be used to obtain supplemental information about the expert or the report, such as:

- Educational background
- Professional designations
- Prior experience testifying as an expert witness
- Prior business valuation experience that is not litigation-related
- Books or articles written by the expert
- Clarification of facts recited in the report and the source of those facts

By using interrogatories, a party who is not entitled to a written report can inquire regarding all of the above-listed information, as well as require the other party to:

- Identify each expert expected to testify at trial
- State the subject matter of the testimony
- State the facts relied on by the expert
- State the substance of the expert's opinions
- Provide a summary of the grounds for each opinion

23. Fed. R. Civ. P. § 45.

24. Seventeen jurisdictions have both of these limitations: Alabama, Arkansas, Delaware, District of Columbia, Indiana, Maine, Massachusetts, Minnesota, Mississippi, Montana, Nebraska, New Mexico, New York, North Carolina, South Dakota, Guam, and Puerto Rico.

Timing of Service

Under FRCP 33(a) and 26(d), and the rules of four other jurisdictions—Colorado, Nevada, Utah, and the Virgin Islands—a party may serve interrogatories at any time after the parties have met and conferred on a plan of discovery and have filed a case conference report (i.e., plan of discovery). Most jurisdictions[25] allow a party to serve interrogatories on the plaintiff at any time after commencement of the action or on any other party with or after service of the summons and complaint on that party. In other jurisdictions, timing for service of interrogatories by plaintiff varies and may be:

- Ten days after service on or appearance by defendant (California)
- At any time after the return day (Connecticut)
- After all defendants have appeared (Illinois)
- After defendant's time for serving a responsive pleading (New York)
- Sixty days after service of summons and complaint upon the party (Rhode Island)
- After the summons and copy of the complaint have been served upon the defendant or the complaint filed (Washington)
- At any time (Maryland and New Hampshire)

Limits on Number of Interrogatories That Can Be Served

Many jurisdictions limit the number of interrogatories that can be served on another party. These limitations should be kept in mind when deciding what information is most important to obtain about a business valuation expert. Limitations can be modified by leave of court or written stipulation of the parties.

Under FRCP 33(a), a party can serve "no more than 25 written interrogatories, including all discrete subparts. Leave to serve additional interrogatories may be granted to the extent consistent with Rule 26(b)(2)." Two other jurisdictions—Utah and the Virgin Islands—follow the Federal Rules limitation. The number of interrogatories allowed in other jurisdictions includes:

- Sixty (Hawaii)
- Fifty (Georgia, Minnesota, Montana, Nebraska, New Hampshire, New Mexico, and North Carolina)

25. Alabama, Alaska, Arizona, Arkansas, Delaware, District of Columbia, Florida, Georgia, Hawaii, Idaho, Indiana, Iowa, Kansas, Kentucky, Louisiana, Maine, Massachusetts, Michigan, Minnesota, Mississippi, Missouri, Montana, Nebraska, New Jersey, New Mexico, North Carolina, North Dakota, Ohio, Oklahoma, Pennsylvania (permits service prior to service of complaint for purpose of preparing the complaint), South Carolina, South Dakota, Tennessee, Vermont, Virginia, West Virginia, Wisconsin, Guam, and Puerto Rico.

- Fifty in addition to the standard interrogatories (South Carolina)
- Forty (Alabama, Arizona, District of Columbia, Idaho, Nevada, Ohio, and West Virginia)
- Thirty-five (Louisiana)
- Thirty-five specially prepared and any additional form interrogatories (California)
- Thirty (Alaska, Colorado, Florida, Illinois, Kentucky, Maine, Maryland, Massachusetts, Mississippi, Oklahoma, Rhode Island, Virginia, and Wyoming)

Form of Response

Some states have started to require that responses to discovery requests are made in electronic format. Indiana requires that the party making a discovery request serve the request or response in an electronic format (either on a disk or as an electronic document attachment) in any commercially available word-processing software system or certify by verified statement that the party does not have the equipment necessary to comply with this rule. Similarly, with respect to interrogatories, Ohio requires a party to provide the party served with both a printed and an electronic copy of the interrogatories or seek leave of court to be relieved of this requirement if it is unable to comply.

Depositions: Timing of Request and Special Rules

Frequently, a lawyer will want to depose a business appraiser that the other party has hired. The deposition is often the most important event during the course of business litigation because most cases settle before trial based on the opposing lawyer's evaluation of the testimony and the demeanor of witnesses.[26] Several issues must be considered: whether the appraiser will be called as an expert at trial, the timing of the request for deposition, limitations upon the taking of depositions, and whether the jurisdiction allows depositions of expert witnesses.

Federal Rules of Civil Procedure 26(b)(4), 30, and 31

Under FRCP 26(b)(4)(A), a party may depose a business appraisal expert whose testimony may be offered at trial. However, the deposition of an expert may be taken only after the parties have met and conferred regarding a plan of discovery as required by FRCP 26(f) and any required written report has been provided, unless leave of court is granted to depose sooner or the parties so stipulate. Other limitations on depositions of testifying experts under FRCP 30 (oral depositions) and 31 (deposi-

26. Brian Brinig, *Business Valuation Litigation: Developing, Documenting, Presenting and Defending Your Opinion*, BVResearch, June 22, 2000, *available at* www.bvlibrary.com.

tions by written questions) require leave of court or stipulation of the parties to conduct a deposition if the proposed deposition would result in more than 10 depositions by the party; the person to be deposed already has been deposed in the case; or the party seeks to take the deposition before the time specified in FRCP 26(d)—generally only after the parties have conferred under FRCP 26(f)—unless the party certifies in the notice, with supporting facts, that the deponent is expected to leave the United States and will be unavailable for examination in this country after that time.

Under FRCP 26(b)(4)(B), if a party hires a business appraiser in anticipation of litigation or preparation for trial, but does not intend to offer the testimony or opinion of that expert at trial, then the other parties may depose that expert only "on showing exceptional circumstances under which it is impracticable for the party to obtain facts or opinions on the same subject by other means."

Only five U.S. jurisdictions—Alaska, Colorado, Nevada, Utah, and the Virgin Islands—follow the Federal Rules of Civil Procedure in requiring the parties to meet and confer to develop a plan of discovery (also referred to as a case management order or case conference report) before depositions may be taken. In many jurisdictions, if the plaintiff seeks to take a deposition prior to the expiration of a certain number of days after service of the summons and complaint upon any defendant or related service, leave of court, granted with or without notice, is required except that leave is not required: (1) if a defendant has served a notice of taking deposition or otherwise sought discovery or (2) if the plaintiff provides a notice that states that the person to be examined is about to go out of the state or out of the country and will be unavailable for examination unless the person's deposition is taken before expiration of the period and sets forth facts to support the statement. Time limitations on the plaintiff for serving a request for deposition in various jurisdictions, irrespective of whether the jurisdiction also requires a court order for the taking of an expert's deposition, are:

- Thirty days after service of summons and complaint (Alabama, Arizona, Arkansas, Delaware, District of Columbia (70 days in any case involving the District of Columbia or its officer or agency, or the United States or its officer or agency), Florida, Georgia, Guam, Hawaii, Idaho, Kansas, Kentucky, Maine, Massachusetts, Minnesota, Mississippi, Missouri, Montana, Nebraska, New Mexico, North Carolina, North Dakota, Oklahoma, South Carolina, South Dakota, Tennessee, Vermont, Washington, West Virginia, and Wyoming)
- Thirty-five days after service (New Jersey)

- Twenty-eight days after service or before the defendant has had a reasonable time to obtain an attorney (Michigan)
- Twenty days after service or return day (California, Connecticut, Indiana, New Hampshire, and Puerto Rico)
- Fifteen days after service (Louisiana)

Any of these time limits can be shortened by leave of court or if the defendant seeks discovery earlier. Four jurisdictions—Maryland, New York and Virginia (due date for defendant's pleading), and Iowa (10 days after due date for defendant's pleading)—base the time limitations for serving a request for deposition on the date on which the defendant is required to file and serve the first responsive motion, answer, or other pleading. These jurisdictions also allow earlier depositions upon leave of court.

Five jurisdictions—District of Columbia, Hawaii, Utah, Wyoming, and the Virgin Islands—limit the total number of depositions that may be taken by a party to 10. A party may be allowed more depositions with leave of court or stipulation of the parties. Twelve jurisdictions—Alaska, Colorado, District of Columbia, Hawaii, Kansas, Maryland, Nevada, Oklahoma, Rhode Island, South Carolina, Utah, and Wyoming—require leave of court to depose an expert witness who already has been deposed in the same case. In Maryland, however, such leave is not required if there have been substantive changes to the deposition transcript. Some states put a limit on the number of independent expert witnesses that may testify about the same issue.[27]

States That Do Not Allow Depositions of Expert Witnesses as a Matter of Course

The right to depose an expert witness may be viewed as a matter of course. However, 18 U.S. jurisdictions[28] do not allow taking the deposition of an expert witness expected to testify at trial without a court order for further discovery beyond interrogatories. Three jurisdictions—Kentucky, Oklahoma, and Rhode Island—require interrogatories to be served before the deposition of an expert witness may be taken; one—Ohio—requires a showing of exceptional circumstances to take the deposition of an expert witness; and one—Oregon—does not allow a deposition of an expert witness under any circumstances.

Ensuring an Expert Is Deposition-Ready

It goes without saying that any expert who will provide a deposition must be thoroughly prepared to do so. However, as *Phase 2 Developers, Corp. v. Citicorp Real*

27. *E.g.*, Alaska (3); Arizona (1).

28. Alabama, Arkansas, Delaware, District of Columbia, Indiana, Maine, Massachusetts, Minnesota, Mississippi, Montana, Nebraska, New Mexico, New York, North Carolina, Pennsylvania, South Dakota, Guam, and Puerto Rico.

Estate[29] illustrates, an unprepared expert can torpedo an entire valuation case. In that case, the expert had prepared his report four years prior to being deposed. At his deposition, the expert testified that "he had not done any preparation for the deposition and had not looked at the material in the opinion binder since [preparing the report]." As a result of his being ill-prepared, the expert was not able to provide meaningful responses to questions about his assumptions and other valuation matters. Thereafter, the opposing party filed a motion *in limine* to exclude this expert's testimony and further sought nonsuit, if the testimony was stricken. The trial court, determining that the expert's inability to testify at deposition regarding his opinion was sufficient to exclude his testimony, granted both motions.

On appeal, the party retaining the expert argued that the expert's inability to give adequate deposition testimony resulted from the four-year delay between the completion of the report and the deposition and that, in any event, the answers to all the questions asked by the opposing party at deposition could be found in the expert's report, which had been supplied to it. The appellate court rejected these arguments, stating that "the delay in taking the deposition does not eliminate the expert's obligation to be prepared adequately for the deposition." Moreover, it stated, "it is not sufficient for an expert to produce work papers and tell the opposing party to search through them for the answers to questions." Thus, it determined that absent meaningful deposition testimony, the trial court properly excluded this expert.

Timely Disclosure and Duty to Supplement

If requested disclosure is not timely made, although it could be, the court may not permit a subsequent disclosure to remedy the original deficiency. In *AMP Enterprises v. Price Pfister, Inc.*,[30] the plaintiffs sought economic damages. The defendants sought information pertaining to the amount and calculation of the independent sales representatives' damages. The plaintiffs, however, did not provide any information relating to damages, except to indicate that they were engaging an economic expert. Supplemental responses to the defendants' interrogatories were not forthcoming and, eventually, the defendants brought a motion for summary judgment on the basis that the plaintiffs could not establish the amount of damages, a required element to their claim. In response to this motion, the plaintiffs provided the court with a declaration from their economic expert. This declaration listed the documents utilized and people interviewed in connection with the report. It further reported the amount of damages in terms of lost profit and lost value of business. The defendants moved to exclude the expert's declaration as without sufficient basis because it did not include any informa-

29. Phase 2 Developers Corp. v. Citicorp Real Estate, 2004 Cal. App. Unpub. 117 (Cal. Ct. App. 2004).

30. AMP Enters. v. Price Pfister, Inc., 2003 Cal. App. Unpub. LEXIS 10830 (Cal. Ct. App. 2003).

tion on how the damages were calculated. The plaintiffs countered this argument by claiming that the insufficiency of the declaration went to the weight of the evidence rather than to admissibility. The trial court agreed with the plaintiffs that the expert's declaration was insufficient to overcome its motion for summary judgment because it did not provide sufficient detail. It particularly noted that the declaration did not explain the formulas or methods used to calculate the loss, disclose the time period used to assess lost profits, or indicate whether the amounts were gross or net profits. Only then did the plaintiffs provide the court with an amended declaration from their expert, including the missing data. The court declined to reopen the matter because it found no reason why the missing data could not have been provided in the original declaration from the expert. On appeal, the appellate court affirmed.

In *Estate of Perry,*[31] the appraisal expert was timely disclosed, but the expert's report was not, and was provided to counsel three weeks after the due date for its disclosure. Counsel moved to extend the disclosure deadline for the report, arguing that it was late as a result of the unexpected illness of one of the parties and a language barrier. Counsel also argued there was no failure of due diligence, and the opposing parties would suffer neither prejudice nor unfair surprise given that the trial was 73 days away and there was ample time to respond to the report. Nonetheless, counsel for the opposing party objected to the motion, claiming this did not constitute good cause for the late disclosure. The trial court agreed with the opposing party, denied the motion, and precluded the expert from testifying at trial. The court concluded that good cause for delaying docket deadlines does not exist simply because there is a lack of surprise to the other side or counsel inadvertently misjudges the need for an appraiser. Here, the court reasoned that the appraiser had commenced work on the report, could have supplied a draft by the disclosure deadline, and could have subsequently amended the draft. On appeal, the appellate court affirmed, holding that given the failure to comply in any fashion with the disclosure time limits—and given the "wide latitude" afforded a trial court to maintain its trial docket and discovery orders—there was no abuse of discretion in precluding the expert.

In *Hammers v. Hammers,*[32] a marital dissolution action, the trial court excluded the husband's valuation expert on the grounds that the expert had been disclosed too late—one week, rather than 60 days, before trial. Early on, the wife disclosed that she had engaged a business appraiser to value the marital business. The expert's report was submitted by the discovery deadline. After reviewing the business appraisal submitted by the wife, the husband realized that he needed a business appraiser and notified the wife's attorneys that he would secure an independent business appraisal. However, it was not until the week before trial that the husband designated his valu-

31. Estate of Perry, 2007 Tex. App. LEXIS 6465 (Tex. Ct. App. 2007).
32. Hammers v. Hammers, 890 So. 2d 944 (Miss. Ct. App. 2004).

ation expert. The trial court excluded the husband's valuation expert for failure to timely disclose the expert, and, on appeal, the appellate court affirmed. The appellate court reasoned that the husband could have petitioned the lower court to amend the discovery deadline but instead chose to wait until the week before trial. Accordingly, the court concluded that the wife would be prejudiced if the husband were permitted to bring the expert in on such short notice.

Similarly, in *In re Letendre,*[33] the trial court excluded the husband's valuation expert's report. Prior to trial, the wife requested disclosure of the husband's valuation expert, but the husband did not comply. Subsequently, the wife moved *in limine* to preclude the husband from presenting an appraisal or valuation expert's report or testimony not disclosed by the discovery deadline. The trial court granted the motion and the husband did not provide any expert information to the wife prior to the close of discovery. On appeal, the husband contended that he had disclosed his expert's identity to the wife's attorney nearly a year before trial and, therefore, the wife had ample opportunity to depose him. He also contended that he believed that the discovery deadline was meant "as the date to exchange expert reports provided the exchange was mutual." The state's highest court ruled that the trial court's decision to exclude the husband's expert from testifying was sustainable on the record because he did not comply with the discovery deadline mandated by the trial court and because, even if he misunderstood the meaning of the discovery date, he failed to comply with the wife's repeated requests for information in violation of discovery rules. The court concluded that the husband's failure to provide the wife with complete information bearing directly on the valuation of the business prevented the wife from adequately preparing for trial.

Many jurisdictions require a party who has made a disclosure—or who has responded to an interrogatory, request for production, or request for admission—to supplement or correct its disclosure or response in a timely manner if the party learns that in some material respect the disclosure or response is incomplete or incorrect, and if the additional or corrective information has not otherwise been made known to the other parties during the discovery process or in writing or as ordered by the court. FRCP 26(e) provides that for an expert whose report must be disclosed under FRCP 26(a)(2)(B), the party's duty to supplement extends both to information included in the report and to information given during the expert's deposition. Any additions or changes to this information must be disclosed by the time the party's pretrial disclosures under FRCP 26(a)(3) are due. Iowa, for example, expressly requires supplementation as to experts, as soon as practicable, but in no event less than 30 days prior to the beginning of trial except on leave of court.

33. *In re* Letendre, 815 A.2d 938 (N.H. 2002).

If required supplemental disclosure is not timely made, a court has broad discretion to craft appropriate sanctions for such failure, up to and including the exclusion of the expert's testimony, or it may make such orders in regard to the nondisclosure as are just. In *Linsell v. Applied Handling, Inc.,*[34] the Michigan Court of Appeals affirmed a trial court's decision to not strike a party's expert even though the party had failed to timely supplement interrogatory answers regarding the expert witness. The trial court had ruled that the moving party was not prejudiced because the documents that formed the basis of the expert's testimony were supplied by the moving party, and the appellate court agreed. It concluded that the trial court had not abused its discretion where not only had the documents relied on by the expert been provided by the moving party, but the expert's charts were provided to the moving party shortly after they had been completed, and the trial court had given the moving party an opportunity to depose the expert.

In *Sharp v. Chase Manhattan Bank,*[35] 350 B.R. 520, 2005 Bankr. LEXIS 3045 (Bankr. N.D. Okla. 2005), the court determined that a business valuation expert's efforts to revise her reports and calculations through supplementation did not necessarily render her methods or opinions unreliable. The court found that no adverse inferences were to be drawn about the quality of her work product under FRCP 26(e) because, in an effort to provide complete and accurate disclosures, she satisfactorily explained the cause of mathematical errors in her business valuation and the basis for revising her calculations through proper and timely supplementation, which did not alter her ultimate opinion that the debtor businesses were insolvent. To the contrary, the court was impressed with the expert's diligence in seeking to ensure that her opinion was based upon demonstrable facts (some of which were overlooked in prior reports or only came to light after the reports were issued), that her reports were internally consistent and consistent with each other, and that her analysis could withstand a rigorous review. As a result of her explanations, the court concluded that the corrections were not of the type to cause suspicion that the expert was influenced by the need to reach a particular result for the purpose of the litigation.

Scope of Discovery—Some Specific Examples

- *Postvaluation date events.* In *Maxon v. Mirror Show Management, Inc.,* the New York Supreme Court ruled that discovery of postvaluation date events was appropriate in a breach of fiduciary case involving the valuation of a corporation.[36]

34. Linsell v. Applied Handling, Inc., 697 N.W.2d 913 (Mich. Ct. App. 2005).

35. Sharp v. Chase Manhattan Bank, 350 B.R. 520, 2005 Bankr. LEXIS 3045 (Bankr. N.D. Okla. 2005).

36. Maxon v. Mirror Show Mgmt., Inc., 7 Misc. 3d 1015A; 801 N.Y.S.2d 236; 2005 N.Y. Misc. LEXIS 795 (N.Y. Sup. 2005).

- *Confidentiality of underlying data and methodologies.* In *Estate of Manship v. United States,* a federal district court ruled that pre-IPO studies relied on by a valuation expert to value a corporation for estate tax purposes were discoverable, finding that there was nothing confidential about them.[37] In another federal case, *U.S. v. Batchelor-Robjohns,*[38] the court ruled that the government's refusal to disclose certain valuation models underlying its expert's valuation opinion would require exclusion of that opinion. In that case, the government's valuation expert provided a valuation of the taxpayer's assets and an opinion concerning the taxpayer's income-generating capacity, but the government refused to disclose information concerning the allegedly proprietary computer models used to value the assets. Finding that the government had failed to substantively justify its failure to disclose, the court excluded the expert's opinion, reasoning that neither the court nor transferees to whom the assets had been transferred were able to test the reliability of the valuation opinion in the absence of the data and methodology upon which the opinion was based. In addition, the court concluded that admission of the expert's opinion would clearly have prejudiced the transferees' ability to cross-examine the expert and rebut his opinion. Finally, the court excluded the reports and testimony of other government valuation experts to the extent they had relied on the opinion based on the nondisclosed models.
- *Waiver of attorney-client privilege.* In a case related to *Estate of Manship,* but brought in a different jurisdiction, the federal district court held that documents disclosed by an appraiser, who obtained them from the estate's attorney, although initially covered by the work product or attorney-client privilege, lost the privilege and were discoverable because (1) the estate waived the privilege by voluntarily disclosing the documents and because (2) by listing the appraiser as a testifying expert, FRCP 26(a)(2)(B) permitted discovery of "all documents 'considered' by those experts in rendering their valuation opinions" "regardless of when those materials were received, generated, reviewed and/or used."[39] The court also noted that because the estate placed the valuation in issue and intended to rely on it at trial, any privilege connected with the reports and related documents submitted by the estate in connection with the estate tax return was waived. Lastly, the court noted that the IRS would be unable to adequately cross-examine or present rebuttal expert testimony without full access to the documents that the estate's appraiser consid-

37. Estate of Manship v. United States, 2006 U.S. Dist. LEXIS 96334 (N.D. Ga. 2006).
38. United States v. Batchelor-Robjohns, 2005 U.S. Dist. LEXIS 13552 (S.D. Fla. 2005).
39. Estate of Manship v. United States, 236 F.R.D. 291; 2006 U.S. Dist. LEXIS 43219; 2006-1 U.S. Tax Cas. (CCH) ¶ 50,331 (M.D. La. 2006).

ered in forming his opinion of value. In a subsequent proceeding,[40] the court ruled that, where yet a different court had ruled that the estate's rebuttal witness (the valuation expert) could not claim the attorney-client privilege as to consulting work the expert had conducted for the estate, because even though the expert would only testify at trial to criticize the methodology employed by the United States' valuation expert, the subject matter of that trial testimony involved the "same topics on which he was engaged in a consulting capacity dealing with the same properties," a protective order should issue to limit the government's questions to those (1) concerning the expert's consulting agreement with the estate (which were questions the expert had refused to answer on grounds of privilege during his previous deposition) and (2) questions arising out of documents produced by the estate related to the prior consulting engagement.

- *Distinguishing opinion from work product.* In *Greenlight Capital Qualified, L.P. v. Emerging Communications, Inc.*,[41] the Delaware Court of Chancery ruled in a fair value case that a deposition of a valuation witness may be taken even though the valuation report was protected from discovery under work-product immunity. The court concluded that "as a logical matter it would seem that the 'bottom line' valuation range, and any intermediate data and calculations leading thereto, would not contain such protected information. Accordingly, I perceive no reason why Emerging's counsel would be unable to frame deposition questions that will elicit the discoverable information . . . without eliciting, directly or indirectly, 'disclosure of an attorney's mental impressions or theories of the case.'"
- *Postproduction assertions of privilege.* Minnesota has a rule dealing with assertions of privilege that are made following production of information in discovery. The rule creates a mandatory obligation to return, sequester, or destroy information that is produced in discovery if the producing party asserts that it is subject to a privilege or work-product protection. The information cannot be used for any purpose until the privilege claim is resolved. The rule provides a mechanism for the receiving party to have the validity of the privilege claim resolved by the court. The rule does not create any presumption or have any impact on the validity of the claim of privilege, nor does it excuse the inadvertent or regretted production. If the court determines that that production waived an otherwise valid privilege, then the information should be ordered for production or release from sequestration of the information.

40. Estate of Manship v. United States, 2007 U.S. Dist. LEXIS 81922 (M.D. La. 2007).

41. Greenlight Capital Qualified, L.P. v. Emerging Communications, Inc., C.A. 16943 (Del. Ct. ch. Feb. 23, 2001).

- *Discovery of draft reports and e-mail.* The defendants in *University of Pittsburgh v. Townsend*[42] sought to exclude the testimony of plaintiff's experts on the grounds that they had destroyed prior drafts of their expert reports as well as e-mail with counsel, on a theory of spoliation and destruction of evidence. The defendants had requested the plaintiff to produce "[a]ll [d]ocuments provided to or by [y]ou to, revised by, relied upon, or otherwise used in consultation with or as a basis for consultation with, any expert witness identified by [y]ou pursuant to Fed. R. Civ. Proc. 26(a)(2)." In its response, the plaintiff objected to this request as premature and stated that "[r]esponsive documents will be produced in accordance with Federal Rule of Civil Procedure 26(a)(2) and the Case Management Order applicable to this matter." Around a year and a half later, the defendants deposed the experts, subpoenaing "any and all" documents related to the preparing of their reports, including all drafts and correspondence with the attorneys. However, the experts had, on counsel's advice, destroyed all prior drafts up to that point as well as e-mail they had had with counsel. Accordingly, the defendants contended that FRCP 26(a)(2) imposes an affirmative duty upon an expert "to preserve all documents, including e-mails and drafts of a report." The defendants also contended that because the plaintiff's experts and counsel destroyed discoverable evidence, the plaintiff should be sanctioned by precluding the experts from testifying at trial.

  The plaintiff countered that until the subpoenas were served on the plaintiff's experts shortly before their depositions, there was no outstanding discovery request asking for the drafts of any expert reports and that no documents were destroyed once the subpoenas were served. Furthermore, the plaintiff contended that the requested e-mail communications and draft reports were not "evidence" and raised inherent issues of privilege and work product. Finally, the plaintiff argued that the defendants had not suffered any prejudice because they had the opportunity to fully depose the plaintiff's experts and the experts specifically identified the portions of their reports where they received assistance or input from counsel.

  As to the discovery of the draft reports, the court ruled that FRCP 26(a)(2) does not impose an "affirmative duty" upon experts to preserve "all documents," particularly draft reports, and that experts are not obligated to provide copies of draft reports as part of their required 26(a)(2)(B) disclosures. The court added, however, that although draft reports are not "technically" required to be disclosed, they are "certainly discoverable." The question was one of timing. The defendants' discovery request was too "awkwardly worded"

42. Univ. of Pittsburgh v. Townsend, 2007 U.S. Dist. LEXIS 24620 (E.D. Tenn. 2007).

to clearly require the production of draft reports, but even a more specific request would have been "unreasonable." Served more than a year before the FRCP 26(a)(2)(B) deadlines, the request would have imposed a "continuing obligation on a party to disclose any document from an expert—whether it be a letter or a draft—as it is received through the consultation process." Moreover, "such a requirement would virtually nullify the expert disclosure deadline established by the Court." Because the defendants clearly requested the draft reports in their deposition subpoenas, "[o]nly at that point were the experts under a duty to retain any drafts and produce them," and because the experts had destroyed the drafts prior to the subpoenas, they would not be subject to sanctions.

As for the e-mail, the court reasoned that because FRCP 26(a)(2)(B) requires the disclosure of "the data or information considered by the [expert] in forming the opinions," to the extent that correspondence between counsel and the experts contained any factual assumptions or background used in the reports, such correspondence had to be disclosed. Because such data or information expressly is not immune from disclosure by any privilege or work-product protection, it was improper "for plaintiff's counsel to have instructed and/or otherwise suggested to the experts that such communications should be destroyed." Nonetheless, the court found no fraudulent intent (plaintiff's counsel, had, in fact apologized for erroneously instructing the experts to destroy the communications). The court also concluded that the defendants were not prejudiced by the destruction of these communications, for the defendants were able to fully cross-examine the witnesses, both during depositions and at a *Daubert* hearing, on the substance of these communications and, particularly, counsel's input into their respective reports. Furthermore, the court noted that any prejudice that might have incurred (essentially depriving the defendants of a document with which to cross-examine and possibly impeach these experts) was minimal, given the collateral nature of the issue involved. For these reasons, the court declined to impose the harsh sanction of excluding the experts.

Some states have expressly addressed the discoverability of expert draft reports. Louisiana provides that the expert's drafts of a report, if required by motion, and communications, including notes and electronically stored information or portions thereof that would reveal the mental impressions, opinions, or trial strategy of the attorney for the party who has retained the expert to testify, shall not be discoverable except, in either case, on a showing of exceptional circumstances under which it is impractical for the party seeking discovery to obtain facts or opinions on the same subject by other means.

Involving the Business Valuation Expert in Discovery[43]

Many lawyers don't involve their business appraisal expert in the discovery process in cases involving the value of a business or practice. However, there are several ways in which the business appraiser can provide support in the discovery process that will assist in refuting the opposing expert's position.

Preparing Discovery Requests

An important service of the business appraiser is the preparation of discovery requests for the information necessary for the appraisal. The appraiser usually will know what to request for companies in the industry or line of practice involved.

The lawyer does not want to be in the position of not having requested some information that would be pertinent to a good appraisal and then not being able to obtain it. On the other hand, an overly broad discovery demand gives the other side excuses for delay and objections about the request being unreasonably onerous.

Preparing Deposition and Interrogatory Questions

As mentioned previously, depending on the nature of the business or practice and the rules of the jurisdiction, in addition to the site visit and management interviews, there may be depositions involving employees, outside advisors (e.g., bankers, CPAs), and, especially, the opposing expert. The business appraisal expert can help formulate the initial questions to ask these individuals, as well as general lines of inquiry that will help elicit important information about the opposing expert's valuation conclusion. Depositions generally are preferable to interrogatories because of their interactive nature. The answer to one question may well lead to another question or series of questions. In circumstances where interrogatories are the only option, however, it is even more critical that the business appraiser be involved in formulating the questions to be sure important information is obtained.

Presence at Opposing Expert's Deposition

If you are deposing an opposing expert, having your expert present usually is a huge benefit. This will help to evaluate the other expert's valuation work product and glean the information needed for effective cross-examination and rebuttal testimony.

Your expert can study the opposing expert's work papers (which you will have demanded be produced via subpoena) and develop questions that delve into the technical nature of what was covered in the appraisal. Your expert can provide follow-up questions, depending on the answers given to the basic questions that already were anticipated.

43. This section was adapted with permission from Shannon P. Pratt, *Involve Your Business Appraiser in Discovery*, DEFENSIBLE BUSINESS VALUATIONS™, Fall 2007.

Many lawyers do not have the financial expertise to totally probe exactly what was determined by the other expert, in a technical sense, to evaluate the strengths and weaknesses of the work and prepare effective cross-examination and rebuttal. Having your expert present should overcome this problem.

Involving Your Own Expert in Depositions of Opposing Experts

The primary purpose of depositions of opposing experts is to find out the opinions and the details of the information and procedures they relied on to reach those opinions. There are a number of topics that should be addressed in the deposition, including the appraiser's qualifications, who the appraiser interviewed, and what other information the expert needs to finish or double-check his or her report.[44] Because opposing experts are relying on specialized knowledge, it usually requires the input of someone with comparable specialized knowledge to formulate initial and follow-up questions, and to determine when the line of questioning has been answered sufficiently for a complete understanding of the expert's opinion and the basis for it.

At the conclusion of the deposition, your expert should be able to replicate the work of the opposing expert and identify any flaws that may be present.

Normally, this necessitates your expert not only reading the opposing report and filling you in on what needs to be covered, but also being present at the deposition of the opposing expert. The reason for this is that it is nearly impossible to create a complete list of deposition questions; follow-up questions are almost always necessary, depending on the answers to the initial questions—often a series of technical questions on details about which the lawyer is unlikely to possess the necessary specialized knowledge.

To take it to the extreme, consider the following:

Q: Why did your sales decline 25 percent in 2008 from 2007?
A: We had a bad year. Customers just didn't seem to be willing to part with their money.

You haven't learned anything. This needs to be probed in detail. In a more technical sense:

Q: Where did you get your guideline public company information?
A: SEC filings.

---

44. *See* Gerald Nissenbaum, *Seven 'knockout punch' questions for cross-examining appraisal experts,* Judges & Lawyers Business Valuation Update, Feb. 2000, at 1–3.

This is totally inadequate. Someone knowledgeable about Securities and Exchange Commission filings needs to ask which forms, which dates (which are likely to vary from company to company), and what medium was used to obtain the filings. It is even better if such information (and, indeed, the expert's whole file) is available at the deposition so that your expert can examine it and raise questions that may never otherwise have been considered. Such questions may include, for example, why did you use the sources and dates that you did? Also, *why didn't* you use ___? Generally, only an expert would know what to ask about what the other expert *didn't* use or procedures *not* performed.

Your expert may be the expert you plan to use to present your primary valuation case at trial. Alternatively, it might be a consulting expert to help prepare you and your testifying expert for trial. Another plan that often works well is to have the expert who assists with the opposing expert's deposition be the one to present the rebuttal expert testimony at trial.

Another big advantage of a thorough technical probing at deposition is that it often facilitates settlement. Once the expert's differences are totally clarified, there is at least a framework to try to resolve them.

Rebutting the Opposition

The two primary ways that the expert can help refute the opposition are by:

1. Helping the lawyer prepare effective cross-examination and
2. Providing rebuttal testimony.

The weaknesses of the opposition's expert should be brought to the court's attention. Your expert can help to identify these weaknesses by listening to the other expert and helping the lawyer to formulate questions that will educate the court convincingly about such weaknesses.

It is often true that effective rebuttal of an opposing expert's testimony contributes more toward winning a case than your own expert's direct testimony. Having your expert hear the opposing expert and provide rebuttal testimony can be crucial in getting a fair outcome for your client. I have seen far too many valuation cases where one side's weak, or even clearly erroneous, testimony carried the day because it was allowed to stand without challenge.

Sometimes, if the case is large enough, you may want to have a rebuttal expert separate from your direct testimony expert. This provides several advantages. For one, it lessens the possibility that the court may feel a taint of bias on the part of your direct expert because of his or her criticism of the opponent's expert's work. Secondly, your rebuttal expert may have extra credibility with the court by "outcredentialing" the opposing expert. Also, the rebuttal expert may lend extra support to the methodology employed by your direct testimony expert.

Summary

Discovery is an important and powerful tool both for learning what the other parties intend to present as evidence of the value of a business interest and for obtaining information to assist your business appraiser in his or her analysis of value. It should not be conducted lightly or haphazardly; careful thought always should be given to every discovery request to ensure that it is both comprehensive and relevant. It is tempting to use form requests to save time, but in the case of valuation issues, such use may miss the mark on much relevant and useful information or may lead to sustained resistance if it is overbroad.

Giving depositions (that is, having one's own expert deposed) is an opportunity to establish the strength of one's case, with a view to encouraging an earlier and more favorable settlement. The conventional instruction to experts is "Just answer the question; don't volunteer information beyond what is asked." However, if you have a strong case and a strong expert, giving your expert leeway to use judgment in volunteering information sometimes helps lead to a settlement.

Also, it is beneficial to use the business appraiser to formulate discovery requests and cross-examination questions, as well as to rebut the other side's experts.

Chapter 28

Buy-Sell Agreements

There are millions of buy-sell agreements in existence, which clients and their attorneys will have to deal with when some triggering event occurs, and there are still many buy-sell agreements to be written.

Many attorneys that have clients with buy-sell agreements could do their clients a large favor by reviewing the agreement in light of this chapter and modifying the agreement if necessary.

This chapter focuses on three aspects of buy-sell agreements:

1. Drafting a good agreement, with emphasis on the valuation portions.
2. Dealing with the agreement when the triggering event occurs.
3. The effect of the buy-sell agreement on valuation for purposes other than the agreement itself.

Types of Agreements

Entity Purchase Agreements

Under entity purchase agreements, the company buys the interest from the departing owner. Unless the entity resells the interest, the proportionate interests of all the remaining owners are increased.

Cross-Purchase Agreements

Under cross-purchase agreements, one or more individuals or entities buys the interest from the departing owner. These can become very complex as the number of owners increases.

Hybrid Agreements

Hybrid agreements can take on a variety of forms, but usually give the entity the first right of refusal to buy the interest of the departing owner. If the entity declines, the interests usually are offered to other owners, generally, but not always, on a pro rata basis. If the other owners decline, the entity still may buy the shares. It may or may not be binding on the entity to purchase if others decline.

Tag-Along Rights

If a company has "tag-along rights," minority owners have the right to sell on the same price and terms if the controlling owner sells. These are gaining popularity in recent years.

Types of Valuation Provisions

Fixed Price

The parties may agree on a fixed price at which the ownership interests will be purchased.

Formula

It is almost impossible to create a formula that will be fair to all parties at the time of the triggering event.

Negotiation Among Parties

Some agreements provide for a periodic (usually annual) meeting among the parties to agree on a price that will prevail for a defined period of time (generally a year) if a triggering event occurs. Such agreements need a provision for how the value will be determined in case the parties cannot agree on a price in their meeting or (what happens most often) they fail to meet.

"Shotgun" Agreements

Under "shotgun" agreements, the party can offer to buy (or sell) ownership interests to another party and the other party has the right (or obligation) to sell (or buy) the interest at the price offered.

Independent Outside Appraisal

Perhaps the most prevalent type of valuation provision is what Christopher Mercer calls a "process agreement," in which case one or more independent appraisers determines the price when the triggering event occurs.[1] He further subdivides the "process agreements" into single-appraiser agreements and multiappraiser agreements.

Drafting a Good Buy-Sell Agreement

The authors highly recommend that the lawyers retain a few hours of a business appraiser's time at the drafting stage of the buy-sell agreement. Many pitfalls can be avoided by gaining the insight of those who have dealt with resolving the valuations under many diverse wordings of buy-sell agreements.

The authors also recommend that the appraiser be present at the signing of the agreement to answer questions about the valuation provisions. We recommend that not only parties to the agreement but also spouses be present at the signing meeting. One source of animosity among the participants can be removed by being sure that all parties to the agreement understand the implications of the valuation language going into the agreement.

Definition of Value

Perhaps the most critical element of the valuation provisions is the definition of value. (See Chapter 1 for definitions of value.) The most prevalent standard (definition) of value is fair market value. This generally is desirable, because fair market value is the most widely used and understood standard of value.

However, once fair market value has been specified, it still is necessary to define the *level of value* (see Exhibit 28-1), that is, is it a proportionate share of the fair market value of the equity as a whole or is it the fair market value of minority shares? If it is the fair market value of minority shares, there would be a minority interest discount. Furthermore, if it is a closely held company, there very likely would be a discount for lack of marketability. As shown in Chapter 15, "Discounts and Premiums," these discounts could total more than 50 percent. (The Levels of Value chart was presented in Chapter 2 but is repeated here for convenience.)

1. Christopher Mercer, Buy-Sell Agreements: Ticking Time Bombs or Reasonable Resolutions? (Peabody Publishing 2007).

Exhibit 28-1
"Levels of Value" in Terms of Characteristics of Ownership

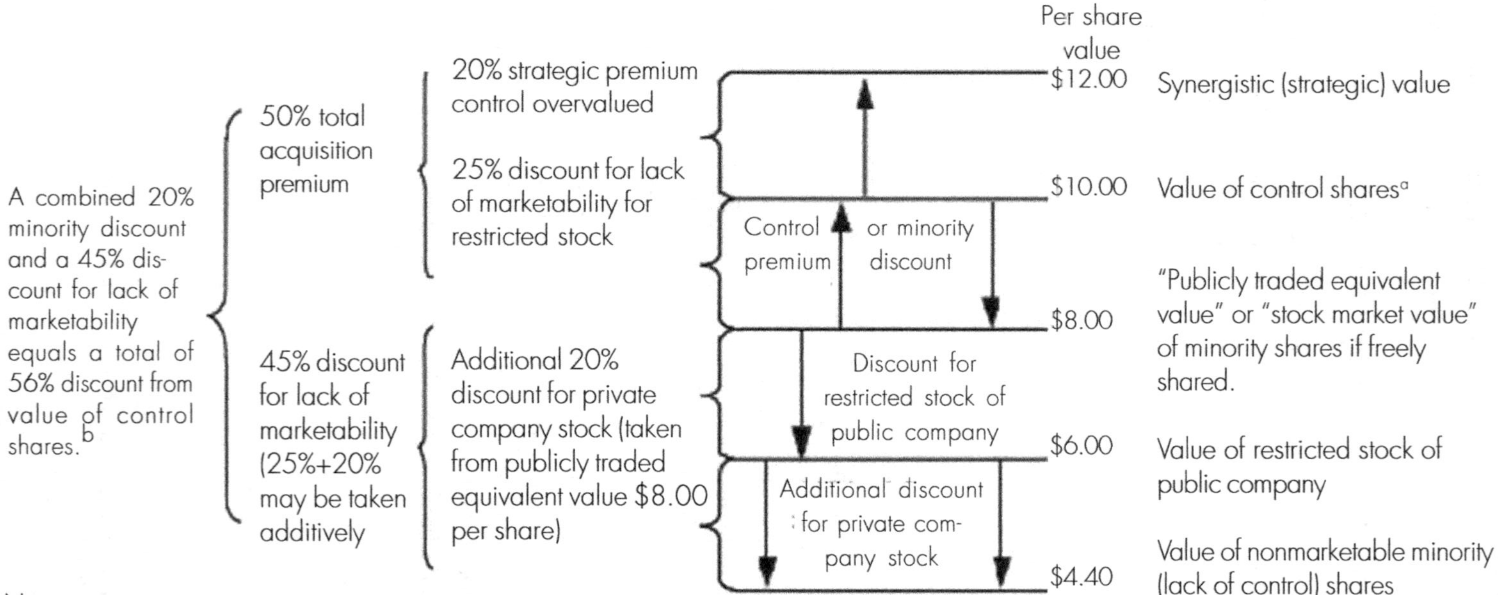

Notes:

a Control shares in a privately held company may also be subject to some discount for lack of marketability, but usually not nearly as much as minority shares.

b Minority and marketability discounts normally are multiplicative rather than additive. That is, they are taken in sequence:

$10.00	Control Value
−2.00	Less: Minority interest discount (.20 x $10.00)
$ 8.00	Marketable minority value
−3.60	Less lack of marketability discount (.45 x $8.00)
$ 4.40	Per-share value of nonmarketable minority shares

Source: Jay E. Fishman, et al., *PPC's Guide to Business Valuations*, 19th ed.

Most clients think of fair market value as a proportionate share of the value of the company as a whole. One of the biggest problem with buy-sell agreements is when the agreement says "the fair market value of the shares" and the person who is the subject of the triggering event is shocked to learn that that means a large discount from a pro rata value of the company as a whole!

The valuation provisions may be different for different triggering events. For example, the definition of value for death or normal retirement may be a pro rata proportion of the fair market value of the equity as a whole, while the value under any other triggering event would be discounted by some percentage from that value.

The "As of" Date

The date as of which the interest is to be valued is a critical piece of information in the buy-sell agreement. The values of companies and interests in them can change drastically, even in a short time, because of both internal and external factors (e.g., stock market conditions).

It is common to have as the valuation date the date of the triggering event. However, the authors suggest, as a matter of convenience in the valuation, the valuation date should be set on a date when financial statements normally would be prepared, such as the end of the month prior to the triggering event.

Appraiser Qualifications

If the buy-sell agreement is a "process agreement," it is important that the agreement addresses appraiser qualifications. There are four organizations that accredit business appraisers in the United States and one in Canada (see Chapter 30, "Business Valuation Standards and Credentials"). Specifying that the appraisers have credentials from one or more of these organizations should go a long way toward avoiding an outlandish outcome in the appraisal processes.

Appraiser Selection and Procedures

Single-Appraiser Scenario

If there is to be a single appraiser, he or she might be named in the buy-sell agreement itself. Most practitioners believe that it is preferable to name a firm rather than an individual because the individual may have a higher likelihood of being unavailable when the triggering event occurs.

Of course, there needs to be a process by which the appraiser can be chosen in the event that the named firm or individual is not available. The authors recommend choice by a neutral party, such as a judge, the state's corporation commissioner, or the head of a regulatory body. For example, for a bank, it might be the state banking commissioner.

If the parties don't want to name a firm or individual in the agreement, a common procedure is, when the triggering event occurs, to have each side submit several qualified nominees (either firms or individuals) and to come to an agreement. Sometimes, this requires multiple submissions to arrive at one that is common to both sides. Of course, there still has to be a procedure in the agreement to break a deadlock.

In all the accrediting organizations, the credentials are held by individuals, not by the firms. Thus, if a firm is named, it is essential that the lead appraiser be accredited.

There also should be a time limit on the selection process. This can be enforced in the agreement in one of two ways: (1) The side not meeting the time requirement defers by default to the side that does or (2) If the time deadline is not met, the selection process automatically reverts to the named neutral party. Of course, these provisions can be subject to modification by mutual agreement of the parties.

Multiappraiser Scenario

Two Appraisers and a Third Only if Necessary. Some agreements call for two appraisers (one appointed by each side) and a third to be appointed by the final two only if the first two are apart by some percentage. In most buy-sell agreements, the percentage limit usually is set at 10 percent. Then the average of the two sets the price.

The authors suggest that the percentage limits be set a little more broadly, perhaps at 15 percent, 20 percent, or even 25 percent, because it is unusual for two business appraisers to come within 10 percent of each other. The 10 percent probably is workable for real estate appraisal, but business appraisal is far more complex than is real estate appraisal.

The authors also suggest that the selection of the third appraiser be made at the outset of the process before it becomes apparent that it will be necessary. There is much greater likelihood of quick agreement at this stage than later on, when the choice may be more contentious.

The authors also suggest that the choice of the third appraiser be left to the sole judgment of the first two appraisers. Making the choice subject to client approval usually delays the process, sometimes substantially, and can cause increased contentiousness between the parties.

The role of the third appraiser varies, but the third appraiser usually is provided access to the work of the first two and generally is allowed to contact them.

Sometimes the value arrived at by the third appraiser is the final value. At times, it is bounded by the high and low values of the first two appraisers. Sometimes the value of the third appraiser is averaged with the closer one of the first two appraisers.

Three-Appraiser Panel. Sometimes a three-appraiser (or more) panel is appointed at the outset. In this case, it is usually common for each side to select a qualified appraiser and the two to select a third qualified appraiser. The same admonitions apply as in the previous section.

When a three-appraiser (or more) panel is selected, often it is possible to reach unanimous agreement, especially if the suggestions in the chapter on arbitration (Chapter 29) are followed. If a unanimous consensus cannot be reached, usually a majority opinion can be reached. If this is not possible, then the average of the closest two may constitute the final value.

A valuation pursuant to a buy-sell agreement is tantamount to an arbitration. In fact, in some cases, it actually may consist of an arbitration. The authors suggest that the appraisers appointed by each side enter the process with open minds rather than being biased toward their client's interest. They also suggest following the procedures recommended for arbitration (see Chapter 29).

Funding and Payment Mechanisms

Payment terms must be spelled out in the buy-sell agreement, including the rate of interest, if anything is on any extended terms. If the agreement is funded by life insurance, it is common to have a lump-sum payment up to the net proceeds of the life insurance and extended payments on the balance. When not funded by life insurance, the company usually has the option to extend payments for anywhere from three to 10 years, sometimes with and sometimes without a down payment. In any case, the company usually has the right to prepay the extended payments, generally without penalty.

If funded by life insurance, the buy-sell agreement should specify whether or not the insurance proceeds are a corporate asset. Exhibit 28-2 demonstrates an example of the difference.

Exhibit 28-2
Treatment of Life Insurance Proceeds in Valuation

Treatment of Life Insurance Proceeds in Valuation
The overview indicated that there are two opposing treatments of life insurance proceeds in valuations for purposes of buy-sell agreements.

- *Treatment 1*—Proceeds Are Not a Corporate Asset. One treatment would not consider the life insurance proceeds as a corporate asset for valuation purposes. This treatment would recognize that life insurance was purchased on the lives of shareholders for the specific purpose of funding a buy-sell agreement. Under this treatment, life insurance proceeds, if considered as an asset in valuation, would he offset by the company s liability to fund the purchase of shares. Logically, under this treatment, the expense of life insurance premiums on a deceased shareholder would be added back into income as a nonrecurring expense.
- *Treatment 2*—Proceeds Are a Corporate Asset. Another treatment would consider the life insurance proceeds as a corporate asset for valuation purposes. In the valuation, the proceeds would be treated as a nonoperating asset of the company. This asset, together with all other net assets of the business, would be available to fund the purchase of shares of a deceased shareholder, Again, under this treatment, the expense of life insurance premiums on a deceased shareholder would be added back into income as a nonrecurring expense.

The choice of treatment of life insurance proceeds can have a significant, if not dramatic, effect on the resulting position of a company following the receipt of life insurance proceeds and the repurchase of shares of a deceased shareholder. The choice of treatment also has an impact on the resulting position of any remaining shareholders. Consider the following hypothetical example (which is not really so hypothetical, since it was prompted by a real-world experience):

- Harry and Sam own 50% interests of High Point Software, and have been partners for many years.
- The buy-sell agreement states that the company will purchase the shares of stock owned by either Harry or Sam in the event of the death of either. The agreement is silent with respect to the treatment of life insurance proceeds. The agreement calls for the company to be appraised by Mercer Capital (wishful thinking, perhaps, but this is our example).
- The company owns term life insurance policies on the lives of Harry and Sam in the amount of $6 million each. Assume for simplicity that there are no corporate income taxes due or that this figure is net of income taxes.

- Now assume that Harry is killed in an accident. Assume that the company is worth $10 million based on Mercer Capital's appraisal prior to consideration of the proceeds of term life insurance owned by the company on the lives of Harry and Sam, and that earnings have been normalized in the valuation to adjust for the expense of the term policies.
- Before finalizing our appraisal, we carefully review the buy-sell agreement for direction on the treatment of life insurance proceeds. It is silent on the issue. We call a meeting of Sam and the executor of Harry's estate to discuss the issue, because we know that the choice of treatment will make a significant difference to Harry's estate, the company, and to Sam personally as the remaining shareholder.

The valuation impact of each treatment is developed below in the context of the High Point Software example.

Treatment I—Proceeds Are Not a Corporate Asset

Figure 17 summarizes the pre– and post–life insurance values and positions for High Point Software, Harry's estate, and Sam if life insurance proceeds are not considered as a corporate asset in valuation.

FIGURE 17
Proceeds Are Not a Corporate Asset

		Company	Harry (Estate)	Sam
1.	Stock Ownership (Shares)	100.0	50.0	50.0
2.	Stack Ownership (%)	100.0%	50.0%	50.0%
3.	Pre- and Post-Life Insurance Value ($m)	$10,000.0	$5,000.0$	5,000.0
4.	Life Insurance Proceeds	$6,000.0		
5.	Repurchase Liability	($5,000.0)		
6.	Post-Life Insurance Value	$11,000.0		
7.	Repurchase Stock	($5,000.0)	$5,000.0	
8.	Retire/Give Up Stock	(50.0)	(50.0)	
9.	Remaining Stock	50.0	0.0	50.0
10.	New Stock Ownership (%)	100.0%	0.0%	100.0%
11.	Post-Life Insurance Value of Co.	$11,000.0	$0 0	$11,000.0
12.	Post Life Insurance Proceeds		$5,000.0	
13.	Net Change in Value from Repurchase	$1,000.0		

On Line 3, we see that High Point Software is worth $10 million before consideration of life insurance, and both Harry and Sam have 50% of this value, or $5 million each. Upon Harry's death, the company receives $6 million of life insurance and recognizes the liability of $5 million to repurchase Harry's stock. The post–life insurance value is $11 million (Lines 4-6).

Lines 7–10 reflect the repurchase and retirement of Harry's shares. The remaining company value, after repurchasing Harry's shares for $5 million, is $11 million. Since Sam owns all 50 shares now outstanding, his post-transaction value is $11 million. Harry's estate has received the $5 million of life insurance proceeds from the sale of 50 shares for $5 million.

Treatment 2— Proceeds Are a Corporate Asset

Figure 18 summarizes the pre– and post–life insurance values and positions for High Point Software, Harry's estate and Sam if life insurance proceeds are considered as a corporate asset in valuation.

FIGURE 18
Proceeds Are a Corporate Asset

1. Stock Ownership (Shares)	100.0	50.0	50.0
2. Stack Ownership (%)	100.0%	50.0%	50.0%
3. Pre–Life Insurance Value ($m)	**$10,000.0**	**$5,000.0**	**$5,000.0**
4. Life Insurance Proceeds	$6,000.0	$3,000.0	$3,000.0
5. Post–Life Insurance Value ($m)	$16,000.0	**$8,000.0**	$8,000.0
6. Repurchase Liability	($8,000.0)		
7. Post–Life Insurance Value	**$8,000.0.0**		
8. Repurchase Stock	($8,000.0)	$8,000.0	
9. Retire/Give Up Stock	(50.0)	(50.0)	
10. Remaining Stock	50.0	0.0	50.0
11. New Stock Ownership (%)	100.0%	0.0%	100.0%
12. Post–Life Insurance Value of Co.	$8,000.0	$0 0	**$8,000.0**
13. Post–Life Insurance Proceeds		**$8,000.0**	
14. Net Change in Value from Repurchase	**$2,000.0**		

Line 3 shows the same pre–life insurance value of $10 million as in the treatment where life insurance is not a corporate asset. Now, however, the $6 million of proceeds is treated as a nonoperating asset and is added to value, raising the post–ife insurance value to $16 million, and the interests of Harry's estate and Sam to $8 million each (Lines

4–5). After recognizing the repurchase liability of Harry's shares ($8 million) the post-life insurance value of High Point Software is $8 million (Lines 6–7).

The shares are repurchased and new ownership positions are calculated on Lines 9–11. Harry's ownership goes to zero, and Sam's rises to 100% of the now 50 shares outstanding. This result is the same as above. However, Harry's estate receives $8 million as a result of the purchase of his shares, rather than $5 million. Note that the company's value has been reduced from the pre-death value of $10 million to a post-death value of $8 million. The decrease in value is the result of Harry's value of $8 million, which is in excess of the life insurance proceeds of $6 million, suggesting that the company had to issue a note to Harry's estate for the remaining $2 million. So the company is in a more leveraged position as result of the buy-sell transaction than it was before. Sam, on the other hand, owns 100% of the remaining value, or $8 million, rather than $11 million in the prior treatment.

Source: Christopher Mercer, *Buy-Sell Agreements: Ticking Time Bombs or Reasonable Resolutions?* 171–75 (Peabody Publishing, 2007).

The buy-sell agreements also should specify how the appraisers are to be paid. Sometimes the company pays the entire bill of the appraiser(s). More commonly, in a multiappraiser scenario, each side pays the appraiser it selects and the company pays the third appraiser.

Dealing with the Agreement When the Triggering Event Occurs

Hopefully, if all the foregoing steps in drafting the agreement have been followed, when the triggering event occurs, the appraisal will go forward without any problems. More commonly, however, there are ambiguities in the existing buy-sell agreement that must be resolved.

Appraisers should be instructed to resolve any ambiguities before they start the actual valuation process (except for preparing the engagement letter specifying that the appraisal is in accordance with the buy-sell agreement as of a given date and document specification). Attorneys and/or the parties should make every effort to resolve the ambiguities among themselves and give the appraisers instructions. Otherwise, the appraisers are left to interpret the agreement for themselves, which may lead to unintended consequences.

Roger Grabowski recently said, "I really don't like the idea that you've got pushed into the position of playing as a lawyer where that is not really what we're supposed to be doing." His solution: "I've been putting this in engagement letters anytime that

I believe that I am going to be asked or forced into making a legal decision . . . I have the right to legal counsel separate and apart and get reimbursed for it."[2]

Once any ambiguities are resolved, the appraisers should proceed in accordance with the procedures for arbitration (see Chapter 29).

The Effect of the Agreement on Valuations for Purposes Other Than the Agreement Itself

As noted elsewhere in this book (Chapter 17, "Valuation for Federal Tax Matters"), the buy-sell agreement valuation may be binding for other purposes, may be given no weight at all, or may be given some weight along with other approaches and methods of valuation. We've seen situations where the buy-sell agreement was binding on the estate and the IRS valued the interest so much higher that the estate had to pay more in taxes than it received for selling the interest back to the company.

The most important factor in determining the weight accorded to a buy-sell agreement is whether it was negotiated on an arm's-length basis. Alternatively, if the buy-sell agreement is among family members, would unrelated parties have been agreeable to the same terms?

Section 2703 of IRS Code Chapter 14, enacted October 8, 1990, requires that in order to be binding for estate, gift, or generation-skipping tax purposes, any buy-sell agreement created or significantly modified after that date must meet the following criteria:

1. It is a bona fide business arrangement.
2. It must not be a device to transfer the property to the natural objects of the transferor's bounty (such as family members) for less than adequate and full consideration in money or money's worth.
3. Its terms must be comparable to similar arrangements entered into by persons in an arm's-length transaction.

References

Bogdanski, John A. "Hard Times for Buy-Sell Agreements." *Estate Planning* (June 1998): 235–39.

_____. "Buy-Sell Agreements and Marketability Discounts." *Estate Planning* (December 2004).

2. Buy-Sell Agreements: Opportunities and Challenges for BV Appraisers. Teleconference featuring Christopher Mercer, Jim Hitchner & Roger Grabowski, July 19, 2007, presented by BVResources.com.

Business Valuation Resources. *Buy-Sell Agreements: Opportunities and Challenges for BV Appraisers.* Teleconference Featuring Christopher Mercer, Jim Hitchner, and Roger Grabowski, July 19, 2007, presented by BVResources.com, available on CD and/or written transcript.

Business Valuation Resources. *The Planner's Role in Buy-Sell Agreements.* Teleconference featuring Christopher Mercer, L. Paul Hood, Jr., Esq., and John H. Brown, Esq., June 14, 2007, presented by BVResources.com, available on CD and/or written transcript.

Business Valuation Resources. *You'll Never Think about Buy-Sell Agreements the Same Way Again.* Teleconference featuring Christopher Mercer, May 24, 2007, presented by BVResources.com, available on CD and/or written transcript.

"Buy-Sell Agreement Ignored in Valuing Decedent's Stock." *Estate Planning* (January 1998): 32–35.

Drake, Dwight J., Kent Whiteley, and Timothy J. McDevitt. "The Ten Most Common Mistakes of Buy-Sell Agreements." *Journal of Financial Planning* (July 1992): 104-12.

Ellentuck, Albert B. "Establishing the Estate Value of Stock by Using a Buy-Sell Agreement." *The Tax Adviser* (September 1998): 637–38.

_____. "Reviewing a Buy/Sell Agreement." *The Tax Adviser* (November 1999): 809–12.

Hall, Lance S. "Lack of Outside Appraisal Dooms Buy-Sell Formula Value Fix for Estate Tax Purposes." *Valuation Strategies* (March/April 2005).

Howitt, Idelle A. "Estate of Cameron W. Bommer." *Valuation Strategies* (September/October 1998): 38–39, 42.

Mercer, Christopher. *Buy-Sell Agreements: Ticking Time Bombs or Reasonable Resolutions?* Peabody Publishing, 2007.

Porter, John W. "Buy-Sell Agreements: True Provision Does Not Control Value for Estate Tax Purposes." *Business Valuation Alert* (April 2005).

Zuckerman, Michael H., and John G. Grall. "Corporate Buy-Sell Agreements as Estate and Business Planning Tools." *Estate Planning* (December 2001).

Chapter 29

Alternative Dispute Resolution

Alternative dispute resolution (ADR) is rising in popularity as a way to avoid going to court and is becoming used more frequently to settle valuation issues. The two primary types of alternative dispute resolution are arbitration and mediation, each with many variations. Private judging, a hybrid of traditional litigation and ADR, also has had success in resolving certain types of matters.[1]

Another vehicle is a minitrial, which generally follows no formal rules of procedure or evidence but rather depends on commonsense arguments and a few key witnesses. This process is most successful for business disputes in which the person hearing the matter is experienced in the business affected.

Disputes over the value of an interest in a business lend themselves particularly well to arbitration because there is a single, clear-cut issue: What is the amount of money needed to settle the case? Some areas where arbitration has worked well are marital dissolution, corporate and partnership dissolution, dissenting stockholder actions, and damage cases.

The senior author has been involved extensively in arbitration, especially in shareholder disputes, and to a limited extent in mediation of business valuation disputes. The results generally have been quite good, providing there are qualified business valuation experts on the arbitration or mediation panels. However, there have been some lopsided valuation decisions when the panels were made up of lawyers and/or industry people rather than qualified business appraisers.

The current status of ADR was summarized by Steven Weiss, a business litigator, in an article in *Business Law Today:*

---

1. Shiela Nagaraj, *The Marriage of Family Law and Private Judging in California*, 116 YALE L.J. 1615 (May 2007).

> ADR resolution is being used more and more to avoid what is perceived as the courts' inability to efficiently resolve business disputes. Since the vast majority of cases settle before trial, it makes sense to try to resolve the case partway through the litigation process, rather than on the eve of trial. Similarly, for those cases that would otherwise go to trial, binding arbitration can achieve a final resolution, generally more quickly and inexpensively than the courts. As alternative dispute resolution becomes more accepted, and the arbitrators and mediators become more successful in resolving disputes, we will probably see even more dispute resolution. It makes sense to embrace ADR and use it as a tool to help your clients obtain better results, more efficiently.[2]

Weiss adds the following observations on mediation and arbitration:

> I am a fan of mediation. The author's experience is that if the parties go to mediation with a real desire to have it be successful, the result will be a settlement. Consequently, the client receives a faster, less expensive resolution of the dispute. A happy client is a repeat client. The times that the author has seen mediation fail are when either one party is not negotiating in good faith, or where the mediator is not very good. Although it is possible for mediation to fail because the parties, in good faith, have a disagreement as to the value of the case, that is generally not the problem.
>
> Binding arbitration is also a useful tool, especially where a relatively quick resolution is required. Binding arbitration, without the right to appeal, usually ends a dispute. The only exception is where one side or the other attacks the procedure itself (for example, based on an undisclosed bias), or attacks the contractual provision requiring arbitration. The "fairness" of the arbitration, and whether it is better or worse than litigation, depends on the ability of the arbitrator.
>
> I generally do not favor nonbinding arbitration. In fact, the author cannot recall a case of mine in which it was successful. If the arbitrator's ruling supports your client's view of the case, your client normally endorses it fully and will not budge from a previous settlement position. On the other hand, if the arbitrator's ruling is contrary to your client's position, the client normally views the arbitrator as incompetent, or comes up with some other reason why the result at trial will be different.[3]

2. Steven A. Weiss, *ADR: A Litigator's Perspective,* Bus. L. Today, Mar./Apr. 1999 at 34. The issue contains a special 17-page section on ADR with articles by several authors.

3. *Id.*

Alternative Dispute Resolution Act of 1998

The practice of ADR was further bolstered by the enactment of House Resolution 3528, the Alternative Dispute Resolution Act of 1998. The act directs every federal district court to establish its own ADR program by local rule and requires litigants in each case to consider the use of ADR. As we go to press, it is too early to evaluate results of the act on situations involving business valuation.

Advantages of Arbitration versus Litigation

The following are the primary advantages of arbitration over litigation (that is, a court trial):

1. Usually less formal and less stressful on all participants, especially the principals to the controversy.
2. Scheduling generally can be made more convenient for all parties.
3. Less likelihood of a lopsided result—in favor of one side over the other—assuming the arbitrators are qualified valuation professionals.
4. Usually takes less elapsed time from start to finish.
5. Usually costs less. Lawyers' time is reduced considerably and experts' fees usually are less than for a court trial. (The appraisal process itself, however, may not be less expensive.)
6. The award of the arbitrators in most situations is final and binding, and it can be confirmed in court.

Under the Uniform Arbitration Act, an arbitrator's award is subject to attack only on the following grounds:

- The award was procured by corruption, fraud, or other undue influence.
- An arbitrator was partial or used corruption or misconduct, which prejudiced the rights of either party.
- The arbitrator exceeded his or her authority.
- The arbitrator refused to postpone the hearing although sufficient cause for postponement was shown, or the arbitrator refused to hear material evidence or failed to conduct the hearing, which resulted in substantial prejudice to a party.
- There was no agreement to arbitrate and the objection was raised during the arbitration.[4]

4. Uniform Arbitration Act § 12(a) (1997).

Choosing Arbitrators or Mediators

Steven Weiss offers the following observations on selecting arbitrators and mediators:

> In arbitration, as opposed to litigation, you have the luxury of choosing someone who has knowledge in the particular area of law or fact involved in your dispute. Conversely, a mediator's technical legal competence and familiarity with the business area of the dispute is less important than in arbitration where the arbitrator must render a decision.
>
> The focus on mediation should be on a mediator with good experience and skills in mediation, regardless of his or her knowledge of the specific area of law. It is helpful for the mediator to be knowledgeable enough to ask questions and point out weaknesses in each party's position, but since mediation is nothing more than a formalized settlement procedure, the real value of a mediator is being able to bring the parties together and in suggesting alternative solutions to the dispute.[5]

Arbitrators

Given the rather complex and technical nature of business valuation, the arbitrators in business valuation disputes should be well-qualified, seasoned business appraisers. It is rare to see an unfair decision in a business valuation arbitration when the arbitrator (or a majority of a panel of arbitrators) was a qualified business appraiser. However, there have been inequitable results when industry experts, economists, accountants, and lawyers lacking the technical training to deal professionally with esoteric business valuation issues dominate the arbitration decision.

Mediators

It is also desirable to have senior business appraisal expertise involved in mediating business valuation disputes. The problem here is that there are only a few business appraisers who are trained and experienced in mediation skills.

The solution to this problem is to employ an excellent mediator and a top-level business appraisal expert as a comediator, even if the appraiser has never before been involved in a mediation.

Process for Selecting Arbitrators

In the case of a sole arbitrator, the person usually is agreed on by the parties. There should be a mechanism in place for appointment by a neutral party if the parties to the

5. Weiss, *supra* note 2, at 33.

action can't come to agreement. The neutral party may be a court or some government official (for example, the state banking commissioner in the case of appraising a financial institution).

When the parties are deadlocked and one party submits a list of qualified business appraisers and the other party submits industry people or others without business appraisal expertise, the neutral party, as far as the author is personally aware, has always selected from the list with business appraisal expertise.

It is common for each party to appoint one arbitrator and have the two arbitrators select a third. That selection should not be subject to the parties' approval, which could delay the process unduly. If possible, the arbitration agreement should specify that the third arbitrator is a qualified business appraiser. To avoid arguments about "qualified," the agreement should specify one or more credentials, such as Accredited Senior Appraiser, as discussed in Chapter 30.

Again, in the event that the two arbitrators cannot agree on a third, there should be a procedure in place to break the deadlock. If one party insists on selection from a group of qualified business appraisers with no conflicts and the other side wants someone else, it is highly unlikely that the neutral party would not pick from the list of qualified appraisers.

Instructions to Arbitrators

Business appraisers generally advocate giving business valuation arbitrators as much flexibility to set their own rules as possible. However, certain factors should be specified to the arbitrators. They are:

- Definition of the property to be appraised
- The effective valuation date
- The standard (definition) of value (see Chapter 1)
- Any legal aspects of the case that the appraisers need to be aware of
- What constitutes a conclusion by the arbitrators, such as:
  - Agreement by a majority (most common)
  - Average of two closest to each other
  - The conclusion of the third (neutral) arbitrator (somewhat akin to a "special master" situation)
- The written report format and procedure for rendering the conclusion
- Some guidance on timing (may require some flexibility)

It may be helpful to have an appraiser experienced in arbitration assist in drafting the arbitration agreement and/or instructions. Obviously, the documents controlling the arbitration should be as clear and complete as possible. However, there should be a provision to request clarification if there are questions after the arbitrators have finished their initial review of the controlling documents.

The following factors typically are left to the arbitrators' discretion:

- Procedures to communicate with each other and scheduling of work and meetings (within the specified timing guidance)
- The valuation approaches, methods, and procedures to apply (within the confines of the designated definition of value and anything mandated in controlling documents)
- The extent to which each arbitrator considers it necessary to develop information independently or is willing to rely on information provided by the company or parties or by another member of the arbitration panel
- Rules regarding contacting the parties or their lawyers (although some lawyers are uncomfortable about giving up control of contacts with the parties)

Communications with Parties and Lawyers

It is often desirable to be very liberal in allowing arbitrators to communicate with parties and lawyers. However, if one learns a fact that might be considered material to the valuation, that information should be shared with the other arbitrators as soon as practically possible.

Field Visit

In most cases, arbitrators will want to visit the operating premises and interview relevant principals and/or management. This works out best if the arbitrators can conduct this field trip together rather than separately so that they will see the same things at the same time and benefit from hearing each other's questions and answers firsthand. A joint field trip also gives the arbitrators an opportunity to address any items not fully covered in their previous communications and gives any previously unacquainted arbitrators an opportunity to get to know each other and to form a basis for working together.

Hearings

The arbitrators should offer each party the opportunity to present oral and written information and opinions if they so desire. It frequently is convenient to hold a meeting to accommodate such input in conjunction with the field trip. This meeting may be conducted with the parties jointly or separately.

Reporting an Arbitration Conclusion

If there is a sole arbitrator, the parties can specify how they wish the conclusion presented. This can range from a single sentence to a full report in accordance with the Uniform Standards of Professional Appraisal Practice or other professional business valuation standards.

However, if there is a panel of arbitrators, the report is usually a brief letter that says that the arbitrators have completed their work in accordance with the arbitration agreement and states the conclusion that was reached. The letter, called an *award* in the parlance of arbitration, is signed by the arbitrators concurring in the conclusion.

In many cases, the principals on both sides want a brief report explaining how the valuation conclusion was reached. In arbitration parlance, this is called an *opinion* and it is usually the sole responsibility of the third appraiser. To make such a report a joint effort of two or more arbitrators, each of whom probably judged various factors a little differently, would most likely be an unnecessarily complicated and costly exercise.

It is most desirable to come to a conclusion that can be endorsed as fair by all members of the arbitration panel. This usually can be achieved if all the arbitrators are qualified professional business appraisers. If unanimous agreement cannot be reached, the arbitrator in the minority position may render a dissenting opinion for the record, if he or she so desires.

Alternative Dispute Resolution in Marital Dissolution

Arbitration has been used successfully to resolve financial issues in marital dissolution[6]:

> Generally speaking, the cases have held that property division may be arbitrated and the result will be final and binding on the parties.[7] The general rationale upon which this conclusion is based is that parties may release property rights by contract.[8] Because parties agree by contract to arbitration, the agreement concerning the process can be enforced. The decision (or award) resulting from arbitration has limited review and limited appeal rights, not unlike arbitration awards in other areas.

---

6. Elizabeth A. Jenkins, Annotation, *Validity and Construction of Provisions for Arbitration of Disputes as to Alimony or Support Payments or Child Visitation or Custody Matters*, 38 A.L.R. Fed. 5th 69, 78–79 (1996).

7. *See, e.g.*, Spencer v. Spencer, 494 A.2d 1279 (D.C. 1985); *In re* T.B.H.-H., 188 S.W.3d 312 (Tex. Ct. App. 2006) (trial court has limited authority when reviewing an arbitration award in a property settlement case; the courts are limited to analyzing the integrity of the arbitration, not the award itself). [Footnote not in original quote.]

8. Alves v. Alves, 262 A.2d 111, 118 (D.C. 1970).

> Awards by arbitrators of spousal support, maintenance, and/or alimony are almost always final and binding because they, too, are contracts to determine an adult property right. Such arbitration decisions, consistent with other arbitration awards, are subject to limited review and appeal rights.[9]

In fact, some states regulate such arbitration by statute,[10] and the American Academy of Matrimonial Lawyers has promulgated a model family law arbitration act.[11]

As one author had indicated, "ADR is great for promoting property division agreements by (a) facilitating the exchange of relevant information regarding property and debts, (b) helping spouses together apply the [state's] property division model to their own marital estate, and (c) providing a means for couples to tailor their divorce economics to meet the family's specific needs and use their resources most effectively."[12] For these reasons, arbitration in most divorce matters has gained increased acceptance and use.[13]

While many see the final and binding nature of arbitration as a benefit of that procedure, all family law courts may not necessarily view it as final and binding. While approving the concept of arbitration of alimony and property division, a Massachusetts intermediate appellate court held that any "award must, of course, be subject to review by the judge, who has the authority and the obligation . . . , to make a fair and equitable distribution of property."[14]

Alternative Dispute Resolution in Federal Tax Disputes

The IRS Office of Chief Counsel issued Notice N(35)000-135 dated October 13, 1995, "to outline general considerations for the use of mediation to resolve Tax Court cases." Although there have been only a few such mediations, they generally have been resolved successfully.

---

9. Joan F. Kessler Kessler et al., *Why Arbitrate Family Law Matters?* 14 J. AM. ACAD. MATRIM. L. 341 (1997).

10. *See, e.g.,* Michigan's Domestic Relations Arbitration Act, MICH. COMP. LAWS § 600.5070 *et seq.* (2009); Indiana's Family Law Arbitration provisions, IND. CODE ANN. § 34-57-5 *et seq.* (2009); North Carolina's Family Law Arbitration Act, N.C. GEN. STAT. § 50-41 *et seq.* (2009).

11. The Model Family Law Arbitration Act, promulgated in 2005, is meant to be a companion to the Revised Uniform Arbitration Act, drafted by the National Conference of Comm'rs on Uniform State Laws, focusing on civil law matters, which has been adopted in at least eight states and is under consideration in several more.

12. William C. Darrah, *ADR Spotlight: A Divorce ADR Primer for the Non-Family Law Attorney*, HAW. B. J., November 2006.

13. *See, e.g.,* George K. Walker, *Arbitrating Family Law Cases by Agreement*, 18 J. AM. ACAD. MATRIM. LAW. 429 (2003); Hon. R. Mark Browning & James K. Hoenig, *Hawaii's Family Court Promotes Innovative Divorce Resolutions*, HAW. B. J., July 2006.

14. Reynolds v. Whitman, 40 Mass. App. Ct. 315 (Mass. App. Ct. 1996).

Even after a case has been calendared for trial in the U.S. Tax Court, the court may grant an extension based on an agreement between the taxpayer and IRS District Counsel to submit the matter to nonbinding mediation.

The IRS, in Rev. Proc. 2002-44, formally established an appeals mediation procedure, which is a nonbinding process that uses the services of a mediator to help the IRS's Office of Appeals (Appeals) and the taxpayer reach a negotiated settlement. The mediator acts as a facilitator to assist in defining the issues and promote settlement negotiations. He or she will not have settlement authority and will not render a decision regarding any issue in dispute. The goal of this mediation process is to resolve issues while they are in the jurisdiction of the Appeals office and may only be used after Appeals settlement discussions are unsuccessful and, generally, when all other issues are resolved but for the issue to be mediated.

In addition to the mediation program discussed in Rev. Proc. 2002-44, which occurs at the Appeals level, there are two other mediation programs available to certain qualifying taxpayers at the compliance level. They are the "fast-track settlement" (FTS) mediation programs for certain small businesses and self-employeds (see IRB 2006-36, Announcement 2006-61) and the FTS program for large and midsize businesses (see Rev. Proc. 2003-40). The program for small businesses and self-employeds enables taxpayers who currently have unagreed issues in at least one open year under examination to work together with the compliance section and Appeals to resolve outstanding disputed issues while the case is still in compliance jurisdiction. The FTS process is used to resolve factual and legal issues and may be initiated at any time after an issue has been fully developed, preferably before the issuance of a 30-day letter or equivalent notice. The FTS program for large and midsize businesses offers qualifying taxpayers a way to resolve audit issues during the examination process in less than 120 days. Working with the compliance section and Appeals, taxpayers can use the settlement authority and mediation skills of Appeals to shorten their overall experience with the IRS by as much as two years.[15]

The senior author gained new appreciation and respect for a well-done mediation by participating as an expert witness in one such process. The arbitration succeeded because of a mediation team consisting of a lawyer highly skilled in mediation and a senior business valuation expert. There were also well-prepared expert witnesses on both sides.

15. For additional IRS guidance, see IRS Publication 4167, Appeals: Introduction to Alternative Dispute Resolution.

Alternative Dispute Resolution References

Books and Publications

American Academy of Matrimonial Lawyers. 1990. *Rules for Arbitration of Financial Issues.* A copy can be obtained from AAML, (312) 263-6477.

Brinig, Brian P., et al. "Alternative Dispute Resolution." In *Guide to Litigation Support Services,* 11th Ed., Ch. 12. Fort Worth, Texas: Practitioners Publishing Company, 2006.

Diana, James C. 1995. "The New Mediation Procedure in Appeals: The Latest Development in the IRS' ADR Initiative." *Tax Management Memorandum* (November 13): 331–39.

Fiore, Nicholas. 1996. "Pros and Cons of the New IRS Mediation Program." *Journal of Accountancy* (May): 36.

Ford, David J. "CPAs and ADR: A Civilized Alternative to Litigation." *CPA Litigation Service Counselor* (February 2000): 1–5.

Iwanyshyn, Deborah. "Mediation as a Form of Dispute Resolution." In Shannon Pratt, *Business Valuation Update,* October 1998, 5–6.

Kaufman, Steve. 1992. "See You Out of Court: Mediation Used in Resolving Business Disputes." *Nation's Business* (June): 58–60.

Klinefelter, Stanard T., and Sandra P. Gohn. 1995. "Alternative Dispute Resolution: Its Value to Estate Planners." *Estate Planning* (May/June): 147–54.

Kratchman, D. Michael, and William P. Walsh. 1995. "Mediation Instead of Litigation for Resolution of Valuation Disputes." *Michigan Business Law Journal* (Winter): 15–17.

Pratt, Shannon P., and Alina V. Niculita. 2008. "Arbitration and Mediation." In *Valuing a Business,* 5th Ed., Ch. 42. New York: McGraw-Hill.

Saltzman, Michael I. 1996. "Tax Court Mediation: A Case Study." *Tax Executive.* (November/December): 449–53.

Professional Arbitration and Mediation Organizations

American Arbitration Associates
1633 Broadway, 10th Flr., New York, NY 10019
(212) 716-5800, (fax) (212) 716-5905, www.adr.org

American Bar Association Section of Dispute Resolution
740 15th St. N.W., Washington, D.C. 20005-1009
(202) 662-1680, (fax) (202) 662-1683, www.abanet.org/dispute

Association for Conflict Resolution
5151 Wisconsin Ave., NW, Ste. 500, Washington, D.C. 20016
(202) 464-9700, (fax) (202) 464-9720, www.acrnet.org

Association of Family and Conciliation Courts
6525 Grand Teton Pl., Madison, WI 53719
(608) 664-3750, (fax) (608) 664-3751, www.afccnet.org

CPR, The International Institute for Conflict Prevention and Resolution
575 Lexington Ave., 21st Flr., New York, NY 10022
(212) 949-6490, (fax) (212) 949-8859, www.cpradr.org
Publishes training modules, videotapes, and books.

Jams/Endispute, Inc.
1920 Main St., Ste. 300, Irvine, CA 92614
(800) 352-5267, www.jamsadr.com

Mediation and Conflict Management Services (Robert D. Benjamin)
3246 S.W. Cascade Terr., Portland, OR 97205
(503) 417-2655, rbenjamin@mediate.com, www.rbenjamin.com

The Keystone Center (Peter Adler)
1628 St. John Rd., Keystone, CO 80435
(970) 513-5841, www.keystone.org

Chapter 30

Business Valuation Standards and Credentials

Organizations Offering Professional Accreditation

Four major professional organizations in the United States and one in Canada offer courses and examinations leading to accreditation in terms of a professional designation in business valuation. The comparative accreditation requirements are shown in Exhibit 30-1.

More detailed information on each of the organizations is shown in Appendix B. All the organizations publish membership directories, either in print or online, which may be obtained for a nominal charge. (Note: All members are not necessarily accredited.)

The course curricula of these five organizations lean primarily toward valuation of closely held businesses (businesses with no public trading market for their securities), partial interests in closely held businesses, and intangible assets. In many instances, they also address matters such as discounts for fractional interests in tangible assets such as real estate.

All the organizations also sponsor continuing-education seminars. The seminars tend to focus on narrower issues in greater depth than do the basic courses, examination of issues about which professional controversy exists, and updated reports on matters such as changes in law and regulation, new precedential case law, and new and expanded sources of empirical data used in valuation. Each organization has continuing-education and recertification requirements, as shown in Appendix B.

Exhibit 30-1
Professional Accreditation Criteria

Organization	Certification	Prerequisites	Course/Exam	Reports	Experience/Other
American Institute of Certified Public Accountants (AICPA)	ABV—Accredited in Business Valuation	Be a member in good standing of the AICPA. Hold a valid and unrevoked CPA certificate or license issued by a legally constituted state authority.	Pass a full-day two-section comprehensive business valuation examination containing multiple-choice and case studies with multiple-choice answers.	None	Substantial involvement in at least 10 business valuation engagements or provide evidence of 150 hours that demonstrate substantial experience.
American Society of Appraisers (ASA)	AM—Accredited Member	Obtain a four-year college degree or equivalent.	Complete four Principle of Valuation courses of three days each and pass one half-day examination following each course, and complete a one-hour Ethics examination and a 15-hour USPAP course, which is followed by a one-hour USPAP examination.	Submit two narrative appraisal reports (three for Real Property–Residential) that were completed within the past two years. These reports must be actual reports that were produced for clients.	Two years of full-time or equivalent experience (e.g., five years of 400 hours business appraisal work per year equals one year full-time equivalent). One full year of requirement is granted to anyone who has CPA, CFA, or CBI (Certified Business Intermediary) designation with five years of practice held.
	ASA—Accredited Senior Appraiser	Meet AM requirements, plus three additional years of full-time or equivalent experience.			Five years of full-time or equivalent experience, including two years for AM.
	FASA—Fellow of the American Society of Appraisers	Meet ASA requirements, plus be voted into the College of Fellows on the basis of technical leadership and contribution to the profession or the society.			

Exhibit 30-1 (continued)
Professional Accreditation Criteria

Organization	Certification	Prerequisites	Course/Exam	Reports	Experience/Other
Institute of Business Appraisers (IBA)	CBA—Certified Business Appraiser	Complete a four-year college degree or equivalent. Complete IBA's 16-hour course 1010 (Report Writing). Be a member in good standing of the IBA.	Complete a four-hour, proctored, CBA written examination. Applicants may be exempt from the examination if they hold the ASA, ABV, CVA, or AVA designation.	Submit two Demonstration Reports demonstrating a high degree of skill, knowledge, and judgment as a business appraiser.	Successfully complete 90 hours of upper-level course work. At least 24 hours of this coursework must have been in courses offered by the IBA. Or the applicant may demonstrate 10,000 hours of active experience as a business appraiser. Provide four satisfactory references, two references as to personal character and two references as to professional competence as a business appraiser.
	MCBA—Master Certified Business Appraiser	Obtain a four-year college degree and a two-year postgraduate degree or equivalent; held the Certified Business Appraiser designation for not less than 10 years; must have 15 years of full-time experience as a business appraiser; and hold one other designation (ASA, CVA, or ABV).			Fifteen years of full-time practice. Provide three references from MCBAs with personal knowledge of applicant's work.

Exhibit 30-1 (continued)
Professional Accreditation Criteria

Organization	Certification	Prerequisites	Course/Exam	Reports	Experience/Other
Institute of Business Appraisers (IBA)	AIBA—Accredited by IBA	Complete a four-year college degree or equivalent; possess a business appraisal designation from peer organizations recognized by the Institute of Business Appraisers, upon application to the IBA, or complete IBA eight-day Appraisal Workshop IBA course 8001.	Complete comprehensive written examination.	Submit one report for peer review.	Provide four references of character and fitness.
	BVAL—Business Valuator Accredited for Litigation	Obtain business appraisal designation from IBA, AICPA, ASA, NACVA or CBA candidate who has passed the exam.	Attend five days of IBA course 7001, for 40 CPE hours; complete prereading and all course assignments (16 CPE hours); and pass four-hour written examination.		Demonstrate presentation and process competency during the testimony clinics. Provide letters of reference from two attorneys or complete 16 hours of education in the area of law in which the appraiser will testify.
	ABAR—Accredited in Business Appraisal Review	Be IBA members in good standing, and possess a 4-year university degree or equivalent. Hold a business appraisal designation awarded by IBA, AICPA, ASA, CICBV or NACVA or must have achieved a passing grade on the CBA written examination.	Successfully complete IBA Course 1044— Critiquing Business Valuation Reports and achieve a passing grade on a comprehensive examination.	Submit two appraisal reviews, which will be peer-reviewed to determine if the reviews meet professional standards of competence.	Provide two professional and two personal references. Demonstrate 10,000 hours of experience in appraisal review or 90 hours of appraisal education. Twenty-four of these hours must have been earned through education sponsored by the IBA.

Exhibit 30-1 (continued)
Professional Accreditation Criteria

Organization	Certification	Prerequisites	Course/Exam	Reports	Experience/Other
Institute of Business Appraisers (IBA)	FIBA—Fellow of the Institute of Business Appraisers	Meet all CBA requirements, plus be voted into the College of Fellows on the basis of technical leadership and contribution to the profession and the institute.			
National Association of Certified Valuation Analysts (NACVA)	AVA—Accredited Valuation Analyst, includes prior GVA designation	Complete optional five-day course; pass a comprehensive two-part examination. Part One is a five-hour proctored exam. Non-CPA applicants without a background in accounting fundamentals may be subject to another half-day examination. Part Two is a take-home/in-office examination that incorporates a standardized case study.	Complete optional five-day course; pass a comprehensive two-part examination. Part One is a five-hour proctored exam. Non-CPA applicants without a background in accounting fundamentals may be subject to another half-day examination. Part Two is a take-home/in-office examination that incorporates a standardized case study.		Two years of full-time or equivalent business valuation or related experience or 10 or more business valuations. Provide three personal references, three business references, and a minimum of one letter of recommendation from an employer or another CPA.

Exhibit 30-1 (continued)
Professional Accreditation Criteria

Organization	Certification	Prerequisites	Course/Exam	Reports	Experience/Other
National Association of Certified Valuation Analysts (NACVA)	CVA—Certified Valuation Analyst	Have a college degree, an unrevoked CPA license, and be a member in good standing of the NACVA.	Complete optional five-day course; pass two-part examination; Part One is a four-hour proctored examination. Part Two is a take-home/in-office examination that requires performing a complete business valuation.		Two years of experience as a CPA. Provide three personal references and three business references.
	CFFA—Certified Financial Forensic Analyst, including prior CFD (Certified Fraud Deterrence Analyst) designation	Possess one of the following designations: CVA, AVA, ABV, AM, ASA, CBA, CBV, CFA, CFE, CMA, CPA, or CA; have a bachelor's degree in a business field from an accredited university/college or, alternatively, a master's degree or doctorate in a field of business; be a Practitioner, Academic, or Government member of the NACVA.	Complete two-week course and eight days of training at NACVA's Forensic Institute; pass two-part examination, one for the specialty area being pursued and one to demonstrate a command of litigation fundamentals.		Provide one business and two legal references. Must show proof of having provided services in the applicable field in which candidate wishes to specialize.

Exhibit 30-1 (continued)
Professional Accreditation Criteria

Organization	Certification	Prerequisites	Course/Exam	Reports	Experience/Other
The Canadian Institute of Chartered Business Valuators (CICBV)	CBV—Chartered Business Valuator	Have a college degree or equivalent— accounting or finance encouraged.	Successfully complete six courses, including assignments and examinations for each course plus the required experience, followed by writing the Membership Entrance Examination.		Have accumulated 1,500 hours of business and securities valuation experience. The experience should be attested to by a sponsor. The required practical experience should be attained within five years of applying to write the Membership Entrance Examination.
	FCBV—Fellow of the Canadian Institute of Chartered Business Valuators	Be a member; have rendered outstanding service to the business valuation profession or have earned distinction and brought honor through achievements in professional life or in the community.			

Each organization also publishes one or more journals and/or newsletters, as shown in Appendix B. These sources (as well as many others) are abstracted regularly in *Business Valuation Update*™ and can be searched by keyword at www.BVLibrary.com.℠

Other Organizations Offering Business Valuation Guidance

In addition to the five organizations discussed above, several other organizations offer various forms of education and guidance in aspects of business valuation. Of particular importance is the CFA Institute (formerly the Association for Investment Management and Research (AIMR)), which awards the professional designation of Chartered Financial Analyst (CFA®). This designation requires passing three rigorous all-day examinations dealing primarily with analyzing and managing publicly traded securities. The curriculum also includes some segments on valuing closely held businesses.

A few hundred of the CFA Institute's 94,000-plus members indicate a specialty in closely held business valuation. Some of these also hold the designation of ASA (Accredited Senior Appraiser of the American Society of Appraisers). This cross-designation may be especially relevant in actions such as when a private company is being acquired by a public company, a public company is going private, or dissenting stockholder actions involve public companies. CFA® members are concentrated in the United States and Canada, but there are members throughout the world.

The other often-mentioned group is the International Business Brokers Association® (IBBA®), which is the largest international nonprofit association operating exclusively for the benefit of people and firms engaged in the various aspects of business brokerage and mergers and acquisitions. Today, the IBBA has more than 1,800 cooperative business brokers and intermediaries across Canada, Mexico, Asia, Europe, Australia, and the United States.

The IBBA® has about 1,500 members who act as intermediaries in the sales of businesses. Some members also offer business appraisal services. The IBBA® awards the professional designation of Certified Business Intermediary (CBI®). The courses required for this designation include two days on valuation and establishing company sale prices.

The ESOP Association consists of companies that have Employee Stock Ownership Plans and companies that provide various advisory services to them, including business appraisers. The ESOP Association does not issue any standards nor does it offer any accreditation. It does publish materials containing valuation guidance for ESOP shares developed by its Advisory Committee on Valuation, which consists of experienced ESOP share appraisers. The ESOP Association also offers continuing-education seminars, including sessions on ESOP valuation issues.

Exhibit 30-2 is a quick reference list of the various professional designations offered by the organizations discussed in this chapter.

Exhibit 30-2
Professional Accreditation Quick Reference List

ABAR	Accredited in Business Appraisal Review (Institute of Business Appraisers)
AIBA	Accredited by IBA (Institute of Business Appraisers)
AM	Accredited Member (American Society of Appraisers)
ARM	Appraisal Review and Management (American Society of Appraisers)
ASA	Accredited Senior Appraiser (American Society of Appraisers)
AVA	Accredited Valuation Analyst (National Association of Certified Valuation Analysts)
BVAL	Business Valuator Accredited for Litigation (Institute of Business Appraisers)
CBA	Certified Business Appraiser (Institute of Business Appraisers)
CBI	Certified Business Intermediary (International Business Brokers Association)
CBV	Chartered Business Valuator (The Canadian Institute of Chartered Business Valuators)
CFA	Chartered Financial Analyst (CFA Institute)
CFFA	Certified Financial Forensic Analyst, including prior CFD (Certified Fraud Deterrence Analyst) designation (National Association of Certified Valuation Analysts)
CPA/ABV	Certified Public Accountant Accredited in Business Valuations (American Institute of Certified Public Accountants)
CVA	Certified Valuation Analyst (National Association of Certified Valuation Analysts)
FASA	Fellow of the American Society of Appraisers (American Society of Appraisers)
FCBI	Fellow Certified Business Intermediary (International Business Brokers Association)
FCBV	Fellow of the Canadian Institute of Chartered Business Valuators
FIBA	Fellow of the Institute of Business Appraisers (Institute of Business Appraisers)
GVA	Government Valuation Analyst (National Association of Certified Valuation Analysts)
MCBA	Master Certified Business Appraiser (Institute of Business Appraisers)

Business Valuation Professional Standards

Uniform Standards of Professional Appraisal Practice (USPAP)

The most widely recognized and cited set of professional standards for appraisal is the *Uniform Standards of Professional Appraisal Practice (USPAP),* published by the Appraisal Foundation.

The Appraisal Foundation was founded in 1987 by a group of the leading professional appraisal organizations serving all appraisal disciplines, including real estate, personal property, and business and intangible asset appraisal. It is funded by Congress, member organizations, donations, and proceeds from sales of publications.

The Appraisal Foundation is governed by a 27-member board of trustees consisting of appointees of sponsoring organizations and trustees at large. The trustees appoint two boards, the Appraisal Standards Board (ASB) and the Appraiser Qualifications Board (AQB), each of which then acts autonomously in developing and promulgating appraisal standards and appraiser qualifications. The Appraisal Standards Board develops the *Uniform Standards of Professional Appraisal Practice.*

The *USPAP* contains four basic components:

1. Prefatory material (definitions, preamble, ethics, competency rule, jurisdictional exceptions).
2. Standards Rules 1 through 10 (9 and 10 apply specifically to business and intangible asset appraisals).
   - Standard 9 includes requirements for procedures and comprehensiveness in conducting an appraisal of a business, business interest, or intangible asset.
   - Standard 10 states what needs to be included in a report of an appraisal of a business, business interest, or intangible asset.
3. Statements on Appraisal Standards, which contain further elaboration on points made in the standards themselves. Compliance with the Statements on Appraisal Standards is mandatory for appraisals that purport to conform to the *USPAP.* However, there are few Statements on Appraisal Standards that actually apply to business and intangible asset valuations.
4. Advisory Opinions, which contain commentary that is advisory in nature. Again, there is little in the Advisory Opinions that is applicable to business or intangible asset appraisals.

The *USPAP* is updated biannually by the Appraisal Standards Board, with each edition usually released in November and applicable to appraisals performed in the following tax calendar years. Note that the edition of *USPAP* that applies is the edition for the year in which the appraisal is performed, which may be a later year than the year of the effective valuation date if an appraisal is performed retrospectively.

Compliance with the *USPAP* is legally mandatory for real estate transactions of more than $250,000 involving federally related agencies and for conversions of mutual savings and loans to stock companies; otherwise, as of this writing, compliance with the *USPAP* is legally required only if so stipulated in the engagement agreement between the appraiser and the client. Nevertheless, whether legally required or not, the *USPAP* is widely accepted in the professional appraisal community. Most leading appraisal authorities consider it a valid set of standards against which to measure the minimum requirements for an appraisal.

Biannual editions of the *USPAP*, usually published in November, cost $75. Contact The Appraisal Foundation, 1155 15th St. N.W., Ste. 1111, Washington, D.C. 20005, (202) 347-7722, info@appraisalfoundation.org, www.appraisalfoundation.org. You also can access its online version free at commerce.appraisalfoundation.org.

The foundation's other board, the Appraiser Qualifications Board (AQB), has promulgated qualifications for real estate appraisers and personal property appraisers. As of this writing, the AQB has no plans to develop qualifications for appraisers of businesses and intangible assets.

Other Professional Organization Standards

All five of the professional associations listed in the first section of this chapter have promulgated professional business valuation standards of their own. These may be ordered free of charge from the address shown in each association's respective information (see Appendix B).

None of the individual associations' standards are in conflict with the *USPAP*. In general, each set of standards goes into more detail than does the *USPAP*.

Internal Revenue Service Authority

Rightly or wrongly, Revenue Rulings issued by the Internal Revenue Service often are cited as authority for business valuation standards. The most commonly cited ruling is Revenue Ruling 59-60, on valuation of stocks and bonds.

Revenue Rulings certainly contain some business valuation wisdom. However, three caveats are important:

1. Revenue Rulings are not the law, they are merely the IRS's position. They are usually, but not always, upheld when tested in court.
2. Revenue Rulings reflect conditions as of the time they were written and are not always (or even usually) updated to reflect current conditions (for example, Revenue Ruling 59-60 was written in 1959).

3. Revenue Rulings are written for valuations for tax purposes (for example, estate and gift taxes, charitable contributions, income taxes) and these reflect valuation in the context of the legal standard of fair market value as defined by the U.S. Treasury Department. In valuations for other purposes under other legal definitions of value (for example, fair value for a shareholder dispute), some aspects of Revenue Rulings may not be applicable.

In 2004, the IRS issued *IRS Business Valuation Guidelines.* This guidance is very similar to the *USPAP.* The latest version of the *IRS Business Valuation Guidelines* (2006) can be found online at www.bvresources.com.

Chapter 31

Cross-examining a Business Valuation Expert

This is a generalized chapter in the sense that it does not distinguish between deposition questions and trial questions. However, the questions are largely designed to find out what the expert has produced, so they are appropriate for deposition. On the basis of the deposition testimony, the attorney probably will choose to concentrate on some areas and leave others alone at trial.

If reports are exchanged ahead of the deposition, the attorney's expert can give the attorney a great deal of help in suggesting what areas to drill down in and specific questions to ask. In any case, the deposition should enable the attorney's expert to replicate the work of the opposing expert. This is the best way to enable the attorney's expert to identify weakness in the opposing expert's work that can be brought out at trial.

We should be present or have a member of our professional staff present during the deposition of the opposing expert. This accomplishes two purposes. First, the answer to one question may lead to another question that may not occur to the attorney. Second, it is useful in preparing for court, both in helping the attorney prepare our expert's examination and helping the attorney prepare the cross-examination of the opposing expert. For preparation for court, we always should read the deposition of the opposing expert(s) as well as our own deposition.

Background and Qualifications (Chapter 30)

Education

School attended with dates
Degrees earned
Majors or special emphasis

Note: There are many people practicing business valuation whose academic education has nothing to do with business valuation. Also, an accounting degree has no business valuation content whatsoever (that is why the AICPA created the additional designation CPA/ABV, Accredited in Business Valuation) and a major in economics may have little or no content in business valuation.

Professional Credentials

- American Society of Appraisers (ASA)
  - FASA
  - ASA
  - AM
  - ARM
- American Institute of Certified Public Accountants (AICPA)
  - CPA/ABV
- Institute of Business Appraisers (IBA)
  - MCBA
  - CBA
  - AIBA
  - BVAL
  - ABAR
  - FIBA
- National Association of Certified Valuation Analysts (NACVA)
  - CVA
  - AVA
  - CFFA
- Institute of Chartered Financial Analysts (ICFA)
  - CFA
- Canadian Institute of Certified Valuation Analysts (CICBV)
  - CBV
  - FCBV
- Others

Note: The above are the primary recognized credentials in business valuation. Courts are becoming increasingly aware of these designations and increasingly critical of experts without them. It usually is very helpful to be able to demonstrate that your expert is more qualified than is the opposing expert.

Experience

Company, job description, dates
(The attorney may want to explore how much of each position is related to business valuation.)

Valuations in similar industries/types of properties

Note: This is nice but not necessary. See *Guang Dong v. ACI International, Inc.*, *Physicians Dialysis Ventures, Inc. v. Griffith,* and *Popovich v. Sony Music Entertainment, Inc.,* where the court said industry experience was not a necessary qualification.

Prior testimony

Note: It can be especially helpful if prior testimony can be found that can be considered contradictory to the testimony in the case at hand.

Assignment (Chapters 1 and 2)

When were you retained?

Who retained you?

What was the assignment?
- Valuation date or dates
- Property to be appraised
  - Name of entity
  - Property within entity to be appraised
  - (e.g., shares of voting common stock out of shares outstanding—if there is other equity in capital structure, should designate that)
  - State of incorporation or registration

What definition of value did you use for this appraisal assignment (for example, fair market value, defined as " . . .")?

What is the source of that definition?

Why is that definition of value appropriate for this valuation assignment (for example, statutory definition, definition from precedential case(s) [which should be cited if relied on as authority], definition from binding contractual agreement)?

Is your appraisal based on a going-concern premise, a liquidation premise, or some combination of going concern and liquidation? Why?

Written documentation of assignment (e.g., engagement letter)

Any changes to assignment?

Work Done

Total number of hours

Hourly rates

Hours by testifying expert

Hours by others (specify)

Who did what?

Total billing

Total payment received to date

Overdue amounts

Unbilled amounts

What other work anticipated?

Sources of Information

Economic and Industry Information (Chapter 14)

To assess the *recent status of the national economy,* what data was referenced and which sources were used? What was the basis for using this information for this purpose?

Which sources were used to form an opinion about the *national economic outlook?*

At the valuation date, which leading indicators and other factors were being emphasized in the national economic forecasts? Why?

To assess the *recent status of the relevant industry,* what data was referenced and which sources were used? What was the basis for using this information for this purpose?

Did these sources include the periodicals from one or more relevant trade associations? If not, why not?

Which aspects of the national economy were emphasized when assessing the performance of the industry? Why?

What other factors (such as developing technology, emerging substitute products, changes in the composition of the industry, foreign competition) were cited as having a current and potential influence on the industry? Why?

Was there any reason to believe the industry benchmarks derived from composite company data may have been biased in some fashion (such as including too few firms, firms with extreme characteristics, or firms that are largely unrepresentative of the subject company's product line)? If so, what steps were taken to deal with the bias?

What ratios and/or other measures were identified by analysts as being particularly relevant in the analysis of the industry or the individual companies making up the industry? Why?

How were the factors identified in the above questions incorporated into the analysis supporting the future projections for the subject company?

To what extent was regional analysis used in assessing the future projections for the subject company? Why or why not?

How was the economic and industry information taken into account in the valuation?

Company Information

Site visits (who, where, and when). How long did your site visit take? How many times did you visit the company?
Interviews (who, where, and when)
Financial statements (what statements, who prepared, compiled, reviewed, or audited)
Tax returns (what periods)
Articles of incorporation, organization
What contracts (noncompete/employment agreements, buy-sell agreements, supplier/customer contracts, union contracts)
Company literature

Financial Statement Adjustments (Chapter 12)

Did you make any adjustments to the subject company's balance sheets? To the income statements? Please describe each adjustment, the reasons for it, and how you quantified the amount of each.

(If the market approach was used) Did you make any adjustments to the statements of any of the guideline companies' financial statements? Please describe. If not, why not? (When guideline public companies are used, either daily market trades or mergers and acquisitions, it is a common error to adjust the subject company's statements and overlook whether any comparable adjustments to the guideline companies' statements should be considered.)

Were there any adjustments for which there would be tax implications? (If so, how did you take the tax implications into account?)

(If valuing a minority interest) Were all your adjustments of a "normalizing nature" (for example, eliminate nonrecurring items to put accounting on a basis comparable with guideline companies or industry standards) or were some of the adjustments things that only a control owner could change? (It is a common error, when valuing minority interests, to make adjustments that only a control owner could cause to happen and that do not reflect the actual expected ongoing operations of the company.)

Comparative Financial Statement Analysis (Chapter 13)

What ratio or trend analysis, if any, did you undertake? For the subject company? For guideline companies? For industry averages?

What unusual occurrences were brought to light by using horizontal analysis (comparing financial statements from one year to the next) over the recent history? What explanations were given for these occurrences?

Have common-sized financial statements been prepared for the subject company over a period of five years or more (if possible)?

What significant changes have been noted in the proportionate composition of the subject company's assets, liabilities, and equity, and income statement over the period for which common-sized financial statements were prepared? What explanations have been given for these changes?

How do the current common-sized financial statements of the subject company compare to the industry benchmarks? What explanations have been given for any significant differences noted?

Which ratios have been used to assess the subject company's profitability? How have these changed over the recent past and how do they compare to the industry benchmarks?

Which ratios have been used to assess the subject company's liquidity? How have these changed over the recent past and how do they compare to the industry benchmarks?

Which ratios have been used to assess the subject company's long-term solvency? How have these changed over the recent past and how do they compare to the industry benchmarks?

Was there any bias in the calculations of the amounts or percentages by which sales or profits have increased over the recent past, such as giving undue weight to exceptionally good or bad years?

What part of the analysis of the subject company's recent financial history is relevant to the assessment of its future performance? Why?

What part of the analysis of the subject company's recent financial history is *not* relevant to the assessment of its future performance? Why?

Where in your report do you show how the financial statement analysis impacted your valuation conclusion?

Note: Some analysts go through an elaborate financial statement analysis and never again refer to it.

Did you do the ratio/trend analysis on the statements before or after the adjustments?

Note: The analysis usually should be done on the statements after adjustments. But doing the ratio analysis before adjustments can be very helpful in identifying performance measurements that appear unusual and require additional inquiry.

Overall Valuation Methodology (Chapter 3)

What approaches did you use (income, market, asset)?

Why did you choose the approaches you used? Why did you not use . . . ?

Did you do the valuation on an enterprise or equity basis or both? Why? (If the answer is different for different approaches, specify which and why.)

Within the valuation approach, what method or methods did you use? Why is this (are those) better than any alternative method(s) for the purpose of the valuation?

Income Approach (Chapter 5)

Did you conduct your income approach on an equity basis or on an invested capital basis? Why is that basis more appropriate for this assignment?

(If on an invested capital basis) What components did you include in your capital structure? Why?

What economic income variable did you use in the income approach (e.g., net cash flow, net income, pretax income, etc.)? Why?

What method(s) did you use (e.g., discounted cash flow, capitalized cash flow)? Why?

Note: Usually either a discounting or a capitalizing method is used, but not both because capitalizing is just a short version of discounting. If both methods were used, this is usually a sign of lack of sophistication on the part of the analyst.

How did you project your net cash flow (or other economic income variable) that you discounted or capitalized?

What were the assumptions?

What did you do (if anything) to check for the reasonableness of the assumptions and resulting forecasts?

If discounting, how did you develop the discount rate? If capitalizing, how did you develop the capitalization rate? Why did you do it in that way?

Note: The capitalization rate equals the discount rate minus the growth rate in perpetuity. If a capitalization rate was developed some other way, the witness should have a good explanation.

If either discounting or capitalizing, how did you estimate the growth rate, if any? Why did you choose that particular growth rate?

Note: Growth rates are in perpetuity, which is a long time. Growth rates in excess of forecasted GNP growth plus inflation (3 percent to 5 percent most of the time) are very likely unsustainable in the long run.

What level of value did your income approach produce (e.g., control, minority marketable)?

Note: The control or minority level of value usually is determined by the level of cash flow projected; i.e., if the cash flows are what a control owner would expect to get, the result would be a control value; if the cash flows would be what a minority owner would expect, the result would be a minority value. (Once in a while, if the company is operated efficiently and all owners are treated in proportion to their ownership interests, the control and minority values might be equal or close to equal.)

The reason that the minority value would be marketable is that if using either the CAPM or buildup method to estimate the discount or capitalization rate, these rates are developed from public market data.

What procedure did you use to estimate your terminal value? (This usually will be a capitalization of constant income, a constant growth model, or a market multiple of some income variable.) (If a market multiple) Why is that procedure better than a capitalized income model? (If a capitalized income procedure) Why is that procedure better than a market multiple model? What percentage of your total present value is attributable to your terminal value?

Will you please define in simple terms exactly what a *discount rate* is? (This question tests the analyst's knowledge and understanding of what the discounting method is all about, and whether the analyst thinks that he or she has captured what he or she should in the rate, that is, *the total rate of return that the market would demand* to place money in this investment, apart from liquidity considerations.)

(If an invested capital procedure was used) Please explain exactly how you computed your Weighted Average Cost of Capital (WACC).

What percentage weight was assigned to each component of your capital structure? How did you arrive at these weights? Are the weights based on book value of equity or market value of equity? (If book value, the WACC is virtually meaningless, but this is a common error.) What source list did you use to derive the weights you used for each component of the capital structure? (If some comparative financial statement source, such as Robert Morris Associates' *Financial Statement Studies* or the *Almanac of Business and Industrial Financial Ratios,* was used and the equity percentage was at market value, there will be a problem, because those sources are at book value.) Why are these weights appropriate to use in this particular valuation assignment? (If the analyst is valuing a minority interest and uses some weights other than the company's own actual weights—for example, some industry average weights—he or she has injected an element of control into the valuation, because the minority stockholder cannot cause a change in the company's capital structure. (This generally would not be appropriate under the standard of fair market value and may or may not be appropriate under other standards of value.)

Did you apply any premiums or discounts to your indicated value from the income approach? Why or why not?

Market Approach (Chapter 6)

What method(s) did you use within the market approach (e.g., guideline public company method, transaction method, past transactions, buy/sell agreements)? For each method, why or why not?

For the guideline public company and transaction methods, what criteria did you use for the selection of guideline companies? What was the population of companies that you searched to make your selections? Why? What steps did you take to make sure that there were no guideline companies in the selected population that met your criteria but were omitted?

Why did you not use (*EDGAR, BIZCOMPS, Pratt's Stats,* or other references listed in this chapter or suggested by opposing expert)?

What steps did you take to determine whether there were any prior transactions, offers to buy, or buy-sell agreements regarding ownership of the company or interests in it?

Did it ever acquire a subsidiary?

What steps did you take to investigate the arm's-length nature of these transactions and what did you find out?

What use did you make of these transactions?

What sources did you use for developing fundamental financial information for your guideline companies?

What adjustments, if any, did you make to the financial statements of your subject company for comparison with the guideline companies? (Explain and justify adjustments; if none, what procedures did you employ to determine that none were necessary?)

What adjustments, if any, did you make to the financial statements of the guideline companies for comparison with your subject company? (Explain and justify adjustments; if none, what procedures did you employ to determine that none were necessary?) If guideline companies were private, there rarely is enough information to make meaningful adjustments. However, if guideline companies were public, whether based on stock market transactions or acquisitions of public companies, there often is information that would suggest adjustments, such as removing a nonrecurring gain or loss even though it was not technically "extraordinary" under the rules of generally accepted accounting principles. Failing to make this analysis is a common error. This is one of the reasons it is better to use SEC filings than more condensed secondary sources for public guideline companies.

What market multiples did you choose to use? Why? How did you decide where within the range of observed multiples the subject company should fall? How did you weight the indications of value from the various multiples? Why?

If you used multiple methods within the market approach, how did you weight the respective methods? Why?

Did you apply any premiums or discounts to the results indicated by any of the market methods? Why?

The Asset Approach (Chapter 7)

What methods did you use within the asset approach (e.g., adjusted net asset value, excess earnings method)? Why?

What assets did you adjust on the balance sheet? For each adjustment, why did you make the adjustment and how did you arrive at the amount of the adjustment? Did you bring any off-balance-sheet assets or liabilities onto the balance sheet? For each, why, and how did you arrive at the amount?

For the excess earning method (Chapter 8), how did you estimate the required return on tangible assets? How did you estimate the capitalization rate for intangibles? What checks for reasonableness, if any, did you perform?

Did you apply any discounts or premiums? Why?

Discounts and/or Premiums (Chapter 15)

Did you apply a minority discount or control premium? Why or why not? What database(s) did you use to help you estimate the amount of the discount/premium? Why did you use that particular database? Describe the data from which the database is compiled and the mechanism of computation.

Note: Many analysts use databases blindly, that is, without knowing what does or does not go into them or how they are constructed. Analysts should be able to explain any data they are using. It often is helpful to the attorney's case to test this knowledge (or lack of it).

How did you estimate the amount of the control premium or lack of control discount?

Did you apply a discount for lack of marketability? If so, the same questions that are listed for the control/minority issue are appropriate. There are many databases regarding discounts for lack of marketability and this is the most common area for widely divergent opinions in business valuation cases. Frequently, a good line of questioning is "Why didn't you use_____ database?" especially if your expert used it and the opposing expert did not. This may bring out some points to be defended in response to rebuttal.

Did you apply any other discounts or premiums (e.g., key person, "portfolio," trapped-in capital gains, contingent liabilities, blockage, voting versus nonvoting)? If so, use the same line of questioning.

Synthesis and Conclusion of Value (Chapter 16)

If only one approach/method was used, why was that approach/method the best and why did you not use other approaches/methods?

If multiple approaches/methods were used, what weight was given to each and why?

If you were advising a client about selling or buying the subject interest, would you advise him or her to sell/buy at the price that you concluded for this appraisal?

If in deposition, what else that I haven't asked about is relevant to your opinion of value?

Appendix A

Glossary of Business Valuation Terms

Terms with an asterisk are from *The International Glossary of Business Valuation Terms* as jointly approved by the AICPA, ASA, CICBV, NACVA, and IBA.

Reference abbreviations are as follows:

VAB5— Shannon P. Pratt with Alina V. Niculita, *Valuing a Business*, 5th ed., McGraw-Hill, 2008.

Guide—Jay E. Fishman, Shannon P. Pratt, J. Clifford Griffith, and James R. Hitchner, *PPC's Guide to Business Valuations,* 19th ed., Thomson Tax & Accounting, 2009.

VT—Internal Revenue Service *Valuation Training for Appeals Officers Coursebook*, 1997 ed., available online at http://onlinestore.cch.com.

Acquisition Premium
The difference between transaction price and the unaffected price before the transaction.

Source: Shannon P. Pratt, *Valuing a Business*, Fifth Edition.
References: VAB5 383–95

Adjusted Book Value
The book value that results after one or more asset or liability amounts are added, deleted, or changed from their respective book amounts.

Source: American Society of Appraisers Business Valuation Standards

Adjusted Book Value Method*
A method within the asset approach whereby all assets and liabilities (including off-

balance sheet, intangible, and contingent) are adjusted to their fair market values. [Note: In Canada on a going-concern basis]

References: VAB5 352

Adjusted Net Asset Method*

See: Adjusted Book Value Method

Appraisal

The act or process of estimating value.

Source: Uniform Standards of Professional Appraisal Practice

Appraisal Approach*

See: Valuation Approach

Appraisal Date*

See: Valuation Date

Appraisal Method*

See: Valuation Method

Appraisal Procedure*

See: Valuation Procedure

Arbitrage Pricing Theory*

A multivariate model for estimating the cost of equity capital, which incorporates several systematic risk factors.

References: VAB5 205–207, 214

Asset (Asset-Based) Approach*

A general way of determining a value indication of a business, business ownership interest, or security using one or more methods based on the value of the assets net of liabilities.

References: VAB5 62–64, 540–541, 951

Beta*

A measure of systematic risk of a stock; the tendency of a stock's price to correlate with changes in a specific index.

References: VAB5 160, 187–89, 293; Guide 503.11

Blockage Discount*
An amount or percentage deducted from the current market price of a publicly traded security to reflect the decrease in the per share value of a block of stock that is of a size that could not be sold in a reasonable period of time given normal trading volume.

Book Value*
See: Net Book Value

Business Enterprise*
A commercial, industrial, service, or investment entity (or a combination thereof) pursuing an economic activity.

Business Equity
The interests, benefits, and rights inherent in the ownership of a business enterprise or a part thereof in any form (including but not necessarily limited to capital stock, partnership interests, cooperatives, sole proprietorships, options, warrants).
Source: Uniform Standards of Professional Appraisal Practice
References: VAB5 36

Business Risk*
The degree of uncertainty of realizing expected future returns of the business resulting from factors other than financial leverage. See Financial Risk.
References: VAB5 160–161

Business Valuation*
The act or process of determining the value of a business enterprise or ownership interest therein.

Capital Asset Pricing Model (CAPM)*
A model in which the cost of capital for any stock or portfolio of stocks equals a risk-free rate plus a risk premium that is proportionate to the systematic risk of the stock or portfolio.
References: VAB5 160, 185–193

Capital Market Theory
A body of economic theory that divides risk into two components: systematic and unsystematic. This theory assumes that investors hold, or have the ability to hold, common stocks in large, well-diversified portfolios, which eliminate the unsystem-

atic risk attached to an individual company's stock. Therefore, the only risk pertinent to a study of capital asset pricing theory is systematic risk.

Source: Shannon P. Pratt, *Valuing a Business*, Fifth Edition

References: VAB5 185

Capital Structure*

The composition of the invested capital of a business enterprise, the mix of debt and equity financing.

Capitalization*

A conversion of a single-period stream of economic benefits into value.

References: VAB5 238

Capitalization Factor*

Any multiple or divisor used to convert anticipated economic benefits of a single period into value.

Capitalization Rate*

Any divisor (usually expressed as a percentage) used to convert anticipated economic benefits of a single period into value.

References: VAB5 238, 240

Cash Flow*

Cash that is generated over a period of time by an asset, group of assets, or business enterprise. It may be used in a general sense to encompass various levels of specifically defined cash flows. When the term is used, it should be supplemented by a qualifier (for example, "discretionary" or "operating") and a specific definition in the given valuation context.

Cash Flow Analysis

A study of the anticipated movement of cash into or out of an investment.

Source: Uniform Standards of Professional Appraisal Practice

References: VAB5 510–2

Client

The party or parties who engage an appraiser (by employment or contract) in a specific assignment.

Source: Uniform Standards of Professional Appraisal Practice

Coefficient of Variation

The standard deviation divided by the mean.

Source: Shannon P. Pratt, *Valuing a Business*, Fifth Edition

References: VAB5 160, 292

Common-Size Statements*

Financial statements in which each line is expressed as a percentage of the total. On the balance sheet, each line item is shown as a percentage of total assets, and on the income statement, each item is expressed as a percentage of sales.

References: VAB5 155

Control*

The power to direct the management and policies of a business enterprise.

References: VAB5 38, 65–67, 254, 275

Control Premium*

An amount or a percentage by which the pro rata value of a controlling interest exceeds the pro rata value of a non-controlling interest in a business enterprise, to reflect the power of control. [Confusingly, however, Delaware decisions have also used the phrase "control premium" with two other meanings (in addition to the inverse of the minority discount). The phrase has been used by the Delaware Court of Chancery not only to describe the inverse of the minority discount, but also to portray the premium above the Financial Control Value that would be paid by a synergistic buyer for control of a company.]

References: VAB5 386–388

Cost Approach*

A general way of determining a value indication of an individual asset by quantifying the amount of money required to replace the future service capability of that asset.

References: VAB5 358

Cost of Capital*

The expected rate of return that the market requires in order to attract funds to a particular investment.

References: VAB5 61, 207–216; Guide Ch.5

Discount for Lack of Control*
An amount or percentage deducted from the pro rata share of the value of 100% of an equity interest in a business to reflect the absence of some or all of the powers of control.
References: VAB5 398–405

Discount for Lack of Marketability*
An amount or percentage deducted from the value of an ownership interest to reflect the relative absence of marketability.
References: VAB5 419–425, 446–448

Discount for Lack of Voting Rights*
An amount or percentage deducted from the per share value of a minority interest voting share to reflect the absence of voting rights.

Discount Rate*
A rate of return used to convert a future monetary sum into present value.
References: VAB5 70, 182–6, 238, 240; Guide 501.2

Discounted Cash Flow Method*
A method within the income approach whereby the present value of future expected net cash flows is calculated using a discount rate.
References: VAB5 57, 516–519, 533

Discounted Future Earnings Method*
A method within the income approach whereby the present value of future expected economic benefits is calculated using a discount rate.

Economic Benefits*
Inflows such as revenues, net income, net cash flows, etc.

Economic Income
Any inflow into an economic unit in exchange for goods, services, and capital.
Source: Shannon P. Pratt, *Valuing a Business*, Fifth Edition
References: VAB5 249

Economic Life*
The period of time over which property may generate economic benefits.

Economic Obsolescence

A type of external obsolescence that occurs when there is a deterioration in the level of operating income or the rates of return on investment that is attributable to factors external to the property itself.

Source: Shannon P. Pratt, *Valuing a Business*, Fifth Edition.

References: VAB5 884–888

Effective Date*

See: Valuation Date

Employee Stock Ownership Plan (ESOP)

A statutorily defined qualified employee pension benefit plan designed to invest primarily in the employer's securities, thus providing a means for employees to have an ownership interest in the company for which they work.

Source: Shannon P. Pratt, *Valuing a Business*, Fifth Edition.

References: VAB5 8, 28, 47, 90, 268, 813–818, 829

Enterprise*

See: Business Enterprise

Equity*

The owner's interest in property after deduction of all liabilities.

References: VAB5 163–164, 249

Equity Net Cash Flows*

Those cash flows available to pay out to equity holders (in the form of dividends) after funding operations of the business enterprise, making necessary capital investments, and increasing or decreasing debt financing.

Equity Risk Premium*

A rate of return added to a risk-free rate to reflect the additional risk of equity instruments over risk-free instruments (a component of the cost of equity capital or equity discount rate).

References: VAB5 207–210; Guide 502.6

Excess Earnings*

That amount of anticipated economic benefits that exceeds an appropriate rate of return on the value of a selected asset base (often net tangible assets) used to generate those anticipated economic benefits.

References: VAB5 331–348; 352; Guide Section 705; VT Lesson 7

Excess Earnings Method*

A specific way of determining a value indication of a business, business ownership interest, or security determined as the sum of (a) the value of the assets derived by capitalizing excess earnings and (b) the value of the selected asset base. Also frequently used to value intangible assets. See Excess Earnings.

External Obsolescence

A reduction in the value of the subject property due to the effects, events, or conditions that are external to, and not controlled by, the current use or condition of the property. The impact of external obsolescence is typically beyond the control of the property owner. For that reason, external obsolescence is usually considered incurable. There are two types of external obsolescence: location obsolescence and economic obsolescence.

Source: Shannon P. Pratt, *Valuing a Business*, Fifth Edition

References: VAB5 884–888

Fair Market Value*

The price, expressed in terms of cash equivalents, at which property would change hands between a hypothetical willing and able buyer and a hypothetical willing and able seller, acting at arms length in an open and unrestricted market, when neither is under compulsion to buy or sell and when both have reasonable knowledge of the relevant facts. (**Note:** In Canada, the term "price" should be replaced with the term "highest price.")

References: VAB5 41, 386–387, 946, 964

Fair Value

A judicial concept, defined differently in different states and countries. It refers to an equitable, just, and reasonable value for property determined without reference to a simulated or real market transaction, since the property holder has no interest in entering the market at all. In a Delaware appraisal, fair value is the value of a a company with no premium for control and no discount for minority interest or liquidity.

Source: Shannon P. Pratt, *Valuing a Business*, Fifth Edition.

References: VAB5 45–46, 387–388, 906, 946, 964, 1006; Guide 201.5

Fairness Opinion*

An opinion as to whether or not the consideration in a transaction is fair from a financial point of view.

Financial Risk*

The degree of uncertainty of realizing expected future returns of the business resulting from financial leverage. *See* Business Risk.

Forced Liquidation Value*

Liquidation value, at which the asset or assets are sold as quickly as possible, such as at an auction.

Going Concern*

An ongoing, operating business enterprise.

References: VAB5 47, 64, 276

Going Concern Value*

The value of a business enterprise that is expected to continue to operate in the future. The intangible elements of going concern value result from factors such as having a trained work force, an operational plant, and the necessary licenses, systems, and procedures in place.

Goodwill*

That intangible asset arising as a result of name, reputation, customer loyalty, location, products, and similar factors not separately identified.

References: VAB5 949, 971–983

Goodwill Value*

The value attributable to goodwill.

Guideline Public Company Method*

A method within the market approach whereby market multiples are derived from market prices of stocks of companies that are engaged in the same or similar lines of business, and that are actively traded on a free and open market.

References: VAB5 270–290

Income (Income-Based) Approach*

A general way of determining a value indication of a business, business ownership interest, security, or intangible asset using one or more methods that convert anticipated economic benefits into a present single amount.

References: VAB5 173–235; Guide 203.3; VT lesson 1

Intangible Assets*

Non-physical assets such as franchises, trademarks, patents, copyrights, goodwill, equities, mineral rights, securities and contracts (as distinguished from physical assets) that grant rights and privileges, and have value for the owner.

References: VAB5 7, 131; Guide Chapter 17, Section 1100, Section 1103; VT Lesson 13

Internal Rate of Return*

A discount rate at which the present value of the future cash flows of the investment equals the cost of the investment.

Intrinsic Value*

The value that an investor considers, on the basis of an evaluation or available facts, to be the "true" or "real" value that will become the market value when other investors reach the same conclusion. When the term applies to options, it is the difference between the exercise price or strike price of an option and the market value of the underlying security.

Invested Capital*

The sum of equity and debt in a business enterprise. Debt is typically (a) all interest bearing debt or b) long-term interest bearing debt. When the term is used, it should be supplemented by a specific definition in the given valuation context.

Invested Capital Net Cash Flows*

Those cash flows available to pay out to equity holders (in the form of dividends) and debt investors (in the form of principal and interest) after funding operations of the business enterprise and making necessary capital investments.

Investment Risk*

The degree of uncertainty as to the realization of expected returns.

References: VAB5 186, 213–214

Investment Value*

The value to a particular investor based on individual investment requirements and expectations. (**Note:** In Canada, the term used is "Value to the Owner.")

References: VAB5 43, 907–8; Guide 201.8

Key Person Discount*
An amount or percentage deducted from the value of an ownership interest to reflect the reduction in value resulting from the actual or potential loss of a key person in a business enterprise.
References: VAB5 460–461, 681

Letter Stock
Stock identical to a freely traded stock of a public company except that a letter stock is restricted from trading on the open market for a certain period of time.
Source: Shannon P. Pratt, *Valuing a Business*, Fifth Edition.
References: VAB5 419

Levered Beta*
The beta reflecting a capital structure that includes debt.
References: VAB5 190–192

Liquidity*
The ability to quickly convert property to cash or pay a liability.
References: VAB5 417–418

Liquidation Value*
The net amount that would be realized if the business is terminated and the assets are sold piecemeal. Liquidation can either be "orderly" or "forced."
References: VAB5 47, 64

Locational Obsolescence
A type of external obsolescence related to the physical environment or neighborhood in which the property is located.
Source: Shannon P. Pratt, *Valuing a Business*, Fifth Edition.
References: VAB5 884–888

Majority Control*
The degree of control provided by a majority position.

Majority Interest*
An ownership interest greater than fifty percent (50%) of the voting interest in a business enterprise.

Market (Market-Based) Approach*
A general way of determining a value indication of a business, business ownership interest, security, or intangible asset by using one or more methods that compare the subject to similar businesses, business ownership interests, securities, or intangible assets that have been sold.

Market Capitalization of Equity*
The share price of a publicly traded stock multiplied by the number of shares outstanding.

Market Capitalization of Invested Capital*
The market capitalization of equity plus the market value of the debt component of invested capital.

Market Multiple*
The market value of a company's stock or invested capital divided by a company measure (such as economic benefits, number of customers).

Marketability*
The ability to quickly convert property to cash at minimal cost.
References: VAB5 39, 66, 417–419, 555–556; Guide Section 803

Marketability Discount*
See: Discount for Lack of Marketability.

Merger and Acquisition Method*
A method within the market approach whereby pricing multiples are derived from transactions of significant interests in companies engaged in the same or similar lines of business.

Mid-Year Discounting*
A convention used in the Discounted Future Earnings Method that reflects economic benefits being generated at mid-year, approximating the effect of economic benefits being generated evenly throughout the year.
References: VAB5 220–221, 249–251, 253–254; Guide 505.60

Minority Discount*
A discount for lack of control applicable to a minority interst.

Minority Interest*

An ownership position less than fifty percent (50%) of the voting interest in a business enterprise.

References: VAB5 398

Multiple*

The inverse of the capitalization rate.

Net Assets

Total assets less total liabilities.

Source: American Society of Appraisers Business Valuation Standards

Net Book Value*

With respect to a business enterprise, the difference between total assets (net of accumulated depreciation, depletion, and amortization) and total liabilities as they appear on the balance sheet (synonymous with Shareholder's Equity). With respect to a specific asset, the capitalized cost less accumulated amortization or depreciation as it appears on the books of account of the business enterprise.

Net Cash Flow*

When the term is used, it should be supplemented by a qualifier. See Equity Net Cash Flows and Invested Capital Net Cash Flows.

Net Income

Revenue less expenses and taxes.

Source: American Society of Appraisers Business Valuation Standards.

References: VAB5 179–181

Net Present Value*

The value, as of a specified date, of future cash inflows less all cash outflows (including the cost of investment) calculated using an appropriate discount rate.

Net Tangible Asset Value*

The value of the business enterprise's tangible assets (excluding excess assets and nonoperating assets) minus the value of its liabilities.

References: VAB5 334

Net Working Capital
Current assets less current liabilities.
Source: Shannon P. Pratt, *Valuing a Business*, Fifth Edition.
References: VAB5 158

Non-operating Assets*
Assets not necessary to ongoing operations of the business enterprise. (**Note:** In Canada, the term used is "Redundant Assets.")
References: VAB5 146, 298

Non-reporting Company
A company whose stock is publicly traded over-the-counter but that is not subject to the same reporting requirements as a reporting company.
Source: Shannon P. Pratt, *Valuing a Business*, Fifth Edition.
References: VAB5 422

Normalized Earnings*
Economic benefits adjusted for nonrecurring, non-economic, or other unusual items to eliminate anomalies and/or facilitate comparisons.

Normalized Financial Statements*
Financial statements adjusted for non-operating assets and liabilities and/or for nonrecurring, non-economic, or other unusual items to eliminate anomalies and/or facilitate comparisons.
References: VAB5 338–339, 345; Guide Section 404

Orderly Liquidation Value*
Liquidation value at which assets are sold over a reasonable period of time to maximize proceeds received.

Pass-Through Entities
Businesses that pass earnings through to their owners, subject only to federal taxation at the owner's personal income tax rate.
Source: Shannon P. Pratt, *Valuing a Business*, Fifth Edition.
References: VAB5 613–624

Physical Obsolescence
The reduction in the value of an asset due to wear and tear resulting from continued use. Also called physical depreciation.
Source: Shannon P. Pratt, *Valuing a Business*, Fifth Edition.
References: VAB5 370

Portfolio Discount*

An amount or percentage deducted from the value of a business enterprise to reflect the fact that it owns dissimilar operations or assets do not fit well together.

References: VAB5 300; Guide 803.51

Portfolio Management Theory

A normative theory that describes how investors should behave, under a given set of assumptions, in selecting common stocks for their portfolios.

Source: Shannon P. Pratt, *Valuing a Business*, Fifth Edition.

References: VAB5 185

Preemptive Right

Stockholders' privilege to subscribe to new issues of voting stock, usually the common stock or securities convertible into voting stock, before such offerings are made to nonstockholders. Also known as a privileged subscription right.

Source: Shannon P. Pratt, *Valuing a Business*, Fifth Edition.

References: VAB5 400

Premise of Value*

An assumption regarding the most likely set of transactional circumstances that may be applicable to the subject valuation; e.g. going concern, liquidation.

References: VAB5 41, 47–48

Present Value*

The value, as of a specified date, of future economic benefits and/or proceeds from sale, calculated using an appropriate discount rate.

Price/Earnings Multiple*

The price of a share of stock divided by its earnings per share.

Put Option

An option which gives the holder the right to sell the underlying stock by a certain date at a certain price.

Source: Shannon P. Pratt, *Valuing a Business*, Fifth Edition.

References: VAB5 587

Range

A measure of dispersion that is defined as the spread between the highest and lowest observations.

Source: Shannon P. Pratt, *Valuing a Business*, Fifth Edition.

References: VAB5 292

Rate of Return*
An amount of income (loss) and/or change in value realized or anticipated on an investment, expressed as a percentage of that investment.

Redundant Assets*
See: Non-operating Assets

Replacement Cost New*
The current cost of a similar new property having the nearest equivalent utility to the property being valued.
References: VAB5 369–370

Report
Any communication, written or oral, of an appraisal, appraisal review, or appraisal consulting service that is transmitted to the client upon completion of an assignment.
Source: Uniform Standards of Professional Appraisal Practice.
References: VAB5 49–50, 485–499, 535–544; Guide Ch. 9, VT Lesson 16

Report Date*
The date on which conclusions are transmitted to the client.

Reproduction Cost
Classification which contemplates the construction of an exact replica of the subject asset.
Source: Shannon P. Pratt, *Valuing a Business*, Fifth Edition.
References: VAB5 370; VT Lesson 13

Reproduction Cost New*
The current cost of an identical new property.
References: VAB5 370

Required Rate of Return*
The minimum rate of return acceptable by investors before they will commit money to an investment at a given level of risk.

Residual Value*
The value as of the end of the discrete projection period in a discounted future earnings model.

Return/Rate of Return
The total yield to the investor, reflecting all dividends, interest, or other cash and cash equivalents received, plus or minus any realized or unrealized appreciation or depreciation in the investment's value.
Source: Shannon P. Pratt, *Valuing a Business*, Fifth Edition.
References: VAB5 182

Return on Equity*
The amount, expressed as a percentage, earned on a company's common equity for a given period.
References: VAB5 166–167

Return on Investment*
See: Return on Invested Capital and Return on Equity.

Return on Invested Capital*
The amount, expressed as a percentage, earned on a company's total capital for a given period.
References: VAB5 168–169

Risk
The degree of uncertainty as to the realization of expected future returns.
Source: Shannon P. Pratt, *Valuing a Business*, Fifth Edition.
References: VAB5 160–162; Guide Section 502

Risk-Free Rate*
The rate of return available in the market on an investment free of default risk.
References: VAB5 61, 207

Risk Premium*
A rate of return added to a risk-free rate to reflect risk.

Rule of Thumb*
A mathematical formula developed from the relationship between price and certain variables based on experience, observation, hearsay, or a combination of these; usually industry specific.

Special-Interest Purchasers*
Acquirers who believe they can enjoy post-acquisition economies of scale, synergies, or strategic advantages by combining the acquired business interest with their own.

Standard of Value*

The identification of the type of value being used in a specific engagement; e.g., fair market value, fair value, investment value.

References: VAB5 41–47; Guide Section 1202

Strategic Acquisition

A purchase by a buyer who expects to benefit from synergies with the purchased company, such as horizontal and vertical integration, elimination of redundant overhead, or better prices through reduced competition.

Source: Shannon P. Pratt, *Valuing a Business*, Fifth Edition.

References: VAB5 384

Strategic Control Premium

That premium, over and above the standard control premium, associated with a unique buyer and a unique seller that would relate to a unique set of beneficial synergies or circumstances between that buyer and seller.

Source: Shannon P. Pratt, *Valuing a Business*, Fifth Edition.

References: VAB5 383–95

Sustaining Capital Reinvestment*

The periodic capital outlay required to maintain operations at existing levels, net of the tax shield available from such outlays.

Systematic Risk*

The risk that is common to all risky securities and cannot be eliminated through diversification. The measure of systematic risk in stocks is the beta coefficient.

References: VAB5 185–187

Tangible Assets*

Physical assets (such as cash, accounts receivable, inventory, property, plant and equipment, etc.).

Technical Obsolescence

A decrease in the value of an asset due to improvements in technology that make an asset less than an ideal replacement for itself.

Source: Shannon P. Pratt, *Valuing a Business*, Fifth Edition.

References: VAB5 370

Terminal Value*

See: Residual Value.

References: VAB5 219–220, 251–254

Transaction Method*

See: Merger and Acquisition Method

Unlevered Beta*

The beta reflecting a capital structure without debt.

References: VAB5 190–192

Unsystematic Risk*

The risk specific to an individual security that can be avoided through diversification.

References: VAB5 185–187

Valuation*

The act or process of determining the value of a business, business ownership interest, security, or intangible asset.

Valuation Approach*

A general way of determining a value indication of a business, business ownership interest, security, or intangible asset using one or more valuation methods.

Valuation Date*

The specific point in time as of which the valuator's opinion of value applies (also referred to as "Effective Date" or "Appraisal Date").

References: VAB5 947, 969–971

Valuation Method*

Within approaches, a specific way to determine value.

Valuation Procedure*

The act, manner, and technique of performing the steps of an appraisal method.

Valuation Ratio*

A factor in which a value or price serves as the numerator and financial, operating, or physical data serves as the denominator.

Value to the Owner*

See: Investment Value

Voting Control*

De jure control of a business enterprise.

Weighted Average Cost of Capital (WACC)*

The cost of capital (discount rate) determined by the weighted average, at market value, of the cost of all financing sources in the business enterprise's capital structure.

References: VAB5 249, 217, 218, 532; Guide Section 506

Working Capital

The amount by which current assets exceed current liabilities.

Source: American Society of Appraiser Business Valuation Standards

Appendix B

Business Appraisal Professional Organizations

American Institute of Certified Public Accountants (AICPA)

Parkway Corporate Center
1230 Parkway Avenue, Ewing, NJ 08628
Phone: (609/671–2930)
Web site: *www.aicpa.org*

Date formed: 1887

Ownership: Organization sponsored

Description: Recognizes business valuation as a CPA service niche and confers an accreditation reflecting this recognition for those in public practice, industry, government, and education.

Certification offered:

> ***CPA/ABV—Accredited in Business Valuation***
>
> **Prerequisite:** Be a member in good standing of the AICPA; hold a valid and unrevoked CPA certificate or license issued by a legally constituted state authority.

Courses/exams: Half-day exam for those holding CVA, CBA, or CFA credentials. Full-day exam for those not certified by a recognized organization. No exam for CPAs with an ASA credential.

Experience requirement: Substantial involvement in at least six business valuation engagements, or provide evidence of 150 hours that demonstrate substantial experience.

Life-long learning: Must earn a minimum of 15 points in life-long learning. Providing 45 hours of qualifying CPE (continuing professional education) credits will allow the candidate to meet the minimum life-long learning requirement.

Advanced Courses: A five-day BV School, plus a variety of one-day advanced courses; three-day ABV exam review course

Seminars and conferences: Annual National Business Valuation Conference; many professional education programs

Publications: *CPA Expert*, a quarterly newsletter; also publishes an extensive list of consulting service publications, generally referred to as "practice aids" or "special reports."

American Society of Appraisers (ASA)

555 Herndon Parkway, Suite 125
Herndon, VA 20170
Phone: (703) 478-2228 · Fax: (703) 742-8471
Web site: *www.appraisers.org*

Date formed: 1936

Ownership: Owned by members

Description: Multidisciplinary professional organization offering courses and exams leading to designations in the appraisal of real estate, machinery and equipment, personal property, gems and jewelry, businesses and business interests (including intangible assets), and certain technical specialties.

Certifications offered:

AM—Accredited Member

Educational requirement: College degree or equivalent

Courses/exams: Completion of four courses of three days each, with successful completion of one half-day exam following each of the three courses, or successful completion of an all-day challenge exam; successful completion of an ethics exam and a USPAP exam.

Reports: Submission of two actual appraisal reports to satisfaction of board examiners.

Experience requirement: Two years full-time or full-time-equivalent work (e.g., five years of 400 hours business appraisal work per year equals one year full-time equivalent).

Related experience offset: One full year of the experience requirement is granted to anyone who has any of the following three designations with five years of practice in that respective field: certified public accountant (CPA), chartered financial analyst (CFA), or certified business intermediary (CBI).

ASA—Accredited Senior Appraiser
Has met all requirements listed above plus an additional three years of full-time or full-time-equivalent experience.

FASA—Fellow of the American Society of Appraisers
Has met all requirements listed plus is voted into the college of fellows on the basis of technical leadership and contribution to the profession and the society.
Courses: The introductory-level courses (numbered 201) in each of the disciplines provide the basics in general valuation theory and terminology, discipline-specific theory and terminology and aspects of appraising as a profession.

The *higher-level* courses (numbered 202-204, with Real Property also having a 205) cover research and analysis methodologies, case studies, government regulations, report writing and professional standards.

Each of these courses has a final 3-4 hour objective question exam, with a minimal passing score of 75 percent. Continuing education hours may be awarded for each course completed.

- Business Valuation
- Gems & Jewelry
- Machinery and Equipment
- Personal Property
- Real Property

Seminars and conferences: Seminars on specialized topics lasting from two hours to two days are sponsored by various groups within the ASA.

- Annual interdisciplinary meeting with two and a half days of technical presentations on each of the society's appraisal disciplines
- Annual Advanced Business Valuation Conference with two or two and a half days of advanced business valuation papers, presentations, and discussion

Publications: *Business Valuation Review,* a quarterly professional journal published by the Business Valuation Committee. *ASA Professional,* the quarterly magazine of the American Society of Appraisers. *Newsline,* published monthly by ASA from 1997 through 2003.
Local chapters: Chapters with regular monthly meetings in 87 cities throughout the United States and Canada.

Institute of Business Appraisers (IBA)

P.O. Box 17410, Plantation, FL 33318
Phone: (954) 584-1144
Fax: (954) 584-1184
Web site: *www.instbusapp.org*

Date formed: 1978

Ownership: Florida not-for-profit corporation (privately owned)

Description: Offers programs of interest to members whose business valuation activities are less than full-time and/or whose practice includes valuation of small to midsize businesses.

Certifications offered:

AIBA—Accredited by IBA
Educational requirement: Complete four-year college degree or equivalent; possess business appraisal designation from compeer organizations recognized by The Institute of Business Appraisers, upon application to the IBA, or complete IBA eight-day Appraisal Workshop IBA course 8001.
Course/Exams: Complete comprehensive written exam.
Reports: Submit one report for peer review.
Experience requirement: Provide four references of character and fitness.
Continuing education: Submit proof of continued professional development with 24 hours of advanced BV education every 24 months OR submit another report for peer review OR pass CBA exam and enter CBA review process OR demonstrate completion of ten business appraisal assignments in two years.

CBA—Certified Business Appraiser
Educational requirement: Complete four-year college degree or equivalent. Complete IBA's 16-hour course 1010 (Report Writing). Be a member-in-good standing of the Institute of Business Appraisers.
Courses/exams: Complete a 6 hour, proctored, CBA written examination. Applicants may be exempt from the exam if they hold the ASA, ABV, CVA, or AVA designation.
Reports: Submit two Demonstration Reports demonstrating a high degree of skill, knowledge and judgment as a Business Appraiser.
Experience requirement: Successfully complete 90 hours of upper-level course work. At least 24 hours of this coursework must have been in courses offered by the Institute of Business Appraisers. Or the applicant may demonstrate 10,000 hours active experience as a business appraiser. Provide four satisfactory refer-

ences, two references as to personal character; and two references as to professional competence as a business appraiser.

MCBA—Master Certified Business Appraiser

Obtain four-year college degree and two-year postgraduate degree or equivalent; held the Certified Business Appraiser designation for not less than ten years, and must have fifteen-years full-time experience as a business appraiser; and hold one other designation (ASA, CVA, or ABV). Provide three references from MCBAs with personal knowledge of applicant's work.

ABAR—Accredited in Business Appraisal Review

Educational requirement: Be IBA members in good standing, and possess a 4-year university degree or equivalent. Hold a business appraisal designation awarded by IBA, AICPA, ASA, CICBV, or NACVA or must have achieved a passing grade on the CBA written examination.

Courses/exams: Successfully complete IBA Course 1044 - Critiquing Business Valuation Reports, and achieve a passing grade on a comprehensive examination.

Reports: Submit two appraisal reviews, which will be peer reviewed to determine if the reviews meet professional standards of competence.

Experience requirement: Provide two professional and two personal references. Demonstrate 10,000 hours' experience in appraisal review, or 90 hours of appraisal education. Twenty-four (24) of these hours must have been earned through education sponsored by IBA.

BVAL—Business Valuator Accredited for Litigation

Educational requirement: Obtain business appraisal designation from IBA, AICPA, ASA, NACVA, or CBA candidate who has passed the exam. **Course/exams:** Attend 5 days of IBA course 7001, for 40 CPE hours; complete prereading and all course assignments (16 CPE hours); and pass four-hour written exam.

Experience requirement: Demonstrate presentation and process competency during the testimony clinics. Provide letters of reference from two attorneys or complete 16 hours of education in the area of law in which the appraiser will testify.

FIBA—Fellow of the Institute of Business Appraisers

Meet all CBA requirement, plus be voted into College of Fellows on basis of technical leadership and contribution to the profession and the Institute.

Courses:

Eight-day workshop, offered two to four times a year, in various locations
Two-day course on valuing small businesses using IBA market database
Seven-day workshop on litigation support and expert testimony
See www.go-iba.org/load.php?t=education_new for course listings

Seminars and conferences: Seminars on business valuation held at various locations around the United States; annual business valuation conference

Publications: *Business Appraisal Practice,* semiannual professional journal with peer-reveiwed articles on practical aspects of business valuation and litigation support..

Local Chapters: A few at present, including Mid-Altlantic, North Central, Northeast, Northwest, South Central, Southeast, and Southwest.

National Association of Certified Valuation Analysts (NACVA)

1111 Brickyard Road, Suite 200
Salt Lake City, UT 84106-5401
Phone: (801) 486-0600
Fax: (801) 486-7500
Web site: *www.nacva.com*

Date formed: 1991

Ownership: Group of shareholders

Description: The National Association of Certified Valuation Analysts (NACVA) is a 4,000-member association of professionals consisting of Certified Public Accountants (CPAs), lawyers, government-employed valuators, and other professionals who provide business valuation and litigation support services. Its purpose is to promulgate the members' status, credentials, and esteem in the field of performing valuations of closely held businesses.

Certifications offered:

AVA—Accredited Valuation Analyst

Educational requirement: Obtain business degree and/or an MBA or higher; member in good standing of NACVA.

Course/exams: Complete optional five-day course; Pass a comprehensive two-part examination. Part One is a five-hour proctored exam. Non-CPA applicants without a background in accounting fundamentals may be subject to another half-day exam.

Reports: And Part Two is a take-home/in-office exam that incorporates a standardized case study.

Experience requirements: Two years full-time or equivalent business valuation or related experiece, or ten or more business valuations. Provide three personal references, three business references, and a minimum of one letter of recommendation from an employer or another CPA.

CVA—Certified Valuation Analyst

Educational requirement: Have college degree, unrevoked CPA license, and be a member in good standing of NACVA.

Course/exams: Complete optional five-day course; pass two-part exam; Part One is a four-hour proctored exam.

Reports: And Part Two is a take-home/in-office exam that requires performing a complete business valuation.

Experience requirements: Two years experience as a CPA. Provide three personal references and three business references.

CFFA— Certified Financial Forensic Analyst, including prior CFD designation

Educational requirement: Possess one of the following designations: CVA, AVA, ABV, AM, ASA, CBA, CBV, CFA, CFE, CMA, CPA, or CA; A bachelor's degree in a business field from an accredited university/college, or, alternatively, a master's or doctorate in a field of business; be a Practitioner, Academic, or Government member of NACVA.

Course/exams: Complete two-week course and eight days of training at NACVA's Forensic Institute; pass two-part exam; one for the specialty area he/she is pursuing, and one to demonstrate a command of litigation fundamentals.

Experience requirements: Provide one business and two legal references.Must show proof of having provided services in the applicable field in which they wish to specialize

Courses/seminars: A five-day Certification Training Center (TC) is offered as prerequisite training prior to certification.

Days 1 & 2:	Fundamentals, Techniques, and Theory
Day 3:	Case Analysis No. 1 and Report Writing
Day 4—Two Parts:	Using Valuation Master 4.0 Software
Day 5—Two Parts:	Working Effectively in the Litigation Environment

Seminars and conferences: Two conferences held annually. Semi-annual one-and-a-half day seminars on business valuation topics. Also one- and two-day seminars on key valuation topics, including symposiums.

Publications: *The Valuation Examiner*™—a bimonthly magazine.

Local chapters: State chapters presently in 38 states and one in Mexico City.

The Canadian Institute of Chartered Business Valuators (CICBV)

277 Wellington Street West
Toronto, Ontario, Canada M5V 3H2
Phone: (416) 977-1117, Fax: (416) 977-7066
E-mail: *admin@cicbv.ca*
Web site: *www.cicbv.ca*

Date formed: 1971

Ownership: Nonprofit federally incorporated corporation owned by members

Description: The CICBV is the largest professional valuation organization in Canada. It was established to promote high standards in business and securities valuations. Members are entitled to use the professional designation CBV (Chartered Business Valuator) following completion of rigorous study and practical experience requirements. The institute's members and students provide a broad range of business valuation services to Canada's business, legal, investment banking, and governmental communities. The institute has a Code of Ethics and issues Valuation Practice Standards and Discipline Procedures.

Designation offered:

CBV—Chartered Business Valuator

Educational requirement: Have college degree or equivalent: accounting or finance encouraged.

Courses/Exams: Successful completion of a program of six courses including assignments and examinations for each course plus the required experience. This is followed by the writing of the Membership Entrance Examination (MEE) (final examination).

Experience requirement: Have accumulated 1,500 hours of business & securities valuation experience. The experience should be attested by a sponsor. The required practical experience should be attained within five years of applying to write the Membership Entrance Examination

FCBV—Fellow of Canadian Institute of Chartered Business Valuators

Recognizes members who have rendered outstanding service to the business valuation profession, or whose achievements in their professional lives or in the community have earned them distinction and have brought honor to the profession. Designation is granted only upon receipt of a nomination, recommendation by the Fellowship Selection Committee, and approval by the Board.

Courses: The program of studies is offered by distance education and includes mandatory assignments with proctored examinations.

Core Courses

Introductory Business and Securities Valuation
Intermediate Business and Securities Valuation
Advanced Business and Securities Valuation
Law and Tax in Business Valuation

Electives Courses

Litigation I (On-Line Course)
Litigation II
Advanced Open Market Transactions
Private Company Finance (On-Line Course)
Restructuring (On-Line Course)
Public Companies (On-Line Course)
Introduction to Valuation for Financial Reporting (On-Line Course)

Subscription: Subscription service is available for a yearly fee, which entitles the subscriber to receive all publications issued by the institute and maintained on a mailing list to receive other mailings.

Seminars & conferences:

- Seminars and workshops offered monthly in major cities across Canada
- Biennial National Conference (two full days)
- Regional conferences—one to one and one-half days

Publications:

- *The Valuation Law Review* is published once a year with three sections: Corporate Securities Law, Family Law, and Taxation.
- *Business Valuation Digest* is a published twice yearly and consists of articles on business valuations.
- *The Journal of Business Valuation* contains the proceedings of the institute's biennial conferences.
- *The Business Valuator* is a quarterly publication dealing with the activities of the institute.

Appendix C

General Bibliography

Books

An Introduction to ESOP Valuations. Washington, D.C.: The ESOP Association, 2005.

Ash, Merri E., Virginia J. Bartlett, et al. 1996. *The ESOP Association Administration Handbook.* Washington, D.C.: The ESOP Association.

Bateman, Tracy A. 2000. *Divorce and Separation: Consideration of Tax Consequences in Distribution of Marital Property.* 9 A.L.R. 5th ed., 568. Lawyers Cooperative Publishing Co.

Bellatti, Robert M., and Shari L. West. 1999. *Estate Planning for Farms and Other Qualified Family-Owned Businesses.* Covers Section 2032A and Section 2057 special use valuations.

Bernstein, Ron, David Binns, Marshal Hyman, and Martin Staubus. 2001. *Transitioning Ownership in the Private Company: The ESOP Solution.*

Bogdanski, John. 1996. *Federal Tax Valuation*, plus annual supplements.

Brinig, Brian P., et al. 2006. "Alternative Dispute Resolution" in *Guide to Litigation Support Services*, 11th ed. Fort Worth, Texas: Practitioners Publishing Co.

BVR's Guide to Fair Value in Shareholder Dissent, Oppression, and Marital Dissolution. Business Valuation Resources. 2009. Portland, Ore.

BVR's Guide to Personal v. Enterprise Goodwill. Business Valuation Resources. 2009. Portland, Ore.

"Closely Held Corporations—Financial Analysis" in *IRS Valuation Guide for Income, Estate and Gift Taxes,* 6-1 to 6-14. Internal Revenue Service, 1994.

Cohen, Harriet N. 2003. "Using Rules of Thumb in Valuation" in *101+ Practical Solutions for the Family Lawyer*, 2d ed. Gregg Herman. Chicago: American Bar Association.

Cook, Larry R. 2005. *Financial Valuation of Employee Stock Ownership Plan Shares.* Hoboken, N.J.: John Wiley & Sons.

Cory, Jacques. 2004. *Business Ethics: The Ethical Revolution of Minority Shareholders*. New York: Springer.

Desmond, Glenn M. 1993. *Handbook of Small Business Valuation Formulas and Rules of Thumb*, 3d ed.

ESOP Accounting Standards. Washington, D.C.: The ESOP Association, 2005.

ESOP Repurchase Obligations. Washington, D.C.: The ESOP Association, 2004.

Feder, Robert, ed. 1997. *Valuation Strategies in Divorce*, 4th ed. New York: Aspen Law & Business.

Feld, Daniel E. 2002. *Estate and Gift Tax Digest*, 4th ed. Boston: Warren, Gorham & Lamont.

Fishman, Jay E., Shannon P. Pratt, James Hitchner & J. Clifford Griffith. 2009. *PPC's Guide to Business Valuations*, 19th ed. Fort Worth, Texas: Practitioners Publishing Co.

_____, Shannon P. Pratt & William J. Morrison. 2007. *Standards of Value: Theory and Applications*. Hoboken, N.J.: John Wiley & Sons.

Frisch, Robert A. 2001. *ESOP: The Ultimate Instrument in Succession Planning*, 2nd ed. Hoboken, N.J.: John Wiley & Sons.

_____. 2002. *ESOP Workbook: The Ultimate Instrument in Succession Planning*. Hoboken, N.J.: John Wiley & Sons.

Goldberg, Barth, and Barry A. Schatz. *Valuation of Divorce Assets*. 1984 plus 1999 supplement. Pages 335–552 of the 1999 supplement and pages 443–85 of 1984 volume are case summaries on valuation of closely held corporations and partnerships; pages 176–217 of 1999 supplement and 198–227 of 1984 volume are on valuation of professional entities, goodwill, and license agreements.

Gold-Biken, Lynne Z., Steven A. Kolodny, Adam R. Koritzinsky & Barbara A. Stark. 1994. *Divorce Practice Handbook*. Charlottesville, Va.: Michie Co.

Hitchner, James R. 2006. *Financial Valuation: Applications and Models*, 2d ed. Hoboken, N.J.: John Wiley & Sons.

How the ESOP Really Works. Washington, D.C.: The ESOP Association, 1997.

IRS Appeals Officer Valuation Training Course. Internal Revenue Service, 1997.

Kasper, Larry J. 1997. "Federal Tax Valuations" in *Business Valuations, Advanced Topics*, 211–58. Westport, Conn.: Greenwood Publishing.

Kleeman, Robert E., Jr., James R. Alerding & Benjamin D. Miller. 1999. *The Handbook for Divorce Valuations*. New York: John Wiley & Sons.

Laro, David, and Shannon P. Pratt. 2005. "Valuation of S Corporations and Other Pass-Through Tax Entities: Minority and Controlling Interests" in *Business Valuation and Taxes: Procedure, Law, and Perspective*. Hoboken, N.J.: John Wiley & Sons.

Matthews, Gilbert E. "Fairness Opinions" in *Business Valuations for the Legal Practitioner*. American Bar Association Center for Continuing Legal Education, 2001.

Mercer, Z. Christopher. 2007. *Buy-Sell Agreements: Ticking Time Bombs or Reasonable Resolutions?* Peabody Publishing.

______. 2005. *Valuing Shareholder Cash Flows: Quantifying Marketability Discounts*, E-Book.

______, 1997. "Overview of Tax Court Decisions" and "Tax Court Case Summary" in *Quantifying Marketability Discounts*, 95–154, 465–82.

Mueller, Susan L., and Judith C. Gehr. 1999. "Valuation Issues in Multi-Investor ESOP LBOs" in *ESOP Valuation*. Scott S. Rodrick, ed. Oakland, Cal.: The National Center for Employee Ownership.

Oldham, L. Thomas. 1999. "The Closely Held Business" in *Divorce, Separation and the Distribution of Property*, 10-1 to 10-5.

O'Neal, F. Hodge, and Robert B. Thompson. 1998. *O'Neal's Oppression of Minority Shareholders: Protecting Minority Rights in Squeeze-Outs, and Other Intracorporate Conflicts*, 2d ed. St. Paul, Minn.: West Group.

Penman, Stephen H. 2001. *Financial Statement Analysis & Security Valuation*. New York: McGraw-Hill.

Phillips, Perry. 2001. *Employee Share Ownership Plans: How to Design and Implement an ESOP in Canada*. Mississauga, Ont.: John Wiley & Sons Canada.

Pratt, Shannon P., and Alina V. Niculita. 2008. *Valuing a Business*, 5th ed. New York: McGraw-Hill.

_____, and Alina V. Niculita. 2006. *The Market Approach to Valuing Businesses Workbook*, 2d ed. New York: John Wiley & Sons.

_____, and Roger J. Grabowski. 2008. *Cost of Capital: Applications and Examples*, 3d ed. New York: John Wiley & Sons.

_____. 2003. *Business Valuation Body of Knowledge*, 2d ed. New York: John Wiley & Sons.

_____. 2009. *Business Valuation Discounts and Premiums*, 2d ed. New York: John Wiley & Sons.

Report on Valuation Considerations for Leveraged ESOPs. Washington, D.C.: The ESOP Association. 1998.

Rodrick, Scott S., ed. 2005. *Leveraged ESOPs and Employee Buyouts*. Cal.: The National Center for Employee Ownership.

_____. 1999. *ESOP Valuation*. Oakland, Cal.: The National Center for Employee Ownership.

Rosen, Corey. 2000. *Understanding ESOP Valuation*. Oakland, Cal.: The National Center for Employee Ownership.

_____, John Case, and Martin Staubus. 2005. *Equity: Why Employee Ownership Is Good for Business*. Cambridge, Mass.: Harvard Business School Press.

Rules for Arbitration of Financial Issues. American Academy of Matrimonial Lawyers. 1990. A copy can be obtained from AAML, (312) 263-6477.

Saltzman, Michael J. 2006. *IRS Practice and Procedure*, revised 2d ed. Boston: Warren, Gorham & Lamont.

Smiley, Robert W., Ronald J. Gilbert, and David M. Binns. 1998. *Employee Stock Ownership Plans, 1998 Yearbook*. Boston: Warren, Gorham & Lamont of the RIA Group.

_____, and Ronald J. Gilbert, eds. 1991. *Employee Stock Ownership Plans: Business Planning, Implementation, and Law and Taxation*. New York: Warren, Gorham & Lamont, supplemented annually.

Solomon, Lewis D., and Lewis J. Saret. 1998. "General Rules of Valuation: Tax Perspective" in *Valuation of Closely Held Businesses*, 67–104. New York: Panel Publishers.

Staubus, Martin, David Binns, and Ron Bernstein. 2005. *Transitioning Ownership in the Private Company: The ESOP Solution*, 2d ed. La Jolla, Cal.: The Beyster Institute.

Structuring Leveraged ESOP Transactions. Washington, D.C.: The ESOP Association, 1999.

The Ownership Advantage. Washington, D.C.: The ESOP Association, 2005.

Trugman, Gary. 2002. *Understanding Business Valuations*, 2nd ed. New York: American Institute of Certified Public Accountants.

West, Tom. 2008. "Rules of Thumb" in *The Business Reference Guide 2008*, 18th ed.

Wild, John J., K. R. Subramanyam & Robert F. Halsey. 2006. *Financial Statement Analysis*, 9th ed. New York: McGraw-Hill.

Valuing ESOP Shares. Washington, D.C.: The ESOP Association. Revised Edition. 1994.

Valuing ESOP Shares. Washington, D.C.: The ESOP Association, 2005.

Articles

Ackerman, David. "Technical Issues under the New S Corporation ESOP Laws." *Journal of Employee Ownership Law and Finance*, Winter 1999, pp. 3–19.

Austin, Douglas V. "Beware of Your ESOP." *Hoosier Banker*, vol. 84, no. 4, April 30, 2000, pp. 9–10.

Bishop, David M. "Reconciling the Indicated Values." *Business Valuation Review*, March 1998, pp.13–15.

______. "Trapped-in Capital Gains: Where Do We Go From Here?" *Business Valuation Review*, June 1999, pp. 64–68.

Bogdanski, John A. "Hard Times for Buy-Sell Agreements." *Estate Planning*, June 1998, pp. 235–39.

______. "Buy-Sell Agreements and Marketability Discounts." *Estate Planning,* December 2004.

Brewer, Wilbur, Jr. "Minority Shareholder Rights." A 17-page paper on rights of minority shareholders in closely held corporations, available on *www.BVLibrary.com.*

Brown, Karen W. "Payment of Control Premiums by ESOPs." *ESOP Report,* November/December1993, pp. 6–8.

Buckley, Allen, Lynda M. Crouse & Greg Kniesel. "S Corporation ESOPs in Dispositive Sales and Reorganization Transactions." *Valuation Strategies*, January/February 2001, pp. 20–29, 46–48.

"Business Valuation Resources' Guide to Personal v. Enterprise Goodwill," 2009. Introduction by David Wood, with contributions by Jay Fishman, Mark Dietrich, James Alerding, Shannon Pratt, Noah Gordon, and Kevin Yeanoplos.

"Buy-Sell Agreement Ignored in Valuing Decedent's Stock." *Estate Planning*, January 1998, pp. 32–35.

Crow, Matthew R. "Developing Valuation Multiples Using Guideline Companies." *CPA Litigation Service Counselor*, September 1999, pp. 8-9

Diana, James C. "The New Mediation Procedure in Appeals: The Latest Development in the IRS' ADR Initiative." *Tax Management Memorandum,* Nov. 13, 1995, pp. 331–39.

Dietrich, Mark. "Identifying and Measuring Personal Goodwill in a Professional Practice." *CPA Expert,* Part 1, Spring 2005; Part 2, Summer 2005.

Drake, Dwight J., Kent Whiteley & Timothy J. McDevitt. "The Ten Most Common Mistakes of Buy-Sell Agreements." *Journal of Financial Planning*, July 1992, pp. 104–12.

Eggart, James. "Replacing the Sword with a Scalpel: The Case for a Bright-Line Rule Disallowing Application of Lack of Marketability Discounts in Shareholder Oppression Cases." *Arizona Law Review*, vol. 44, no. 1, 2002, pp. 213–246.

Ellentuck, Albert B. "Establishing the Estate Value of Stock by Using a Buy-Sell Agreement." *The Tax Adviser*, September 1998, pp. 637–38.

_____. "Reviewing a Buy/Sell Agreement." *The Tax Adviser*, November 1999, pp. 809–12.

Emory, John D., Jr. "The Role of Discounts in Determining 'Fair Value' under Wisconsin's Dissenters' Rights Statutes: The Case for Discounts." *Wisconsin Law Review, 1995,* no. 5 (March 1996), pp. 1155–75. Although specifically oriented to Wisconsin, the article references statutes and cases throughout the United States.

Etkind, Steven M., and Joseph E. Godfrey III. "ESOPs Rediscovered: Tax Advantages and Recyclable Refunding." *The CPA Journal*, vol. 72, no. 4, April 30, 2002, pp. 60–61.

Fannon, Nancy. "Rates of Return: Don't Ignore Public Market or Transactional Data." *Business Valuation Update*, September 2007, available at *BVResources.com.*

_____. "Valuing Controlling Versus Minority Interests in S Corporations." *Business Valuation Review,* March 2008, vol. 26, no. 4.

Fiore, Nicholas. "Pros and Cons of the New IRS Mediation Program." *Journal of Accountancy,* May 36, 1996.

Ford, David J. "CPAs and ADR: A Civilized Alternative to Litigation." *CPA Litigation Service Counselor*, February 2000, pp. 1–5.

Fowler, Bradley, A. "How Do You Handle It?" *Business Valuation Review*, September 1996, pp. 136–37.

"Goodwill Hunting in Divorce, Business Valuation Resources." 2007. A state-by-state summary of the leading U.S. court cases deciding the disposition of goodwill in marital dissolution.

Goeldner, Richard W. "Bridging the Gap between Public and Private Market Multiples." *Business Valuation Review*, September 1998, pp. 97–101.

Hall, Lance S. "Lack of Outside Appraisal Dooms Buy-Sell Formula Value Fix for Estate Tax Purposes." *Valuation Strategies,* March/April 2005.

Hamilton, Janet. "Marketability Discounts in the Courts, 1991–1996." Published as a supplement to the March 1997 issue of *Shannon Pratt's Business Valuation Update*. Covers cases of all types.

Hirschfeld, Christopher. "ESOPs as an Estate Planning Vehicle for Business Owners." *Journal of Financial Planning*, vol. 15, no. 11, Nov. 30, 2002, pp. 92–97.

Howitt, Idelle A. "Estate of Cameron W. Bommer." *Valuation Strategies*, September/October 1998, pp. 38–39, 42.

Iwanyshyn, Deborah. "Mediation as a Form of Dispute Resolution." *Shannon Pratt's Business Valuation Update*, October 1998, pp. 5–6.

Jacobs, Jack B. 1999. "Adjudicating Statutory Appraisal and Breach of Fiduciary Duty Valuations in the Delaware Court of Chancery" (interview with Shannon Pratt). *Judges & Lawyers Business Valuation Update* (September), pp. 1, 3–4.

Julius, J. Michael. "ESOP Appraisals and Non-ESOP Shareholders." *CPA Litigation Service Counselor*, July 1998, pp. 9–10.

Kaufman, Steve. "See You Out of Court: Mediation Used in Resolving Business Disputes." *Nation's Business,* June 1992, pp. 58–60.

Klinefelter, Stanard T., and Sandra P. Gohn. "Alternative Dispute Resolution: Its Value to Estate Planners." *Estate Planning,* May/June, 1995. pp. 147–54.

Kober, John A. "A Tool for Shareholder Liquidity, Estate Planning and Management Succession Planning." White paper (1999), available on *www.BVLibrary.com.*

Korschot, John. "Valuation Issues." *BV Papers*, December 2001. Available at *www.BVLibrary.com.*

Kratchman, D. Michael, and William P. Walsh. "Mediation Instead of Litigation for Resolution of Valuation Disputes." *Michigan Business Law Journal,* Winter 1995, pp. 15–17.

Kubersky, Andrew S. "Marketability Discounts and ESOP Acquisitions of Minority Share Interests." *Journal of Employee Ownership Law and Finance*, Fall 1998, pp. 97–103.

Lannom, Allan L. R. "Valuing Non-ESOP Shares in ESOP Companies—Some Empirical Evidence." *Business Valuation Review,* March 1994, pp. 19–21.

Lee, M. Mark, and Gilbert E. Matthews. "How Should Trapped-In Capital Gains Taxes Be Valued?" *Business Valuation Update*, August 2004.

Lee, M. Mark. "Control Premiums and Minority Discounts: the Need for Economic Analysis." *Business Valuation Update*, August 2001.

______. "The Ratio of Depreciation and Capital Expenditures in DCF Terminal Values." *Financial Valuation and Litigation Expert*, August-September 2007, pp. 7–8.

Lippert-Gray, Carol. "An ESOP's Tale." *Financial Executive,* vol. 16, no. 1, Feb. 28, 2000, pp. 40–42.

"Multiattribute Utility Model Accepted in Allocating Personal/Enterprise Goodwill." *Business Valuation Update*, December 2006 (case abstract of *In re Marriage of Alexander,* 2006 Ill. App. LEXIS 836 (Ill. Ct. App. 2006)).

Malick, S.A. "Oppression of and Relief for Minority Shareholders: Cases and Commentaries." *Golden Books Centre*, 2000.

Mantese, Gerard V. and Ian Williamson. "Minority Shareholder Oppression: From Estes to Franchino." *Michigan Bar Journal*, August 2005, pp. 16–20.

Matthews, Gilbert E. "Misuse of Control Premiums in Delaware Appraisals." *Business Valuation Review*, Summer 2008.

______. "A Review of Valuations in Delaware Appraisal Cases, 2004–2005." *Business Valuation Review,* Summer 2006, pp. 44–63.

______. "When Averaging Multiples, Apply the Harmonic Mean." *Business Valuation Update*, June 2006.

______. "The Superiority of the Harmonic Mean as a Method for Averaging Multiples of Guideline Companies and Acquisitions." *Financial Valuation and Litigation Expert,* June/July 2008, pp. 12–15.

______. "CapX = Depreciation Is Unrealistic Assumption for Most Terminal Values." *Shannon Pratt's Business Valuation Update*, March 2002.

______. "Pitfalls in Fairness Opinion Valuations." *Judges & Lawyers Business Valuation Update*, April 2001.

May, Richard C., Robert L. McDonald & Brad Van Horn. "Valuation Issues in Leveraged ESOPs." *Journal of Employee Ownership Law and Finance,* Summer1994. pp. 61–82.

McConaughy, Daniel L., and Bordi, Lorena. "The Long-Term Relationships between Capital Expenditures and Depreciation Across Industries: Important Data for Capitalized Income Based Valuations." *Business Valuation Review*, March 2004. pp. 14–24.

Miller, Karren L. "Using an ESOP to Let Go." *Central Penn Business Journal*, vol. 16, no. 23, June 9, 2000, p. 3.

Moll, Douglas K. "Minority Oppression and the Limited Liability Company: Learning (or Not) from Close Corporation History." *Wake Forest Law Review*, Vol. 40, 2005, p. 883.

Mueller, Susan L. "An Introduction to ESOP Appraisal Controversies." *Journal of Employee Ownership Law and Finance*, Winter 1998, pp. 89–96.

Nath, Eric W. "How Public Guideline Companies Represent 'Control' Value for a Private Company." *Business Valuation Review*, December 1997, pp. 167–71.

Peters, Jerry O. "Adjusting Price/Earnings Ratios for Differences in Company Size." *Business Valuation Review*, June 1999, pp 71–85.

Porter, John W. "Buy-Sell Agreements: *True* Provision Does Not Control Value for Estate Tax Purposes." *Business Valuation Alert*, April 2005.

Pratt, Shannon P., and Noah J. Gordon. "Trustee and Appraiser Duties in ESOP Valuations—Recent Judicial Decisions." *ESOP Report Magazine*, June/July 2007, pp. 65–66.

Pratt, Shannon P., "Shareholder Suit Valuation Criteria Vary from State to State." *Valuation Strategies*, January/February 1999, pp. 12–15.

______. "Controversies Involving the Market Approach to Business Valuation; Raising the Issues, Soliciting Feedback." *Shannon Pratt's Business Valuation Update*, November 2000.

______. "Practitioners disagree strongly on excess earnings methodology" (results of a survey of business appraisers). *Shannon Pratt's Business Valuation Update*, April 1997, pp. 1–3.

Regnitz, Timothy J. "Understanding the ESOP Repurchase Obligation." *The Journal of Employee Ownership Law and Finance*, Winter 1999, pp. 21–34.

Ross, Franz. "'Just One Thing': The Most Reliable Variable for Use in the Market Approach." *Shannon Pratt's Business Valuation Update*, August 2004.

Saltzman, Michael I. "Tax Court Mediation: A Case Study." *Tax Executive*, November/December 1996, pp. 449–53.

Shartsis, Arthur, Jr. "Dissolution Actions Yield Less Than Fair Market Enterprise Value." *Judges & Lawyers Business Valuation Update*, January 1999, p. 5.

Sheeler, Carl L. "The Market Approach: A Neglected and Misunderstood Aspect of Business Value." *Journal of Financial Planning*, May 2004, Article 7.

_____. "A Misunderstood Aspect of Business Value: The Market Approach." *The CPA Journal*, October 2004.

Slee, Rober T. "Is the Subject Company Similar?" *Valuation Strategies*, May/June 1998, pp. 4–7, 34.

Suhre, Karen K. "Should the ESOP-Owned Company Elect to Become an S Corporation?" *Benefits Law Journal*, Spring 1998.

"To ESOP or Not to ESOP?" *The Tax Adviser*, May 2004.

Torolopoulos, Sam G. "Valuation of ESOP Shares: Opportunities and Challenges." *CPA Expert*, Fall 2005, pp. 9–12.

Trugman, Gary. "Guideline Public Company Method—Control or Minority Value?" *Shannon Pratt's Business Valuation Update*, December 2003.

_____. "Guideline Public Company Method: Control or Minority Control Position?" *BVPapers,* February 2005. Available at *www.BVLibrary.com.*

Wise, Richard. "Application of the Market Approach in Valuing a Canadian Business." *BVPapers*, February 2005. Available at *www.BVLibrary.com.*

_____. "Caveats for Market Approach." *CA Magazine,* January-February 2004.

_____. "Multiple-of-Revenues as a Valuation Method." *Business Valuation Digest*, October 1996, pp. 1–4.

Wood, David, "'MUM's the Word': A Formal Method to Allocate Blue Sky Value in Divorce." *Business Valuation Update*, March 2007.

Zuckerman, Michael H., and John G. Grall. "Corporate Buy-Sell Agreements as Estate and Business Planning Tools." *Estate Planning,* December 2001.

Periodicals

American Business Law Journal. Quarterly. Academy of Legal Studies in Business, c/o Daniel J. Herron, Dept. of Finance, 120 Upham Hall, Miami University, Oxford, OH 45056; phone: (513) 529-2945, fax: (513) 529-6992.

American Journal of Family Law. Quarterly. Aspen Law and Business, 1185 Avenue of the Americas, New York, NY 10036; phone: (888) 859-8081.

ASA Professional. Quarterly. American Society of Appraisers, Box 17265, Washington, D.C. 20041-0265.

Business Law Today. Bimonthly (five times a year). American Bar Association Section of Business Law, ABA Service Center, 541 N. Fairbanks Court, Chicago, IL 60611.

Business Valuation Review. Monthly. American Society of Appraisers, P.O. Box 17265, Washington, D.C. 20041; phone: (703) 478-2228; fax: (703) 472-8471.

Business Valuation Update. Monthly. Business Valuation Resources, 1000 S.W. Broadway, Suite 1200, Portland, OR 97205; phone: (888) 287-8258.

Canadian Tax Highlights. Monthly. Canadian Tax Foundation, 1200-595 Bay St., Toronto, ON M5G 2N5, Canada; phone: (416) 599-0283; fax: (416) 599-9283.

Control Premium Study. Quarterly. FactSet Mergerstat, LLC, 2150 Colorado Ave., Suite 150, Santa Monica, CA 90404; phone: (310) 315-3100. *www.mergerstat.com.*

CPA Expert. Quarterly. American Institute of Certified Public Accountants, Harborside Financial Center, 201 Plaza Three, Jersey City, NJ 07311-3881; phone: (888) 777-7077 or (201) 938-3000.

CPA Litigation Service Counselor. Monthly. Hartcourt Brace Professional Publishing, Subscription Fulfillment, 6277 Sea Harbor Dr., Orlando, FL 32887; phone: (800) 831-7799.

Delaware Journal of Corporate Law. Three times per year. Widener University, School of Law, Box 7286, Wilmington, DE 19803; phone: (302) 477-2145; fax: (302) 477-2042.

E-Law Business Valuation Perspective. Twenty times per year. Mercer Capital Management, 5850 Ridgeway Center Pkwy., Suite 410, Memphis, TN 38120; *www.bizval.com.*

Estate Planning (New York). Base volume (plus semiannual updates). Warren, Gorham & Lamont of the RIA Group, 90 Fifth Ave., New York, NY 10011; phone: (212) 645-4800; fax: (212) 337-4280.

Fair$hare: The Matrimonial Law Monthly. Monthly. Aspen Law & Business, 1185 Avenue of the Americas, 37th Fl., New York, NY 10036; phone: (212) 597-0200 or (800) 638-8437; fax: (212) 597-0338.

Family Advocate. Quarterly. Section of Family Law, American Bar Association, 321 N. Clark St., Chicago, IL 60654; phone: (312) 988-6113; *www.abanet.org/family/advocate.*

Family Law Quarterly. Section of Family Law, American Bar Association, 321 N. Clark St., Chicago, IL 60611; phone: (312) 988-5000; *www.abanet.org/family/advocate.*

Federal Tax Valuation Digest. Howitt, Idelle A., ed. New York: Warren, Gorham & Lamont. Updated annually.

Fordham Law Review. Bimonthly. Fordham University, School of Law, Lincoln Center, 140 W. 62nd St., Rm. 04, New York, NY 10023; phone: (212) 636-6876; fax: (212) 636-6965.

Journal of the American Academy of Matrimonial Lawyers. Annually. American Academy of Matrimonial Lawyers, University of Wisconsin–Madison Law School, 150 N. Michigan Ave., #2040, Chicago, IL 60601; phone: (312) 263-6477.

Journal of Accountancy. Monthly. American Institute of Certified Public Accountants, Harborside Financial Center, 201 Plaza Three, Jersey City, NJ 07311; phone: (201) 938-3796 or (888) 777-7077; fax: (201) 329-1112.

Journal of Business Valuation. Annually. The Canadian Institute of Business Valuators, 277 Wellington Street West, 5th Floor, Toronto, Ontario M5V 3H2; phone: (416) 204-3397; fax: (416) 977-8585; e-mail: admin@cicbv.va; Web site: *www.businessvaluators.com*

Journal of Employee Ownership Law and Finance. Quarterly. National Center for Employee Ownership, 1201 Martin Luther King Jr. Way, Oakland, CA 94612; phone: (510) 272-9461; fax: (510) 272-9510.

Journal of Pension Planning and Compliance. Panel Publishers c/o Aspen Law and Business, 1185 Avenue of the Americas, New York, NY 10036; phone: (212) 597-0200 or (800) 638-8437; fax: (212) 597-0338.

Matrimonial Strategist. Monthly. American Lawyer Media, d.b.a. Leader Publications, 345 Park Ave. S., New York, NY 10010; phone: (212) 545-6170; fax: (212) 969-1848.

Mergers & Acquisitions. Bimonthly. Securities Data Publishing, 40 W. 57th St., 11th fl., New York, NY 10019; phone: (212) 765-5311; fax: (212) 765-6123.

Mergerstat Review. Annual. FactSet Mergerstat, LLC, 2150 Colorado Ave., Suite 150, Santa Monica, CA 90404; phone: (310) 315-3100; *www.mergerstat.com.*

Michigan Business Law Journal. State Bar of Michigan, 306 Townsend St., Lansing, MI 48933; phone: (517) 372-9030.

Nation's Business. Monthly. U.S. Chamber of Commerce, 1615 H St. N.W., Washington, D.C. 20062-2000; phone: (202) 659-6000.

National Law Journal. Weekly. American Lawyer Media, d.b.a. Leader Publications, 345 Park Ave. S., New York, NY 10010; phone: (212) 779-9200.

New York Law Journal. Quarterly. American Lawyer Media, d.b.a. Leader Publications, 345 Park Ave. S., New York, NY 10010; phone: (212) 779-9200.

The Review of Securities & Commodities Regulation. Semimonthly (22 issues per year). Standard & Poor's of McGraw-Hill Companies, 25 Broadway, New York, NY 10004; phone: (212) 208-8650; fax: (212) 412-0240.

The ESOP Report. Monthly. ESOP Association, 1726 M St. N.W., Suite 501, Washington, D.C. 20036; phone: (202) 293-2971; fax: (202) 293-7568.

The Federal Tax Course Letter. Monthly. Aspen Law & Business, 1185 Avenue of the Americas, 37th fl., New York, NY 10036; phone: (212) 597-0200 or (800) 638-8437; fax: (212) 597-0338.

The Journal of Taxation. Monthly. Warren, Gorham & Lamont of the RIA Group, 90 Fifth Ave., New York, NY 10011; phone: (212) 645-4800; fax: (212) 337-4280.

The Tax Adviser. Monthly. American Institute of Certified Public Accountants, Harborside Financial Center, 201 Plaza Three, Jersey City, NJ 07311-9808; phone: (201) 938-4796 or (800) 862-4272; fax: (201) 329-1112.

The Tax Executive. Bimonthly. Tax Executives Institute, 1200 G St. N.W., No. 300, Washington, D.C. 20005-3814; phone: (202) 638-5601; fax: (202) 638-5607.

The Tax Lawyer. Quarterly. Section of Taxation, American Bar Association, 321 N. Clark St., Chicago, IL 60654; *www.abanet.org/tax.*

Tax Management Memorandum. Biweekly. Tax Management, 1231 25th St. N.W., Washington, D.C. 20037; phone: (202) 785-7191 or (800) 223-7270; fax: (202) 785-7195.

Taxation for Accountants. Monthly. Warren, Gorham & Lamont of the RIA Group, 90 Fifth Ave., New York, NY 10011; phone: (212) 645-4800; fax: (212) 337-4280.

Taxation for Lawyers. Bimonthly. Warren, Gorham & Lamont of the RIA Group, 90 Fifth Ave., New York, NY 10011; phone: (212) 645-4800; fax: (212) 337-4280.

Taxes, The Tax Magazine. Monthly. CCH, 2700 Lake-Cook Rd., Riverwoods, IL 60015; phone: (847) 267-7000.

Trusts & Estates. Ten issues per year. Monitor Press Ltd., Suffolk House, Church Field Rd., Sudbury, Suffolk CO10 6YA, England; phone: 44-1787-378607; fax: 44-178-881147.

Valuation Strategies. Bimonthly. RIA Group, 31 St. James St., Boston, MA 02116; phone: (800) 431-9025.

Wisconsin Law Review. Bimonthly. University of Wisconsin at Madison, Law School, 975 Bascom Mall, Madison, WI 53706-1399; phone: (608) 262-5815, fax: (608) 262-5485.

Conference Papers

Berka, Jack W. "An ESOP Update Review of Current Issues." Presentation to the International Conference of the American Society of Appraisers, June 1997. Available on *www.BVLibrary.com.*

"Buy-Sell Agreements: Opportunities and Challenges for BV Appraisers." Business Valuation Resources, Teleconference featuring Christopher Mercer, Jim Hitchner, and Roger Grabowski, July 19, 2007, presented by BVResources.com, available on CD and/or written transcript.

"Calculating Goodwill: What is Personal and What is Professional?" Business Valuation Resources, Teleconference January 18, 2006, with Ron Seigneur, R. James Alerding, Mark Dietrich, and Kevin Yeanoplos, presented by BVResources.com, available on CD and/or written transcript.

Goeldner, Richard W. "Adjusting Market Multiples of Guideline Companies." Presentation to the 18th Annual Advanced Business Valuation Conference of the American Society of Appraisers, October 29, 1999. Available on *www.BVLibrary.com.*

"Minority Shareholder Disputes." Minnesota Institute of Legal Education, Minneapolis. Several hundred pages of conference papers in three-ring binder. Although primarily oriented to Minnesota, the papers reflect national research on the issues.

Ostermueller, Ralph E. "Reasonable Executive Compensation." AICPA National Business Valuation Conference, Dec 3, 2006.

"The Planner's Role in Buy-Sell Agreements." Business Valuation Resources, Teleconference featuring Christopher Mercer, L. Paul Hood, Jr., and John H. Brown, June 14, 2007, presented by BVResources.com, available on CD and/or written transcript.

"You'll Never Think about Buy-Sell Agreements the Same Way Again." Business Valuation Resources, Teleconference featuring Christopher Mercer, May 24, 2007, presented by BVResources.com, available on CD and/or written transcript.

Databases

Almanac of Business and Industrial Financial Ratios. CCH, 2700 Lake-Cook Rd., Riverwoods, IL 60015. (800) 248-3248. tax.cchgroup.com.

BIZCOMPS. Asset Business Appraisal, P.O. Box 97757, Las Vegas, NV 89193. (858) 457-0366. Available online at www.BVResources.com.

BVUpdate™, Deluxe BVUpdate™, and *BVLaw™* are available online at www.BVLibrary.com. Portland, Ore.: Business Valuation Resources, LLC.

Compustat, Analyst's Handbook, and other Standard & Poor's Products, Standard & Poor's Corp., available at www.compustat.com and www.standardandpoors.com. (800) 523-4534.

Directory of Companies Required to File Annual Reports with the Securities and Exchange Commission under the Securities Exchange Act of 1934. U.S. Government Printing Office. (202) 512-1800. Available at www.gpo.gov.

Direct Investments Spectrum Newsletter. Partnership Profiles, Inc., 1300 Lakeside Ct., Argyle, TX 76226-6393. (940) 455-2173; www.partnershipprofiles.com. The May/June issue each year is a compilation of empirical data concerning discounts from net asset value at which minority interests in real estate partnerships trade in the informal resale market.

Done Deals. Thomson PPC, P.O. Box 966, Fort Worth, TX 76101-0966. (800) 323-8724.

EDGAR Database. Securities and Exchange Commission. Available at www.sec.gov/cgi-bin/srch-edgar and www.sec.gov/edgar/searchedgar/webusers.htm.

Emory & Co. Pre-IPO Studies. Emory & Co., 611 N. Broadway, Suite 210, Milwaukee, WI 53202. (800) 252-5984; www.emorybizval.com. It is also available from www.bvlibrary.com.

Factiva. Available at www.factiva.com. (800) 369-0166.

FactSet Mergerstat. FactSet Mergerstat LLC, 2150 Colorado Ave., Suite 150, Santa Monica, CA 90404. (310) 315-3100. Database includes *Mergerstat Review* (annual), *Flashwire Monthly, Online Transaction Roster, Flashwire Weekly, Control Premium Study,* and *M&A Decade Library* (CD-ROM).

IBA Market Database. Institute of Business Appraisers. P.O. Box 17410, Plantation, FL 33318. (954) 584-1144.

Industry Norms and Key Business Ratios. The D&B Corp., 103 JFK Parkway, Short Hills, NJ 07078. (973) 921-5500. www.dnb.com.

Integra Data and Report. Integra Information: A Division of MicroBilt Corp. 1-800-780-2660. www.integrainfo.com.

Mergent (previously Moody's). Available at www.mergent.com. (888) 369-0166.

Mergerstate/BVU's Control Premium Study. Business Valuation Resources, LLC, 1000 S.W. Broadway, Suite 1200, Portland, OR 97205. (888) 287-8258. A Web-based tool used to quantify minority discounts and control premiums used in the business valuation, business appraisal, venture capital, and merger and acquisition professions. Available online at www. BVResources.com.

Morningstar®. Ibbotson Associates®, 225 N. Michigan Ave., Ste. 700, Chicago, IL 60601, (312) 616-1620, publishes series of data dealing with cost of capital:

- *Stocks, Bonds, Bills & Inflation,* Valuation Edition, published annually. Provides equity risk premium series, small stock premium series, and other data to develop cost of equity capital.
- *Cost of Capital Yearbook and Quarterly Updates,* published annually with quarterly update. Contains cost of equity by both CAPM and DCF procedures and Weighted Average Cost of Capital by Industry, as well as capital structure at market value by industry.
- *Beta Book,* published semiannually. Several computations of beta for over 5,000 publicly traded stocks.
- *Cost of Capital Center,* online service for all of above data on per-inquiry basis, corporate.morningstar.com.

OneSource (a division of *InfoUSA*). Available at www.onesource.com. (978) 318-4300.

Pratt's Stats. Business Valuation Resources, 1000 S.W. Broadway, Suite 1200, Portland, OR 97205. (888) 287-8258. Available online at www.BVResources.com.

RMA Annual Statement Studies. The Risk Management Association, 1801 Market St., Suite 300, Philadelphia, PA 19103; phone: (215) 446-4000; fax: (215) 446-4101. www.rmahq.org.

Risk Premium Report. Duff & Phelps LLC, 55 East 52nd St., 31st Floor, New York, NY 10055. (212) 871-2000. Published annually and available at www.bvresources.com and corporate.morningstar.com

SDC Platinum (previously Securities Data Corp.). Thomson Financial, 195 Broadway, New York, NY 10007. (800) 782-5555.

The FMV Restricted Stock Study™. Business Valuation Resources, LLC, 1000 S.W. Broadway, Suite 1200, Portland, OR 97205. (888) 287-8258. www.bvmarketdata.com.

The LiquiStat™ Database. Pluris Valuation Advisors, LLC, 17 Battery Place, Ste. 1343, New York, NY 10004. (212) 248-4500. www.plurisvaluation.com.

Thomson Financial. (800) 843-7747. Available at www.thomson.com/solutions/financial and www.dialog.com.

Valuation Advisors' Lack of Marketability Discount Study™. Business Valuation Resources, LLC, 1000 S.W. Broadway, Suite 1200, Portland, OR 97205. (888) 287-8258. www.bvmarketdata.com.

Table of Cases

Index

A

B

C

D

E

G

H

I

N

O

P

Q

R

U

V

W

Y

Z